BIG DATA
IN
PSYCHOLOGICAL
RESEARCH

BIG DATA
IN
PSYCHOLOGICAL
RESEARCH

EDITED BY
SANG EUN WOO, LOUIS TAY, AND ROBERT W. PROCTOR

AMERICAN PSYCHOLOGICAL ASSOCIATION

Published by
American Psychological Association
750 First Street, NE
Washington, DC 20002
https://www.apa.org

Order Department
https://www.apa.org/pubs/books
order@apa.org

In the U.K., Europe, Africa, and the Middle East, copies may be ordered from Eurospan
https://www.eurospanbookstore.com/apa
info@eurospangroup.com

Typeset in Meridien and Ortodoxa by Circle Graphics, Inc., Reisterstown, MD

Printer: Sheridan Books, Chelsea, MI
Cover Designer: Beth Schlenoff, Bethesda, MD

Library of Congress Cataloging-in-Publication Data

Names: Woo, Sang Eun, editor. | Tay, Louis (Psychologist) editor. |
   Proctor, Robert W., editor.
Title: Big data in psychological research / edited by Sang Eun Woo, Louis
   Tay, and Robert W. Proctor.
Description: Washington : American Psychological Association, 2020. |
   Includes bibliographical references and index.
Identifiers: LCCN 2019054296 (print) | LCCN 2019054297 (ebook) |
   ISBN 9781433831676 (hardcover) | ISBN 9781433832338 (ebook)
Subjects: LCSH: Psychology—Research—Data processing. |
   Psychology—Research—Methodology.
Classification: LCC BF76.6.I57 B54 2020 (print) | LCC BF76.6.I57 (ebook) |
   DDC 150.72—dc23
LC record available at https://lccn.loc.gov/2019054296
LC ebook record available at https://lccn.loc.gov/2019054297

http://dx.doi.org/10.1037/0000193-000

Printed in the United States of America

10 9 8 7 6 5 4 3 2 1

CONTENTS

CONTRIBUTORS

Mohammad Adibuzzaman, PhD, Regenstrief Center for Healthcare Engineering, Purdue University, West Lafayette, IN

Sara Aghajanzadeh, MSc candidate, Purdue University, West Lafayette, IN

Talya N. Bauer, PhD, School of Business Administration, Portland State University, Portland, OR

Elisa Bertino, PhD, Department of Computer Science, Purdue University, West Lafayette, IN

Andrew B. Blake, doctoral candidate, Department of Management, Texas Tech University, Lubbock

Grant Brady, PhD, School of Business, Portland State University, Portland, OR

Roberto De La Rosa, doctoral candidate, Department of Experimental Psychology, Texas Tech University, Lubbock

Sidney K. D'Mello, PhD, Institute of Cognitive Science, Department of Computer Science, University of Colorado, Boulder

David S. Ebert, PhD, Electrical and Computer Engineering, Purdue University, West Lafayette, IN

Michael T. Ford, PhD, Department of Management, University of Alabama, Tuscaloosa

James A. Grand, PhD, Department of Psychology, University of Maryland, College Park

Paul M. Griffin, PhD, Regenstrief Center for Healthcare Engineering, Purdue University, West Lafayette, IN

Kevin J. Grimm, PhD, Department of Psychology, Arizona State University, Tempe

Brian D. Haig, PhD, School of Psychology, Speech and Hearing, University of Canterbury, Christchurch, New Zealand

Ivan Hernandez, PhD, Department of Psychology, Virginia Tech, Blacksburg

Ross Jacobucci, PhD, Department of Psychology, University of Notre Dame, Notre Dame, IN

Randall K. Jamieson, PhD, Department of Psychology, University of Manitoba, Winnipeg, Canada

Andrew T. Jebb, MA, Department of Psychological Sciences, Purdue University, West Lafayette, IN

Brendan T. Johns, PhD, Department of Psychology, McGill University, Montreal, Quebec, Canada

Mark P. Jones, DPhil, Department of Computer Science, Portland State University, Portland, OR

Michael N. Jones, PhD, Cognitive Science Program, Indiana University, Bloomington

Morteza Karimzadeh, PhD, Department of Geography, University of Colorado, Boulder

Margaret L. Kern, PhD, Graduate School for Education, University of Melbourne, Melbourne, Australia

Daniel I. Lee, MA, Social/Personality Psychology, University of California, Riverside

Yifan Li, MSc, School of Electrical and Computer Engineering, Purdue University, West Lafayette, IN

Mengqiao Liu, PhD, Development Dimensions International, Pittsburgh, PA

Laura F. Long, Department of Psychological Sciences and Department of Statistics, Purdue University, West Lafayette, IN

Yung-Hsiang Lu, PhD, School of Electrical and Computer Engineering, Purdue University, West Lafayette, IN

Frederick L. Oswald, PhD, Department of Psychological Sciences, Rice University, Houston, TX

Alexandra Paxton, PhD, Department of Psychological Sciences, Center for the Ecological Study of Perception and Action, University of Connecticut, Storrs

Robert W. Proctor, PhD, Department of Psychological Sciences, Purdue University, West Lafayette, IN

Sarfaraz Serang, PhD, Department of Psychology, Utah State University, Logan

Ryne A. Sherman, PhD, Hogan Assessment Systems, Tulsa, OK

Luke S. Snyder, Purdue University, West Lafayette, IN

Q. Chelsea Song, PhD, Department of Psychological Sciences, Purdue University, West Lafayette, IN

Padmini Srinivasan, PhD, Department of Computer Science, University of Iowa, Iowa City

Gabriela Stegmann, PhD, Department of Psychology, Arizona State University, Tempe

Joshua A. Strauss, BA, Department of Psychology, University of Maryland, College Park

Chen Tang, School of Labor and Employment Relations, University of Illinois at Urbana-Champaign, Champaign

Louis Tay, PhD, Department of Psychological Sciences, Purdue University, West Lafayette, IN

George K. Thiruvathukal, PhD, Department of Computer Science, Loyola University, Chicago, IL, and Argonne National Laboratory, Argonne, IL

Donald M. Truxillo, PhD, Department of Work and Employment Studies, Kemmy Business School, University of Limerick, Limerick, Ireland

Guizhen Wang, Electrical and Computer Engineering, Purdue University, West Lafayette, IN

Sang Eun Woo, PhD, Department of Psychological Sciences, Purdue University, West Lafayette, IN

Aiping Xiong, PhD, College of Information Sciences and Technology, The Pennsylvania State University, University Park

Jieqiong Zhao, MS, Electrical and Computer Engineering, Purdue University, West Lafayette, IN

BIG DATA
IN
PSYCHOLOGICAL
RESEARCH

Introduction

Sang Eun Woo, Louis Tay, and Robert W. Proctor

We live in an exciting time for psychology. In this digital age, the power of technology enables us to collect and store a massive amount of data in a way that is faster, more plentiful, and more diverse than once imagined. These new data streams contain potentially useful information about human cognition, emotion, attitudes, and behavior that used to be prohibitively difficult—or even impossible—to capture using traditional research methods (Adjerid & Kelley, 2018). This limitation was due in part to costs but also a lack of technological infrastructure (e.g., smartphones, social media). Not only have technological advancements led to an abundance of new data streams, repositories, and computational power, they also have resulted in advances in statistical and computational techniques that have proliferated widespread analysis of such data in multiple domains (e.g., business, education, health care), improving our ability to predict psychological and societal outcomes. This is the era of *big data* for psychological research, which broadly refers to multiplying multiform data (e.g., structured, unstructured) and their supporting technological infrastructure (i.e., capture, storage, processing) and analytic techniques that can enhance psychological research (cf. Adjerid & Kelley, 2018; Harlow & Oswald, 2016).[1]

---

[1]Although we believe this is a broad enough definition that captures a reasonably large portion of "big data" discussions to date, it is important to note that there is little to no consensus on what the term *big data* exactly means; it is defined and conceptualized in a variety of different ways depending on the specific purposes and context of a given discussion.

http://dx.doi.org/10.1037/0000193-001
Big Data in Psychological Research, S. E. Woo, L. Tay, and R. W. Proctor (Editors)

The rapid emergence of big data has been met with enthusiasm in many different fields—especially within applied settings. Although big data hold promise for psychology, there remains hesitancy and even skepticism about this approach. These attitudes stem not from Luddite mindsets but emerge from grounded concerns—apprehensions that arise from issues our field has had to tackle over its history. There are legitimate concerns about the loss of theoretical depth and specificity when big data advocates call for a moratorium on theory (e.g., Anderson, 2008). Psychologists are concerned with using data not only to maximize one's ability to predict meaningful outcomes but also to develop and further establish theories that explain the observed relationships. In this regard, more thoughtful and contextualized discussions are needed about what theoretical and scientific advancements can and cannot be achieved through the collection and analysis of big data. For example, an empirical finding that languages posted on social media can reliably predict the users' self-reported personality should not be immediately accepted as direct evidence for social media language's validity as a "measure" of personality; doing so would require philosophical and theoretical justification of the equivalence between prediction and causal explanation by personality constructs (for further discussions, see Woo, Tay, Hickman, & Saef, 2019).

Further, there are methodological and empirical questions as to the reliability, validity, and utility of big data for psychology. For one, the conditions under which the data are collected are largely uncontrolled (from an experimentalist's perspective, this is a major limitation). For another, there is limited evidence to date that machine learning algorithms that are currently used in applied and commercialized settings (e.g., recruitment and selection) can improve our ability to predict the outcomes of interest to psychologists (e.g., individual attributes that may be captured using traditional methods during selection, job performance, turnover; cf. Hickman, Tay, & Woo, 2019). Going beyond the prediction accuracy, another notable problem with using machine learning algorithms in hiring is the perpetuation of potential biases in the assessment and decision-making processes. For instance, Amazon had to halt their machine learning tool for sifting through applicant resumes when they observed that the algorithm had a preference for men over women (Dastin, 2018). These potential problems in control, prediction, and bias apply broadly to a vast array of psychological research and have to be better understood and clarified.

These questions occur at a time of deep self-reflection and self-criticism in psychology as psychologists work through the challenges of replication and reproducibility even in our well-established traditional research designs and methods. In this light, big data are intuitively appealing because the large swathes of data used have a greater statistical power to detect phenomena and yield more accurate statistical estimates. Yet, these same big data may introduce new issues or magnify old ones in replication and reproduction. These include aspects such as the way data are collected and cleaned, the type of hardware used, the expertise of the researcher, and the choice of analytic techniques. Big data may also continue to underrepresent certain demographic groups, and analyses on subgroup differences may not be as robust.

Finally, there is the inevitable association of big data with "big brother" and digital surveillance. Where data are being collected at scale without informed consent for a specific research question, there are questions as to when and how these types of data can be used, to what extent informed consent is necessary, and how the privacy of individuals can be protected in the analytic and research process. The emergence of such data requires our field to work through ethical challenges of confidentiality and privacy as they pertain to big data.

Our desire to organize this handbook is twofold. We seek to showcase the opportunities of big data and its related methodologies for psychologists to study human behavior and cognition. At the same time, we believe that the key to unlocking this possibility requires addressing many of these concerns and challenges. For individual researchers to decide whether to incorporate some of these technology-driven ways of collecting and analyzing data into their existing methodological toolkits, there has to be a systematic and comprehensive understanding of big data in psychological research—both conceptually and methodologically. More broadly, our field requires a consolidated resource to continue informed conversations about the prospect of big data for psychology. This edited volume aims to address these needs.

In May 2018, we (the three editors of this book, Woo, Tay, and Proctor) organized a symposium, sponsored by Purdue University's Department of Psychological Sciences, to which we invited 20 leading scholars and practitioners not only from different domains in psychology but also from other key related disciplines such as computer science, data science, philosophy of science, management, health care, and education. The goal of the symposium was to assess the current state of the big data movement critically in terms of its scientific value to the psychology community to address the conceptual, methodological, and ethical challenges and to identify areas in which future research is most needed. We sought to obtain a broad array of opinions on a wide variety of issues associated with the use of big data in psychology, which sparked a number of significant discussions and new insights. The current edited volume closely follows the structure and content of the symposium. Many of the symposium presenters have contributed a chapter to this edited volume, and we added several other authors to supplement the overall content coverage of the book.

As such, the overarching goal of this edited book is to provide readers with a bird's-eye view of what big data mean for psychological research—new opportunities for collecting and analyzing psychological data, as well as challenges that may come with such possibilities. The book consists of four main parts, bookended by this introduction (by the editors) and the concluding chapter by Oswald (Chapter 19).

Part I, Background and Overview, features three chapters that discuss how big data have been (and should be) conceptualized and discussed in psychology and other fields, addressing the "big picture," conceptual questions from the perspectives of philosophy of science and research methodology. This section lays out the broad rationale for big data in psychology and discusses potential concerns of theoretical implications, research designs, and measurement reliability and validity.

In Chapter 1, Haig presents his scientific realist perspective (in terms of both global and local realism) on big data science, laying down a key philosophical foundation for understanding the role of science and scientific methods. He then explains inductive and abductive modes of science, in contrast with the hypothetico-deductive method, as alternative methodological paradigms for big data science. In particular, Haig proposes that the abductive method offers a useful framework for a broad array of big data inquiries because it guides not only the initial process of phenomena detection (on which the inductive method focuses) but also the subsequent efforts toward theory construction where researchers generate, develop, and appraise theories. Importantly, Haig warns against the antirealist claims that have been endorsed by some "big data enthusiasts" who completely dismiss the importance of theory and causal explanations. In doing so, he returns us to a more nuanced discussion of what constitutes a "theory" in the first place and points to the different interpretations of causation that exist in the literature.

In Chapter 2, Proctor and Xiong discuss how various aspects of big data present new opportunities and challenges for research in the experimental psychology tradition. They provide an impressive historical sweep of the experimental tradition and show how big data can contribute to experimental designs that have greater scale and representativeness. Critically, this enables research designs and analyses that would more directly account for environmental and contextual compatibilities and constraints on human cognition and behavior, providing a broader human–environment systems approach. This broader applicability has been one of the goals of experimentalists, and the big data approach can serve to complement existing approaches.

In Chapter 3, Woo, Tay, Jebb, Ford, and Kern offer an integrative overview of the different ways in which specific sources of big data (i.e., social media, wearable sensors, Internet behavior, public network cameras, smartphones) may be used for enhancing the measurement quality of psychological research in capturing affective and attitudinal states, personality traits, and interpersonal relationships. Specifically, the authors discuss issues of content relevance (as well as content deficiency and contamination), response processes, internal (factorial) structure, nomological net, and reliability as they relate to each of these data sources. In doing so, they provide psychologists with an analysis of the key considerations in reliability and validity for different big data sources.

Part II, Innovations in Large-Scale Data Collection and Analysis Techniques, contains five chapters that discuss tangible opportunities and strategies for using big data to enhance existing methods of data collection and analysis within psychology. These chapters also present specific challenges and future research directions.

In Chapter 4, Ford reviews the current state of psychological research that uses Internet behavior data. Specifically, he discusses major topics of interest covered in research to date on searches and page selections and views as captured by Google Trends and Wikipedia (i.e., physical health and disease; mental health; legal and illicit drugs; health behavior; consumer, economic, and financial market behavior; and policy and politics). He also presents some preliminary evidence for the criterion-related validity of these data in predicting psychologically meaningful outcomes. There is a substantial opportunity here for psychologists to collect and use such data for understanding and predicting behavior at the aggregate level.

In Chapter 5, Aghajanzadeh, Jebb, Li, Lu, and Thiruvathukal discuss the promise of using public network cameras for collecting observational data of human behaviors around the world. After reviewing the literature illustrating the value of using video data of public human behavior for psychological research, the authors introduce recent technological advances in computer science that enable researchers to access and analyze such video data. Specifically, CAM², a software platform built at Purdue University, can serve as a useful research tool for retrieving and analyzing data from worldwide network cameras, presenting psychologists with (largely unexplored) possibilities for capturing public human behavior on a large scale.

In Chapter 6, Blake, Lee, De La Rosa, and Sherman demonstrate the utility of wearable cameras in capturing the natural environments people encounter in their daily lives on a moment-to-moment basis. After providing a theoretical background for the importance of measuring situational cues and characteristics, the authors discuss the practical, legal, and ethical complexities of using wearable cameras in psychological research (e.g., privacy, obtrusiveness). In an illustrative example, the authors present a recent study that used wearable camera data analyzed with machine vision. This chapter clearly delineates the steps and protocols required for conducting such research.

In Chapter 7, Karimzadeh, Zhao, Wang, Snyder, and Ebert provide an overview of human-guided visual analytics that will be useful for psychological research using big data approaches. With the abundance and complexity of data, there is a need to visually present information in an interactive manner aligned with known perceptual and cognitive principles to enable more effective use and parameterization of big data for research and decision making. The implication is that advances in psychology (e.g., perception, information processing, decision making) can, in turn, contribute to this field of big data visual analytics. Further, the adoption of visual analytics in various application domains creates opportunities for psychological research on the use of such technologies in real-world scenarios and how such use modifies or is affected by human behavior.

In Chapter 8, Srinivasan describes the overall landscape of various text-mining approaches, organized into three broad categories: information extraction, information inferencing, and literature-based discovery. Given that a substantial amount of the work in psychology focuses on the use of lexicon approaches (e.g., dictionary approaches) in information extraction,

Srinivasan discusses the limitations of lexicons and how information extraction can be enhanced through template approaches that provide greater precision in identifying relevant sources of information. Several examples—including belief surveillance, personality perceptions, and life satisfaction—are used to illustrate this. This substantially more accurate approach requires psychologists to provide a priori content specification and operational definitions, highlighting the importance of construct and measurement validity.

Part III, Applications, contains six chapters that summarize how big data have been (and may be) used in specific subdisciplines of psychological sciences and other related fields. These areas include learning and education (Chapter 9), social psychology (Chapter 10), health care (Chapter 11), language and cognition (Chapter 12), developmental psychology (Chapter 13), and industrial and organizational psychology (Chapter 14).

In Chapter 9, D'Mello provides a compelling case for the promise of data-driven, technology-enabled approaches to advancing the science of learning. His examples of such approaches range from innovations in formative assessment techniques (e.g., Bayesian knowledge tracing, additive factor models) to various analytic techniques for dealing with transactional, sequential, linguistic, and multisensory-multimodal behavioral data in education research. Clearly, the field of educational research is embracing the promise and possibilities of big data.

In Chapter 10, Hernandez begins by briefly discussing how four defining characteristics of big data (i.e., volume, velocity, variety, veracity) may complement social psychological research. After extensively cataloging the sources of big data commonly used in social psychology (e.g., website messages, profile information, wearable sensors), he reviews the social psychology literature for key trends in big data research—organized by 12 focal topic areas of social psychology (e.g., attitudes, culture, diversity, motivation, groups). He also offers a summary of the linkages between key social psychological constructs and big data measures. This will serve as an important resource for not only social psychologists but also psychologists from different fields.

In Chapter 11, Adibuzzaman and Griffin note that the progress of big data research in health care has been slow, despite its significant promise. The authors offer helpful insights into reasons behind such delays, such as multi-layered issues of patient privacy in storing, managing, and sharing electronic health records and the limitations of drawing causality (as normally done in health care research through randomized controlled trials) from retrospective observational data. One implication here is that integrating and digitizing different threads of data for an entire field is a significant undertaking requiring careful consideration and coordination.

In Chapter 12, Johns, Jamieson, and Jones describe how big data approaches can be (and have been) applied to understanding human cognition, focusing on the case of building, testing, and validating computational models of natural language using large text corpora. They explain how the ability to store and analyze large amounts of data has enabled the development of better and more diverse sources of language characteristics. Johns and coauthors highlight the fact that the precision provided by large-scale data sets allows researchers to test cognitive models at the level of individual items. The authors emphasize the importance of theory in guiding the scientific progress in this domain and suggest that theoretical insights gained from the abductive development of theories from big data must be accompanied by deductive verification under more controlled experimental conditions.

In Chapter 13, Grimm, Stegmann, Jacobucci, and Serang discuss the importance of longitudinal forms of big data in developmental psychology to understand growth. They focus on machine learning approaches for modeling explanations for growth trajectories in longitudinal panel data. These methods can help researchers explore and identify explanatory variables, which is especially useful in typical scenarios where there are too many variables for researchers to theoretically deduce the optimal set of explanations. The detailed explanation and application of these models to the Early Childhood Longitudinal Study—Kindergarten Cohort of 1998/1999 provide researchers a practical step-by-step guide to model selection and interpretation.

In Chapter 14, Song, Liu, Tang, and Long describe the rapid integration of big data into the field of industrial and organizational psychology to better understand and improve workplaces. There have been substantial advances made in both research and applied settings on topics that range from recruitment and selection (due to online platforms that provide new sources of data and advanced analytics to assess worker attributes for predicting performance) to diversity and inclusion (through multiobjective optimization techniques). They also detail the sources of data that organizational psychologists are integrating and using (e.g., enterprise data, social media data) and the various algorithms that are used to analyze those data (e.g., machine learning, text mining). This chapter showcases the extensive adoption of big data in the field of industrial and organizational psychology and the benefits it provides.

Part IV, Recommendations for Responsible and Rigorous Use of Big Data, addresses practical and ethical challenges associated with big data methods such as privacy, data security and storage, data sharing, and replicability and reproducibility issues. By providing information on technical advances and ethical considerations pertaining to big data, this provides guidance to psychologists undertaking big data research.

In Chapter 15, Paxton discusses key ethical principles of conducting human subject research as described in the Belmont Report, as well as their implications for today's psychological science dealing with big data. She introduces issues and open questions for readers to consider, which go beyond the scope of the Belmont Report (e.g., how to achieve a balance between requirements of open science and protection of participant rights, securing computational pipelines). In doing so, the chapter serves as a helpful guide for shaping the field's discussion about big data research ethics. We expect this work to be informative for updating our ethical principles in light of big data.

In Chapter 16, Strauss and Grand discuss key characteristics of robust and reliable science (e.g., relevant, rigorous, replicable and cumulative, transparent and open, theory oriented), providing a useful framework for evaluating big data science in psychology. This is especially timely given that the fashionability of big data methods can lead to the relaxing of research standards when evaluating such work. They discuss extensions of the topics—HARKing, questionable research practices, and replicability and reproducibility—to big data, providing recommendations to enhance the rigor of big data science.

In Chapter 17, Bauer, Truxillo, Jones, and Brady address issues of privacy and cybersecurity as they relate to the specific context of big data application: personnel selection via online application systems. Considering both the benefits and concerns for multiple stakeholders in this context, the authors provide a set of practical recommendations for online job applicants, employers, developers and providers of online job application tools, and policymakers. They also highlight areas in which best-practice recommendations do not yet exist and thus need further research.

In Chapter 18, Bertino itemizes the numerous ways that the privacy of individuals can be compromised in the collection, storage, and analysis of big data. Her chapter is organized around privacy enhancing techniques that are also consistent with maintaining a high level of data security. She describes specific computer science techniques for addressing privacy and security concerns and identifies several remaining challenges in reconciling security with privacy. These challenges relate to data confidentiality (for which the emphasis is control of access) and data privacy (for which the major issue is that unforeseen information can be obtained about individuals and populations by correlating multiple big data sets). She also briefly discusses data transparency—a key requirement in today's big data era. Although much is being done to ensure the security and privacy of data, big data researchers have to understand that it is a complex problem.

In the closing chapter, Oswald summarizes key themes that emerge across the different chapters in the book. Although there is considerable promise in big data, particularly in allowing investigation of complex human behavior, there are also limitations that psychology can potentially help overcome. The limitations include the interpretability of data models, which can benefit from a substantive grounding in psychology; predictive biases that can profit from psychologists' engagement in open science practices that seek to balance transparency and privacy; and the privacy concerns themselves, which can be addressed through ethical and legal frameworks in psychology. Oswald also suggests multiple future research directions to evaluate the effectiveness of psychological science in improving the quality of big data projects (e.g., measurement, interpretation, research design, transparency) and data science teams (e.g., training and evaluation of teams).

To summarize, our goal in preparing this edited volume has been to provide frank discussions of the many potential benefits for psychological researchers opened up by big data, as well as possible pitfalls. As such, the book is intended for students (undergraduates and graduates), researchers, and practitioners who are interested in what the future of psychology holds in light of the "fourth industrial revolution" (i.e., digital technology). We hope that readers will come away with an appreciation for various ways in which they may be able to incorporate big data research into their research programs and into the multidisciplinary research programs in which they engage.

REFERENCES

Adjerid, I., & Kelley, K. (2018). Big data in psychology: A framework for research advancement. *American Psychologist, 73,* 899–917. http://dx.doi.org/10.1037/amp0000190

Anderson, C. (2008, June 23). The end of theory: The data deluge makes the scientific method obsolete. *Wired.* Retrieved from https://www.wired.com/2008/06/pb-theory/

Dastin, J. (2018). Amazon scraps secret AI recruiting tool that showed bias against women. *Reuters.* Retrieved from https://www.reuters.com/article/us-amazon-com-jobs-automation-insight/amazon-scraps-secret-ai-recruiting-tool-that-showed-bias-against-women-idUSKCN1MK08G

Harlow, L. L., & Oswald, F. L. (2016). Big data in psychology: Introduction to the special issue. *Psychological Methods, 21,* 447–457. http://dx.doi.org/10.1037/met0000120

Hickman, L., Tay, L., & Woo, S. E. (2019). Validity investigation of off-the-shelf language-based personality assessment using video interviews: Convergent and discriminant relationships with self and observer ratings. *Personnel Assessment and Decisions.* Retrieved from https://www.researchgate.net/publication/332544721_Validity_Investigation_of_Off-the-Shelf_Language-Based_Personality_Assessment_using_Video_Interviews_Convergent_and_Discriminant_Relationships_with_Self_and_Observer_Ratings

Woo, S. E., Tay, L., Hickman, L., & Saef, R. (2019). *More questions about the validity of machine-learning approaches to personality assessment: A case of social media text mining.* Manuscript submitted for publication.

BACKGROUND
AND OVERVIEW

1

Big Data Science

A Philosophy of Science Perspective

Brian D. Haig

The advent of big data and its place in science has recently received consideration in both science studies and popular literatures. And in the past 2 or 3 years, articles on big data analysis have started to appear in psychology's methodological literature (e.g., Harlow & Oswald, 2016; McAbee, Landis, & Burke, 2017; Oswald & Putka, 2016; Tonidandel, King, & Cortina, 2018). In this chapter, I am not concerned with big data as such (i.e., with the collection, curation, and analysis of large data sets) but with big data science or, as it is sometimes called, *data-intensive* science. Dealing with data is of major importance to science, of course, but my focus is on the nature of science more broadly construed. Big data science is sometimes claimed to be a new paradigm that provides us with a revolutionary conception of scientific methodology (Hey, Tansley, & Tolle, 2009), one that analyzes large data sets for correlations rather than causes, uses an inductive rather than hypothetico-deductive method, and eschews theories that make reference to causal mechanisms.

Consideration of methodological matters such as these in big data science center on metascientific concepts that are the stock-in-trade of philosophers of science. Contemporary philosophy of science gives considerable attention to scientific practice and is now well positioned to help us understand the nature and status of science. My purpose in this chapter is to make use of relevant philosophical literatures and undertake a critical conceptual examination of a number of central claims made by methodologists about big data science.

http://dx.doi.org/10.1037/0000193-002
Big Data in Psychological Research, S. E. Woo, L. Tay, and R. W. Proctor (Editors)

I begin by evaluating the provocative claims that the advent of big data science spells the end of both scientific method and theory as we understand them. In doing so, I identify the different roles of inductive and abductive methods in an altered understanding of both big data and small data science and go on to identify different types of theory and their relevance for both conceptions of science. I also ask whether it is viable for big data science to emphasize correlational research at the expense of causal explanatory research. I suggest that big data science has to accommodate a number of different conceptions of causality.

Many of the challenges facing big data science are challenges faced by science more generally. Accordingly, the chapter emphasizes the commonalities between big data science and other forms of science. It also proceeds on the assumption that the philosophical work on big data biology has relevance for psychological science. Thus far, most of the emerging research on the philosophy of big data science is to be found in the philosophy of biology. In this respect, I will have particular regard for the work of Sabina Leonelli (2016), Emanuele Ratti (2015), and Wolfgang Pietsch (2015, 2016, 2018). There are instructive lessons for psychology in works such as these, apart from the fact that parts of psychology can reasonably be construed as biological science (Bunge, 1990). At the end, I summarize the chapter and briefly suggest that future work on the philosophy of big data science should draw from a realist philosophy of science. For the purpose of this chapter, it will suffice to understand *realism* in minimalist terms as a commitment to the belief that there exists a real world of which we are part and that both observable and unobservable features of the world can be known by the proper use of scientific methods. A detailed treatment of realist philosophy in relation to social science inquiry can be found in Haig and Evers (2016).

SCIENTIFIC METHOD AND BIG DATA SCIENCE

Modern science is a complex ensemble of different parts. It simultaneously pursues aims, uses methods, fashions theories, and is embedded in institutions, but scientific method is undoubtedly its centerpiece. The centrality of method to science stems from the fact that it provides scientists with the primary form of guidance in their quest to obtain knowledge about the world.

Much of our understanding of the nature and place of methods in science comes in the form of theories of scientific method. Undoubtedly, the two most prominent of these are the hypothetico-deductive and inductive accounts of method. Much less known, but just as important for science, is a third theory of method, sometimes called the abductive theory of method (Curd, 1980; Haig, 2014). By privileging inductive inference, the inductive method has often been associated with narrow forms of empiricist thinking that urge us to stay close to the facts. The hypothetico-deductive method gives sole attention to testing hypotheses and theories and fits comfortably within the more liberal philosophy of logical empiricism. It has been, and continues to be, the method of choice for most scientists. The abductive method, with its emphasis on explanatory reasoning, it should be emphasized, is tailor-made for realist theorizing about hidden entities. Given my focus on big data science, I largely restrict my attention here to the inductive and abductive accounts of method. However, I believe that all three theories of method can be productively used in a methodologically pluralist conception of science.

Big data science is often presented as having strong revisionist implications for our understanding of scientific inquiry, and commentaries about these implications have focused on the first two of these three theories of scientific method. For example, in his well-known pronouncements about big data science, Chris Anderson (2008) declared, "The scientific method is based around testable hypotheses. . . . But faced with massive data, this approach to science—hypothesis, model, test—is becoming obsolete" (para. 8–10). In effect, this is to suggest that we should abandon the hypothetico-deductive method as we know it. The most common recommendation is that big data science should use an inductive conception of scientific method in its place.

In renouncing the tacit realist philosophy of most working scientists, some advocates of inductive inquiry in big data science speak of a new era of empiricism in which big data analytic techniques allow the data to speak for themselves in a theory-free manner (Kitchin, 2014). Further, among big data scientists with realist preferences, one rarely encounters the suggestion that big data science needs an abductive conception of scientific method in which data-driven research leads beyond data patterns and empirical generalizations to explanatory hypotheses about the patterns of interest extracted from the data. Clearly, what is said about big data and scientific method deserves our critical scrutiny.

In considering the place of inductive and abductive accounts of scientific method in big data science, I endeavor to provide a fuller explication of the methods than big data proponents have typically provided and say what goals they serve in the production of scientific knowledge.

Inductive Method and Big Data Science

In the absence of an accompanying elaboration and justification, Anderson's (2008) assertion that big data science is simply inductive has little more than shock value. One has to look elsewhere for a decent treatment of the topic. In philosophy, Chalmers (2013) offered an accessible and informative account of inductive method in which scientists are portrayed as reasoning by enumerative induction from established statements about particular observed events to laws or theories. These inductions are commonly regulated by an overarching principle of inductive inference. Correct inductive reasoning is said to create and justify theories concurrently, thus removing the need for later empirical testing.

This inductive account of scientific method has been criticized for bestowing too much confidence in the resources of observation and inductive generalization and for thinking that induction by enumeration exhausts the domain of scientific inference. B. F. Skinner's radical behaviorist psychology is a clear example of a research program that subscribes to an inductive theory of scientific method (Skinner, 1984). For Skinner, the primary goal of science is to fashion claims about empirical phenomena and, only then, to systematize those regularities by formulating nonexplanatory theories. Radical behaviorism is an empiricist philosophy, but because it subscribes to an instrumentalist conception of theories as nonexplanatory organizational devices, it is not dust bowl empiricism. This latter form of empiricism is typically characterized as being decidedly atheoretical. Psychologists McAbee, Landis, and Burke (2017) provided an assessment of the value of big data science for organizational psychology and recommended a measured inductive perspective for such research to counter the hegemony of hypothetico-deductive theorizing.

Despite extensive criticism by advocates of hypothetico-deductive and abductive accounts of method, the inductive theory of method rightly emphasizes the importance to science of discovering empirical generalizations through inductive reasoning. In the next section, I outline an abductive theory of scientific method. This method also can be understood as endorsing a form of reasoning by enumerative induction ("induction by generalization") as a means of detecting empirical phenomena before promoting the construction of explanatory theories by abductive means.

A final point to be made here is that enumerative inductive methods are not the only type of inductive method used in science. In the later section dealing with causation and big data science, I draw attention to Wolfgang Pietsch's (2015, 2016, 2018) use of eliminative inductive methods to establish causal claims.

Abductive Method and Big Data Science

It is well known that science makes use of both inductive and deductive forms of inference. Less well known is the fact that science also makes considerable use of a third type of reasoning known as *abductive inference*, a form of inference that is sometimes confused with inductive inference. Briefly, abductive inference is explanatory inference, and in science, it involves reasoning about hypotheses, models, and theories in a manner that explains the relevant facts (Haig, 2005, 2014; Magnani, 2001). There are different species of abductive reasoning having to do with the generation, development, and comparative appraisal of hypotheses and theories, and I come to these shortly.

Given that my focus is on scientific method and big data science, it should be emphasized at the outset that different forms of scientific reasoning should not be equated with different accounts of scientific method. Theories of scientific method are primarily structuring devices that involve the efficient, systematic ordering of inquiry. As such, they describe ordered sequences of actions that comprise strategies designed to achieve research goals that are explicitly concerned with the acquisition of knowledge (Haig, 2014; Nickles,

1987). To reach their goals, some theories of scientific method use more than one form of inference. I turn now to consider the abductive theory of scientific method. Here, I follow my formulation of the method (Haig, 2005, 2014), which is described in capsule form as follows:

> Guided by evolving research problems that comprise packages of empirical, conceptual, and methodological constraints, sets of data are analyzed in order to detect robust empirical regularities, or phenomena. Once detected, these phenomena are explained by abductively inferring the existence of underlying causal mechanisms responsible for their production. Here, abductive inference involves reasoning from phenomena, understood as presumed effects, to their theoretical explanation in terms of underlying causal mechanisms. Upon positive judgments of the initial plausibility of the explanatory theories about these causes, attempts are made to elaborate on the nature of the causal mechanisms in question. This is done by constructing plausible models of those mechanisms by analogy to relevant ideas in domains that are already well understood. When the theories are well developed, they are assessed against their rivals with respect to their explanatory goodness. This assessment involves making judgments of the best of competing explanations. (Haig, 2005, p. 373)

Phenomena Detection

Scientists use various strategies to ensure that data provide reliable grounds for the existence of empirical phenomena. One way of understanding the process of phenomena detection is in terms of a statistical model of data analysis (Haig, 2005). The model described here has four stages: In Stage 1, initial data analysis, the concern is with ascertaining the quality of the data; in Stage 2, exploratory data analysis, the focus is on the detection of patterns in the data; in Stage 3, close replication, the researcher looks to confirm the data patterns revealed in Stage 2; and in the fourth stage, constructive replication, the task is to ascertain whether, and to what extent, empirical generalizations can be obtained. As noted earlier, phenomena detection is a process of enumerative induction, in that one establishes empirically, on the basis of case-by-case replications, the scope of the empirical generalizations, or phenomena.

It is worth pointing out that phenomena detection adopts a reliabilist approach to justification. *Reliabilism* maintains that knowledge claims receive their justification to the extent that they are acquired by reliable processes or methods. For example, the data-analytic stages of close and constructive replication just mentioned are, in effect, consistency tests that are used to help show, on reliabilist grounds, that empirical phenomena exist.

Theory Construction

There are three phases of theory construction in the abductive theory of method: theory generation, theory development, and theory appraisal. The first two phases are temporal. The abductive theory maintains that all three phases of theory construction are abductive but that the nature of abductive inference in each case is different.

Theory generation in the abductive theory of method takes place through a process known as *existential abduction*. The name derives from the fact that the existence, although not the nature, of the causal mechanisms are postulated as plausible explanations of their relevant empirical phenomena. The method of exploratory factor analysis is perhaps psychology's clearest example of a method that uses existential abduction. It does this to generate nascent theories about latent factors that are thought to underlie patterns of correlations in manifest variables (Haig, 2014).

It is important to appreciate that, in the context of theory generation, existential abduction confers a generative justification on the theories it helps produce. In effect, generative justification provides assessments of the soundness of the abductive reasoning used in arriving at new hypotheses. Judgments of the initial plausibility of the hypotheses provide the warrant for investigating the hypotheses further.

The abductive theory of scientific method is also a method for "theories-in-the-making." It owes the existence of its theory development phase to the fact that the hypotheses and theories obtained through theory generation often fall short of specifying the nature of the sought-after causal mechanisms. In looking to specify the nature of these mechanisms further, the abductive method requires the construction of models of those mechanisms by reasoning to them from knowledge of the nature of mechanisms that are well known. That is to say, the researcher constructs an analogical model of the unknown causal mechanisms, which is based on the nature and behavior of the known source models. Because analogical modeling is used to develop explanatory theories further, the reasoning process involved is termed *analogical abduction*. The credibility of Darwin's theory of natural selection was increased by its analogical relation to the known process of artificial selection.

We have seen that assessments of the initial plausibility of hypotheses in the theory generation phase of the abductive theory are subsequently augmented by judgments of the plausibility of appropriate analogical models in the theory development phase. It remains to consider a fuller, and comparative, appraisal of well-developed explanatory theories in the so-called phase of theory appraisal.

In systematically appraising well-developed theories, the abductive theory of method uses yet another abductive strategy, known as *inference to the best explanation*. True to its name, inference to the best explanation involves accepting a theory when it is deemed to afford a better explanation of the relevant evidence than its rivals. With the abductive theory of method, inference to the best explanation gets cashed out in terms of the theory of explanatory coherence (Thagard, 1992). The following gloss on the theory of explanatory coherence is derived from Haig (2005).

The theory of explanatory coherence gets its name from the fact that it takes inference to the best explanation to be centrally concerned with making assessments of explanatory coherence, where the explanatory coherence of the propositions of a theory "hold together" because of their explanatory relations.

Three criteria are used to determine the explanatory coherence of a theory: explanatory breadth, simplicity, and analogy. The most important criterion for choosing the best explanation is explanatory breadth. This criterion captures the insight that a more explanatorily powerful theory will explain a greater range of facts than its rivals. The second criterion, simplicity, is committed to the idea that theories that make fewer special or simplifying assumptions should be given preference. The criterion of analogy is considered an important component of explanatory coherence because, with analogical abduction, explanations based on credible analogies receive additional justificatory force. Relations of explanatory coherence are established through the operation of a number of principles and a computer program (see Thagard, 1992, for details). The theory of explanatory coherence provides a rational reconstruction of the reasoning Darwin used in judging his theory of evolution to be superior to its creationist rival.

True to its name, the theory of explanatory coherence adopts a coherentist approach to justification, which contrasts with the reliabilist approach to justification used when justifying claims about empirical phenomena. As noted earlier, coherence justification, too, is a realist methodological principle.

I maintain that the abductive theory of scientific method has the methodological resources to help us understand and evaluate a good part of the structure of big data inquiry. There are several points to be made in this regard:

- The advocates of big data science are correct in claiming that not all scientific inquiry has to conform to the stricture of hypothetico-deductive hypothesis testing, though, as will be mentioned later, the hypothetico-deductive method may form part of a more expansive view of data-intensive science. The abductive theory of method is quite different from the hypothetico-deductive method because it promotes a data-before-theory sequence of inquiry, seeks to generate explanatory theories by methodological means, and appraises theories in terms of their explanatory goodness, not in terms of their predictive success.

- The abductive theory of method provides a detailed methodological account of the discovery of empirical phenomena, typically in the form of empirical generalizations. When advocates of big data inquiry speak favorably about adopting an inductive conception of inquiry, they say little about the nature of the inductive reasoning involved. By contrast, the abductive theory gives a detailed methodological account of the process of enumerative induction involved in phenomena detection and the statistical methods and scientific strategies that can be used in so doing. The role of eliminative inductive inference in an alternative conception of big data inquiry is yet to be considered.

- Although most proponents of big data science speak in favor of inductive research, they occasionally suggest that data-intensive science should be thought of as abductive (e.g., Fox & Hendler, 2014), but they do not elaborate on the claim (Chapter 12, this volume, is an exception). The abductive theory of method takes its name from the fact that it emphasizes the importance of abduction in science, conceives the theory construction process as abductive through and through, and provides a detailed characterization of several abductive methods and strategies that can be used to further that theory construction process.

- Phenomena detection is a relatively autonomous part of scientific inquiry, and it is an important scientific goal in its own right. But it also provides a natural stimulus for theory construction, which is equally important in science. Big data scientists who want to go no further than a concern with data analytics have given no convincing reason for eliminating or downplaying the importance of theory construction in science.

- Rob Kitchin (2014) suggested, "Data-driven science . . . is more open to using a hybrid combination of abductive, inductive and deductive approaches to advance the understanding of a phenomenon" (p. 5), though his sequencing of these elements is difficult to discern. The abductive theory of method advocates a combination of inductive and abductive methods, where the sequence is, in specific terms, enumerative induction (phenomena detection), existential abduction (theory generation), analogical induction (theory development), and inference to the best explanation (comparative theory appraisal). Note also that the abductive theory of method can be profitably regarded as an overarching framework into which an array of more particular research methods can be deployed to give the parent theory its operational bite.

To conclude this section, I suggest that it is a merit of the abductive theory of scientific method that it clearly distinguishes between inductive and abductive inference and assigns a different research goal to each. Some advocates of inductive theory building mix up the two. Edwin Locke (2015), for example, characterized induction as moving from the particular to the general yet, at the same time, seems to understand it as taking us to mediating causal mechanisms. However, inductive inference is descriptive inference, countenancing more entities of the same kind, whereas it is abductive inference that enables us to reason about entities that are different from those to be found in their evidential base (Haig, 2014).

THE PLACE OF THEORY IN BIG DATA SCIENCE

The End of Theory?

As was noted earlier in this chapter, Anderson (2008) maintained that the advent of big data science renders the very idea of theory obsolete. He made this claim in the following forthright manner:

> Out with every theory of human behavior, from linguistics to sociology. Forget taxonomy, ontology, and psychology. Who knows why people do what they do? The point is that they do it, and we can track and measure it with unprecedented fidelity. With enough data, the numbers speak for themselves. (p. 3)

This quotation serves as a useful stepping-off point to examine the extent to which, and in what forms, theory has a role in a credible view of big data science. I begin by rejecting Anderson's (2008) claim that the end of theory is nigh. I then outline and discuss Sabina Leonelli's (2016) novel view that classificatory theories play an indispensable role in data-intensive science. Finally, I argue that scientific theories have no uniform nature or canonical structure, there being a variety of different types of theory serving different purposes in science.

Anderson's (2008) proclamation that the advent of big data spells the end of theory as we know it in science is highly implausible and can be dealt with quickly. The first, and obvious, point to make is that observations (data, facts) are theory-laden, a general conclusion reached in the middle of the last century by prominent philosophers of science such as N. R. Hanson, Thomas Kuhn, and Paul Feyerabend. The theory-ladenness arises unavoidably from various sources, such as human interests, research questions, scientific methods, and theoretical assumptions. Mindful that there are different types of theory-ladenness, it is also useful to distinguish between being theory informed and theory driven. Leonelli (2016) used this distinction to argue that data-centric biology is theory informed but not theory driven, in the sense that it is not concerned with the testing of theories but with the formation of theories that arise out of data-analytic work. Pietsch (2015) similarly argued that frequently used algorithms, such as classificatory trees and nonparametric regression, are theory laden but not in a way that raises questions about the causal structure of the phenomena being examined.

It is worth pointing out here that in his haste to dismiss theory altogether, Anderson (2008) failed to consider the possibility that an instrumentalist conception of scientific theory that does not invoke causal explanations, and that is constructed after the facts are in, might well suit his strong empiricist preferences. As noted in the previous section, B. F. Skinner (1984) did precisely this, while adopting an inductive conception of scientific method.

Classificatory Theories for Big Data Science

As part of her extensive philosophical examination of data-centric biology, Leonelli (2016) argued for the importance of classificatory theories in the field. Although data-centric biology is not coextensive with big data biology, what Leonelli said about classificatory theories has a direct bearing on how one might think about theory in big data science. Rejecting the naive idea that data-intensive science is a theory-free inductive process, she suggested that data curators, in fact, perform the important role of constructing classificatory theories to enable data to "travel" between scientists within, and across, disciplines. For this to happen, "ontologies," or labeling devices (e.g., the "Gene Ontology" project in bioinformatics), based on biological entities and processes used in research, are created to provide the stability needed to search, retrieve, and transport data from databases.

Although Leonelli (2016) sometimes spoke of classificatory theories as networks of ordered terms, she intended them to be understood as networks of interconnected propositions that refer to biological entities and processes. The descriptive sentences contained in the bio-ontologies have the same epistemic function as testable hypotheses. Classificatory theories themselves may be likened to the "bottom-theory" that emerges from the practices of data handling. In this sense, they do not involve theoretical terms that refer to new entities.

Classificatory theories, then, differ from other, more familiar forms of scientific theory, such as those that center on law-like propositions and those that focus on claims about causal mechanisms. Nonetheless, they have several features that philosophers of science identify as the good-making features of theories, even though these features are understood somewhat differently. Leonelli (2016) identified and discussed four important features of classificatory theories: generality, unification, explanation, and synthesizing frameworks. Classificatory theories aim for generality in the form of restricted generalizations that apply locally to narrowly defined domains. They also have unifying power, which is reductive rather than universal, in that they seek commonality among phenomena without embedding them in an overarching conceptual structure. Further, classificatory theories are explanatory in the sense that they answer "how" questions without appeal to law-like statements or mechanisms. However, this criterion for a good classificatory theory is said by Leonelli to be a secondary epistemic virtue, with precedence being given to virtues such as empirical accuracy, breadth of understanding, and heuristic value. However, these three just-mentioned virtues are, in fact, often held to be highly desirable properties of an explanatory theory. Finally, classificatory theories provide perspectives for guiding research that are methodological rather than conceptual; that is, they identify the methodological commitments of specific research programs, rather than broad visions for biological knowledge.

To conclude this brief consideration of classificatory theories, we can say that their presence in data-intensive biology adds to our understanding of theories beyond the more familiar explanatory conceptions of theories discussed by philosophers of science. They also help us to appreciate just how unrealistic it is to portray data-centric and, therefore, big-data science as theory-free inductive undertakings. Finally, the role played by classificatory theories in science is the result of extending the "new experimentalism" in the philosophy of science to a concern with data curation. Before that extension, theory was primarily seen as an explanatory undertaking that only came after a focus on the role that experimental data played as evidence for the establishment of empirical phenomena.

Theories Are Networks With No Canonical Structure

Heavily influenced by Cronbach and Meehl's (1955) groundbreaking paper on construct validity, psychology remains in thrall to the idea that scientific theories are nomological networks—that is, networks of propositions containing laws, with implicit definitions that coordinate observational and theoretical terms. However, this conception of theory, a product of the now outdated mid-20th-century logical empiricist philosophy of science, is ill-suited to psychology. Two reasons for this are that most of psychology does not have genuine laws and that it does not use implicit definitions to coordinate observational and theoretical terms in the network.

More realistically, scientific theories can be conceived as networks of claims about empirical phenomena, models of causal mechanisms, and coherence relations between propositions in the theories. This is the conception of theories that results from using the abductive theory of scientific method. This, too, is a network view of theories, but it is not the nomological network view. Its components are those we find in much scientific theorizing today. Of course, other network formulations of theories are possible, such as those depicted in structural equation models and complex network theory. It is important to appreciate that Leonelli's (2016) classificatory view of theories is explicitly understood by her as a network conception of theories. Cronbach and Meehl (1955) and the logical empiricists were wrong to think that scientific theories could be given a canonical formulation as nomological nets. A more realistic portrayal points to the need for local conceptions of theories that are tailored to a discipline's various natures and achievements, whether that discipline be psychology or not.

CAUSATION, CORRELATION, AND BIG DATA SCIENCE

The idea that modern science frequently makes causal inferences based on correlational data is anathema to some big data science enthusiasts. Well known in this regard is Anderson's (2008) provocative, and cryptic, contention, "Correlation supersedes causation, and science can advance even without coherent models, unified theories, or really mechanistic explanation at all" (para. 18). More recently, and in like manner, Viktor Mayer-Schönberger and Kenneth Cukier (2013) argued that big data science involves a "move away from the age-old search for causality" (p. 14) to correlation.

The claim that correlation supersedes causation will strike many scientists as wrongheaded for the fairly obvious reason that knowledge of causes is a major means by which we come to explain empirical phenomena and increase our understanding of them. Further, knowledge of relevant causes is often found to be useful in applying the findings of science.

When delving into the extensive literature on the nature of causation and its place in science, one is struck by the variety of accounts on offer; there is nothing like a consensus on how we should characterize this important idea. However, rather than seeing this variety as a conflicting diversity, it would be better to think of these accounts as an "amiable jumble" that sustains a realistic attitude of causal pluralism, whereby different accounts of causation are suited to different purposes (Godfrey-Smith, 2009). In what follows, I consider three different accounts of causation, all of which are relevant for understanding big data science. These are the regularity, difference-making, and mechanistic theories of causation.

Causes as Regularities

The idea that correlation supersedes causation was strongly expressed by Karl Pearson, the author of the product-moment correlation, dearly beloved by psychologists. With a strong interest in the philosophy of science, and influenced in particular by the British empiricist philosophers of his day, Pearson (1911) rejected, as metaphysically unacceptable, the idea that causes produce their effects. Instead, he embraced the idea that association, or correlation, was all that there was; functional relations were to be taken as the mark of a mature science. Anderson (2008) was quick to dismiss causation, but one might imagine that Pearson's attitude to causation, and his successor concept of correlation, fit quite well with Anderson's stated rejection of causation in big data science.

Although psychologists make heavy use of Pearson's product-moment correlation, they invariably go beyond its strictures and explicitly engage in causal reasoning. Their causal reasoning follows the dictates of the regularity theory of causation (Harré & Madden, 1975). According to this theory, a causal relation is an actual, or hypothetical, regularity between different variables or events. Further, three conditions are said to be jointly necessary and sufficient for a relationship between variables to be properly judged as causal. In the simple two-variable case: (a) X must precede Y in time, (b) X and Y must covary, and (c) no additional factors can enter into, and confound, the X–Y relationship (e.g., Kenny, 1979). Enshrined in its textbooks, the regularity theory might well be considered psychology's official view of causation. Interestingly, in presenting their considered conception of big data science for organizational science, McAbee, Landis, and Burke (2017) appeared to subscribe to this regularity view of causation.

It is worth pointing out that the third condition of this regularity theory imposes an odd restriction on the causal thinking of its users (Haig, 2003). In ruling out alternative causal interpretations to a direct causal relationship between X and Y, it is simultaneously maintained that the cause, X, in the X–Y relationship must be a direct and, presumably, observed cause. Yet in establishing this requirement, the existence of confounding third variables in causal fields must be considered a genuine possibility. Oddly, these often-unobserved causes are taken to be causally relevant but only for the purpose of discounting their existence! The oddity here lies in the fact that implementing the regularity theory of causation requires the researcher to provisionally step outside its bounds and momentarily adopt a more liberal generative theory of causation (Harré & Madden, 1975), where the third variables are considered as potential productive forces. Despite this oddity, something like the regularity theory of causation might well appeal to those big data scientists who do not want to go beyond the confines of empirical regularities and fathom the workings of underlying causal mechanisms.

Causes as Difference Makers

The second conception of causation expands on the idea that causes are things that make a difference. Happily, one formulation of this account has been explicitly formulated with data-intensive science in mind. In a series of papers, Wolfgang Pietsch (2015, 2016, 2018) developed a philosophically rigorous conception of data-intensive science that subscribes to a difference-making account of causation and an eliminative-inductive conception of scientific method that together help produce useful scientific knowledge about empirical phenomena.

Central to a number of different approaches to causation is the idea that a cause is something that makes a difference to its effects, although there are different accounts of how this idea should be unpacked. One prominent account explicates difference making in terms of claims about counterfactual relationships. In this view, a cause makes a difference to an effect in the sense that if the cause had occurred, so would the effects, and if it had not occurred, the effects would not have occurred either.

Traditional counterfactual approaches to causation determine the truth value of counterfactuals in terms of the rarefied notion of possible world semantics, which is far removed from the practice of actual science. By contrast, Pietsch's (2016) difference-making account of causation is determined by the scientific practice of using the inductive method of difference or its twin, the direct method of agreement. Of relevance for psychological researchers here is the fact that J. S. Mill's joint method of agreement and difference lies behind Fisherian analysis of variance. In his own words, Pietsch brings the scientific method of eliminative induction into play as follows:

> The best known and arguably most effective method is the so-called *method of difference* that establishes causal relevance of a boundary condition CX by comparing two instances which differ only in CX and agree in all other circumstances C. If in one instance, both CX and A are present and in the other both CX and A are absent, then CX is causally relevant to A. There is a twin method to the method of difference, called the *strict method of agreement*, which establishes causal irrelevance, if the change in CX has no influence on A. (p. 8)

Two important points about this gloss on Pietsch's (2016) difference-making account of causation should be made here. First, his account is based on eliminative induction, which focuses on boundary conditions, and it does not lead to a regularity view of causation. The regularity theory, by contrast, is founded on enumerative induction, which is concerned with establishing the number of confirming or disconfirming instances. Second, Pietsch's account of causation is concerned with the causal structure of claims about empirical phenomena and thereby serves a conception of data-intensive science that is concerned with making predictive inferences without appeal to knowledge of underlying causal processes. As I remark in the concluding section, Pietsch's conception of data-intensive science is a new form of empiricism.

Causes as Mechanisms

A third, and important, approach to causation focuses not on difference making but on tracing the causal processes involved in the production of effects. We saw earlier that Anderson's (2008) presentation of big data science eschewed a concern with causal mechanisms. And we have just seen that Pietsch (2016) was clear that his focus on difference making excludes appeal to such processes. However, I submit that one can adopt a defensible perspective on data-intensive science that does concern itself with causal processes. This possibility brings us naturally to mechanistic theories of causation.

Today, mechanistic theories of causation occupy a prominent place in the philosophical literature on causation. Glennan (1996) succinctly characterized the mechanistic approach by declaring that "a relation between two events (other than fundamental physical events) is causal when and only when these events are connected in the appropriate way by a mechanism" (p. 56). As such, the mechanistic account goes well beyond the strictures of the regularity account of causation; the mechanisms and their components are, by their very nature, productive of change. About the idea of a mechanism itself, Bechtel and Abrahamsen (2005) said, "A mechanism is a structure performing a function in virtue of its component parts, component operations, and their organization. The orchestrated functioning of the mechanism is responsible for one or more phenomena" (p. 423).

In psychology, the adoption of the explanatory practice of identifying complex mechanisms to help explain psychological phenomena is more widespread than is generally realized. Generically, the research strategy involves the decomposition of hierarchically organized systems into their components and operations and then building models to understand better the organization that comprises the mechanisms' activities. The rise of the information-processing perspective in psychology explicitly adopted this mechanistic strategy at the level of the person, with the test-operate-test-exit unit being a clear case in point. More recent examples from cognitive psychology that focus on subpersonal mechanisms can be found in Wright and Bechtel (2007).

From Data to Mechanisms: A Hybrid Model

The received view in the philosophy of biology depicts molecular biology as using strategies and methods that facilitate the discovery of causal mechanisms (Craver & Darden, 2013). Today, molecular biology is home to the most concerted debates about whether the advent of big data has ushered in a new data-driven view of science that replaces its traditional search for causal mechanisms (Leonelli, 2016). One instructive reconstruction of some parts of contemporary biological research is offered by Ratti (2015), who rejected the view that the two approaches represent separate lines of inquiry. Instead, he presented a hybrid model that combines both data-driven and hypothesis-driven approaches.

The idea is that, first, data-driven strategies are used to generate hypotheses. Then, hypotheses are developed and tested with methods that enable the discovery of causal mechanisms. This hybrid formulation of data-driven and hypothesis-driven research comprises three phases: (a) the initial formulation of a set of competing hypotheses; (b) the elimination of false, or less probable, hypotheses; and (c) the testing or validation of hypotheses that have not been eliminated in the second phase. Taken together, the first two phases constitute a strategy involving eliminative inference in which implausible hypotheses are discarded. In addition to discarding hypotheses, the second phase involves the prioritization of hypotheses that seem worth retaining and submitting them to stronger testing in the third phase. A sophisticated view of the hypothetico-deductive method has a legitimate role to play in this third phase.

It should be made clear that not all data-driven research fits this hybrid model of inquiry. For instance, data-mining studies, in the form of exploratory experiments, do not directly form part of the hybrid model, although they might provide guidelines for eliminative inference that is itself used in the hybrid model (Ratti, 2015). Further, the data-driven–hypothesis-driven sequence is just one way in which researchers attempt to get a purchase on causal mechanisms. Finally, this composite research strategy, with mechanistic causation as the focus of its third phase, can be understood more deeply by placing it within the broader framework of the philosophy of science known as the "new mechanical philosophy," a philosophy that centers on historically informed scientific practices to do with discovery, modelling, and explanation (Craver & Darden, 2013). Moreover, this philosophy might naturally be considered something of a local realist philosophy of science for big data science.

Some big data science enthusiasts claim that causation should be jettisoned and that correlational information alone is sufficient for science ("correlation supersedes causation"). However, we have seen that some sophisticated philosophical analyses of big data science do, in fact, make explicit use of causal thinking and thereby join with other modes of scientific research in claiming that causal inferences can be based on correlational data ("correlation implies causation"). Because different accounts of causation have different positive features, I think that big data science should accommodate a plurality of conceptions of causation, including regularity and mechanistic theories, but also conceptions of causality that do not appeal to causal mechanisms, such as the difference-making account.

CONCLUSION

In discussing big data science from a philosophy of science perspective, I have presented many different ideas. I conclude by summarizing the main points before offering some closing remarks.

- The three revolutionary claims, frequently mentioned in discussions of big data science, that it should eschew scientific method, explanatory theory, and causal knowledge, are implausible. All three endeavors remain vitally important for successful science.

- The abductive theory of scientific method can provide a useful methodological perspective for big data science. Further, the alternative perspectival accounts of scientific method of Pietsch (2016) and Ratti (2015) should also be understood as having decent, but different, philosophical justifications that can be used to support their adoption.

- Inductive, abductive, and hypothetico-deductive theories of scientific method can each be used to help meet their appropriate and different research goals in both big and small data science. Inductive method plays an important role in the detection of empirical phenomena, different abductive methods combine to enable the construction of explanatory theories, and a modified hypothetico-deductive account of method can be used to test knowledge claims produced by the implementation of big data research strategies.

- There is no canonical formulation of scientific theories. Instead, there are different conceptions of theories, expressed as networks of propositions, each of which has a legitimate claim to representing knowledge claims. The idea of classificatory theories is an important addition to our inventory of scientific theories that comes directly from the field of data-intensive biology.

- A pluralist attitude to big data science that allows different conceptions of causation to operate is needed to contribute to the variety of causal claims made in scientific research. At a minimum, this will include the regularity, difference-making, and mechanistic theories.

I bring this concluding section to an end with three briefly stated thoughts. First, we have seen that big data science has a variety of defensible formulations. So, it is inappropriate to characterize it as a new paradigm, at least in Kuhn's (1970) sense of that idea. Like the rest of science, it is multiparadigmatic and, therefore, theoretically pluralist.

Second, the ability to fashion realist construals of big data science allows us to understand "flattened," seemingly empiricist, characterizations of big data science as locally realist in character. For example, Leonelli's (2016) philosophical treatment of data-centric biology, with its sponsorship of classificatory theories, is nonetheless seen by her as consistent with Hasok Chang's (2012) brand of scientific realism, a form of realism that endorses a strong form of methodological pluralism and rejects the standard realist view that truth is paramount in science in favor of an emphasis on scientific progress. However, given Pietsch's (2016) reluctance to go beyond empirical phenomena, his take on data-intensive science is better seen as a limited brand of local empiricism.

Finally, it is a significant truism that science, as we know it, is a human endeavor and that human judgment is unavoidably involved in the production of its knowledge claims. At the same time, the emergence of big data science helps us to see that, as more science is carried out automatically through the use of electronic devices, parts of it can be seen as less of a human activity (Lyon, 2016). This trend can be viewed as one aspect of the evolutionary march of science for "limited beings," a conception of science for which William Wimsatt's (2007) local realist philosophy is explicitly devised. However, it should be appreciated that this is a perspectival realism, in the sense that science cannot rise above our human cognitive framework. Werner Callebaut (2012) also said that perspectival realism is the most appropriate philosophy for big data biological science. For both philosophers, perspectival realism has the value of emphasizing the complex, pluralist, and pragmatist nature of science. Future work on the conceptual foundations of big data science would do well to consider seriously this important formulation of realism.

REFERENCES

Anderson, C. (2008, June). The end of theory: The data deluge makes the scientific method obsolete. *Wired Magazine*. Retrieved from http://www.wired.com/science/discoveries/magazine/16-07/pb_theory

Bechtel, W., & Abrahamsen, A. (2005). Explanation: A mechanist alternative. *Studies in History and Philosophy of Biological and Biomedical Sciences, 36*, 421–441. http://dx.doi.org/10.1016/j.shpsc.2005.03.010

Bunge, M. (1990). What kind of discipline is psychology: Autonomous or dependent, humanistic or scientific, biological or sociological? *New Ideas in Psychology, 8*, 121–137. http://dx.doi.org/10.1016/0732-118X(90)90002-J

Callebaut, A. F. W. (2012). Scientific perspectivism: A philosopher of science's response to the challenge of big data biology. *Studies in History and Philosophy of Biological and Biomedical Sciences, 43*, 69–80. http://dx.doi.org/10.1016/j.shpsc.2011.10.007

Chalmers, A. F. (2013). *What is this thing called science?* (4th ed.). St. Lucia, Australia: University of Queensland Press.

Chang, H. (2012). *Is water H₂O? Evidence, realism, and pluralism.* Dordrecht, The Netherlands: Springer. http://dx.doi.org/10.1007/978-94-007-3932-1

Craver, C. F., & Darden, L. (2013). *In search of mechanisms.* Chicago, IL: University of Chicago Press. http://dx.doi.org/10.7208/chicago/9780226039824.001.0001

Cronbach, L. J., & Meehl, P. E. (1955). Construct validity in psychological tests. *Psychological Bulletin, 52*, 281–302. http://dx.doi.org/10.1037/h0040957

Curd, M. (1980). The logic of discovery: An analysis of three approaches. In T. Nickles (Ed.), *Scientific discovery, logic, and rationality* (pp. 201–219). Dordrecht, The Netherlands: Reidel. http://dx.doi.org/10.1007/978-94-009-8986-3_8

Fox, P., & Hendler, J. (2014). The science of data science. *Big Data, 2*, 68–70. http://dx.doi.org/10.1089/big.2014.0011

Glennan, S. (1996). Mechanisms and the nature of causation. *Erkenntnis, 44,* 50–71. http://dx.doi.org/10.1007/BF00172853

Godfrey-Smith, P. (2009). Causal pluralism. In H. Beebee, P. Menzies, & C. Hitchcock (Eds.), *The Oxford handbook of causation* (pp. 326–337). New York, NY: Oxford University Press.

Haig, B. D. (2003). What is a spurious correlation? *Understanding Statistics, 2,* 125–132. http://dx.doi.org/10.1207/S15328031US0202_03

Haig, B. D. (2005). An abductive theory of scientific method. *Psychological Methods, 10,* 371–388. http://dx.doi.org/10.1037/1082-989X.10.4.371

Haig, B. D. (2014). *Investigating the psychological world: Scientific method in the behavioral sciences.* Cambridge, MA: MIT Press. http://dx.doi.org/10.7551/mitpress/9780262027366.001.0001

Haig, B. D., & Evers, C. W. (2016). *Realist inquiry in social science.* Los Angeles, CA: Sage.

Harlow, L. L., & Oswald, F. L. (2016). Big data in psychology: Introduction to the special issue. *Psychological Methods, 21,* 447–457. http://dx.doi.org/10.1037/met0000120

Harré, R., & Madden, E. H. (1975). *Causal powers: A theory of natural necessity.* Oxford, England: Basil Blackwell.

Hey, A. J. G., Tansley, S., & Tolle, K. (2009). *Jim Gray on escience: A transformed scientific method.* In A. J. G. Hey, S. Tansley, & K. Tolle (Eds.), *The fourth paradigm: Data-intensive scientific discovery* (pp. xvii–xxxi). Redmond, WA: Microsoft Research.

Kenny, D. (1979). *Correlation and causation.* New York, NY: Wiley.

Kitchin, R. (2014). Big data, new epistemologies, and paradigm shifts. *Big Data & Society, 1,* 1–12. http://dx.doi.org/10.1177/2053951714528481

Kuhn, T. S. (1970). *The structure of scientific revolutions* (2nd ed.). Chicago, IL: University of Chicago Press.

Leonelli, S. (2016). *Data-centric biology: A philosophical study.* Chicago, IL: University of Chicago Press. http://dx.doi.org/10.7208/chicago/9780226416502.001.0001

Locke, E. A. (2015). Theory building, replication, and behavioral priming: Where do we need to go from here? *Perspectives on Psychological Science, 10,* 408–414. http://dx.doi.org/10.1177/1745691614567231

Lyon, A. (2016). Data. In P. Humphreys (Ed.), *The Oxford handbook of philosophy of science* (pp. 738–758). New York, NY: Oxford University Press.

Magnani, L. (2001). *Abduction, reason, and science: Processes of discovery and explanation.* New York, NY: Kluwer/Plenum. http://dx.doi.org/10.1007/978-1-4419-8562-0

Mayer-Schönberger, V., & Cukier, K. (2013). *Big data: A revolution that will transform how we live, work, and think.* Boston, MA: Houghton Mifflin Harcourt.

McAbee, S. T., Landis, R. S., & Burke, M. I. (2017). Inductive reasoning: The promise of big data. *Human Resource Management Review, 27,* 277–290. http://dx.doi.org/10.1016/j.hrmr.2016.08.005

Nickles, T. (1987). Methodology, heuristics, and rationality. In J. C. Pitt & M. Pera (Eds.), *Rational changes in science* (pp. 103–132). Dordrecht, The Netherlands: Reidel. http://dx.doi.org/10.1007/978-94-009-3779-6_5

Oswald, F. L., & Putka, D. J. (2016). Statistical methods for big data: A scenic tour. In E. B. King & J. M. Cortina (Eds.), *Big data at work: The data science revolution and organizational psychology* (pp. 43–63). New York, NY: Routledge.

Pearson, K. (1911). *The grammar of science* (3rd ed.). London, England: Adam & Charles Black.

Pietsch, W. (2015). Aspects of theory-ladenness in data-intensive science. *Philosophy of Science, 82,* 905–916. http://dx.doi.org/10.1086/683328

Pietsch, W. (2016). The causal nature of modeling with big data. *Philosophy & Technology, 29,* 137–171. http://dx.doi.org/10.1007/s13347-015-0202-2

Pietsch, W. (2018). *Big data: The new science of complexity.* Unpublished manuscript.

Ratti, E. (2015). Big data biology: Between eliminative inferences and exploratory experiments. *Philosophy of Science, 82,* 198–218. http://dx.doi.org/10.1086/680332

Skinner, B. F. (1984). Methods and theories in the experimental analysis of behavior. *Behavioral and Brain Sciences, 7,* 511–523. http://dx.doi.org/10.1017/S0140525X00026996

Thagard, P. (1992). *Conceptual revolutions.* Princeton, NJ: Princeton University Press. http://dx.doi.org/10.1515/9780691186672

Tonidandel, S., King, E. B., & Cortina, J. M. (2018). Big data methods: Leveraging modern data analytic techniques to build organizational science. *Organizational Research Methods, 21,* 525–547. http://dx.doi.org/10.1177/1094428116677299

Wimsatt, W. (2007). *Re-engineering philosophy for limited beings: Piecewise approximations to reality.* Cambridge, MA: Harvard University Press.

Wright, C., & Bechtel, W. (2007). Mechanisms and psychological explanation. In P. Thagard (Ed.), *Philosophy of psychology and cognitive science* (pp. 31–79). Amsterdam, The Netherlands: Elsevier. http://dx.doi.org/10.1016/B978-044451540-7/50019-0

2

From Small-Scale Experiments to Big Data

Challenges and Opportunities for Experimental Psychologists

Robert W. Proctor and Aiping Xiong

In 2000, 25% of the world's information was stored electronically, whereas, by 2013, this value was 98% (Cukier & Mayer-Schoenberger, 2013). Moore's Law estimated that the density of transistors on an integrated circuit board was doubling every 2 years (Moore, 1965). The growth rate of the networked, digitized, and sensor-laden data volumes in the current information age is estimated to be even faster (Coffman & Odlyzko, 2002; National Institute of Science and Technology [NIST], 2014). *Big data*, a term coined and made popular by John Mashey (1998), is a buzzword that has come to be used with increasing frequency over the past 2 decades (Cukier & Mayer-Schoenberger, 2013). It refers in general to large data sets, but there is little agreement as to exactly what the term means and whether it even has a meaning on which almost everyone can agree (e.g., Boyd & Crawford, 2012; Gandomi & Haider, 2015; Ward & Barker, 2013). Beyond that, there is no clear definition or understanding of the role of big data in the psychological sciences. What are the opportunities that it affords? What methodological tools does a researcher in psychology have to know to be able to exploit those opportunities? How can big data research be integrated with smaller-scale experimental research? These and other questions have to be answered satisfactorily if its scientific value to the psychological research community is to be realized.

In this chapter, we address those questions and other issues from the perspective of experimental psychologists—more specifically, empirically oriented cognitive psychologists who take a human information-processing approach in contemporary psychology. Experimental psychology was at the forefront of establishing psychology as a scientific discipline because the control in

http://dx.doi.org/10.1037/0000193-003
Big Data in Psychological Research, S. E. Woo, L. Tay, and R. W. Proctor (Editors)

laboratory settings affords the highest internal validity. Early experimental research primarily examined and reported data of a few individual participants (e.g., Hall & Motora, 1887). However, in the mid 20th century, there was a shift to an emphasis on group designs with relatively small samples of participants in which comparisons between conditions were made using inferential statistics (Danziger, 1994). Although small-scale laboratory experiments continue to be the rule, online research platforms, large databases, and the rapidly increasing interconnectivity of devices of all types open unprecedented opportunities for experimental psychologists to conduct research for situations with higher external and ecological validity, using larger samples or population-level data (Lazer et al., 2009). We briefly describe the evolution of research methodology in the experimental tradition and use it as a mirror to reflect how to construct the language and tools appropriate for the "big data" era.

RESEARCH METHODOLOGY IN THE EXPERIMENTAL TRADITION

Single-Subject Research

Among the earliest research that can be classified as experimental psychology are the psychophysical studies of Ernst H. Weber (1834, 1851, 1996) and Gustav T. Fechner (1860/1966). Their psychophysical methods, variants of which continue to be used, focused on obtaining thresholds or other measurements from individual well-trained observers to specify relations between physical stimuli and their sensations (Gescheider, 1997). The observer in the psychophysical studies of the 1800s was often the experimenter. For example, Weber (1996) said, in his investigations of the tactile senses, "My propositions are tested more extensively by the many observations I have performed on my own body" (p. 33). Psychophysical research continues to the present day, with an emphasis on fitting models to data from individual participants (e.g., Dyre & Hollands, 2016).

Chronometric studies using reaction time as the dependent measure also were conducted in the latter half of the 1800s. Franciscus C. Donders (1868/1969) performed analyses of reaction time in simple (one response to one stimulus; *a* reaction), choice (one response to one stimulus, another response to the other stimulus; *b* reaction), and go–no-go (one response to one of two stimuli; *c* reaction) reaction tasks to estimate the time required for elementary mental processes. In some cases, he tested only himself and a graduate student. For example, he subtracted the reaction time to repeat a single, known vowel sound spoken by the experimenter from the reaction time to repeat one or the other of two possible vowel sounds (p. 420) to estimate the combined time required for stimulus identification and "expression of the will" (i.e., response selection; p. 423). For other experiments, Donders presented results from three to five participants, sometimes averaged across the participants.

Wilhelm M. Wundt and his students continued the chronometric tradition of measuring reaction times, adopting a set-up in which three persons rotated through the roles of subject, experimenter, and observer (Robinson, 2001).

They added a *d* reaction (discrimination) for which the trained subject was to make a single response when the stimulus that occurred was discriminated from the alternatives (i.e., identified). This subjective decision was intended to be a measure of the time for what Wundt called "apperception." Wundt also used a method of controlled introspection in which the trained subjects made simple judgments of internal perception such as size, intensity, or duration of basic sensory stimuli (Danziger, 1994; Wundt, 1897). Hermann Ebbinghaus (1885/1964) laid the groundwork for the study of human learning and memory by memorizing lists of nonsense syllables himself and examining how various factors such as number of repetitions affected their retention when tested later.

In the first decade of the 20th century, Oswald Külpe and the psychologists of the Würzburg school extended the laboratory introspective methods to study preparatory processes and higher-level thought processes (Ach, 1905/1964; Hoffmann, Stock, & Deutsch, 1996). Introspection under controlled conditions was also promulgated in the United States during the same period by Edward B. Titchener, who, like Külpe, used it to study memory, thought, and feelings, as well as sensory elements. Titchener (1903) said, "The method of psychology is the method of experimental introspection. Only by looking inward can we gain knowledge of mental processes; only by looking inward under standard conditions can we make our knowledge scientific" (p. 32). Use of the method produced detailed reports of individual participants under various experimental conditions (e.g., Geissler, 1912; see also Pratt, 1924). However, introspection fell out of favor as the primary research method from about 1915 onward, particularly in the United States, as behaviorism came to predominate (Weiss, 1924).

The primary point of this section is that the initial experimental research in psychological science focused mainly on data obtained from individual participants in situations that differed in the types and volumes of data that were produced. All required relatively sophisticated methods for analysis and interpretation.

Group Designs and the Analysis of Variance

Coinciding with the decrease in emphasis on introspection, an increase in reports of group data occurred in the middle of the 20th century. Although single-subject research continues to be conducted to this day, group designs predominate. Danziger (1994) found that for three major experimental psychology journals (*American Journal of Psychology*, *Psychological Monographs*, *Journal of Experimental Psychology*), reports of individual data predominated in the period 1914–1916, whereas by 1949–1951 only about 20% of articles reported any individual data, even as secondary to group data. Researchers summarized the results from these group research designs in a variety of ways, and the designs often used only a single independent variable (e.g., Lambert & Ewart, 1932). Thus, research data had increased from measures of individual participants to more complex group designs by the early 1950s.

Of importance, Ronald Fisher (1925, 1935) wrote influential books on statistics and experimental methods, targeted for agricultural researchers, which introduced the analysis of variance (ANOVA). In those books, Fisher advocated the use of factorial experimental designs in which the separate and combined effects of two or more variables can be examined together. His books also provided the means and logic for null hypothesis testing, which became customary in experimental psychology. Rucci and Tweney (1980) noted that the ANOVA was used in the early 1940s in only a few psychology studies, but by 1952 almost all published articles reported ANOVAs. Since then, small group designs and inferential statistical tests like the ANOVA have predominated. Typically, the null hypothesis is that there is no effect of an independent variable, and rejection of the null hypothesis allows the researcher to rule out that chance alone was operating. Gigerenzer and Murray (1987) called this shift to hypothesis testing in group designs the *inference revolution*. Although debates about the adequacy of null hypothesis testing have been ongoing for years (e.g., Tijmstra, 2018), its logic continues to be followed in most psychological research.

The Information-Processing Revolution

The inference revolution was one of three pillars of a larger revolution in the language and methods of psychology that occurred during 1940–1955 (Xiong & Proctor, 2018). Although this revolution is often called the cognitive revolution, we argue that it is more aptly labeled the *information-processing revolution*. As Mandler (2007) emphasized, cognitive psychology existed before the 20th century and continued throughout the first half of that century, when behaviorism directed most research in the United States. The key change that occurred in the 1950s that resulted in the rise in prominence of cognitive psychology was the advent of the information-processing approach in experimental psychology. The central aspect of the information-processing revolution was the adoption of a new language of concepts and analytical methods, including those provided by probability theory and inferential statistics.

The most important pillar in the revolution is the concept of control systems, which formed the heart of *cybernetics*, an interdisciplinary approach spearheaded by Norbert Wiener (1948). A central thesis of cybernetics is that information is essential to communication and that levels ranging from basic physiology to society can be characterized in terms of control systems with feedback loops. Ashby (1956) and MacKay (1956) put more emphasis on the role of feedforward control as means for the anticipation of future events and actions, which is increasingly incorporated into models of selection and control of action (e.g., Lu, Bilaloglu, Aluru, & Raghavan, 2015). The framework of control systems forms the basis for analyzing human information processing. Closely related to the cybernetics pillar is that of information theory, or communication theory, founded by Claude Shannon (1948), that quantified information in terms of the amount of entropy, or uncertainty, which in simplified form is often given as $\log_2 N$ bits, with N being the number of equally likely alternatives. Shannon's information metric captured the relation that the more uncertainty that existed, the greater the information conveyed by an event. Cybernetics and information theory laid the foundation for psychologists to begin conceiving of humans as information-processing systems that could themselves be thought of as subsystems of larger systems with machines, other humans, and societal organizations of various types.

The pillar of statistical inference is of particular relevance to psychological research. As noted, Fisher's ANOVA provided the tool for partitioning variance in multifactor group designs, allowing for the systematic study of interactions between variables. Also, as Gigerenzer et al. (1989) emphasized, the effects on psychological research were far reaching: "When psychologists adopted inference statistics as a tool of the trade, they also came to view the same technique as models of the mind" (p. xv). Methodological tools were among the many offspring of statistical decision theory and probability. These include signal detection theory for analyzing decision processes (Green & Swets, 1966), additive factors analysis of reaction times to identify the processing stages affected by specific variables (Sternberg, 1969), and probabilistic accumulation models of reaction times and errors (Donkin, Brown, Heathcote, & Wagenmakers, 2011). It is fair to say that the information-processing approach and sampling designs to which inferential statistics are applied have predominated in experimental psychology from the 1950s to the present.

The information-processing revolution has several implications for the current big data era. First, the advances that led to the revolution in psychology (e.g., inferential statistics, cybernetics, and information theory) were interdisciplinary and largely outside of psychology. The impact of those advances occurred through their being incorporated into psychology and elaborated by psychologists for their purposes. Second, the three pillars provided conceptual language that allowed communication between psychologists and nonpsychologists, as well as effective ways to frame and articulate the research questions. Third, the advances in inferential statistics and experimental design, and information theory, provided specific analytical tools for quantifying uncertainty. The former allowed interactions of variables in controlled experiments to be examined and extracted, whereas the latter provided a formal means for calculating information based on entropy. In total, the information-processing revolution provided an appropriate psychology for the information age. As we enter the big data era, this depiction suggests that (a) interdisciplinary work should be key for psychologists to understand big data, (b) the goals of cognitive psychology should be borne in mind for its effective use, and (c) appropriate conceptual language and analytical tools have to be formalized.

EXPERIMENTAL PSYCHOLOGY IN THE ERA OF BIG DATA

What Is Big Data?

To evaluate the possible value of big data to experimental psychologists, it is necessary to define first what the concept of big data means in general and for psychologists. The International Standards Organization defined big data as follows:

> Big Data is a data set(s) with characteristics (e.g., *volume, velocity, variety, variability, veracity* [emphasis added], etc.) that for a particular problem domain at a given point in time cannot be efficiently processed using current/existing/established/traditional technologies and techniques in order to extract value. (ISO/IEC, 2015, p. 8)

To represent a fundamental change in the architecture needed to handle current data sets efficiently, *volume* refers to the magnitude of data, with big data typically reported in multiple terabytes, petabytes (10^3 terabytes equals to 1 petabyte), and exabytes (10^3 petabytes). It was predicted that in the next few years, the volume of data will increase to zettabytes due to the increased use of mobile devices and social media (Katal, Wazid, & Goudar, 2013). *Variety* refers to the structural heterogeneity in a data set (e.g., structured or unstructured data from multiple repositories, domains, or type). Whetsel and Qu (2017) noted that, unlike volume, variety is not easily quantifiable and proposed a measure of the impact of variety on a big data set based on Kolmogorov's (1968) complexity theory, which is derived from information theory and probability theory. *Velocity* refers to the rate at which data are generated and the speed at which those data should be analyzed and acted on. *Variability* represents the change in other characteristics (e.g., variation in the data flow rates), whereas *Veracity* refers to imprecision and uncertainty in data.

With regard to psychology, opportunities are embedded within each of the characteristics of big data. First, the volume of the big data affords the collection of measures from larger and more diverse samples than can be studied in traditional laboratory experiments (e.g., college students). For example, Thorstad and Wolff (2018) conducted a large-scale analysis of Twitter users' tweets to measure future thinking, noting that the level of education, gender composition, income level, and urban versus rural residence of Twitter users are representative of the broader population. Their initial study established "a link between future thinking and decision-making at the population level in showing that US states with citizens having relatively far future sightedness, as reflected in their tweets, take fewer risks than citizens in states having relatively near future sightedness" (p. 1). They reported additional studies that investigated this relation in more detail, providing evidence that the influence of future sightedness on decisions may be through its causing the future to be perceived as more connected to the present.

For variety, information about human behavior can be recorded along many dimensions (e.g., text, audio, video), which enables investigation of factors that cannot be considered within the laboratory. Variety also opens the opportunity for collaboration across laboratories and platforms to expand the understanding of those potential measures. The velocity with which data can be collected provides opportunities to investigate human behaviors in larger spatial and time scales than in laboratory settings, allowing location-dependent and time-dependent comparisons as well. As an example, the variety and velocity of data on social media platforms offer opportunities for investigations of sentiment analysis of people's thoughts, for which data are classified into positive, negative, and neutral categories (Andrade & Santos, 2017; Poria, Cambria, Howard, Huang, & Hussain, 2016). Poria et al. (2016) noted that sentiment analysis has typically been conducted through natural language processing but emphasized that it can benefit from fusing audio, visual, and textual clues from multimodal content on social media platforms.

As another example, the number of devices worldwide connected to the Internet (called the Internet of Things) is predicted to increase from about 15 billion in 2015 to 30 billion in 2020 and 75 billion in 2025 (Dull, 2014; Statista, 2018), providing a vast variety of data. This increase in volume from devices is mainly data collected by cameras, sensors, radar, and lidar (which measures distances by illuminating a target with pulsed laser light). These data primarily concern people's interactions with the physical world. Using sufficiently detailed traces, the cyber-physical system can establish a human behavior model to improve human well-being. For example, sensors embedded in the home environment can monitor the physical environment and a person's activities within it. The collected data can provide a record for algorithms to learn the relative frequencies of different behavioral patterns (Dahmen, Thomas, Cook, & Wang, 2017) to control the home environment and home security, as well as provide data for research purposes.

For variability and veracity, an opportunity is to examine probabilistic aspects of human behavior in specific situations, uncovering the ecological validity that is difficult to study within laboratory settings. For example, how do the veracity (noise), variety (data heterogeneity), and velocity (rapidly changing data) of the data influence decisions that people make based on big data (Janssen, van der Voort, & Wahyudi, 2017)?

Despite those opportunities afforded by big data, the data explosion raises significant challenges for experimental psychologists due to its various characteristics. For the value of big data to be unearthed, experimental psychologists should address the issues accompanying data collection, data analysis, and data inference and application.

Obtaining and Using Big Data

The analytic processes of big data, collectively known as *data science*, refer to the extraction of actionable knowledge directly from data through a process of discovery, or hypothesis formulation about data patterns and testing them (NIST, 2014). Therefore, proper conduct of big data analysis requires awareness of the source and origin of the data, the appropriateness and accuracy of the transformation on the data, and the interplay of the transformation algorithm with processes and data storage mechanisms.

Nowadays, big data are typically collected and maintained by diverse companies and platforms (e.g., Amazon, Facebook, Google). Although those data are of much interest to cognitive psychologists, how to get access to those data is not transparent or sometimes difficult due to concerns such as privacy (see Chapter 18, this volume). Moreover, recently, those companies reduced their sharing of data, as did Twitter.

As expressed previously, Twitter provides a rich source of people's comments concerning various issues and events. Many researchers who might be able to make use of data from Twitter are probably unaware of how to acquire the data. Littman (2017) listed four ways: (a) retrieve data from the Twitter public application programming interface (API), (b) locate a preexisting Twitter data set, (c) purchase a data set from Twitter, or (d) access or purchase a data set from a Twitter service provider. Several tools exist for retrieving data from the public API that simplify the process and analysis of the data. Data sets for topics such as the federal government exist that can be used in research. However, whereas Twitter previously provided access to several APIs for researchers at major universities, Twitter recently reduced the sampling of existing APIs such that researchers increasingly question its utility for basic social science (Pfeffer, Mayer, & Morstatter, 2019). For example, free, standard APIs from Twitter include only filtered and sampled tweets from the past 7 days (Twitter, 2018). Although those data allow researchers to address some problems in which they are interested, it becomes difficult for researchers to analyze the problems as thoroughly as they may want to. The two options of purchasing data sets may be useful, but they are also limited to researchers who are able to pay the costs.

A viable alternative that has become popular with experimental psychologists in recent years is crowdsourcing sites such as Amazon Mechanical Turk and CrowdFlower (Figure Eight), which allow a more general population of computer users worldwide to participate in studies. These populations are larger and more varied than an undergraduate student population within a single university, and the velocity with which data can be collected is greater (Keith, Tay, & Harms, 2017). Crowdsourcing research has been widely accepted and put to many uses by experimental psychologists in, for example, studies of sequential action (e.g., Behmer & Crump, 2017) and memory (e.g., Weinstein, Nunes, & Karpicke, 2016). The main attractions of crowdsourcing research for experimental psychologists are that independent variables can still be manipulated, and large amounts of data can be collected quickly relative to similar studies conducted in the laboratory (though with more variation in settings).

The relatively large amounts of data can allow factors to be examined that could not be meaningfully measured in small-scale laboratory experiments. For example, Yang, Li, Chowdhury, Xiong, and Proctor (2016) conducted a study evaluating performance in generating and recalling passwords using various mnemonic strategies, for which a total of 6,236 participants were tested in two experiments. The large number of participants allowed examination of the relative frequency of "collisions" of passwords—that is, those created by more than one user—for each strategy. This measure is important for cybersecurity purposes because entropy is reduced as the redundancy among passwords increases. The success of crowdsourcing research depends on adequate consideration of its unique methodological concerns (Buhrmester, Talaifar, & Gosling, 2018), especially incomplete information about the participants' behaviors (e.g., whether to-be-remembered words were written down) and the research environment (e.g., details of the presentation platform).

Researchers could also create platforms themselves to collect big data. For example, Stafford and Dewar (2014) examined skill learning in a sample of more than 850,000 players of an online game called Axon. This game was designed with code that registered the identity of a machine each time the game was loaded on it and recorded the date and time of play, as well as the score. This massive data set allowed the researchers to "slice" the data to examine subsets of individuals that met various conditions and to use boot-strapping methods to test sophisticated null hypotheses. They were able to confirm lawful relations established in the experimental literature and show that greater variation in performance across initial sessions was related to better subsequent performance.

For data analysis, the challenges start from the processing and cleaning of big data's content and structure into formats usable for research purposes (Endel & Piringer, 2015). At the same time, the collected behavioral and environmental data may be incomplete and possibly erroneous, which requires methods to detect and deal with the issues appropriately. Also, the traditional null hypothesis testing at .05 alpha level loses its meaning because very small and practically insignificant effects can be statistically significant due to the large sample sizes. Thus, one obvious accompanying challenge is how to extract meaningful information and prediction from the mass of data. One solution is to place more emphasis on computational modeling. Psychologists have started to apply modeling methods that developed at the intersection of statistics and computer sciences, such as data mining (Stanton, 2013) and machine learning (e.g., Jones, Willits, Dennis, & Jones, 2015; see Hussain, Cambria, Schuller, & Howard, 2014, for other applications).

Traditionally, psychological research relies heavily on hypothesis testing, an approach including deductive reasoning, empirical testing, and theory confirmation (Haig, 2014) and falsification (Popper, 1962). In contrast, the available big data research requires researchers to pursue, at least in part, a bottom-up approach, in which insights are generated from learning about the data. Abductive reasoning, which can use an iterative combination of inductive and deductive reasoning, has been proposed to formalize theories and test hypotheses using big data to inform the development of psychology (see Chapter 1, this volume, for a detailed discussion).

Role of Big Data From Experimentalists' Perspective

In the prior section, we discussed different opportunities and challenges of big data for experimental psychology from big data's perspective. Nevertheless, from a system viewpoint, the scientific psychologist should have unambiguous research goals for which analyses of big data seem to inform the ultimate quest of cognitive psychology. Specifically, using big data to address the issues or limitations of current cognitive psychology research may make big data research more informative than it would be otherwise. For example, Griffiths (2015, p. 22) called for a new cognitive revolution, stating, "Ubiquitous records of human behavior offer the potential to study human cognition at a scale and level of validity that could never be achieved in the laboratory." Goldstone and Lupyan (2016) emphasized the potential benefit of big data research for virtually all areas of human experimental psychology, stating, "When creatively interrogated, a diverse range of large, real-world data sets provides powerful diagnostic tools for revealing principles of human judgment, perception, categorization, decision-making, language use, inference, problem solving, and representation" (p. 548).

Contemporary cognitive psychology is mainly developed through means of controlled experiments conducted in the laboratory. Researchers have isolated effects of specific variables on task performance and neurophysiological measures, increasing understanding of perception, cognition, and action. Although much of the research has used group designs, the increase in understanding has occurred mainly at the level of the individual—for example, how working memory limitations affect performance. Typically, the generalizability of cognitive psychology principles outside of the lab has been challenged because the majority of laboratory research is not representative of the natural environment (i.e., having low ecological validity) and there is a lack of consideration of social factors beyond the individual that may affect behaviors (e.g., Hirst & Manier, 1995). However, the principles have proved to be useful for the development of designed systems with human-machine and human-computer interactions (Proctor & Vu, 2010), as well as for understanding many other aspects of human behavior (Healy & Bourne, 2011).

Newell (1990) proposed a categorization of human action that differentiates bands in different time scales (see Table 2.1). Note that the third column

TABLE 2.1. Categorization of Human Action

Scale (in seconds)	Time units	System	Band
10^7	months		Social
10^6	weeks		
10^5	days		
10^4	hours	Task	Rational
10^3	10 min	Task	
10^2	min	Task	
10^1	10 s	Unit task	Cognitive
10^0	1 s	Operations	
10^{-1}	100 ms	Deliberate act	
10^{-2}	10 ms	Neural circuit	Biological
10^{-3}	1 ms	Neuron	
10^{-4}	100 us	Organelle	

Note. From *Unified Theories of Cognition* (p. 122), by A. Newell, 1990, Cambridge, MA: Harvard University Press. Copyright 1990 by Harvard University Press. Adapted with permission.

from the left is labeled *System*, in agreement with the view that the cybernetic system approach is relevant to all time scales of human action. Most knowledge acquired by experimental psychologists concerns the cognitive band of 100 milliseconds to 10 seconds (e.g., attentional limits, stimulus-response compatibility effects on response selection, decision making), and some involve the rational band of minutes to hours (e.g., problem solving).

However, the approach based on laboratory experiments is of limited applicability to what Newell called the *social* band of days and months, as illustrated by the blank region under the system column at the social band level. The increasing availability of big data concerning many aspects of human behavior provides not only an opportunity for experimental psychologists to expand knowledge at the levels of the cognitive and rational bands but also an opportunity to extend their understanding of human action to the social band. The social band may provide much crucial knowledge about the dynamic aspects of human behavior across time, places, and interactions with other persons, allowing a better understanding of the influence of dynamics on humans' perception, cognition, and action. Therefore, our emphasis on the social band here does not mean that experimental psychologists should focus mainly on social psychology but that they should consider the dynamic mechanisms of human perception, cognition, and action over larger time scales. Egon Brunswik (1952, 1956) argued that to understand and predict behavior outside of the laboratory, within psychology research, the natural physical environment should be given equal weighting to that given to the mediating psychological processes of the person. This is a less extreme view of the position of ecological psychologists in the tradition of Gibson (1979).

Brunswik (1943, p. 257) defined the sum of the natural conditions in which individuals live as a "population" of situations. Here, we borrow the term from Brunswik and use *situation* to fill in the blanks that Newell left in the system column for the social band of Table 2.1. When the system escalates from task to situation, the information increases extensively. In other words, individuals deal with physical big data daily. Thus, the critical control within the upper system is to find what is needed and when it is needed to satisfy specific goals. The idea of situation has also been incorporated into human factors research in the concept of *situation awareness*, defined initially by Endsley (1988) as "the perception of elements in the environment within a volume of time and space, the comprehension of their meaning and the projection of their status in the near future" (p. 97).

Although Endsley (2000) characterized situation awareness in terms of the person's explicit knowledge about a dynamic environment at a given time and place, an alternative approach puts more emphasis on the processes people use to attain awareness (Vu & Chiappe, 2015). How people coordinate their actions to achieve various goals seems more informative than just their awareness of the current state with regard to their adapting to the complex and dynamic environment. With a nod to Brunswik (1943), we suggest that the concept of situation, which integrates human information processing with ecological approaches, should play a more central role in investigating behavior than it does currently. For example, when people generate passwords for online accounts, two goals (i.e., usability and security) are involved. Typically, people sacrifice the security of the password to make it easy to use. Nowadays, we mainly study password generation within specific tasks. Varying the situations in which users generate passwords may inform researchers and designers not only as to why users who express security concerns devote limited time and effort to security-related actions but also how to help them bring security back into alignment with their goals.

Development of a Language and Tools Applicable to Big Data

The major reason for the success of the information-processing approach to cognitive psychology is that it provided a language of concepts that was based in communications engineering, inferential statistics, and computer science (Broadbent, 1959; Posner, 1986; Xiong & Proctor, 2018). This language was developed through interdisciplinary efforts of the researchers advocating cybernetics and information theory and the artificial intelligence and computer simulation work that issued forth from those efforts. The information-processing framework provided a common language for research psychologists in areas such as perception, memory, attention, problem solving, and motor control to characterize alternative theories and hypotheses, which could be tested empirically. It also provided a means of communication vertically between the four bands identified by Newell (1990), from social to neuronal.

The development of an interdisciplinary language applicable to big data seems necessary, as well. At present, most of the terminology in the area of big data and data science comes mainly from computer scientists and data scientists. This may make it difficult for researchers in psychology and other domains, as well as everyday users, to understand key concepts and communicate with those at the forefront of developing big data and data science. Psychologists themselves will have to have a good understanding of what value they may get out of big data if they are to contribute to the development of the new language. More critically, because the big data are largely direct or indirect traces of human behavior, humans have to be put at the center of big data research. Psychologists should play a major role in developing the language and tools of big data and how to communicate those effectively to researchers and other stakeholders.

One thing that becomes apparent as research moves from controlled experiments in which a few independent variables are manipulated separately to the uncontrolled region of the cyber-physical world is that the researcher must deal with a mass of correlated data from users coping with environments full of uncertainties. This fact was highlighted by Brunswik (1952, 1956) many years ago. To understand human-environment relations, Brunswik proposed three key concepts to understand human behavior within different situations: probabilistic functionalism, lens model, and representative design (see reviews of Dhami, Hertwig, & Hoffrage, 2004; and Hammond, 1966).

Probabilistic functionalism theory focuses on the probabilistic coupling of human-environment systems. On the one hand, the human system has to adapt to the environment when there is uncertainty in the environment. On the other hand, an individual can change the environment to achieve their goals through different means. The core idea of probabilistic functionalism is depicted by the lens model, in which cues from the environment are processed through a lens to deal with the environment's uncertainties. Figure 2.1 illustrates a double convex lens, showing a collection of proximal cues diverging from a distal criterion in the environment. The proximal effects may be used as cues by humans for achieving the distal variable and so converge at the point of a response in the human side. Thus, the crucial achievement of the human lens is to shift between interchangeable paths to reach a distal goal, which Brunswik (1952, 1956) called *vicarious functioning*.

For Brunswik (1952), the primary aim of psychological research was to discover probabilistic laws that describe an organism's adaptation in terms of a distal variable to the causal texture of its environment. Brunswik proposed to measure the ecological or predictive validity by the correlation between the proximal cues and the distal variable.

FIGURE 2.1. The Double Convex Lens Model

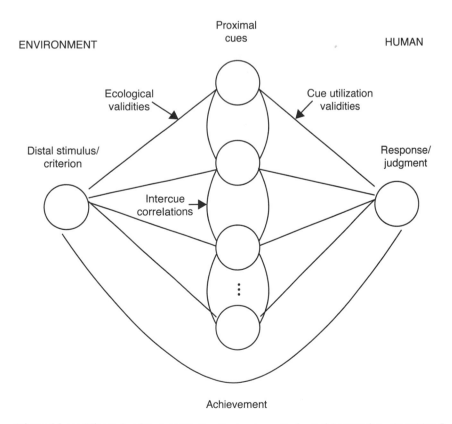

REPRESENTATIVE DESIGN

ENVIRONMENT ⸻ Proximal cues ⸻ HUMAN

Ecological validities — Cue utilization validities

Distal stimulus/ criterion — Response/ judgment

Intercue correlations

Achievement

Adapted from "The Role of Representative Design in an Ecological Approach to Cognition," by M. K. Dhami, R. Hertwig, and U. Hoffrage, 2004, *Psychological Bulletin*, *130*, p. 961. Copyright 2004 by the American Psychological Association.

Despite the fact that Brunswik worked in the area of perception, whereas the famous cognitive behaviorist Edward C. Tolman (1948) worked in the area of animal learning, Tolman and Brunswik (1935) derived a common viewpoint about the causal texture of the environment in which the joint function of perception and action of an organism is combined into one picture. This work was done before Brunswik (1952, 1956) developed his lens model to explain human perception. Subsequently, the use of the lens model has expanded into investigations of information integration in judgment and decision making (Dhami et al., 2004; Gigerenzer & Kurz, 2001; Hammond, 1966). Consistent with Tolman and Brunswik's lead, Leary (1987) added a behavioral lens to Brunswik's perceptual lens and used this expanded lens model to describe daily activities such as drinking coffee. Specific actions are seen as means to reach goals, which are represented by the behavioral lens.

More recently, beyond human behaviors, Scholz (2017) proposed to broaden the lens model to incorporate sustainable transitions of human-environment systems. Following up on that proposal, Hoffrage (2018) added a planning lens to unfold the interaction between the perceptual and behavioral lenses within a complex social context (see Figure 2.2). Also, Hoffrage replaced the term *objects* with *systems*, consistent with Brunswik's (1956) opinion that the organism and environment are equal partners from a system viewpoint. Although Hoffrage explained the model by using the case of teamwork, the planning lens can be treated as a lens of cognitive processes, with which experimental cognitive psychologists have been concerned from the beginning.

Generally, the lens model builds up the connection between the environment and human perception, cognition, and action and can be used as a tool to expand the statistical properties of the cognitive mechanism over a subject population to understand the statistical texture of the environment. With the information about the environment afforded by big data, experimental psychologists should seize the opportunity to place the understanding of human cognition within the environment.

FIGURE 2.2. Hoffrage's Extension of the Lens Model to Cognition and Action

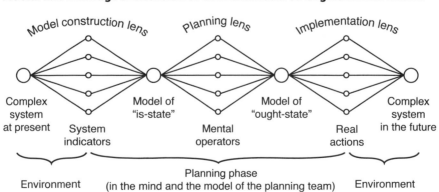

From "From Representation via Planning to Action: An Extension of Egon Brunswik's Theory of Probabilistic Functionalism," by U. Hoffrage, 2017, *Environment Systems and Decisions*, *38*, p. 71. Copyright 2018 by Springer Nature. Reprinted with permission.

Besides the conceptual framework of probabilistic functionalism and the lens model, Brunswik (1952, 1956) also developed methodological procedures called representative design to guide how to conduct experiments. Brunswik highlighted two major limitations of the common experimental procedure in which experimenters manipulate several variables independently: (a) It does not allow participants to show the natural vicarious-functioning processes, and (b) it does not enable the ecological generalization of the findings from an experiment beyond the laboratory (Dhami et al., 2004). Thus, besides sampling the individuals to be representative of the population, situations should be sampled to be representative of the environment.

With representative design methods, the researcher tries to retain all the relevant environmental variables in the design and identify their effects on decisions after the fact through correlational statistical analyses. The representative design method has been used for research on overconfidence (e.g., Gigerenzer, Hoffrage, & Kleinbölting, 1991) and on hindsight bias (e.g., Hoffrage, Hertwig, & Gigerenzer, 2000). In the sports domain, Travassos, Duarte, Vilar, Davids, and Araújo (2012) investigated the effects of varying the number of action possibilities in a futsal (a variant of soccer and football) passing task with eight male senior futsal players to understand the representativeness of practice tasks designs. Travassos et al. found that the regularity (i.e., the consistency of passing speed) and accuracy of passes executed by experienced futsal players tended to vary as a function of the representativeness of the practice task. When the task required passes to be executed in conditions with predetermined passing options (less representative task), the accuracy of passes increased, and ball speed became more regular compared with the passes observed in a competitive game. In contrast, the passes performed in practice scenarios where there were a greater number of passing options (more representative task) tended to be a closer match to those observed in competition, exhibiting reduced accuracy and more irregular ball speed. Thus, with the representativeness of the environment increased, the behaviors' fidelity also improved.

Although practical difficulties for representative design made it a seldom-used method in the past (Dhami et al., 2004), we think big data will make the goal of representative design more attainable for experimental psychology. Big data allows research to capture various details of people's environment, often in an ongoing manner, which can be used by psychologists to analyze information structure in the environment. This understanding of the environment can be brought downward to further analyze human behavior in more controlled laboratory settings. Given Brunswik's (1956) emphasis on the environmental structure, it is not surprising that perhaps the greatest contributions of big data approaches in cognitive psychology have been in the area of natural language processing. That is, word corpora have "allowed for a systematic analysis of the connection between the statistical structure of the environment and human behavior" (Chapter 12, this volume, p. 278). We conjecture that increasing use of the representative design method will accompany the use of big data in experimental psychology.

Contributions of Applied and Engineering Psychologists to Big Data

The focus of our chapter has been on the purposes to which experimental psychologists can put big data, but another intersection of interests is the role that psychologists can play in the implementation and use of big data. As noted, to date, computer scientists, engineers, and data scientists have been the main forces driving the development of how big data are coded, stored, and protected. Yet, the potential of big data has to be mined by other disciplines. Therefore, the generalization of the data analytic tools and methods to other disciplines is a major issue, as is the usability of the tools for specific user groups. Systematic application of principles of human information processing to the design of the tools and methods is crucial, as are studies assessing usability and user experience of the targeted end users. In other words, because people are ultimately the ones who have to use the information contained in big data, their information-processing capabilities will have to be taken into consideration.

The main challenge for psychologists and others is to be able to extract meaningful information from the increasingly large amounts of data. It is already established that people have difficulty extracting information from much smaller amounts of data than are typically considered to be big data. Data visualization techniques have been developed to assist researchers in comprehending higher order features of data sets (see Chapter 7, this volume). For example, Kreuz, Mulansky, and Bozanic (2015) described a user-friendly graphical user interface to assist in identifying similarity patterns in neuronal spike train data. Also, people often rely on heuristics to make fast decisions requiring little mental effort, rather than analyzing the data in detail. For instance, Gigerenzer and Kurz (2001) presented an argument in terms of Brunswik's (1952, 1956) lens model that for binary choices among alternatives that have multiple cues to consider, people adopt a take-the-best heuristic: They select the single cue with the highest validity, base their decision on that cue alone if it discriminates the alternatives, and proceed to the next best cue if it does not. In fact, users will often rely on salient cues of relatively low validity to make decisions, such as judging a website's validity on the basis of its appearance (Fogg et al., 2001).

Big data must be coded and organized in ways that are useful for researchers if their potential for understanding human behavior is to be realized. This is true not only for research but also for applied decisions that must be made on large amounts of data, including examining system log files of a computer system to determine whether a security breach has occurred and making agile business decisions from big data.

Pitfalls of Big Data Oriented Research

As with small-scale experimental research, and any research method for that matter, big data research has its limits and pitfalls. That the amount of data is "big" does not necessarily mean that the data are better for research purposes or representative of the entire user population for the research question. For example, online social media users are popular with younger age groups, suggesting that big data obtained from online social media platforms may not provide valid insights for people in older age groups (Anderson & Perrin, 2017). Also, the data sets collected in real-world situations do not allow tight control of variables, as is typically desired in scientific investigations of fundamental human processing, including perception, cognition, and action. Also, the real-world data sets are not necessarily random and are prone to missing data and errors due to a lack of control of the data-collection process (Wu, Zhu, Wu, & Ding, 2014). For example, knowing how many people "shared" or "retweeted" fake news is not sufficient to gain insights about users' information processing of fake news online unless one also knows how many people saw the articles without sharing them with others.

We also note that data do not speak themselves, no matter the size, and the specific methods chosen for data processing, analyses, and interpretation are subjective decisions, which are susceptible to bias. Moreover, correlations in big data may lend themselves to particular causal explanations that have high face validity but are incorrect. If inferential hypotheses generated from the big data focus on such explanations, this may occur at the expense of considering alternative hypotheses that may provide better explanations. In other words, hypotheses can be generated in many different ways, and creativity in the generation of hypotheses to test may be biased if they are driven mainly by big data.

Historically, technologies and data analytic tools have had a significant role in shaping the world in which we use them, as well as how people think about the world. For example, in cognitive psychology, the computer metaphor (Gentner & Grudin, 1985) and probabilistic thinking (Gigerenzer, 1991) have been extremely influential in the information age. As for all previous research methods, big data research is a new possible source of information, which requires that specialized tools be added to the toolbox of science. With so many tools on hand, researchers should choose the tool or combine several tools based on the pros and cons to solve the problems or questions in which they are interested.

CONCLUSION

Science typically develops from simple to complex and from controlled to less controlled (Newell, 1989). Although human behavior has been the major focus of experimental psychology since the information-processing revolution in the 1950s, the rise of big data will allow experimental psychologists to understand human behavior by placing it into a larger and/or more complex system. Big data are included in each band that Newell (1990) identified (see Figure 2.3). However, from experimental psychology's perspective, the dimension of different time scales is more critical to exploit big data in

FIGURE 2.3. Big Data Categorization With Time Scale of Human Action

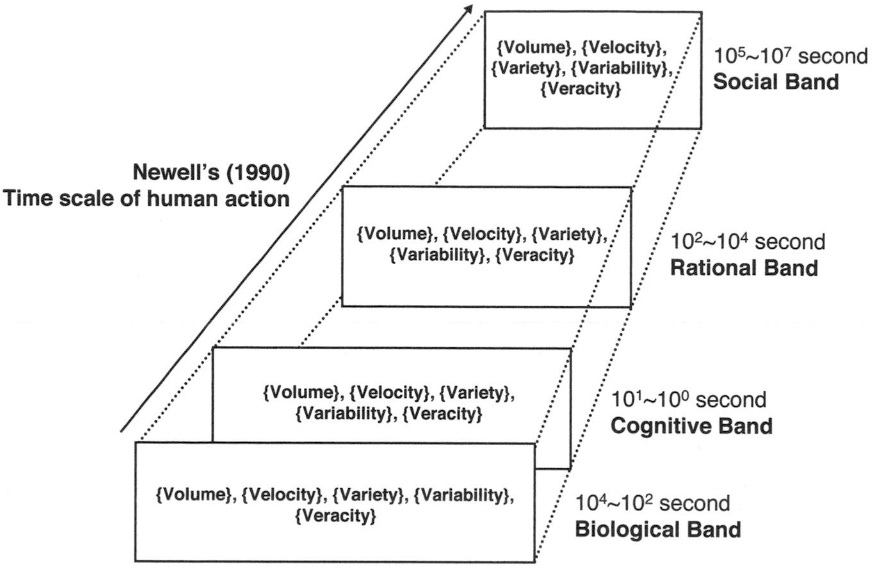

Four different bands (biological band, cognitive band, rational band, social band), with big data for each band broken down into different dimension vectors (e.g., volume, velocity, variety, variability, veracity). Data from Newell (1990).

understanding human behavior. Experimental psychologists should not only focus on using big data to improve our understanding of human behavior in the cognitive and rational bands but also attend to the upper and lower bands, especially the use of big data to escalate our understanding of human behavior at the social band.

To achieve this goal, human information processing should be placed within the situations encountered over the time scales of days, weeks, and months. Brunswik's (1952, 1956) lens model and representative design provide tools for experimental psychologists to investigate human behavior in different situations. We also emphasized that experimental psychologists should take an interdisciplinary approach and work together with computer scientists, data scientists, and others, both to advance the use of big data in experimental psychology and ensure the usability of big data for a range of end users.

REFERENCES

Ach, N. S. (1964). *Über die Willenstätigkeit und das Denken* [Determining tendencies]. In J. M. Mandler & G. Mandler (Eds.), *Thinking: From association to Gestalt* (pp. 201–207). New York: Wiley. (Original work published 1905)

Anderson, M., & Perrin, A. (2017). *Technology use among seniors.* Retrieved from http://www.pewinternet.org/2017/05/17/technology-use-among-seniors/

Andrade, C. S., & Santos, M. Y. (2017). Sentiment analysis with text mining in contexts of big data. *International Journal of Technology and Human Interaction, 13,* 47–67. http://dx.doi.org/10.4018/IJTHI.2017070104

Ashby, W. R. (1956). *An introduction to cybernetics.* London, England: Chapman & Hall. http://dx.doi.org/10.5962/bhl.title.5851

Behmer, L. P., & Crump, M. J. (2017). The dynamic range of response set activation during action sequencing. *Journal of Experimental Psychology: Human Perception and Performance*, *43*, 537–554. http://dx.doi.org/10.1037/xhp0000335

Boyd, D., & Crawford, K. (2012). Critical questions for big data: Provocations for a cultural, technological, and scholarly phenomenon. *Information, Communication & Society*, *15*, 662–679. http://dx.doi.org/10.1080/1369118X.2012.678878

Broadbent, D. E. (1959). Information theory and older approaches in psychology. *Acta Psychologica*, *15*, 111–115. http://dx.doi.org/10.1016/S0001-6918(59)80030-5

Brunswik, E. (1943). Organismic achievement and environmental probability. *Psychological Review*, *50*, 255–272. http://dx.doi.org/10.1037/h0060889

Brunswik, E. (1952). *The conceptual framework of psychology*. Chicago, IL: University of Chicago Press.

Brunswik, E. (1956). *Perception and the representative design of experiments*. Berkeley: University of California Press.

Buhrmester, M. D., Talaifar, S., & Gosling, S. D. (2018). An evaluation of Amazon's Mechanical Turk, its rapid rise, and its effective use. *Perspectives on Psychological Science*, *13*, 149–154. http://dx.doi.org/10.1177/1745691617706516

Coffman, K. G., & Odlyzko, A. M. (2002). Internet growth: Is there a "Moore's Law" for data traffic? In J. Abello, P. M. Pardalos, & M. G. C. Resende (Eds.), *Handbook of massive data sets* (pp. 47–93). Boston, MA: Springer. http://dx.doi.org/10.1007/978-1-4615-0005-6_3

Cukier, K., & Mayer-Schoenberger, V. (2013). The rise of big data: How it's changing the way we think about the world. *Foreign Affairs*, *92*, 28–40.

Dahmen, J., Thomas, B. L., Cook, D. J., & Wang, X. (2017). Activity learning as a foundation for security monitoring in smart homes. *Sensors*, *17*, 737. http://dx.doi.org/10.3390/s17040737

Danziger, K. (1994). *Constructing the subject: Historical origins of psychological research*. New York, NY: Cambridge University Press.

Dhami, M. K., Hertwig, R., & Hoffrage, U. (2004). The role of representative design in an ecological approach to cognition. *Psychological Bulletin*, *130*, 959–988. http://dx.doi.org/10.1037/0033-2909.130.6.959

Donders, F. C. (1969). On the speed of mental processes. In W. G. Koster (Ed. & Trans.), *Attention and performance II* (pp. 412–431). Amsterdam, Netherlands: North Holland. (Original work published 1868)

Donkin, C., Brown, S., Heathcote, A., & Wagenmakers, E. J. (2011). Diffusion versus linear ballistic accumulation: Different models but the same conclusions about psychological processes? *Psychonomic Bulletin & Review*, *18*, 61–69. http://dx.doi.org/10.3758/s13423-010-0022-4

Dull, T. (2014, December). Big data and the Internet of Things: Two sides of the same coin? *Smart Data Collective*. https://www.smartdatacollective.com/big-data-and-internet-things-two-sides-same-coin/

Dyre, B. P., & Hollands, J. G. (2016). The psychophysical function and separable model forms in joint magnitude estimation. *Journal of Mathematical Psychology*, *75*, 218–230. http://dx.doi.org/10.1016/j.jmp.2016.06.005

Ebbinghaus, H. (1964). *Über das Gedächtnis. Untersuchungen zur experimentellen Psychologie* [Memory: A contribution to experimental psychology] (H. A. Ruger & C. E. Bussenius, Trans.). New York, NY: Dover. (Original work published 1885)

Endel, F., & Piringer, H. (2015). Data wrangling: Making data useful again. *International Federation of Automatic Control*, *48*, 111–112.

Endsley, M. R. (1988). Design and evaluation for situation awareness enhancement. *Proceedings of the Human Factors Society Annual Meeting*, *32*, 97–101. http://dx.doi.org/10.1177/154193128803200221

Endsley, M. R. (2000). Theoretical underpinnings of situation awareness: A critical review. In M. R. Endsley & D. J. Garland (Eds.), *Situation awareness analysis and measurement* (pp. 3–32). Mahwah, NJ: Erlbaum.

Fechner, G. T. (1966). *Elements of psychophysics* (Vol. 1, H. E. Adler, D. H. Howes, & E. G. Boring, Trans.). New York, NY: Holt, Rinehart & Winston. (Original work published 1860)

Fisher, R. A. (1925). *Statistical methods for research workers*. London, England: Oliver & Boyd.

Fisher, R. A. (1935). *The design of experiments*. London, England: Oliver & Boyd.

Fogg, B., Marshall, J., Laraki, O., Osipovich, A., Varma, C., Fang, N., . . . Treinen, M. (2001). What makes Web sites credible? A report on a large quantitative study. *Proceedings of the SIGCHI Conference on Human Factors in Computing Systems*, 61–68. http://dx.doi.org/10.1145/365024.365037

Gandomi, A., & Haider, M. (2015). Beyond the hype: Big data concepts, methods, and analytics. *International Journal of Information Management, 35*, 137–144. http://dx.doi.org/10.1016/j.ijinfomgt.2014.10.007

Geissler, L. R. (1912). Analysis of consciousness under negative instruction. *The American Journal of Psychology, 23*, 183–213. http://dx.doi.org/10.2307/1412840

Gentner, D., & Grudin, J. (1985). The evolution of mental metaphors in psychology: A 90-year retrospective. *American Psychologist, 40*, 181–192. http://dx.doi.org/10.1037/0003-066X.40.2.181

Gescheider, G. (1997). *Psychophysics: The fundamentals* (3rd ed.). Mahwah, NJ: Erlbaum.

Gibson, J. J. (1979). *The ecological approach to visual perception*. Boston, MA: Houghton Mifflin.

Gigerenzer, G. (1991). From tools to theories: A heuristic of discovery in cognitive psychology. *Psychological Review, 98*, 254–267. http://dx.doi.org/10.1037/0033-295X.98.2.254

Gigerenzer, G., Hoffrage, U., & Kleinbölting, H. (1991). Probabilistic mental models: A Brunswikian theory of confidence. *Psychological Review, 98*, 506–528. http://dx.doi.org/10.1037/0033-295X.98.4.506

Gigerenzer, G., & Kurz, E. M. (2001). Vicarious functioning reconsidered: A fast and frugal lens model. In K. R. Hammond & T. R. Stewart (Eds.), *The essential Brunswik: Beginnings, explications, applications* (pp. 342–347). New York, NY: Oxford University Press.

Gigerenzer, G., & Murray, D. J. (1987). *Cognition as intuitive statistics*. Mahwah, NJ: Erlbaum.

Gigerenzer, G., Swijtink, Z., Porter, T., Daston, L., Beatty, J., & Krüger, L. (1989). *The empire of chance: How probability changed science and everyday life*. New York, NY: Cambridge University Press. http://dx.doi.org/10.1017/CBO9780511720482

Goldstone, R. L., & Lupyan, G. (2016). Discovering psychological principles by mining naturally occurring data sets. *Topics in Cognitive Science, 8*, 548–568. http://dx.doi.org/10.1111/tops.12212

Green, D., & Swets, J. (1966). *Signal detection theory and psychophysics*. New York, NY: Wiley.

Griffiths, T. L. (2015). Manifesto for a new (computational) cognitive revolution. *Cognition, 135*, 21–23. http://dx.doi.org/10.1016/j.cognition.2014.11.026

Haig, B. D. (2014). *Investigating the psychological world: Scientific method in the behavioral sciences*. Cambridge, MA: MIT Press. http://dx.doi.org/10.7551/mitpress/9780262027366.001.0001

Hall, G. S., & Motora, Y. (1887). Dermal sensitiveness to gradual pressure changes. *The American Journal of Psychology, 1*, 72–98. http://dx.doi.org/10.2307/1411232

Hammond, K. R. (Ed.). (1966). *The psychology of Egon Brunswik*. New York, NY: Holt, Rinehart and Winston.

Healy, A. F., & Bourne, L. J. (2011). Applied cognitive psychology. In P. R. Martin, F. M. Cheung, M. C. Knowles, M. Kyrios, L. Littlefield, J. B. Overmier, & J. M. Prieto (Eds.), *IAAP handbook of applied psychology* (pp. 559–572). Chichester, England: Wiley-Blackwell. http://dx.doi.org/10.1002/9781444395150.ch23

Hirst, W., & Manier, D. (1995). Opening vistas for cognitive psychology. In L. W. Martin, K. Nelson, E. Tobach, L. W. Martin, K. Nelson, & E. Tobach (Eds.), *Sociocultural psychology: Theory and practice of doing and knowing* (pp. 89–124). New York, NY: Cambridge University Press. http://dx.doi.org/10.1017/CBO9780511896828.007

Hoffmann, J., Stock, A., & Deutsch, R. (1996). The Würzburg school. In J. Hoffman & A. Sebald (Eds.), *Cognitive psychology in Europe: Proceedings of the ninth conference of the European society for cognitive psychology* (pp. 147–172). Lengerich, Germany: Pabst Science.

Hoffrage, U. (2018). From representation via planning to action: An extension of Egon Brunswik's theory of probabilistic functionalism. *Environment Systems & Decisions, 38,* 69–73. http://dx.doi.org/10.1007/s10669-017-9660-7

Hoffrage, U., Hertwig, R., & Gigerenzer, G. (2000). Hindsight bias: A by-product of knowledge updating? *Journal of Experimental Psychology: Learning, Memory, and Cognition, 26,* 566–581. http://dx.doi.org/10.1037/0278-7393.26.3.566

Hussain, A., Cambria, E., Schuller, B., & Howard, N. (2014). Affective neural networks and cognitive learning systems for big data analysis. *Neural Networks, 58,* 1–3. http://dx.doi.org/10.1016/j.neunet.2014.07.010

ISO/IEC. (2015). *Big data: Preliminary report 2014.* Geneva, Switzerland: International Standards Organization.

Janssen, M., van der Voort, H., & Wahyudi, A. (2017). Factors influencing big data decision-making quality. *Journal of Business Research, 70,* 338–345. http://dx.doi.org/10.1016/j.jbusres.2016.08.007

Jones, M. N., Willits, J., Dennis, S., & Jones, M. (2015). Models of semantic memory. In J. R. Busemeyer, Z. Wang, J. T. Townsend, & A. Eidels (Eds.), *Oxford handbook of mathematical and computational psychology* (pp. 232–254). New York, NY: Oxford University Press. http://dx.doi.org/10.1093/oxfordhb/9780199957996.013.11

Katal, A., Wazid, M., & Goudar, R. H. (2013). Big data: Issues, challenges, tools and good practices. In *Proceedings of the Sixth International Conference on Contemporary Computing* (pp. 404–409). Piscataway, NJ: IEEE.

Keith, M. G., Tay, L., & Harms, P. D. (2017). Systems perspective of Amazon Mechanical Turk for organizational research: Review and recommendations. *Frontiers in Psychology, 8,* 1359. http://dx.doi.org/10.3389/fpsyg.2017.01359

Kolmogorov, A. (1968). Logical basis for information theory and probability theory. *IEEE Transactions on Information Theory, 14,* 662–664. http://dx.doi.org/10.1109/TIT.1968.1054210

Kreuz, T., Mulansky, M., & Bozanic, N. (2015). SPIKY: A graphical user interface for monitoring spike train synchrony. *Journal of Neurophysiology, 113,* 3432–3445. http://dx.doi.org/10.1152/jn.00848.2014

Lambert, J. F., & Ewart, P. H. (1932). Part I: The effect of verbal instructions upon stylus maze learning. *Journal of General Psychology, 6,* 377–399. http://dx.doi.org/10.1080/00221309.1932.9711879

Lazer, D., Pentland, A. S., Adamic, L., Aral, S., Barabasi, A. L., Brewer, D., . . . Van Alstyne, M. (2009, February 6). Computational social science. *Science, 323*(5915), 721–723. http://dx.doi.org/10.1126/science.1167742

Leary, D. E. (1987). From act psychology to probabilistic functionalism: The place of Egon Brunswik in the history of psychology. In M. G. Ash & W. R. Woodward (Eds.), *Psychology in twentieth-century thought and society* (pp. 115–142). Cambridge, England: Cambridge University Press.

Littman, J. (2017, September). *Where to get Twitter data for academic research.* https://gwu-libraries.github.io/sfm-ui/posts/2017-09-14-twitter-data

Lu, Y., Bilaloglu, S., Aluru, V., & Raghavan, P. (2015). Quantifying feedforward control: A linear scaling model for fingertip forces and object weight. *Journal of Neurophysiology, 114,* 411–418. http://dx.doi.org/10.1152/jn.00065.2015

MacKay, D. M. (1956). Towards an information-flow model of human behaviour. *British Journal of Psychology, 47*, 30–43. http://dx.doi.org/10.1111/j.2044-8295.1956.tb00559.x

Mandler, G. (2007). *A history of modern experimental psychology: From James and Wundt to cognitive science*. Cambridge, MA: MIT Press.

Mashey, J. (1998). *Big data . . . and the next wave of infrastress*. Retrieved from http://static.usenix.org/event/usenix99/invited_talks/mashey.pdf

Moore, G. (1965). Moore's law. *Electronics Magazine, 38*, 114–119.

National Institute of Science and Technology. (2014). *NIST Big Data interoperability framework: Volume 1, definitions* (NIST Special Publication 1500-1). Retrieved from https://bigdatawg.nist.gov/_uploadfiles/NIST.SP.1500-1r1.pdf

Newell, A. (1989). Put it all together. In D. Klahr & K. Kotovsky (Eds.), *Complex information processing: The impact of Herbert A. Simon* (pp. 399–440). Hillsdale, NJ: Erlbaum.

Newell, A. (1990). *Unified theories of cognition*. Cambridge, MA: Harvard University Press.

Pfeffer, J. Mayer, K., & Morstatter, F. (2019). *Twitter tampered samples: Limitations of big data sampling in social media*. Retrieved from http://blogs.biomedcentral.com/on-society/2019/01/28/twitters-tampered-samples-limitations-of-big-data-sampling-in-social-media/

Popper, K. R. (1962). *Conjectures and refutations: The growth of scientific knowledge*. New York, NY: Basic Books.

Poria, S., Cambria, E., Howard, N., Huang, G., & Hussain, A. (2016). Fusing audio, visual and textual clues for sentiment analysis from multimodal content. *Neuro-computing: An International Journal, 174*, 50–59.

Posner, M. I. (1986). Overview. In K. R. Boff, L. I. Kaufman, & J. P. Thomas (Eds.), *Handbook of perception and human performance: Vol. 2. Cognitive processes and performance* (pp. V-1–V-10). New York, NY: Wiley.

Pratt, C. C. (1924). The present status of introspective technique. *Journal of Philosophy, 21*, 225–231. http://dx.doi.org/10.2307/2014871

Proctor, R. W., & Vu, K.-P. L. (2010). Cumulative knowledge and progress in human factors. *Annual Review of Psychology, 61*, 623–651. http://dx.doi.org/10.1146/annurev.psych.093008.100325

Robinson, D. K. (2001). Reaction-time experiments in Wundt's institute and beyond. In R. W. Rieber & D. K. Robinson (Eds.), *Wilhelm Wundt in history: The making of a scientific psychology* (pp. 161–204). New York, NY: Kluwer Academic/Plenum. http://dx.doi.org/10.1007/978-1-4615-0665-2_6

Rucci, A. J., & Tweney, R. D. (1980). Analysis of variance and the "second discipline" of scientific psychology: A historical account. *Psychological Bulletin, 87*, 166–184. http://dx.doi.org/10.1037/0033-2909.87.1.166

Scholz, R. W. (2017). Managing complexity: From visual perception to sustainable transitions—contributions of Brunswik's Theory of Probabilistic Functionalism. *Environment Systems & Decisions, 37*, 381–409. http://dx.doi.org/10.1007/s10669-017-9655-4

Shannon, C. E. (1948). A mathematical theory of communication. *The Bell System Technical Journal, 27*, 379–423. http://dx.doi.org/10.1002/j.1538-7305.1948.tb01338.x

Stafford, T., & Dewar, M. (2014). Tracing the trajectory of skill learning with a very large sample of online game players. *Psychological Science, 25*, 511–518. http://dx.doi.org/10.1177/0956797613511466

Stanton, J. M. (2013). Data mining: A practical introduction for organizational researchers. In J. M. Cortina & R. S. Landis (Eds.), *Modern research methods for the study of behavior in organizations* (pp. 225–256). New York, NY: Routledge.

Statista. (2018). *Internet of Things (IoT) connected devices installed base worldwide from 2015 to 2025 (in billions)*. https://www.statista.com/statistics/471264/iot-number-of-connected-devices-worldwide/

Sternberg, S. (1969). The discovery of processing stages: Extensions of Donders' method. *Acta Psychologica, 30*, 276–315. http://dx.doi.org/10.1016/0001-6918(69)90055-9

Thorstad, R., & Wolff, P. (2018). A big data analysis of the relationship between future thinking and decision-making. *PNAS, 115*, E1740–E1748. https://doi.org/10.1073/pnas.1706589115

Tijmstra, J. (2018). Why checking model assumptions using null hypothesis significance tests does not suffice: A plea for plausibility. *Psychonomic Bulletin & Review, 25*, 548–559. http://dx.doi.org/10.3758/s13423-018-1447-4

Titchener, E. B. (1903). *A primer of psychology* (rev. ed.). New York, NY: Macmillan.

Tolman, E. C. (1948). Cognitive maps in rats and men. *Psychological Review, 55*, 189–208. http://dx.doi.org/10.1037/h0061626

Tolman, E. C., & Brunswik, E. (1935). The organism and the causal texture of the environment. *Psychological Review, 42*, 43–77. http://dx.doi.org/10.1037/h0062156

Travassos, B., Duarte, R., Vilar, L., Davids, K., & Araújo, D. (2012). Practice task design in team sports: Representativeness enhanced by increasing opportunities for action. *Journal of Sports Sciences, 30*, 1447–1454. http://dx.doi.org/10.1080/02640414.2012.712716

Twitter. (2018). *New developer requirements to protect our platform*. Retrieved from https://blog.twitter.com/developer/en_us/topics/tools/2018/new-developer-requirements-to-protect-our-platform.html

Vu, K.-P. L., & Chiappe, D. (2015). Situation awareness in human systems integration. In D. A. Boehm-Davis, F. T. Durso, & J. D. Lee (Eds.), *APA handbook of human systems integration* (pp. 293–308). Washington, DC: American Psychological Association. http://dx.doi.org/10.1037/14528-019

Ward, J. S., & Barker, A. (2013). *Undefined by data: A survey of big data definitions*. Retrieved from http://citeseerx.ist.psu.edu/viewdoc/download?doi=10.1.1.705.9909&rep=rep1&type=pdf

Weber, E. H. (1834). *De Tactu* [Concerning touch]. Leipzig, Germany: Koehler.

Weber, E. H. (1851). Der *Tastsinn und das Gemeingefühl* [The sense of touch and the common sensibility]. Brunswick, Germany: Vieweg.

Weber, E. H. (1996). *E. H. Weber on the tactile senses* (2nd ed., Helen E. Ross & D. J. Murray, Trans.). Hove, England: Erlbaum/Taylor & Francis.

Weinstein, Y., Nunes, L. D., & Karpicke, J. D. (2016). On the placement of practice questions during study. *Journal of Experimental Psychology: Applied, 22*, 72–84. http://dx.doi.org/10.1037/xap0000071

Weiss, A. P. (1924). Behaviorism and behavior, II. *Psychological Review, 31*, 118–149. http://dx.doi.org/10.1037/h0069345

Whetsel, R. C., & Qu, Y. (2017). Quantifying the impact of big data's variety. In *Proceedings of the Third IEEE International Conference on Computer and Communications* (pp. 2299–2303). Piscataway, NJ: IEEE.

Wiener, N. (1948). *Cybernetics or control and communication in the animal and the machine*. New York, NY: Wiley.

Wu, X., Zhu, X., Wu, G. Q., & Ding, W. (2014). Data mining with big data. *IEEE Transactions on Knowledge and Data Engineering, 26*, 97–107. http://dx.doi.org/10.1109/TKDE.2013.109

Wundt, W. (1897). *Outlines of psychology* (C. H. Judd, Trans.). New York, NY: Gustav E. Stechert. http://dx.doi.org/10.1037/12908-000

Xiong, A., & Proctor, R. W. (2018). Information processing: The language and analytical tools for cognitive psychology in the information age. *Frontiers in Cognitive Science*. Retrieved from https://www.frontiersin.org/articles/10.3389/fpsyg.2018.01270/full

Yang, W., Li, N., Chowdhury, O., Xiong, A., & Proctor, R. W. (2016). An empirical study of password generation strategies. *Proceedings of the 2016 ACM SIGSAC Conference on Computer and Communications Security* (pp. 1216–1229). New York, NY: ACM.

3

Big Data for Enhancing Measurement Quality

Sang Eun Woo, Louis Tay, Andrew T. Jebb,
Michael T. Ford, and Margaret L. Kern

Through technology, it is becoming easier to gather a large volume of data at a fast pace in a variety of forms (i.e., *big data*; McAfee & Brynjolfsson, 2012). Although numerous articles and books have considered the general value of big data, it is necessary to delineate further the distinct sources of big data to develop a robust framework for how different types of big data may be useful for psychological research and under what circumstances. With this in mind, in this chapter, we discuss several specific sources of big data that are potentially useful to psychological research. After extensively reviewing the existing literature (academic, practice oriented, news articles), we identified three major sources of big data as most frequently mentioned or used in current psychological research: social media (e.g., Twitter, Facebook), wearable sensors (e.g., sociometric badges, Fitbit), and Internet activities (e.g., Internet searches, page views). In addition, we consider two other emergent data sources that provide an increasing amount of accessible data: public network cameras and smartphones. We review these sources, the types of information they contain, and consider ways they have been used in psychological research, providing a foundation for creating a robust big data framework.

Although these sources of big data hold broad promise for psychological science, issues specifically related to measurement quality have not yet received the level of attention that is necessary for rigorous scientific work (Adjerid & Kelley, 2018). To fill this void, the bulk of this chapter is devoted to delineating how each specific source of big data might help and/or limit psychologists' efforts to improve measurement validity and reliability (American Educational Research Association [AERA], American Psychological Association, & National

http://dx.doi.org/10.1037/0000193-004
Big Data in Psychological Research, S. E. Woo, L. Tay, and R. W. Proctor (Editors)

Council on Measurement in Education, 2014; Guion, 2002). We review the fast-emerging big data literature in psychology (both conceptual and empirical) for evidence of their validity and reliability and identify areas in which future research can shed light on lesser understood issues.

In considering each of the big data methodologies, we first discuss which psychological constructs may be better captured through big data versus existing methods, speaking to the content relevance of measures, as well as to possible issues of content deficiency and contamination. In doing so, we focus on three broad types of commonly measured psychological constructs: affective and attitudinal states (e.g., mood, life satisfaction), personality traits (e.g., extraversion, agreeableness), and interpersonal relationships (e.g., social networks). For the first two, we also consider the level of analysis—whether the information about a given construct is being gathered at the individual or group level and what has to be done to generalize the findings and subsequent theoretical interpretations about the construct across different levels (i.e., psychometric isomorphism and homology of multilevel constructs; Tay, Woo, & Vermunt, 2014).

We then discuss three additional ways in which the validity of big data measurements can be evaluated: (a) response processes (i.e., the congruence between the construct and the nature of response engaged in by respondents; AERA et al., 2014, p. 12), (b) internal (factorial) structure, and (c) nomological net—relations to other variables. Last, we consider issues related to reliability, the consistency across repeated measurements, which can be evaluated from various perspectives such as classical test theory (Allen & Yen, 2002); generalizability theory (Cronbach, Gleser, Nanda, & Rajaratnam, 1972); and/or item response theory (Hambleton, Swaminathan, & Rogers, 1991).

A few cautionary remarks are necessary: We discuss opportunities and challenges associated with these big data sources compared with more "traditional" data sources (e.g., surveys, assessment centers, interviews), which typically are much smaller in size, more slowly generated, and less technological. At the same time, we acknowledge that "small" and "big" data range on a continuum rather than represent two distinct categories. The boundaries between the two are often fuzzy in reality (e.g., personnel records vs. electronic personnel records, smartphone-assisted experience sampling surveys vs. big data smartphone methods), and as such, any differences we discuss here should be understood on a continuum. Big data do not replace traditional approaches but can be used to address different questions; fitting the type of data to the research purpose remains crucial. Also, "more" data do not automatically improve the quality of measurement; different types of data are advantageous for capturing different aspects of a given phenomenon, as we highlight throughout this chapter. Last, although this chapter does not go into details about ethical and legal issues related to big data measurement approaches, such topics are extremely important to consider; we direct interested readers to other chapters of this edited volume for relevant discussions (e.g., Chapters 15, 17, 19).

SOCIAL MEDIA

The most dominant source of big data used in psychological research arguably comes from social media platforms (e.g., McFarland & Ployhart, 2015). These sites are

> web-based services that allow individuals to (1) construct a public or semi-public profile within a bounded system, (2) articulate a list of other users with whom they share a connection, and (3) view and traverse their list of connections and those made by others within the system. (Boyd & Ellison, 2007, p. 211; see also Kietzmann, Hermkens, McCarthy, & Silvestre, 2014; McFarland & Ployhart, 2015)

Social media sites comprise some of the most visited websites on the Internet ("Alexa—the Top 500 Sites on the Web," n.d.) and include Facebook, YouTube, Instagram, Twitter, WhatsApp, WeChat, Snapchat, and Reddit (Lenhart, Purcell, Smith, & Zickuhr, 2010). Despite their common functions, different social media sites contain different components that allow for expressive behavior. For example, Facebook (http://www.facebook.com) currently includes sections describing the user, a place to post short to long "updates," a timeline of events, albums of photos and videos, a directory of friends, social groups, and the ability to "like" other posts. Twitter (http://www.twitter.com) includes brief posts ("tweets"), the ability to follow and be followed by others, photos and videos, and likes. The components help construct and define the culture of the platform and the way people interact with it and use it. They are also constantly changing, making it important for researchers to stay updated on the available features and typical user constellations and ways of using and interacting with the platform.

To date, social science research with social media data has focused primarily on Facebook and Twitter. This is driven in part by the popularity of these sites and because the data have been made accessible to social scientists who are increasingly aware of big data methodologies. Although other social media sites (e.g., YouTube, Pinterest) provide other forms of data such as video and images, they have not been as widely utilized by psychologists. Given this, we reference primarily Facebook and Twitter in our discussion of social media (unless noted otherwise), whereas the general ideas and principles presented may be applicable to other sites and platforms. It is also important to note that these two sites will continue to evolve as public interest and constraints around data access shift. For instance, over the past 5 years, Facebook and Twitter have dominated public interest, with billions of users each year (Greenwood, Perrin, & Duggan, 2016). As a result of this growth, the dynamic nature of user characteristics and demographics has to be continually revisited. Also, until recently, Facebook data were relatively accessible, and Twitter data were publicly available, making ethical issues easier to address. But as public concern over user privacy has risen, social media platforms are tightening constraints around access (see Chapters 15 and 18, this volume).

Constructs and Content Relevance

A number of studies have used social media data to capture a variety of psychological variables. First, various forms of data extracted from social media sites offer the possibility of capturing momentary behavioral traces of personality as it manifests in everyday life (Gosling, Augustine, Vazire, Holtzman, & Gaddis, 2011; Kosinski, Stillwell, & Graepel, 2013). Although personality research has relied considerably on broad trait classifications that can be captured through trait descriptions (predominantly via survey), personality is manifested behaviorally through a variety of situational contexts. Many studies have demonstrated that text data from social media can indeed be used to capture broad dimensions of (normal) personality, such as extraversion, conscientiousness, and openness (Kern et al., 2014; Park et al., 2015), as well as the "dark" traits, such as narcissism (e.g., Akhtar, Winsborough, Ort, Johnson, & Chamorro-Premuzic, 2018; Sumner, Byers, Boochever, & Park, 2012). In addition to words, profile photo choices and other types of social media activities (e.g., number of posts, friends, and groups on Facebook) have been also used to predict users' personality traits (Bachrach, Kosinski, Graepel, Kohli, & Stillwell, 2012; Gosling et al., 2011; Kosinski et al., 2013; Liu, Preotiuc-Pietro, Samani, Moghaddam, & Ungar, 2016). Not surprisingly, video blogging on YouTube has also been found to be a source of personality expression (Biel & Gatica-Perez, 2013).

Second, online textual data can capture attitudinal and affective constructs such as stress, affect, mood, and sentiment (e.g., Coviello et al., 2014; Golder & Macy, 2011; Thelwall, Buckley, & Paltoglou, 2011; Wang, Hernandez, Newman, He, & Bian, 2016). Recent research has also found that emojis of faces and objects are used to express and communicate emotion states (Riordan, 2017).

Last (and perhaps most obvious), because social media are defined by interactions with others (hence the word *social*), a number of studies have utilized social networks data distilled from social media (based on the patterns of likes, comments, and replies, etc.) to measure constructs related to interpersonal relationships. Such constructs include tie strength, communication patterns, and network structures (e.g., Gilbert & Karahalios, 2009; Manago, Taylor, & Greenfield, 2012).

Social media enables easy access to a large number of self-reports on behavioral incidents, feelings, thoughts, and interpersonal relationships, which are often generated in situ by users around the world over multiple time points. As such, a major advantage of social media is the ability to capture the multilevel extension of a given psychological attribute or phenomenon as it appears in near real time in the real world. For example, researchers have sought to examine the aggregate life satisfaction of communities from individual-level Twitter data (L. Smith et al., 2016). Others have proposed and used social media data over time to understand longer term societal trends such as popular topics, disruptive events, and public opinion (Cvijikj & Michahelles, 2011; Sobkowicz, Kaschesky, & Bouchard, 2012).

One common criticism of social media is the potential for social desirability biases, with the idea that people actively manage their online presence to maintain certain images. Because communication does not take place instantaneously, individuals are allowed to "manage their self-presentations more strategically than in face-to-face situations" (Krämer & Winter, 2008, p. 106). To be fair, this phenomenon of impression management is hardly new; it has challenged self-report research for decades, resulting in the development of scales that try to detect and account for its occurrence (e.g., the Marlow-Crowne Social Desirability Scale; Crowne & Marlowe, 1960). The added challenge of social media, however, is to determine whether such impression management (which is allegedly easier to do online) further distorts what would have been observed in offline settings.

Despite concerns over self-presentation biases, research to date suggests that features on personal social networking sites such as Facebook reflect the user's actual personality, more so than their ideal self-images (Back et al., 2010), and that even less desirable, dark sides of personality traits can be reliably inferred via social media (e.g., Akhtar et al., 2018; Sumner et al., 2012). Studies clearly find personality-based differences in how people use social media (Kern et al., 2014; Kosinski et al., 2013). At the same time, when specifically motivated (e.g., placed in a job application setting), individuals are capable of—and do engage in—manipulating their social media profile features and activities to present themselves in a more positive light (Roulin & Levashina, 2016). Whether the self-promotion is honest or deceptive, this points to the potential for content contamination.

Relatedly, another (perhaps more fundamental) question can be posed: Can human behaviors and personality traits observed or inferred online be construed as an extension of their offline counterparts, or do they tap into a distinct sphere of social–psychological phenomena altogether? As people spend a considerable number of waking hours online, they become known through the image they place online, whether or not that reflects their self-image. A number of daily events and human behaviors readily observed in offline settings (e.g., driving to work, having small talks with a neighbor, washing dishes while listening to a podcast) do not show up on social media because they are too mundane to share, whereas atypical, extraordinary events and behaviors get posted more often. Furthermore, not all significant moments and experiences are shared on social media—whether or not to post something on Facebook and Twitter likely depends on the individual user characteristics and motivations related to affiliation, self-promotion, information sharing, and privacy. The discrepancy between online and offline repertoires of behavioral episodes and events in representing a given psychological construct, not only pertains to the issue of content deficiency and contamination but also to that of response processes through which measurements are taken.

Response Processes

In social media data, response processes comprise the psychological processes that underlie individuals' social media behaviors. Actions taking place within social media are just like other forms of behavior: They are determined by the psychological states, motivations, and attributes of the actor. For instance, if a person is upset or angry and chooses to post online, they might express that emotion through words and emoticons. We can also infer various stable traits based on the content of the posts (e.g., negative affectivity) and the individuals' decision to make these posts public (e.g., low self-monitoring, high extraversion, low neuroticism) across multiple posts. As such, "social media language is rich in psychological content" (Park et al., 2015, p. 942).

Zywica and Danowski (2008) looked at two motives for social media use: social enhancement (to expand one's good popularity) and social compensation (to improve inadequate popularity). Individuals who were higher in extraversion and self-esteem were more likely to use social enhancement, whereas those low in extraversion and self-esteem were more likely to compensate. Quan-Haase and Young (2010) factor analyzed the needs met by Facebook, finding six dimensions of gratifications: pastime, affection, fashion, sharing problems, sociability, and social information. Although the response processes are similar to other forms of behavior, there is a unique emphasis on social motives and needs.

Still, the extent to which social media data can indeed be used to approximate psychological content rests on the assumption of congruence. How well this assumption holds has to be tested and continually revisited as user behavior shifts and evolves. Social media platform also has its own culture, and the extent to which response processes differ across platforms has to be established.

Internal Structure

One of the challenges of integrating big data within psychological research is the overwhelming number of features (e.g., words, images, sensor inputs) that could be analyzed. For instance, Kern et al. (2014) analyzed language associated with the Big Five personality factors (i.e., Extraversion, Agreeableness, Conscientiousness, Emotional Stability, Openness); 69,000 respondents created 452 million words and phrases. As such, it is necessary to reduce the number of dimensions. Just as it is necessary in traditional survey-based studies to reduce a large number of items into a smaller number of dimensions (e.g., factor analysis of a set of items resulting in a smaller number of latent factors, represented by individual items), it is necessary to reduce the data to a more manageable number.

One approach is to use a top-down, closed data approach by counting the number of times each category occurs. For example, with language, the 2015 version of the Linguistic Inquiry Word Count program (Pennebaker, Boyd, Jordan, & Blackburn, 2015) consists of over 72 preestablished categories that run through the text and count each time a word in that category is used. Alternatively, specific behaviors can be counted, such as likes, image features, and number of friends. However, several problems arise with this approach. First, social media data commonly include features that are not included in preconstructed categories, such as emoticons, misspellings, and abbreviations. Second, stemming (e.g., sleep* includes sleep, sleeps, sleeping, etc.) at times is appropriate, but other times there are meaningful differences between words with different endings. Third, categories may be completely driven by one or two words, which can change the meaning of the category. For instance, *sick* could indicate somatic symptoms, but is also used by youth to indicate that something is "cool." Thus, it might appear that many people are sick when it is actually an expression of positive emotion. Fourth, categories are generally based on single words, which can have different meanings than phrases. For example, counting the occurrence of "merry" makes Christmas look like a happy day, but this is simply capturing the popular expression "Merry Christmas," regardless of how some individuals may actually feel on that day (e.g., "holiday blues").

Part of the power of big data comes from the potential for using machine learning approaches to identify coherent factors and patterns in the data (e.g., through open-vocabulary approaches; Schwartz et al., 2013). For example, language topics (or groups of commonly co-occurring words) can be identified using approaches such as latent Dirichlet allocation (Blei, Ng, & Jordan, 2003), which identifies a prespecified number of latent clusters, much like different factors are identified in factor analysis. Words receive a weighting as to how strongly they load on that factor. From our experience, some topics are easily interpretable (e.g., a food topic), whereas others appear rather meaningless. Just as factor analysis involves judgments about the right number of topics, human raters are needed to monitor automatically created results to determine which topics are meaningful and which are noise.

The large number of users and features makes it possible to split the data randomly into smaller samples, allowing some subsets to be used to train models and other subsets to be used to test those models, making it possible to replicate findings within the same study. The accuracy of automatic models can also be compared with human annotations of a subset of data (e.g., Park et al., 2015), providing an additional indication of accuracy.

Nomological Net

Just as the validity of any psychological construct measured with surveys is evaluated in part through correlations with measures of other constructs (Cronbach & Meehl, 1955; John & Benet-Martínez, 2014), constructs measured with social media data are validated by comparison with other variables containing meaningful psychological content. Standard practice at this time is to correlate linguistic features with self-report questionnaire data, assuming the self-report to be the "ground truth." Park et al. (2015) presented a particularly rigorous evaluation, testing language-based assessments (LBAs) of the Big Five personality traits (i.e., predicted values of personality-based or linguistic features extracted from social media data). The authors first demonstrated validity evidence by correlating LBAs with conventional self-reported personality traits measured by items from the International Personality Item Pool (Goldberg et al., 2006), showing correlations were substantially larger between the two measures of same traits (average $r = .38$) than between those of different traits. They also compared LBAs with reports from third-party informants, finding similar results. In addition, they showed that LBAs predicted self-report after controlling for informant ratings. Finally, the authors examined 14 criterion variables (e.g., life satisfaction, recent days sick), comparing the relations in social media with those found with self-report. Patterns of correlations were compared using multiple complementary methods: (a) *sign agreement*, that the estimates were consistent in sign; (b) *correlation magnitudes*, tests for differences in the value of the correlations; and (c) *column-vector correlations*, the correlation of the correlations.

Reliability

Reliability estimates can be calculated on various parts of the data analysis process. If raters are used (e.g., indicating the extent to which a set of Facebook posts represents extraversion), reliability can be calculated using typical interrater reliability statistics (e.g., kappa, intraclass correlation coefficient). For data-driven features (e.g., topics, predictive words), sets of data can be randomly sampled, and the extent to which results replicate (e.g., the same words are predictive of a particular trait) can be assessed. For instance, Kern et al. (2014) found an average split-half correlation of $r = .84$. Alternatively, as social media usually contains time stamps, the data can be split across several time points, and correlations across time sets indicate the cross-time consistency, in the same way that participants can respond to a survey at multiple time points, and cross-time consistency can be established. For instance, Kern et al. (2014) split data across two periods, finding that 79% of most predictive words were equivalent across the two periods. Park et al. (2015) generated multiple predictions of traits across six time points for each individual and then correlated the time-adjacent scores. Each time point was separated by six months, and the average correlation was $r = .70$, compared with self-report surveys that ranged from $r = .65$ to $r = .85$.

WEARABLE SENSORS

The second major type of big data comes from wearable sensors (e.g., sociometric badges, Fitbits), defined here as sensors with Internet connectivity that can provide a continual stream of data (as opposed to nonconnected sensors, such as hearing aids; Swan, 2012). Virtually any type of sensor could be embedded in wearables to collect specific streams of information (e.g., stretch and pressure sensors, chemical sensors; Bandodkar & Wang, 2014), but forms that have been included in social science research are accelerometers, microphones, infrared sensors, and Bluetooth sensors (Chaffin et al., 2017; Olguín et al., 2009). Each of these sensors can capture a unique form of physical behavior, including location, posture, and movement (e.g., sitting, standing, walking, running); speech frequency, duration, and loudness; frequency and duration of face-to-face interactions; and physical proximity to other sensors

(Chaffin et al., 2017; Kim, McFee, Olguín, Waber, & Pentland, 2012; Olguín & Pentland, 2007). These technologies are ever expanding, and new types of sensors that capture unique types of behavioral data (especially for the medical and health care field) to date have been less accessible to researchers due to privacy and confidentiality concerns, costs, and practical limitations. As technology continues to develop, a growing number of sensors, which are increasingly time and resource efficient, will become available to researchers.

Constructs and Content Relevance

To date, wearable sensors have been used most often in the social science literature to capture constructs related to interpersonal relationships and group-level social phenomena. Traditionally, interpersonal relationships have been assessed using retrospective self-reports from group members, which bring multiple biases and inaccuracies (Donaldson & Grant-Vallone, 2002). Wearable sensors, however, have been used to capture a variety of interpersonal and group-level social phenomena "as they unfold." These phenomena include individuals' boundary-spanning behaviors and leadership emergence within groups (Chaffin et al., 2017), group problem-solving performance (Dong & Pentland, 2010), co-influence of individual and group behaviors (Dong, Lepri, & Pentland, 2011), interteam collaboration integration of new members within teams (Kim et al., 2012), amount of communication (Olguín et al., 2009), knowledge transfer and network cohesion (Wu, Waber, Aral, Brynjolfsson, & Pentland, 2008), social capital in creative teams (Gloor et al., 2012), and group flow among jazz musicians (Gloor, Oster, & Fischbach, 2013).

Sensors can be highly useful for supplementing traditional measures of human behaviors in a specific context. For example, behaviors such as physical movement and verbal activity may be key aspects of individual and team functioning in certain organizational and work domains, such as the military, the technology industry, and the service industry. Also, wearable sensors are useful for behavioral constructs related to health (e.g., exercise), providing a method to monitor and promote health outcomes. The ability of sensors to capture physical behaviors such as posture and movement is important given concerns of physical inactivity in developed nations (World Health Organization, 2018). A particular benefit of wearable sensors, from a motivational perspective, is that many report data back to users, allowing them to monitor their activity and compare their efforts with others, thus increasing interest in incorporating physical activity throughout their day (Malik, Blake, & Suggs, 2014).

Extant studies have measured physical movements, physical strain and demands, and seated posture. For example, Pärkkä et al. (2006) showed that automatic classification of activities for walking, running, and cycling exceeded 80% accuracy. Dunne, Walsh, Hermann, Smyth, and Caulfield (2008) used sensors to monitor posture and found that it was capable of discriminating good versus bad posture comparable with the analysis of experts. More recently, Betti and colleagues (2018) developed a wearable physiological sensors system that can measure and monitor levels of stress. Massive amounts of sensor data have been generated over the past 5 to 10 years, such that numerous other studies are possible using already existing data.

Although sensors adequately capture actual behavior and activity, traits and affective or attitudinal constructs are less likely to be measured well. Some technologies are attempting to monitor mood through sensors measuring, for example, skin temperature and heart rate variability, much like a mood ring, but it remains unclear what such sensors are capturing. Traits, in particular, are less likely to be captured through sensors, as they comprise complex, high-level patterns of the mind and behavior that cannot be derived from simple behaviors alone. Continued technological advances most likely will continue to open new opportunities to connect physiological elements to emotion and other characteristics, and in combination with other measures, such sensors might provide information about physiological manifestations of various traits in everyday contexts.

Aside from problems related to the technological accuracy in capturing physical movements (Chaffin et al., 2017), a number of questions remain regarding how the physical behaviors (measured by wearable sensors) can represent the constructs of interest. For instance, is colocation a reasonable indicator of team cohesion? Does movement indicate proactivity or engagement in tasks? Can speech frequency represent leadership proactivity and traits such as extraversion? Does speech loudness indicate social dominance? Linking specific attributes and patterns of physical movements to underlying psychological constructs often entails a careful a priori theoretical justification. However, as we noted earlier, one may also choose to take an inductive route in exploring the (systematic and robust) relations between sensor-derived variables and various measures of theoretical constructs that are already established in the literature.

Response Processes

For sensors that capture readily observable behaviors (e.g., walking, talking), the response processes are assumed to be the psychological factors that cause the measured behaviors. For instance, constructs such as dominance, team collaboration, and leadership emergence can be theorized or assumed as the psychological determinants of acting in a dominant manner, collaborating with others, and engaging in leadership activities, respectively. If a particular construct is known to give rise to the measured behaviors, the inference can be justified, but the extent to which this is true must be analyzed within the paradigm of expected nomological relationships. For sensors capturing physiological responses (e.g., heart rate, galvanic skin response), an empirical connection has to be established between physiological responses and underlying or co-occurring psychological experiences (Horvath, 1979). Just as neurological studies have created interest in understanding neurophysiological traces of characteristics and behaviors, data is messy and often contradictory. Although there is considerable excitement over the physiological signals that can be detected with sensors, the practical meaning of such patterns is unclear. Establishing these links becomes especially important if the sensors are to be used as unobtrusive ways of measuring and monitoring respondents that could impact subsequent actions. For instance, if a person is struggling with a mental disorder, sensors potentially could be used to monitor mood, establishing when emotions change and informing the therapist about what happens between sessions. But if those indicators are not correctly capturing emotions, they could misguide treatment. This is an area where close collaboration between computer scientists (with skills to analyze sensor data) and social scientists (with theories and understandings of human attitudes, emotions, behaviors, cognitions, and characteristics) will be useful for making sense of what information is valuable, where technology has to go to create valuable information, and what observed patterns actually mean.

Internal Structure

Studies with sensors have typically used single indicators, or the indicators simply provide an operational measure (Chaffin et al., 2017). In these cases, concerns about internal structure have less relevance. However, just as traditional studies find that combining multiple indicators most likely provide a more consistent representation of a construct (e.g., Credé, Harms, Niehorster, & Gaye-Valentine, 2012), the combination of multiple sensors, or a sensor with other types of information, may be more informative. Like combining multiple survey items to represent a single psychological construct, two or more behavioral indicators from a sensor may be used together to represent a single psychological construct. For instance, leadership behavior and team communication might be captured by verbal sounds, proximity to others, and movement patterns. In these cases, exploratory or confirmatory factor models can be specified and tested for goodness of fit. It is also important to consider whether indicators are reflective of underlying constructs or whether they are formative (Edwards & Bagozzi, 2000). For example, verbal sounds, proximity, and movement patterns alone might be inadequate markers of leadership, but when they occur together, they do indicate leadership (MacKenzie, Podsakoff, & Jarvis, 2005).

Given that sensor data provide multivariate time series data, longitudinal or dynamic factor models have to be developed and implemented to validate the use of indicators over time, at time scales that are both manageable (in terms of handling and analyzing the data) and appropriate for capturing the construct under consideration (Molenaar, 1985). Methodological work in this area is not at a mature stage. In addition, work is needed on best-practice approaches for capturing complex constructs such as teamwork and leadership.

Nomological Net

A number of studies have successfully used social network indicators measured by sensors to make predictions for other psychological constructs. For instance, Gloor et al. (2012) found that network centrality predicted extraversion, whereas the number of signals between badges predicted statements of distrust. Olguín et al. (2009) found that the amount of interpersonal communication (both face-to-face and electronic) was related to employee satisfaction. Other studies have reported similar evidence (e.g., Aharony, Pan, Ip, Khayal, & Pentland, 2011; Dong & Pentland, 2010; Kim et al., 2012).

Although these results are encouraging, the behaviors captured via wearable sensors may predict criteria due to the multifaceted, compound nature of the construct–indicator relations. In other words, sensor-based behavioral data likely reflect a variety of psychological constructs that are not necessarily the same as the target construct. For example, a consistent pattern of fast movements synchronized within a work team may reflect situational requirements, physical fitness of the members, and/or shared affective experiences such as excitement, urgency, or fear. Thus, it is important to examine both convergent and divergent associations across a range of potentially relevant constructs. To date, such evidence is sparse. One example, however, can be found in Chaffin et al. (2017), who showed that convergent correlations for some constructs (e.g., speaking dominance) were acceptable, while also finding that results were contingent on the specific methodologies used (e.g., signal strength cutoff, speech detection algorithm).

Reliability

Chaffin et al. (2017) recently scrutinized the reliability of sensor data by conducting four studies on the use of wearable sensors for capturing behavioral constructs at the individual and group levels. The authors discriminated between two sources of measurement error: (a) sensitivity differences between sensors (e.g., Sensor A may be slightly more sensitive than Sensor B) and (b) differences within the same sensor across time. Both are caused by differences in sensor sensitivity, but they differ in how it manifests. The latter, within-sensor variability, is the more innocuous of the two because it essentially induces a small source of random error that generally averages out across the many assessments made by the sensors. Indeed, Chaffin et al. found that changes in within-sensor sensitivities accounted for merely 1.4% of the variance in colocation, 1.2% of raw volume, and < 1% of filtered amplitude. By contrast, between-sensor differences represent a systematic source of error that may accumulate over time, given the repeated measurements of the sensors. Accordingly, the authors found that sensitivity differences between sensors accounted for 8% of the variance in colocation, 23% of raw volume, and 3.8% of filtered amplitude variance. These results suggest that researchers have to be careful in making inferences about differences between individuals because these differences may arise because of differences in sensors themselves (i.e., sensitivity, condition, etc.).

INTERNET BEHAVIOR

The third major form of big data is Internet behavior, which refers to online actions commonly captured in web searches, page views, clicks, and time spent online (Agichtein, Brill, & Dumais, 2018; Bucklin & Sismeiro, 2009; Hölscher & Strube, 2000; see also Chapter 4, this volume). The automatic recording of such behaviors through Internet logs generates a massive number of in-the-moment data points. Given that Internet behaviors are most often information seeking based on interests (Powell & Clarke, 2006; Savolainen & Kari, 2004), data on these forms of behavior are widely used in marketing to assess levels and trends in the interests of groups and individuals (e.g., Goel, Hofman, Lahaie, Pennock, & Watts, 2010). Other social science studies have been conducted on searches of various topics, such as bitcoins (Kristoufek, 2013), unemployment claims (Choi & Varian, 2012), cancer screening (Schootman et al., 2015), and suicide (McCarthy, 2010).

Constructs and Content Relevance

Internet search and page view behavior (e.g., number of clicks on terms related to "retirement," "stress," or "vacation") may directly reflect an interest in the topic searched or viewed or at least a momentary curiosity. Further, such interests can potentially signal the co-occurring psychological traits and states of the Internet users. For example, a high frequency of Google search terms like "coping with job stress" and "how to deal with frustration with boss" may reflect actual experiences and dispositional tendencies, although what state is being indicated may not always be fully clear. For instance, searching for "job stress" might reliably reflect the presence of stress, but searching for "love" might reflect a lack of (but desire for) romantic engagement. On the whole, Internet behaviors are arguably less relevant for the study of interpersonal relationships than other forms of big data.

Although performed anonymously and/or in private, Internet behavior can be easily aggregated into units based on time and location, allowing researchers to monitor how interest in a topic (and underlying psychological states) changes over time. Due to practical, ethical, and legal constraints, it is unusual for a researcher to have access to an individual's Internet behavior over time because search behavior data are typically maintained by large organizations, such as Google and Microsoft, and access is impossible unless one collaborates directly with these companies. Still, the same companies are increasingly making aggregate sets of the data publicly available (e.g., Google, IBM, and Bloomberg; see Emerging Technology From the arXiv, 2010) and are driving crowdsourced approaches to data analytics. For instance, public hackathons provide access to such data in a supported competition centered on specific research questions.

Internet behavior data may supplement traditional self-reported survey methods for assessing people's collective attitudes, emotions, and interests at the community level or aggregate location level over time. Traditional approaches for assessing psychological states across time and location involve representative surveys such as the General Social Survey (https://gss.norc.org/) and the Gallup-Healthways daily tracking survey (https://www.gallup.com/analytics/213701/us-daily-tracking.aspx), which are typically conducted over the phone, mail, or e-mail. Internet search and page view behavior data can help to quickly and inexpensively address questions about how attitudes, well-being, and interests are related to and influenced by seasonal patterns, public policy (e.g., minimum wage increases), local and national economic productivity, regional and national culture, and local market conditions, among other things.

Response Processes

The process of searching for information about a term on the Internet is qualitatively different from responding to a survey item because the search depends on the motives behind the search behavior. This is where knowledge about the motivations that drive people, developed across decades of research in social science, is particularly useful. Search behavior is often driven by an information gap (cf. Broder, 2002), and it could be assumed that individuals who enter a search term or look for a Wikipedia page are interested in that topic, at least for that moment. However, the underlying reasons for such an interest may be unclear. For example, a person who searches for information about a particular emotional term may be experiencing that emotion and motivated to alleviate it (e.g., depression, anxiety, stress), seeking that emotion (e.g., happiness, calmness), or simply investigating the topic for nonpersonal reasons (e.g., writing a research report on different emotion words).

In the interdisciplinary field of human-computer interaction, several theoretical models have been proposed to explicate the cognitive, information-seeking processes that underlie individuals' web search activities (see Kammerer & Gerjets, 2011, for an overview). These models are helpful in organizing different types of web search activities into distinct stages or elements of the information problem-solving or information-foraging process. As such, they provide a useful framework for understanding how each search entry or page view fits into an overall process of resolving the initial information gap. Building from these models, psychologists may identify and delineate different non-cognitive, motivational factors that cause the information gap in the first place, as well as factors influencing the specific types of search activities. For example, with regard to the search term *depression*, would people with a long history of experiencing the emotion (and thus motivated to find remedial strategies) be more likely to search for other related terms and/or engage in different cognitive strategies and information-seeking tasks (e.g., deep processing; Hölscher & Strube, 2000) compared with those interested in the topic for research purposes? Using the technology directly, a question could be displayed directly after the search term is entered to gauge the underlying motive that triggered the behavior. Experience sampling methods and/or experimental methods can also be used to illuminate what situational triggers prompt a person to search for certain terms, while also capturing concurring psychological experiences.

Internal Structure

To our knowledge, little consideration has been given within studies to the internal structure of Internet behaviors. Its features suggest similarities to approaches possible with social media and wearable sensor data. Search terms or specific behaviors (e.g., number of pages related to a topic visited) can be used as individual variables, in which case the internal structure is not an issue. One recent study examined how positive and negative emotion Google search terms in the Positive and Negative Affect Schedule (Watson, Clark, & Tellegen, 1988) hang together and only found weak evidence of the expected two-factor structure because positive and negative emotion searches were not strongly unidimensional (Ford, Jebb, Tay, & Diener, 2018). Researchers could also determine the number of search terms that an Internet user enters before proceeding to individual pages, providing insight into how well the search algorithms are capturing the initial intention. If users are immediately moving to pages suggested by the search engine, this might indicate that the search engine's algorithms are accurately meeting the user's interests, whereas additional searches would suggest that the algorithm is wrong.

However, like social media, a broad range of words, misspellings, and terms might be used by different users to reflect the same construct, or the same term might indicate a number of different constructs. Single words can be misclassified because of multiple semantic meanings. For instance, a search term that is also part of a popular movie title (e.g., *Up in the Air*, *The Time Traveler's Wife*) might be misclassified as an interest in travel. To improve accuracy, similar terms can be grouped together, and topics can be identified (e.g., a travel topic might include "airline tickets," "Airbnb," "hotels," "rental cars") using either the top-down or bottom-up approaches discussed earlier. For example, searches for "job stress" should correlate with searches for "job burnout" or "frustration at work" because they reflect the general construct of negative work-related affect.

Search data often contain additional markers beyond the term itself, such as the location of the user and the time and date of the search. This means that studies can compare, for instance, search behaviors across locations or time. We note, however, that the unit of measurement can place constraints on the analysis. For example, if a researcher is analyzing searches at the U.S. state level, they are limited to 50 units of analysis, compared with the U.S. county level, which includes over 3,000 units. If units of analysis are separated over time, more units are available, just as multiple assessments of an individual over time increase power.

One practical challenge with searches is that access to the data is dependent on the search platform (e.g., Google, Apple). For example, Google has made search data available through Google Trends (https://trends.google.com/trends/). However, researchers do not always have full flexibility to know how scores are calculated or to manipulate the types of searches we want to target. In addition, the issues of whether these page views or searches are formative or reflective indicators (as discussed earlier) should also be considered (Edwards & Bagozzi, 2000).

Nomological Net

Although the three aforementioned forms of validity evidence have received little empirical attention, there has been extensive research on the associations between Internet behavior scores and external criteria. Indeed, early studies reported that search data could measure flu trends better than the Centers for Disease Control and Prevention (Ginsberg et al., 2009) and that H1N1 influenza and other ailments could be detected through Internet behaviors (e.g., Chew & Eysenbach, 2010; Salathé, Freifeld, Mekaru, Tomasulo, & Brownstein, 2013; Seifter, Schwarzwalder, Geis, & Aucott, 2010). These studies fueled much of the current interest in public policy in using online data as a public health initiative. From a public health standpoint, if Internet behavior can successfully predict meaningful economic and/or health outcomes, the analysis of such behavior provides a much more efficient and cost-effective approach relative to traditional epidemiological surveys. However, more recent work suggests that Google Flu Trends may not be as accurate (Butler, 2013), and prediction performance is not favorable for contexts such as Latin America. Prediction accuracies have to be established and regularly revisited, especially because how users engage with and use technology continues to shift and evolve.

One type of validity evidence can be evaluated by examining convergent relationships with known measures of psychological constructs that are thought to be relevant, such as content-specific interests and related psychological states, typically measured using self-reported surveys and aggregated across users. For instance, research might investigate associations between Internet searches and page view behaviors over time and other indices of job satisfaction, such as those gathered by Gallup-Healthways and the General Social Survey. It may be that increased job search behavior, for example, corresponds with lower job satisfaction. Relatedly, Internet behavior might be used to predict changes in economic productivity and rates of health problems at the state or location level. When individuals are searching for information about job burnout or stress, they may be experiencing those mental states and, in turn, be less productive (Gilboa, Shirom, Fried, & Cooper, 2008) and more likely to need mental health treatment (Ganster & Rosen, 2013). Other research might investigate Internet search and page view behavior as correlates of economic conditions at the temporal (e.g., monthly, yearly) and location (e.g., state, metro area) level.

To the extent that survey responses are available in the aggregate at the location and/or temporal (e.g., yearly, monthly) level, these scores can be correlated with search and page view scores as the convergent validity evidence for those scores, as a number of studies have done. Examples include correlations of searches on depression, anxiety, and fatigue with coronary heart disease (Ford et al., 2018), depression and anxiety searches with indicators of economic distress (Ayers, Althouse, Allem, Rosenquist, & Ford, 2013), depression searches with seasonal variation (Yang, Tsai, Huang, & Peng, 2011), searches for a variety of topics with stock market activity (Curme, Preis, Stanley, & Moat, 2014), and searches for products with corresponding consumer behavior (Goel et al., 2010). Several other studies have investigated search terms related to health and health-related criteria in the population (for a review, see Nuti et al., 2014). The variety of search terms and the continuous availability of new data offers opportunities to investigate these and other questions in the aggregate that were generally not possible in the past.

However, although some studies find the expected correlations, not all correlate with external criteria as expected. For example, McCarthy (2010) found that searches related to suicide were negatively related to suicide behavior, leading the author to suggest that perhaps suicide searches reflect help-seeking that successfully prevents suicide behavior. There has also been little research on page view counts, such as those of Wikipedia topics, as predictors of criteria, representing an opportunity for further research.

Reliability

Like other forms of big data, Internet search and page views generate considerable data, but it is difficult to index the reliability of these scores by traditional means. Past research on search query scores suggests that these have little random noise; much of the fluctuation in scores reflect seasonal patterns and real changes in the world (Zhu, Wang, Qin, & Wu, 2012). But some search query scores are based on a sampling strategy; if this varies over time, it may contribute to random fluctuation. This appears to be the case for the Google Trends data (T. W. Smith, 2013), which represent the largest data source on Internet search behavior. Still, even a sample of these data represents a large number of observations, suggesting that the scores should be reliable enough to consider questions of validity further.

Scale reliability of the search terms and page views will have to be sensitive to the unit of analysis. As mentioned, most of the frequency information on searches is based on higher level units (e.g., U.S. states or countries) due to the need to protect individual anonymity. However, with individual searches on a website, one may be able to track which pages users frequently covisit at an individual level. The calculation of scale reliability will have to account for the number of units available. With fewer units, one should also seek to include data over time to examine variability attributable to indicators, units, and time. Finally, a unique issue for Internet searches is that many searches have a relatively lower base rate, which can lower the covariation between indicators and lead to lower scale reliability.

NEW POSSIBILITY 1: PUBLIC NETWORK CAMERAS

One of the upcoming possible sources of big data is public surveillance cameras installed in public spaces (e.g., lounge or lobby areas in commercial or governmental buildings, parks, shopping malls) and connected to networks (see Chapter 5, this volume, and Tay, Jebb, & Woo, 2017, for more detailed introductions). Since the 1950s, video cameras have been used as an unobtrusive and informative method of data collection in the behavioral sciences, including education, sociology, anthropology, economics, and psychology (Adolph, 2016; Ash, 2003). More recently, video data have been frequently discussed in contemporary academic discussions about methodological innovation (e.g., Congdon, Novack, & Goldin-Meadow, 2018; Hindmarsh & Llewellyn, 2018; Jarrett & Liu, 2018) and have also been used in empirical work in the psychological sciences (Bodenmann et al., 2015; Fan, Liberman, Keysar, & Kinzler, 2015; Plötner, Over, Carpenter, & Tomasello, 2015).

Video data allow for the analysis of various human behaviors (e.g., body language, gestures, appearance, posture) that have been shown to communicate emotions (Bailenson et al., 2008), cognitive function (Smyth, 1996), development (Franchak, Kretch, Soska, & Adolph, 2011), personality traits (Asendorpf, Banse, & Mücke, 2002), and behavioral effectiveness (Fan et al., 2015; Travassos et al., 2012). Although video data available through public cameras usually have insufficient image resolution for fine-grained, individual-level behavioral analyses, they can still be used to capture meaningful patterns of individual, interpersonal, and group behaviors in public spaces, such as standing in line at a bus stop, loitering, and helping versus bystanding (e.g., Mazerolle, Hurley, & Chamlin, 2002; Plötner et al., 2015). They can also capture movement through a city, pointing to interconnectivity, neighborhood walkability, and other dynamic location-based metrics that are hard to capture through other big data approaches.

For psychological research, public network camera data can be used to supplement the measurement of psychological states, traits, and interpersonal relationships, traditionally done with self- and other reports, with directly observable behavioral indicators. For example, with the extant analytic technologies for capturing human emotions from facial patterns, cameras positioned in public spaces have been used to infer group-level emotions such as smiles (von Bismarck, 2008). Also, massive video data aggregated across time and compared across locations can capture meaningful differences in those constructs across physically separated clusters of individuals that are socially and/or professionally connected (Stigler, Gallimore, & Hiebert, 2000).

There are at least three psychometric issues with using public network cameras for psychology research where future work is needed. First, the reliability and validity of public camera data in measuring the aforementioned psychological constructs will depend heavily on the resolution and position of the camera (similar to the case of wearable sensors), which has to be systematically examined. Researchers often have little control over the positioning and resolution of many of the public network cameras. Many cameras may be facing a roadway, be located too far away to detect faces, capture faces that are obscured by shadows, or capture movement away from the camera. For cameras that are outdoors, weather conditions will affect the quality of the images collected. All of these result in less usable data despite the large proliferation of public network cameras.

Second, proper video-analytic technologies have yet to be developed to automate the coding and real-time analysis of human behaviors at a fine-grained level, such as facial expressions, which constrains the immediate utility of camera data for psychological research at this point. We note, however, that this is an area of key interest to computer scientists, and methods are rapidly improving, such that in the near future, this might be a valid and useful approach (Gosling, Redi, Sherman, & Kosinski, 2017).

Third, evaluating public camera data's psychometric properties requires careful a priori decisions on the appropriate unit of analysis for assessing the constructs of interest and boundaries around the time frame and what aspects of the image are included or excluded. For example, consider using counts of individuals smiling to measure group-level positive affect within a given region. Moving toward a real-time analysis of group-level affect via camera data will require deciding whether a certain group of individuals has to be uniquely within the scene over time; if not, an algorithm will have to weight and aggregate specific individuals' emotions over a prespecified period.

NEW POSSIBILITY 2: SMARTPHONES

Smartphones can be conceived as a big data approach that captures a variety of fine-grained temporal data, including several of the types described earlier as related to social media, searches, and sensors. As of 2018, 77% of American adults owned an Internet-enabled smartphone (Pew Research Center, 2018), and that number continues to rise. Many people are continually connected to their phones, such that nearly a continuous stream of in-the-moment behaviors, thoughts, voice recordings, photos, and survey responses are produced (see a review by Harari et al., 2016). The proliferation of applications (apps) installed on many phones creates endless possibilities of types of data potentially being collected across a large number of individuals (Miller, 2012).

Combining many of the same features found in other big data types mentioned in this article, smartphone data can assess a broad range of momentary psychological experiences ranging from cognitive, affective, and attitudinal states recorded and shared through sensors, apps, and plug-ins (e.g., mood, cognitive functioning) to various interpersonal activities captured through the phone use (e.g., voice or video call, texting). In psychology, smartphones are used in experience sampling studies, although these typically capture only survey responses over time, and many of the reliability and validity issues discussed in previous reviews are relevant here (Csikszentmihalyi &

Larson, 1987; Fisher & To, 2012; Harari et al., 2016). What may be a unique advantage of smartphones is that they enable researchers to triangulate survey data with behavioral (and often multimedia) data recorded and shared through smartphone sensors, apps, and plug-ins to capture a holistic account of one's psychological states and more (Harari et al., 2016).

The general discussions of reliability and validity of psychological measurements using smartphone data have been recently offered (Harari et al., 2016), and we guide the reader to the discussions there. Research using smartphones will be dependent on the accessibility of data; best-practice approaches for accessing and managing such data will have to be carefully considered in the future (Miller, 2012).

CONCLUSION

Big data offers a new frontier for psychological research. As computer science and psychology collide together over an inconceivable amount of information, it opens the door to pushing the edge of research and application. Big data approaches complement rather than replace traditional measurement approaches, providing a cost-effective and efficient method for collecting information on a previously unimaginable number of people, with a much broader reach than typical psychology studies. But more data are not necessarily better, and traditional psychological approaches often are needed to establish the validity, accuracy, and usefulness of the data.

A growing number of data collection and analysis tools are available, and early psychological research in this area has made some significant contributions. Nevertheless, it is time for research to go to a deeper level, pushing the boundaries of identifying and investigating what is and is not possible with big data. One particular challenge with regard to using big data for psychological measurement is to understand the appropriate levels of analysis and theoretical interpretation as data are collected across geographical units and time. Also, as highlighted in this chapter, much more empirical work is needed to assess what big data can do for the scientific progress of psychological research via enhanced measurement. Although we have offered a number of possibilities and ideas here, the actual evidence of reliability and validity of these big data sources, along with a complete framework of relevant big data approaches, must follow.

REFERENCES

Adjerid, I., & Kelley, K. (2018). Big data in psychology: A framework for research advancement. *American Psychologist, 73,* 899–917. http://dx.doi.org/10.1037/amp0000190

Adolph, K. (2016). Video as data: From transient behavior to tangible recording. *APS Observer, 29*(3), 23–25.

Agichtein, E., Brill, E., & Dumais, S. (2018). Improving web search ranking by incorporating user behavior information. *SIGIR Forum, 52*(2), 11–18. http://dx.doi.org/10.1145/3308774.3308778

Aharony, N., Pan, W., Ip, C., Khayal, I., & Pentland, A. (2011). Social fMRI: Investigating and shaping social mechanisms in the real world. *Pervasive and Mobile Computing, 7*, 643–659. http://dx.doi.org/10.1016/j.pmcj.2011.09.004

Akhtar, R., Winsborough, D., Ort, U., Johnson, A., & Chamorro-Premuzic, T. (2018). Detecting the dark side of personality using social media status updates. *Personality and Individual Differences, 132*, 90–97. http://dx.doi.org/10.1016/j.paid.2018.05.026

Alexa—the top 500 sites on the web. (n.d.). Retrieved from https://www.alexa.com/topsites/category/Computers/Internet/On_the_Web/Online_Communities/Social_Networking

Allen, M. J., & Yen, W. M. (2002). *Introduction to measurement theory.* Long Grove, IL: Waveland Press.

American Educational Research Association, American Psychological Association, & National Council on Measurement in Education. (2014). *Standards for educational and psychological testing.* Washington, DC: American Educational Research Association.

Asendorpf, J. B., Banse, R., & Mücke, D. (2002). Double dissociation between implicit and explicit personality self-concept: The case of shy behavior. *Journal of Personality and Social Psychology, 83*, 380–393. http://dx.doi.org/10.1037/0022-3514.83.2.380

Ash, D. (2003). Dialogic inquiry in life science conversations of family groups in a museum. *Journal of Research in Science Teaching, 40*, 138–162. http://dx.doi.org/10.1002/tea.10069

Ayers, J. W., Althouse, B. M., Allem, J.-P., Rosenquist, J. N., & Ford, D. E. (2013). Seasonality in seeking mental health information on Google. *American Journal of Preventive Medicine, 44*, 520–525. http://dx.doi.org/10.1016/j.amepre.2013.01.012

Bachrach, Y., Kosinski, M., Graepel, T., Kohli, P., & Stillwell, D. (2012). Personality and patterns of Facebook usage. In *Proceedings of the 4th Annual ACM Web Science Conference* (pp. 24–32). New York, NY: ACM. http://dx.doi.org/10.1145/2380718.2380722

Back, M. D., Stopfer, J. M., Vazire, S., Gaddis, S., Schmukle, S. C., Egloff, B., & Gosling, S. D. (2010). Facebook profiles reflect actual personality, not self-idealization. *Psychological Science, 21*, 372–374. http://dx.doi.org/10.1177/0956797609360756

Bailenson, J. N., Pontikakis, E. D., Mauss, I. B., Gross, J. J., Jabon, M. E., Hutcherson, C. A. C., . . . John, O. (2008). Real-time classification of evoked emotions using facial feature tracking and physiological responses. *International Journal of Human-Computer Studies, 66*, 303–317. http://dx.doi.org/10.1016/j.ijhcs.2007.10.011

Bandodkar, A. J., & Wang, J. (2014). Non-invasive wearable electrochemical sensors: A review. *Trends in Biotechnology, 32*, 363–371. http://dx.doi.org/10.1016/j.tibtech.2014.04.005

Betti, S., Lova, R. M., Rovini, E., Acerbi, G., Santarelli, L., Cabiati, M., . . . Cavallo, F. (2018). Evaluation of an integrated system of wearable physiological sensors for stress monitoring in working environments by using biological markers. *IEEE Transactions on Biomedical Engineering, 65*, 1748–1758. http://dx.doi.org/10.1109/TBME.2017.2764507

Biel, J., & Gatica-Perez, D. (2013). The YouTube lens: Crowdsourced personality impressions and audiovisual analysis of vlogs. *IEEE Transactions on Multimedia, 15*, 41–55. http://dx.doi.org/10.1109/TMM.2012.2225032

Blei, D. M., Ng, A. Y., & Jordan, M. I. (2003). Latent Dirichlet allocation. *Journal of Machine Learning Research, 3*, 993–1022.

Bodenmann, G., Meuwly, N., Germann, J., Nussbeck, F. W., Heinrichs, M., & Bradbury, T. N. (2015). Effects of stress on the social support provided by men and women in intimate relationships. *Psychological Science, 26*, 1584–1594. http://dx.doi.org/10.1177/0956797615594616

Boyd, D. M., & Ellison, N. B. (2007). Social network sites: Definition, history, and scholarship. *Journal of Computer-Mediated Communication, 13*, 210–230. http://dx.doi.org/10.1111/j.1083-6101.2007.00393.x

Broder, A. (2002). A taxonomy of web search. *SIGIR Forum, 36*(2), 3–10. http://dx.doi.org/10.1145/792550.792552

Bucklin, R. E., & Sismeiro, C. (2009). Click here for Internet insight: Advances in click-stream data analysis in marketing. *Journal of Interactive Marketing, 23*, 35–48. http://dx.doi.org/10.1016/j.intmar.2008.10.004

Butler, D. (2013). When Google got flu wrong. *Nature, 494*, 155–156. http://dx.doi.org/10.1038/494155a

Chaffin, D., Heidl, R., Hollenbeck, J. R., Howe, M., Yu, A., Voorhees, C., & Calantone, R. (2017). The promise and perils of wearable sensors in organizational research. *Organizational Research Methods, 20*, 3–31. http://dx.doi.org/10.1177/1094428115617004

Chew, C., & Eysenbach, G. (2010). Pandemics in the age of Twitter: Content analysis of Tweets during the 2009 H1N1 outbreak. *PLoS One, 5*(11), e14118. http://dx.doi.org/10.1371/journal.pone.0014118

Choi, H., & Varian, H. (2012). Predicting the present with Google Trends. *The Economic Record, 88*, 2–9. http://dx.doi.org/10.1111/j.1475-4932.2012.00809.x

Congdon, E. L., Novack, M. A., & Goldin-Meadow, S. (2018). Gesture in experimental studies: How videotape technology can advance psychological theory. *Organizational Research Methods, 21*, 489–499. http://dx.doi.org/10.1177/1094428116654548

Coviello, L., Sohn, Y., Kramer, A. D. I., Marlow, C., Franceschetti, M., Christakis, N. A., & Fowler, J. H. (2014). Detecting emotional contagion in massive social networks. *PLoS One, 9*(3), e90315. http://dx.doi.org/10.1371/journal.pone.0090315

Credé, M., Harms, P., Niehorster, S., & Gaye-Valentine, A. (2012). An evaluation of the consequences of using short measures of the Big Five personality traits. *Journal of Personality and Social Psychology, 102*, 874–888. http://dx.doi.org/10.1037/a0027403

Cronbach, L. J., Gleser, G. C., Nanda, H., & Rajaratnam, N. (1972). *The dependability of behavioral measurements: Theory of generalizability for scores and profiles.* New York, NY: Wiley.

Cronbach, L. J., & Meehl, P. E. (1955). Construct validity in psychological tests. *Psychological Bulletin, 52*, 281–302. http://dx.doi.org/10.1037/h0040957

Crowne, D. P., & Marlowe, D. (1960). A new scale of social desirability independent of psychopathology. *Journal of Consulting Psychology, 24*, 349–354. http://dx.doi.org/10.1037/h0047358

Csikszentmihalyi, M., & Larson, R. (1987). Validity and reliability of the experience-sampling method. *Journal of Nervous and Mental Disease, 175*, 526–536. http://dx.doi.org/10.1097/00005053-198709000-00004

Curme, C., Preis, T., Stanley, H. E., & Moat, H. S. (2014). Quantifying the semantics of search behavior before stock market moves. *PNAS, 111*, 11600–11605. http://dx.doi.org/10.1073/pnas.1324054111

Cvijikj, I. P., & Michahelles, F. (2011). Monitoring trends on Facebook. In *2011 IEEE Ninth International Conference on Dependable, Autonomic and Secure Computing* (pp. 895–902). Sydney, Australia: IEEE. http://dx.doi.org/10.1109/DASC.2011.150

Donaldson, S. I., & Grant-Vallone, E. J. (2002). Understanding self-report bias in organizational behavior research. *Journal of Business and Psychology, 17*, 245–260. http://dx.doi.org/10.1023/A:1019637632584

Dong, W., Lepri, B., & Pentland, A. (Sandy). (2011). Modeling the co-evolution of behaviors and social relationships using mobile phone data. In *Proceedings of the 10th International Conference on Mobile and Ubiquitous Multimedia* (pp. 134–143). New York, NY: ACM. http://dx.doi.org/10.1145/2107596.2107613

Dong, W., & Pentland, A. (2010). Quantifying group problem solving with stochastic analysis. In *International Conference on Multimodal Interfaces and the Workshop on Machine Learning for Multimodal Interaction* (pp. 40:1–40:4). New York, NY: ACM. http://dx.doi.org/10.1145/1891903.1891954

Dunne, L. E., Walsh, P., Hermann, S., Smyth, B., & Caulfield, B. (2008). Wearable monitoring of seated spinal posture. *IEEE Transactions on Biomedical Circuits and Systems, 2*(2), 97–105. http://dx.doi.org/10.1109/TBCAS.2008.927246

Edwards, J. R., & Bagozzi, R. P. (2000). On the nature and direction of relationships between constructs and measures. *Psychological Methods, 5,* 155–174. http://
dx.doi.org/10.1037/1082-989X.5.2.155

Emerging Technology From the arXiv. (2010, December 3). *The 70 online databases that
define our planet.* Retrieved from https://www.technologyreview.com/s/421886/
the-70-online-databases-that-define-our-planet/

Fan, S. P., Liberman, Z., Keysar, B., & Kinzler, K. D. (2015). The exposure advantage:
Early exposure to a multilingual environment promotes effective communication.
Psychological Science, 26, 1090–1097. http://dx.doi.org/10.1177/0956797615574699

Fisher, C. D., & To, M. L. (2012). Using experience sampling methodology in organizational behavior. *Journal of Organizational Behavior, 33,* 865–877. http://dx.doi.org/
10.1002/job.1803

Ford, M. T., Jebb, A. T., Tay, L., & Diener, E. (2018). Internet searches for affect-related
terms: An indicator of subjective well-being and predictor of health outcomes
across US states and metro areas. *Applied Psychology: Health and Well-Being, 10,* 3–29.
http://dx.doi.org/10.1111/aphw.12123

Franchak, J. M., Kretch, K. S., Soska, K. C., & Adolph, K. E. (2011). Head-mounted eye
tracking: A new method to describe infant looking. *Child Development, 82,* 1738–1750.
http://dx.doi.org/10.1111/j.1467-8624.2011.01670.x

Ganster, D. C., & Rosen, C. C. (2013). Work stress and employee health: A multidisciplinary review. *Journal of Management, 39,* 1085–1122. http://dx.doi.org/
10.1177/0149206313475815

Gilbert, E., & Karahalios, K. (2009). Predicting tie strength with social media. In *Proceedings of the 27th International Conference on Human Factors in Computing Systems*
(p. 211). Boston, MA: ACM Press. http://dx.doi.org/10.1145/1518701.1518736

Gilboa, S., Shirom, A., Fried, Y., & Cooper, C. (2008). A meta-analysis of work demand
stressors and job performance: Examining main and moderating effects. *Personnel
Psychology, 61,* 227–271. http://dx.doi.org/10.1111/j.1744-6570.2008.00113.x

Ginsberg, J., Mohebbi, M. H., Patel, R. S., Brammer, L., Smolinski, M. S., & Brilliant, L.
(2009). Detecting influenza epidemics using search engine query data. *Nature, 457,*
1012–1014. http://dx.doi.org/10.1038/nature07634

Gloor, P. A., Grippa, F., Putzke, J., Lassenius, C., Fuehres, H., Fischbach, K., & Schoder, D.
(2012). Measuring social capital in creative teams through sociometric sensors.
International Journal of Organisational Design and Engineering, 2, 380–401. http://
dx.doi.org/10.1504/IJODE.2012.051442

Gloor, P. A., Oster, D., & Fischbach, K. (2013). JazzFlow—analyzing "group flow"
among jazz musicians through "honest signals." *Künstliche Intelligenz, 27*(1), 37–43.
http://dx.doi.org/10.1007/s13218-012-0230-3

Goel, S., Hofman, J. M., Lahaie, S., Pennock, D. M., & Watts, D. J. (2010). Predicting
consumer behavior with Web search. *PNAS, 107,* 17486–17490. http://dx.doi.org/
10.1073/pnas.1005962107

Goldberg, L. R., Johnson, J. A., Eber, H. W., Hogan, R., Ashton, M. C., Cloninger, C. R.,
& Gough, H. G. (2006). The international personality item pool and the future of
public-domain personality measures. *Journal of Research in Personality, 40,* 84–96.
http://dx.doi.org/10.1016/j.jrp.2005.08.007

Golder, S. A., & Macy, M. W. (2011). Diurnal and seasonal mood vary with work, sleep,
and daylength across diverse cultures. *Science, 333,* 1878–1881. http://dx.doi.org/
10.1126/science.1202775

Gosling, S. D., Augustine, A. A., Vazire, S., Holtzman, N., & Gaddis, S. (2011). Manifestations of personality in online social networks: Self-reported Facebook-related
behaviors and observable profile information. *Cyberpsychology, Behavior and Social
Networking, 14,* 483–488. http://dx.doi.org/10.1089/cyber.2010.0087

Gosling, S. D., Redi, M., Sherman, R., & Kosinski, M. (2017). *Automated image analysis:
The next frontier in psychological research?* Symposium conducted at the meeting of the
Society for Personality and Social Psychology, San Antonio, TX.

Greenwood, S., Perrin, A., & Duggan, M. (2016, November 11). Social media update 2016. *Pew Research Center.* Retrieved from http://www.pewinternet.org/2016/11/11/social-media-update-2016/

Guion, R. M. (2002). Validity and reliability. In S. G. Rogelberg (Ed.), *Handbook of research methods in industrial and organizational psychology* (pp. 57–76). Malden, MA: Blackwell.

Hambleton, R. K., Swaminathan, H., & Rogers, H. J. (1991). *Fundamentals of item response theory.* Thousand Oaks, CA: Sage.

Harari, G. M., Lane, N. D., Wang, R., Crosier, B. S., Campbell, A. T., & Gosling, S. D. (2016). Using smartphones to collect behavioral data in psychological science: Opportunities, practical considerations, and challenges. *Perspectives on Psychological Science, 11*, 838–854. http://dx.doi.org/10.1177/1745691616650285

Hindmarsh, J., & Llewellyn, N. (2018). Video in sociomaterial investigations: A solution to the problem of relevance for organizational research. *Organizational Research Methods, 21*, 412–437. http://dx.doi.org/10.1177/1094428116657595

Hölscher, C., & Strube, G. (2000). Web search behavior of Internet experts and newbies. In *Proceedings of the 9th International World Wide Web Conference on Computer Networks: The International Journal of Computer and Telecommunications Networking* (pp. 337–346). Amsterdam, The Netherlands: North-Holland.

Horvath, F. (1979). Effect of different motivational instructions on detection of deception with the psychological stress evaluator and the galvanic skin response. *Journal of Applied Psychology, 64*, 323–330. http://dx.doi.org/10.1037/0021-9010.64.3.323

Jarrett, M., & Liu, F. (2018). "Zooming with": A participatory approach to the use of video ethnography in organizational studies. *Organizational Research Methods, 21*, 366–385. http://dx.doi.org/10.1177/1094428116656238

John, O. P., & Benet-Martínez, V. (2014). Measurement: Reliability, construct validation, and scale construction. In H. T. Reis & C. M. Judd (Eds.), *Handbook of research methods in social and personality psychology* (2nd ed., pp. 473–503). New York, NY: Cambridge University Press.

Kammerer, Y., & Gerjets, P. (2011). Searching and evaluating information on the WWW: Cognitive processes and user support. In K. P.-L. Vu & R. W. Proctor (Eds.), *Handbook of human factors in Web design* (pp. 288–307). Boca Raton, FL: CRC Press.

Kern, M. L., Eichstaedt, J. C., Schwartz, H. A., Dziurzynski, L., Ungar, L. H., Stillwell, D. J., . . . Seligman, M. E. P. (2014). The online social self: An open vocabulary approach to personality. *Assessment, 21*, 158–169. http://dx.doi.org/10.1177/1073191113514104

Kietzmann, J., Hermkens, K., McCarthy, I. P., & Silvestre, B. (2014). *Social media? Get serious! Understanding the functional building blocks of social media* (SSRN Scholarly Paper No. ID 2519365). Rochester, NY: Social Science Research Network.

Kim, T., McFee, E., Olguín, D. O., Waber, B., & Pentland, A. (2012). Sociometric badges: Using sensor technology to capture new forms of collaboration. *Journal of Organizational Behavior, 33*, 412–427. http://dx.doi.org/10.1002/job.1776

Kosinski, M., Stillwell, D., & Graepel, T. (2013). Private traits and attributes are predictable from digital records of human behavior. *PNAS, 110*, 5802–5805. http://dx.doi.org/10.1073/pnas.1218772110

Krämer, N. C., & Winter, S. (2008). Impression management 2.0: The relationship of self-esteem, extraversion, self-efficacy, and self-presentation within social networking sites. *Journal of Media Psychology: Theories, Methods, and Applications, 20*, 106–116. http://dx.doi.org/10.1027/1864-1105.20.3.106

Kristoufek, L. (2013). BitCoin meets Google Trends and Wikipedia: Quantifying the relationship between phenomena of the Internet era. *Scientific Reports, 3*, 3415. http://dx.doi.org/10.1038/srep03415

Lenhart, A., Purcell, K., Smith, A., & Zickuhr, K. (2010). Social media & mobile Internet use among teens and young adults. Millennials. *Pew Internet & American Life Project.* Retrieved from https://eric.ed.gov/?id=ED525056

Liu, L., Preotiuc-Pietro, D., Samani, Z. R., Moghaddam, M. E., & Ungar, L. (2016). *Analyzing personality through social media profile picture choice.* Retrieved from https://www.aaai.org/ocs/index.php/ICWSM/ICWSM16/paper/view/13102/12741

MacKenzie, S. B., Podsakoff, P. M., & Jarvis, C. B. (2005). The problem of measurement model misspecification in behavioral and organizational research and some recommended solutions. *Journal of Applied Psychology, 90,* 710–730. http://dx.doi.org/10.1037/0021-9010.90.4.710

Malik, S. H., Blake, H., & Suggs, L. S. (2014). A systematic review of workplace health promotion interventions for increasing physical activity. *British Journal of Health Psychology, 19,* 149–180. http://dx.doi.org/10.1111/bjhp.12052

Manago, A. M., Taylor, T., & Greenfield, P. M. (2012). Me and my 400 friends: The anatomy of college students' Facebook networks, their communication patterns, and well-being. *Developmental Psychology, 48,* 369–380. http://dx.doi.org/10.1037/a0026338

Mazerolle, L., Hurley, D., & Chamlin, M. (2002). Social behavior in public space: An analysis of behavioral adaptations to CCTV. *Security Journal, 15,* 59–75. http://dx.doi.org/10.1057/palgrave.sj.8340118

McAfee, A., & Brynjolfsson, E. (2012, October 1). Big data: The management revolution. *Harvard Business Review.* Retrieved from https://hbr.org/2012/10/big-data-the-management-revolution

McCarthy, M. J. (2010). Internet monitoring of suicide risk in the population. *Journal of Affective Disorders, 122,* 277–279. http://dx.doi.org/10.1016/j.jad.2009.08.015

McFarland, L. A., & Ployhart, R. E. (2015). Social media: A contextual framework to guide research and practice. *Journal of Applied Psychology, 100,* 1653–1677. http://dx.doi.org/10.1037/a0039244

Miller, G. (2012). The smartphone psychology manifesto. *Perspectives on Psychological Science, 7,* 221–237. http://dx.doi.org/10.1177/1745691612441215

Molenaar, P. C. M. (1985). A dynamic factor model for the analysis of multivariate time series. *Psychometrika, 50,* 181–202. http://dx.doi.org/10.1007/BF02294246

Nuti, S. V., Wayda, B., Ranasinghe, I., Wang, S., Dreyer, R. P., Chen, S. I., & Murugiah, K. (2014). The use of google trends in health care research: A systematic review. *PLoS ONE, 9*(10), e109583.

Olguín, D. O., & Pentland, A. (2007). *Sociometric badges: State of the art and future applications.* Retrieved from https://vismod.media.mit.edu/tech-reports/TR-614.pdf

Olguín, D. O., Waber, B. N., Kim, T., Mohan, A., Ara, K., & Pentland, A. (2009). Sensible organizations: Technology and methodology for automatically measuring organizational behavior. *IEEE Transactions on Systems, Man, and Cybernetics. Part B, Cybernetics, 39,* 43–55. http://dx.doi.org/10.1109/TSMCB.2008.2006638

Park, G., Schwartz, H. A., Eichstaedt, J. C., Kern, M. L., Kosinski, M., Stillwell, D. J., . . . Seligman, M. E. P. (2015). Automatic personality assessment through social media language. *Journal of Personality and Social Psychology, 108,* 934–952. http://dx.doi.org/10.1037/pspp0000020

Pärkkä, J., Ermes, M., Korpipää, P., Mäntyjärvi, J., Peltola, J., & Korhonen, I. (2006). Activity classification using realistic data from wearable sensors. *IEEE Transactions on Information Technology in Biomedicine, 10,* 119–128. http://dx.doi.org/10.1109/TITB.2005.856863

Pennebaker, J. W., Boyd, R. L., Jordan, K., & Blackburn, K. (2015). *The development and psychometric properties of LIWC2015.* Austin: University of Texas at Austin.

Pew Research Center. (2018). *Mobile fact sheet.* Retrieved from http://www.pewinternet.org/fact-sheet/mobile/

Plötner, M., Over, H., Carpenter, M., & Tomasello, M. (2015). Young children show the bystander effect in helping situations. *Psychological Science, 26*, 499–506. http://dx.doi.org/10.1177/0956797615569579

Powell, J., & Clarke, A. (2006). Internet information-seeking in mental health: Population survey. *The British Journal of Psychiatry, 189*, 273–277. http://dx.doi.org/10.1192/bjp.bp.105.017319

Quan-Haase, A., & Young, A. L. (2010). Uses and gratifications of social media: A comparison of Facebook and instant messaging. *Bulletin of Science, Technology & Society, 30*, 350–361. http://dx.doi.org/10.1177/0270467610380009

Riordan, M. A. (2017). Emojis as tools for emotion work: Communicating affect in text messages. *Journal of Language and Social Psychology, 36*, 549–567. http://dx.doi.org/10.1177/0261927X17704238

Roulin, N., & Levashina, J. (2016). Impression management and social media profiles. In R. N. Landers & G. B. Schmidt (Eds.), *Social media in employee selection and recruitment: Theory, practice, and current challenges* (pp. 223–248). Cham, Switzerland: Springer International.

Salathé, M., Freifeld, C. C., Mekaru, S. R., Tomasulo, A. F., & Brownstein, J. S. (2013). Influenza A (H7N9) and the importance of digital epidemiology. *The New England Journal of Medicine, 369*, 401–404. http://dx.doi.org/10.1056/NEJMp1307752

Savolainen, R., & Kari, J. (2004). Placing the Internet in information source horizons. A study of information seeking by Internet users in the context of self-development. *Library & Information Science Research, 26*, 415–433. http://dx.doi.org/10.1016/j.lisr.2004.04.004

Schootman, M., Toor, A., Cavazos-Rehg, P., Jeffe, D. B., McQueen, A., Eberth, J., & Davidson, N. O. (2015). The utility of Google Trends data to examine interest in cancer screening. *BMJ Open, 5*(6), e006678. http://dx.doi.org/10.1136/bmjopen-2014-006678

Schwartz, H. A., Eichstaedt, J. C., Kern, M. L., Dziurzynski, L., Ramones, S. M., Agrawal, M., . . . Ungar, L. H. (2013). Personality, gender, and age in the language of social media: The open-vocabulary approach. *PLoS One, 8*(9), e73791. http://dx.doi.org/10.1371/journal.pone.0073791

Seifter, A., Schwarzwalder, A., Geis, K., & Aucott, J. (2010). The utility of "Google Trends" for epidemiological research: Lyme disease as an example. *Geospatial Health, 4*, 135–137. http://dx.doi.org/10.4081/gh.2010.195

Smith, L., Giorgi, S., Solanki, R., Eichstaedt, J., Schwartz, H. A., & Abdul-Mageed, M. . . . Ungar, L. (2016). Does 'well-being' translate on Twitter? In *Proceedings of the 2016 Conference on Empirical Methods in Natural Language Processing* (pp. 2042–2047). Austin, TX: Association for Computational Linguistics.

Smith, T. W. (2013). Survey-research paradigms old and new. *International Journal of Public Opinion Research, 25*, 218–229. http://dx.doi.org/10.1093/ijpor/eds040

Smyth, M. M. (1996). Interference with rehearsal in spatial working memory in the absence of eye movements. *Quarterly Journal of Experimental Psychology A: Human Experimental Psychology, 49*, 940–949. http://dx.doi.org/10.1080/713755669

Sobkowicz, P., Kaschesky, M., & Bouchard, G. (2012). Opinion mining in social media: Modeling, simulating, and forecasting political opinions in the web. *Government Information Quarterly, 29*, 470–479. http://dx.doi.org/10.1016/j.giq.2012.06.005

Stigler, J. W., Gallimore, R., & Hiebert, J. (2000). Using video surveys to compare classrooms and teaching across cultures: Examples and lessons from the TIMSS Video Studies. *Educational Psychologist, 35*, 87–100. http://dx.doi.org/10.1207/S15326985EP3502_3

Sumner, C., Byers, A., Boochever, R., & Park, G. J. (2012). Predicting dark triad personality traits from Twitter usage and a linguistic analysis of tweets. In *2012 11th International Conference on Machine Learning and Applications* (Vol. 2, pp. 386–393). Boca Raton, FL: IEEE. http://dx.doi.org/10.1109/ICMLA.2012.218

Swan, M. (2012). Sensor mania! The Internet of Things, wearable computing, objective metrics, and the quantified self 2.0. *Journal of Sensor and Actuator Networks, 1*, 217–253. http://dx.doi.org/10.3390/jsan1030217

Tay, L., Jebb, A. T., & Woo, S. E. (2017). Video capture of human behaviors: Toward a big data approach. *Current Opinion in Behavioral Sciences, 18*, 17–22. http://dx.doi.org/10.1016/j.cobeha.2017.05.026

Tay, L., Woo, S. E., & Vermunt, J. K. (2014). A conceptual framework of cross-level isomorphism: Psychometric validation of multilevel constructs. *Organizational Research Methods, 17*, 77–106.

Thelwall, M., Buckley, K., & Paltoglou, G. (2011). Sentiment in Twitter events. *JASIST, 62*, 406–418. http://dx.doi.org/10.1002/asi.21462

Travassos, B., Araújo, D., Davids, K., Vilar, L., Esteves, P., & Vanda, C. (2012). Informational constraints shape emergent functional behaviours during performance of interceptive actions in team sports. *Psychology of Sport and Exercise, 13*, 216–223. http://dx.doi.org/10.1016/j.psychsport.2011.11.009

von Bismarck, J. (2008). *Stimmungsgasometer/Fühlometer*. Retrieved from https://www.digitalartarchive.at/database/general/work/stimmungsgasometer-fuehlometer.html

Wang, W., Hernandez, I., Newman, D. A., He, J., & Bian, J. (2016). Twitter analysis: Studying US weekly trends in work stress and emotion. *Applied Psychology, 65*, 355–378. http://dx.doi.org/10.1111/apps.12065

Watson, D., Clark, L. A., & Tellegen, A. (1988). Development and validation of brief measures of positive and negative affect: The PANAS scales. *Journal of Personality and Social Psychology, 54*, 1063–1070. http://dx.doi.org/10.1037/0022-3514.54.6.1063

World Health Organization. (2018). *Physical activity*. Retrieved from https://www.who.int/news-room/fact-sheets/detail/physical-activity

Wu, L., Waber, B. N., Aral, S., Brynjolfsson, E., & Pentland, A. (2008). *Mining face-to-face interaction networks using sociometric badges: Predicting productivity in an IT configuration task* (SSRN Scholarly Paper No. ID 1130251). Rochester, NY: Social Science Research Network.

Yang, A. C., Tsai, S.-J., Huang, N. E., & Peng, C.-K. (2011). Association of Internet search trends with suicide death in Taipei City, Taiwan, 2004–2009. *Journal of Affective Disorders, 132*, 179–184. http://dx.doi.org/10.1016/j.jad.2011.01.019

Zhu, J., Wang, X., Qin, J., & Wu, L. (2012). *Assessing public opinion trends based on user search queries: Validity, reliability, and practicality*. Retrieved from https://wapor2012.hkpop.hk/doc/papers/ConcurrentSessionsI/IC/IC-5.pdf

Zywica, J., & Danowski, J. (2008). The faces of Facebookers: Investigating social enhancement and social compensation hypotheses; predicting Facebook™ and offline popularity from sociability and self-esteem, and mapping the meanings of popularity with semantic networks. *Journal of Computer-Mediated Communication, 14*, 1–34. http://dx.doi.org/10.1111/j.1083-6101.2008.01429.x

INNOVATIONS IN LARGE-SCALE DATA COLLECTION AND ANALYSIS TECHNIQUES

4

Internet Search and Page View Behavior Scores

Validity and Usefulness as Indicators of Psychological States

Michael T. Ford

ata automatically produced by the searches and page selections of Internet users are voluminous and have the potential to offer insights into the thoughts and affections of individuals throughout the world. People typically view and search for information on the Internet based on their interests and information gaps and do so within the apparent privacy of their machines and locations, revealing psychological states that may otherwise be difficult to detect. When aggregated to regional units such as cities, states, provinces, or nations, Internet behavior can be indicative of differences in what is on the minds of Internet users across those locations. Internet behavior data also have finer temporal resolution than is typically possible with more traditional methods of psychological assessment. Nonetheless, alongside these advantages and opportunities, there are challenges in the use of Internet behavior data for research in psychology with respect to the meaning of the scores generated, the multidisciplinary nature of the perspectives used to inform the methods and theories behind the research, and the ethics of aggregating data on private behavior.

The purpose of this chapter is to summarize scholarship on the usefulness of Internet search and page view behavior as indicators of psychological states when aggregated to time and place. To this end, I review examples of Internet data that are relevant to psychology and can be easily and inexpensively collected. This is followed by a review of theory and research on the validity of Internet search and page view data as indicators of human interests, emotions, and behavioral intentions. Finally, there will be a consideration of the

http://dx.doi.org/10.1037/0000193-005
Big Data in Psychological Research, S. E. Woo, L. Tay, and R. W. Proctor (Editors)

challenges, limitations, and opportunities posed by Internet search and page view data for the purpose of psychological research.

It should be noted that the focus of this chapter, Internet search and page view behavior, differs from other forms of Internet behavior that involve self-expression, the most popular being Twitter postings, Facebook profiles, and other forms of social media in which individuals explicitly share information. Internet search and page views, by contrast, are not intentionally shared by their users and can potentially yield new information beyond social media. Also, Internet search and page view behavior is motivated by information seeking, which is different from the motive of self-expression associated with other forms of Internet behavior, particularly social media.

INTERNET SEARCH AND PAGE VIEW BEHAVIOR DATA SOURCES AND CONTENT

I focus on two large sources of Internet and page view data in this review: Google Trends and Wikipedia page views. The first, Google Trends (http:// trends.google.com—formerly Google Insights), provides normalized and aggregated scores for term and phrase popularity across time and place among searches on the Google search engine. The scores are based on the proportion of Google search queries that include the term or phrase of interest. Because Google represents approximately two thirds of all Internet search activity in the United States, these data, although not from an exhaustive sample of Internet searches, have the potential to yield information about many individuals in aggregate form. Scores from Google Trends are at the level of time and place, meaning that each place is given a score at each particular time span of interest. Places can be countries, states, and metro areas, and the time span can be a particular day, month, or year or a specific span of days, months, or years of the researcher's choosing. Scores are normed such that for any given search term or phrase, the place and/or time with the largest proportional search frequency in a particular data draw receives a score of 100 and all other times and places receive scores relative to 100 based on proportional search frequency relative to the time and place for which that search was most frequent. For example, if the largest proportion of searches for *unemployment* among states during 2014 occurred in the state of Wisconsin, the score for Wisconsin would be 100 and all other U.S. states would have scores for 2014 that are normalized as a proportion of 100 based on the proportion of searches for *unemployment* within those states relative to that in Wisconsin in 2014.

The second source of Internet and page view data reviewed in this chapter, the website Wikipedia, also counts page views and thus provides a source of page view behavior that may be relevant to psychology. Wikipedia is an electronic encyclopedia with information on most topics and individuals of public interest and significance, and the raw number of page views are made publicly available at the daily level. People tend to view specific Wikipedia pages out of an interest in the topic, thus potentially revealing information about their interests and other psychological states. Both Google Trends and Wikipedia page view data are publicly and freely available.

Research that has been conducted on Google Trends and Wikipedia has primarily used scores that are based on search entries, relative search frequency, and page view counts. In psychology, there has been little investigation into other forms of Internet behavior, such as the amount of time spent on a page, the links that a person clicks on once entering a page, or where the person is viewing the page from (e.g., a public or private computer or a mobile device). To the extent that more data of this type become available, they may provide additional information on the depth at which one is processing the information on the website or thinking about the topic.

The content of this chapter may apply to other search data and views of other popular websites where people seek information. For example, Baidu is a popular search engine in China and may yield similar information about individuals' thoughts, preferences, and interests. Page views for specific pages on medical information websites such as WebMD may also yield information about psychological conditions that are described on particular web pages. For example, views of pages on the topic of depression may reflect depressive states experienced by those viewing the pages. Thus, although I focus on Google and Wikipedia, data on search and page view behavior on other websites and search engines should have similar value.

The content and constructs most relevant to psychology that Google search and Wikipedia page view data can provide insight into include emotions, mental health conditions, interests, and behavioral intentions. Emotions that Internet searches can reveal include fear, stress, loneliness, and anxiety (Ford, Jebb, Tay, & Diener, 2018), whereas mental health conditions such as depression and burnout may be the subject of searches among individuals who are experiencing these afflictions (e.g., Ayers, Althouse, Allem, Rosenquist, & Ford, 2013). Interests and behavioral intentions that go beyond one's emotions and psychological states can also be revealing. These include particular products that one is interested in learning more about or purchasing (e.g., Hu, Du, & Damangir, 2014), as well as other services, activities, and career-related terms such as *unemployment, stock buying*, or *medical care* that might reveal information about one's behavioral intentions (e.g., Choi & Varian, 2012; Heiberger, 2015) or the physical symptoms one is experiencing (e.g., O'Keeffe, 2017). Searches and page views for terms related to many of these issues are frequent enough to yield reliable differences across time and place, potentially providing insight into variance in psychological states.

THE MEANING OF INTERNET BEHAVIOR AS INDICATORS OF PSYCHOLOGICAL STATES

To better understand the meaning of Internet search and page view behavior, it is worth considering existing theories of Internet behavior, which typically treat Internet behavior as a dependent variable. To the extent that these theories are accepted, we can assume that differences in Internet behavior reflect differences in psychological states across time and place to some degree.

One popular theory that has been used in several studies to predict Internet behavior is the theory of planned behavior (TPB; Ajzen, 1991). According to the TPB, the most immediate predictor of behavior is intentions, which capture the motivation to engage in a particular behavior. Intentions vary as a function of attitudes, subjective norms, and perceived control. In the context of Internet use, search behaviors reflect the intention to search, which is predicted by attitudes toward, subjective norms for, and perceived control over search behavior. If we apply the TPB to Internet behavior and unpack its elements, Internet behavior scores are based on (a) searchers' interests in a particular topic and their belief that Internet search will yield valuable information (i.e., attitudes toward search behavior), (b) the perception of whether others do this (i.e., subjective norms about search behavior), and (c) the extent to which searchers perceive they are capable of searching for information and have the freedom to do so (i.e., perceived control over one's search behavior). Of these three categories, that which is most likely to explain differences in relative search term frequency across time and place is (a). Given the proliferation of the Internet, subjective norms about Internet use and the perceived ability to use the Internet should be relatively constant across time and place, or if not, at least show constant differences across different search terms. However, one can expect systematic differences in topical interests across time and place.

Other research has focused on information seeking and problem solving as drivers of Internet search and page view behavior (e.g., Powell & Clarke, 2006). From this perspective, Internet searches and page views reflect problems that individuals are trying to solve related to the content they are seeking. At the collective level, Internet behavior of this type can also reflect issue salience in the population (e.g., Mellon, 2014), which means that issues that are related to search terms on a particular topic are more prominent when and where searches or page views on a particular topic are more common.

These perspectives suggest that differences across time and place in Internet search and page view behavior are driven by the prominence of an issue, problems that are occurring in people's lives, and a need or desire for information. Of course, not everyone interested in a topic is going to search or view a web page on that topic. However, at an aggregate level, places and/or times in which more people are searching for or viewing pages on a topic are likely to have more people who are interested in that topic.

To the extent that Internet search and page view behavior is driven by the need and desire for information, searches for topics related to emotions (e.g., anxiety, fears) have the potential to yield information about emotions that people are experiencing. Negative emotions and related conditions such as depression, stress, fear, anxiety, and burnout are unpleasant and may inspire a subset of individuals experiencing these emotions to search for information about how to cope with and escape these troubling states. Individuals may also search for information about these terms when they believe that individuals near to them are experiencing negative emotional states. Also, searchers experiencing negative emotional states may search for information related to positive emotions (e.g., happy, excited) to gain knowledge about how to experience these emotions. Users in a positive emotional state may also search for positive emotion terms to identify mood-congruent subjects (e.g., happy songs or events). Thus, Google search queries that include terms relevant to these affective states might reflect the experience of these psychological states in the population. Similarly, variance in views of Wikipedia pages on such topics may reflect variance in the experience of emotions in the population over time.

Search and page view data can also yield information on the interests people have in other topics and behaviors. For example, in places where people are entering search terms related to finding work (e.g., *jobs, part-time work*), there are people who are thinking about and intending to find a new job. Places where people search for information about certain types of automobiles may have more people who are interested in those products than do other areas. Interests in topics such as these have the potential to predict behaviors at the aggregate level.

In summary, there are good reasons to believe that differences in Internet search and page view activity across time and place reveal, at least to some degree, differences in emotions, psychological conditions, interests, and behavioral intentions. Whether scores based on Internet search and page views yield meaningful and useful information also depends on the extent to which the scores predict or correlate with expected outcomes and do so beyond other available indices.

RESEARCH ON THE PREDICTIVE AND CRITERION VALIDITY OF INTERNET BEHAVIOR SCORES

A number of studies published between 2005 and 2010 began to explore the usefulness of Internet search behavior for assessing and predicting behavior and interests. Since 2010, empirical papers using data from Google Trends have proliferated and covered an increasingly diverse set of topics. Some of this work has treated search scores as independent variables to test the extent to which these scores predict outcomes of interest at the temporal, state, and/or regional level. Other work has positioned Google search scores as outcome variables, based on the assumption that the scores are meaningful indicators of interest in a topic. In some cases, researchers have focused on seasonality in search behavior, whereas in other cases, researchers have studied the effect of current events or advertising campaigns on search behavior. This work has come from a variety of disciplines, including public health, economics, political science, marketing, and psychology, among others. In the next section, I review the primary topics researchers have studied and some of the evidence relevant to the predictive or criterion validity of Internet search scores.

Health and Disease

The most popular subject of research using Google Trends data has been physical health and disease. Some studies have investigated the extent to which search scores for topics such as cancer, the flu, Lyme disease, and epileptic seizures covary with other criteria of interest at the state or temporal level. Perhaps most notable have been efforts to predict influenza outbreaks. Efforts to predict influenza emergency room visits and laboratory-confirmed cases with Google search queries for influenza-related terms have had some success (Ginsberg et al., 2009; Malik, Gumel, Thompson, Strome, & Mahmud, 2011). The specific methods and precision used to determine the search queries that are part of the predictive algorithm have received criticism due to (a) overfitting a small number of cases, resulting in false-positive correlations between influenza and structurally irrelevant search terms, and (b) instability in the search algorithms across time (Lazer, Kennedy, King, & Vespignani, 2014). However, it does appear that search queries related to influenza reflect an interest in the disease and its symptoms, and scholars who have been critical of Google's original approach to assessing flu trends have argued that search data can be useful when combined with other surveillance data (Lazer et al., 2014). Searches for information related to skin cancer and melanoma at the state level have also been shown to correlate with melanoma mortality but not incidence, suggesting that interest is driven not by detection or early prevention but by individuals and families severely affected (Bloom, Amber, Hu, & Kirsner, 2015). Other research has focused on how search queries for health-related information increase in response to expected seasonal patterns, such as those for leg cramps (O'Keeffe, 2017) and Lyme disease (Seifter, Schwarzwalder, Geis, & Aucott, 2010).

These and other studies generally suggest that times or places with a greater proportion of searches for information about a specific health issue tend to have more people that are interested in that health issue. This may reflect a greater incidence of the disease and its symptoms. Although not psychological per se, health-related topics in Internet search queries may be of interest to health psychology researchers studying how interest in health topics responds to events or advertising campaigns. There have also been several studies on public interest in medical treatments (Dahele & Tol, 2017) that might be of value to psychologists studying patients with cancer and other severe illnesses.

Mental Health

Also popular in research on Google Trends has been public interest in mental health topics such as depression, suicide, and psychiatric disorders. There have been several studies on the relationship between suicide-related search queries at the aggregate level and actual suicide rates. At the U.S. state level, searches for *commit suicide*, *suicide prevention*, and *how to suicide* have been found to correlate with suicide rates (Gunn & Lester, 2013). Similarly, searches related to suicide and depression have been found to correlate over time with actual suicide rates in Taiwan (Yang, Tsai, Huang, & Peng, 2011).

Other work has focused more on depression and its correlates. Research has shown predictable seasonal patterns in searches for information about depression, with increases during colder times of the year and cycles in the northern and southern hemispheres that mirror each other (Ayers et al., 2013; Yang, Huang, Peng, & Tsai, 2010). Other research has found that searches for *depression* at the state and metro area levels correlate with incidents of depression as measured by the U.S. Centers for Disease Control and Prevention's Behavioral Risk Factor Surveillance System (Ford et al., 2018).

Additional studies have focused on other issues related to trends in the search frequency for suicide and mental health-related terms, under the assumption that these represent changes in public interest. Although it is not always possible to determine what is causing differences in interest in mental health issues over time and place, the criterion-related evidence suggests the interest in searches reflects, to some degree, differences in the symptoms that individuals are experiencing across temporal and spatial units.

Legal and Illicit Drugs

A considerable body of literature has used Google Trends data to study interest in legal as well as illicit drugs, some of which have rapidly increased in popularity. Much of this work has studied interest in new synthetic or emerging drugs, with some of this research likely motivated by the difficulty in tracking interest in and use of such drugs using other data collection methods. For example, one analysis (Bright, Bishop, Kane, Marsh, & Barratt, 2013) found that searches for *Kronic*, a form of synthetic cannabis that gained notoriety in Australia, correlated with news stories on the topic. A similar study on mephedrone-related searches found similar associations with news stories (Forsyth, 2012). Searches for *dabbing*, an emergent method of marijuana use, have also been shown to be higher in U.S. states that have legalized medical and/or recreational marijuana (Zhang, Zheng, Zeng, & Leischow, 2016). Other research in Russia found that searches for *krokodil* or *desomorphine* on the Yandex search engine, a popular search engine in Russia, correlated strongly with desomorphine-related court appearances at the oblast (i.e., province) level (Zheluk, Quinn, & Meylakhs, 2014). Searches for specific drugs such as amoxicillin have been shown to correlate with use as assessed by the Medical Expenditure Panel Survey (Simmering, Polgreen, & Polgreen, 2014). Meanwhile, comparisons across drugs suggests that the popularity of drugs, as measured by the number of websites with that drug as a keyword, correlates with search frequency (Jankowski & Hoffmann, 2016). Interestingly, researchers have also investigated the potential impact of policy changes in drug interest. For example, one analysis of Japanese search data found that tobacco price increases were associated with spikes in searches for information about smoking cessation (Tabuchi, Fukui, & Gallus, 2018).

These are examples of studies that have correlated drug-related searches with other measures of use, news coverage, and public policy. Several other studies have looked at similar effects or focused solely on trends in search frequency as indicators of interest in a particular drug. These aforementioned studies suggest that search frequency is an indicator, albeit imperfect, of relative interest in various drugs across time and place. Although most of this work has been conducted by scholars of public health or researchers from specific industry topic areas (e.g., pharmacy), health and clinical psychologists might find this method of studying interest in drugs to be useful.

Health Behavior

Closely related to the topics already covered in this chapter, Google Trends can also be used to study interest in health behavior. This includes interest in dieting, exercise, fitness, smoking cessation, and health screening. Searches for information on common lifestyle-related factors in health, such as weight, dieting, and fitness, have been shown to be highest in January and to decrease throughout the year, conforming to expected seasonal patterns associated with the so-called "New Year's resolutions" (Carr & Dunsiger, 2012). Furthermore, searches related to dieting have been found to correlate with state-level obesity rates (Markey & Markey, 2013), suggesting that searches for health behavior change reflect an interest that is driven by needs and seasonal exposure. Searches for information about vaccination and other preventive measures have also been shown to correlate with external indices. Searches for *H1N1* and *vaccine* were found to be related to H1N1 vaccination coverage at the state level, whereas searches for *vaccine* were also related to HPV vaccination coverage (Kalichman & Kegler, 2015). Searches for information about HIV testing increased in response to celebrity Charlie Sheen's HIV disclosure and, in turn, predicted sales of OraQuick, a rapid in-home HIV test kit (Allem et al., 2017).

This research further supports the validity and usefulness of Google search activity relevant to health behavior change. Researchers interested in health behavior might consider Google search data as indicators of interest in health behavior change that correlate with events, economic conditions, public service announcement campaigns, and/or seasonal factors.

Consumer, Economic, and Financial Market Behavior

Several analyses have investigated the ability of Google search data to predict consumer behavior, including purchasing behavior, the behavior of stock traders, and movement in the stock market. Some of this work has studied the impact of advertising on interest in particular products, whereas other research has looked into hypotheses about the effects of economic and social context on public interests.

Several studies have looked at search behavior as a predictor of consumer purchases. For example, one study found that searches related to travel to specific regions of Switzerland correlated with between-region differences in overnight stays (Siliverstovs & Wochner, 2018). Similarly, Google searches for movie-related terms have been found to predict cinema admissions (Hand & Judge, 2012), whereas searches for automotive-related terms have been shown to predict sales of motor vehicles and parts (Choi & Varian, 2012). Many other demonstrations of similar effects exist. Some comparisons have also found Google search volume scores to make superior predictions about consumer behavior relative to survey-based indicators (Vosen & Schmidt, 2011).

Other research has looked at the stock market and other economic factors such as unemployment. For example, searches for information about a company can be an indicator of negative news and financial risk (Heiberger, 2015). On a similar note, other researchers found that investor attention, as indicated by Google searches, is a predictor of stock market volatility (Hamid & Heiden, 2015), whereas additional work suggests that searches for keywords related to financial markets predict market decreases (Preis, Moat, & Stanley, 2013). More complex patterns have been found for Bitcoin-related search behavior, with an apparent bidirectional temporal relationship between search queries and Bitcoin prices (Kristoufek, 2013). Finally, searches related to unemployment have been shown to predict unemployment claims (Choi & Varian, 2012). On the whole, these results suggest that Internet search behavior scores have some validity as predictors of financial markets and macroeconomic conditions.

Google Trends data on consumer interests have also been used to test substantive psychological theories and hypotheses. For example, studies have found that income inequality at the national and state level is correlated with searches for high-status or positional goods such as designer brands or expensive jewelry (Walasek & Brown 2015, 2016). Other research has combined Google Trends data with experiments to study the importance of scarcity and popularity cues in purchasing decisions (Wu & Lee, 2016). In their set of studies, Wu and Lee (2016) first analyzed Google trends data and found that searches for *limited edition* were more frequent than searches for *best selling*. However, when incorporating the term *gifts* into the search, searches for *best selling* became more frequent, suggesting that people are more sensitive to scarcity cues when purchasing for themselves but more sensitive to popularity cues when purchasing for others. They followed up this analysis with four experiments in which they manipulated scarcity and popularity cues and assessed purchasing intentions, finding that scarcity cues were more important when people were looking to purchase for themselves, and popularity cues were more important when purchasing for others. Future papers of this nature in which researchers combine Internet search or page view data with more traditional methods may shed new light on psychological theories as they operate at different levels of analysis.

Politics and Policy

Interest in political issues, elections, and public policy has also been the subject of research using Google Trends data. One study, for example, showed that search volume predicted a candidate's share of the two-party vote in U.S. Senate elections (Swearingen & Ripberger, 2014), whereas another analysis found that searches for racist terms negatively predicted the share of votes received by Barack Obama in 2008 and 2012 (Stephens-Davidowitz, 2014). Other research has found that the salience of issues measured by Gallup surveys correlates with Google search volume (Mellon, 2014). Searches for *Obamacare* were also found to be more frequent in metro areas with large numbers of uninsured individuals, as one might expect (Gollust et al., 2017). As with other areas of study, data suggest that Google Trends provides useful and predictive information about interest in political and policy topics.

Other Topics of Interest to Psychology

Google search data may have some usefulness and validity as indicators of interest in other topics relevant to psychology researchers, including morality, religion, sexuality, and cognitive ability. For example, one analysis found that search volume for major illness-related topics, in particular, *cancer*, *diabetes*, and *hypertension*, predicted searches for religious terms, in particular, *God*, *Jesus*, and *prayer*, with the religious search terms also corresponding to religious holidays, as expected (Pelham et al., 2018). Other research has found that state-level religiosity is correlated with sex- and gay porn-related searches (MacInnis & Hodson, 2015). An additional analysis found that searches for morally relevant terms such as *corrupt* and *ethics* were less frequent after losing 1 hour of sleep due to the time change in the United States (Barnes, Gunia, & Wagner, 2015). This finding was combined with findings from an experiment and field study to suggest that sleep loss reduces moral awareness. These studies are examples of analyses that researchers have conducted using Google Trends data to study different topics of interest to psychologists and, in some cases, to test theoretically based predictions.

Summary of Criterion-Related Research on Google Search Scores

As shown here, a wide variety of topics have been studied using Google Trends data. Although I reviewed the most popular topics for research using these data, others have been studied as well. Research has generally supported the conclusion that differences in search scores across time and place reflect differences in interest. These differences also tend to correlate with and predict relevant criteria to some degree, sometimes beyond other more traditional measures of interest or issue salience. If we assume that search behavior at the aggregate level does indeed reflect interest in a topic, this opens the door to a number of potential research questions that treat search behavior as an independent variable, dependent variable, and/or mediator.

CRITERION VALIDITY OF WIKIPEDIA PAGE VIEW SCORES

Wikipedia makes available the raw number of page views for each page on a daily basis, allowing researchers to test for variability in interest over time on a daily or a broader temporal level. The locations from which Internet users are viewing the pages are not freely available, limiting the testing of differences across regions. Despite the fine temporal resolution of page view data, there has been less research on the extent to which Wikipedia page views predict or correlate with criteria of interest.

Nonetheless, researchers have used Wikipedia page views to investigate some of the same topics that have been studied using Google search data. One of the studies cited earlier (Kristoufek, 2013) investigated the relationship between Wikipedia page views for the Bitcoin page and found that when Bitcoin prices were going up, Wikipedia views predicted a stronger increase, and when Bitcoin prices were going down, Wikipedia views predicted a stronger decrease. Also, as was the case with Google Trends, Wikipedia page view increases for financial-related pages tended to predict market decreases (Moat et al., 2013). Other studies have investigated Wikipedia page views as a method for surveillance of disease. As with Google Trends scores, Wikipedia page views have been shown to have some utility in estimating and predicting influenza trends (McIver & Brownstein, 2014). Meanwhile, recent analyses also provide initial evidence that Wikipedia page views on topics related to mental illness show predictable seasonal patterns (Dzogang, Lansdall-Welfare, & Cristianini, 2017).

Although there has been no research to my knowledge directly comparing Wikipedia page views with Google search scores as sources of information about interest in a topic, there is a reason to believe that these data sources may complement each other. Google search data reflect a larger volume of activity than Wikipedia scores reflect and thus may generate more accurate estimates of population interest, particularly when separated across time and location. However, Wikipedia page views are more precise than Google searches in the interest that they reflect because the pages are specific to a topic of interest, whereas search terms may reflect different interests. Internet users might include a search term for reasons unrelated to the term itself, whereas a Wikipedia page view is less likely to reflect random or extraneous interests. For example, a Google user may include *stress* in a search for information about an establishment or song that has the word *stress* in it. The most popular searches of this kind can be eliminated from the score, but it is difficult to clean all such searches out. However, there is a specific Wikipedia page for *psychological stress*, meaning it is likely that individuals who view this page are interested in mental stress and not something extraneous.

Given this preliminary evidence, it appears that Wikipedia page views may yield information about phenomena similar to those reflected in search behavior, namely issue salience, the need for information, and problems that people are experiencing. Wikipedia data also have potential advantages in the precision with which they reflect interest in a topic. Future research might further investigate the usefulness of Wikipedia page view data for studying daily, weekly, and more long-term trends in the interests people have in topics relevant to psychology such as health behavior, well-being, morality, and politics.

CHALLENGES AND OPPORTUNITIES FOR RESEARCH USING INTERNET BEHAVIOR

Internet search and page view data offer opportunities for future research and application in a number of areas. The greatest advantages of these data are (a) the ease with which they can be collected through a simple download from the Internet, (b) the large number of topics that can be studied, and (c) the timeliness and temporal resolution of the data produced. As such, new data will continue to be produced and updated, and these data may be useful in marking trends and changes in society at large.

Nonetheless, there are still significant challenges and reasons for caution in using Internet behavior data for psychological science research. One issue is that, although there are theoretical reasons and growing empirical evidence to support the meaningfulness of the scores that are based on Internet searches and page views, the validity of these scores as indicators of psychological states is still not as clear as would be expected for more traditional measures of these variables (e.g., paper and pencil or telephone surveys). Do scores for searches related to an issue reflect differences in thoughts and emotions? Which thoughts and emotions are reflected? Researchers might conduct further analyses examining the factor structure of search behavior scores to identify clusters of search behavior that reflect constructs at the aggregate level. It is also possible that autonomous or semiautonomous machines can manipulate or skew Internet behavior data in ways that result in outliers that are difficult to explain or understand. Researchers should investigate outliers for this possibility.

Related to concerns about construct validity, search and page view data are only available at the aggregate level and cannot be used to represent individual-level constructs. More important, this means that these data are not ideal for testing and building individual-level theories. The well-known ecological fallacy occurs when inferences are made about individual-level relationships using data from variables that have been aggregated to the group level. In some cases, group-level variables may carry a different meaning than individual-level variables. Stress at the individual level, for example, may exert different effects on health than stress at the collective level, which reflects not only the stress one is experiencing alone but also the stress experienced by others in the community. As such, researchers have to be cautious about applying individual-level theories to understand relationships that are uncovered with Internet search and page view data.

At the same time, this is not a reason to dismiss correlations at the aggregate level, which have other advantages for understanding collective phenomena (see Schwartz, 1994). Researchers might also combine studies that use search or page view data with traditional laboratory or field research to conceptually replicate or triangulate on theoretical relationships at the individual and collective level. For example, research on the influence of resource scarcity in consumer behavior might manipulate or measure resource scarcity and consumer behavior at the individual level in one study and then use aggregate data on Internet behavior and resource scarcity at the collective level to test relationships at different levels of analysis and generalizability. Other research might examine correlations between economic factors such as unemployment rates with Google search-related indicators of psychological well-being. This research could be combined with individual-level surveys to test the effects of economic factors on well-being. Such approaches can assemble the advantages of laboratory research for causal inference, individual-level field research for measurement precision, and Internet behavior data for volume and generalizability to behavior in a broader population. Also, Internet search data can yield findings that researchers might then follow up on using more traditional techniques.

An additional challenge for research using the Google search data, in particular, is the lack of information about how the search scores are computed. Although the search scores are known to be based on the relative proportion of searches that include a search term, the precise algorithm through which the scores are computed is not clear. The search scores can also change slightly across time due to changes in the algorithm used, making it challenging to reproduce precisely one's research results. Still, most attempts to reproduce analyses should produce similar results even if not exact. Going forward, it will be important for researchers to document when they collected their search scores. Researchers should also be willing to share the data sets they downloaded if needed to reproduce or extend their findings.

A final challenge to interpreting and integrating research on Internet search and page view behavior is the variety of disciplines that are using these data. With this variety of disciplines comes a diversity of statistical and methodological approaches. Some researchers take a more theoretical approach using theories from their own discipline, whereas others use more data-driven techniques. The data analysis techniques that are used also vary considerably across disciplines (e.g., psychology, economics, political science). As of now, research using Internet behavior data has resulted in little communication or reference across these disciplines. In the future, researchers from different disciplines may be able to combine their efforts and techniques to build on the strengths of each.

ETHICAL ISSUES IN THE USE OF INTERNET SEARCH AND PAGE VIEW DATA

Two distinct ethical issues should be considered when using Internet search and page view data, one involving privacy and the other involving scientific approach and philosophy. The first ethical issue is that these data are based on private behavior. This is advantageous for understanding thoughts and interests that are relatively unfiltered compared with public behavior. However, the data are also based on the monitoring of behavior that is not public and is not preceded by any informed consent. Of course, the data are only available to researchers at the aggregate level, meaning it is not possible to monitor individual-level private behavior. Nonetheless, researchers have to be cautious about opportunities to access data of this nature that are more identifiable.

The second ethical issue I raise here, which is a broader issue of scientific approach and philosophy, is in the choice of search terms and pages on which to collect data. Because it is relatively easy to collect some forms of Internet behavior data, researchers have opportunities to explore many different terms and pages, resulting in the potential for more Type I errors. It is, therefore, important for researchers to be transparent about their choices of content. These choices can be a priori and based on logic and theory, or they can be empirically determined to maximize prediction. There are advantages to both approaches, but in either case, it is important for researchers to be transparent about which strategy they take.

FUTURE DIRECTIONS FOR RESEARCH

Despite these challenges and limitations, Internet search and page view data offer opportunities to develop new knowledge and theory about psychological states. There are many possible ways to explore how Internet searches predict and forecast outcomes of interest at the collective level beyond those reviewed here. In addition, these data can be used to surveil regions of the country or world for information about how people are thinking and feeling, supplementing more traditional phone and mail surveys that are expensive and increasingly difficult to execute. The effects of macroeconomic factors on psychological states and behavior intentions can also be explored in new ways by linking data at the metro, state, and/or national level over time. As of now, theories connecting macro-level conditions to psychological outcomes (or vice versa) are not well developed and could be informed and enhanced through careful analysis of Internet search and page view data. Researchers can also develop or retest theories about seasonality in affective states and interests while taking a dynamic approach to other interests. Finally, Internet search and page view data might be combined and correlated with other forms of big data (e.g., social media) that are also aggregated to similar temporal and spatial levels of analysis (e.g., Ford et al., 2018).

The Internet search and page view data that are collected at the collective level, although not ideal for testing individual-level theories, may be useful for studying individual behavior at the collective level and for understanding and targeting behavior change attempts. First, researchers can monitor collective Internet search and/or page view behavior to quickly identify times and places in which an issue of concern is most prominent; this monitoring can help in targeting resources where they are most needed. Researchers might also investigate how search behavior, which predicts consumption and other forms of behavior relevant for health and well-being, responds to health or other advertising campaigns (e.g., smoking cessation, hypertension awareness), providing timely data before more concrete behavioral data become available. Public health professionals may also monitor Internet content in an attempt to ensure and improve the accuracy of the information for which people can search. Research is still needed on the usefulness of Internet search and page view data for these purposes, but they offer the potential to supplement traditional methods for monitoring and evaluating psychological and other health-related phenomena.

In addition to the potential for studying phenomena at the collective level, more detailed information about the behavior of Internet users may provide additional information about their psychological states. In particular, the intensity of interest in a topic may differ from its popularity, and this may be reflected in differences between (a) search query or page view frequency and (b) the depth of engagement with a search query or website. More specifically, it would be interesting to know when people enter a search query how many links they actually click on and how many pages of search results they browse. Similarly, it would be useful to know the collective time that interested users spend on a website, which should differ in meaning from the raw number of views. Whereas number of views may reflect the popularity of the topic, the time spent on a page by those viewing it may reflect the depth of interest in those who do view the page. The number of pages that a Google user visits after searching for a topic may also yield information that is useful for assessing the intensity of the interest among individuals who search for a topic. Also, the links that people click on when they enter a website may provide information about the more specific interests of people who are interested in a general topic. In the case of Wikipedia, the links that individuals click on when viewing a page might also provide insight into how topical interests are related. Individual lab studies (e.g., Rains & Tukachinsky, 2015) have used these types of Internet behavior in controlled settings as indicators of information-seeking depth, and if such data become available at a mass scale, it would be useful for assessing the depth of interest at the collective level.

CONCLUSION

In summary, Internet search and page view behavior data have the potential to contribute to knowledge about human emotions, thoughts, interests, and behavioral intentions in a variety of domains. Such data have limitations that have to be considered, and researchers have to be cautious about using these data to draw theoretical inferences at the individual level. Still, there is empirical evidence from research on a number of topics indicating that Internet search and page view data reveal meaningful information about psychological states, offering an opportunity to study these states at the aggregate level in new ways that inform, complement, and expand on more traditional methods of psychological research.

REFERENCES

Ajzen, I. (1991). The theory of planned behavior. *Organizational Behavior and Human Decision Processes, 50,* 179–211. http://dx.doi.org/10.1016/0749-5978(91)90020-T

Allem, J.-P., Leas, E. C., Caputi, T. L., Dredze, M., Althouse, B. M., Noar, S. M., & Ayers, J. W. (2017). The Charlie Sheen effect on rapid in-home human immunodeficiency virus test sales. *Prevention Science, 18,* 541–544. http://dx.doi.org/10.1007/s11121-017-0792-2

Ayers, J. W., Althouse, B. M., Allem, J.-P., Rosenquist, J. N., & Ford, D. E. (2013). Seasonality in seeking mental health information on Google. *American Journal of Preventive Medicine, 44,* 520–525. http://dx.doi.org/10.1016/j.amepre.2013.01.012

Barnes, C. M., Gunia, B. C., & Wagner, D. T. (2015). Sleep and moral awareness. *Journal of Sleep Research, 24,* 181–188. http://dx.doi.org/10.1111/jsr.12231

Bloom, R., Amber, K. T., Hu, S., & Kirsner, R. (2015). Google search trends and skin cancer: Evaluating the U.S. population's interest in skin cancer and its association with melanoma outcomes. *JAMA Dermatology, 151,* 903–905. http://dx.doi.org/10.1001/jamadermatol.2015.1216

Bright, S. J., Bishop, B., Kane, R., Marsh, A., & Barratt, M. J. (2013). Kronic hysteria: Exploring the intersection between Australian synthetic cannabis legislation, the media, and drug-related harm. *International Journal on Drug Policy, 24,* 231–237. http://dx.doi.org/10.1016/j.drugpo.2012.12.002

Carr, L. J., & Dunsiger, S. I. (2012). Search query data to monitor interest in behavior change: Application for public health. *PLoS ONE, 7,* e48158. http://dx.doi.org/10.1371/journal.pone.0048158

Choi, H., & Varian, H. (2012). Predicting the present with Google Trends. *The Economic Record, 88,* 2–9. http://dx.doi.org/10.1111/j.1475-4932.2012.00809.x

Dahele, M., & Tol, J. (2017). Google Trends can provide objective data on the impact of radiation oncology related media events and the level of interest in specific types of treatment. *Radiotherapy and Oncology, 124,* 182–183. http://dx.doi.org/10.1016/j.radonc.2017.06.015

Dzogang, F., Lansdall-Welfare, T., & Cristianini, N. (2017, December). *Seasonal fluctuations in collective mood revealed by Wikipedia searches and Twitter posts.* Paper presented at the IEEE 16th International Conference on Data Mining Workshops, Barcelona, Spain.

Ford, M. T., Jebb, A. T., Tay, L., & Diener, E. (2018). Internet searches for affect-related terms: An indicator of subjective well-being and predictor of health outcomes across U.S. states and metro areas. *Applied Psychology: Health and Well-Being, 10,* 3–29. http://dx.doi.org/10.1111/aphw.12123

Forsyth, A. J. M. (2012). Virtually a drug scare: Mephedrone and the impact of the Internet on drug news transmission. *International Journal on Drug Policy, 23,* 198–209. http://dx.doi.org/10.1016/j.drugpo.2011.12.003

Ginsberg, J., Mohebbi, M. H., Patel, R. S., Brammer, L., Smolinski, M. S., & Brilliant, L. (2009, February 19). Detecting influenza epidemics using search engine query data. *Nature, 457,* 1012–1014. http://dx.doi.org/10.1038/nature07634

Gollust, S. E., Qin, X., Wilcock, A. D., Baum, L. M., Barry, C. L., Niederdeppe, J., . . . Karaca-Mandic, P. (2017). Search and you shall find: Geographic characteristics associated with Google searches during the Affordable Care Act's first enrollment period. *Medical Care Research and Review, 74*, 723–735. http://dx.doi.org/10.1177/1077558716660944

Gunn, J. F., III, & Lester, D. (2013). Using Google searches on the internet to monitor suicidal behavior. *Journal of Affective Disorders, 148*, 411–412. http://dx.doi.org/10.1016/j.jad.2012.11.004

Hamid, A., & Heiden, M. (2015). Forecasting volatility with empirical similarity and Google Trends. *Journal of Economic Behavior & Organization, 117*, 62–81. http://dx.doi.org/10.1016/j.jebo.2015.06.005

Hand, C., & Judge, G. (2012). Searching for the picture: Forecasting UK cinema admissions using Google Trends data. *Applied Economics Letters, 19*, 1051–1055. http://dx.doi.org/10.1080/13504851.2011.613744

Heiberger, R. H. (2015). Collective attention and stock prices: Evidence from Google Trends data on Standard and Poor's 100. *PLoS ONE, 10*, e0135311. http://dx.doi.org/10.1371/journal.pone.0135311

Hu, Y., Du, R. Y., & Damangir, S. (2014). Decomposing the impact of advertising: Augmenting sales with online search data. *Journal of Marketing Research, 51*, 300–319. http://dx.doi.org/10.1509/jmr.12.0215

Jankowski, W., & Hoffmann, M. (2016). Can Google searches predict the popularity and harm of psychoactive agents? *Journal of Medical Internet Research, 18*, e38. http://dx.doi.org/10.2196/jmir.4033

Kalichman, S. C., & Kegler, C. (2015). Vaccine-related Internet search activity predicts H1N1 and HPV vaccine coverage: Implications for vaccine acceptance. *Journal of Health Communication, 20*, 259–265. http://dx.doi.org/10.1080/10810730.2013.852274

Kristoufek, L. (2013). *BitCoin* meets *Google Trends* and *Wikipedia*: Quantifying the relationship between phenomena of the Internet era. *Scientific Reports, 3*, 3415. http://dx.doi.org/10.1038/srep03415

Lazer, D., Kennedy, R., King, G., & Vespignani, A. (2014). The parable of Google Flu: Traps in big data analysis. *Science, 343*, 1203–1205. http://dx.doi.org/10.1126/science.1248506

MacInnis, C. C., & Hodson, G. (2015). Do American states with more religious or conservative populations search more for sexual content on google? *Archives of Sexual Behavior, 44*, 137–147. http://dx.doi.org/10.1007/s10508-014-0361-8

Malik, M. T., Gumel, A., Thompson, L. H., Strome, T., & Mahmud, S. M. (2011). "Google flu trends" and emergency department triage data predicted the 2009 pandemic H1N1 waves in Manitoba. *Canadian Journal of Public Health, 102*, 294–297. http://dx.doi.org/10.1007/BF03404053

Markey, P. M., & Markey, C. N. (2013). Annual variation in Internet keyword searches: Linking dieting interest to obesity and negative health outcomes. *Journal of Health Psychology, 18*, 875–886. http://dx.doi.org/10.1177/1359105312445080

McIver, D. J., & Brownstein, J. S. (2014). Wikipedia usage estimates prevalence of influenza-like illness in the United States in near real-time. *PLoS Computational Biology, 10*, e1003581. http://dx.doi.org/10.1371/journal.pcbi.1003581

Mellon, J. (2014). Internet search data and issue salience: The properties of Google Trends as a measure of issue salience. *Journal of Elections, Public Opinion, and Parties, 24*, 45–72. http://dx.doi.org/10.1080/17457289.2013.846346

Moat, H. S., Curme, C., Avakian, A., Kenett, D. Y., Stanley, E., & Preis, T. (2013). Quantifying *Wikipedia* usage patterns before stock market moves. *Scientific Reports, 3*, 1801. http://dx.doi.org/10.1038/srep01801

O'Keeffe, S. T. (2017). Summertime blues? A re-examination of the seasonality of web searches for restless legs and leg cramps. *Sleep Medicine, 37*, 119–123. http://dx.doi.org/10.1016/j.sleep.2017.06.017

Pelham, B. W., Shimizu, M., Arndt, J., Carvallo, M., Solomon, S., & Greenberg, J. (2018). Searching for God: Illness-related mortality threats and religious search volume in Google in 16 nations. *Personality and Social Psychology Bulletin, 44*, 290–303. http://dx.doi.org/10.1177/0146167217736047

Powell, J., & Clarke, A. (2006). Internet information-seeking in mental health: Population survey. *The British Journal of Psychiatry, 189*, 273–277. http://dx.doi.org/10.1192/bjp.bp.105.017319

Preis, T., Moat, H. S., & Stanley, H. E. (2013). Quantifying trading behavior in financial markets using *Google Trends. Scientific Reports, 3*, 1684. http://dx.doi.org/10.1038/srep01684

Rains, S. A., & Tukachinsky, R. (2015). An examination of the relationships among uncertainty, appraisal, and information-seeking behavior proposed in uncertainty management theory. *Health Communication, 30*, 339–349. http://dx.doi.org/10.1080/10410236.2013.858285

Schwartz, S. (1994). The fallacy of the ecological fallacy: The potential misuse of a concept and the consequences. *American Journal of Public Health, 84*, 819–824. http://dx.doi.org/10.2105/AJPH.84.5.819

Seifter, A., Schwarzwalder, A., Geis, K., & Aucott, J. (2010). The utility of "Google Trends" for epidemiological research: Lyme disease as an example. *Geospatial Health, 4*, 135–137. http://dx.doi.org/10.4081/gh.2010.195

Siliverstovs, B., & Wochner, D. S. (2018). Google Trends and reality: Do the proportions match? Appraising the informational value of online search behavior: Evidence from Swiss tourism regions. *Journal of Economic Behavior & Organization, 145*, 1–23. http://dx.doi.org/10.1016/j.jebo.2017.10.011

Simmering, J. E., Polgreen, L. A., & Polgreen, P. M. (2014). Web search query volume as a measure of pharmaceutical utilization and changes in prescribing patterns. *Research in Social & Administrative Pharmacy, 10*, 896–903. http://dx.doi.org/10.1016/j.sapharm.2014.01.003

Stephens-Davidowitz, S. (2014). The cost of racial animus on a black candidate: Evidence using Google search data. *Journal of Public Economics, 118*, 26–40. http://dx.doi.org/10.1016/j.jpubeco.2014.04.010

Swearingen, C. D., & Ripberger, J. T. (2014). Google Insights and U.S. Senate elections: Does search traffic provide a valid measure of public attention to political candidates? *Social Science Quarterly, 95*, 882–893. http://dx.doi.org/10.1111/ssqu.12075

Tabuchi, T., Fukui, K., & Gallus, S. (2018). Tobacco price increases and population interest in smoking cessation in Japan between 2004 and 2016: A Google Trends analysis. *Nicotine & Tobacco Research, 21*, 475–480. http://dx.doi.org/10.1093/ntr/nty020

Vosen, S., & Schmidt, T. (2011). Forecasting private consumption: Survey-based indicators vs. Google Trends. *Journal of Forecasting, 30*, 565–578. http://dx.doi.org/10.1002/for.1213

Walasek, L., & Brown, G. D. A. (2015). Income inequality and status seeking: Searching for positional goods in unequal U.S. States. *Psychological Science, 26*, 527–533. http://dx.doi.org/10.1177/0956797614567511

Walasek, L., & Brown, G. D. A. (2016). Income inequality, income, and internet searches for status goods: A cross-national study of the association between inequality and well-being. *Social Indicators Research, 129*, 1001–1014. http://dx.doi.org/10.1007/s11205-015-1158-4

Wu, L., & Lee, C. (2016). Limited edition for me and best seller for you: The impact of scarcity versus popularity cues on self versus other-purchase behavior. *Journal of Retailing, 92*, 486–499. http://dx.doi.org/10.1016/j.jretai.2016.08.001

Yang, A. C., Huang, N. E., Peng, C.-K., & Tsai, S.-J. (2010). Do seasons have an influence on the incidence of depression? The use of an Internet search engine query data as a proxy of human affect. *PLoS ONE, 5*, e13728. http://dx.doi.org/10.1371/journal.pone.0013728

Yang, A. C., Tsai, S.-J., Huang, N. E., & Peng, C.-K. (2011). Association of Internet search trends with suicide death in Taipei City, Taiwan, 2004–2009. *Journal of Affective Disorders, 132,* 179–184. http://dx.doi.org/10.1016/j.jad.2011.01.019

Zhang, Z., Zheng, X., Zeng, D. D., & Leischow, S. J. (2016). Tracking dabbing using search query surveillance: A case study in the United States. *Journal of Medical Internet Research, 18,* e252. http://dx.doi.org/10.2196/jmir.5802

Zheluk, A., Quinn, C., & Meylakhs, P. (2014). Internet search and krokodil in the Russian Federation: An infoveillance study. *Journal of Medical Internet Research, 16,* e212. http://dx.doi.org/10.2196/jmir.3203

5

Observing Human Behavior Through Worldwide Network Cameras

Sara Aghajanzadeh, Andrew T. Jebb, Yifan Li,
Yung-Hsiang Lu, and George K. Thiruvathukal

In recent years, many organizations, such as departments of transportation, restaurants, universities, and shopping centers, have deployed network cameras and made the streaming data publicly available on the Internet. These cameras provide opportunities for gathering real-time visual data that can be used for observing a range of human behaviors, such as walking, sitting, talking, or eating. The data can enable researchers—psychologists and other social scientists—to observe and analyze human behavior in real time across different geographical locations simultaneously. This data opportunity handles two major hurdles associated with research in psychology: (a) the lack of diversity and breadth in its samples (Ceci, Kahan, & Braman, 2010; Henrich, Heine, & Norenzayan, 2010) and (b) experimental studies being too carefully orchestrated to be generalizable (Grant & Wall, 2009; McGuire, 1973). All of the data from these kinds of network cameras will be correlational, but in this way, video big data can contribute by adding to the traditional correlational and experimental approaches and may reveal unknown patterns or validate

The authors would like to thank the organizations that provide the camera data. This project is supported in part by National Science Foundation OAC-1535108, IIP-1530914, OISE-1427808, and CNS-0958487; a Lynn Computer Science and Engineering Fellowship; Amazon; Microsoft; Google; and Facebook. We thank Intel and Argonne National Laboratory for access to computational clusters, and the owners of the camera data. Any opinions, findings, and conclusions or recommendations expressed in this material are those of the authors and do not necessarily reflect the views of the sponsors.

http://dx.doi.org/10.1037/0000193-006
Big Data in Psychological Research, S. E. Woo, L. Tay, and R. W. Proctor (Editors)
Copyright © 2020 by the American Psychological Association. All rights reserved.

psychological theories at a larger scale. These network camera data may also be integrated and/or cross-referenced with other data sources that also index different geographic locations, such as large-scale survey data, social media data, or other forms of big data (e.g., Internet search queries; Yang, Tsai, Huang, & Peng, 2011). In this chapter, we present an overview of the opportunities from video data available in worldwide network cameras and a research tool, called CAM², for obtaining and analyzing visual data at a large scale.

To date, network camera data has already been useful for observing human behaviors and internal psychological states. For example, Hernandez, Hoque, Drevo, and Picard (2012) tracked the number of smiles on four different campuses for 10 weeks using network cameras. They found that the number of smiles was correlated with certain events (e.g., graduation, weekends, exams). Mazerolle, Hurley, and Chamlin (2002) used video data to track individual prosocial and antisocial behaviors in a U.S. city over several months.

Another domain for which network cameras can provide opportunities is in the study of large crowds. The typical units of study in psychology are individuals or small groups (e.g., dyads, teams, families). However, large groups (i.e., crowds) are another class of social grouping that frequently occur (at airports, transportation areas, malls, stadiums, etc.) and have unique psychological dynamics. Both macro- and microlevels (i.e., the whole crowd vs. individuals) and their interactions have long been of interest to psychology (e.g., Wilder, 1977; Yamori, 1998).

Recently, researchers have been developing methods for estimating the physical properties of crowds, such as the size, density, and flow and events and anomalies of crowds (Liya, 2016; Saleh, Suandi, & Ibrahim, 2015). Psychologically, the collective emotions of crowds can also be estimated (Urizar, Barakova, Marcenaro, Regazzoni, & Rauterberg, 2017), which can be used for examining important phenomena such as emotional contagion (Hatfield, Cacioppo, & Rapson, 1993). Individuals or smaller groups can also be tracked within crowds (Aggarwal & Ryoo, 2011), providing a way to observe how individuals interact with the greater whole (e.g., adopting the behavior of the crowd; Milgram, Bickman, & Berkowitz, 1969) and detecting individual-level personality traits (see Favaretto, Dihl, Musse, Vilanova, & Costa, 2017).

Another domain in which video data can be particularly prominent is in the study of consumer behavior (Summers & Hebert, 2001). Video can reveal consumers' walking speed and direction, pausing to view items of interest, looking for help, waving of hands, and waiting for assistance. The video can show a variety of events such as walking, resting, or talking, as well as other information about the people (e.g., being alone or in groups). It can serve to estimate how often people walk by a particular store and how the pattern varies at different times during the day, as well as comparing weekdays and weekends. More important, it is possible to calculate how long people spend in the store and observe their facial expressions when they leave the store. These examples suggest that visual data is a rich resource for understanding human behavior and can provide insights about consumers, as well. Unfortunately, examples of such data could not be published in this book; thus, they are not included in this chapter.

Most notably, Tay, Jebb, and Woo (2017) suggested that video data can enable behavioral detection (e.g., frequency, patterns), capture behavioral change, understand development over time (e.g., episodes, interactions, life span), and inform the contexts in which behaviors are enacted, facilitated, or constrained (i.e., locations, countries). Such observation may be used for studying specific psychological research questions. For example, using the traffic camera in Figure 5.1a, it is possible to analyze accidents and improve safety. In another example, using the camera in Figure 5.1b, one can examine crowd behaviors (e.g., demographics, walking speed, proximities).

In the past, public human behavior was commonly watched and analyzed by humans. In recent years, the significant progress in machine learning technologies have made possible the use of computer programs in observing human behavior (Margineantu, Wong, & Dash, 2010). Video analytics have been deployed in cashier-less stores (e.g., Amazon Go). Machine learning techniques can detect and track human movement or summarize a sequence of activities (Gandomi & Haider, 2015). Despite the great promise of using video to understand human behaviors, acquiring data in natural settings has been a challenge. The video streams on the Internet from network cameras can be potential sources propelling the progress.

In this chapter, we start by providing an overview of computer technologies for analyzing human behaviors from video data, followed by a discussion of how various human behaviors are classified and the challenges in creating analysis software. We use several examples as sources of data (i.e., network cameras) from which it would be possible to observe human behaviors. We then introduce a software infrastructure built at Purdue University, called CAM² (Continuous Analysis of Many CAMeras; http://cam2project.net), as a

FIGURE 5.1. Observation of Pedestrian Activities

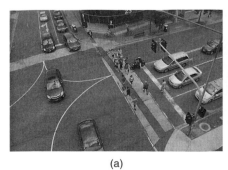 

(a)   (b)

(a) Reprinted from "*Intersection view from above*," by philip.mallis (https://ccsearch. creativecommons.org/photos/f7fc6938-6344-4c0d-8871-1c288b3115a9). CC BY-SA 2.0.
(b) Reprinted from "*Crowds at 57th and Broadway*," by tweber1 (https://ccsearch. creativecommons.org/photos/35d7a2e2-ad79-477b-8850-6adcb5dbaf9a). CC BY-SA 2.0.

general-purpose computing platform for retrieving and analyzing visual data from many sources across the globe.

VIDEO ANALYTICS FOR HUMAN BEHAVIOR

Stages for Video Analytics

Humans can usually recognize behaviors that are recorded in videos. Creating computer software to recognize human behaviors ("behavior recognition"), however, is much more difficult. Fortunately, significant progress in machine learning has made behavior recognition possible. Behavior recognition usually involves the following steps: (1) segmentation, (2) motion detection, (3) object classification, and (4) motion tracking (Gowsikhaa, Abirami, & Baskaran, 2014). These stages are shown in Figure 5.2. Motion detection, object classification, and motion tracking (left column) are all low-level processing techniques that are currently all machine based (i.e., involve machine learning algorithms). By contrast, behavior recognition, behavior analysis, and behavior classification (right column) are high-level processing techniques that can be either machine and/or human based because they are not yet fully automated.

The first step, *segmentation*, classifies pixels into different regions that are called *segments*. Pixels in the same segment belong to the same object.

After segmentation, the second stage, *motion detection*, identifies moving pixels and distinguishes them from the pixels that belong to the background. In this process, *background modeling* extracts a background from a sequence of successive frames, and the pixels that do not belong to this background (i.e., those that are moving) are identified as foreground. The foreground is then separated, and noise is eliminated. Figure 5.3 shows how the moving foreground pixels are shown in blobs that represent human silhouettes.

After identifying foreground (moving) pixels, the blobs are classified and labeled as objects (humans, vehicles, furniture, etc.) in the step *object classification*. Object classification only considers whether objects are humans or not (a binary decision); in this chapter, we discuss human behavior. Object classification may use features such as shapes of objects or type of motion to identify what has been observed (Ko, 2008). The next step, *motion tracking*, follows objects from one frame to another to determine the objects' new locations as the video progresses, as shown in Figure 5.4.

Human Behavior Classification

Once the initial stages of video analysis have been completed, human behaviors can then be classified. First, human behaviors can be placed into a category based on who is involved in the interaction: (a) single-person activities, (b) single-person interactions with objects, (c) two-person interactions, and

FIGURE 5.2. Video Analytics Procedure for Understanding Human Behavior

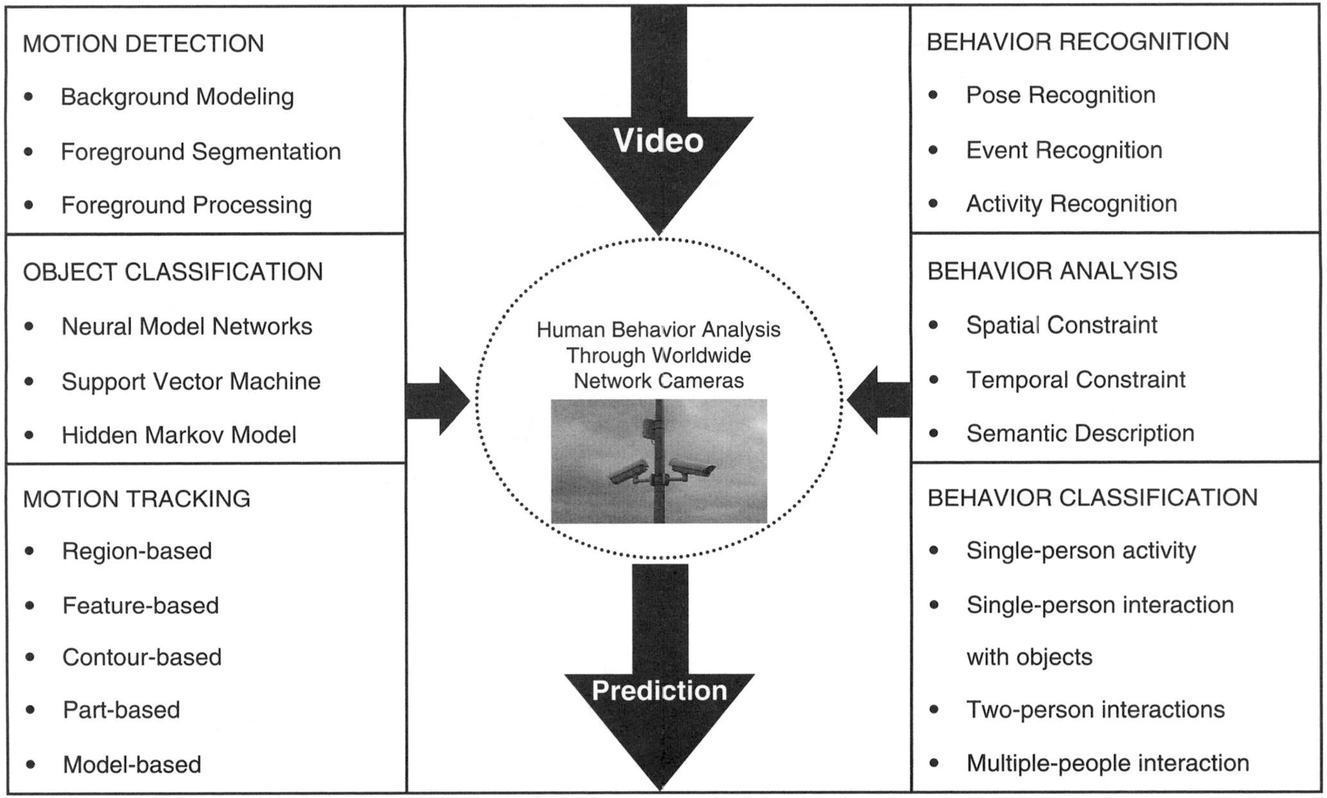

Video

Human Behavior Analysis Through Worldwide Network Cameras

Prediction

MOTION DETECTION
- Background Modeling
- Foreground Segmentation
- Foreground Processing

OBJECT CLASSIFICATION
- Neural Model Networks
- Support Vector Machine
- Hidden Markov Model

MOTION TRACKING
- Region-based
- Feature-based
- Contour-based
- Part-based
- Model-based

BEHAVIOR RECOGNITION
- Pose Recognition
- Event Recognition
- Activity Recognition

BEHAVIOR ANALYSIS
- Spatial Constraint
- Temporal Constraint
- Semantic Description

BEHAVIOR CLASSIFICATION
- Single-person activity
- Single-person interaction with objects
- Two-person interactions
- Multiple-people interaction

FIGURE 5.3. Moving Object Detection

Original video frames (top), extracted foreground (middle), and extracted silhouette after denoising (bottom). Adapted from "Human Silhouette Extraction Using Background Modeling and Subtraction Techniques," by S. Sulaiman, A. Hussain, N. Tahir, S. A. Samad, and M. M. Mustafa, 2008, *Information Technology Journal, 7,* p. 157.

(d) multiple-people interactions. Once the number of persons involved in the interaction is known, behaviors can be broadly classified into two groups: (a) poses and (b) events (Gowsikhaa et al., 2014). *Poses* are basic body positions such as sitting, standing, and lying. There are several methods to predict the pose, such as classifiers or rule-based methods. Lao, Han, and deWith (2010) used the coordinates of various body parts to classify different poses. Another method uses a rectangular bounding box (used to represent a region of interest) to calculate the height and width of the object and ratio between them and then compare the ratio with a range of thresholds to find out the exact pose. Sometimes, an inaccurate body ratio may result because the box binds the human along with objects they may be holding, such as a purse or a shopping bag. As an alternative to a bounding box, Foroughi, Yazdi, Pourreza, and Javidi (2008) used an approximated ellipse of the person to obtain more

FIGURE 5.4. Examples of Tracking

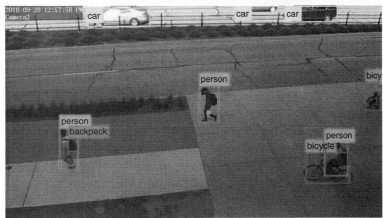

Objects are detected, classified, and tracked by a computer.

precise poses. Similarly, a method by Park and Aggarwal (2004) detected the body parts first and then constructed an ellipse separately for each body part before combining them to determine the pose.

Once a pose is determined, human behavior that can be classified as an *event* can be identified (walk, run, sleep, etc.). Variables such as speed can be used to distinguish walking from running. More complex events can be identified using *spatial–temporal constraints*. A *spatial constraint* refers to the location and distance between objects, whereas a *temporal constraint* refers to the duration between actions (Brémond, Thonnat, & Zúñiga, 2006). For instance, when two people approach each other, the distance between them decreases from one frame to the next. Consequently, the preceding actions from the previous frames and the current action from the current frame will be correlated and allow the behavior to be predicted. Once the actions (poses or events) are recognized, a classifier is used to predict the behavior with the help of semantic descriptions. For example, Foroughi et al. (2008) defined "forward fall" behavior with a "falling on knees, chest, or arms" semantic description or "backward fall" behavior with a "falling caused by slipping" semantic description. In another example, Park and Aggarwal (2004) defined "handshaking" behavior with a "hands clasped as in intimacy or affection" semantic description.

Challenges in Analyzing Human Behavior From Video

Many studies about human behavior focus on detecting "abnormal behaviors" in surveillance video (e.g., Popoola & Wang, 2012). Despite decades of research, many challenges remain in the automatic recognition and interpretation of human behavior by computer programs. First, human behaviors have to be understood within a context. This context may or may not be easily determined from where the behavior occurs. For example, individuals fighting on the street would be considered abnormal, whereas individuals fighting in a boxing ring would be expected. Here, the context can be deduced from the location. In another example, people running on a street may be anomalous if it is in response to something dangerous or alarming. However, running is expected in the event of a city marathon. In this case, the location itself does not provide enough context to interpret the behavior. The second challenge is that many applications require understanding individuals' behaviors in crowds when many other people are moving, which is difficult for humans, let alone computer programs, to do. Third, some applications have to identify the same individuals captured by multiple cameras, which is currently a challenge in computer vision. Fourth, there are constraints in using existing infrastructure because the cameras may not provide a high-quality recording and are not always located ideally for behavioral captures (e.g., facing the road instead of a sidewalk; Tay et al., 2017).

Data From Worldwide Network Cameras

As mentioned in the introduction, machine learning is a promising solution in the analysis of video for understanding human behavior. Machine learning, however, encounters two major challenges: (a) training and testing machine learning algorithms on data in realistic settings and (b) labeling the human behaviors in video data to be used for prediction by machine learning algorithms. We suggest using data from network cameras (a) because they provide video footage from realistic settings just in time and using the context to alleviate the burden and (b) because labeling done by human raters is expensive and prone to error. Thus, we introduce semiautomatic labeling in the following section.

Public Network Cameras

Many cities, restaurants, universities, and hotels deploy network cameras and make the data available to the public. Figure 5.5 shows four examples.

Figure 5.5a shows Old Faithful in Yellowstone National Park. The video can be used to count the number of visitors and how long they stay watching the eruptions. The street camera in Figure 5.5b may be used to see how fast

**FIGURE 5.5. Observing Human Behavior Using Network Cameras
in Different Locations**

(a)   (b)

(c)   (d)

(a) Old Faithful in Yellowstone National Park, (b) a street in the United States,
(c) a university campus, and (d) a computer lab. The image of Yellowstone is from
https://www.npr.gov/yell/learn/photosmiltimedia/webcams.htm. In the public domain.
The rest of the images are from https://engineering.purdue.edu/ECN/WebCam.
Reprinted with permission from the Office of Legal Counsel, Purdue University.

people drive or how often drivers change lanes. Figure 5.5c is a university
campus, and Figure 5.5d is a computer laboratory; students can use the real-
time data to determine whether the laboratory is too crowded and they
should go to another laboratory. The data can also help the university understand the usage patterns, such as when the laboratory is most used and when
the laboratory is empty.

Some studies have been conducted to understand pedestrian behavior,
including their walking speeds and road crossing strategies. Traditionally, the
studies were conducted using methods such as surveys and direct observation with trained observers (e.g., Levine & Norenzayan, 1999). In surveys,
self-reported questionnaires can suffer from inaccuracy and/or respondents
may not be fully cognizant enough of their behaviors to report them. Direct
observation is usually labor-intensive and expensive, and it cannot be easily
applied to a multiplicity of geographic regions over long periods, leading to
problems of generalizability. There are also limitations in terms of attentional

bandwidth that make it difficult for observers to account for certain behaviors in crowded public areas.

Traffic camera data is crucial first-hand evidence for analyzing pedestrian behavior in public areas. Compared with traditional methods mentioned earlier, analysis conducted using camera data is relatively cost-efficient and less labor-intensive. For instance, Chen, Ning, Zhou, Wu, and Zhang (2014) used a camera installed in a metro station to count pedestrians and measure the flow volume of passengers. Because the installed camera was close to pedestrians, they were able to improve pedestrian detection accuracy by using face detection. Zaki, Sayed, Tageldin, and Hussein (2013) studied pedestrian violations against the street-crossing rules in an urban area by applying computer vision techniques on traffic camera videos. Their system can automatically detect jaywalkers and measure jaywalking rates and frequency of vehicle–pedestrian conflict.

It is frequently asked whether the data captured by these network cameras violate the privacy of its subjects. Widen (2008) created a matrix to determine whether privacy is protected according to the subject's and observer's location. Briefly, if both are in public properties, privacy is not protected, and data can be recorded without violation. In the United States, the privacy of online multimedia can be considered part of the Fourth Amendment to the U.S. Constitution, which restricts government activities such as searches (Lu, Cavallaro, Crump, Friedland, & Winstein, 2017). Currently, the Fourth Amendment does not legally restrict an individual from video recording another individual in a public place. Thus, the network cameras in public locations do not violate known privacy laws or court cases in the United States.

Using Context for Data Labeling

Despite rapid progress in machine learning technologies for understanding human behaviors in videos, computer programs are still inferior to humans in many tasks. As a result, computer programs still rely on labels made by humans (called *supervised learning*, with the assumption that humans act as "supervisors"). Kamar, Hacker, and Horvitz (2012) and Wang and Hua (2011) suggested using interactions between humans and machine learning to reduce the labeling efforts.

Network cameras can potentially use "context" to reduce the labeling efforts because these cameras have fixed locations (some have pan–tilt–zoom), and the data are real-time. Consequently, it is possible to cross-reference other sources of data or prior knowledge to label the data. For example, a computer laboratory is expected to see many students near the end of each semester and few (or no) students during semester breaks. In another example, a shopping mall is expected to see no customers when the mall is closed. The context (e.g., location and time) may reduce but does not necessarily eliminate the need for human labeling. Thus, this is considered as semi-automatic labeling.

A RESEARCH TOOL USING NETWORK CAMERAS IN UNDERSTANDING HUMAN BEHAVIOR

Continuous Analysis of Many CAMeras Built at Purdue University

Recognizing the potential of using network cameras in understanding human behaviors, a team at Purdue University has been building a research tool called CAM^2. CAM^2 has the following major components: (a) a database of more than 100,000 network cameras with an application programming interface, (b) a runtime system that can retrieve and analyze data from the network cameras, (c) a web user interface, and (d) a manager for allocating computing resources. In the following sections, we explain the camera database and the resource manager.

Camera Database and Application Programming Interface

The foundation of CAM^2 is a database that stores the descriptions of more than 100,000 network cameras whose data is publicly available on the Internet. IHS Markit estimated that more than 245 million surveillance cameras have been deployed worldwide (Jenkins, 2015). Many of these cameras' data are available on the Internet without password protection. Even though the data from each camera provides intrinsic value, the true potential of real-time data is fully exploited when the data from multiple streams are aggregated using a camera database.

On the basis of the protocols for retrieving data, the database classifies network cameras into two categories: (a) IP (Internet Protocol) cameras and (b) non-IP cameras. Each IP camera has a unique IP address that allows direct communication with the camera itself. IP cameras usually have built-in web servers and can respond to HTTP GET requests. The hypertext transfer protocol (HTTP) works as a request–response protocol between a client (browser) and a server. A non-IP camera does not have a unique IP address for direct access. Instead, a non-IP camera is connected through a computer. A webcam is an example of a non-IP camera. Many departments of transportation have websites on which the data streams from multiple cameras are aggregated. There is no standard method for retrieving data from these aggregation sites. CAM^2 makes all available cameras accessible through its interface. The CAM^2 database also stores additional information about each camera (known as *metadata*) that includes the camera's location, city, state, country, frame rate, and owner.

Resource Manager

Video analytics is computationally expensive; analyzing multiple data streams from worldwide sources can require many computers running simultaneously. To solve this problem, CAM^2 uses cloud computing to analyze the data. Many factors can affect the types, locations, and numbers of computers needed (Kaseb, Mohan, Koh, & Lu, 2017). Some analytics programs require large amounts of computation, whereas others require more memory. In some cases, the network distance (measured by round trip time) can affect the video's frame rates (Mohan, Kaseb, Lu, & Hacker, 2016). Consequently, computation should be performed geographically near the sources of data by selecting the right data centers for cloud instances because cloud vendors have data centers in many different countries.

The resource management problem can be modeled as a multiple-dimension, multiple-size integer bin-packing problem. The resource requirements for analyzing one particular video stream are expressed as a multidimensional vector. The capability (e.g., number of cores, amount of memory, presence of graphics processing unit) of each type of cloud instance is modeled as a bin of the same dimension. Each type of cloud instance has a cost per hour. The resource manager's responsibility is to determine the types and numbers of cloud instances (i.e., bins) so that all data streams can be analyzed and the overall cost minimized. The integer bin-packing problem is computationally intractable; thus, heuristic solutions are adopted.

Using Worldwide Network Cameras to Understand Human Behavior

CAM^2 can be used to study human behaviors in two ways: online analysis or offline analysis. Online analysis requires analysis programs that use CAM^2's programming interface and runtime system. These programs will set the desired frame rates (which must be lower than the cameras' refresh rates) and select the network cameras whose data will be analyzed. The programming interface is event-driven: When new frames are acquired from network cameras, callback functions are invoked to analyze the frames. The programs may store multiple recent frames if the analyses need recent data. The advantage of online analysis is that valuable information can be obtained immediately when the data is captured. The challenge here, however, is writing the analysis programs that can process the incoming data as fast as the specified frame rates. Offline analyses save the data and can be more flexible. The analysis programs do not have stringent performance requirements, and the data can also be inspected by humans. CAM^2 is open to researchers using network cameras in their studies. Registration is available on the website.

CONCLUSION

In sum, in this chapter, we presented an overview of the opportunities from video data available in the worldwide network of cameras and the CAM^2 research tool for obtaining and analyzing visual data on a large scale. Video data can be a rich source of human behavior. Behavioral researchers use video cameras to capture contextual information, human facial and body information, and social interactions. Meanwhile, there are continued technical and ethical challenges that have to be tackled as we embark on drawing on such data.

REFERENCES

Aggarwal, J. K., & Ryoo, M. S. (2011). Human activity analysis: A review. *ACM Computing Survey, 43*(3), 1–43.

Brémond, F., Thonnat, M., & Zúñiga, M. (2006). Video-understanding framework for automatic behavior recognition. *Behavior Research Methods, 38*, 416–426. http://dx.doi.org/10.3758/BF03192795

Ceci, S. J., Kahan, D. M., & Braman, D. (2010). The WEIRD are even weirder than you think: Diversifying contexts is as important as diversifying samples. *Behavioral and Brain Sciences, 33*(2–3), 87–88. http://dx.doi.org/10.1017/S0140525X10000063

Chen, Y. Y., Ning, C., Zhou, Y. Y., Wu, K. H., & Zhang, W. W. (2014). Pedestrian detection and tracking for counting applications in metro station. *Discrete Dynamics in Nature and Society, 2014*, 712041.

Favaretto, R. M., Dihl, L., Musse, S. R., Vilanova, F., & Costa, A. B. (2017). *Using Big Five personality model to detect cultural aspects in crowds.* Retrieved from https://arxiv.org/pdf/1903.01688.pdf

Foroughi, H., Yazdi, H. S., Pourreza, H., & Javidi, M. (2008). *An eigenspace-based approach for human fall detection using integrated time motion image and multi-class support vector machine.* Retrieved from shorturl.at/hjtA2

Gandomi, A., & Haider, M. (2015). Beyond the hype: Big data concepts, methods, and analytics. *International Journal of Information Management, 35*, 137–144. http://dx.doi.org/10.1016/j.ijinfomgt.2014.10.007

Gowsikhaa, D., Abirami, S., & Baskaran, R. (2014). Automated human behavior analysis from surveillance videos: A survey. *Artificial Intelligence Review, 42*, 747–765. http://dx.doi.org/10.1007/s10462-012-9341-3

Grant, A. M., & Wall, T. D. (2009). The neglected science and art of quasi-experimentation: Why-to, when-to, and how-to advice for organizational researchers. *Organizational Research Methods, 12*, 653–686. http://dx.doi.org/10.1177/1094428108320737

Hatfield, E., Cacioppo, J. T., & Rapson, R. L. (1993). Emotional contagion. *Current Directions in Psychological Science, 2*(3), 96–100. http://dx.doi.org/10.1111/1467-8721.ep10770953

Henrich, J., Heine, S. J., & Norenzayan, A. (2010). The weirdest people in the world? *Behavioral and Brain Sciences, 33*, 61–83. http://dx.doi.org/10.1017/S0140525X0999152X

Hernandez, J., Hoque, M. E., Drevo, W., & Picard, R. W. (2012, September). *Mood meter: Counting smiles in the wild.* Paper presented at the 2012 ACM Conference on Ubiquitous Computing, Pittsburgh, PA.

Jenkins, N. (2015, June 11). 245 million video surveillance cameras installed globally in 2014. *IHS Markit Technology.* Retrieved from https://technology.ihs.com/532501/245-million-video-surveillance-cameras-installed-globally-in-2014

Kamar, E., Hacker, S., & Horvitz, E. (2012). *Combining human and machine intelligence in large-scale crowdsourcing.* Retrieved from http://www.ifaamas.org/Proceedings/aamas2012/papers/3C_3.pdf

Kaseb, A., Mohan, A., Koh, Y., & Lu, Y. (2017). *Cloud resource management for analyzing big real-time visual data from network cameras.* Retrieved from https://pdfs.semanticscholar.org/902f/7452e7c576c729434dbc074bc1778d9eaf45.pdf

Ko, T. (2008, October). *A survey on behavior analysis in video surveillance applications.* Paper presented at the IEEE Applied Imagery Pattern Recognition Workshop, Washington, DC.

Lao, W., Han, J., & deWith, H. N. P. (2010). Flexible human behavior analysis framework for video surveillance applications. *International Journal of Digital Multimedia Broadcasting, 2010,* 920121.

Levine, R. V., & Norenzayan, A. (1999). The pace of life in 31 countries. *Journal of Cross-Cultural Psychology, 30,* 178–205. http://dx.doi.org/10.1177/0022022199030002003

Liya, R. (2016). Motion tracking & detection of anomalous events in the crowd based on intelligence video surveillance. *International Journal of Computer Science and Mobile Computing, 5*(8), 254–261.

Lu, Y., Cavallaro, A., Crump, C., Friedland, G., & Winstein, K. (2017). *Panel: Privacy protection in online multimedia.* Mountain View, CA: ACM Multimedia.

Margineantu, D., Wong, W., & Dash, D. (2010). Machine learning algorithms for event detection: A special issue of machine learning. *Machine Learning, 79,* 257–259. http://dx.doi.org/10.1007/s10994-010-5184-9

Mazerolle, L., Hurley, D., & Chamlin, M. (2002). Social behavior in public space: An analysis of behavioral adaptations to CCTV. *Security Journal, 15,* 59–75. http://dx.doi.org/10.1057/palgrave.sj.8340118

McGuire, W. J. (1973). The yin and yang of progress in social psychology: Seven koan. *Journal of Personality and Social Psychology, 26,* 446–456. http://dx.doi.org/10.1037/h0034345

Milgram, S., Bickman, L., & Berkowitz, L. (1969). Note on the drawing power of crowds of different size. *Journal of Personality and Social Psychology, 13,* 79–82. http://dx.doi.org/10.1037/h0028070

Mohan, A., Kaseb, A., Lu, Y., & Hacker, T. (2016). Location based cloud resource management for analyzing real-time video from globally distributed network cameras. In J. Cardoso, D. Ferguson, V. M. Muñoz, & M. Helfert (Eds.), *Proceedings of the IEEE International Conference on Cloud Computing Technology and Science* (pp. 176–183). Lda, Portugal: Science and Technology Publications.

Park, S., & Aggarwal, J. K. (2004, June–July). *Semantic-level understanding of human actions and interactions using event hierarchy.* Paper presented at the IEEE Computer Society Conference on Computer Vision and Pattern Recognition Workshop, Washington, DC.

Popoola, O., & Wang, K. (2012). Video-based abnormal human behavior recognition—A review. *IEEE Transactions on Systems, Man, and Cybernetics, Part C (Applications and Reviews), 42,* 865–878.

Saleh, S. A. M., Suandi, S. A., & Ibrahim, H. (2015). Recent survey on crowd density estimation and counting for visual surveillance. *Engineering Applications of Artificial Intelligence, 41,* 103–114. http://dx.doi.org/10.1016/j.engappai.2015.01.007

Sulaiman, S., Hussain, A., Tahir, N., Samad, S. A., & Mustafa, M. M. (2008). Human silhouette extraction using background modeling and subtraction techniques. *Information Technology Journal, 7,* 155–159. http://dx.doi.org/10.3923/itj.2008.155.159

Summers, T., & Hebert, P. (2001, November). Shedding some light on store atmospherics: Influence of illumination on consumer behavior. *Journal of Business Research, 54*(2), 145–150. http://dx.doi.org/10.1016/S0148-2963(99)00082-X

Tay, L., Jebb, A. T., & Woo, S. (2017). Video capture of human behaviors: Toward a Big Data approach. *Current Opinion in Behavioral Sciences, 18,* 17–22. http://dx.doi.org/10.1016/j.cobeha.2017.05.026

Urizar, O. J., Barakova, E. I. L., Marcenaro, L., Regazzoni, C. S., & Rauterberg, M. (2017, July). *Emotion estimation in crowds: A survey.* Paper presented at the 8th International Conference of Pattern Recognition Systems, Madrid, Spain.

Wang, M., & Hua, X. (2011, February). Active learning in multimedia annotation and retrieval: A survey. *ACM Transactions on Intelligent Systems and Technology, 2*(2), 10. http://dx.doi.org/10.1145/1899412.1899414

Widen, W. (2008). Smart cameras and the right to privacy. *Proceedings of the IEEE, 96,* 1688–1697.

Wilder, D. A. (1977). Perception of groups, size of opposition, and social influence. *Journal of Experimental Social Psychology, 13,* 253–268. http://dx.doi.org/10.1016/0022-1031(77)90047-6

Yamori, Y. (1998). Going with the flow: Micro-macro dynamics in the macro behavioral patterns of pedestrian crowds. *Psychological Review, 105,* 530–557. http://dx.doi.org/10.1037/0033-295X.105.3.530

Yang, A. C., Tsai, S.-J., Huang, N. E., & Peng, C.-K. (2011). Association of Internet search trends with suicide death in Taipei City, Taiwan, 2004–2009. *Journal of Affective Disorders, 132,* 179–184. http://dx.doi.org/10.1016/j.jad.2011.01.019

Zaki, M., Sayed, T., Tageldin, A., & Hussein, M. (2013). Application of computer vision to diagnosis of pedestrian safety issues. *Transportation Research Record, 2393*(1), 75–84. http://dx.doi.org/10.3141/2393-09

6

Wearable Cameras, Machine Vision, and Big Data Analytics

Insights Into People and the Places They Go

Andrew B. Blake, Daniel I. Lee, Roberto De La Rosa, and Ryne A. Sherman

The use of big data in psychological research expands the boundaries of the classical lab environment by providing access to behaviors and scenarios previously thought unreachable (Kosinski & Behrend, 2017). One possible method of big data collection is the use of wearable cameras to examine social interaction in a naturalistic setting (Tay, Jebb, & Woo, 2017). This chapter demonstrates the utility of wearable cameras in a psychological study of daily life and offers practical advice for implementation and future research using wearable cameras. We begin with a brief introduction and theoretical background of the relationships between person and situation. Second, a brief literature review provides insight into the recent history and direction of the measurement of daily life. Third, we offer practical advice for the implementation of wearable cameras in a psychological study, including how the cameras work, where to purchase a wearable camera, legal and ethical concerns, and the overall obtrusiveness of the camera perceived by participants. Fourth, we discuss a study that used wearable cameras and machine vision. Finally, we present recommendations for research opportunities.

PERSON AND SITUATION THEORETICAL BACKGROUND

Kurt Lewin (1951) is often credited as being the first to posit the idea that human behavior (B) is a function of the person (P) and their environment (E). Although Lewin's equation, $B = f(P, E)$, did not necessarily imply such a

http://dx.doi.org/10.1037/0000193-007
Big Data in Psychological Research, S. E. Woo, L. Tay, and R. W. Proctor (Editors)

divide, decades of research were spent debating which of the two forces, persons or situations, were more important for explaining human behavior (Bem & Allen, 1974; Block, 1977; Bowers, 1973; Epstein, 1979; Mischel, 1968). As the science of psychology matured, researchers moved away from the view that human behavior stems from one of two dichotomous sources (Funder, 2006, 2009; Hogan, 2009; Johnson, 1999, 2009). Indeed, it is now widely accepted that the characteristics of both persons and situations influence behavior (Kenrick & Funder, 1988) and that it is often an interaction of both persons and situations that best describes the causes of said behaviors (Schmitt et al., 2013). Persons, situations, and behaviors are now considered to be a complex interwoven triad of elements that we concluded could be analyzed in greater depth by the measurement of daily life (Funder, 2006, 2008; Wagerman & Funder, 2009).

MEASURING DAILY LIFE

The most fundamental purpose of any psychological study is to describe and explain human behavior. Perhaps the most popular psychological method for understanding human behavior is the laboratory experiment. Indeed, decades of research purporting the power of situations come from precisely such experiments. However, laboratory experiments offer a limited perspective in terms of how people live their daily lives (Reis, 2012). For example, laboratory experiments cannot speak to the temporal series of events an individual experiences in his or her daily life because they do not measure it. Thus, although we can observe and measure human behavior in laboratories or psychological surveys, such behavior is circumscribed and not necessarily a reflection of a person's behavior in daily life. As such, it is sensible to study human behavior where it occurs, in daily life (Reis, 2012).

The limitations of laboratory experiments have been known for decades. However, the lack of available technology has hampered research that attempts to go far beyond the laboratory. For example, Craik (2000) hired a professional video recording team to follow a few volunteers around for 24 hours. Although this study was principally used to demonstrate how traits, goals, and situations are intertwined in a person's daily life, it is not feasible to conduct such a study on a large group of participants. Further, the size and obvious presence of the recording team and equipment increases the likelihood of measurement reactivity (e.g., biased data due to the act of being measured; Barta, Tennen, & Litt, 2012). Such reactivity could sacrifice the ecological validity supposedly gained by conducting research in the real world.

However, recent advances in technology have continued to improve the ability to study psychological processes as they naturally occur (Bolger, Davis, & Rafaeli, 2003). Before the 1980s, perhaps the most useful method for studying daily psychological processes was the daily diary method. The daily diary method required participants to record entries about their daily lives in a diary or journal, usually once a day (Wilhelm, Perrez, & Pawlik, 2012). Of course, although the daily diary has the advantage of repeated assessments, such assessments are dependent on the participant's ability to recall his or her entire day and do not capture psychological processes in real time. The experience-sampling method (ESM; Csikszentmihalyi & Larson, 1987), which requires participants to answer questionnaires several times a day after being prompted by a mobile electronic device (e.g., a pager), allowed researchers to capture psychological processes in real time. Ecological momentary assessment, which collected psychological and physiological moment-by-moment data using handheld devices such as palmtop computers, began around the same time (Stone & Shiffman, 1994). Although these types of devices can capture psychological processes in vivo, limitations such as survey fatigue and response bias may have influenced participants' self-report survey responses (Podsakoff, MacKenzie, Lee, & Podsakoff, 2003). More critically, although participant perceptions are useful, there are still many small moments and natural activities in daily living that are difficult to capture with self-reports. Technologies that can objectively capture such experiences bring researchers closer to the lives of their participants (Reis, 2012) and provide a more representative understanding of human behavior.

Several daily life methods provide objective assessments of a participant's environment and their behaviors within it. One of the oldest is the electronically activated recorder (EAR; Mehl, Pennebaker, Crow, Dabbs, & Price, 2001), a digital voice recorder a participant wears that periodically records brief intervals of their ambient sounds. From these recordings, conversations can be transcribed, and other social and environmental data can also be coded. However, with the advent of smartphones, voice recorders have become obsolete. Mobile sensing using smartphones is a more modern approach to unobtrusively collect naturalistic behavior (Dufau et al., 2011; Harari et al., 2016). As in ESM, participants can be prompted to answer queries randomly throughout the day. However, mobile sensing discretely tracks a participant's physical location, their sent and received communications (e.g., texts), their physical activity, and much more (Harari et al., 2016). As more people use smartphones, mobile sensing provides incredible access to different aspects of human behavior.

Although the EAR and other advances in mobile sensing capture important aspects of a person's natural environment, they miss the visual component. For example, the EAR captures sound from a participant's natural environment, such as watching a film (Mehl et al., 2001); however, it provides no information about the lighting of the environment or what the participant may be watching. With mobile sensing, movements and locations can be specified, but it provides no visual sense of what the person has encountered or how a setting may have changed. A wearable camera can provide raw, unfiltered, and objective information about an individual's visual environment and can fill this gap in the collection of naturalistic behavior.

WEARABLE CAMERAS

Wearable cameras provide a unique opportunity for studying daily life and people's natural environments. They allow researchers to see the world that their participants encounter on a moment-to-moment basis in their daily lives. For example, wearable cameras can investigate memory recall (Sellen et al., 2007), personal behavior, and well-being (Doherty et al., 2013), or autism diagnoses in children (Marcu, Dey, & Kiesler, 2012). Specifically, Sellen et al. (2007) found that using images collected from a SenseCam (a wearable camera from Microsoft) increased experiential memory recall relative to participants who did not have images of past events available. At the time of this writing, however, the use of wearable cameras in social and personality research has been limited to the data we present here. In the next section, we discuss perspective selection for wearable cameras, how wearable cameras work, where to buy them and how much they cost, and ethical and legal concerns, and we report participant obtrusiveness ratings from a recently completed wearable camera study.

Perspective Selection for Wearable Cameras

Currently, there are a plethora of wearable cameras that allow a person to capture a variety of perspectives, which include in front, behind, or above them. Wearable cameras worn on the chest or head can capture what is in front of the person, which can provide a relatively close representation of a first-person perspective. In contrast, there are wearable devices that can be worn on the head that capture images of the activity transpiring behind the wearer. There are also wearable cameras that are attached to a harness that can provide a third-person perspective, which may provide more nuance to the wearer's activity or situation. We encourage researchers to consider their specific research question to optimize device selection and data relevance. For this study, we selected a wearable camera that is small and can be worn on the chest to provide an unobtrusive look at the situations the participants experienced from day to day (i.e., the things they see that are in front of them).

How Wearable Cameras Work

Wearable cameras are small, portable electronic devices that can be worn on the outermost layer of clothing to record the person's environment visually. Such cameras can be purchased from a number of vendors (see the next section), but they generally operate in a similar fashion. Most of our experience pertains to the Narrative Clip (https://www.getnarrative.com), and thus we focus on it here. Initial configuration of the Narrative Clip requires connecting to a personal computer via USB (included in the box), downloading software, and creating an account (for cloud storage). This process creates a docking station for the camera that allows the device to charge and upload captured images to the computer and/or optional cloud service automatically.

Once the camera is disconnected from the docking station, it begins to capture images automatically every 30 seconds. The image capture process is controlled by a light sensor inside the device such that placing it in your pocket would halt the camera from taking pictures. Plugging the camera into a docking station triggers the camera to automatically upload stored images to a designated directory on the computer and remove those images from the camera to free storage space.

Where to Get a Wearable Camera

Wearable cameras are designed with the consumer in mind. Unfortunately, the lack of demand by consumers has made the Narrative Clip difficult to find and purchase. Currently, Narrative lists their devices as "temporarily out of stock" with no definitive time frame for availability. However, depending on need and functionally requirements (motion capture, battery life), there are other viable alternatives to Narrative Clip that offer similar functionality. For example, the Frontrow wearable device (https://www.frontrow.com) offers a story mode setting that automatically captures images at a 3-, 5-, 8-, 10-, or 20-second intervals. Another alternative is Google Clips (store.google.com), which captures small video clips (without audio) when motion is detected. The price of these devices ranges from USD $199 to $400. As the technology for wearable cameras evolves, we anticipate that the specifics of each device will change and that new cameras will come onto the market.

Legal and Ethical Considerations

When considering the viability of adding wearable cameras to a potential study, the researcher should carefully consider the possible legal and ethical challenges (see Chapter 15, this volume). The legality of image recording others in even public settings may vary according to local governments. Ethical considerations generally fall into two categories: protecting participant privacy and the privacy of nonparticipants. We discuss each in turn here.

Privacy of Participant

As with almost any psychological study, signed consent from the participant to voluntarily participate will eliminate much of the risk of privacy violation for the participant. The consent should specify who can access the available data from the study (e.g., research team—graduate students, research assistances, collaborators) and require anyone on the team to sign confidentiality agreements. For image data, images transferred from the camera to the computer should only be done via USB (or alternative wired transfer) because transferring data wirelessly has possible security risks that wired connections do not (see Vanhoef & Piessens, 2017, for an example of a major Wi-Fi security issue). Once all pictures are downloaded from the camera, participants should be able to screen and delete any images they do not want the research team to see (a procedure similar to that used by Mehl et al., 2001). Next, precautions should be implemented to protect the image data from being seen by anyone outside the research team. Therefore, it is necessary to password-protect the computers and hard drives where the images are being stored. And, if possible, we suggest encrypting all image data concurrently. These steps will ensure maximum privacy security for the participant.

Privacy for Others

The possibility of the wearable camera capturing an image that includes bystanders is almost certain. Therefore, it is appropriate to address this possibility and its legal and ethical concerns. In the United States, the laws for recording audio of bystanders without consent vary by state. However, image recording laws are generally more lenient and emphasize the bystanders' reasonable expectation of privacy. For example, one would not expect much privacy at a public park or public event. However, entering a private residence or private dormitory, one would certainly expect a certain level of privacy. Therefore, the participant (camera wearer) should be instructed to communicate that he or she is wearing a camera when entering a situation in which privacy is expected and to remove the camera in clearly private environments (e.g., a restroom or locker room). Further, the participant should also remove the camera on request if there are any comfortability issues being communicated about recording images of others. If the participant forgot to mention the camera in a private environment, they should be allowed to screen and delete any of the images they did not have permission to photograph. This is an effective form of compliance because participants actively remove images based on the concern of others' privacy (Hoyle, Templeman, Anthony, Crandall, & Kapadia, 2015).

People may be concerned that the Narrative Clip is a surveillance device or spy camera. However, the Narrative Clip is a poor device for surveillance when compared with other such devices on the market. First, the battery life is less than 24 hours, which prevents sustained observation. Second, because the Narrative Clip uses light sensing to turn itself off and on, it has poor performance in low-light conditions. Finally, the unpredictable image capture time makes it difficult to intentionally capture any single image as one might wish to do for surveillance purposes. Thus, although there are legitimate concerns about the use of surveillance devices, the wearable cameras discussed here are not designed for, or much good at, surveillance.

Obtrusiveness

In a recently completed wearable camera study (Brown, Blake, & Sherman, 2017), participants were asked to rate the obtrusiveness of wearing a Narrative Clip for 1 day. As seen in Table 6.1, participants indicated that wearing the camera was not uncomfortable or an impediment to their day, and it did not influence their behavior or that of others. However, participants also reported that they were relatively aware of the camera, and others were aware of the camera as well. Overall, although participants and bystanders were

TABLE 6.1. Descriptive Statistics for the Obtrusiveness Questionnaire

	M	*SD*	Med	Min	Max
Obtrusiveness for participant					
To what degree . . .					
were you generally aware of the Narrative?	3.03	1.30	3	1	5
did you feel uncomfortable wearing the Narrative?	1.86	1.31	1	1	5
did the Narrative impede your daily activities?	1.42	0.82	1	1	5
did the Narrative change your actual behavior?	1.34	0.74	1	1	4
did the Narrative influence places you went?	1.42	0.87	1	1	5
Obtrusiveness for others					
To what degree . . .					
were people around you aware of the Narrative?	3.14	1.30	3	1	5
did you talk to people around you about the Narrative?	2.94	1.29	3	1	5
did the Narrative influence the behavior of the people around you?	1.99	1.18	2	1	5

Note. N = 281. The average intercorrelation among the item is .17 (*SD* = .13, median = .15, min = −.03, max = .55). From "A Snapshot of the Life as Lived Wearable Cameras in Social and Personality Psychological Science," by N. A. Brown, A. B. Blake, and R. A. Sherman, 2017, *Social Psychological and Personality Science*, *8*, p. 596. Copyright 2017 by Sage. Adapted with permission.

aware of and talked about the Narrative Clip, the camera itself only slightly influenced the participants' and bystanders' typical behavior.

Wearable Camera Data

Images captured from the wearable camera are time stamped, which makes sorting a situation or entire day straightforward. In addition to images, most wearable cameras collect metadata from sensors built into the device. For example, the Narrative clip includes GPS and magnetometer sensors that record the location and the direction the camera was facing (north, south, east, or west) when an image was captured. Taken together, images and metadata recorded from the Narrative Clip provide a detailed description of what the wearer was doing and where they were at the time of the photo (or sequence of photos).

STUDYING SITUATIONS IN EVERYDAY LIFE

To best illustrate the capabilities of wearable cameras and how to leverage the collected data, we now turn to a recently conducted wearable camera study investigating the relationship between persons, situations, and behaviors as they interact in the participants' everyday lives. We present the methodological steps, followed by a detailed description of the application of machine vision software to image data, and we end with the results and discussion of the study.

Students from Florida Atlantic University ($N = 298$) were recruited to participate in a study in which they were asked to wear a Narrative Clip for 1 full waking day. Initially, participants were asked to complete the Big Five Aspect Scale measurement of personality (DeYoung, Quilty, & Peterson, 2007). We then gave every participant instructions on how to use a Narrative Clip, which included instructions to remove the camera in potentially private situations (e.g., restrooms, others' living quarters, locker rooms). After wearing the camera for a full waking day, participants then returned to the lab. During this visit, photos taken from the cameras were uploaded onto a password-protected computer. Before researchers viewed the pictures, participants were allowed to review and delete any images they did not wish to share with the research team. The photos were divided into situations by the participants (i.e., when one situation stopped and another started) who then provided a brief description of each situation (e.g., "I was walking back to my room by myself" or "Leaving Walmart with my boyfriend and driving back to our house"). Once the description for each situation was completed, the participants rated the situation on the DIAMONDS (Duty, Intellect, Adversity, Mating, pOsitivity, Negativity, Deception, Sociality) situation measurement using the S8-I (Rauthmann & Sherman, 2016) and their behavior on a semantic differential Big Five Aspects Scale.

Machine Vision Data Collection

After participant data collection ended, we began to investigate how the cues of participants' situations connected with how they perceived the situations (situation characteristics). The investigation began by partnering with Clarifai (https://www.clarifai.com/), a commercial software company whose focus is on machine vision and the detection of objects within photos. Specifically, the software first analyzes a given image, then provides a list of the 20 most probable objects within that image. We then used R (https://www.R-project.org/) to automatically process the uploading of images to Clarifai and the downloading of object lists for each photo (this can also be done through Python and Javascript). For this study, the object image data set for all 254,208 images was completed in around 48 hours (this depends on Internet and computer speed).

In total, 2,388 unique objects (or situation cues) were identified by the Clarifai software as appearing in at least one photo. However, many of these objects appeared extremely infrequently (e.g., only once). As such, we reduced the object image data set by removing objects that appeared less than once per 10 images. This reduced the total number of objects to 901. To further reduce the total number of objects, a principal components analysis of these 901 objects was conducted. Using a step-up approach (Rosenthal & Rosnow, 2008), we ultimately extracted 15 orthogonal and interpretable components. The 15 components were named as follows: Outdoors, Food, Dark Versus Light, Car/Driving, Music, Patterns, People Present, Shopping, Computing, Paper, Ground, Home Versus Commuting, Equipment, Classroom, and Bathroom. These dimensions of situation cues should not be considered a comprehensive taxonomy of cues that can be found in an individual's situation. Instead, they are a convenient and representative set of situation cues encountered by participants in our study. Each of the 254,208 images was scored on these 15 dimensions (using component scoring), and these scores were aggregated (averaged) up to the situation level for further analyses.

We then analyzed these data in two ways. First, we examined the relationship between personality traits and the 15 object components derived from the cues identified with Clarifai's machine vision software. Second, we examined the relationship between participants' perceptions of the characteristics of situations and the cues present in those situations (15 object components).

How Is Personality Related to the Objective Features of Situations That People Encounter in Their Daily Life?

We used multiple linear regression to predict person-level aggregates of the aforementioned cue components from personality trait scores. Table 6.2 presents the unstandardized regression coefficients. Overall, the pattern of relationships shown in Table 6.2 does not appear to be consistent or logically coherent. That is, although there are some statistically significant relationships between personality and situation cues, the associations are haphazard and show no discernible pattern. For example, Neuroticism was negatively related to People Present ($b = -.22$, $t = -2.04$) and Classroom ($b = -.22$, $t = -2.14$). Extraversion was weakly associated with the cue components Music ($b = -.14$, $t = -1.82$), Computing ($b = .18$, $t = 1.76$), and Home Versus Commuting ($b = -.20$, $t = -1.90$). Openness was related to Car/Driving ($b = .14$, $t = 1.90$) and Equipment ($b = .17$, $t = 1.97$). Agreeableness was marginally related to Dark Versus Light ($b = .12$, $t = 1.66$). Conscientiousness was related to the components Dark Versus Light ($b = .23$, $t = 2.85$) and Music ($b = -.17$, $t = -2.34$).

How Are Situation Cues Related to Situation Characteristics?

Theoretically, situation characteristics ought to be made up of situation cues (Rauthmann, Sherman, & Funder, 2015). To test this, we computed linear mixed-effects regressions predicting each DIAMONDS situation characteristic from all 15 cue components (see Rauthmann et al., 2014, for a complete overview of DIAMONDS situation measurement). Table 6.3 displays the associations between situation cues and characteristics. Table 6.3 indicates that the relationships between cues and characteristics are widespread and conceptually sensible. For example, Duty (does work need to be done?) was positively associated with Computing, Paper, and Classroom and negatively related to Dark Versus Light and Car/Driving. Overall, these paint the prototypical Duty situations as being well-lit and containing materials typically associated with work (e.g., computing equipment, documents).

Similarly, Intellect (is deep thinking required?) was positively related to Computing, Paper, Music, and Classroom and negatively related to Dark Versus Light, Outdoors, Food, Ground, and Cars/Driving. The overlap between the cues associated with Duty and Intellect indicates that, for our sample, situations characterized by Duty and Intellect occur in similar object

TABLE 6.2. Model Parameters for Predicting Personality Traits From Situational Cues

Personality trait	Intercept	b	LL	UL	t
Neuroticism	2.61		2.52	2.69	60.89
Outdoors		−0.09	−0.36	0.18	−0.65
Food		0.07	−0.24	0.38	0.47
Dark versus light		−0.06	−0.26	0.13	−0.64
Car/driving		−0.05	−0.26	0.16	−0.47
Music		0.03	−0.15	0.21	0.34
Patterns		−0.05	−0.26	0.15	−0.53
People present		−0.22	−0.43	−0.01	−2.04
Shopping		0.18	−0.14	0.50	1.12
Computing		−0.02	−0.27	0.22	−0.19
Paper		−0.08	−0.44	0.28	−0.42
Ground		0.01	−0.23	0.25	0.10
Home versus commuting		0.12	−0.12	0.36	1.01
Equipment		−0.01	−0.25	0.23	−0.08
Classroom		−0.22	−0.42	0.37	−2.14
Bathroom		−0.04	−0.45	0.37	−0.20
Extraversion	3.68		3.61	3.76	101.74
Outdoors		0.11	−0.12	0.34	0.93
Food		−0.04	−0.30	0.22	−0.28
Dark versus light		0.12	−0.04	0.29	1.46
Car/driving		−0.01	−0.18	0.17	−0.07
Music		−0.14	−0.29	0.01	−1.82
Patterns		0.12	−0.05	0.29	1.36
People present		0.08	−0.10	0.26	0.90
Shopping		−0.16	−0.43	0.11	−1.15
Computing		0.18	0.02	0.39	1.76
Paper		0.10	−0.20	0.41	0.68
Ground		−0.12	−0.32	0.08	−1.21
Home versus commuting		−0.20	−0.40	0.01	−1.90
Equipment		0.07	−0.13	0.27	0.69
Classroom		0.11	−0.06	0.28	1.25
Bathroom		0.07	−0.28	0.42	0.69
Openness	3.83		3.77	3.90	126.66
Outdoors		−0.12	−0.32	0.07	−1.29
Food		−0.71	−0.40	0.05	−1.54
Dark versus light		0.04	−0.10	0.18	0.52
Car/driving		0.14	−0.00	0.29	1.90
Music		−0.02	−0.14	0.11	−0.30
Patterns		0.06	−0.08	0.21	0.89
People present		0.08	−0.07	0.22	1.01
Shopping		−0.10	−0.33	0.13	−0.89
Computing		0.00	−0.17	0.18	0.07
Paper		−0.04	−0.30	0.21	−0.33
Ground		0.05	−0.12	0.22	0.58
Home versus commuting		−0.09	−0.26	0.08	−1.06
Equipment		0.17	0.00	0.34	1.97
Classroom		0.04	−0.10	0.19	0.60
Bathroom		−0.02	−0.31	0.28	−0.10

TABLE 6.2. Model Parameters for Predicting Personality Traits From Situational Cues (*Continued*)

Personality trait	Intercept	b	LL	UL	t
Agreeableness	3.99		3.93	4.05	133.10
Outdoors		0.10	−0.08	0.29	1.09
Food		0.11	−0.11	0.33	0.99
Dark versus light		0.12	−0.02	0.26	1.66
Car/driving		0.09	−0.05	0.24	1.25
Music		−0.06	−0.19	0.06	−1.04
Patterns		−0.06	−0.20	0.08	−0.82
People present		0.03	−0.11	0.18	0.44
Shopping		0.03	−0.19	0.26	0.28
Computing		0.12	−0.05	0.29	1.35
Paper		−0.04	−0.29	0.21	−0.30
Ground		−0.10	−0.27	0.06	−1.21
Home versus commuting		0.07	−0.09	0.24	0.87
Equipment		−0.06	−0.22	0.11	−0.65
Classroom		−0.05	−0.20	0.08	−0.79
Bathroom		−0.04	−0.33	0.25	−0.27
Conscientiousness	3.50		3.43	3.57	101.41
Outdoors		0.02	−0.20	0.24	0.20
Food		−0.04	−0.29	0.21	−0.32
Dark versus light		0.23	0.07	0.39	2.85
Car/driving		−0.04	−0.22	0.12	−0.53
Music		−0.17	−0.31	−0.03	−2.34
Patterns		−0.05	−0.21	0.12	−0.57
People present		−0.03	−0.20	−0.14	−0.30
Shopping		−0.19	−0.45	0.07	−1.44
Computing		0.07	−0.13	0.26	0.68
Paper		0.02	−0.27	0.31	0.13
Ground		−0.08	−0.27	0.11	−0.85
Home versus commuting		−0.02	−0.21	0.18	−0.18
Equipment		−0.16	−0.35	0.04	−1.60
Classroom		0.12	−0.05	0.28	1.39
Bathroom		0.23	−0.10	0.56	1.36

Note. $N = 266$, as such situation cues are aggregated to the person level. *b*'s are in unstandardized regression coefficients. LL and UL respectively represent lower and upper limits for 95% confidence intervals based on $K = 500$ bootstrapped samples. All predictors were entered simultaneously.

environments. Given that the sample is drawn from a student population, it does seem sensible to see a high overlap between Duty and Intellect because "work" for students often means "school work."

pOsitivity (is the situation pleasant?) was positively related to People Present, Food, and Dark Versus Light and negatively related to Bathroom, Paper, Computing, and Equipment. Unsurprisingly, Negativity (can negative feelings ensue?) had a similar pattern of results but with the opposite valence, having positive relationships with Computing, Classroom, and Paper and negative relationships with Food, Outdoors, Ground, and Shopping. Overall, this suggests that people experience more pOsitivity and less Negativity in situations that are less well-lit (perhaps in the evening); include other people, food, and shopping activities; and do not include work-related materials (e.g., computers, documents).

TABLE 6.3. Mixed Effects Models of Characteristics Predicted by Cue Components

Situation characteristic	Intercept	b	<LL	UL	t
Duty	3.94		3.80	4.08	54.66
Outdoors		−0.03	−0.09	0.03	−1.01
Food		0.16	−0.22	−0.09	−4.69
Dark versus light		−0.27	−0.32	−0.20	−8.46
Car/driving		−0.07	−0.12	−0.00	−2.24
Music		−0.04	−0.01	0.11	1.65
Patterns		−0.04	−0.10	0.02	−1.26
People present		−0.13	−0.18	−0.06	−4.06
Shopping		0.02	−0.04	0.08	0.53
Computing		0.25	0.19	0.30	8.15
Paper		0.20	0.14	0.27	6.68
Ground		−0.00	−0.06	0.06	−0.03
Home versus commuting		−0.08	−0.14	−0.02	−2.62
Equipment		0.09	0.03	0.14	2.95
Classroom		0.18	0.12	0.24	5.72
Bathroom		0.11	0.06	0.17	3.91
Intellect	3.10		2.99	3.23	49.73
Outdoors		−0.17	−0.22	−0.12	−6.61
Food		−0.15	−0.20	−0.09	−5.00
Dark versus light		−0.18	−0.24	−0.13	−6.66
Car/driving		−0.08	−0.14	−0.03	−2.98
Music		0.08	0.04	0.13	3.10
Patterns		−0.04	−0.09	0.02	−1.56
People present		−0.00	−0.06	0.05	−0.13
Shopping		−0.02	−0.07	0.03	−0.73
Computing		0.37	0.31	0.41	13.79
Paper		0.28	0.22	0.33	10.30
Ground		−0.13	−0.18	−0.08	−4.82
Home versus commuting		−0.05	−0.10	0.00	−1.78
Equipment		−0.03	−0.08	0.03	−1.09
Classroom		0.29	0.23	0.34	10.12
Bathroom		0.00	−0.04	0.05	0.29
Adversity	1.44		1.35	1.52	33.39
Outdoors		−0.02	−0.04	0.00	−1.41
Food		−0.02	−0.05	0.01	−1.0
Dark versus light		0.04	0.01	0.08	3.08
Car/driving		0.01	−0.02	0.04	0.85
Music		0.02	−0.01	0.04	1.24
Patterns		−0.00	−0.03	0.02	−0.08
People present		0.02	−0.01	0.05	1.31
Shopping		0.00	−0.03	0.02	−0.29
Computing		−0.01	−0.01	0.05	1.33
Paper		0.01	−0.02	0.04	0.43
Ground		−0.01	−0.04	0.02	−0.67
Home versus commuting		0.01	−0.02	0.04	0.84
Equipment		−0.02	−0.05	0.00	−1.57
Classroom		0.02	−0.01	0.05	1.39
Bathroom		−0.01	−0.04	0.01	−0.75

TABLE 6.3. Mixed Effects Models of Characteristics Predicted by Cue Components (*Continued*)

Situation characteristic	Intercept	b	<LL	UL	t
Mating	1.98		1.82	2.13	25.21
Outdoors		−0.02	−0.06	0.02	−0.76
Food		0.07	0.02	0.11	2.93
Dark versus light		0.08	0.03	0.12	3.40
Car/driving		0.00	−0.04	0.04	0.10
Music		0.02	−0.05	0.02	−0.85
Patterns		0.00	−0.04	0.05	0.23
People present		0.02	−0.02	0.07	1.12
Shopping		0.02	−0.01	0.07	1.78
Computing		−0.00	−0.04	0.04	−0.02
Paper		0.00	−0.04	0.05	0.23
Ground		−0.01	−0.06	0.03	−0.56
Home versus commuting		−0.07	−0.12	−0.03	−3.41
Equipment		0.01	−0.03	0.05	0.39
Classroom		0.04	−0.00	0.08	1.58
Bathroom		−0.03	−0.07	0.01	−1.59
pOsitivity	4.62		4.46	4.75	69.69
Outdoors		0.01	−0.04	0.06	0.44
Food		0.16	0.10	0.22	5.80
Dark versus light		0.01	0.04	0.14	3.39
Car/driving		−0.00	−0.06	0.05	−0.16
Music		0.04	−0.01	0.09	1.55
Patterns		−0.02	−0.08	0.03	−0.95
People present		0.19	0.14	0.24	6.94
Shopping		0.03	−0.01	0.08	1.30
Computing		−0.06	−0.11	−0.01	−2.25
Paper		−0.06	−0.11	−0.01	−2.38
Ground		0.02	−0.04	0.07	0.79
Home versus commuting		0.03	−0.02	0.09	1.27
Equipment		−0.05	−0.10	−0.00	−1.96
Classroom		0.01	−0.05	0.06	0.45
Bathroom		−0.01	−0.16	−0.06	−4.41
Negativity	2.05		1.94	2.16	36.77
Outdoors		−0.06	−0.10	−0.02	−2.81
Food		−0.07	−0.11	−0.02	−2.93
Dark versus light		−0.04	−0.09	0.01	−1.76
Car/driving		0.03	−0.02	0.07	1.29
Music		−0.02	−0.06	0.02	−0.99
Patterns		0.00	−0.04	0.04	0.16
People present		−0.04	−0.08	0.01	−1.71
Shopping		−0.04	0.09	−0.00	−2.10
Computing		0.12	0.08	0.17	5.89
Paper		0.09	0.04	−0.133	4.11
Ground		−0.04	−0.09	−0.00	−2.11
Home versus commuting		−0.03	−0.07	0.01	−1.30
Equipment		−0.00	−0.05	0.04	−0.14
Classroom		0.10	0.06	0.15	4.61
Bathroom		−0.00	−0.04	0.04	−0.03

(*continues*)

TABLE 6.3. Mixed Effects Models of Characteristics Predicted by Cue Components (*Continued*)

Situation characteristic	Intercept	b	<LL	UL	t
Deception	1.32		1.25	1.41	30.08
Outdoors		−0.01	−0.03	0.01	−1.00
Food		−0.01	−0.03	0.01	−0.74
Dark versus light		0.00	−0.02	0.03	0.52
Car/driving		0.00	−0.02	0.02	0.33
Music		0.00	−0.02	0.02	0.22
Patterns		0.00	−0.02	0.02	0.08
People present		0.01	−0.01	0.02	0.81
Shopping		−0.01	−0.03	0.03	−1.16
Computing		0.00	−0.02	0.01	0.54
Paper		0.00	−0.01	0.03	0.44
Ground		−0.01	−0.03	0.02	−0.86
Home versus commuting		0.01	−0.02	0.03	0.57
Equipment		−0.01	−0.03	0.01	−0.95
Classroom		0.02	−0.00	0.04	1.70
Bathroom		−0.01	−0.03	0.01	−0.76
Sociality	4.33		4.19	4.48	58.19
Outdoors		−0.03	−0.08	0.04	−0.87
Food		0.12	0.06	0.19	3.49
Dark versus light		−0.01	−0.07	0.05	−0.34
Car/driving		−0.10	−0.17	−0.03	−3.12
Music		−0.06	−0.12	−0.01	−2.03
Patterns		−0.18	−0.24	−0.12	−5.41
People present		0.17	0.11	0.24	5.18
Shopping		0.20	0.14	0.26	6.40
Computing		−0.12	−0.19	−0.06	−3.78
Paper		−0.08	−0.14	−0.01	−2.52
Ground		0.09	0.03	0.16	2.84
Home versus commuting		−0.10	−0.16	−0.04	−3.13
Equipment		−0.09	−0.16	−0.03	−2.97
Classroom		0.40	0.32	0.47	−11.69
Bathroom		−0.05	−0.11	0.00	−1.73

Note. $N = 281$ participants, with 4878 observations. *b*'s are in unstandardized mixed effects regression coefficients. LL and UL respectively represent the lower and upper 95% confidence intervals from $K = 500$ bootstrapped samples. All predictors were entered simultaneously.

Sociality (is social interaction present or important?) was related to 12 of the 15 components, including positive relationships with Classroom, Shopping, People Present, Food, and Ground and negative relationships with Patterns, Computing, Home Versus Commuting, Car/Driving, Equipment, Paper, and Music. These results seem quite consistent with the concept of Sociality, which emphasizes the presence of others.

Although Adversity (is someone being threatened?), Mating (is the situation sexually or romantically charged?), and Deception (are there issues of trust or mistrust?) had either few or no significant relationships with the cue components in these data, the pattern of results for each seemed conceptually sensible. For example, Adversity was positively related to the cue component Dark Versus Light, suggesting a greater presence of Adversity at night. A similar result was found in a study measuring situational characteristics via social media use (Serfass & Sherman, 2015). The situational characteristic Mating, which refers to the presence of potential romantic partners, was found to be positively related to Dark Versus Light and Food and negatively associated with Home Versus Commuting. This pattern suggests that romantic opportunities are more likely to occur in the evening, when food is present, and on the road rather than in one's home (e.g., on a date). The final characteristic, Deception, was not related to any of the cue components, indicating that there may be few environmental cues related to Deception and that perceptions of others' behaviors may be more telling of this situation characteristic.

CONCLUSION

Overall, we found persuasive evidence that more granular situational information (i.e., situation cues) is related to molar, psychological interpretations of situations. People report that situations are higher on Sociality when more people are present, higher on Duty when work-related materials are nearby, higher on Adversity and Negativity at night, and so forth. Such findings are consistent with theoretical models of situation perception (e.g., Rauthmann, Sherman, & Funder, 2015) that posit situation cues as the raw stimuli that must be perceived to create psychological meaning.

However, we did not find compelling evidence that personality is related to the kinds of situation cues that people encounter during a waking day. This is inconsistent with perspectives on situation selection suggesting that personality plays a role in the kinds of situations in which people find themselves (Larsen, Diener, & Emmons, 1985; Snyder & Ickes, 1985). A possible conclusion one might draw from this result is that the situation selection hypothesis is wrong. Indeed, the original studies on situation selection relied on self-reports of both personality and situational information. As a result, it is not possible to separate situation selection from situation construal in those studies (Sherman, Nave, & Funder, 2013; Rauthmann, Sherman, & Funder, 2015; Rauthmann, Sherman, Nave, & Funder, 2015). Thus, although the results of the original studies on situation selection were interpreted as evidence of situation selection, for methodological reasons, such interpretations may not be accurate. In contrast, the study reported in this chapter used objective measures of situations and is not subject to such confounds. Therefore, the lack of connection between personality and situation cues must be interpreted as contra the situation selection hypothesis. Nonetheless, it would be too hasty to declare, on the basis of the evidence reported here, that the situation selection hypothesis is incorrect.

One plausible explanation for the lack of relationship between personality and situation cues is the limited number of situation cues gathered on each person. Although more than 800 photographs per person (on average) with 20 cues each may sound like a lot, in the grand scheme of all of the possible situation cues in the universe that a person may encounter in daily life, this study may not have gathered enough information about the kinds of cues a person typically encounters. That is, the measurement of situation cues only took place over a single day. It is possible that with increased sampling of situation cues by gathering data for a longer period (e.g., a week), relationships between personality and situation cues may become more apparent. On balance, the results of this study should give us some pause regarding the situation selection hypothesis and suggest that it needs further investigation.

The current use of wearable cameras in personality and social psychology literature is limited to, as far as we know, only the study reported here. On the surface, wearable cameras are most effective for capturing images (and videos) from everyday life. Therefore, the possibilities are expansive. As previously mentioned, memory (Sellen et al., 2007), behavior, well-being (Doherty et al., 2013), and autism diagnoses (Marcu et al., 2012) are just a few possible applications. An important aspect to keep in mind is what information can be extracted from these images automatically. For example, the accuracy of computer facial analysis software has improved immensely (Martinez & Valstar, 2016). One example is the software OpenFace (Baltrušaitis, Mahmoud, & Robinson, 2015), which automatically detects the presence and intensity of Facial Action Units originally develop by Ekman and Rosenberg (1997). Researchers could use these technologies in tandem to understand aspects of nonverbal communication in close relationships and interdependent behavior. Another possible avenue of research is behavior classification. For example, Kerr and colleagues (2013) used wearable cameras with accelerometers to identify objective sedentary behavior. Researchers should also consider the type of device being used in the study. Google Clips, mentioned earlier in this chapter, is equipped with artificial intelligence that can automatically recognize and record events with important people (to the wearer) through face recognition. This would be useful in research that investigates the frequency of interaction with important people (close relationships) and how these interactions change over time or between people. Overall, wearable cameras, in conjunction with advances in machine vision and big data analytics, have the potential to transform personality and social psychological research because they make people's natural environments more accessible.

Technological advancements in mobile sensing have changed the way psychologists do research, and these changes are poised to continue. We now have the capability to capture the sights and sounds of people's daily environments as they encounter them like never before. We believe that these advances make it the right time for psychologists to dive deeply into age-old questions about the role that situations play on behavior and how situations transact and interact with personality.

REFERENCES

Baltrušaitis, T., Mahmoud, M., & Robinson, P. (2015, May). *Cross-dataset learning and person-specific normalisation for automatic action unit detection.* Paper presented at the Automatic Face and Gesture Recognition IEEE International Conference, Ljubljana, Slovenia.

Barta, W. D., Tennen, H., & Litt, M. D. (2012). Measurement reactivity in diary research. In M. R. Mehl & T. S. Conner (Eds.), *Handbook of research methods for studying daily life* (pp. 108–123). New York, NY: Guilford Press.

Bem, D. J., & Allen, A. (1974). On predicting some of the people some of the time: The search for cross-situational consistencies in behavior. *Psychological Review, 81,* 506–520. http://dx.doi.org/10.1037/h0037130

Block, J. (1977). Advancing the psychology of personality: Paradigmatic shift or improving the quality of research? In D. Magnusson & N. S. Endler (Eds.), *Personality at the crossroads: Current issues in interactional psychology* (pp. 37–63). Hillsdale, NJ: Erlbaum.

Bolger, N., Davis, A., & Rafaeli, E. (2003). Diary methods: Capturing life as it is lived. *Annual Review of Psychology, 54,* 579–616. http://dx.doi.org/10.1146/annurev.psych.54.101601.145030

Bowers, K. S. (1973). Situationism in psychology: An analysis and a critique. *Psychological Review, 80,* 307–336. http://dx.doi.org/10.1037/h0035592

Brown, N. A., Blake, A. B., & Sherman, R. A. (2017). A snapshot of the life as lived: Wearable cameras in social and personality psychological science. *Social Psychological and Personality Science, 8,* 592–600. http://dx.doi.org/10.1177/1948550617703170

Craik, K. H. (2000). The lived day of an individual: A person–environment perspective. In W. B. Walsh, K. H. Craik, & R. H. Price (Eds.), *Person–environment psychology: New directions and perspectives* (pp. 233–266). Mahwah, NJ: Erlbaum.

Csikszentmihalyi, M., & Larson, R. (1987). Validity and reliability of the experience-sampling method. *Journal of Nervous and Mental Disease, 175,* 526–536. http://dx.doi.org/10.1097/00005053-198709000-00004

DeYoung, C. G., Quilty, L. C., & Peterson, J. B. (2007). Between facets and domains: 10 aspects of the Big Five. *Journal of Personality and Social Psychology, 93,* 880–896. http://dx.doi.org/10.1037/0022-3514.93.5.880

Doherty, A. R., Hodges, S. E., King, A. C., Smeaton, A. F., Berry, E., Moulin, C. J., . . . Foster, C. (2013). Wearable cameras in health: The state of the art and future possibilities. *American Journal of Preventive Medicine, 44,* 320–323. http://dx.doi.org/10.1016/j.amepre.2012.11.008

Dufau, S., Duñabeitia, J. A., Moret-Tatay, C., McGonigal, A., Peeters, D., Alario, F. X., . . . Grainger, J. (2011). Smart phone, smart science: How the use of smartphones can revolutionize research in cognitive science. *PLoS ONE, 6,* e24974. http://dx.doi.org/10.1371/journal.pone.0024974

Ekman, P., & Rosenberg, E. L. (1997). *What the face reveals: Basic and applied studies of spontaneous expression using the Facial Action Coding System (FACS).* New York, NY: Oxford University Press.

Epstein, S. (1979). The stability of behavior: I. On predicting most of the people much of the time. *Journal of Personality and Social Psychology, 37,* 1097–1126. http://dx.doi.org/10.1037/0022-3514.37.7.1097

Funder, D. C. (2006). Towards a resolution of the personality triad: Persons, situations, and behavior. *Journal of Research in Personality, 40,* 21–34. http://dx.doi.org/10.1016/j.jrp.2005.08.003

Funder, D. C. (2008). Persons, situations and person–situation interactions. In O. P. John, R. Robins, & L. Pervin (Eds.), *Handbook of personality* (3rd ed., pp. 568–580). New York, NY: Guilford Press.

Funder, D. C. (2009). Persons, behaviors and situation: An agenda for personality psychology in the postwar era. *Journal of Research in Personality, 43,* 120–126. http://dx.doi.org/10.1016/j.jrp.2008.12.041

Harari, G. M., Lane, N. D., Wang, R., Crosier, B. S., Campbell, A. T., & Gosling, S. D. (2016). Using smartphones to collect behavioral data in psychological science: Opportunities, practical considerations, and challenges. *Perspectives on Psychological Science, 11*, 838–854. http://dx.doi.org/10.1177/1745691616650285

Hogan, R. (2009). Much ado about nothing: The person-situation debate. *Journal of Research in Personality, 43*, 249. http://dx.doi.org/10.1016/j.jrp.2009.01.022

Hoyle, R., Templeman, R., Anthony, D., Crandall, D., & Kapadia, A. (2015, April). *Sensitive lifelogs: A privacy analysis of photos from wearable cameras.* Paper presented at the 33rd Annual ACM Conference on Human Factors in Computing Systems, Seoul, Republic of Korea.

Johnson, J. A. (1999). Persons in situations: Distinguishing new wine from old wine in new bottles. *European Journal of Personality, 13*, 443–453. http://dx.doi.org/10.1002/(SICI)1099-0984(199909/10)13:5<443::AID-PER358>3.0.CO;2-9

Johnson, J. A. (2009). Wrong and right questions about persons and situations. *Journal of Research in Personality, 43*, 251–252. http://dx.doi.org/10.1016/j.jrp.2008.12.022

Kenrick, D. T., & Funder, D. C. (1988). Profiting from controversy: Lessons from the person-situation debate. *American Psychologist, 43*, 23–34. http://dx.doi.org/10.1037/0003-066X.43.1.23

Kerr, J., Marshall, S. J., Godbole, S., Chen, J., Legge, A., Doherty, A. R., . . . Foster, C. (2013). Using the SenseCam to improve classifications of sedentary behavior in free-living settings. *American Journal of Preventive Medicine, 44*, 290–296. http://dx.doi.org/10.1016/j.amepre.2012.11.004

Kosinski, M., & Behrend, T. (2017). Editorial overview: Big data in the behavioral sciences. *Current Opinion in Behavioral Sciences, 18*, iv–vi. http://dx.doi.org/10.1016/j.cobeha.2017.11.007

Larsen, R. J., Diener, E. D., & Emmons, R. A. (1985). An evaluation of subjective well-being measures. *Social Indicators Research, 17*, 1–17. http://dx.doi.org/10.1007/BF00354108

Lewin, K. (1951). *Field theory in social science.* New York, NY: Harper.

Marcu, G., Dey, A. K., & Kiesler, S. (2012, September). *Parent-driven use of wearable cameras for autism support: A field study with families.* Paper presented at the ACM Conference on Ubiquitous Computing, Pittsburgh, PA.

Martinez, B., & Valstar, M. F. (2016). Advances, challenges, and opportunities in automatic facial expression recognition. In M. Kawulok, M. E. Celebi, & B. Smolka (Eds.), *Advances in face detection and facial image analysis* (pp. 63–100). Cham, Switzerland: Springer. http://dx.doi.org/10.1007/978-3-319-25958-1_4

Mehl, M. R., Pennebaker, J. W., Crow, D. M., Dabbs, J., & Price, J. H. (2001). The Electronically Activated Recorder (EAR): A device for sampling naturalistic daily activities and conversations. *Behavior Research Methods, Instruments & Computers, 33*, 517–523. http://dx.doi.org/10.3758/BF03195410

Mischel, W. (1968). *Personality and assessment* (pp. 13–39). New York, NY: Wiley.

Podsakoff, P. M., MacKenzie, S. B., Lee, J.-Y., & Podsakoff, N. P. (2003). Common method biases in behavioral research: A critical review of the literature and recommended remedies. *Journal of Applied Psychology, 88*, 879–903. http://dx.doi.org/10.1037/0021-9010.88.5.879

Rauthmann, J. F., Gallardo-Pujol, D., Guillaume, E. M., Todd, E., Nave, C. S., Sherman, R. A., . . . Funder, D. C. (2014). The Situational Eight DIAMONDS: A taxonomy of major dimensions of situation characteristics. *Journal of Personality and Social Psychology, 107*, 677–718. http://dx.doi.org/10.1037/a0037250

Rauthmann, J. F., & Sherman, R. A. (2016). Ultra-brief measures for the Situational Eight DIAMONDS domains. *European Journal of Psychological Assessment, 32*, 165–174. http://dx.doi.org/10.1027/1015-5759/a000245

Rauthmann, J. F., Sherman, R. A., & Funder, D. C. (2015). Principles of situation research: Towards a better understanding of psychological situations. *European Journal of Personality, 29*, 363–381. http://dx.doi.org/10.1002/per.1994

Rauthmann, J. F., Sherman, R. A., Nave, C. S., & Funder, D. C. (2015). Personality-driven situation experience, contact, and construal: How people's personality traits predict characteristics of their situations in daily life. *Journal of Research in Personality*, *55*, 98–111. http://dx.doi.org/10.1016/j.jrp.2015.02.003

Reis, H. T. (2012). Why researchers should think "real-world": A conceptual rationale. In M. R. Mehl & T. S. Connor (Eds.), *Handbook of research methods for studying daily life* (pp. 3–21). New York, NY: Guilford Press.

Rosenthal, R., & Rosnow, R. L. (2008). *Essentials of behavioral research: Methods and data analysis*. New York, NY: McGraw-Hill.

Schmitt, M., Gollwitzer, M., Baumert, A., Blum, G., Gschwendner, T., Hofmann, W., & Rothmund, T. (2013). Proposal of a nonlinear interaction of person and situation (NIPS) model. *Frontiers in Psychology*, *4*, 499. http://dx.doi.org/10.3389/fpsyg.2013.00499

Sellen, A. J., Fogg, A., Aitken, M., Hodges, S., Rother, C., & Wood, K. (2007). *Do lifelogging technologies support memory for the past? An experimental study using SenseCam*. Copenhagen, Denmark: ACM Press. http://dx.doi.org/10.1145/1240624.1240636

Serfass, D. G., & Sherman, R. A. (2015). Situations in 140 characters: Assessing real-world situations on Twitter. *PLoS ONE*, *10*, e0143051. http://dx.doi.org/10.1371/journal.pone.0143051

Sherman, R. A., Nave, C. S., & Funder, D. C. (2013). Situational construal is related to personality and gender. *Journal of Research in Personality*, *47*, 1–14. http://dx.doi.org/10.1016/j.jrp.2012.10.008

Snyder, M., & Ickes, W. (1985). Personality and social behavior. In G. Lindzey & E. Aronson (Eds.), *Handbook of social psychology* (3rd ed., pp. 883–948). New York, NY: Random House.

Stone, A. A., & Shiffman, S. (1994). Ecological momentary assessment (EMA) in behavioral medicine. *Annals of Behavioral Medicine, 16*, 199–202. http://dx.doi.org/10.1093/abm/16.3.199

Tay, L., Jebb, A. T., & Woo, S. E. (2017). Video capture of human behaviors: Toward a Big Data approach. *Current Opinion in Behavioral Sciences, 18*, 17–22. http://dx.doi.org/10.1016/j.cobeha.2017.05.026

Vanhoef, M., & Piessens, F. (2017). *Key reinstallation attacks: Forcing nonce reuse in WPA2*. Retrieved from https://papers.mathyvanhoef.com/ccs2017.pdf

Wagerman, S. A., & Funder, D. C. (2009). Situations. In P. J. Corr & G. Matthews (Eds.), *Cambridge handbook of personality psychology* (pp. 27–42). Cambridge, England: Cambridge University Press. http://dx.doi.org/10.1017/CBO9780511596544.005

Wilhelm, P., Perrez, M., & Pawlik, K. (2012). Conducting research in daily life: A historical review. In M. R. Mehl & T. S. Conner (Eds.), *Handbook of research methods for studying daily life* (pp. 62–86). New York, NY: Guilford Press.

7

Human-Guided Visual Analytics for Big Data

Morteza Karimzadeh, Jieqiong Zhao, Guizhen Wang,
Luke S. Snyder, and David S. Ebert

In this chapter, we provide an overview of the research and practice in visual analytics with a specific focus on decision-support systems that facilitate generating useful information from big, unstructured, and complex data. We first define what is usually referred to as *big data* and its unique characteristics. We then define visual analytics and human–computer collaborative decision-making (HCCD) environments, compare and contrast human-in-the-loop analysis methods with automated algorithms such as machine learning models, and explain how these approaches complement each other for real-world problem solving. To ground our discussions, we provide an overview of four exemplar visual analytics systems with applications in various domains, including humanitarian relief, social media analytics, critical infrastructure vulnerability modeling, resource allocation, and performance evaluation using multidimensional data.

MOTIVATION AND OPPORTUNITY

Advanced analytics and computational algorithms enable the transformation of the evolving deluge of digital data into useful and actionable information. However, as data sets continue to increase in size and complexity in the digital

We wish to acknowledge the work of Calvin Yau, Junghoon Chae, Jiawei Zhang, Sungahn Ko, Abish Malik, Ross Maciejewski, Kelly Gaither, William Ribarsky, and Isaac Cho for their contributions to the systems and research overviewed in this chapter.

http://dx.doi.org/10.1037/0000193-008
Big Data in Psychological Research, S. E. Woo, L. Tay, and R. W. Proctor (Editors)

age, analytics become more computationally demanding, time consuming, and less clear to human analysts, and the analytics output produces large amounts of information that can overwhelm the human user. Some complex algorithms, such as machine learning models, are designed to reduce the massive amounts of complex data to manageable sizes and dimensions. However, the complexity and, at times, lack of transparency of the algorithms result in humans being unable to understand and trust the results (Burrell, 2016). This contradicts the original value of computing, as noted by Hamming (1962): The ultimate purpose of computing is to gather insights into the dynamic processes of the world instead of merely generating numbers.

These problems are exacerbated with big data, where the data is large or complex in one or more of three aspects: volume (size), variability (number of variables or types of data), and velocity (rate of incoming data—e.g., real-time, streaming; Zikopoulos & Eaton, 2011; see Chapter 2, this volume). Big data poses additional challenges for analysis techniques and human ability to synthesize, explore, and distill big data into significant and relevant information. Visualization that is combined and interlinked with data analytics can help alleviate these challenges. Moreover, visualization that is integrated within the analytics pipeline can help confirm the expected and discover the unexpected (Thomas & Cook, 2006). As pointed out by Tay et al. (2017), visualization is key to solving many big data analysis problems if the following four issues are carefully considered in the design: (a) identification (isolating and highlighting relevant data and patterns), (b) integration (combining different data sources and different models to reveal new insights), (c) immediacy (streaming, real-time, and time-sensitive data), and (d) interactivity (user manipulation and exploration to inductively uncover and identify new patterns). The field of visual analytics expands on previous work in these areas to assist researchers, analysts, and decision makers in their use of data for effective discovery, monitoring, analysis, and decision making. In this chapter, we explore the background, potential, challenges, exemplar techniques, and applications of human-guided big data visual analytics, specifically in HCCD environments.

WHAT IS BIG DATA?

The term *big data* has emerged in the last decade to describe data that can be characterized by large volume, variety, or velocity (Zikopoulos & Eaton, 2011). *Volume*, intuitively, refers to the large size of the data that have to be stored, queried, analyzed, and visualized. Large volumes make storing and querying on traditional system architectures challenging. Infrastructures such as Apache Hadoop[1] are used to distribute computational operations on a network or cluster of computers to enable processing large amounts of data. Modern

---

[1]https://hadoop.apache.org/

graphical processing units (GPUs) also enable speeding up compute-intensive algorithms by parallelizing computations simultaneously into hundreds of thousands of computational threads. Approximate query techniques in visual analytics (Fisher, Popov, Drucker, & Schraefel, 2012; A. Kim et al., 2015) enable interactive data exploration by reducing the data volume in the computation process and providing users approximate results with bounded errors.

Variety in big data refers to the heterogeneity of the data being collected, such as text, numeric, geographic location, and temporal data. Different data structures that are collected at different speeds and sampling rates make drawing connections and identifying patterns a challenging task, and traditional automatic data analysis makes the fusion of information hard, whereas visual analytics systems take advantage of human ability to find patterns and identify connections.

Velocity refers to the speed at which data is being collected (e.g., streaming social media data). Data collected at streaming rates require methods with low computational complexity that can process the incoming data at the same speed. Visual interfaces should be able to use open (and usually two-way, between the user interface and the server) communication technologies such as WebSocket[2] to seamlessly update the user interface with incoming data (or the real-time result of analysis and processing of the incoming data) to enable visual analytics of data with high velocity.

Big data includes items that are interdependent, such as social network data with links including follower and followee, repost, quote, spatial proximity, or topical relatedness. Interdependence of data items are usually recorded in different data structures with different analytical needs (e.g., social network data or spatial coordinates data for social media users and posts), making pure computational analysis more challenging. Humans, however, can find patterns and relationships in heterogeneous data while connecting it to the context that might not necessarily be captured in data, especially if human users are presented with appropriate visualizations.

WHAT IS VISUAL ANALYTICS?

Visual analytics is defined as the science of analytical reasoning facilitated by interactive visual interfaces (Thomas & Cook, 2006). Visual analytics enhances the cognitive abilities of humans by maximizing the use of their perceptual and cognitive capabilities in an integrated visual analysis and exploration environment (Eick & Wills, 1993; S. Kim et al., 2013; Stasko, Görg, & Liu, 2008; Zhao, Chevalier, Pietriga, & Balakrishnan, 2011). The primary goal of visual analytics is to provide insight into various phenomena to enable more effective research, analysis, and decision making. As data size and complexity have grown in the era of big data, the role of visual analytics has become

---

[2]https://developer.mozilla.org/en-US/docs/Web/API/WebSockets_API

increasingly important. HCCD environments effectively and efficiently combine the experience, contextual information, and expertise of the human user with the power of human-guided computational analysis, which, in turn, enhances the human-centered decision-making process.

Visual analytics is the intelligent evolution of visualization, bringing the fundamental understanding of perception and human cognition used in visualization to the realm of analysis of data using and through interactive visualization, instead of merely using visual techniques to communicate the analytical results to users. To achieve this, visual analytics incorporates the principles of design and cognitive science to identify appropriate visual metaphors for data or analytical results, with a strong emphasis on creating perceptually effective representations at the appropriate cognitive level for each analytical task (see the examples in the Opportunities and Examples subsection).

As discussed earlier, new analytical techniques and technologies are being adopted to gain insights and steer decision making in various fields, leveraging the vast amounts of complex data, which are growing at exponential speeds since the emergence of the Internet. In particular, machine learning and artificial intelligence algorithms are being applied to generate information from data and predict future states. Generally, these methods involve sophisticated calculations and numerous input parameters. Visual analytics helps incorporate human domain knowledge through the users' iterative refinement of inputs using visual interfaces to improve the calculated results. More important, without visual techniques, it is difficult and at times impossible (depending on the models used) for users to understand the causality relationship between inputs and derived results. Oftentimes, users may suspect the reliability of the generated results due to the overly complex design of the algorithms. Visual analytics can bridge the gap between the results derived by these automatic algorithms and reasonable interpretation through model-integrated visualization techniques. In other words, visual analytics not only improves data analytics (through the incorporation of human domain knowledge, expertise, and analytical abilities) but also increases trust in, and therefore, the adoption of, the analytical results.

The usefulness of a visual analytics system can be characterized by its utility and usability (Ellis & Dix, 2006). *Utility* refers to the ability of the system to support users in completing the required tasks, and *usability* describes the ease of use of the system in completing the same required tasks. Therefore, utility is more or less an objective measure, whereas usability is related to the subjective satisfaction and user experience, describing the success of a system in terms of intuitive design, ease of learning, efficiency of use, and memorability (Usability.gov, n.d.-a). To ensure a system's utility and usability, visual analytics researchers usually adopt the user-centered design paradigm (Usability.gov, n.d.-b), and work closely with stakeholders at various stages of design and development. *User-centered design* usually entails identifying the context of use, specifying requirements, and creating design solutions. This last stage itself is typically an iterative process in which multiple design ideas are presented to users (via sketches, mockups, or actual implementations of the system), feedback is sought and intermediate "formative" evaluations are conducted, leading to refining the design and presenting the system again for more feedback (Roth, Ross, & MacEachren, 2015). After a system implementation is finished, researchers conduct final "summative" evaluations through various evaluation protocols (Ellis & Dix, 2006) to scientifically report on the usability and/or utility of the system (for the particular target purpose and particular target users).

Visual analytics has been successfully applied and reported on to support (a) advance research and scientific activities or (b) domain users for practical needs outside academia or industry. For instance, MacEachren, Stryker, Turton, and Pezanowski (2010) reported on HEALTH GeoJunction, a visual analytics application for exploring health-related scientific publications using place–time–theme queries (e.g., studies about Ebola in Africa in 2010). Diakopoulos, Naaman, and Kivran-Swaine (2010) created and evaluated a system for journalists to sift quickly through large amounts of social media traffic about events of interest to identify public sentiment. Wade and Nicholson (2010) reported on the successful use of visual analytics in the aviation safety engineering industry, leading to changes in flight training manuals. Jaiswal et al. (2011) used GeoCAM in computational linguistics research to interpret human-generated route directions. Karimzadeh, Pezanowski, MacEachren, and Wallgrün (2019) described the successful application of a semiautomatic visual analytics platform to create annotated textual data sets (Wallgrün, Karimzadeh, MacEachren, & Pezanowski, 2018) to support the development of automated algorithms for geolocating (i.e., mapping) textual documents. Wagner et al. (2019) reported on the successful evaluation and application of KAVAGait, a system for clinicians to support clinical analysis of patients' gait using complex data sets while incorporating clinicians' domain knowledge. Throughout the rest of this chapter, we also address the design and capabilities of a few other visual analytics systems, elaborating on their use by end-users.

VISUAL ANALYTICS TO TACKLE BIG DATA

Traditional big data analytics may leave out some context in modeling the complex world. Data is rarely complete, and it does not incorporate all the relevant information necessary in decision making (Brooks, 2013). Decision making (by humans) always happens within context; policy makers or executives rarely rely merely on numbers to make decisions. They contextualize analytical results within the broader context of society, risks, and long-term outcomes and, at times, may even go against the analytical (quantitative) results to have more favorable broader impacts when considering every aspect that may not be reflected in analysis. Visual analytics enhances computational algorithms by incorporating humans' extensive information, experience, and domain knowledge that may not be collected in the data used for analysis.

Further, data analysis relies heavily on quantifiable data. For instance, in population dynamics modeling, projections of the population in the future are generated on the basis of the spatiotemporal measurements and dynamics of the current population (Uhl et al., 2018; Zoraghein, Leyk, Ruther, & Buttenfield, 2016). Qualitative information, fuzzy data, and social aspects (decisions, emotions, connections, or opinions), although intuitive to humans, are difficult and, at times, impossible to quantify and analyze. As another example, novel sentiment analysis methods may underperform in determining the affective states and subjective information of statements that include exaggerations, sarcastic remarks, jokes, and negations (e.g., "The whole house is flooded. How great!" may confuse a sentiment detection algorithm because the author is using *great* sarcastically). Such naive cases are easier for human readers to identify; therefore, humans in the loop can improve the computational results and alleviate the potential of biased results.

Big data introduces another challenge in data analysis: As the number of data items increases, so does the number of statistically significant relationships. Many of such significant relationships may be misleading or irrelevant. This overwhelms an analyst's ability to find meaningful relationships due to a high ratio of noise to signal. Visual analytics provides interactive querying, sorting, detail on demand, and contextual information to help users focus on actionable data and patterns that matter the most.

Finally, real-world big problems are complex and multifaceted with multiple parameters and interdependencies. Whereas in classic statistics, a controlled or observational study is conducted, many real-world problems cannot be solved by trial and error or analysis of retroactive observations, and results from one experiment are not generalizable to another case. For instance, no two natural events are the same. No "earthquake drill" can simulate the impacts of an earthquake; therefore, traditional data analysis cannot be used to simulate the impacts of one event. Real-time, context-enabled, multifaceted sensing, modeling, and decision-making environments are necessary for human users to evaluate and respond to any specific earthquake and natural disaster.

CHALLENGES IN USING MACHINE LEARNING

Machine learning-based approaches have certain limitations for use in some real-world problem-solving scenarios, where visual analytics is well-positioned to make significant contributions. In this section and the next one, we review the potential and limitations of machine learning and point out situations in which visual analytics can help remedy some of the limitations for real-world use cases.

Machine learning approaches can be generally categorized into supervised or unsupervised learning methods (Alpaydin, 2009). In *supervised learning,* a model is trained with labeled data for different prediction tasks such as classification (e.g., pictures classified into "dog" or "cat" categories) or regression. The goal of supervised learning algorithms is to find the relationships or structures in the input data that allow a model to generate correct output labels. These correct outputs are determined according to training data. *Training data* includes examples for which input and output are known, usually through the process of human manual annotation of input data (e.g., labeling a cat picture with *cat*). The way the training data is sampled and the method using it is annotated influence the generated automated models and may introduce the sampler's assumptions or bias, especially if such a sample represents a snapshot in time, space, or event type. Most important, training data that do not reflect the real world may lead to erroneous results that may go unnoticed (unless the assumptions and results are visually displayed to users with domain knowledge), and any sampling, by nature, introduces the biases and perceptions of the samplers (Wallgrün et al., 2018). Furthermore, dynamic phenomena, such as various characteristics of human behavior, do not lend themselves to a one-off training of a machine learning model because such characteristics change due to human agency and interdependence of actions. Models generated for one particular event, time, or place may not work as well in other places. Overfitting to training data is always a challenge, too, meaning that the model can predict excellent results for the test data set but not for unseen input data.

Machine learning, like traditional data analysis, may struggle to model human and social contexts that cannot be easily collected in data and, therefore, lacks the ability to generate the narratives that a human analyst can produce using sequences of events, external forces, their relationships, and context. Once such context changes, machine learning algorithms still perform according to the initial model training, whereas humans can base their understanding on the existing model results but also draw the necessary connections with the new context, identify the potential differences and significance in the outcome, and make appropriate inferences or decisions.

Unsupervised learning does not require labeled data or pretrained models. Instead, the training algorithm directly learns from current data. For example, the K-means clustering algorithm finds the natural categories of data by maximizing "within-cluster" similarity and minimizing "inter-cluster" similarity. It can be used, for instance, to identify clusters of grades earned in a class (i.e., the natural grouping of grades that are similar to each other). Still, K-means requires the upfront knowledge of the number of clusters (information that humans with domain knowledge may have a better understanding of, even in the case of some unsupervised methods that can identify a purely computationally optimum number of clusters). Also, the generated clusters are shifted significantly if outliers exist in the data. Again, humans, if equipped with the right tools, visuals, and information, are more reliable at identifying erroneous outliers or natural extreme values depending on the context.

Regardless of whether supervised or unsupervised methods are used, human involvement can ensure relevant results for changing context or dynamic phenomena. Visual analytics provides the infrastructure for human experts to adjust input and hyperparameters (e.g., model configurations and structure, as in Das, Cashman, Chang, & Endert, 2019), monitor a model performance (for precision or speed, as in Zhao et al., 2019), compare results against context, and correct the erroneously generated output labels to provide real-time examples for online (real-time) learning (e.g., retraining or incremental training of models, where new labels are used to improve the existing models, as in Snyder, Lin, Karimzadeh, Goldwasser, & Ebert, 2019). Most important, visual analytics enables the use of machine learning within what-if scenarios, where users can see the outputs based on different input parameters that reflect different human decisions, assumptions, or policies. We describe examples of such cases throughout the rest of this chapter.

THE DEEP LEARNING PROMISES AND OVERPROMISES

Deep learning is a specific type of artificial neural network with many layers (thus called *deep*) that has partly been revitalized due to the recent advancements in hardware (LeCun, Bengio, & Hinton, 2015). Specifically, input values (e.g., pixel values in images) are multiplied by weights (which are ultimately optimized) and added many times with constants to generate the desired output values (e.g., digit labels for images containing handwritten digits). With the advent of strong GPUs and even commercial deep-learning accelerators (e.g., Nvidia DGX-1), it is possible more than ever to apply deep learning to various domains for classification purposes. Deep learning has provided much better performance in some fields such as computer vision and has shown great promise in other domains, such as natural language processing, though not to the same level of maturity yet.

Deep learning relies heavily on large amounts of training data. The gold standard (ground truth) examples are used in optimizing the weights and constants in the neural network and generating a model that can predict labels for the "testing" data with acceptable accuracy (and, therefore, unseen data). Testing data also usually are manually annotated by humans to ensure that the generated models can produce labels for examples that were not used during the training phase of optimization.

Deep learning models require a high number of training examples for acceptable outputs (much higher compared with statistical machine learning), given that many weights and constants in all the layers have to be optimized. In other words, deep learning models' performance depends heavily on training and testing gold standard data, which is neither cheap nor easy to generate. However, as introduced in the previous section, training and testing data may only represent a snapshot of a time, space, phenomenon, or event; for example, a traffic congestion detection model that works for particular modes of transportation may suffer inaccuracies if new modes of transportation are introduced or new policies are put in place. Building up a new representative training data set is costly and laborious and, again, would only capture the variation of the real world made on hard assumptions of sampling at the time.

In certain scenarios, deep learning alone may suffer from the issues discussed in the previous section: the inability of users to adjust input parameters dynamically (to account for what-if scenarios of dynamic phenomena that need flexible inputs), detaching results from the context, and being specific to the training data instead of accommodating spatial or temporal variability in the phenomenon. Visual analytics systems integrated with online learning models provide a great opportunity for alleviating these problems. We discuss systems adopting this approach in the following sections.

EXPLAINABLE ARTIFICIAL INTELLIGENCE

Deep learning models are essentially classification methods, where input values are mapped to output values or labels. Unlike traditional statistics, deep learning models are not geared for "explaining" the relative importance or significance of input parameters, and therefore, deep learning models are not "explanatory." For instance, a simple linear regression model can explain the contribution of the "number of cars" or "price of gas" (as independent variables) to the "number of traffic jam incidents" (as the dependent variable). After the regression model is solved, the analyst can examine the generated coefficients and significance values of independent variables and infer how much a unit increase—for instance, in the price of gas—would translate into a decrease (or increase) in traffic jams and if that value is in fact significant. Deep learning models, however, primarily focus on predicting the number of traffic jams without directly explaining the relative contribution of independent variables. This poses a problem for decision makers and policymakers who do not just have to use the classification system but have to understand the underlying phenomenon for planning and policy making.

Moreover, a user's ability to trust the conclusions of machine learning models may be affected negatively by the lack of transparency in the models. Although deep learning and other statistical machine learning models have made significant progress on many challenges, many are opaque black boxes with limited explanatory capabilities.

Explainable artificial intelligence (XAI) is an emerging field of research that seeks to enhance traditional machine learning techniques with explanatory metrics. For instance, current classification models and neural networks can be difficult to understand and unclear with regard to how classification and clustering decisions are made. In other words, it is unclear which specific characteristics of the input data (or independent variables) cause an item to be classified into a certain class. As a result, users may struggle to trust AI outputs. XAI seeks to address this problem by providing explainable models that directly indicate what decisions were made and why, allowing users to more effectively understand and act on the models' outputs (Gunning, 2017). Such explanatory models can be presented and generated in many forms. For instance, some approaches use auxiliary integrated machine learning models that seek to identify the discriminatory features of input data (that distinguish a certain class) and assign a natural language or visual cue to such discriminatory features, effectively explaining (in human language or visual cues) what specific parameters in the input data led to the machine learning model decision. Such approaches either use ground truth training data that humans have annotated with both labels and (natural language or visual) explanations of the discriminatory features (Rajani & Mooney, 2018) or automatically harvested corpora of such explanations (e.g., image captions sourced from the web; Venugopalan, Hendricks, Mooney, & Saenko, 2016).

Other XAI approaches leverage interactive visualizations to focus on the computational components of a machine learning model with the goal of (a) increasing performance through hyperparameter[3] optimization or (b) reducing the computational time necessary for computation-heavy models (Zhao et al., 2019). Such models do not necessarily need extra annotated explanations for training. Instead, they focus on model parameters, model structure, computation time for each stage, bottlenecks, or functions that lead to higher model performance (Kahng, Andrews, Kalro, & Chau, 2018; Wongsuphasawat et al., 2018).

HUMAN–COMPUTER COLLABORATIVE MACHINE LEARNING FOR BIG DATA

In the first half of this chapter, we discussed the importance of human involvement in analytical tasks to incorporate domain knowledge, social and changing context for dynamic phenomena, adjusting input variables, and monitoring model performance. However, human involvement in big data analytics problems can be beneficial from a computational standpoint, as well. Processing the entire big data to get accurate results could be a lengthy process, even with advanced computational architectures that use more computational resources, because the growth of data has significantly surpassed that of hardware resources (Mozafari, 2017).

Involving humans in big data analysis can reduce computational latencies efficiently and effectively because, in many situations, approximate results of analysis on fewer representative data points can satisfy the analytical requirements of end users (Fisher et al., 2012). One preliminary experiment (Wu & Nandi, 2015) indicated that a query to estimate the average of a data set can eliminate the need for sampling 10^4 more data through a reduction in the perceptually perceived error by 10–5. Researchers across both the database and visualization fields have devised a series of approximate query methods and integrated visual analytics approaches to facilitate the decision making of end users using approximate query processing. Researchers in the database field have explored novel approximate data query techniques to generate samples with the specific consideration of human perception of the generated samples. For instance, Park, Cafarella, and Mozafari (2016) proposed a spatial

---

[3]Hyperparameters is a model configuration parameters (e.g., number of hidden layers in a deep learning approach) whose value is set before the learning process.

sampling method that improves the perceptual accuracy of generated visualizations. In a similar vein, Ding, Huang, Chaudhuri, Chakrabarti, and Wang (2016) proposed an approach to assist end users in specifying the approximate query accuracies in "Group By" aggregation queries (in which an approximate aggregate of an attribute for several data items is retrieved). A. Kim et al. (2015) advocated a ranking-aware sampling method to generate data samples through which approximate results of "Group By" queries keep the same ranking order as the exact results from the analysis of the entire data.

In the visual analytics field, a series of proposed approaches allow end users to analyze big data through providing quick approximate results using fewer data items and progressively improving the accuracy of the analytical results until the accuracy satisfies the analytical requirements (Fisher et al., 2012; Mozafari, 2017). Considering the uncertainty of approximate results for end users to make decisions, these visual analytics approaches assist end users to understand better the accuracy of approximate results via customized visual designs that encode statistical measurements of approximate accuracies. In one of our preliminary works in this area, for instance, we proposed a user-driven spatiotemporal big data sampling approach for data residing in remote servers (Wang et al., 2017). Through the well-designed spatial and temporal data indexing, our method focuses on data within the spatial and temporal query ranges expected by users to avoid sampling data outside the query range as much as possible. As a result, a visual analytics system built on this approach loads data from the servers in real time and reduces data transfer and sampling latencies.

Aside from improving the computation time, human-in-the-loop machine learning can help circumvent the need for training data. Attributed to the mixed-initiative user interfaces, these approaches seek to aid the interactive visual exploration process through a combination of machine learning and user domain knowledge. The premise is to enable users to provide interactive feedback to the system for retraining the underlying machine learning model parameters (Badam, Zhao, Sen, Elmqvist, & Ebert, 2016; Wall et al., 2018). Users play a central role in guiding the workflow, and auxiliary machine learning algorithms provide shortcuts by generating candidate results from which users can choose. Over time, the mixed-initiative visual analytics systems leverage newly added (e.g., sensed) data and user feedback into the simulation models (active learning). The interoperation of data and the various machine learning models, along with user feedback, enhances the underlying models and reduces the overall reliance on the need for additional data.

Mixed-initiative visual analytical systems use direct human-user manipulation of the desired results to update the parameters of automatic computational models through interfaces while trying to achieve fluid interactions to represent cognitive processes with externalized cognitive artifacts (Elmqvist et al., 2011; Horvitz, 1999). Users can investigate the model outputs dynamically and iteratively. The analysis process is a reasoning procedure that involves information foraging, formulating hypotheses, and validating results. The system provides instant feedback based on user input. Thus, users have opportunities to correct their outcome if the results do not match their expectations. However, it is challenging to understand users' actions through learning of trivial and repetitive user interactions. Human-in-the-loop and mixed-initiative visual analytics create new opportunities to collect user behavioral information (e.g., eye gazing, mouse interactions) and analyze that information with machine learning algorithms to understand the semantics of the interactions (intention of performing a specific interaction; Endert, Chang, North, & Zhou, 2015) or predict future interactions (Heer, Hellerstein, & Kandel, 2015).

It is important to recognize that the human-in-the-loop may introduce their own biases in the analysis process. The core idea central to visual analytics is to use the complementary powers of humans and machines. Thus, it is imperative that bias is quantified, visualized (i.e., externalized), and present to the human user as much as possible. For instance, Zhao et al. (2019) demonstrated how an expert human user could modify the features and (hyper) parameters in machine learning models and view the resulting accuracies on the fly with the ultimate goal of selecting optimal models, which are results of data-driven models and the human's contextual knowledge. In such a scenario, if the human user relies too much on their assumptions (i.e., a misconception on strong discriminatory power of a certain hyperspectral index), the resulting performance drop—as quantified and visualized by the system—indicates to the users that their knowledge is biased or not applicable to the current context. Related to the idea of bias and systematic errors is that visualizing uncertainty is an active area of research that strives to address the positivist aspects of visualization by explicitly conveying the risks ensuing in the use of imprecise data or human-introduced errors during analysis (Spiegelhalter, Pearson, & Short, 2011), using which users can steer the analysis and decision-making path.

HUMAN–COMPUTER COLLABORATIVE DECISION-MAKING ENVIRONMENTS

An HCCD typically consists of an interactive front-end application (through which the user interacts with the system), as well as data-driven and model-integrated back ends. HCCDs usually include simulation capabilities for what-if scenarios that enable end users to see the outcomes, patterns, and trends in the information based on the decisions and assumptions they introduce into the system. In this section, we describe exemplar systems that exhibit HCCD characteristics with simple integrated models.

The Visual Analytics for Simulation-based Action (VASA) system (Ko et al., 2014) shown in Figure 7.1,[4] is a visual analytics platform for modeling the

---

[4]The images in this chapter were generated in systems that use color, though they are printed in black and white here. For color images with more information, see http://pubs.apa.org/books/supp/woo

FIGURE 7.1. VASA System Overview, With Calendar View on the Left, Event View on the Top, Map (Geographical) View in the Center, and Advanced Filtering and Querying Panels on the Right (Ko et al., 2014)

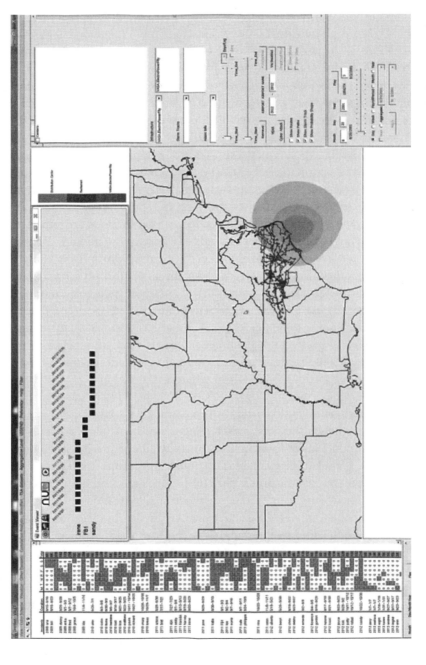

This figure shows the simulation of the landfall of Hurricane Irene in North Carolina. In this simulation, power generation units are hit by up to 34-knot winds. The hurricane proxy estimates the impacted restaurants and distribution centers. The system also allows identifying the power outage areas and out-of-service roads, which can be used in computing new food delivery paths. This image was generated in a system that uses color, though it is printed in black and white here. For a color image with more information, see http://pubs.apa.org/books/supp/woo

impact of various kinds of threats (e.g., natural threats such as hurricanes or human-caused threats such as cyberattacks) on critical infrastructure, such as supply chain systems, road networks, cyber networks, and power grids. VASA includes a set of components encapsulating high-fidelity (i.e., realistic) simulation models for each type of threat and infrastructure that together form a system of systems of individual simulations.

VASA (Figure 7.1) provides a critical infrastructure module that allows analysts to identify vulnerabilities in critical infrastructures (e.g., maritime supply chain networks, power plants, management command centers) in case they are compromised by adverse elements (e.g., cyberattacks). This component, shown in Figure 7.2, models a hierarchical network (e.g., power grid, supply chain), where the nodes (e.g., power generators) are connected with edges (e.g., transmission lines). This model simulates the impacts of the closure of a node and provides information on the other impacted regions in the network (e.g., power outage areas). It helps analysts answer questions such as, "When a main network node is compromised, how do the effects propagate through the network? What other nodes connected to the affected node are impacted, and thus, which critical areas are vulnerable to threats?" The VASA framework provides analysts with the ability to input different models and can be used to study the effects of different cyber threat vectors on critical maritime infrastructures to detect vulnerabilities. Further, the incorporation of multiple displays in the visual analytics environment enhances monitoring capabilities. For instance, cyberattacks combined and cascaded with other natural events (e.g., severe weather) and cyber threats (e.g., attacking systems to disable ports) could drastically exacerbate damages, and multiple displays help users integrate the information from different simulations.

For example, let us examine a scenario where a cyberterrorist has disabled a power generation plant. This scenario is shown in Figure 7.2 (leftmost), where the analyst first disables the plant by selecting a power plant shown as a red rectangle. The model instantly estimates the affected operational facilities in the network (second left, Figure 7.2). The simulation results are rendered by a polygon that represents the area where all facilities are shut down (second right, Figure 7.2). The right-most image provides magnification of the result.

We have obtained initial feedback about the system from various groups. For instance, food chain experts stated that the VASA system helped them identify alternative routes in extreme weather through simulations of hurricanes and the resulting impact on societal infrastructure, as well as the impact on local stores. The regional Federal Emergency Management Agency personnel appreciated the simulation pipeline provided by VASA, which enables proactive planning for severe weather conditions (Ko et al., 2014).

cgSARVA (Malik, Maciejewski, Maule, & Ebert, 2011) is another exemplar visual analytics system that helps users use customized simulation results in a decision-making software environment (seen in Figure 7.3). The system, which was developed for the U.S. Coast Guard Ninth District and Atlantic Area Commands, gives expert analysts a method of interactively analyzing the historical performance of their search and rescue (SAR) operations and

FIGURE 7.2. An Example of a Cyberattack Simulation Using the VASA System

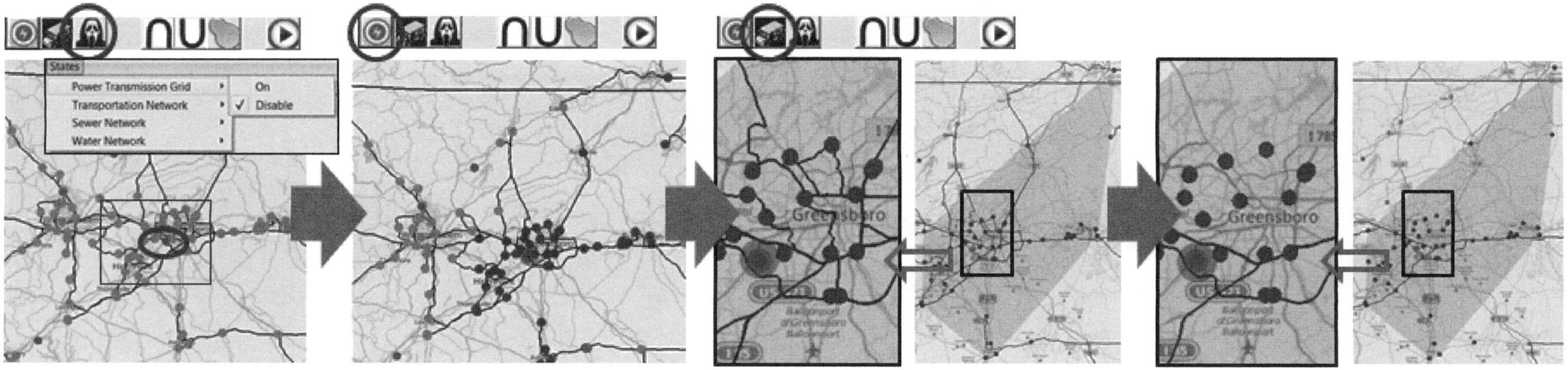

The analyst selects the option to disable a power plant to simulate a cyberattack on that plant and selects a region shown using the red rectangle to indicate the area of interest (left). One main plant (purple dot) falls within this rectangle (second left). The integrated models estimate the affected subsidiary plants and workstations (red dots, second right). Finally, network-disabled regions are represented by a polygon and along with updated routes (right). This image was generated in a system that uses color, though it is printed in black and white here. For a color image with more information, see http://pubs.apa.org/books/supp/woo

FIGURE 7.3. cgSARVA User Interface

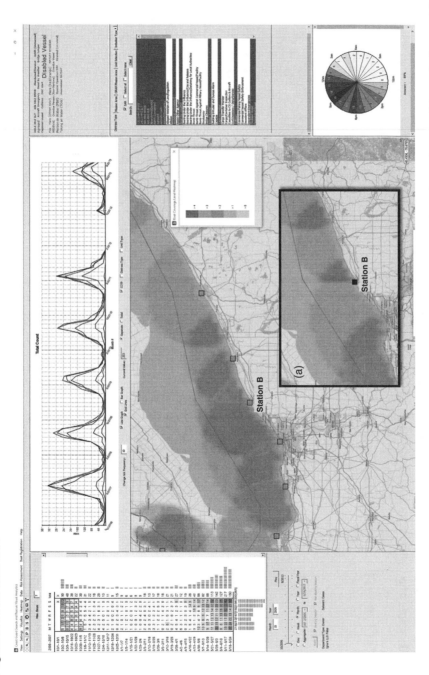

The calendar view at the top left counts incidents in the day-of-week layout to assist temporal analysis of incidents, the time slider at the bottom left allows users to interactively filter data in a variety of temporal granularities, the time series view at the top center counts incidents by the user-specified granularity (e.g., by year, month, or week), the clock view at the bottom right visualizes incident counts per hour. The view at the top right shows the keywords of incident reports. The view in the middle right allows users to filter data by multiple attributes (e.g., incident types or rescue stations). The map view at the bottom center shows the spatial analysis of incidents and rescue resources. Here, the map view visualizes the water area safety by the number of available boats. The subfigure (a) visualizes the water area safety with the assumption that Station B is closed and its boats are out of operation. The colors show boat coverage level, with green showing low and red showing higher boat coverage levels. This image was generated in a system that uses color, though it is printed in black and white here. For a color image with more information, see http://pubs.apa.org/books/supp/woo

assessing potential risks in the maritime environment (e.g., the spatiotemporal trends of cases or water area safety coverage of stations). For instance, the system provides risk assessment functions such as station closure analysis to identify the potential risks if one or multiple auxiliary stations are closed due to budgetary shortages or natural disasters that render a station dysfunctional. The goal of this analysis is to optimize resource allocation, whose cost depends significantly on where stations are located.

cgSARVA provides several types of risk assessments. Here, we describe two for station closure analysis, namely the distance for rescue teams to arrive at incident scenes and boat coverage in the water area. The distance between the geographical location of a case and its closest station (which provides the rescue assets) contributes to the "level of risk" for a case (because it determines the time and distance required to attend to that case). On the basis of their domain knowledge and potential policies and commands (e.g., to prepare for natural hazards or maintenance or budgetary shutdowns), the analyst interactively selects a target station for a specific temporal range in the visual interface to indicate a hypothetical closure for that station. The system automatically determines the nearest station for each case that would have been handled by the hypothetically closed station and the shortest distance between a case and the newly assigned station. After that, cgSARVA visualizes the distance assessment results in three aspects, including the distance distribution, the number of cases each station would take over, and intuitive representation of cases and related stations on the map (see Figure 7.4). The map view at the bottom center of Figure 7.3 shows the safe areas through the boat coverage in the water. The visualization shows the longest distance that boats can reach with their fuel limits from base stations. Figure 7.3 (a) shows the updated view if Station B is closed and its boats are not operational. The interactive analysis process enables an analyst to assess effectively and efficiently the potential risks caused by a particular station closure.

cgSARVA was accredited for use by the United States Coast Guard (USCG). Vice Admiral Robert C. Parker (Ret.), Commander, U.S. Coast Guard in Atlantic Area, described the system as "especially helpful in guiding operations and resource decisions by carefully analyzing data in a way that ensures the best return on investment" (Venere, 2013, para. 6). According to the Government Accountability Office, the permanent closure of stations that duplicate the services of nearby stations (without tangibly improving SAR efficiency) could result in up to $290 million in cost savings over 20 years. cgSARVA was successfully used by the USCG to right size the USCG SAR resources in the Great Lakes region, and it was used to avoid resource relocation costs following Super Storm Sandy along the eastern seaboard. The output from cgSARVA demonstrated that the number of anticipated SAR missions would be low because of colder fall and winter temperatures and the number of private boats damaged during the storm. Although the USCG's ability to respond was diminished due to the storm damage, the requirement for SAR response was also lower. cgSARVA demonstrated that a lower cost solution than shifting

FIGURE 7.4. Distance Risk Assessment in cgSARVA When a Station Is Hypothetically Closed (Malik et al., 2011)

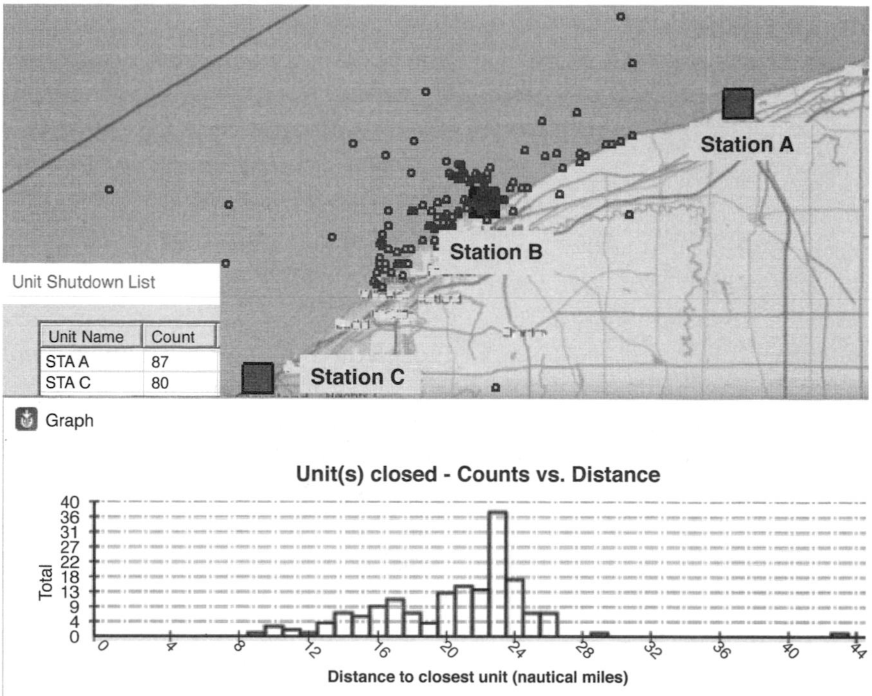

In this case, a simulation is run assuming that Station B is shut down. As a result, all cases in Station B between 2006–2013 would be handled by the other nearest stations: 87 cases in Station A and 80 in Station C (shown in Unit Shutdown List). In the map view, blue dots are Station B's cases. The histogram shows the frequency of case distances for the Coast Guard to have rescue resources on the scene for response from the newly assigned stations. This image was generated in a system that uses color, though it is printed in black and white here. For a color image with more information, see http://pubs.apa.org/books/supp/woo

USCG assets from other regions was possible. cgSARVA was also used to analyze swimmer deaths and provided information for the USCG swimmer and boating safety public information campaign in 2011. Also, the cgSARVA analysis provided input to determine the number of patrols used in 2011, leading to a significant decrease in deaths in 2011.

cgSARVA was used to determine the allocation of resources during Hurricane Irene, which occurred along the east coast in the summer of 2011. The USCG initially discussed diverting resources from the Great Lakes area to the east coast, but the data from cgSARVA indicated that there was a demonstrable need to keep the Great Lakes region fully resourced at that time and to draw the resources from another region. Similarly, cgSARVA was used to analyze the effects of closing Port Arthur, Texas, in 2011, including the economic impact and the effectiveness of alternative mitigation strategies.

HUMAN–COMPUTER COLLABORATIVE DECISION-MAKING ENVIRONMENTS FOR BIG DATA

HCCDs are interactive and integrated discovery environments that balance human cognition with automated data analytics methods. Computerized analysis is designed and integrated within HCCDs to amplify human cognition (e.g., helping human users identify patterns and relationships among salient data items). The ultimate goal of HCCDs is to enable discovery or facilitate informed decision making by providing transparent, reliable, and reproducible evidence. In an HCCD, the different data flows and parameters for the simulation modules and analytical methods are configurable through the visual interface. A real-time calculation or approximation of each simulation module enables an interactive visual discourse, which allows users to use the HCCD tool even while simulations are computing. In what follows, we expound on the most important characteristics of HCCDs, namely, interactivity and integrated models.

VISUALIZATION TECHNIQUES AND INTERACTIVITY FOR BIG DATA

The analysis of big data poses unique challenges in volume, variety, and velocity that must be accommodated and considered for data and visual analytics. Here, we briefly review how the interactivity of visual analytics interfaces helps address the unique characteristics of big data.

Most notably, big data includes large volumes of data, making identification of particular data points, groups of data points, or patterns difficult. Identification involves isolating or highlighting data that is relevant to the analysis question or phenomena of interest. Visual analytics systems use interactive dynamics such as selection, view coordination, sorting, or real-time querying for identification while enabling the users to correct the system-generated identified data items (unlike traditional sampling). Identification has another purpose too—determining the appropriate scale of analysis for any phenomena. Usually, data is aggregated in various units (spatial units, such as census tracts, counties, or states, or temporal units, such as days, weeks, or months). Using interactive dynamics, automated aggregating mechanisms, and iterative refinement of views, users can identify the relevant scale of analysis according to the data and context at hand (Klein & Kozlowski, 2000).

Interactivity helps with addressing the integration of various types of data (which is another characteristic of big data) though giving the users the ability to select, switch, swap, and combine different data types on visual interfaces for gaining insight into a complex phenomenon of interest. Furthermore, interactivity helps with the analysis of data that have high velocity (e.g., streaming data), by giving the users the ability to view and sort through the incoming data (which is added incrementally to the interactive and dynamic interface) for identifying key insights. Real-time visual analytics enables users to identify important dynamic changes over time using both incoming and historical data.

These interactive dynamics are especially important for big data analytics because the goal of big data analytics is usually not to just validate known hypotheses but to unveil new patterns. In traditional data analysis (e.g., statistics), hypotheses are formed beforehand and tested for validity during analysis, and visualization is used for communicating the analysis results. In big data visual analytics, however, data visualization is used as a means of exploration and pattern identification (Kirk, 2012).

As far as visualization techniques are concerned, individual big data analytics techniques are not inherently different from small data visualization techniques. Given that familiarity and memorability are key to successful visualizations, it is common to renovate and reenvision familiar visualizations and integrate them within complex visual analytics systems with added interactivity, linked views, and bushing techniques (Robinson, 2011). For instance, the same visualizations for summarization (e.g., bar graphs, pie charts, line graphs) are used for big data but with more interactive features that can render additional elements and details on demand. Innovative data visualizations are more common with unstructured novel data sources such as text. Even though the majority of all data in digital form is in unstructured, free-form text, leveraging text in research and analysis has become common only in the social media age (Karimzadeh et al., 2013; Savelyev et al., 2014; Wallgrün et al., 2018). Various novel techniques such as Themerivers (Havre, Hetzler, Whitney, & Nowell, 2002) or overlaid tag-clouds (Bateman, Gutwin, & Nacenta, 2008; Zhang et al., 2018) are used in interactive settings to visualize textual content in time or space, respectively.

Last, interactivity is essential in incorporating user input in what-if scenarios, such as the discussed examples of cgSARVA and VASA. The interactivity of HCCD and visual analytics systems also allows stakeholder feedback for the coupled, data-driven methods for correction or adjustment. In other words, interactive visualizations are not used just for adjusting parameters and introducing what-if scenarios but also to correct the integrated (machine learning or biophysical) models.

OPPORTUNITIES AND EXAMPLES

In this section, we review the visual design, features, and application of two proven visual analytics systems for big and high-dimensional data, leveraging computational algorithms and user input for two different domains: social media analysis for situational awareness and organizational performance evaluation. These systems highlight the capabilities of visual analytics and integrated HCCD environments described throughout this chapter.

Social Media Analytics

Social media data have become increasingly popular due to the ability to provide useful information on people's attitudes, opinions, and behavior. Social media has enabled researchers and practitioners to have access to real-time data at unprecedented rates and resolutions, essentially using humans as sensors on the ground, enhancing "situational awareness." Of specific relevance to our discussions on visual analytics of big data is the widely used platform, SMART (Social Media Analytics and Reporting Toolkit—Figure 7.5), which exemplifies our efforts in machine learning-based visual analytics to support humanitarian assistance and disaster response (Zhang, Chae, Surakitbanharn, & Ebert, 2017; Snyder, Karimzadeh, Stober, & Ebert, 2019). SMART provides users with scalable, real-time, and interactive social media data (e.g., Twitter and Instagram) visual analytics. SMART allows analysts to customize classifiers to monitor trending topics as well as unusual anomalies in the online discourse. SMART combines advanced statistical modeling, text analytics, and novel anomaly detection techniques augmented by human expertise. It provides users with the ability to search, examine, and further investigate relevant social media messages from the streaming big social media data by using natural language processing, topic modeling, advanced filtering techniques, and visual summarization techniques. The system uses several semiautomated text analysis and probabilistic event detection tools together with traditional zooming, interaction, and exploration to enable the detection and exploration of tending and abnormal topics. Web and news media sources are also incorporated into the system so that users can search for relevant news articles of interest to further corroborate intelligence acquired from social media data.

SMART leverages text classifiers to sift through large amounts of social media posts (with a low signal-to-noise ratio) for advanced yet intuitive visualizations to present users with the most relevant information on the disaster or event in question. To ensure that these classifiers do not generate false positives (posts that are not relevant to the analyst's interests) due to content that includes various meanings of certain keywords (e.g., "I feel on fire tonight; everything is going great"), we have supplemented the system with human-in-the-loop deep learning classifiers that leverage context to identify relevant (or irrelevant) content (Snyder, Lin, et al., 2019).

One of SMART's visualizations is the topic model view (see Figure 7.6). The topic model view uses latent Dirichlet allocation (Blei, Ng, & Jordan, 2003) to discover, define, and prioritize the primary topics in the social media data. Within each topic, associated keywords are displayed in a word cloud visualization, where each word's size and color jointly encode its usage frequency. By clicking on any of the words, the user can immediately view the tweets containing them on the map and in the geo-message table, allowing for the rapid discovery of social media posts on particular trending topics.

In addition, the content lens feature (see Figure 7.7) complements the topic model view by allowing the user to hover over an area on the map and view the most frequently used words among the tweets within that area. The topic model view and content lens together enable users to quickly detect and learn important content information about specific areas and topics. This shows the strong potential of coupled computational models such as latent Dirichlet allocation, natural language processing, and text and spatial data visualization for sifting through massive amounts of social media to identify important insights during various events of interest.

FIGURE 7.5. SMART's Main User Interface Summarizing Hurricane-Related Twitter and Instagram Posts for Hurricane Florence

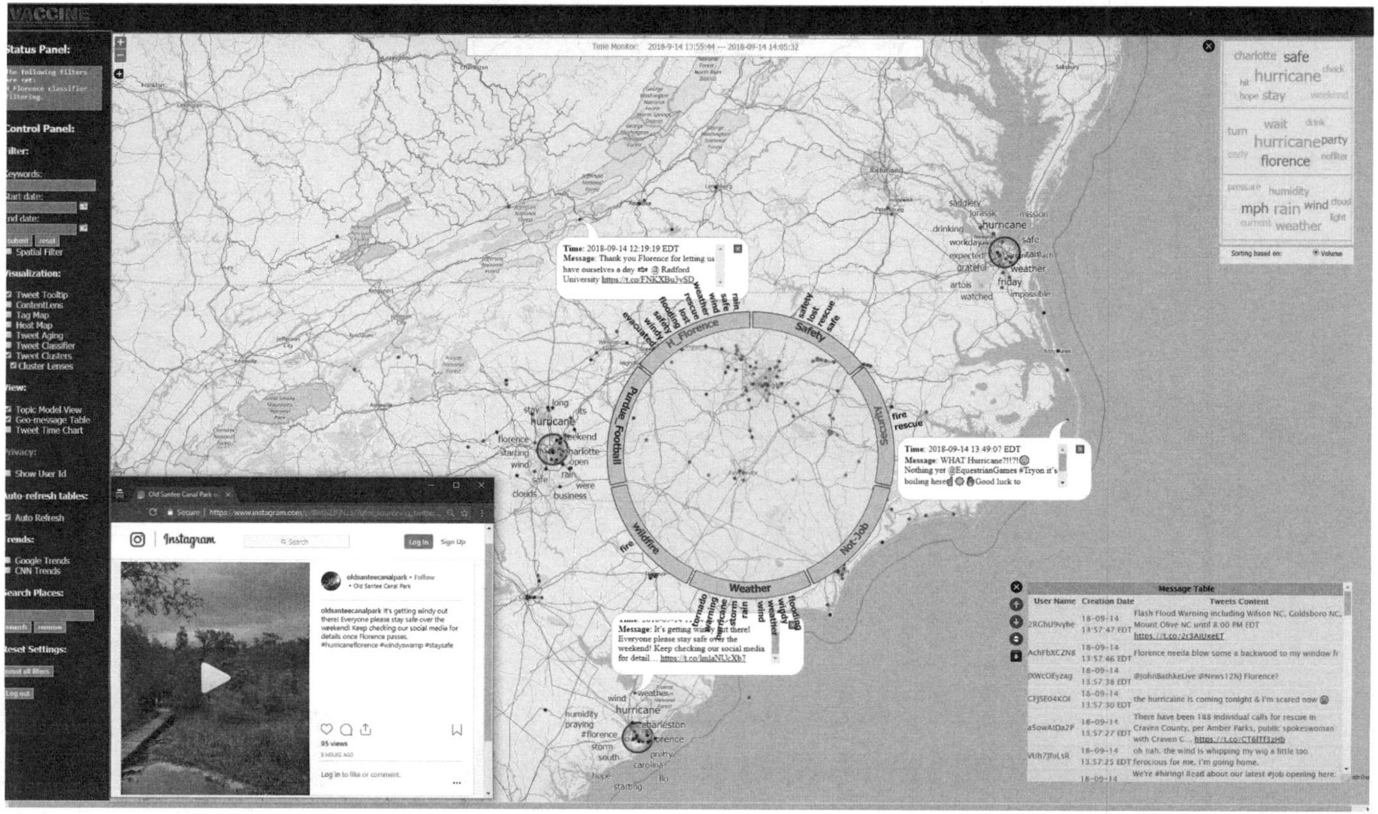

The topic lens (center) helps analysts identify different categories of posts (e.g., weather, Hurricane Florence, safety) according to user-defined classifiers and machine learning models, content lenses (three lenses placed on the map) showing different human-generated first-hand reports in the north (e.g., "WHAT Hurricane?!!?!") and the south (e.g., "It's getting windy out here!"), and relevant information extracted through Instagram posts such as real-time videos and reports on the weather. This image was generated in a system that uses color, though it is printed in black and white here. For a color image with more information, see http://pubs.apa.org/books/supp/woo

FIGURE 7.6. Topic View, Showing Words in Each Detected Topic Using Latent Dirichlet Allocation

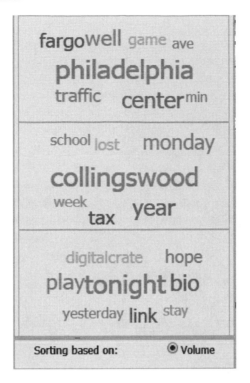

The size and color of words show their frequency in each topic. Users can click on any word to narrow down the visualization in other views to topical contents represented by those words. This image was generated in a system that uses color, though it is printed in black and white here. For a color image with more information, see http://pubs.apa.org/books/supp/woo

To narrow down the sea of incoming text data from social media, SMART also allows users to interactively define and apply semantic text classification filters, such as ones for "Safety," "Security," and "Weather" (see Figure 7.8), which can provide increased detection of contextually relevant data on the fly. Moreover, the cluster lens visualization (see Figure 7.9) aggregates a specific geographic area and populates the topical keywords that the social media posts used for each classifier.

Together, SMART's classification and cluster lens are incredibly powerful tools that provide users with situational awareness for effective decision making based on the situation on the ground, as sensed by human users. Particularly, emergency responders can rapidly identify user posts pertaining to disaster-related, life-threatening, or hazardous events for further investigation or resource deployment. When combined with geographic coordinates and supplementary human knowledge, responders can use information from SMART to efficiently determine the best course of action and act appropriately.

FIGURE 7.7. Content Lens of SMART, Combining Spatial Aggregation With Latent Dirichlet Allocation for Topic Modeling, Showing the Top Topics and Keywords for Any Area of Interest Represented by User-Placed Circles on the Map View

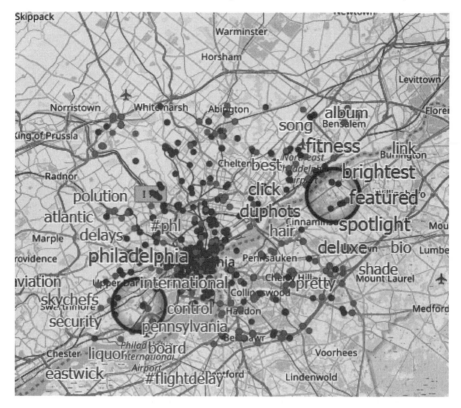

This image was generated in a system that uses color, though it is printed in black and white here. For a color image with more information, see http://pubs.apa.org/books/supp/woo

SMART has been used successfully by over 50 agencies across the country, including first responders, nongovernmental organizations, and government agencies for situational awareness and hurricane response and recovery (Snyder, Karimzadeh, et al., 2019). The USCG has used SMART to maintain situational awareness for safety during several significant events (e.g., San Francisco Fleet Week, Cincinnati Riverfest 2017 and 2018, Thunder-Over-Louisville, multiple hurricanes during the 2017 and 2018 hurricane seasons, and the Republican National Convention held in Cleveland in July 2016). Overall, SMART provides a wide range of use cases, such as monitoring planned events or detecting unexpected issues, that might otherwise be difficult due to the vast amount of social media data.

Performance Evaluation for Law Enforcement Agencies

The performance evaluation of individuals, teams, and organizations requires the combination of multidimensional performance metrics that are objectively

FIGURE 7.8. Creating New Classifiers in SMART

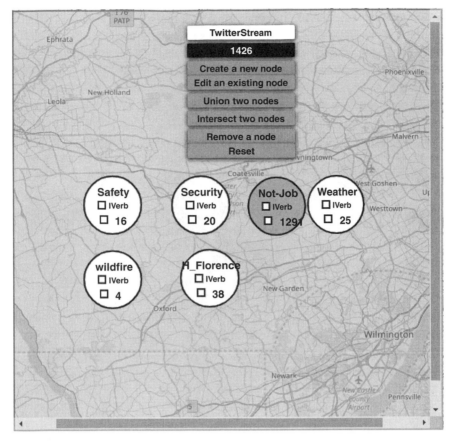

Users can associate certain keywords with different categories for further filtering down of posts related to those classifiers, creating a union or intersection of different classifiers. This image was generated in a system that uses color, though it is printed in black and white here. For a color image with more information, see http://pubs.apa.org/books/supp/woo

measured, flexible structure for incorporating various kinds of tasks and organizational dynamics, and supervisors' domain knowledge of the importance of various metrics. The visual analytics approach has been applied in the field of organizational performance evaluation, which is a fundamental topic in organizational psychology (Cleveland, Murphy, & Williams, 1989). In this section, we provide an example of such an approach from our previous work on a performance evaluation tool kit designed for medium to large-sized law enforcement agencies. The approach and the visualization techniques presented, however, are generalizable to other kinds of organizations.

With the assistance of computer-aided dispatch systems, law enforcement agencies can take advantage of digitized incident logs to analyze officer response. Importantly, digitized records can allow police department chiefs and supervisors to examine more effectively officer productivity for performance

FIGURE 7.9. Cluster Lens in SMART, Using Spatial Aggregation and Topic Modeling to Show Important Keywords for Each Category (Resulting From a User-Defined Text Classifier) on Any Area of Interest

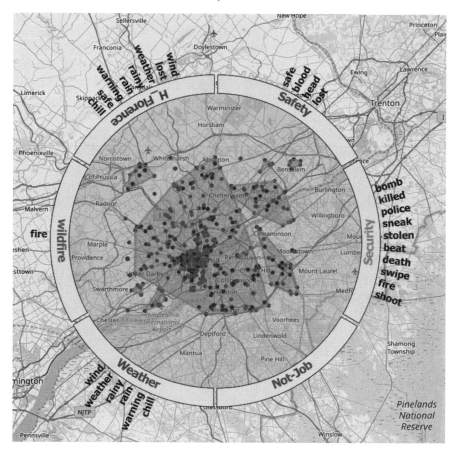

The cluster lens in this example signifies the presence of important social media content for the Security, Weather, and Safety classifiers. This image was generated in a system that uses color, though it is printed in black and white here. For a color image with more information, see http://pubs.apa.org/books/supp/woo

improvement across departments. To facilitate this process, we designed a visual analytics application called MetricsVis that supports data-driven, multi-criteria performance evaluation of employees (Zhao et al., 2017). Specifically, the system allows supervisors to both interactively customize evaluation metrics by defining what data characteristics constitute exemplar performance and discover influential factors that can improve resource allocation, strategic planning, and operational decision making.

MetricsVis uses multi-attribute vectors, which are obtained from stored relational database records to represent employee performance. Within the context of law enforcement, different types of incidents (e.g., theft, murder, arson) each represent an attribute, and an officer's number of responses to a given incident represents the numeric value for that attribute. Overall performance can then be computed as the sum of an officer's attributes, with each attribute weighted by the user according to its importance. However, the large number of dimensions and extensive data can cause difficulty in comparing performance between employees or for specific tasks. Thus, MetricsVis adopts an interactive reorderable matrix (see Figure 7.10b) that effectively demonstrates the details of each data item in one view. Users can dynamically adjust weights and filter attributes to understand performance from different perspectives and gain insight into improving and maintaining organizational achievements. As a result, supervisors can better understand employee performance on an individual, team, and organizational level. The police chief and commanders at the Lafayette police department have confirmed the usefulness of the matrix visualization for obtaining a holistic view of all officers' effectiveness for each incident category, as well as the overall performance of the entire department.

CONCLUSION

Advanced automated methods, such as deep learning models, provide great promise in gleaning insight from big data. Dynamic, changing, and context-dependent phenomena, however, require human knowledge, expertise, and reasoning for decision making. Humans' natural ability to identify patterns in disparate sources of data and to contextualize analytical results in a broader social context complement automated methods in generating useful, actionable information for real-world problems. Extending the traditional visualization paradigm that communicates the analysis results through storytelling, visual analytics enables further exploration and analysis of data and discovering unknown stories and patterns in data. For these systems to be successful, though, they have to ensure that they amplify the cognitive and analytical processes of the human while not increasing the user's cognitive load or reducing their effectiveness.

Machine learning models generate results that depend heavily on the training data or configuration parameters, potentially leading to biased results that reflect the choices made in the sampling of training data (or the real-world conditions captured in the training data as a snapshot) or the choice of configuration parameters. Integrating machine learning models within interactive systems allows researchers to elicit feedback from human users to correct erroneously generated results and provide additional training data, resulting in models that reflect real-world conditions. This interactive, visual, and explainable machine learning offers the greatest promise for the successful adoption and use of machine learning.

In addition, HCCD environments enable the integration of various computational models with interactive user interfaces for generating simulation results that facilitate testing various what-if scenarios for optimal decision making. HCCDs integrate sensed data, models (e.g., environmental, energy, or decision models), and interactive analysis, exploration, and prediction

FIGURE 7.10. The Overview of the Organizational Performance Evaluation Visual Analytics Application

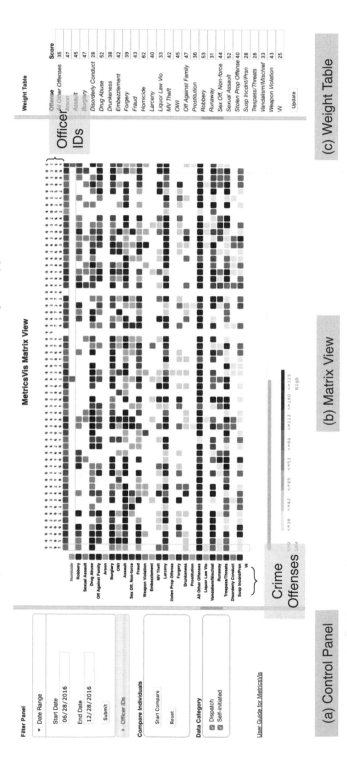

(a) Control Panel   (b) Matrix View   (c) Weight Table

(a) A control panel includes options for selecting a temporal range and filtering by incident types (e.g., dispatched vs. self-initiated). (b) A matrix visual representation shows the crime offense categories in rows and individual officers in columns. The colored blue cells demonstrate the product of [number of incidents that were responded to by an officer in one crime offense category] and the [weight assigned to the particular crime offense category by the system user]. Users can change the weight for each category interactively according to the perceived importance and policies for each organization. The red cells in the top headings show the total score of an officer, and the red cells on the left show the total score of a crime offense category. Darker colors mean higher values. (c) A weight table lists the crime offense categories and the corresponding manually assigned weights. The weights usually reflect the priorities of an organization. This image was generated in a system that uses color, though it is printed in black and white here. For a color image with more information, see http://pubs.apa.org/books/supp/woo

capabilities. Users can visualize and manipulate intermediate and final results of the different data-driven and theoretical models for key decision points (within what-if scenarios) to identify optimal solutions, such as balancing resource allocation and response time in disaster management.

As demonstrated in this chapter, visual analytics systems have been in active use and have great potential for problem solving in various domains such as social media analytics, humanitarian relief, disaster preparedness response and mitigation, and resource allocation. Furthermore, visual analytics provides pathways for researchers in various fields, including psychology, to engage in inductive or abductive approaches using the wealth of available data to generate new hypotheses (see Chapters 1 and 12).

Research in computational methods, visualization, and cognitive science can help advance visual analytics by finding solutions that leverage both machines' computational power and humans' cognitive abilities. Specifically, behavioral and cognitive studies can identify the tendencies and biases in ways humans view and use information, approach analysis, and make decisions. This line of research is essential not only to visual analytics but also to computational methods because automated methods are also marked by the choices (and potentially biases) humans introduce when designing algorithms, sampling data, and interpreting the results.

REFERENCES

Alpaydin, E. (2009). *Introduction to machine learning*. Cambridge, MA: MIT press.

Badam, S. K., Zhao, J., Sen, S., Elmqvist, N., & Ebert, D. (2016). *Timefork: Interactive prediction of time series*. Retrieved from http://users.umiacs.umd.edu/~elm/projects/timefork/timefork.pdf

Bateman, S., Gutwin, C., & Nacenta, M. (2008). *Seeing things in the clouds: The effect of visual features on tag cloud selections*. Retrieved from http://www.hci.usask.ca/publications/2008/fp039-bateman.pdf

Blei, D. M., Ng, A. Y., & Jordan, M. I. (2003). Latent Dirichlet allocation. *Journal of Machine Learning Research, 3*, 933–1022.

Brooks, D. (2013, February 18). What data can't do. *The New York Times*. Retrieved from https://www.nytimes.com/2013/02/19/opinion/brooks-what-data-cant-do.html

Burrell, J. (2016). How the machine 'thinks': Understanding opacity in machine learning algorithms. *Big Data & Society*. http://dx.doi.org/10.1177/2053951715622512

Cleveland, J. N., Murphy, K. R., & Williams, R. E. (1989). Multiple uses of performance appraisal: Prevalence and correlates. *Journal of Applied Psychology, 74*, 130–135. http://dx.doi.org/10.1037/0021-9010.74.1.130

Das, S., Cashman, D., Chang, R., & Endert, A. (2019). BEAMES: Interactive multi-model steering, selection, and inspection for regression tasks. *IEEE Computer Graphics and Applications, 39*(5), 20–32. http://dx.doi.org/10.1109/MCG.2019.2922592

Diakopoulos, N., Naaman, M., & Kivran-Swaine, F. (2010). Diamonds in the rough: Social media visual analytics for journalistic inquiry. In A. MacEachren & S. Miksch (Eds.), *2010 IEEE Symposium on Visual Analytics Science and Technology* (pp. 115–122). Piscataway, NJ: IEEE. http://dx.doi.org/10.1109/VAST.2010.5652922

Ding, B., Huang, S., Chaudhuri, S., Chakrabarti, K., & Wang, C. (2016, June–July). Sample + seek: Approximating aggregates with distribution precision guarantee. In *Proceedings of the 2016 International Conference on Management of Data* (pp. 679–694). New York, NY: ACM. http://dx.doi.org/10.1145/2882903.2915249

Eick, S. G., & Wills, G. J. (1993). Navigating large networks with hierarchies. In D. Bergeron & G. Nielson (Eds.), *Proceedings of the 4th Conference on Visualization '93* (pp. 204–209). Washington, DC: IEEE Computer Society.

Ellis, G., & Dix, A. (2006). An explorative analysis of user evaluation studies in information visualisation. In *Proceedings of the 2006 AVI Workshop on BEyond Time and Errors: Novel Evaluation Methods for Information Visualization* (pp. 1–7). New York, NY: ACM. http://dx.doi.org/10.1145/1168149.1168152

Elmqvist, N., Vande Moere, A., Jetter, H., Cernea, D., Reiterer, H., & Jankun-Kelly, T. J. (2011). Fluid interaction for information visualization. *Information Visualization, 10*, 327–340. http://dx.doi.org/10.1177/1473871611413180

Endert, A., Chang, R., North, C., & Zhou, M. (2015). Semantic interaction: Coupling cognition and computation through usable interactive analytics. *IEEE Computer Graphics and Applications, 35*(4), 94–99. http://dx.doi.org/10.1109/MCG.2015.91

Fisher, D., Popov, I., Drucker, S., & Schraefel, M. C. (2012). Trust me, I'm partially right: Incremental visualization lets analysts explore large datasets faster. In *Proceedings of the SIGCHI Conference on Human Factors in Computing Systems* (pp. 1673–1682). New York, NY: ACM. http://dx.doi.org/10.1145/2207676.2208294

Gunning, D. (2017). *Explainable artificial intelligence (XAI)*. Retrieved from https://www.darpa.mil/attachments/XAIProgramUpdate.pdf

Hamming, R. W. (1962). *Numerical analysis for scientists and engineers*. New York, NY: Dover.

Havre, S., Hetzler, E., Whitney, P., & Nowell, L. (2002). Themeriver: Visualizing thematic changes in large document collections. *IEEE Transactions on Visualization and Computer Graphics, 8*, 9–20. http://dx.doi.org/10.1109/2945.981848

Heer, J., Hellerstein, J. M., & Kandel, S. (2015). *Predictive interaction for data transformation*. Retrieved from http://cidrdb.org/cidr2015/Papers/CIDR15_Paper27.pdf

Horvitz, E. (1999). Principles of mixed-initiative user interfaces. In *Proceedings of the SIGCHI conference on Human Factors in Computing Systems* (pp. 159–166). New York, NY: ACM.

Jaiswal, A., Pezanowski, S., Mitra, P., Zhang, X., Xu, S., Turton, I., . . . MacEachren, A. M. (2011). GeoCAM: A geovisual analytics workspace to contextualize and interpret statements about movement. *Journal of Spatial Information Science, 2011*(3), 65–101. http://dx.doi.org/10.5311/JOSIS.2011.3.55

Kahng, M., Andrews, P. Y., Kalro, A., & Chau, D. H. (2018). ActiVis: Visual exploration of industry-scale deep neural network models. *IEEE Transactions on Visualization and Computer Graphics, 24*(1), 88–97. http://dx.doi.org/10.1109/TVCG.2017.2744718

Karimzadeh, M., Huang, W., Banerjee, S., Wallgrün, J. O., Hardisty, F., Pezanowski, S., . . . MacEachren, A. M. (2013). GeoTxt: A web API to leverage place references in text. In C. Jones & R. Purves (Eds.), *Proceedings of the 7th Workshop on Geographic Information Retrieval* (pp. 72–73). New York, NY: ACM. http://dx.doi.org/10.1145/2533888.2533942

Karimzadeh, M., Pezanowski, S., MacEachren, A. M., & Wallgrün, J. O. (2019). GeoTxt: A scalable geoparsing system for unstructured text geolocation. *Transactions in GIS, 23*, 118–136. http://dx.doi.org/10.1111/tgis.12510

Kim, A., Blais, E., Parameswaran, A., Indyk, P., Madden, S., & Rubinfeld, R. (2015). Rapid sampling for visualizations with ordering guarantees. *Proc. VLDB Endow, 8*, 521–532. http://dx.doi.org/10.14778/2735479.2735485

Kim, S., Maciejewski, R., Malik, A., Jang, Y., Ebert, D. S., & Isenberg, T. (2013). Bristle Maps: A multivariate abstraction technique for geovisualization. *IEEE Transactions on Visualization and Computer Graphics, 19*, 1438–1454. http://dx.doi.org/10.1109/TVCG.2013.66

Kirk, A. (2012). *Data visualization: A successful design process*. Birmingham, England: Packt.

Klein, K. J., & Kozlowski, S. W. J. (2000). *Multilevel theory, research, and methods in organizations: Foundations, extensions, and new directions*. San Francisco, CA: Jossey-Bass.

Ko, S., Zhao, J., Xia, J., Afzal, S., Wang, X., & Abram, G., . . . Ebert, D. S. (2014). VASA: Interactive computational steering of large asynchronous simulation pipelines for societal infrastructure. *IEEE Transactions on Visualization and Computer Graphics, 20,* 1853–1862. http://dx.doi.org/10.1109/TVCG.2014.2346911

LeCun, Y., Bengio, Y., & Hinton, G. (2015, May 27). Deep learning. *Nature, 521,* 436–444. http://dx.doi.org/10.1038/nature14539

MacEachren, A. M., Stryker, M. S., Turton, I. J., & Pezanowski, S. (2010). HEALTH GeoJunction: Place-time-concept browsing of health publications. *International Journal of Health Geographics, 9*(1), 23. http://dx.doi.org/10.1186/1476-072X-9-23

Malik, A., Maciejewski, R., Maule, B., & Ebert, D. (2011). A visual analytics process for maritime resource allocation and risk assessment. In *IEEE Conference on Visual Analytics Science and Technology* (pp. 221–230). Washington, DC: IEEE. http://dx. doi.org/10.1109/VAST.2011.6102460

Mozafari, B. (2017). Approximate query engines: Commercial challenges and research opportunities. In *Proceedings of the 2017 ACM International Conference on Management of Data* (pp. 521–524). New York, NY: ACM. http://dx.doi.org/10.1145/3035918.3056098

Park, Y., Cafarella, M., & Mozafari, B. (2016). Visualization-aware sampling for very large databases. In *2016 IEEE 32nd Conference on Data Engineering* (pp. 755–766). Washington, DC: IEEE. http://dx.doi.org/10.1109/ICDE.2016.7498287

Rajani, N. F., & Mooney, R. J. (2018). Ensembling visual explanations. In H. Escalante, S. Escalera, I. Guyon, X. Baró, Y. Güçlütürk, U. Güçlü, & M. van Gerven (Eds.), *Explainable and interpretable models in computer vision and machine learning* (pp. 155–172). Cham, Switzerland: Springer. http://dx.doi.org/10.1007/978-3-319-98131-4_7

Robinson, A. C. (2011). Highlighting in geovisualization. *Cartography and Geographic Information Science, 38,* 373–383. http://dx.doi.org/10.1559/15230406384373

Roth, R. E., Ross, K. S., & MacEachren, A. M. (2015). User-centered design for inter-active maps: A case study in crime analysis. *ISPRS International Journal of Geo-Information, 4,* 262–301. http://dx.doi.org/10.3390/ijgi4010262

Savelyev, A., MacEachren, A. M., Pezanowski, S., Karimzadeh, M., Luo, W., Nelson, J., & Robinson, A. C. (2014). *Report on new methods for representing and interacting with qualitative geographic information, Stage 2: Task Group 4: Message-focused use case.* Retrieved from https://apps.dtic.mil/dtic/tr/fulltext/u2/a616154.pdf

Snyder, L. S., Karimzadeh, M., Stober, C., & Ebert, D. S. (2019, November). *Situational awareness enhanced through social media analytics: A survey of first responders.* Paper presented at the IEEE International Symposium on Technologies for Homeland Security, Woburn, MA.

Snyder, L. S., Lin, Y. S., Karimzadeh, M., Goldwasser, D., & Ebert, D. S. (2019). Inter-active learning for identifying relevant tweets to support real-time situational awareness. *IEEE Transactions on Visualization and Computer Graphics, 1,* 1. Advance online publication. http://dx.doi.org/10.1109/TVCG.2019.2934614

Spiegelhalter, D., Pearson, M., & Short, I. (2011, September). Visualizing uncertainty about the future. *Science, 333*(6048), 1393–1400. http://dx.doi.org/10.1126/science. 1191181

Stasko, J., Görg, C., & Liu, Z. (2008). Jigsaw: Supporting investigative analysis through interactive visualization. *Information Visualization, 7,* 118–132. http://dx.doi.org/ 10.1057/palgrave.ivs.9500180

Tay, L., Ng, V., Malik, A., Zhang, J., Chae, J., Ebert, D., . . . Kern, M. (2017). Big data visualizations in organizational science. *Organizational Research Methods, 21,* 660–688. http://dx.doi.org/10.1177/1094428117720014

Thomas, J. J., & Cook, K. A. (2006). A visual analytics agenda. *IEEE Computer Graphics and Applications, 26,* 10–13. http://dx.doi.org/10.1109/MCG.2006.5

Uhl, J. H., Zoraghein, H., Leyk, S., Balk, D., Corbane, C., Syrris, V., & Florczyk, A. J. (2018). Exposing the urban continuum: Implications and cross-comparison from an interdisciplinary perspective. *International Journal of Digital Earth.* http://dx.doi.org/10.1080/17538947.2018.1550120

Usability.gov. (n.d.-a). *Usability evaluation basics.* Retrieved from https://www.usability.gov/what-and-why/usability-evaluation.html

Usability.gov. (n.d.-b). *User-centered design basics.* Retrieved from https://www.usability.gov/what-and-why/user-centered-design.html

Venere, E. (2013, April 22). U.S. Coast Guard accredits analytical system developed at Purdue. *Purdue University News.* Retrieved from https://www.purdue.edu/newsroom/releases/2013/Q2/u.s.-coast-guard-accredits-analytical-system-developed-at-purdue.html

Venugopalan, S., Hendricks, L. A., Mooney, R., & Saenko, K. (2016). Improving LSTM-based video description with linguistic knowledge mined from text. In *Proceedings of the 2016 Conference on Empirical Methods in Natural Language Processing* (pp. 1961–1966). Austin, TX: Association for Computational Linguistics. http://dx.doi.org/10.18653/v1/d16-1204

Wade, A. T., & Nicholson, R. (2010). *Improving airplane safety: Tableau and bird strikes.* Retrieved from http://de2010.cpsc.ucalgary.ca/uploads/Entries/Wade_2010_InfoVisDE_final.pdf

Wagner, M., Slijepcevic, D., Horsak, B., Rind, A., Zeppelzauer, M., & Aigner, W. (2019). KAVAGait: Knowledge-Assisted Visual Analytics for Clinical Gait analysis. *IEEE Transactions on Visualization and Computer Graphics, 25*, 1528–1542. http://dx.doi.org/10.1109/TVCG.2017.2785271

Wall, E., Das, S., Chawla, R., Kalidindi, B., Brown, E. T., & Endert, A. (2018). Podium: Ranking data using mixed-initiative visual analytics. *IEEE Transactions on Visualization and Computer Graphics, 24*, 288–297. http://dx.doi.org/10.1109/TVCG.2017.2745078

Wallgrün, J. O., Karimzadeh, M., MacEachren, A. M., & Pezanowski, S. (2018). GeoCorpora: Building a corpus to test and train microblog geoparsers. *International Journal of Geographical Information Science, 32*, 1–29. http://dx.doi.org/10.1080/13658816.2017.1368523

Wang, G., Malik, A., Surakitbanharn, C., Florencio de Queiroz Neto, J., Afzal, S., Chen, S., . . . Ebert, D. (2017). *A client-based visual analytics framework for large spatio-temporal data under architectural constraints.* Retrieved from https://www.interactive-analysis.org/papers/2017/Wang-Spatiotemporal-2017.pdf

Wongsuphasawat, K., Smilkov, D., Wexler, J., Wilson, J., Mané, D., Fritz, D., . . . Wattenberg, M. (2018). Visualizing dataflow graphs of deep learning models in TensorFlow. *IEEE Transactions on Visualization and Computer Graphics, 24*, 1–12. http://dx.doi.org/10.1109/TVCG.2017.2744878

Wu, E., & Nandi, A. (2015). *Towards perception-aware interactive data visualization systems.* Retrieved from https://pdfs.semanticscholar.org/0ebf/291393632cc89a786c39a1423892407993ab.pdf

Zhang, J., Chae, J., Surakitbanharn, C., & Ebert, D. S. (2017). *SMART: Social media analytics and reporting toolkit.* Retrieved from https://pdfs.semanticscholar.org/3ec1/49c0cd87e3af3269558b7fc9584e0fb3c334.pdf

Zhang, J., Surakitbanharn, C., Elmqvist, N., Maciejewski, R., Qian, Z., & Ebert, D. (2018). *TopoText: Context-preserving text data exploration across multiple spatial scales.* Retrieved from http://users.umiacs.umd.edu/~elm/projects/topotext/topotext.pdf

Zhao, J., Chevalier, F., Pietriga, E., & Balakrishnan, R. (2011). Exploratory analysis of time-series with ChronoLenses. *IEEE Transactions on Visualization and Computer Graphics, 17*, 2422–2431. http://dx.doi.org/10.1109/TVCG.2011.195

Zhao, J., Karimzadeh, M., Masjedi, A., Wang, T., Zhang, X., Crawford, M. M., & Ebert, D. S. (2019). *FeatureExplorer: Interactive feature selection and exploration of regression models for hyperspectral images.* Retrieved from https://arxiv.org/pdf/1908.00671.pdf

Zhao, J., Malik, A., Zu, H., Wang, G., Zhang, J., Surakitbanharn, C., & Ebert, D. (2017). MetricsVis: A visual analytics framework for performance evaluation of law enforcement officers. In *2017 IEEE International Symposium on Technologies for Homeland Security* (pp. 221–227). Piscataway, NJ: IEEE.

Zikopoulos, P., & Eaton, C. (2011). *Understanding big data: Analytics for enterprise class hadoop and streaming data.* New York, NY: McGraw-Hill Osborne Media.

Zoraghein, H., Leyk, S., Ruther, M., & Buttenfield, B. P. (2016). Exploiting temporal information in parcel data to refine small area population estimates. *Computers, Environment and Urban Systems, 58,* 19–28. http://dx.doi.org/10.1016/j.compenvurbsys.2016.03.004

8

Text Mining

A Field of Opportunities

Padmini Srinivasan

In *text mining*, the goal is to extract or infer valuable information from a text or, as is more often the case, from a collection of texts. There is a wide variety in text mining because of differences in the types of collections selected, what information is in focus, the methods used, and the goals addressed. Text mining efforts also differ in the extent to which novelty is emphasized. At one end, the outcome must be something new, such as an idea or hypothesis that has not yet been explored, at least in the published literature of the domain. At the other end, there are many efforts where the goal is to identify entities or propositions of interest that appear somewhat explicitly in the text. Broadly, there are three flavors of text mining: (a) information extraction, (b) information inferencing, and (c) literature-based discovery. This chapter begins with a brief overview of each, followed by a more detailed description of information extraction research, the most foundational and popular of the three flavors across application domains.

INFORMATION EXTRACTION

Information extraction is about identifying references in texts to concepts of interest—for example, places, persons, restaurants, genes, proteins, patient attributes, and conclusion statements. For example, one may process a news collection and identify all references to cities. There are also second-order information extractions—that is, identifying relationships between entities in

http://dx.doi.org/10.1037/0000193-009
Big Data in Psychological Research, S. E. Woo, L. Tay, and R. W. Proctor (Editors)

texts, such as A is a spouse of B, city C is the capital of country D, or persons P, Q, and R met in Budapest on a particular day. Relationship extraction relies on the correct identification of the underlying entities. The advantage of information extraction is that if we focus on the correct entities and relationships, we know what the text is about. Moreover, when accumulating extractions from large and varied collections, certain observations may unexpectedly become prominent, thus also providing novel outcomes. For example, one may observe that persons P, Q, and R are interacting more often than expected by chance alone or that two seemingly unrelated proteins are implicated in the same disease. Component observations may be extracted from different texts, and their cumulative evidence may be unknown outside of the text mining efforts, thus revealing new insights on some phenomenon of interest.

Standard by-products of information extraction include special-purpose lexicons of entities and collections of relationships in the form of predicates optionally with confidence estimations. A *predicate* is a formal representation of a relationship as, for example, *was_president*(Trump, United States) and *is_located*(Taj Mahal, India, 1.0). The third argument in the second predicate indicates on a scale of (0,1) the extent to which one is certain of that relationship. A *lexicon* is a collection of entries with optional qualifications. For example, a gazetteer may be described as a lexicon, with entries representing place names optionally qualified with geographical coordinates. A listing of gene names associated with their synonyms is another example. The Linguistic Inquiry and Word Count (LIWC) and WordNet are classic examples of lexicons used in psychological research (G. A. Miller, 1995; Tausczik & Pennebaker, 2010). Lexicons may also be collections of relationships—for example, each entry could represent a pairing between a disease and one or more implicated genes, countries and capitals, or words that tend to co-occur meaningfully in a text collection of interest or a semantic group of words that have similar meanings. These automatically built resources may be used by downstream processes to achieve various goals. For example, to identify gene–disease connections, a back-end extraction process may first build a lexicon of genes that occur in the text collection. When studying cyberbullying on social media platforms, being able to identify terms that convey aggression or sarcasm would be most useful. Occurrences of temporal information (time, days, date ranges) mined from a collection of news reports may be used to assist in the downstream extraction of event details from the collection. More modern versions of semantic resources include distributional word embeddings such as word2vec (Mikolov, Chen, Corrado, & Dean, 2013) and GloVe (Pennington, Socher, & Manning, 2014) embeddings built using neural network methods.

INFORMATION INFERENCING

Another significant flavor of text mining is one where the emphasis is on inferring information that may be implicitly conveyed by the text. A classic example is to infer the sentiment, whether positive, negative, or neutral, of a text or its components. *Sentiment* is a challenging concept, given its nuanced connections to *opinion, view, belief, conviction, affect,* and *persuasion.* Several lexicons, such as SentiWordNet (Esuli & Sebastiani, 2006), WordNet-Affect (Strapparava & Valitutti, 2004), and Subjectivity Lexicon (Wilson, Wiebe, & Hoffmann, 2005), and tools, such as LIWC,[1] OpinionFinder (Choi, Cardie, Riloff, & Patwardhan, 2005), and LingPipe,[2] have been developed for inferring sentiment. There are also machine learning algorithms applied to estimate sentiment using a variety of textual features, including n-grams (phrases of length *n* built from contiguous words in texts), part-of-speech (categories such as noun, verb, article), syntax (e.g., noun and prepositional phrases), negation words, and other domain-specific special usage words (e.g., jargon, acronyms)— for example, "ttyl" in the texting community, "stat" in the medical community, and acronyms such as "ESL" (English as a second language). Pang, Lee, and Vaithyanathan (2002) published an early paper comparing features and machine learning algorithms for sentiment analysis. In general, the field of sentiment analysis is ripe, and psychologists may be interested in using its robust tools because sentiment is related to a variety of psychological constructs such as attitude, interest, and affect. For example, elections, debates between candidates, natural or human-made disasters, sporting events, and so forth, make it possible to study affect at a social media scale. The extent to which affect changes over time, event, demographics, and age might be of interest. One could also, for example, use these methods to automatically assess affect in the writings of depressed individuals compared with suitable controls.

Besides sentiment, other inferencing goals have been explored in this text mining category. Currently, there is intense activity to infer latent demographic attributes such as gender, race, age group, and location from an individual's posts (tweets, blogs, reviews, photo uploads, technical papers) and the person's online behavior (likes, friendships, hashtags, URLs). For example, Zheng, Han, and Sun (2017) provided a recent survey of location prediction on Twitter; Aletras and Chamberlain (2018) predicted user socioeconomic attributes; Z. Miller, Dickinson, and Hu (2012) used machine learning with success to predict gender on Twitter using n-grams; and Nguyen et al. (2014) discussed the challenges of gender and age prediction from Twitter. There is also keen interest in inferring other social, health, and psychological attributes, such as personality dimensions, well-being, political leanings, health status, sexual preferences, religiosity, and so on (Choudhury, Kiciman, Dredze, Coppersmith, & Kumar, 2016; Coppersmith, Dredze, Harman, Hollingshead, & Mitchell, 2015; Le, Boynton, Mejova, Shafiq, & Srinivasan, 2017a; Schwartz et al., 2016; Staiano et al., 2012). Some efforts have also garnered public attention in terms of privacy implications as, for instance, in the work of Matz, Kosinski, Nave, and Stillwell (2017). There are good reasons, including

[1]http://liwc.wpengine.com/
[2]http://alias-i.com/lingpipe/

personal safety, that motivate an individual to want attributes such as address, current location, religious practices, gender, and ethnicity to be kept private. In general, we are beginning to observe how these latent (i.e., hidden or subtle) attributes influence an individual's postings and writings. The challenge, which is being met with a surprising level of success, is in developing methods to infer these latent features. Studies focusing on many of the attributes mentioned, such as personality, are of direct interest to research and development in psychological sciences.

LITERATURE-BASED DISCOVERY

A special variety of inferencing in text mining research is one in which the goal is to "laterally" combine evidence obtained from different texts in a way that yields novel ideas. This approach, generally referred to as *literature-based discovery* (LBD), represents a class of methods for which the emphasis is squarely on novelty (i.e., mining hypotheses valuable enough to be explored further by the end user). Methodologically, it is extremely challenging because the algorithm has to identify sensible knowledge that is both previously unknown (though there is some flexibility in this) and justifiable as a promising hypothesis. Starting with the pioneering work of Don Swanson (e.g., Swanson, 1986), LBD has attracted significant interest. Swanson's focus was on manually inferring from the published literature hypotheses of interest to bioscientists conducting bench experiments. Good progress has been made in automating these text-mining procedures in recent decades. A recent review of the field is available (Henry & McInnes, 2017).

There are two broad approaches for LBD: open and closed discovery (for an explanation, see Srinivasan, 2004). In *open discovery*, the algorithm performs transitive inferencing (see Figure 8.1). Typically, this is done involving three concepts, X, Y, and Z. If we know from different parts of the text collection that X and Y are associated and that Y and Z are also associated in meaningful ways, the hypothesis that there is a meaningful relationship between X and Z as well may be generated. This inference is particularly interesting if X and Z have not yet been studied together and if the two connections can be combined to infer a meaningful link between X and Z. This process, which is similar to deductive logic (cf. Woo, O'Boyle, & Spector, 2017), has been labeled in this field as open discovery. The difference between the two is soft: In deductive logic, there is the inclination toward involving general premises (e.g., all men are mortal), whereas, in open discovery, the premises are often specific, such as that of a specific gene causing a specific disease. The transitivity inferencing, in open discovery efforts, may be taken forward several steps as opposed to just two, and there usually are many interconnecting Y concepts, as shown in Figure 8.1. In the second approach, a scientist may have a hunch about two concepts, P and Q, being related, and the goal is to find possible connections between them in the text collection

FIGURE 8.1. Open Discovery Approach

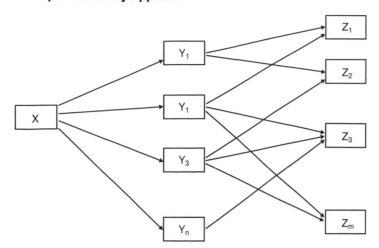

The starting concept *X* leads to a set of intermediate concepts *Y*, which, in turn, lead to a set of terminal concepts *Z*.

through other intermediate concepts using LBD. This process, because it is inward facing in nature, is referred to as *closed discovery*. There could be several ways to connect P and Q, and these could be ranked by the text mining algorithm and presented to the user.

Examples of recent efforts illustrating LBD are presented in Hristovski et al. (2016) and Yang, Ju, Wong, Shmulevich, and Chiang (2017). For example, Hristovski et al. explored genetic connections between drugs and their adverse effects via closed discovery. Essentially, their intuition was that genes connecting a drug with its adverse effect might offer explanations of the negative effect. With this intuition, they mined the biomedical literature to understand further the adverse effects of statins such as atorvastatin (Lipitor) and azathioprine (to prevent organ rejection after a transplant). Yang et al. explored open discovery to repurpose drugs for new treatments. In essence, they went from known disease–gene and known gene–drug relationships reported in the biomedical literature to postulate new disease–drug connections.

An example of possible interest in psychological sciences is exploring an intuition connecting religiosity with life satisfaction. In closed discovery, applied, for instance, to the published literature, the algorithm would process articles to identify connections postulated between the two. A strong algorithm would differentiate between statements asserting possibilities from others asserting greater certainty and thereby qualify the discovered connections with confidence scores. In open discovery, the algorithm starts at a single concept, such as religiosity, and then looks for indirectly connected aspects. Such indirectly connected aspects may include health and family ties. The algorithm would then sift through these to identify connections that are novel with respect to the starting variable (i.e., religiosity). The same strategies may be applied to social media data, and the discovered connections would then reflect discussions in such forums.

INFORMATION EXTRACTION

Information extraction is about identifying explicit occurrences of entities and relationships of interest in a text collection. Although the history of information extraction research extends back to the 1970s, the field was spurred by the Message Understanding Conference (MUC)[3] initiative funded by the Defense Advanced Research Projects Agency in the late 1980s. The initial emphasis was on military themes, such as the extraction of information about terrorist activities from news reports. The emphasis later evolved into extracting information of interest to businesses, such as corporate mergers, while still focusing on news report collections. At this point, information extraction is recognized as a core activity of wide interest, and this clearly includes a special emphasis on information extraction from social media data.

A key challenge in information extraction is semantic ambiguity and identity resolution. For example, the word *Washington* represents several persons and places. Ambiguity is present even in technical domains. For example, in biomedicine, different genes may have the same name: *Frapl* refers to both a mouse gene and a rat gene; *APAH1*, a human gene, is also an alias for the mouse gene *Nudt2*. Sometimes gene names also have meanings in the general English language, such as *BAR*, *GAB*, and *ACT*. Finally, some gene names may have other technical meanings. For example, the gene abbreviation *ACR*, which stands for the gene name *acrosin*, also has other technical meanings: albumin/creatinine ratios, acquired cellular resistance, acute to chronic ratio, and anomalous cosmic rays. Thus, it becomes important to identify the correct meaning behind the appearance of a name in a text. These are some of the challenges when extracting information from texts.

Preprocessing

Given a text collection, the first step in information extraction is to preprocess it to normalize it in different ways. Hickman, Thapa, Tay, Cao, and Srinivasan (2018) provided an introduction to different decisions that are to be made in this step, ensuring that we can handle the different file and record formats (e.g., pdf, Word, XML, HTML, JSON, txt). Once this is accomplished, various preprocessing tasks are undertaken to "normalize" the text: recognizing spelling errors and variations, handling abbreviations and acronyms, managing case differences, and so forth. Part of the preprocessing can include identifying components of the texts so these can be used in different ways. For example, for medical diagnosis, sections in the patient notes pertaining to "present

---

[3]https://www-nlpir.nist.gov/related_projects/muc/index.html

medical status" and "family history" may be the most important. In research papers, the title, abstract, introduction, and conclusion are generally the most important. Being able to identify logical units such as paragraphs, sentences, phrases, and n-grams also can become necessary. In some cases, legends attached to tables and figures can also be important. With tweets, recognizing hashtags, URL references, mentions, tweet timestamp, and user ID from the JSON (JavaScript Object Notation) structure is generally desired. Thus, the ability to identify key components becomes necessary. At this point, the text data is likely ready for the information extraction process. What is key to note is that the preprocessing steps are tailored to the data and the goals. For example, the preprocessing requirements for predicting location using metadata alone and using tweet text alone would differ.

Lexicons Versus Templates

A common approach to extracting relevant information is to use a predefined lexicon of words and phrases. For example, if one were interested in sentences about genes, one could extract all sentences that contain a lexicon entry in a lexicon of gene names and abbreviations. However, these extractions could contain many false positives because of semantic ambiguity. Although research lexicons are currently rarely used as stand-alone devices for specific topics such as gene function, they are still highly favored for areas of broad interest, as in sentiment and affect analysis (Dodds & Danforth, 2010). Unfortunately, in these contexts as well, the presence of lexicon words is no assurance of relevance. Consider the tweet "Happiness and joy elude me always." Individually, two out of the six words exist in a sentiment lexicon with positive polarity, but clearly, an inference of positive sentiment would be incorrect.

These and other limitations described later motivate our template-based approach for information extraction. The use of templates is not new. In fact, we see its usage in the MUC initiative introduced earlier. Templates specifying terrorist activities would include fields such as *Perpetrator*, *Instrument*, *Target*, and *Date*. The task was to fill these templates with data from the text. In the template approach, although lexicons are involved (e.g., words related to *bombing*), there are also key semantic constraints to be satisfied. Overall, the advantage gained is in precision. Precision is particularly important and challenging when working with social media data sets, given their large volume and also the high level of noise.

My emphasis in this chapter is on template-based approaches to information extraction, and I present three template-based extraction projects from our research group. The projects are presented in order of the increasing sophistication of their templates. In each project, the emphasis is primarily on the methodology so that the reader may better gauge their application to the social and psychological sciences. For fuller descriptions of the observations made in each study, the reader is referred to the primary publications.

PROJECT 1: BELIEF SURVEILLANCE ON SOCIAL MEDIA

Inspired in part by studies on disease surveillance using social media, we explored belief surveillance on Twitter (Bhattacharya, Tran, & Srinivasan, 2012; Bhattacharya, Tran, Srinivasan, & Suls, 2012). This is an extraction project because our first step was to extract expressions of support for or opposition to particular ideas related to health care. The second step was to summarize the extractions to make an overall assessment of belief. Generally, *belief* is an acceptance that a statement is true or that something exists. For our purposes, it is convenient to consider specific propositions such as "the earth is round" or "it will rain tomorrow" as statements of interest. A person may express complete or partial belief in a proposition or, conversely, firm disbelief. For a given proposition, belief can vary over people and time. We were interested in belief expressions that may be examined independent of the truth or veracity of a proposition. Of course, the study of belief becomes more interesting in the context of their alignment with proposition veracity.

Curious about the prevalence of health-related myths, we conducted a study of health belief expressions on Twitter. First, as an example, given the proposition, "Fluoride causes liver damage," the tweet "Horrible! Government covering up fluoride—liver problems connection" supports the proposition. The tweet "No, your liver cannot be damaged by fluoride in water" opposes the proposition, and the tweet "What is the status of fluoride–liver problems debate?" is neutral. Last, the tweet "Liver salts, fluoride-free toothpastes for sale" is not relevant to the proposition, though lexically, it has all the key words. Notice too that belief and sentiment are different. In the example, the first tweet carries a negative sentiment, whereas the next two are neutral. If we delete "Horrible!" in the first tweet, it would not change the belief, but the sentiment would become neutral. Adding a smiley icon does not alter the level of belief expressed. Thus, sentiment and belief are not the same; in fact, they are independent aspects.

As an experiment, we assessed beliefs regarding prespecified health-related propositions, including several that are recognized as misconceptions (Bhattacharya, Tran, & Srinivasan, 2012; Bhattacharya, Tran, Srinivasan, & Suls, 2012). Figure 8.2 shows these results. The *y* axis represents the degree of (belief, disbelief, doubt, and a catchall other category); estimation methods are described in Bhattacharya, Tran, and Srinivasan (2012) and Bhattacharya, Tran, Srinivasan, and Suls (2012). There were three groups of propositions (*probes*), those acknowledged by a group of physicians as true (T), false (F), and debatable (D). Ideally, the tweets conveyed a 100% belief in statements that were true, a 100% disbelief in statements that were not true, and a more mixed position for statements that were ambiguous (i.e., debatable). Interestingly, we observed several positions that are not consistent with this ideal.

Most interesting are the observations about the false statements. Belief score is greater than or equal to 0.6 for the first four statements. For the next two false statements, belief exceeds disbelief. When we combine belief and

FIGURE 8.2. Beliefs Result

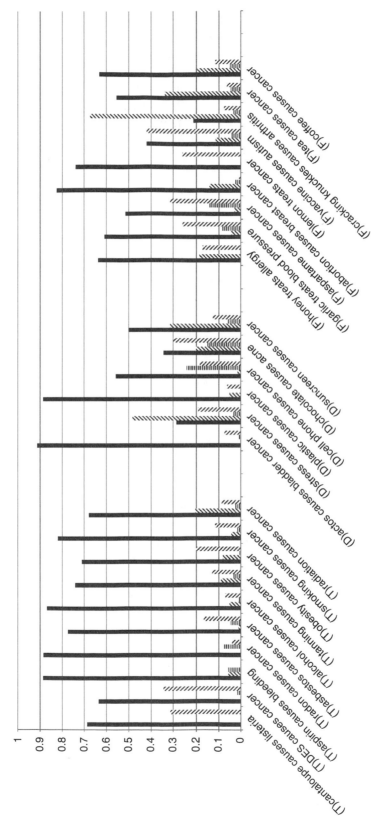

The y axis depicts the degree of belief, disbelief, doubt, or other in regard to a proposition. Propositions marked *T*, *D*, or *F* are considered true, debatable, or false, respectively.

doubt and then compare them with disbelief, the observations are even stronger. Again, in the last three false statements, we see much more disbelief than belief; however, there is also some doubt.

Some observations generated concern, such as the level of belief in thinking that one can get cancer from an abortion or by consuming aspartame (both are false statements). There was also high belief in allergies being treatable with honey. Propositions that were debatable, such as "cell phones cause cancer," yielded strong beliefs. Although this charged notion has attracted much media attention, we anticipated belief and disbelief would appear balanced. In terms of doubt, the proposition that had the lead was "chocolate causes acne." This could be due to the relatively high proportion of young users on Twitter. Finally, sunscreen causing cancer was disbelieved the most—in spite of the prevailing debate about that link.

In a follow-up experiment, Bhattacharya, Tran, Srinivasan, and Suls (2012) mined Twitter data to extract belief expressions related to causes and side effects of specific drugs and treatments of specific diseases. We explored 20 common drugs (e.g., Cialis, Cymbalta) and 30 common chronic diseases (e.g., asthma, osteoporosis). Our template-based methods are illustrated in Figure 8.3. In brief, we retrieved tweets containing a drug name and the word *cause* or *causes*, leaving the effect portion unspecified. We also retrieved tweets containing a disease name and either *treat* or *treats*, leaving the treatment strategy—for example, drug—unspecified. We then processed this high-precision set using MetaMap, a semantic extraction tool, to identify disease names, drug names, side effect terms, and so forth, and the nature of their relationship. We used MetaMap to enforce template-based semantic constraints

FIGURE 8.3. Methodology for Harvesting Probes

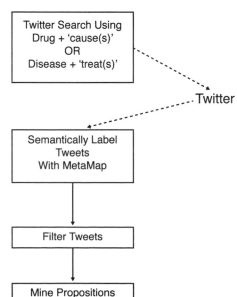

on the relationship between the entities of interest (drugs, side effects, and diseases). Using this filter, we identified propositions from the tweet set.

The harvesting process resulted in mining more than 750 propositions from a Twitter data set built from a search conducted on a single day (see Bhattacharya, Tran, Srinivasan, & Suls, 2012, for details). Examples of mined probes included "Advil treats hangover," "Nyquil causes coma," "Neem treats psoriasis," and "Coffee causes diabetes." This portion of the research is also an example of open discovery in the LBD subfield of text mining (see the section on LBD and, in particular, Figure 8.1). The difference is that the mined text collection is from social media and not the published biomedical literature. Further exploration of these mined probes in the biomedical literature showed that some probes had a few publications supporting them, such as "Curcumin treats multiple sclerosis," whereas others, such as "Gingko treats bronchitis" and "Lyrica causes hair loss" had no support in the published literature. In effect, these may be viewed as *proto hypotheses* that could generate some scientific interest. Mining social media for possible insights is an active area, especially for pharmaceutical companies for drug repurposing goals. The idea here is to mine reports from the public about side effects or unexpected positive effects of a drug.

PROJECT 2: EXTRACTING PERSONALITY PERCEPTIONS OF U.S. PRESIDENTIAL CANDIDATES

In another project (Bhattacharya, Yang, Srinivasan, & Boynton, 2016), which was part of a larger initiative on understanding communications in social media related to U.S. presidential elections, our goal was to identify public perceptions of the personality traits of candidates running for U.S. president both in the 2012 and the 2016 elections. A key task in this work conducted with Twitter data was to extract public opinion on personality traits from posts. After retrieving tweets mentioning a candidate's name, we applied template-based extractors to identify the opinion and the trait being addressed. The templates in this project are more advanced and explicit compared with the belief project presented earlier. Another distinctive aspect is that we adopted a formal approach and built our templates using traits from the Adjective Check List (ACL; Gough & Heilbrun, 1983). Examples of the 300 traits in the ACL include *honest*, *strong*, and *coarse*. These 300 traits (adjectives) have been reduced to a more measurable set of 110 (Simonton, 1986). In a manual study, Simonton (1986) used these 110 adjectives to analyze biographical sentences about 39 American presidents to compare their personalities. To illustrate, T. Roosevelt and Jackson were the least moderate and Jefferson the most brilliant.

Each template devised is, in essence, a semantic pattern specifying a trait, a person, and their semantic connection. When a tweet satisfies a template, we have extracted a predicate with its relevant components that together convey an opinion on a candidate's personality. For example, [P] is [A] [T] is a template which retrieves tweets such as "Obama is surely intelligent," and "Romney is clearly strong." [P] is a placeholder for a person name, [T] for a trait (represented by a set of synonyms), and [A] for an adverb of high certainty. Another template is [P] is [S] not [antonym (T)]. Here, S is an adverb indicating a low level of certainty (such as *maybe, somewhat, sort of*). This template would extract statements such as "Obama is kind of not honest." Although these templates may not extract all the personality expressions about a person, they will extract a high precision subset. Moreover, there is no a priori reason to expect the designed templates to be biased in favor of any individual in comparison studies.

After extracting statements about a trait T for a candidate, we mapped them to points along a continuum of scores for T. The opposite ends of the continuum represented opposing values for the trait (e.g., unfriendly vs. friendly), and these ends also represented high certainty statements. Statements of lower certainty mapped to points in between. Points on the continuum were also scored; the ends had the highest scores of equal magnitude but with opposite signs. A key advantage in our templates is in this mapping to the continuum with numerical scores. To illustrate, the first template described previously maps to the highest value for the trait. The second maps to a score that is still positive but less than the highest value. The exact scores assigned to points in the continuum are less important than their relative strengths, as long as we ensure that the scoring strategy is equivalent for both the negative and positive sides. Given a score for each extracted statement, we summarized these numerically as an estimate of the overall opinion about a candidate regarding a trait. Figure 8.4 provides a sample of trait scores computed for

FIGURE 8.4. Sample of Personality Trait Perceptions for Obama

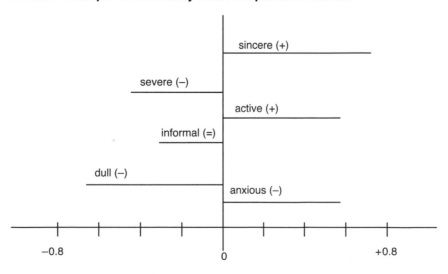

The scores along the *x* axis indicate perceptions of trait presence (positive) and absence (negative). The +, –, and = symbols represent a qualitative assessment of the value of a trait. For example, *active* is a desired trait, whereas *anxious* is an undesired trait.

Obama. It shows, for example, that positive traits perceived as present in Obama included *sincere* and *active*. The negative traits *dull* and *severe* were perceived as absent, whereas in contrast, the negative trait *anxious* was perceived as present. The neutral trait of *informal* was perceived as absent.

Using factor analysis, Simonton (1986) grouped the 110 adjectives into 14 nontrivial personality dimensions. Each component trait has a numerically rated "loading" between −1 and 1. A positive loading indicates that the trait directly contributes to the personality dimension; that is, it has a direct relationship. If negative, the presence of the trait reduces the strength of that personality dimension. The magnitude indicates the (relative) extent of contribution and detraction. Following a parallel strategy, we were able to compare perceptions of candidates along these dimensions. We found, for example, that Romney was perceived as somewhat more forceful than Obama, and Obama was slightly more conservative than Romney. It is key to note here that given their party stances, being perceived as conservative has different connotations for each candidate.

This template-based approach for extracting personality perceptions has been applied in several follow-up studies, especially in the context of the 2012 and 2016 presidential elections and several of its key events (primaries, caucuses, debates). For example, we compared the assessments made about Clinton and Trump over 50 million tweets about the 2016 U.S. presidential elections (Le, Boynton, Mejova, Shafiq, & Srinivasan, 2017b). The data were collected between mid-November 2015 and the end of February 2016. Analysis included comparing personality perceptions across party affiliations. We saw, for example, that only republicans emphasize Trump's conservatism, whereas this was not the case with users identified potentially as independents. Trump also rated higher among republicans on Machiavellianism, Brilliance, and Moderation. Details are in Le et al. (2017b).

When comparing the template-based approach to a baseline lexicon approach, the former fared significantly and observably better. Specifically, we took the five most frequent traits (considering synonyms) and a sample of 800 tweets that mentioned a trait and a candidate name. Judgments by crowd workers indicated that this baseline resulted in *F*-scores of about 0.16, whereas the template strategy obtained an *F*-score of 0.55. An *F*-score is the harmonic mean of recall and precision. Recall is the same as sensitivity, whereas precision is the same as positive predictive value. Its advantage is that it represents a single measure of system performance in contrast to having two measures: recall and precision. When comparing precision and recall scores, the template approach was a clear winner in precision, achieving above 0.9 compared with scores 0.1 and lower. Not surprisingly, the baseline was better in recall. Thus, the constraints imposed by the templates provided a significant and key advantage over a purely lexical approach.

Prediction of election outcomes with social media data is fraught with risk, and this was not the goal of our text mining efforts in the political realm. Our goal instead was to explore and understand the nature of social media communications related to elections. However, consistent with key results reported in the 1960 seminal study *The American Voter* (Campbell, Philip, Warren, & Donald, 1960) and its 2008 follow-up study (Lewis-Beck, Jacoby, Norpoth, & Weisberg, 2008), our social media text mining efforts indicate that personality perceptions continue to be one of three important aspects influencing elections. Our explorations of the other two dimensions of policy and party affiliation are reported in Le et al. (2017a).

PROJECT 3: EXTRACTING LIFE SATISFACTION TWEETS

In this third project illustrating the use of templates for information extraction, we explored life satisfaction on Twitter (Yang & Srinivasan, 2014, 2016). *Life satisfaction* is an assessment of the overall quality of one's life. It is a cognitive assessment and tends to be somewhat stable. It is a component of *subjective well-being*, which, in turn, is the scientific term for happiness. Subjective well-being has another component—*affect*—which represents the extent to which positive and negative emotions remain balanced in daily life. The goal in this project was to study life satisfaction using social media, which had received less attention compared with affect studies with social media.

The project may again be viewed as an extraction project because our first significant task was to extract what social media users were saying about their lives. Once again, we adopted a template-based extraction approach but with increasing sophistication compared with the belief and personality projects. The difference here is threefold: (a) we started in a principled manner with a survey instrument, the Satisfaction With Life Scale (SWLS); (b) we focused on extracting most if not all of the common expressions about life satisfaction (so the emphasis is on both recall and precision); and (c) we involved crowd workers in building templates. Moreover, the resulting templates were far more numerous than the number of templates in our previous projects.

The SWLS is a widely used and respected survey from psychology to rate life satisfaction (Diener, Emmons, Larsen, & Griffin, 1985; Pavot & Diener, 1993). It has five statements, such as, "In most ways my life is close to my ideal." Respondents give a scale-based rating for each statement that indicates the extent to which it applies to their lives. By intent, the survey does not focus on specific satisfaction criteria such as family and health. Thus, a respondent may consider any aspect he or she regards as important. Figure 8.5 shows our overall methodology, which is named *S-to-S* because it starts with a survey of interest and ends in a set of templates. Crowd workers were first engaged to write several statements that were synonymous with the input survey statement. The advantage was that we could expect diversity in crowd results, given the linguistic diversity expected even within English. These crowd statements were generalized, and in parallel, a lexicon of working synonyms was built. The lexicon, combined with the templates, gave us a large set of strategies for extracting life satisfaction posts. Exhibit 8.1 illustrates this process

FIGURE 8.5. S-to-S Methodology

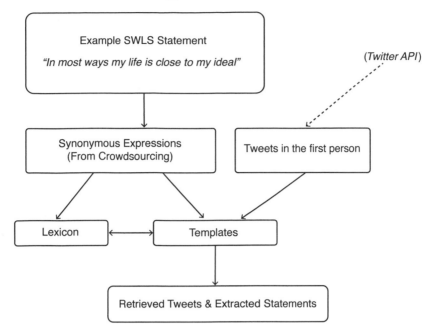

API = application programming interface; SWLS = Satisfaction With Life Scale.

EXHIBIT 8.1

Sample Templates and Lexicon Entries

Phrase entries are in parentheses. Lexicon variable names carry no meaning.

Example 1. Sentence: My life is perfect. Sentence template: my X Y

Lexicon entry X: {life's (life is) (life has) (life has been) (life's been) etc.}

Lexicon entry Y: {amazing adorable awesome beautiful best (the best) blessed bliss blissful brilliant comfortable comfy contended delightful desired dream enjoyable exemplary excellent exciting etc.}

Example 2. Sentence: I live a perfect life. Sentence template: A Y B

Lexicon entry A: {(I have been living) (I've been living) (I am living) (I'm living) (I live) (I have been having) (I've been having) (I am having) (I'm having) (I have) etc.}

Lexicon entry Y: {Shown above.}

Lexicon entry B: {life existence}

Example 3. Sentence: I love my life. Sentence template: D E F

Lexicon entry D: {(I've (I have) (I have been) (I've been) (I've been having) (I have been having) (I am) I'm Im (I'm having) (I am having) I . . .}

Lexicon entry E: {like liking love loving adore adoring enjoy enjoying etc.}

Lexicon entry F: {life existence (my life) (this life) (my existence) (this existence) etc.}

---

with a few examples. Figure 8.6 provides examples of the tweets eventually extracted. It is key to note that we checked for elongated words, such as *Loooove*, slang, and nonword sounds. Although we did not use icons because their use is not restricted to life satisfaction expressions, we found consistencies between the sentiment in life satisfaction and the sentiment in these pictorial symbols, as illustrated in the figure. In validation experiments comparing our approach with survey data and with competing methods, our template method achieved recall, precision, and *F*-scores between 0.59 and 0.65. These were considerably better than standard lexicon-based methods and machine learning methods. Details are in Yang and Srinivasan (2014).

With this template-based methodology, we were able to identify users who were satisfied and users who were dissatisfied with their lives. We did this on the basis of all their posts (to the extent they were accessible) to ensure that there were no changes in these cognitive assessments. Several types of comparisons were then made, for example, using LIWC categories, as shown in Figure 8.7. Dissatisfied users were overall less positive in almost all categories, with marked differences in achievement and home.

Overall, differences between tweets posted by satisfied and dissatisfied users were consistent with survey outcomes in psychology and sociology research. For example, dissatisfied users posted more about death, depression, sadness, anger, anxiety, poor health, and lower social support. Results from Strine, Chapman, Balluz, Moriarty, and Mokdad (2008), for example, indicated an elevated risk of adverse health and declining social support with declining life satisfaction.

Temporal comparisons also revealed interesting differences between the two groups. For instance, the groups differed in the extent to which they talked about depression, as shown in Figure 8.8. In the figure, the trends are centered

FIGURE 8.6. Example Life Satisfaction Extractions

POSITIVE STATEMENTS	NEGATIVE STATEMENTS
I feel good, life's good	I hate my life so much
I love my life	My Entire Life Is A Mess . . . . . .
I looooove this life	I have no life
Life is a bliss	I really have no real life.
I live a very blessed life	I regret my existence
My life is f* amazing honestly	F* my life
I love the life I have built	MY LIFE SUCKS!!!!!!!!!
I love how my life is going rn	My existence: pain. Constantly
life I'm living butter soft	Yoooooo my life is a MESSSSS
I am in love with life	Need a change in my life asap, fed up
Yo I love the life I live seriously	Wow I suck at life :/
My life is already beautiful	I regret my life choices.
Life is so good I am so blessed	I've been doing life wrong.
Great things are happening in my life #blessed	My life is depressing lol.
I couldn't be any more happy with life	I seriously have no life

FIGURE 8.7. Difference Between Life-Satisfied (Solid Bar) and Life-Dissatisfied (Dashed Bar) Users

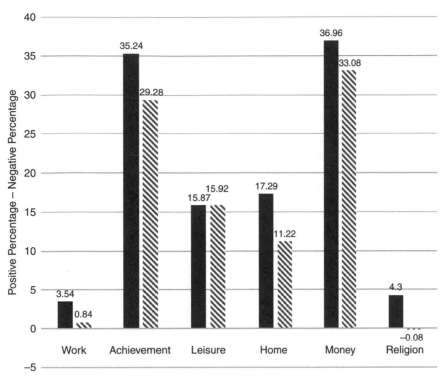

FIGURE 8.8. Posts About Depression

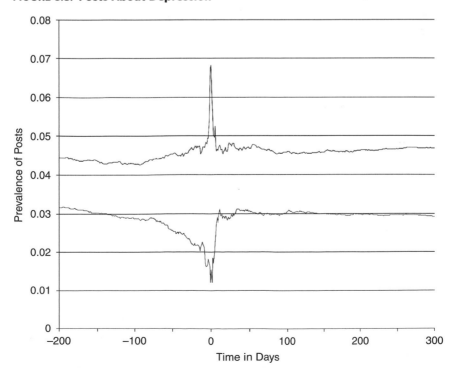

Class D is the upper graph; Class S is the lower graph.

on Day 0, the day when the life satisfaction post was made (we obtained this information from the time stamp given in the tweet). The plot shows trends from several months before to several months after this post was made. The upper line represents Class D, dissatisfied users, and the lower line represents Class S, satisfied users. Besides the gap between the two, the frequency increased around Day 0 for D and dipped for S. Similar comparisons are shown in Yang and Srinivasan (2014) for anger, anxiety, death, health, religion, and so forth. Another interesting conclusion drawn from this previous work is that users who first expressed satisfaction with life and later changed their position look more like users who only expressed life dissatisfaction than those only expressing life satisfaction.

In summary, the template-based text mining strategy, which was validated against survey data, has shown great promise in extracting life satisfaction statements. In particular, it offers the level of precision necessary to make meaningful comparisons between groups of interest.

CONCLUSION

Although the primary emphasis in this chapter has been on the information extraction portion of text mining, the value of the other two major strands, information inferencing and LBD, should be noted. The former is a highly active branch, especially in computational social sciences; the latter is far less studied in the social and psychological sciences.

The three projects presented have in common the use of templates for information extraction. However, they differ most significantly in the level of sophistication of their templates. For example, the life satisfaction project used the S-to-S framework for generating appropriate templates, whereas, for belief surveillance, the templates were generated using intuition and common expectations.

There are several takeaways for the social and psychological sciences. First, these studies show that the intellectual investment in building templates, rather than simply relying on lexicons to extract relevant information, yields strong returns. In each of our studies comparing lexicon and machine learning baselines, the template-based effort achieved significantly and observably better performance. Although lexicons are tremendously useful structures in text mining, their value as stand-alone tools is questionable. Words examined out of context are highly likely to diminish precision, and this is especially true for social media data. We find that the addition of even minimal semantic constraints in the form of templates (as in our belief project) provides a significant boost in precision. With machine learning algorithms, the challenge faced is in the high degree of linguistic variation and the large amount of labeled training data needed to build classifiers that perform well on social media. Perhaps with the advent of deep learning models, we can look forward to scalable classifiers that perform effectively with social media data.

Second, domain expertise is of great value in building such templates. The process of building templates can be simple: A group of experts in psychology, perhaps with the help of linguistic expertise, collaboratively generate templates for the problem addressed. For example, if we were to explore religiosity on social media, we would build templates to find expressions such as those of gratitude tied to religion, postings about prayer meetings, and so on. Alternately, for a more complex topic, one might also make use of crowd workers. In this context, our S-to-S methodology also provides a validated approach for generating templates from well-established survey instruments of interest, ensuring that the templates have theoretical grounding. For example, if we wanted to extract expressions pertaining to physical health, we might use portions of the Centers for Disease Control and Prevention's Behavioral Risk Factor Surveillance System instrument (https://www.cdc.gov/brfss/index.html) on health status, exercise, days unwell, and so on.

Third, even though social media is slanted toward a particular segment of the population (as, for example, in age and economics), the observations we have made, especially in the life satisfaction and personality projects, are consistent with observations made previously by social scientists and political scientists. This augurs well for the continued importance of text mining in these domains.

Finally, projects involving social media data have to consider the legal and ethical implications of data collection and analysis. It is unclear whether users are sufficiently aware of the consequences of participating in social media communications or whether they understand the extent to which their privacy may be invaded. It remains to be seen how these complex aspects will evolve in the future. Chapter 15 of this volume is relevant in that it explores ethics related to the study of social media.

REFERENCES

Aletras, N., & Chamberlain, B. P. (2018). Predicting Twitter user socioeconomic attributes with network and language information. In *Proceedings of the 29th ACM Conference on Hypertext and Social Media* (pp. 20–24). New York, NY: ACM. http://dx.doi.org/10.1145/3209542.3209577

Bhattacharya, S., Tran, H., & Srinivasan, P. (2012, November). *Discovering health beliefs in Twitter*. Paper presented at the AAAI Fall Symposium: Information Retrieval and Knowledge Discovery in Biomedical Text, Arlington, VA.

Bhattacharya, S., Tran, H., Srinivasan, P., & Suls, J. (2012). Belief surveillance with twitter. In *Proceedings of the 4th Annual ACM Web Science Conference* (pp. 43–46). New York, NY: ACM. http://dx.doi.org/10.1145/2380718.2380724

Bhattacharya, S., Yang, C., Srinivasan, P., & Boynton, B. (2016). Perceptions of presidential candidates' personalities in Twitter. *Journal of the Association for Information Science and Technology, 67*, 249–267. http://dx.doi.org/10.1002/asi.23377

Campbell, A., Philip, C., Warren, M., & Donald, S. (1960). *The American voter*. Chicago, IL: University of Chicago Press.

Choi, Y., Cardie, C., Riloff, E., & Patwardhan, S. (2005). Identifying sources of opinions with conditional random fields and extraction patterns. In *Proceedings of the Conference on Human Language Technology and Empirical Methods in Natural Language Processing* (pp. 355–362). Stroudsburg, PA: Association for Computational Linguistics. http://dx.doi.org/10.3115/1220575.1220620

Choudhury, M. D., Kiciman, E., Dredze, M., Coppersmith, G., & Kumar, M. (2016). Discovering shifts to suicidal ideation from mental health content in social media. In *Proceedings of SIGCHI Conference on Human Factors in Computing Systems* (pp. 2098–2110). http://dx.doi.org/10.1145/2858036.2858207

Coppersmith, G., Dredze, M., Harman, C., Hollingshead, K., & Mitchell, M. (2015). Clpsych 2015 shared task: Depression and PTSD on Twitter. In *Proceedings of the 2nd Workshop on Computational Linguistics and Clinical Psychology: From Linguistic Signal to Clinical Reality* (pp. 31–39). Denver, CO: Association for Computational Linguistics.

Diener, E., Emmons, R. A., Larsen, R. J., & Griffin, S. (1985). The Satisfaction With Life Scale. *Journal of Personality Assessment, 49,* 71–75. http://dx.doi.org/10.1207/s15327752jpa4901_13

Dodds, P. S., & Danforth, C. M. (2010). Measuring the happiness of large-scale written expression: Songs, blogs, and presidents. *Journal of Happiness Studies, 11,* 441–456. http://dx.doi.org/10.1007/s10902-009-9150-9

Esuli, A., & Sebastiani, F. (2006). Sentiwordnet: A publicly available lexical resource for opinion mining. In *Proceedings of the 5th Conference on Language Resources and Evaluation* (pp. 417–422). Paris, France: European Language Resources Association.

Gough, H. G., & Heilbrun, A. B. (1983). *The Adjective Check List manual.* Sunnyvale, CA: Consulting Psychologists Press.

Henry, S., & McInnes, B. T. (2017, October). Literature based discovery: Models, methods, and trends. *Journal of Biomedical Informatics, 74,* 20–32. http://dx.doi.org/10.1016/j.jbi.2017.08.011

Hickman, L., Thapa, S., Tay, L., Cao, M., & Srinivasan, P. (2018). *Text preprocessing for text mining in organizational research: Review and recommendations.* Manuscript submitted for publication.

Hristovski, D., Kastrin, A., Dinevski, D., Burgun, A., Žiberna, L., & Rindflesch, T. C. (2016, August). Using literature-based discovery to explain adverse drug effects. *Journal of Medical Systems, 40*(8), 185. http://dx.doi.org/10.1007/s10916-016-0544-z

Le, H., Boynton, G., Mejova, Y., Shafiq, Z., & Srinivasan, P. (2017a). Bumps and bruises: Mining presidential campaign announcements on Twitter. In *Proceedings of the 28th ACM Conference on Hypertext and Social Media* (pp. 215–224). New York, NY: ACM. http://dx.doi.org/10.1145/3078714.3078736

Le, H., Boynton, G. R., Mejova, Y., Shafiq, Z., & Srinivasan, P. (2017b). Revisiting the American voter on twitter. In *Proceedings of the 2017 CHI Conference on Human Factors in Computing Systems* (pp. 4507–4519). New York, NY: ACM. http://dx.doi.org/10.1145/3025453.3025543

Lewis-Beck, M. S., Jacoby, W. G., Norpoth, H., & Weisberg, H. F. (2008). *The American voter revisited.* Ann Arbor: University of Michigan Press. http://dx.doi.org/10.3998/mpub.92266

Matz, S. C., Kosinski, M., Nave, G., & Stillwell, D. J. (2017). Psychological targeting as an effective approach to digital mass persuasion. *PNAS, 114,* 12714–12719. http://dx.doi.org/10.1073/pnas.1710966114

Mikolov, T., Chen, K., Corrado, G., & Dean, J. (2013, May). *Efficient estimation of word representations in vector space.* Paper presented at the International Conference of Learning Representations, Scottsdale, AZ.

Miller, G. A. (1995). Wordnet: A lexical database for English. *Communications of the ACM, 38*(11), 39–41. http://dx.doi.org/10.1145/219717.219748

Miller, Z., Dickinson, B., & Hu, W. (2012). Gender prediction on twitter using stream algorithms with n-gram character features. *International Journal of Intelligence Science, 2,* 143–148. http://dx.doi.org/10.4236/ijis.2012.224019

Nguyen, D.-P., Trieschnigg, R., Dogruoz, A., Gravel, R., Theune, M., Meder, T., & de Jong, F. (2014). Why gender and age prediction from tweets is hard: Lessons from a crowdsourcing experiment. In *Proceedings of the 25th International Conference on*

Computational Linguistics (pp. 1950–1961). Cambridge, MA: Association for Computational Linguistics.

Pang, B., Lee, L., & Vaithyanathan, S. (2002, July). Thumbs up? Sentiment classification using machine learning techniques. In *Proceedings of the Conference on Empirical Methods in Natural Language Processing* (Vol. 10, pp. 79–86). Philadelphia, PA: Association for Computational Linguistics. http://dx.doi.org/10.3115/1118693.1118704

Pavot, W., & Diener, E. (1993). Review of the satisfaction with life scale. *Psychological Assessment, 5,* 164–172. http://dx.doi.org/10.1037/1040-3590.5.2.164

Pennington, J., Socher, R., & Manning, C. D. (2014). GloVe vectors for word representation. In *Proceedings of the Conference on Empirical Methods in Natural Language Processing* (pp. 1532–1543). Stroudsburg, PA: Association for Computational Linguistics.

Schwartz, A., Sap, M., Kern, M. L., Eichstaedt, J. C., Kapelner, A., Agrawal, M., . . . Ungar, L. H. (2016). Predicting individual well-being through the language of social media. *Proceedings of the Pacific Symposium on Biocomputing, 21,* 516–527.

Simonton, D. K. (1986). Presidential personality: Biographical use of the Gough adjective check list. *Journal of Personality and Social Psychology, 51,* 149–160. http://dx.doi.org/10.1037/0022-3514.51.1.149

Srinivasan, P. (2004). Text mining: Generating hypotheses from Medline. *Journal of the American Society for Information Science and Technology, 55,* 396–413. http://dx.doi.org/10.1002/asi.10389

Staiano, J., Lepri, B., Aharony, N., Pianesi, F., Sebe, N., & Pentland, A. (2012). Friends don't lie: Inferring personality traits from social network structure. In *Proceedings of the 2012 ACM Conference on Ubiquitous Computing* (pp. 321–330). New York, NY: ACM.

Strapparava, C., & Valitutti, A. (2004). Wordnet-affect: An affective extension of Wordnet. In *Proceedings of the 4th International Conference on Language Resources and Evaluation* (pp. 1083–1086). Lisbon, Portugal: European Language Resources Association.

Strine, T. W., Chapman, D. P., Balluz, L. S., Moriarty, D. G., & Mokdad, A. H. (2008). The associations between life satisfaction and health-related quality of life, chronic illness, and health behaviors among U.S. community-dwelling adults. *Journal of Community Health, 33,* 40–50. http://dx.doi.org/10.1007/s10900-007-9066-4

Swanson, D. R. (1986). Fish oil, Raynaud's syndrome, and undiscovered public knowledge. *Perspectives in Biology and Medicine, 30,* 7–18. http://dx.doi.org/10.1353/pbm.1986.0087

Tausczik, Y., & Pennebaker, J. (2010). The psychological meaning of words: LIWC and computerized text analysis methods. *Journal of Language and Social Psychology, 29,* 24–54. http://dx.doi.org/10.1177/0261927X09351676

Wilson, T., Wiebe, J., & Hoffmann, P. (2005). Recognizing contextual polarity in phrase-level sentiment analysis. In *Proceedings of the Conference on Human Language Technology and Empirical Methods in Natural Language Processing* (pp. 347–354). Stroudsburg, PA: Association for Computational Linguistics. http://dx.doi.org/10.3115/1220575.1220619

Woo, S. E., O'Boyle, E., & Spector, P. (2017). Best practices in developing, conducting, and evaluating inductive research. *Human Resource Management Review, 27,* 255–264. http://dx.doi.org/10.1016/j.hrmr.2016.08.004

Yang, C., & Srinivasan, P. (2014). Translating surveys to surveillance on social media: Methodological challenges and solutions. In *Proceedings of the 014 ACM Conference on Web Science* (pp. 4–12). Bloomington, IN: ACM.

Yang, C., & Srinivasan, P. (2016). Life satisfaction and the pursuit of happiness on Twitter. *PloS ONE, 11*(3). http://dx.doi.org/10.1371/journal.pone.0150881

Yang, H. T., Ju, J. H., Wong, Y. T., Shmulevich, I., & Chiang, J. H. (2017). Literature-based discovery of new candidates for drug repurposing. *Briefings in Bioinformatics, 18,* 488–497.

Zheng, X., Han, J., & Sun, A. (2017). *A survey of location prediction on Twitter.* Retrieved from https://arxiv.org/pdf/1705.03172.pdf

APPLICATIONS

9

Big Data in the Science of Learning

Sidney K. D'Mello

A couple of years ago, I watched with surprise, amusement, and perhaps even a tinge of horror as my colleague's middle school children completed their math homework with paper and pencil at the dining room table. I thought to myself, "Surely, they have iPads, Chromebooks, or some other fancy technology at their expensive private schools. There is no way they actually turn in their paper homework the next day and get written feedback some days later." As it turned out, this is precisely how it was done. What a waste of data and learning opportunities. The children's behaviors as they completed their math problems—the time spent reading and (re)reading each problem, pauses, failed attempts, fresh starts, eureka moments—were forever lost. All that remained was the completed homework, which told no tales of the underlying learning process, the struggles, despair, and eureka moments. Also missed were the real-time learning opportunities, such as immediate elaborate feedback, just-in-time explanations, and personalized problems. Invaluable insights that teachers could use to improve instruction, such as topics or problems associated with boredom versus bewilderment, were also lost forever.

This research was supported by the National Science Foundation (NSF DUE 1745442, DRL 1235958, IIS 1523091, IIS 1735785), the Institute of Educational Sciences (IES R305A130030, R305A170432, R305C160004), the Walton Family Foundation, the Mindset Scholars Network, the Bill & Melinda Gates Foundation, the Joyce Foundation, the Overdeck Family Foundation, and the Raikes Foundation. Any opinions, findings, and conclusions or recommendations expressed in this material are those of the author and do not necessarily reflect the views of the funding agencies.

http://dx.doi.org/10.1037/0000193-010
Big Data in Psychological Research, S. E. Woo, L. Tay, and R. W. Proctor (Editors)

Fortunately, things are changing. The low cost of mobile computing devices (smartphones, tablets, Chromebooks), coupled with cheap and elastic cloud-based data storage and computing, along with advances in the fields of artificial intelligence and machine learning, has launched a data revolution in the science of learning. But data are abundant. Knowledge is sparse. How do we gain knowledge about how people learn from data on hundreds of thousands of students and their teachers collected across extended time frames? I consider this question in this chapter, starting with a word about the data itself.

BACKGROUND

Tipping Points

The modern (circa the 1990s) intelligent tutoring system (ITS) represents one of the first serious attempts to use data to drive learning and teaching (Sleeman & Brown, 1982). At the heart of the ITS lies the student or learner model (Sottilare, Graesser, Hu, & Holden, 2013)—a computational representation of the students' knowledge and skills that is continually updated as the learning session progresses. The learner model works in conjunction with a model of the knowledge domain, such as physics (the domain model), and a model of pedagogy, such as Socratic dialog learning (tutor model), to adapt the tutoring session to the individual learner. Parameters of the learner model are learned from existing data and then dynamically adjusted to each student. ITSs have been quite effective in promoting learning, with meta-analyses indicating effect sizes that outperform computer-assisted instruction, classroom instruction, textbooks and workbooks, laboratory or homework assignments, and other controls (Kulik & Fletcher, 2016; Ma, Adesope, Nesbit, & Liu, 2014; Steenbergen-Hu & Cooper, 2013, 2014). Their effectiveness is similar to that of novice human tutors (see VanLehn, 2011).

Beyond ITSs, the past decade has witnessed tipping points that have launched the data revolution in education. One is the advent of massive open online courses (MOOCs). By opening up content to millions of learners worldwide, MOOCs have unleashed a tsunami of educational data, logging millions of clicks and views (called clickstream) every second. Traditional MOOCs (xMOOCs), which mainly consist of watching videos, completing auto-graded assessments, and maybe participating in discussions, are a step backward from the sophisticated cognitive models, levels of interactivity, and adaptive learning approach of ITSs. Thus, it is unsurprising that MOOCs have problems with engagement and dropout (Yang, Sinha, Adamson, & Rosé, 2013) and there are few controlled experiments on the effectiveness of MOOCs in increasing learning. Nevertheless, given that we are in the early stages of MOOC development, their true value lies in the sheer volume of real-world distance-learning heterogeneous data they generate daily. Like MOOCs, virtually every university course uses a learning management system, which generates gobs of similar data.

The big textbook publishers (e.g., Pearson, McGraw-Hill, Mifflin Harcourt) are also catching up, each experiencing its own digital education transition. Whereas their earlier efforts primarily focused on digitizing print textbooks, more recent initiatives emphasize blending print and digital materials with embedded assessments, electronic note taking, and multimedia. Some are also moving toward virtual tutoring and more adaptive forms of instruction (e.g., McGraw-Hill recently incorporated the ALEKS [Assessment and Learning in Knowledge] ITS; Canfield, 2001). The result is billions of more data points on page reads, clicks, time on task, and the like.

Never to miss out on the fun, big tech has entered the classroom with gusto. So far, they have mainly provided cloud-based technological solutions to streamline teacher and student communication (e.g., assignment management, file sharing, grading). Another invaluable contribution is the platform for thousands of educational apps, especially educational games that spark engagement. Although their ultimate goal is likely to sell more hardware to school districts and to get the next generation hooked on their free apps, the end result is even more data.

Although the initiatives ushered in by MOOCs, big text, and big tech have resulted in reams of data, the data are quite narrow in scope, consisting mainly of overt actions adduced in clicks, likes, and written text. The fabric of human learning is considerably richer. We smile, gesture, express emotions, communicate with peers, laugh, cry, get distracted, and feel anxious. Save for the lonely graduate student coding them from video, these data streams were previously lost forever. However, the ubiquity of webcams and microphones in everyday devices, the availability of wearable sensing devices (e.g., wristbands for multichannel physiology), consumer off-the-shelf sensors (e.g., Fitbit, Kinect), the ability to sense environmental and social context (e.g., smartphones with GPS), and cost-effective computation and storage in the cloud has afforded the collection of unprecedented amounts of naturalistic multimodal data in the wild. This is a game changer.

Research Communities Involved

We have a ton of data and are collecting a ton more daily. Who makes sense of it all? The traditional research area has been artificial intelligence in education (AIED) whose foray has historically been ITSs but is now broadening in scope to other intelligent educational technologies, such as educational games. With the advent of MOOCs came the Society for Learning Analytics Research (SoLAR) and Learning at Scale. The educational data mining community is a blend of AIED and SOLAR. Whereas these organizations are heavily technology-focused, the International Society of the Learning Sciences and the Society for Text and Discourse emphasize situated learning and text analysis, respectively, in contexts that may or may not involve technology. These two organizations also emphasize collaborative learning in both face-to-face and computer-supported collaborative learning contexts. Along with the European Association of Technology Enhanced Learning, these organizations recently formed the International Alliance to Advance Learning in the Digital Era with a goal of advancing the science of learning in a technological era, much of which is data driven.

Whereas the aforementioned research areas focus mainly on process data—clicks, responses, and text—the emerging field of multimodal learning analytics (Blikstein, 2013) emphasizes the analysis of video, audio, posture, gesture, eye gaze, and peripheral and central physiology. It is also concerned with modeling phenomena beyond cognitive factors, such as engagement, affect, and attention.

There are other data-driven research initiatives with myriad goals, such as improving test preparation, developing more diagnostic test items, improving educational platforms, and selling more products. I do not discuss them further because the primary goal is not to advance knowledge in the science of learning.

HOW IS IT DONE?

How to make sense of all these data? Let us briefly consider some of the key research areas and computational techniques used.

Formative Assessment

One key research area is *formative assessment*, the goal of which is assessing to improve, not evaluate, learning. Stealth assessments, which are integrated into the learning experience rather than occurring summatively, are a popular formative assessment technique (Shute, 2011).

Based on evidence-centered design (Mislevy & Haertel, 2006), stealth assessment begins with a theoretical model of the domain consisting (at a minimum) of things to be learned (competency model) connected to things learners do that can provide evidence of learning (indicators). The competency estimates are continually updated as learners generate evidence through their interactions with the learning environment. The competency and evidence models are represented as a probabilistic graphical model, typically a Bayes net (Shute & Moore, 2017). Model parameters can be initially set based on educated guesses and can be subsequently tuned as data accumulate. The model can be used to estimate competencies for individual students in real time, and the estimates themselves can be used to dynamically adapt the experience to individual learners—for example, by unlocking levels in an educational game.

Assessment also underlies the core component of ITSs—the learner model (called *knowledge components* [KC] in educational data mining and *Q-matrix* in psychometrics), which is the engine of adaptivity. A particularly popular assessment approach used in ITSs called *knowledge tracing* (Corbett & Anderson, 1994; computationally Bayesian Knowledge Tracing or BKT) is derived from

Anderson's (1982) theory of cognitive skill acquisition. The model is formulated as a two-state dynamic Bayesian network or hidden Markov model (HMM), which estimates the probability of mastering a knowledge component (competency) based on responses to the current questions or problems (indicators) as well as past performance (i.e., the model is dynamic). Each knowledge component of standard BKT has four parameters: an estimate of prior knowledge, a probability of learning, a probability of guessing (getting the item correct despite not knowing), and a probability of slipping (getting the item incorrect despite knowing). The model parameters are also fit using existing data and are used for adaptive instruction.

In contrast to the use of graphical models, researchers have also used logistic regression models with a growth term to increase the predicted estimate for a knowledge component each time the student encounters a problem involving that component (from a Q-matrix). The resultant models, called additive factor models (Cen, Koedinger, & Junker, 2006), and their variants, such as the performance factors model (Pavlik, Cen, & Koedinger, 2009) and instructional factors analysis model (Chi, Koedinger, Gordon, Jordon, & VanLahn, 2011), model the log odds of students succeeding on a KC item as a function of student parameters, KC parameters, learning rates, previous success and failure counts on items, and exposure to instructional interventions. Again, the parameters are all learned from data. The Pittsburgh Science of Learning Center DataShop (Koedinger et al., 2010) and its recent extension LearnSphere are massive data repositories to train and experiment with these models.

Supervised, Semisupervised, and Unsupervised Learning

Machine learning is a broad umbrella of techniques that use big data in the learning sciences. "Early warning indicators" are one of the killer applications that use big data and machine learning. In one early study, Macfadyen and Dawson (2010) used logistic regression to predict students who would fail a course using basic features captured from a learning management system (e.g., number of discussion messages sent, assignments completed). Similarly, Aguiar, Ambrose, Chawla, Goodrich, and Brockman (2014) studied patterns of engagement with electronic portfolios to predict retention among first-year engineering students. The basic idea of this type of modeling is to utilize data already logged by learning management systems and/or any type of administrative system to predict important outcomes, with an eye for early intervention to prevent undesirable outcomes. Researchers typically use standard supervised learning methods, such as linear or logistic regression, nearest neighbors, decision trees, Naive Bayes classifiers, support vector machines, feedforward neural networks, and ensemble methods such as random forest.

Supervised learning requires supervision in the form of labeled data (e.g., graduation outcomes, grade point average). These labels can be quite sparse in many domains. For example, consider the task of predicting whether a student would learn the content from video viewing patterns (e.g., pauses, rewinds) based on a voluntarily post-viewing quiz taken by 1% of the students. Instead of discarding the 99% of unlabeled data, researchers could use semisupervised learning techniques, such as self-training or co-training, to utilize the unlabeled data to improve overall model accuracy (Chapelle, Schölkopf, & Zien, 2006). Unfortunately, this is rarely done.

Large-scale data sets are usually heterogeneous, so some grouping based on student characteristics, contextual factors, behavioral snapshots, or action sequences is warranted. There are also situations when we are interested in identifying subgroups with certain characteristics. This is done using unsupervised learning methods—mainly cluster analysis—using standard techniques such as k-means clustering, expectation-maximization, and self-organizing maps (see Vellido, Castro, & Nebot, 2010, for a brief review of clustering applied to educational data).

Relationship Discovery

Educational data are often transactional—that is, multiple "events" occur within a time frame (transaction). For example, students might make certain errors on certain problems, they might select certain subsets of videos to view on a given topic, or they might simultaneously take certain courses within a semester. Much can be learned by identifying "interesting" associations from these transactions. It is particularly informative to identify multivariate associations (e.g., Events A, B, C, and D have a certain likelihood of co-occurring), which are different from multivariate correlational analyses, where two sets of variables are correlated. It is also important to go beyond associations by identifying dependencies (i.e., A implies B, but B does not imply A; e.g., a smile might imply happiness but not vice versa). And because the data can contain millions of transactions, methods to discover associations and dependencies should be computationally efficient. The field of association rule mining (Agrawal & Srikant, 1994) provides such methods to identify multivariate associations and their dependencies (e.g., [A, B, C] → [D, E]; Events A, B, and C co-occur and predict Events D and E).

Sequence Modeling

Educational data are also sequential (e.g., click stream sequences, course taking sequences, turn-taking in student–tutor dialogs). Techniques to analyze sequential data can be grouped into four categories. The first uses dynamical probabilistic graphical models, such as dynamic Bayesian nets (e.g., Conati & Maclaren, 2009), HMMs (e.g., Boyer et al., 2009), conditional random fields, and hierarchical variants of these models. For example, Boyer et al. (2009) used HMMs to discover latent higher order structures in tutorial dialogs called *dialog modes* (Cade, Copeland, Person, & D'Mello, 2008; e.g., modeling, scaffolding) from sequences of lower level dialog acts (or moves; e.g., positive feedback).

The second approach is to use recurrent neural networks (RNNs) for sequence learning. RNNs are variants of feedforward neural networks with recurrent links (e.g., backward links between output neurons and hidden neurons). Traditional RNNs are limited with respect to how much of the past (sequence length) can be modeled due to the so-called vanishing gradient problem (Bengio, Simard, & Frasconi, 1994). Long short-term memory (LSTM) RNNs (Hochreiter & Schmidhuber, 1997) address this problem by incorporating a form of "memory" in the neurons (called memory cells). In one popular study, Piech et al. (2015) used LSTMs to simultaneously model a number of skills (knowledge components) from sequences of prior performance on exercises targeting those skills. The so-called deep knowledge tracing outperformed traditional BKT (see earlier), but Khajah, Lindsey, and Mozer (2016) found equitable performance compared with enhanced versions of BKT.

The third approach is to find associations—frequently occurring subsequences among a set of sequences (e.g., A → B is a subsequence of $\underline{A}$ → $\underline{B}$ → C and also of $\underline{A}$ → J → K → K → C → $\underline{B}$ → L)—using fast algorithms designed for this task (Srikant & Agrawal, 1996). For example, Zhou, Xu, Nesbit, and Winne (2010) investigated self-regulatory processes by identifying frequently occurring candidate sequences from clickstreams generated as students used a digital tracking tool called nStudy.

The fourth approach is to use techniques from time-series analyses, such as lag-sequential analysis, recurrence quantification analysis, growth curve modeling, dynamic time warping, and countless other techniques to investigate the phenomenon of interest.

Content Analysis and Natural Language Processing

Educational data are heavily linguistic, consisting of texts, lecture notes, word problems, student open-ended responses, more formal essays, discussion posts, verbose feedback, and so on. Text analysis plays an important role in a number of applications, for example predicting MOOC completion by analyzing discussion posts (Crossley, Paquette, Dascalu, McNamara, & Baker, 2016), automatic essay grading (Dong, Zhang, & Yang, 2017), assessing student knowledge (Graesser, Penumatsa, Ventura, Cai, & Hu, 2007), investigating reading processes (Mills, Graesser, Risko, & D'Mello, 2017), and analyzing spoken discourse in collaborative learning (Howley, Mayfield, & Rosé, 2012).

There are four major approaches to analyzing textual data. The first consists of using computer programs, such as Coh-Metrix (Graesser, McNamara, & Kulikowich, 2011), to derive higher order features via a multilevel analysis at the word, sentence, paragraph, or text level or even across multiple texts. The second approach, called the closed-vocabulary approach, entails counting occurrences of predefined word categories (e.g., affective terms, future terms) obtained from theoretically grounded and psychometrically validated dictionaries, the most popular being the Linguistic Inquiry and Word Count

(Tausczik & Pennebaker, 2010; but see also the Sentiment Analysis and Social Cognition Engine; Crossley, Kyle, & McNamara, 2017). In contrast, open-vocabulary approaches do not rely on existing word categories but derive language features from the texts themselves, by counting, for example, frequent unigrams (i.e., single words), bigrams and trigrams (i.e., phrases), and topic distributions—clusters of semantically similar words (Blei, Ng, & Jordan, 2003). The fourth major approach, which is gaining increasing popularity in the era of deep learning, is to directly model sequences of words via word embeddings (converting them to real-valued vectors) using deep RNNs like LSTMs (Dong et al., 2017).

Multisensory, Multimodal Modeling

A majority of data-intensive research in the learning sciences focuses on behavioral (e.g., clickstreams, responses to assessment items) and textual data with the main goal of analyzing the cognitive aspects of learning, such as student knowledge and skills. Researchers have been expanding the bandwidth of sensory streams by considering additional modalities, such as facial expressions, gestures, posture, paralinguistics, eye movements, and peripheral and central physiology, to better understand factors that modulate the cognitive aspects of learning, such as motivation, emotion, metacognition, and social relations. Much of the research so far has focused on modeling affective states, such as boredom, confusion, frustration, anxiety, and happiness, because these states are tightly coupled with cognitive processing (D'Mello & Graesser, 2012; Mandler, 1976), operate continually throughout learning (Pekrun & Linnenbrink-Garcia, 2012), and occur quite frequently when learning from digital technologies (D'Mello, 2013).

One key research thrust is to develop objective measures of these mental states to complement self-reports, which is the dominant measurement method despite known limitations (Duckworth & Yeager, 2015). This requires interdisciplinary collaboration from a host of research areas, such as computer vision (to extract information from video), speech processing (to compute paralinguistics), computational psychophysiology (to process physiological signals such as electrodermal response, pupillometry, electromyography, and electrocardiography), and computational neuroscience (for electroencephalography and functional near-infrared spectroscopy [fNIRS]; fMRI is typically not analyzed). Researchers then use machine learning techniques, specifically supervised learning, to build computational models of affective states from these sensing streams (see Calvo & D'Mello, 2010; D'Mello, Dieterle, & Duckworth, 2017; D'Mello, Kappas, & Gratch, 2018; Zeng, Pantic, Roisman, & Huang, 2009, for reviews). The individual modalities can also be combined using multimodal fusion techniques (D'Mello, Bosch, & Chen, 2018) with varying degrees of success, as discussed in D'Mello and Kory (2015). The resultant computational models can be used in a number of ways as a measurement tool to better understand mental states during learning or as a means to trigger real-time interventions that are sensitive to the senses states (see D'Mello, Blanchard, Baker, Ocumpaugh, & Brawner, 2014, for a review).

CASE STUDIES

I now turn to four case studies from our lab to illustrate a broad range of research goals, data, and methods. I direct interested readers to a couple of handbooks (Lang, Siemens, Wise, & Gašević, 2017; Romero, Ventura, Pechenizkiy, & Baker, 2010) and the conference proceedings of the organizations mentioned earlier for other examples.

Scaling Up: Sensor-Free Measurement of Engagement During Online Learning

Most would agree that engagement is necessary for learning. A student who is actively engaged is primed to learn; one who is bored and only superficially attending is not. Engagement is a multicomponent construct involving cognitive, affective, behavioral, motivational, and agentic components (Fredricks, Blumenfeld, & Paris, 2004; Pekrun & Linnenbrink-Garcia, 2012) that play out across multiple time scales and can be analyzed from multiple perspectives, such as person oriented, person in context, or context oriented (Sinatra, Heddy, & Lombardi, 2015).

Progress in understanding engagement is stifled by a lack of measures. Self-report questionnaires, which are the dominant measure of engagement (Fredricks & McColskey, 2012), are easy to administer and are scalable but have several well-known limitations (Duckworth & Yeager, 2015). More objective measures, such as teacher reports, online observations, and video coding, alleviate several of the limitations of self-reports but are labor intensive and do not scale.

What about actions? Because cognition is in the service of action, we should be able to make inferences on cognitive states and their moderating influences (i.e., engagement) from observable behaviors (D'Mello et al., 2017). We adopt this perspective with the goal of modeling the cognitive and affective states (e.g., interest, curiosity, self-regulation) associated with engagement from observable behaviors. These measures can be sensor based, akin to the multisensory, multimodal approach discussed previously, or sensor free, where clickstream data recorded in logs is used for this purpose (Baker & Ocumpaugh, 2015). The basic approach is to train supervised classifiers to associate student activity from log files with human-provided engagement labels (via self- or observer reports) in a manner that generalizes to new learners. Recent efforts have shown considerable progress along this front, with behavior-based engagement models predicting valued outcomes such as standardized test scores (Pardos, Baker, San Pedro, & Gowda, 2013) and college enrollment (San Pedro, Baker, Bowers, & Heffernan, 2013). However, contemporary methods are limited by overfitting models to system-specific activity data (e.g., specific videos watched or items answered), relatively small and insufficiently diverse student samples (typically a few hundred students), and short time frames of a week or less (D'Mello et al., 2017).

Taking a different approach, we focused on generic activity measures with an eye for scalability to tens of thousands of diverse students across extended time frames of an entire school year and beyond (Grafsgaard, Keirn, & D'Mello, 2019). Our generic activity features (e.g., viewing any video lecture vs. Lecture X from Platform Y) were designed to be applicable to additional domains and similar learning environments. We collected these features from a large-scale data set of over 25,000 introductory algebra students who used Algebra Nation, an online math learning platform, as part of their regular math classes for a semester. We used experience sampling to collect self-reports (to train supervised classifiers) of 18 mental states related to engagement. The reports were probabilistically triggered as students interacted with Algebra Nation.

We trained LSTM RNNs and feedforward neural networks to predict these mental states from activity sequences (e.g., video selected → paused → resume → quit → quiz selected) 5 minutes before the self-reports. The models were validated in a student-independent manner such that data from the same student could never be in the training and testing set. The models were (a) most predictive (Spearman's $\rho > 0.3$) of frustration, confusion, and happiness; (b) moderately predictive ($0.2 < \rho < 0.3$) of hopefulness, relief, disappointment, engagement (global measure), contentment, pride, and pleasantness; (c) less predictive ($0.09 < \rho < 0.2$) of mind wandering, anxiety, interest, boredom, sadness, and arousal; and (d) not predictive ($\rho < .04$) of curiosity and surprise.

Although there is considerable room for improvement, these results show the promise of scaling up sensor-free affect detection on the largest and most heterogeneous student sample to date using generic activity features that are not specific to a particular domain or system. We are in the process of customizing these models to particular student cohorts (based on cluster analyses) while studying generalizability to novel subject matter (e.g., Algebra 2 and Geometry) and even other learning environments. We are also considering personalizing the online learning environment based on automatically measured levels of engagement. Stay tuned!

Who Will Make It? Predicting 4-Year College Graduation From Student Applications

There are numerous benefits to earning a college degree. For one, the 2015 median earnings for young U.S. adults (25–34 years of age) with a bachelor's degree were 64% higher than those who had only completed high school, a consistent pattern over the past 15 years (McFarland et al., 2017). In addition to economic gains for the student, college completion also correlates with economic gains for the nation as a whole (Carnevale, Rose, & Cheah, 2011).

It is even more important to graduate on time because it is estimated that every additional year in a 4-year public institution costs an extra $22,826 in college-related expenses and $45,327 in lost wages (Complete College America, 2014). Yet, on-time graduation rates are abysmal—only 40% of first-time, full-time, U.S. students graduated with a bachelor's degree within 4 years (National Center for Education Statistics, 2016; 60% graduated within 6 years). There is also a significant achievement gap, with only 21% of Black and 30% of Hispanic students graduating within 4 years compared with 44% White and 48% Asian and Pacific Islander students (National Center for Education Statistics, 2016). Can big data help?

We addressed this question by leveraging the Common Application-National Student Clearinghouse data set—a 6-year longitudinal de-identified data set of college application data with 4- and 6-year graduation outcomes for 273,196 U.S. high school students. Our first question pertained to how accurately we could predict 4-year graduation solely from the information contained in the college application. Our initial analysis (Hutt, Gardener, Kamentz, Duckworth, & D'Mello, 2018) focused on a subset of 41,359 college applications from all 50 states. Using a combined theory-guided and data-driven approach, we extracted a set of 166 features spanning sociodemographics, institutional graduation rates, academic achievement (e.g., high school grade point average), standardized test scores, honors (e.g., type of honor, level—school vs. state), engagement in extracurricular activities (e.g., type of the activity, time commitment), work experiences (e.g., number of jobs), and ratings by teachers and high school guidance counselors (e.g., students' reaction to setbacks, quality of writing). A random forest classifier successfully predicted 4-year graduation for 71.4% of the students (base rate = 44%) using all 166 features and a split-half validation method.

Next, we used a stochastic hill-climbing (a local optimization algorithm) feature selection procedure to select a minimal set of 37 features while maintaining the same classification accuracy. The retained features consisted of an approximately equal representation of sociodemographics, academics and test scores, and extracurriculars and work experiences. Of particular interest are the extracurriculars and work experiences because they are hypothesized to provide a context for the development and demonstration of key noncognitive characteristics, such as initiative (Larson, Hansen, & Moneta, 2006), identity (Eccles, Barber, Stone, & Hunt, 2003), competence, confidence, and character (Bowers et al., 2010).

In summary, motivated by the maxim that the best predictor of future behavior is past behavior, our big biodata approach successfully predicted 4-year bachelor's graduation with 71% accuracy using application data completed before students spent a single day in college. But prediction is not the same as generating insight (see the next section). We are currently investigating Bayesian structure learning (a method to automatically learn the structure in a Bayesian network; Tsamardinos, Brown, & Aliferis, 2006) to understand causal links between sociodemographics, cognitive ability, and extracurricular engagement in predicting 4-year graduation. We are also clustering students based on affordances of their home, school, and neighborhood environments to tailor insights gleaned from the causal model to specific youth.

Zoning Out? Multimodal Detection of Mind Wandering in Real-World Classrooms

It may be surprising to some to learn that when performing a task, our thoughts often drift toward things completely unrelated to the task at hand (Killingsworth & Gilbert, 2010), a phenomenon called *mind wandering* (more colloquially, daydreaming or zoning out). Mind wandering is perfectly fine for tasks with low attentional demands (e.g., performing household chores, showering) and can even serve as a "mental" escape from our physical environment (Mooneyham & Schooler, 2013) or from the doldrums. People's general propensity to mind wander may even be positively linked with creativity (Baird et al., 2012).

Alas, things go awry when the task at hand requires sustained attention over extended periods. Learning is one such task. Hence, it should come as no surprise that mind wandering is both frequent during learning—occurring about 30% of the time—and is negatively correlated ($r_+ = -.24$) with learning outcomes (based on a selective meta-analysis of 25 studies D'Mello, 2019). Thus, there might be advantages to real-time detection and intervention to mitigate mind wandering.

Whereas previous work attempted mind wandering detection in controlled lab settings (e.g., Faber, Bixler, & D'Mello, 2018; Pham & Wang, 2015), we recently took a stab at doing it in the classroom. We focused on eye gaze because there is a close link between eye movements and attention—the so-called eye–mind link (Rayner, 1998). Our approach uses commercial off-the-shelf (COTS) eye trackers, which retail for as little as $100 (compared with $10K+ for research-grade trackers), to track the locus of students' visual attention. We first tested the feasibility of COTS eye tracking while groups of high-school students ($N = 135$) completed two 30-minute tutorial sessions with a biology ITS called GuruTutor (Olney et al., 2012). The sessions were conducted in students' regular biology classroom during their scheduled class period. We could successfully track eye gaze 75% (both eyes tracked) and 95% (one eye tracked) of the time for the sessions where gaze was successfully recorded (85%).

We asked students to self-report mind wandering by responding to pseudorandom thought probes interspersed throughout the learning session. We computed eye-gaze features (e.g., number of fixations, fixation durations, blinks) in 30-second windows preceding each probe and trained supervised classifiers (Bayesian networks) to discriminate between positive and negative probe responses from the gaze features. The models were specifically trained to avoid overfitting to individual students (i.e., using student-level cross-validation). We were moderately successful in detecting mind wandering, achieving a precision of 55% and a recall of 65%, with a mind wandering F_1 of 0.59 (compared with a chance F_1 of 0.23; Hutt et al., 2017).

We then tested live mind wandering detection on a new sample of 39 students (Hutt et al., 2019). This was done by analyzing eye gaze in real time, running it through the aforementioned offline mind wandering detector and triggering a thought probe based on the observed likelihood of mind wandering (rather than pseudorandomly). We found that the accuracy of real-time mind wandering detection (F_1 = .40) was lower than offline detection accuracy (F_1 = 0.59) but was much better than chance (F_1 = 0.24). Furthermore, both offline and real-time mind wandering detection negatively correlated with learning on a subsequent posttest (Spearman ρ's around −.20), thereby providing some evidence for their predictive validity.

We experimented with a second automated mind wandering detector on the same data, this time using facial expressions automatically extracted from video captured using commercial webcams (Bosch & D'Mello, in press). Although the face-based models (F_1 = 0.35) were less accurate than the gaze models (F_1 of 0.47; different from the previous models), they outperformed chance (F_1 = 0.25). Importantly, we found that combining both models improved accuracy (F_1 = 0.50) when one modality had missing data (Hutt et al., 2019).

Thus, it is possible to collect eye gaze and facial expressions with sufficient fidelity to build "in the wild" automated measures of mind wandering despite the challenges inherent in noisy real-world classrooms. We are currently integrating these models into an attention-aware version of GuruTutor (D'Mello, 2016) that aims to detect mind wandering in real time and respond with dynamic interventions to reengage learners and improve learning outcomes.

Big Data in the Science of Teaching: Automatic Analysis of Real-World Classroom Discourse

Most applications of data science in education are focused on the students. What about the teachers? The little we know about what teachers do in the classroom is derived from the occasional classroom observation, which is usually evaluative rather than formative. Current in-person observational methods are also logistically complex, require observer training, are an expensive allocation of administrators' time, and simply do not scale. Further, teachers rarely get regular, detailed feedback about their classroom practice, and given the importance of feedback to learning (Shute, 2008), it is unsurprising that teaching effectiveness plateaus after 5 years in the profession despite considerable room for growth (The New Teacher Project, 2015).

Can computers help? We think so. As an initial proof of concept, we attempted to automate the collection and analysis of classroom discourse with a specific emphasis on authentic questions. These are open-ended questions without a prescripted response (e.g., Do you think Abigail is going to tell the truth?; Juzwik, Borsheim-Black, Caughlan, & Heintz, 2013, p. 27) that are linked to engagement and achievement growth (Applebee, Langer, Nystrand, & Gamoran, 2003; Nystrand, 1997).

The overall approach proceeded as follows. We first experimented with different recording configurations and microphones to balance a set of technical requirements and constraints (D'Mello et al., 2015). For example, cameras could not be used because of privacy concerns, and students could not be individually miked because of scalability concerns. We selected a wireless Samson AirLine 77 vocal headset system for teachers and a Crown PZM-30D pressure zone microphone to record general classroom activity. We used this setup to record 7,663 minutes of audio, comprising 132, 30 to 90-minute class sessions from 27 classrooms taught by 14 teachers in seven schools over five semesters. At the same time, a trained observer used live coding software to identify (a) instructional activities (e.g., lecture, small group work), (b) teacher and student questions, and (c) question properties (e.g., authenticity). The live annotations were refined offline and checked by a second coder.

We proceeded with data analysis as follows. First, using an amplitude-envelope voice activity detection method we developed for this task (D'Mello et al., 2015), we obtained a total of 45,044 teacher utterances with a median length of 2.26 seconds. The spoken utterances were automatically transcribed using Microsoft Bing Speech, which yielded a speech recognition accuracy of 53.3% (Bing) when word order was considered and 61.5% when it was ignored.

We focused on two subtasks before addressing authenticity detection. First, we trained supervised learning models to automatically identify the five instructional activities (e.g., question and answer, lecture, small group work) that collectively comprised a majority (76%) of the data based on discourse timing (e.g., patterns of speech and rest, length of utterance) and linguistic (e.g., parts of speech, identification of question words) and paralinguistic (e.g., volume, pitch contours) features extracted from teacher audio. We achieved F_1 scores, ranging from .64 to .78, which reflect a substantial improvement over chance (Donnelly et al., 2016a). We subsequently included features from the classroom microphone, which resulted in a further 8% improvement (Donnelly et al., 2016b).

We also trained supervised classifiers to automatically identify individual teacher questions using linguistic features only and achieved an F_1 score of .59, representing a 51% improvement over chance (Blanchard et al., 2016). When averaging the individual predictions across a class session, the automated estimates were strongly correlated (Pearson's $r = .85$) with human-coded question rates. We obtained a further improvement in F_1 (.69) by adding acoustic and contextual features (Donnelly et al., 2017).

Finally, we focused on authentic question detection. Because these questions were rare compared with all teacher utterances (about 3%), we focused on estimating the proportion of authentic questions per class session rather than on identifying individual authentic questions. We experimented with both closed- and open-vocabulary approaches for this task. For the closed-vocabulary approach, we extended a handcrafted set of word and part-of-speech features useful for classifying question types (Olney et al., 2003) to include word-level, utterance-level, and discourse-level features obtained through syntactic and discourse parsing (Manning et al., 2014). Examples included named entity type (e.g., LOCATION), question stems (e.g., "what"), word position and order (e.g., whether the named entity PERSON feature occurred at the first word or the last word), and referential chains (connections across utterances via pronouns and their referents). Using M5P regression trees (a type of random regression tree; Quinlan, 1992), we obtained a 0.602 correlation in predicting authenticity compared with gold standard codes (Kelly, Olney, Donnelly, Nystrand, & D'Mello, 2018). The model was trained in a manner that generalizes to new teachers to prevent overfitting.

For the open-vocabulary approach, we derived frequently occurring words and phrases (unigrams, bigrams, and N-grams) from the transcripts themselves and trained M5P regression trees with these features (Cook, Olney, Kelly, & D'Mello, 2018). Although this did not result in performance improvements over the previous closed-vocabulary approach ($r = 0.613$), a combined model that averaged predictions from the two approaches improved the correlation to 0.686. We replicated these results on a large archival database of text transcripts of approximately 25,000 questions from 451 observations of 112 classrooms (Cook et al., 2018).

Our results confirm the feasibility of fully automated approaches to analyze classroom discourse despite the noisy nature of real-world classroom discourse, which includes conversational speech, multiparty chatter, background noise, and so on. The next step is to integrate the models into technologies that provide feedback to researchers, teachers, teacher educators, and professional development personnel.

FOOD FOR THOUGHT: ETHICAL AND PRACTICAL CONSIDERATIONS FOR RESEARCH

Thus far, I have extolled the many virtues of big data and the computational approach to the science of learning. But, like everything, there are costs associated with the many benefits of big data. One is the cost to privacy and security and, by extension, trust, accountability, and transparency. Data mining in education has been met with concern from parents (rightly so), a joint House subcommittee hearing with perhaps a flair for the dramatic (Committee on Homeland Security, 2014), and calls for a "student privacy bill of rights" (Strauss, 2014). Researchers have responded with best practice guidelines for protecting the privacy and security of student data (Zeide, 2017). I will not repeat this discussion here, except to say that de-identification is often offered as a knee-jerk solution to all privacy concerns. However, one has to be realistic about promises of de-identification because data is technically re-identifiable (Narayanan & Shmatikov, 2010), and some multimodal data inherently contain personally identifiable information in the form of biomarkers (e.g., facial images, vocal patterns).

Researchers have also explored some of the ethical issues that arise in a data-driven world (Prinsloo & Slade, 2017). Let me pose two additional mandates in addition to those covered under general guidelines for behaving ethically. For researchers in academia, let us be at the forefront of ethical issues that are not the main concern of industry, such as issues of equity and equality in education, so we can do our part in closing the achievement gap. For those in industry, especially the hundreds of startups on personalized learning, rather than adopting the tenuous assumption that "usage equals learning," a suggested mandate is to collect and provide high-standard evidence of learning (e.g., https://ies.ed.gov/ncee/wwc/) before selling products to cash-strapped school districts.

Finally, it is worth asking whether the easy availability of data has reduced our creativity and ingenuity. Specifically, much of the modeling approaches in the field are directed toward classification and prediction, leading one to question whether supervised learning is our main "hammer," causing us to conceive all problems as "nails." Supervised learning is invaluable for detecting, identifying, or predicting an outcome of interest but contributes little to nothing in terms of providing actionable insights to manipulate these outcomes. Even worse, researchers sometimes mistakenly bestow causal powers to influential correlates of an outcome even when a more likely cause is lurking in plain sight. We need alternate "tools" to identify causal chains to target interventions on variables with causal agency. We need explanatory modeling where the goal is to discover causal relationships between constructs that can be directly measured or inferred from auxiliary indicators (Liu & Koedinger, 2017). I believe the true power of data comes from combining data-driven and theory-based models, achievable by combining predictive and causal models, though this is rarely done.

In conclusion, we are living in the midst of a data and computation revolution. What happens when enormous quantities of data mesh with unsurpassed computation capabilities and enter the science of learning? It is anybody's guess, but we are the ones who, at least partly, get to decide.

REFERENCES

Agrawal, R., & Srikant, R. (1994). Fast algorithms for mining association rules. In J. B. Bocca, M. Jarke, & C. Zaniolo (Eds.), *Proceedings of the 20th International Conference on Very Large Data Bases* (pp. 487–499). San Francisco, CA: Morgan Kaufmann.

Aguiar, E., Ambrose, G. A. A., Chawla, N. V., Goodrich, V., & Brockman, J. (2014). Engagement vs performance: Using electronic portfolios to predict first semester engineering student persistence. *Journal of Learning Analytics*, *1*(3), 7–33. http://dx.doi.org/10.18608/jla.2014.13.3

Anderson, J. R. (1982). Acquisition of cognitive skill. *Psychological Review, 89,* 369–406. http://dx.doi.org/10.1037/0033-295X.89.4.369

Applebee, A. N., Langer, J. A., Nystrand, M., & Gamoran, A. (2003). Discussion-based approaches to developing understanding: Classroom instruction and student performance in middle and high school English. *American Educational Research Journal, 40,* 685–730. http://dx.doi.org/10.3102/00028312040003685

Baird, B., Smallwood, J., Mrazek, M. D., Kam, J. W., Franklin, M. S., & Schooler, J. W. (2012). Inspired by distraction: Mind wandering facilitates creative incubation. *Psychological Science, 23,* 1117–1122. http://dx.doi.org/10.1177/0956797612446024

Baker, R., & Ocumpaugh, J. (2015). Interaction-based affect detection in educational software. In R. Calvo, S. D'Mello, J. Gratch, & A. Kappas (Eds.), *The Oxford handbook of affective computing* (pp. 233–245). New York, NY: Oxford University Press.

Bengio, Y., Simard, P., & Frasconi, P. (1994). Learning long-term dependencies with gradient descent is difficult. *IEEE Transactions on Neural Networks, 5*(2), 157–166. http://dx.doi.org/10.1109/72.279181

Blanchard, N., Donnelly, P., Olney, A. M., Samei, B., Ward, B., Sun, X., . . . D'Mello, S. K. (2016). Identifying teacher questions using automatic speech recognition in live classrooms. *Proceedings of the 17th Annual SIGdial Meeting on Discourse and Dialogue* (pp. 191–201). Stroudsburg, PA: Association for Computational Linguistics.

Blei, D. M., Ng, A. Y., & Jordan, M. I. (2003). Latent Dirichlet allocation. *Journal of Machine Learning Research, 3,* 993–1022.

Blikstein, P. (2013, April). *Multimodal learning analytics.* Paper presented at the Third International Conference on Learning Analytics and Knowledge, Leuven, Belgium.

Bosch, N., & D'Mello, S. K. (in press). Detecting mind wandering from video in the lab and in the wild. *IEEE Transactions on Affective Computing.*

Bowers, E. P., Li, Y., Kiely, M. K., Brittian, A., Lerner, J. V., & Lerner, R. M. (2010). The Five Cs model of positive youth development: A longitudinal analysis of confirmatory factor structure and measurement invariance. *Journal of Youth and Adolescence, 39,* 720–735. http://dx.doi.org/10.1007/s10964-010-9530-9

Boyer, K., Young, E., Wallis, M., Phillips, R., Vouk, M., & Lester, J. (2009). Discovering tutorial dialogue strategies with hidden Markov models. In V. Dimitrova, R. Mizoguchi, B. Du Boulay, & A. Graesser (Eds.), *Proceedings of the 14th International Conference on Artificial Intelligence in Education* (pp. 141–148). Amsterdam, Netherlands: IOS Press.

Cade, W., Copeland, J., Person, N., & D'Mello, S. K. (2008). Dialogue modes in expert tutoring. In B. Woolf, E. Aimeur, R. Nkambou, & S. Lajoie (Eds.), *Proceedings of the 9th International Conference on Intelligent Tutoring Systems* (pp. 470–479). Berlin/ Heidelberg, Germany: Springer-Verlag.

Calvo, R. A., & D'Mello, S. K. (2010). Affect detection: An interdisciplinary review of models, methods, and their applications. *IEEE Transactions on Affective Computing, 1*(1), 18–37. http://dx.doi.org/10.1109/T-AFFC.2010.1

Canfield, W. (2001). ALEKS: A web-based intelligent tutoring system. *Mathematics and Computer Education, 35,* 152–158.

Carnevale, A. P., Rose, S. J., & Cheah, B. (2011). *The college payoff: Education, occupations, lifetime earnings.* Washington, DC: Georgetown University Center on Education and the Workforce.

Cen, H., Koedinger, K., & Junker, B. (2006). Learning factors analysis—A general method for cognitive model evaluation and improvement. In M. Ikeda, K. D. Ashley, & T.-W. Chan (Eds.), *Proceedings of the 8th International Conference on Intelligent Tutoring Systems* (pp. 164–175). Berlin, Germany: Springer.

Chapelle, O., Schölkopf, B., & Zien, A. (Eds.). (2006). *Semi-supervised learning.* Cambridge, MA: MIT Press. http://dx.doi.org/10.7551/mitpress/9780262033589. 001.0001

Chi, M., Koedinger, K. R., Gordon, G. J., Jordon, P., & VanLahn, K. (2011). Instructional factors analysis: A cognitive model for multiple instructional interventions. In M. Pechenizkiy, T. Calders, C. Conati, S. Ventura, C. Romero, & J. C. Stamper (Eds.), *Proceedings of the 4th International Conference on Educational Data Mining* (pp. 61–70). Boston, MA: International Educational Data Mining Society.

Committee on Homeland Security. (2014). *How data mining threatens student privacy.* Retrieved from https://archive.org/details/gov.gpo.fdsys.CHRG-113hhrg91448

Complete College America. (2014). *Four-year myth.* Indianapolis, IN: Author.

Conati, C., & Maclaren, H. (2009). Empirically building and evaluating a probabilistic model of user affect. *User Modeling and User-Adapted Interaction, 19,* 267–303. http://dx.doi.org/10.1007/s11257-009-9062-8

Cook, C., Olney, A., Kelly, S., & D'Mello, S. K. (2018). An open vocabulary approach for detecting authentic questions in classroom discourse. In *Proceedings of the 11th International Conference on Educational Data Mining* (pp. 116–126). Boston, MA: International Educational Data Mining Society.

Corbett, A., & Anderson, J. (1994). Knowledge tracing: Modeling the acquisition of procedural knowledge. *User Modeling and User-Adapted Interaction, 4,* 253–278. http://dx.doi.org/10.1007/BF01099821

Crossley, S. A., Kyle, K., & McNamara, D. S. (2017). Sentiment Analysis and Social Cognition Engine (SEANCE): An automatic tool for sentiment, social cognition, and social-order analysis. *Behavior Research Methods, 49,* 803–821. http://dx.doi.org/10.3758/s13428-016-0743-z

Crossley, S. A., Paquette, L., Dascalu, M., McNamara, D. S., & Baker, R. S. (2016). Combining click-stream data with NLP tools to better understand MOOC completion. In S. Dawson, H. Drachsler, & C. P. Rosé (Eds.), *Proceedings of the Sixth International Conference on Learning Analytics & Knowledge* (pp. 6–14). New York, NY: ACM.

D'Mello, S. (2013). A selective meta-analysis on the relative incidence of discrete affective states during learning with technology. *Journal of Educational Psychology, 105,* 1082–1099. http://dx.doi.org/10.1037/a0032674

D'Mello, S., Dieterle, E., & Duckworth, A. (2017). Advanced, analytic, automated (AAA) measurement of engagement during learning. *Educational Psychologist, 52,* 104–123. http://dx.doi.org/10.1080/00461520.2017.1281747

D'Mello, S., & Graesser, A. (2012). Dynamics of affective states during complex learning. *Learning and Instruction, 22,* 145–157. http://dx.doi.org/10.1016/j.learninstruc.2011.10.001

D'Mello, S. K. (2016). Giving eyesight to the blind: Towards attention-aware AIED. *International Journal of Artificial Intelligence in Education, 26,* 645–659. http://dx.doi.org/10.1007/s40593-016-0104-1

D'Mello, S. K. (2019). What do we think about when we learn? In K. Millis, J. Magliano, D. Long, & K. Wiemer (Eds.), *Deep comprehension: Multi-disciplinary approaches to understanding, enhancing, and measuring comprehension* (pp. 52–67). New York, NY: Routledge.

D'Mello, S. K., Blanchard, N., Baker, R., Ocumpaugh, J., & Brawner, K. (2014). I feel your pain: A selective review of affect-sensitive instructional strategies. In R. Sottilare, A. Graesser, X. Hu, & B. Goldberg (Eds.), *Design recommendations for adaptive intelligent tutoring systems: Adaptive instructional strategies* (Vol. 2, pp. 35–48). Orlando, FL: U.S. Army Research Laboratory.

D'Mello, S. K., Bosch, N., & Chen, H. (2018). Multimodal, multisensory affect detection. In S. Oviatt, P. Cohen, & A. Krueger (Eds.), *The handbook of multimodal-multisensor interfaces* (pp. 167–202). New York, NY: ACM Books/Morgan Claypool.

D'Mello, S. K., Kappas, A., & Gratch, J. (2018). The affective computing approach to affect measurement. *Emotion Review, 10,* 174–183. http://dx.doi.org/10.1177/1754073917696583

D'Mello, S. K., & Kory, J. (2015). A review and meta-analysis of multimodal affect detection systems. *ACM Computing Surveys, 47,* 43:41–43:46.

D'Mello, S. K., Olney, A. M., Blanchard, N., Samei, B., Sun, X., Ward, B., & Kelly, S. (2015). Multimodal capture of teacher-student interactions for automated dialogic analysis in live classrooms. In *Proceedings of the 2015 ACM on International Conference on Multimodal Interaction* (pp. 557–566). New York, NY: ACM.

Dong, F., Zhang, Y., & Yang, J. (2017). Attention-based recurrent convolutional neural network for automatic essay scoring. In *Proceedings of the 21st Conference on Computational Natural Language Learning* (pp. 153–162). Stroudsburg, PA: Association for Computational Linguistics.

Donnelly, P., Blanchard, N., Olney, A. M., Kelly, S., Nystrand, M., & D'Mello, S. K. (2017). Words matter: Automatic detection of questions in classroom discourse using linguistics, paralinguistics, and context. In X. Ochoa, I. Molenaar, & S. Dawson (Eds.), *Proceedings of the 7th International Learning Analytics and Knowledge Conference* (pp. 218–227). New York, NY: ACM.

Donnelly, P., Blanchard, N., Samei, B., Olney, A. M., Sun, X., Ward, B., . . . D'Mello, S. K. (2016a). Automatic teacher modeling from live classroom audio. In L. Aroyo, S. D'Mello, J. Vassileva, & J. Blustein (Eds.), *Proceedings of the 2016 ACM on International Conference on User Modeling, Adaptation, & Personalization* (pp. 45–53). New York, NY: ACM.

Donnelly, P., Blanchard, N., Samei, B., Olney, A. M., Sun, X., Ward, B., . . . D'Mello, S. K. (2016b). Multi-sensor modeling of teacher instructional segments in live classrooms. In *Proceedings of the 18th ACM International Conference on Multimodal Interaction* (pp. 177–184). New York, NY: ACM.

Duckworth, A. L., & Yeager, D. S. (2015). Measurement matters: Assessing personal qualities other than cognitive ability for educational purposes. *Educational Researcher, 44,* 237–251. http://dx.doi.org/10.3102/0013189X15584327

Eccles, J. S., Barber, B. L., Stone, M., & Hunt, J. (2003). Extracurricular activities and adolescent development. *Journal of Social Issues, 59,* 865–889. http://dx.doi.org/10.1046/j.0022-4537.2003.00095.x

Faber, M., Bixler, R., & D'Mello, S. K. (2018). An automated behavioral measure of mind wandering during computerized reading. *Behavior Research Methods, 50,* 134–150. http://dx.doi.org/10.3758/s13428-017-0857-y

Fredricks, J. A., Blumenfeld, P. C., & Paris, A. H. (2004). School engagement: Potential of the concept, state of the evidence. *Review of Educational Research, 74,* 59–109. http://dx.doi.org/10.3102/00346543074001059

Fredricks, J. A., & McColskey, W. (2012). The measurement of student engagement: A comparative analysis of various methods and student self-report instruments. In S. Christenson, A. Reschly, & C. Wylie (Eds.), *Handbook of research on student engagement* (pp. 763–782). New York, NY: Springer. http://dx.doi.org/10.1007/978-1-4614-2018-7_37

Graesser, A., Penumatsa, P., Ventura, M., Cai, Z., & Hu, X. (2007). Using LSA in AutoTutor: Learning through mixed-initiative dialogue in natural language. In T. Landauer, D. McNamara, S. Dennis, & W. Kintsch (Eds.), *Handbook of latent semantic analysis* (pp. 243–262). Mahwah, NJ: Erlbaum.

Graesser, A. C., McNamara, D. S., & Kulikowich, J. M. (2011). Coh-Metrix: Providing multilevel analyses of text characteristics. *Educational Researcher, 40,* 223–234. http://dx.doi.org/10.3102/0013189X11413260

Grafsgaard, J. F., Keirn, Z., & D'Mello, S. (2019). *Scaling up sensor-free affect detection using generic activity features across extended time frames.* Manuscript in preparation.

Hochreiter, S., & Schmidhuber, J. (1997). Long short-term memory. *Neural Computation, 9,* 1735–1780. http://dx.doi.org/10.1162/neco.1997.9.8.1735

Howley, I., Mayfield, E., & Rosé, C. P. (2012). Linguistic analysis methods for studying small groups. In C. E. Hmelo-Silver, C. A. Chinn, C. K. K. Chan, & A. M. O'Donnell

(Eds.), *The international handbook of collaborative learning* (pp. 184–202). New York, NY: Taylor & Francis.

Hutt, S., Gardener, M., Kamentz, D., Duckworth, A., & D'Mello, S. K. (2018). Prospectively predicting 4-year college graduation from student applications. In S. B. Shum, R. Ferguson, A. Merceron, & X. Ochoa (Eds.), *Proceedings of the 8th International Learning Analytics and Knowledge Conference* (pp. 280–289). New York, NY: ACM.

Hutt, S., Krasich, K., Mills, C., Bosch, N., White, S., Brockmole, J., & D'Mello, S. K. (2019). Automated gaze-based mind wandering detection during computerized learning in classrooms. *User Modeling and User-Adapted Interaction, 4,* 821–867. http://dx.doi.org/10.1007/s11257-019-09228-5

Hutt, S., Mills, C., Bosch, N., Krasich, K., Brockmole, J. R., & D'Mello, S. K. (2017). Out of the Fr-eye-ing pan: Towards gaze-based models of attention during learning with technology in the classroom. In M. Bielikova, E. Herder, F. Cena, & M. Desmarais (Eds.), *Proceedings of the 2017 Conference on User Modeling, Adaptation, and Personalization* (pp. 94–103). New York, NY: ACM.

Juzwik, M. M., Borsheim-Black, C., Caughlan, S., & Heintz, A. (2013). *Inspiring dialogue: Talking to learn in the English classroom.* New York, NY: Teachers College Press.

Kelly, S., Olney, A. M., Donnelly, P., Nystrand, M., & D'Mello, S. K. (2018). Automatically measuring question authenticity in real-world classrooms. *Educational Researcher, 47,* 451–464. http://dx.doi.org/10.3102/0013189X18785613

Khajah, M., Lindsey, R. V., & Mozer, M. C. (2016). How deep is knowledge tracing? In T. Barnes, M. Chi, & M. Feng (Eds.), *Proceedings of the 9th International Conference on Educational Data Mining* (pp. 94–101). Boston, MA: International Educational Data Mining Society.

Killingsworth, M. A., & Gilbert, D. T. (2010). A wandering mind is an unhappy mind. *Science, 330,* 932–932. http://dx.doi.org/10.1126/science.1192439

Koedinger, K. R., Baker, R., Cunningham, K., Skogsholm, A., Leber, B., & Stamper, J. (2010). A data repository for the EDM community: The PSLC DataShop. In C. Romero, S. Ventura, S. R. Viola, M. Pechenizkiy, & R. S. J. Baker (Eds.), *Handbook of educational data mining* (pp. 43–55). Boca Raton, FL: Chapman & Hall/CRC Press. http://dx.doi.org/10.1201/b10274-6

Kulik, J. A., & Fletcher, J. (2016). Effectiveness of intelligent tutoring systems: A meta-analytic review. *Review of Educational Research, 86,* 42–78. http://dx.doi.org/10.3102/0034654315581420

Lang, C., Siemens, G., Wise, A., & Gašević, D. (Eds.). (2017). *Handbook of learning analytics.* Beaumont, Alberta, Canada: Society for Learning Analytics Research. http://dx.doi.org/10.18608/hla17

Larson, R. W., Hansen, D. M., & Moneta, G. (2006). Differing profiles of developmental experiences across types of organized youth activities. *Developmental Psychology, 42,* 849–863. http://dx.doi.org/10.1037/0012-1649.42.5.849

Liu, R., & Koedinger, K. (2017). Going beyond better data prediction to create explanatory models of educational data. In C. Lang, G. Siemens, A. Wise, & D. Gašević (Eds.), *Handbook of learning analytics* (pp. 69–76). Beaumont, Alberta, Canada: Society for Learning Analytics Research. http://dx.doi.org/10.18608/hla17.006

Ma, W., Adesope, O. O., Nesbit, J. C., & Liu, Q. (2014). Intelligent tutoring systems and learning outcomes: A meta-analysis. *Journal of Educational Psychology, 106,* 901–918. http://dx.doi.org/10.1037/a0037123

Macfadyen, L. P., & Dawson, S. (2010). Mining LMS data to develop an "early warning system" for educators: A proof of concept. *Computers & Education, 54,* 588–599. http://dx.doi.org/10.1016/j.compedu.2009.09.008

Mandler, G. (1976). *Mind and emotion.* New York, NY: Wiley.

Manning, C. D., Surdeanu, M., Bauer, J., Finkel, J. R., Bethard, S., & McClosky, D. (2014). The stanford corenlp natural language processing toolkit. In *Proceedings of*

52nd Annual Meeting of the Association for Computational Linguistics: System Demonstrations (pp. 55–60). Stroudsburg, PA: Association for Computational Linguistics.

McFarland, J., Hussar, B., de Brey, C., Snyder, T., Wang, X., Wilkinson-Flicker, S., . . . Hinz, S. (2017). *The condition of education 2017* (NCES 2017-144). Washington, DC: U.S. Department of Education, National Center for Education Statistics.

Mills, C., Graesser, A., Risko, E. F., & D'Mello, S. K. (2017). Cognitive coupling during reading. *Journal of Experimental Psychology: General, 146,* 872–883. http://dx.doi.org/10.1037/xge0000309

Mislevy, R. J., & Haertel, G. D. (2006). Implications of evidence-centered design for educational testing. *Educational Measurement: Issues and Practice, 25*(4), 6–20. http://dx.doi.org/10.1111/j.1745-3992.2006.00075.x

Mooneyham, B. W., & Schooler, J. W. (2013). The costs and benefits of mind-wandering: A review. *Canadian Journal of Experimental Psychology/Revue canadienne de psychologie expérimentale, 67*(1), 11.

Narayanan, A., & Shmatikov, V. (2010). Myths and fallacies of personally identifiable information. *Communications of the ACM, 53*(6), 24–26. http://dx.doi.org/10.1145/1743546.1743558

National Center for Education Statistics. (2016). *Digest of education statistics 2016.* Washington, DC: U.S. Department of Education, National Center for Education Statistics.

The New Teacher Project. (2015). *Confronting the hard truth about our quest for teacher development.* New York, NY: Author.

Nystrand, M. (1997). *Opening dialogue: Understanding the dynamics of language and learning in the English classroom.* New York, NY: Teachers College Press.

Olney, A., D'Mello, A., Person, N., Cade, W., Hays, P., Williams, C., . . . Graesser, A. C. (2012). Guru: A computer tutor that models expert human tutors. In S. Cerri, W. Clancey, G. Papadourakis, & K. Panourgia (Eds.), *Proceedings of the 11th International Conference on Intelligent Tutoring Systems* (pp. 256–261). Berlin/Heidelberg, Germany: Springer-Verlag.

Olney, A., Louwerse, M., Matthews, E., Marineau, J., Hite-Mitchell, H., & Graesser, A. (2003, May). *Utterance classification in AutoTutor.* Paper presented at the HLT-NAACL 03 Workshop on Building Educational Applications Using Natural Language Processing, Philadelphia, PA.

Pardos, Z., Baker, R. S. J. d., San Pedro, M. O. C. Z., & Gowda, S. M. (2013). Affective states and state tests: Investigating how affect throughout the school year predicts end of year learning outcomes. In D. Suthers, K. Verbert, E. Duval, & X. Ochoa (Eds.), *Proceedings of the 3rd International Conference on Learning Analytics and Knowledge* (pp. 117–124). New York, NY: ACM.

Pavlik, P. I., Jr., Cen, H., & Koedinger, K. R. (2009). Performance factors analysis— A new alternative to knowledge tracing. In V. Dimitrova, R. Mizoguchi, B. D. Boulay, & A. C. Graesser (Eds.), *14th International Conference on Artificial Intelligence in Education* (pp. 531–538). Amsterdam, Netherlands: IOS Press.

Pekrun, R., & Linnenbrink-Garcia, L. (2012). Academic emotions and student engagement. In S. Christenson, A. Reschly, & C. Wylie (Eds.), *Handbook of research on student engagement* (pp. 259–282). New York, NY: Springer. http://dx.doi.org/10.1007/978-1-4614-2018-7_12

Pham, P., & Wang, J. (2015). AttentiveLearner: Improving mobile MOOC learning via implicit heart rate tracking. In *Proceedings of the International Conference on Artificial Intelligence in Education* (pp. 367–376). Berlin/Heidelberg, Germany: Springer.

Piech, C., Bassen, J., Huang, J., Ganguli, S., Sahami, M., Guibas, L. J., & Sohl-Dickstein, J. (2015). Deep knowledge tracing. In C. Cortes, N. D. Lawrence, D. D. Lee, M. Sugiyama, & R. Garnett. (Eds.), *Proceedings of the Advances in Neural Information Processing Systems 2015 Conference* (pp. 505–513). New York, NY: Curran Associates.

Prinsloo, P., & Slade, S. (2017). Ethics and learning analytics: Charting the (un) charted. In C. Lang, G. Siemens, A. Wise, & D. Gašević (Eds.), *Handbook of learning analytics* (pp. 49–57). Beaumont, Alberta, Canada: Society for Learning Analytics Research. http://dx.doi.org/10.18608/hla17.004

Quinlan, J. R. (1992, November). *Learning with continuous classes.* Paper presented at the 5th Australian Joint Conference on Artificial Intelligence, Hobart, Tasmania, Australia.

Rayner, K. (1998). Eye movements in reading and information processing: 20 years of research. *Psychological Bulletin, 124,* 372–422. http://dx.doi.org/10.1037/0033-2909. 124.3.372

Romero, C., Ventura, S., Pechenizkiy, M., & Baker, R. (Eds.). (2010). *Handbook of educational data mining.* Boca Raton, FL: Chapman & Hall/CRC Press. http://dx.doi.org/10.1201/b10274

San Pedro, M., Baker, R. S., Bowers, A. J., & Heffernan, N. T. (2013). Predicting college enrollment from student interaction with an intelligent tutoring system in middle school. In S. D'Mello, R. Calvo, & A. Olney (Eds.), *Proceedings of the 6th International Conference on Educational Data Mining* (pp. 177–184). Boston, MA: International Educational Data Mining Society.

Shute, V. (2008). Focus on formative feedback. *Review of Educational Research, 78,* 153–189. http://dx.doi.org/10.3102/0034654307313795

Shute, V. J. (2011). Stealth assessment in computer-based games to support learning. In S. Tobias & J. D. Fletcher (Eds.), *Computer games and instruction* (pp. 503–524). Charlotte, NC: Information Age.

Shute, V. J., & Moore, G. R. (2017). Consistency and validity in game-based stealth assessment. In H. Jiao & R. W. Lissitz (Eds.), *Technology enhanced innovative assessment: Development, modeling, and scoring from an interdisciplinary perspective* (pp. 31–51). Charlotte, NC: Information Age.

Sinatra, G. M., Heddy, B. C., & Lombardi, D. (2015). The challenges of defining and measuring student engagement in science. *Educational Psychologist, 50,* 1–13. http://dx.doi.org/10.1080/00461520.2014.1002924

Sleeman, D., & Brown, J. (1982). Introduction: Intelligent tutoring systems. In D. Sleeman & J. Brown (Eds.), *Intelligent Tutoring Systems* (pp. 1–11). New York, NY: Academic Press.

Sottilare, R., Graesser, A., Hu, X., & Holden, H. K. (Eds.). (2013). *Design recommendations for intelligent tutoring systems: Vol. 1. Learner modeling.* Orlando, FL: U.S. Army Research Laboratory.

Srikant, R., & Agrawal, R. (1996, March). *Mining sequential patterns: Generalizations and performance improvements.* Paper presented at the 5th International Conference on Extending Database Technology, Avignon, France.

Steenbergen-Hu, S., & Cooper, H. (2013). A meta-analysis of the effectiveness of intelligent tutoring systems on K–12 students' mathematical learning. *Journal of Educational Psychology, 105,* 970–987. http://dx.doi.org/10.1037/a0032447

Steenbergen-Hu, S., & Cooper, H. (2014). A meta-analysis of the effectiveness of intelligent tutoring systems on college students' academic learning. *Journal of Educational Psychology, 106,* 331–347. http://dx.doi.org/10.1037/a0034752

Strauss, V. (2014, March 6). Why a "student privacy bill of rights" is desperately needed. *The Washington Post.* Retrieved from https://www.washingtonpost.com/news/answer-sheet/wp/2014/03/06/why-a-student-privacy-bill-of-rights-is-desperately-needed/

Tausczik, Y. R., & Pennebaker, J. W. (2010). The psychological meaning of words: LIWC and computerized text analysis methods. *Journal of Language and Social Psychology, 29,* 24–54. http://dx.doi.org/10.1177/0261927X09351676

Tsamardinos, I., Brown, L. E., & Aliferis, C. F. (2006). The max-min hill-climbing Bayesian network structure learning algorithm. *Machine Learning, 65,* 31–78. http://dx.doi.org/10.1007/s10994-006-6889-7

VanLehn, K. (2011). The relative effectiveness of human tutoring, intelligent tutoring systems, and other tutoring systems. *Educational Psychologist, 46,* 197–221. http://dx.doi.org/10.1080/00461520.2011.611369

Vellido, A., Castro, F., & Nebot, A. (2010). Clustering educational data. In C. Romero, S. Ventura, S. R. Viola, M. Pechenizkiy, & R. S. J. Baker (Eds.), *Handbook of educational data mining* (pp. 75–92). Boca Raton, FL: Chapman & Hall/CRC Press. http://dx.doi.org/10.1201/b10274-8

Yang, D., Sinha, T., Adamson, D., & Rosé, C. P. (2013, December). *Turn on, tune in, drop out: Anticipating student dropouts in massive open online courses.* Paper presented at the 2013 NIPS Data-Driven Education Workshop, Lake Tahoe, NV.

Zeide, E. (2017). Unpacking student privacy. In C. Lang, G. Siemens, A. Wise, & D. Gašević (Eds.), *Handbook of learning analytics* (pp. 327–335). Beaumont, Alberta, Canada: Society for Learning Analytics Research. http://dx.doi.org/10.18608/hla17.028

Zeng, Z., Pantic, M., Roisman, G. I., & Huang, T. S. (2009). A survey of affect recognition methods: Audio, visual, and spontaneous expressions. *IEEE Transactions on Pattern Analysis and Machine Intelligence, 31,* 39–58. http://dx.doi.org/10.1109/TPAMI.2008.52

Zhou, M., Xu, Y., Nesbit, J. C., & Winne, P. H. (2010). Sequential pattern analysis of learning logs: Methodology and applications. In C. Romero, S. Ventura, S. R. Viola, M. Pechenizkiy, & R. S. J. Baker (Eds.), *Handbook of educational data mining* (pp. 107–121). Boca Raton, FL: CRC Press. http://dx.doi.org/10.1201/b10274-10

10

Big Data in Social Psychology

Ivan Hernandez

Social psychology studies how situations and interactions with others affect (often in subtle ways), a person's thoughts, feelings, and behaviors (Gilovich, Keltner, Chen, & Nisbett, 2016). These behavioral, affective, and cognitive outcomes occur in a variety of social contexts with countless possible precursors found in the social environment. As a result of the topic diversity, social psychologists apply a broad array of metrics and use a great deal of creativity in translating hypotheses to a multitude of social contexts. Big data, a new form of data made possible by recent computational advances, has become increasing leveraged by social psychologists to help address existing questions in novel ways.

BIG DATA DEFINED

In the past decade, how much of our daily lives is quantified has drastically increased (Marr, 2018). People interact with technology much more frequently, and those technologies contain more precise ways of recording our daily activity. In the early stages of the Internet, users participated little in creating and modifying web content. Websites consisted mostly of static pages. The website creators provided all the information, and changes to the content happened slowly. Computational limitations, including storage size, Internet speeds, and processing capacity, meant that the webpage content primarily consisted of text and low-resolution images. However, a new age of Internet

http://dx.doi.org/10.1037/0000193-011
Big Data in Psychological Research, S. E. Woo, L. Tay, and R. W. Proctor (Editors)

emerged called "Web 2.0." In this era, web developers adopted technology that could adapt to sudden influxes of data. Examples of these advancements leading to Web 2.0 are structured relational databases (e.g., MySQL, PostgreSQL) and eventually nonrelational databases (e.g., Cassandra, MongoDB), parallel and distributed processing utilities (e.g., Hadoop, Hive), decreased cost of data storage, and multicore processors (O'Reilly, 2005). These technological advances gave the users of the site the power of content creation. Website visitors could simultaneously create new webpages, edit existing pages, add commentary, upload media, and exchange ideas with others. Web developers allowed any person with an Internet connection to record his or her thoughts, feelings, and actions. Further, developers provided other users access to that information instantaneously.

Simultaneously, technology for recording daily activities became cheaper and more widespread. Wearable sensors, cameras, and smartphones became integrated throughout society during the same period that Web 2.0 developed. These connected devices form what is referred to as the *Internet of Things* (Ashton, 2009; Gubbi, Buyya, Marusic, & Palaniswami, 2013). The prevalence of Internet-enabled devices provides additional data on a user's social behaviors, and these devices often directly interface with social media, sharing the user's locations, images, and biometrics to the Internet community. Anyone who could harness the information collected and shared could access a deluge of data. This chapter largely focuses on this special category of newly available information from Web 2.0 Internet and related mobile technologies, which will subsequently be referred to as *big data*.

Although big data can take on many meanings, a commonly used taxonomy of its characteristics is the multiple v's (Laney, 2001). Specifically, big data distinguishes itself from traditional data due to its volume (size), velocity (frequency), variety (complexity), and veracity or validity (authenticity). These defining characteristics of big data complement the defining features of social psychology.

Volume

Volume Defined

Big data distinguishes itself from traditional data, in part, by its relative volume. *Volume* represents both the raw amount of information (i.e., bytes) and the number of cases (i.e., individuals measured) in the data. Historically, social psychological studies have a median sample size of 104 participants (Fraley & Vazire, 2014) and a limited number of variables, depending on the time allotted for data collection. Big data, however, typically contains thousands or millions of individuals, each with hundreds or thousands of measurements, because it represents a comprehensive recording of online user interaction. Every click, post, and request is logged and preserved. These data are normally occurring aspects of a user's daily online experience and, therefore, are less subject to time constraints that traditional studies must manage. Whereas lab and survey studies are obstacles in the way of a user's social life, big data is often integrated into people's daily patterns, representing an essential part of people's lives. Examples of data with high volume are the millions of messages sent every day on Facebook and Twitter from their thousands of users. This vastness of data encompasses not only active users: Those who socialize with and are part of the lives of users are often implicated in the data. Half of Internet users who do not use Facebook themselves live with someone who does (Smith, 2014). This indirect connection allows the lives of the nonusers to be captured through the data posted by their roommate. Thus, big data can offer views of society that capture a multitude of individuals and their interactions.

Volume as a Complement to Social Psychology

The size of big data allows for greater statistical power and precision when examining relationships between variables. Greater statistical power is especially important when studying the subtle effects found in social psychology (Simonsohn, 2014). Likewise, because of the multivariate complexity of the phenomenon, null hypotheses are unlikely to be true, and therefore, social psychology is probably not suited for a null hypothesis significance testing framework (Gelman, 2018). Rather, when the null hypothesis is false, but the effect is potentially small, researchers place greater emphasis on estimation of the effect size. Focusing on the magnitude of the relationship provides a sense of the relative value of the finding. Just as a biologist benefits from using an electron microscope over an optical microscope to study atoms, incorporating big data allows social psychologists to study more subtle phenomena because it provides the necessary precision. The average effect size in social psychology is approximately $r = .21$, with a standard deviation of .15. Further, the effect sizes have a positively skewed distribution, with a mode of $r = .10$ (Richard, Bond, & Stokes-Zoota, 2003). The average effect size in social psychology suggests that typical studies need nearly 200 participants to reject the null hypothesis at 80% power. The modal effect size suggests that the most common sample size social psychological studies would require is nearly 783 participants. In either case, access to large data sets would facilitate studying the existing topics in the field.

Velocity

Velocity Defined

Velocity represents the speed of data collection and transmission over time. Thousands of different individuals create new instances of big data by the second and also longitudinally across the same individuals. Some examples of data with especially high velocity are messages on Twitter where the service exchanges approximately 8,000 messages every second. On Instagram, 900 new photos are posted every second (http://www.internetlivestats.com). Within users, we also see high frequencies of data. On Facebook, users make approximately 18.35 posts per month, which is equivalent to each user making a new post every 1.5 days. This high rate of sampling from people's experiences opens greater possibilities for social psychologists to study behavior.

Velocity as a Complement to Social Psychology

The velocity of big data facilitates studying questions that focus on social dynamics. Growth, change, and dissolution are all examples of phenomena that describe variation over time. Studying these phenomena requires examining their trajectories over multiple time points. Not only are certain research questions inherently dynamic but also even the findings of cross-sectional hypotheses can be considered dynamic. People and the relationships between variables change. People's knowledge of social phenomena can affect their behavior leading to outcomes not originally predicted by the theory. Therefore, it is important to constantly reexamine the phenomenon to determine its stability and the general regularities of human behavior (Schlenker, 1974). Big data's velocity provides quickly collected data, repeatedly measured across individuals. The speed of this data collection allows assessing behavior across multiple time points and temporal settings. By providing measurements from people over time, big data helps researchers understand the generalizability of their findings.

Big data's velocity also creates opportunities and challenges for studying various levels of analysis. By repeatedly recording people, researchers can aggregate behavior across different time spans. Big data researchers have the option of studying users at a daily, weekly, monthly, or yearly level depending on how they group the user's data. This flexibility can also be problematic. Specifically, the number of aggregation options may create difficulties when building theory if the constructs at various levels are not isomorphic. Researchers may inadvertently test an individual-level theory using a higher level conceptualization. That is, researchers may find that a predictor variable aggregated to the group level (e.g., average illness within a state) is positively related to a group-level outcome (average religiosity within a state; Gray & Wegner, 2010). That group-level relationship does not mean that the individual-level predictor (i.e., a person's illness) shares the same relationship with the individual-level outcome (i.e., a person's religiosity; Robinson, 1950). Therefore, it is important to qualify the findings of big data by addressing the levels that the findings apply to and do not apply to and provide multilevel analysis when appropriate. Researchers have suggested specific frameworks on isomorphic validation of multilevel constructs (Tay, Woo, & Vermunt, 2014).

Variety

Variety Defined

Variety refers to the number of forms the data can take or its multiplexity. Users generate data that span the spectrum of formats—text, photos, videos, clicks, ratings, among many others. Webpages can emphasize any combination of data formats, depending on the type of service offered. In addition, within each format is different content that can overlap with the content provided by other formats. Text can include location, age, and current thoughts. Photos can indicate location, age, interests, and feelings. Clicks can represent location (via IP address), agreement, disagreement, and interests. Users can indicate these variables explicitly through emoticons, likings of pages, profile information, and verbal endorsements. Users can also provide this information more subtly through their photographs, networks, and subscriptions. This variety provides the opportunity to examine not only a wide range of constructs but also the various manifestations of a single construct.

Variety as a Complement to Social Psychology

Big data allows users to indicate their emotions, attitudes, class, and ideologies through various indicators. Therefore, big data provides many avenues for aspects of people's traits to manifest in online settings, which can serve as reliable cues to incorporate in research (Back et al., 2010; Gosling, Augustine, Vazire, Holtzman, & Gaddis, 2011). Although social psychology has examined qualitative, mixed media data, its use is often constrained by the labor required to translate the information it contains into structured data. Using big data, researchers can move beyond the limitations historically encountered in analyzing multimedia data. Qualitative data and trace data indirectly assess the construct of interest, and methods such as content analysis or factor analysis provide ways to transform the data into the desired construct. Through machine learning, both supervised and unsupervised, researchers can better utilize the varied forms of data. These association mining techniques require larger sample sizes to perform accurately, which is a key aspect of big data. Therefore, the variety of indicators that big data provides can be analyzed in unique and more scalable ways than traditional data allow.

Social psychologists study not only a wide range of topics but also a wide range of settings and contexts. Social psychology also highlights the importance of the group and context on an individual and on a group's behavior. Certain disciplines in social psychology incorporate group, region, and cultural differences into their explanations of the human experience. This research depends on obtaining samples from diverse populations to study the effect of those settings. Because individuals form communities online and are commonly identified by different higher order grouping variables (location, race, common interest), big data makes it easier to study collective phenomena. Further, even social psychologists who do not explicitly study population differences would be interested in understanding the generalizability of their findings. Recent articles have highlighted the frequent absence of variety in psychological study populations (Henrich, Heine, & Norenzayan, 2010). By accessing diverse populations, big data serves as a means for cross-validating and exploring the boundaries of social psychological theories.

Veracity

Veracity Defined

Veracity (also called *validity*) refers to the trustworthiness of the data. Although not inherently more valid than survey-based measures, big data tends to measure specific user actions with a direct real-world implication. Ratings provided to a product represent an actual experience of engaging with a personally relevant stimulus. Messages sent to other users represent communication with other individuals with actual social connections and consequences. Photos provided by users represent actual memories and meaningful concepts to the user. The question of whether the behavior examined in big data studies replicates in the "real world" is partially addressed because the actions are occurring in the context of everyday, natural interaction.

Veracity as a Complement to Social Psychology

Big data allows behaviors to be studied in situ, keeping the individuals studied within their typical environment. The variables studied are not contrived but often have a direct connection to real-world behavior. A criticism levied against social psychology is that the field relies too heavily on indirect forms of behavior or abstract precursors to behavior (Baumeister, Vohs, & Funder, 2007). Social psychological studies disproportionately involve asking people to report on their thoughts, feelings, memories, and attitudes. If not reporting on a mental state, participants are asked to report on recent or hypothetical actions. Although measuring mental states is important for understanding psychological processes, it is still necessary to study the actual action rather than assume concordance.

One study illustrating this need conducted the same experiment two different ways (West & Brown, 1975). In one condition, people were asked what they would do if an ostensible accident victim standing on the street asked for help paying for medical care. In the other condition, people actually experienced the event on the street. Asked how they would react to such a request, people said they would give fairly generously, but people who experienced the live event donated, on average, approximately 10 cents. Further, the victim's attractiveness did not have a significant effect on hypothetical donations, but it did have a significant effect on real donations. Therefore, mental states cannot be assumed to always correspond to behavioral counterparts and can remove potentially moderating social variables from the context.

A meta-analysis found that social psychology tends to have the least correspondence between effects found in the lab versus the field, suggesting that there is a need for more applied research and testing theories in realistic settings (Mitchell, 2012). Further, big data offers greater transparency of the data collected because the data sources tend to be public and archival. Even if the data were not shared, the methods are clear enough to allow others with a minimum knowledge of programming to easily attempt replication, compared with traditional survey research that requires structured participant recruitment.

Summary of Big Data

As defined, big data falls along a multidimensional continuum, with axes representing the size, frequency, complexity, and authenticity of the data. Data that maximize these properties have become more common and easier to collect with developments in computational hardware and changes in Internet norms. Incorporating data that have these properties offers social psychology a way to address limitations that would otherwise be difficult through traditional measures.

SOURCES OF BIG DATA FOR SOCIAL PSYCHOLOGICAL RESEARCH

There are a variety of sources of big data. I present a categorization that organizes the most commonly used data into smaller overall groups. In addition, historical antecedents of big data are discussed. These precursors to modern big data sources illustrate how researchers have incorporated data with some of the defining characteristics of big data.

Precursors to Big Data Sources

Although *big data* is a relatively new term, social psychologists have long been leveraging data sets that had many of the properties of big data. These data sets, which existed before the availability of the Internet and modern technological development, contained only some of the defining characteristics of big data.

One example of an antecedent to big data in social psychological work is incorporating responses to the U.S. Census and American Community Survey. This data set, collected by the U.S. government and converted into manageable structured files by organizations such as Integrated Public Use Microdata Series USA (Ruggles, Genadek, Goeken, Grover, & Sobek, 2017), optimizes size (containing millions of records) and complexity (recording hundreds of variables) at the expense of frequency (only recorded once a year or once a month) and social context.

Similar to the census, Freedom of Information Act requests allow researchers to gain a comprehensive view of behavior across many individuals and variables. These requests can provide information on employee e-mails or city crime rates. With this information, researchers can uncover patterns in people's social networks or how environmental variables relate to crime (Diesner, Frantz, & Carley, 2005; Hutchings, Bywater, Davies, & Whitaker, 2006).

Other precursors to big data are experience sampling methodology and ecological momentary assessment. *Experience sampling methodology* (ESM) is a systematic approach for capturing experiences and activities of individuals in their ecological context (Csikszentmihalyi, Larson, & Prescott, 1977). ESM emphasizes capturing a people's representative subjective experience across a representative set of activities. Alternatively, *ecological momentary assessment*

(EMA) emphasizes monitoring a specific set of behaviors and activities in a repeated fashion, such as health states (e.g., blood pressure, heart rate), momentary behaviors (e.g., smoking), and psychological states (e.g., anger). Thus, ESM focuses on developing a representative view of various activities throughout a time span, whereas EMA examines the dynamics of specific psychological phenomena. These related methodologies both rely on obtaining multiple measurements of psychological variables at specific points and share the velocity dimension of big data. Historically, participants used paper and pencil measures at specified points. However, this method has increasingly converged with the big data paradigm by incorporating technology to prompt the user and also collect information. Researchers have translated the ESM and EMA methodology to mobile apps (e.g., Expimetrics) that can automate the scheduling, prompting and recording, and analyzing of the participant's experience.

Another example of archival data sets that preceded big data is subscription information, which is similar to how trace data is used online. Cohen (1998) acquired, at the state level from publicly available sources, viewership numbers of violent television programs (estimating the audience for the six most violent TV shows of 1980), readership of violent magazines (involving subscription rates for five violent magazines, such as *Guns and Ammo* or *Shooting Times*), National Guard enrollments and state expenditures, and hunting licenses issued per capita. These counts served as a measure of that state's endorsement of legitimate violence and facilitated studying the regional variation of violence norms.

Modern Sources of Big Data

Website Messages

One of the most widely used sources of big data in social psychology are publicly accessible messages posted by website users on the Internet. These data include blogs, micro-blogs (e.g., tweets, status updates), forum posts, and conversation threads on article comments. Because these data represent a user's shared thoughts and opinions, researchers can code the content for the presence or absence of predefined criteria. Therefore, they allow a great deal of flexibility for assessing psychological constructs because content coding schemes can be generated ad hoc, and multiple criteria can be coded for in the same text. Likewise, message text allows for other variables to be examined beyond the content, such as the writing style, number of grammatical errors, formality, and readability. These additional metrics can serve as proxies for individual differences, education level, respect, and coherence (for a review on automated text analysis, see Schwartz & Ungar, 2015).

Profile Information

Several websites offer users the opportunity to create a webpage that contains basic personal attributes such as their name, location, demographic information, work history, and relationship status. This collection of personal information, often referred to as a *profile*, provides person-level insight into people's self-image. Some examples of services that allow users to create profiles are Facebook, LinkedIn, and dating sites. Unlike messages, where psychological meaning is indirectly inferred, profile information contains clear answers to structured questions. For example, whereas a person's education level could be indirectly inferred through their writing ability, people's education history is often directly stated in their profiles. Therefore, profile information offers a complement to the benefits and limitations of unstructured messages.

Media Repositories

Messages and profiles provide information about a person in text format. However, there are additional ways to infer psychological constructs, such as content analyzing images and videos that people take of their lives and upload to media repositories. Some examples of services that allow users to store their personal media are YouTube, Instagram, and Flickr.

Reviews

Big data also includes the reviews and opinions users have left for products and services. Sites such as Amazon, Yelp, and Glassdoor all offer publicly available comments and ratings that prospective consumers can use to make informed decisions. These data sources provide insight into attitudes (including individuals' affect, behaviors, and cognitions) toward a target (e.g., product, business, employer) through this content.

User Applications

In addition to relying on a platform with existing data to query or scrape, some researchers have also created their own small applications or websites that users interact with, providing their data through those interactions. Examples of this method are applications that offer personality tests, life planners, and cognitive games for anyone online to complete. The application records users' activities while they interact with the service. The applications incentivize users to engage in various ways. Applications provide users feedback on their psychological traits, achievements from games, or personal satisfaction from having helped with scientific research. Applications made within Facebook, such as the "myPersonality" (Stillwell & Kosinski, 2004) or "thisisyourdigitallife" apps, allowed users to take validated psychometric tests. These apps were developed by academic research psychologists to both provide validated psychological insights to the user about their personality and to provide data on social interactions to the researchers. By using these apps, respondents agreed to give access to their profile and social network data, in addition to things they "liked."

Amidst privacy concerns, platforms such as Facebook have become more strict on allowing social and personality applications, specifying that "[apps] that provide (or claim to provide) users with assessments of personality, personal attributes, character traits, behavioral tendencies, or whose core functionality otherwise involves making predictions about who the user is, may not be allowed" (Facebook, 2019, Item 1.10). Despite this scrutiny, applications that record user traits and provide personalized feedback are still pervasive across other platforms, such as Apple's App Store and Google's Play store. These mobile applications can collect a variety of data beyond survey data. The "funf" app, developed at Massachusetts Institute of Technology, asks users to install an application on their phone that records the person's movement, geolocation, and activity (Eagle & Pentland, 2006). These data provide additional insight and reflect a separate dimension of its users' lives by integrating with technology already being used.

Friendship and Follower Networks

Researchers can measure not only individual users but also the social connections between users. Many of the aforementioned sites (e.g., Facebook, Twitter, Instagram, LinkedIn) also show the friends and followers of the users and, therefore, allow the context of the user to be better understood.

Wearable Sensors

Big data can also come from other types of technology that users interact with daily. The greater emphasis on digitizing and networking daily devices, called the Internet of Things, facilitates obtaining data from a wider range of settings. These devices are often ones that users can carry with them regularly. An example of these wearable sensors is an accelerometer-based tracker (e.g., Fitbit), which provides insight into people's health, movement, social engagement, and activities. The sound of people's environment can be captured with environment recording devices, which provide insight into the daily language and interactions between individuals (Mehl, Pennebaker, Crow, Dabbs, & Price, 2001). Another more integrative form of wearable technology is the sociometric badge (Olguin & Pentland, 2007). These devices capture people's interactions more broadly by combining many of the features present in other wearable sensors, such as accelerometers, sound recording, and Bluetooth transmission, into a single miniature device that can be worn around a person's neck like an employee badge.

Traces Queries and Posts

In addition to data that directly represent the action of interest (a communication, ratings, facial expressions), researchers have leveraged *trace data*, or logs of web interaction not intended for public display. These trace data indirectly indicate behaviors by using clicks and queries as proxies for the construct of interest. Search patterns, purchases, and product listings are not generally intended as a form of direct communication to another person, nor do they represent a specific evaluation. Rather, they are a remnant of people's activities. Google Trends is one example of search trace data. Using the frequency with which people search for specific symptoms and diseases in a given region, researchers have been able to detect and monitor disease outbreaks (Carneiro & Mylonakis, 2009; Ginsberg et al., 2009). Similarly, searches about life-threatening illnesses at the country level (e.g., cancer, diabetes, hypertension) predicted searches relating to religious concepts such as "God," and this finding was replicated using search data from 16 different countries (Pelham et al., 2018). These findings are consistent with those derived from Gallup survey data at the U.S. state level (Gray & Wegner, 2010).

APPLICATIONS OF BIG DATA TO SOCIAL PSYCHOLOGY

Although big data can manifest in many different forms, each of the sources described has offered insight into different areas of social psychology. In the following section, I highlight a focal topic area of social psychology, identified by the Society for Personality and Social Psychology. Within that section, I summarize specific instances where one of the types of big data has offered insight into that area.

Attitudes

Attitudes, or people's positive and negative evaluation toward a target (Eagly & Chaiken, 1993), are ubiquitous throughout social psychology—measured throughout various domains such as consumer behavior (attitudes toward products), health (attitudes toward treatments), person perception (attitudes toward new individuals), prejudice (attitudes toward racial groups), and many others. Traditionally, attitudes are measured using self-report Likert scales that ask about the overall general evaluation or about the separate affective, cognitive, and behavioral components regarding a specified target. Social psychologists interested in big data infer these ratings from online indicators that capture positive and negative evaluations. Some websites use structured indicators such as "likes," star ratings, and "upvotes" to measure a user's approval of a defined target (e.g., an event, a product or movie, a news story). In addition to using the structured indicators of attitudes, unstructured data such as reviews, comments, and messages are also used to measure an individual's evaluation via natural language processing of text to construct numeric sentiment scores. These data sources may not have a clear attitudinal rating or target, but the emotional content of the language and the structure of the sentences both provide insight into the person's evaluation.

Because attitudes correlate with intentions and subsequent behaviors, researchers have used the attitudes inferred from big data to predict future behavior with a high degree of precision. Researchers at Hewlett-Packard identified 2.89 million tweets referring to 24 different movies released over 3 months in 2009. The rate at which people discussed a movie the week before the movie opened explained 80% of the variance in the gross opening week box office revenue. Including the rate for each day of the week and the number of theaters at which the movie was playing accounted for 97.3% of the variance in opening weekend revenue. Further, the second-weekend box office gross was better predicted by including the sentiment of the tweets (ratio of tweets with positive content to tweets with negative content) in addition to the tweet rate (Asur & Huberman, 2010).

Attitudes stem from specific antecedents (i.e., affect, behaviors, cognitions). Therefore, understanding a person's attitudes provides insight into these antecedents. Researchers have used people's attitudes on social media to gain insight into their traits and attributes (Kosinski, Stillwell, & Graepel, 2013). By examining users' "likes" on Facebook, collected via the myPersonality app, researchers could infer, better than base rate probabilities, a person's personality traits, ethnicity, sexual orientation, religious and political views, intelligence, happiness, age, or gender.

Culture

Culture represents another critical area of emphasis for social psychologists because it has implications for the generalizability of all other topics. *Culture* is defined as a collection of learned routines of thinking, feeling, and interacting with other people, as well as the assertions and ideas about aspects of the world (Wyer, Chiu, & Hong, 2009). To approximate the complex appreciation of people's collective narrative, researchers use regional boundaries as a proxy for culture (for a brief discussion, see Oyserman & Sorensen, 2009).

Big data facilitates the study of cross-cultural differences through a variety of mechanisms, including comparing samples from international versions of websites. Researchers interested in understanding differences between collectivist and individualist cultures, often use U.S. participants as representatives of individualist cultures and Japanese participants as collectivists. In addition to recruiting participants from American and Japanese universities, researchers used reviews found on U.S. and Japanese versions of Amazon. They coded the reviews for the presence of approach and avoidance content to examine cultural differences (Hamamura, Meijer, Heine, Kamaya, & Hori, 2009). Among American reviews, "approach" content was significantly more prevalent than "avoidance" content, whereas Japanese reviews contained roughly equal amounts of each. In addition, the rated "helpfulness" of the review was negatively correlated with avoidance content for U.S. reviews but uncorrelated among Japanese reviews. These findings allowed researchers to better understand cultural differences in people's sensitivity to approach and avoidance information.

One exciting area of research to which cultural psychologists may consider applying big data is studying intracultural variability. That is, more recent models of culture address the notion that individuals within a culture do not all subscribe to the same cultural script (e.g., honor, face, dignity; Leung & Cohen, 2011; Nowak, Gelfand, Borkowski, Cohen, & Hernandez, 2016). Whether people from cultures that have a modal or prototypical culture (e.g., the "honor" culture in the southern United States) act in accordance with cultural norms depends on the context and their personality. There is also evidence that cultures may share certain norms, but the emphasis of those norms may vary between cultures. That is, although Australia, the United States, China, and Taiwan all find emotions such as joy and affection as desirable to display, pride shows intercultural variability. Individualist cultures tend to view pride as positive, whereas collectivist cultures tend to view pride as undesirable (Eid & Diener, 2001). Because big data more easily allow for collecting data across a nation, they allow observing variation that would be missed if sampling from only one metropolitan area or only examining aggregated data.

Big data also allows the discovery of new cultures, such as regional personality cultures, through dimension reduction of data collected from users from the different parts of the culture. One example of this application is the discovery of regional subcultures within the United States (Rentfrow et al., 2013). Using data collected from websites offering a personality quiz, researchers aggregated respondents' Big Five personality scores to the state level and then performed a cluster analysis to examine whether there were smaller cohesive subgroups of states that shared similar personality profiles. They found three distinct personality subcultures within the United States that also fell along relatively clear geographic boundaries.

Diversity

Personally disclosed locations, geocoded communications, and visual representations of the world allow researchers to understand the geographic context of people's behaviors. Because big data sources often contain location information, they, therefore, contain a proxy for linking users to cities, counties, and states. Knowing a user's location allows researchers to infer other variables present in that user's environment. For example, researchers can infer the diversity of a user's environment from archival information for that area. They can then examine that variable in relation to other hypothesized factors. Nai, Narayanan, Hernandez, and Savani (2018) collected data from 200 metropolitan statistical areas. Each Twitter message was coded for the presence and absence of prosocial content. The racial diversity of that user's metropolitan statistical areas was then coded. A cross-level multilevel analysis of the data revealed that the more diverse a person's area, the more likely they were to mention prosocial content. This effect was only found for racial prosociality and existed above and beyond religious, socioeconomic, or gender diversity.

Emotion

Emotion, or the brief specific psychological and physiological responses that help humans meet social goals, have been inferred through both text-based and visual media sources. From the text, researchers typically find words associated with distinct emotions and, using natural language processing, derive the proportion of emotional content within that text (Pennebaker, Boyd, Jordan, & Blackburn, 2015; Tausczik & Pennebaker, 2010). Applying this methodology to big data allows researchers to examine trends in affect at a scale that would be difficult to examine through traditional means. Patterns of weekly and diurnal variations can be examined across the world by mining people's daily status posts. Researchers who collected people's tweets found consistent changes in positive and negative affect over 2 years. Specifically, emotion data from tweets showed that individuals awaken in a good mood, which decreases throughout the day; positive affect varies with change in day length; and people are happier on weekends (Golder & Macy, 2011).

Drawing from the facial expression literature, researchers use posted images to infer people's emotional states. Prior work in emotional expressions found that each of the primary emotions (e.g., happiness, anger, contempt, sadness, disgust) has a distinct profile of muscular activity, which is consistent across cultures (Ekman, 1993; Ekman & Friesen, 1971). In this research, each possible muscular movement in the face was assigned a numeric ID, called an *action unit*. In the human face, there are 28 main action units, as well as action units for head and eye movement. An example of a facial action unit is AU12, which corresponds to the lip corners being pulled upward by the zygomaticus major muscle. As mentioned, each primary emotion has a distinct myographic profile. The action unit pattern for happiness is the raising of cheeks (AU6) and the pulling of lip corners (AU11). The facial action units that distinguish disgust are nose wrinkling (AU9), lip corners lowering (AU15), and lower lips lowering (AU16). By observing the facial action units present at a given moment, researchers can code how people feel and how those emotions relate to other factors based on only a video recording.

More recently, investigators have adopted computerized facial action coding systems. Machine learning algorithms, such as convolutional neural networks, can reduce an image into its basic structural features (e.g., angles, lines, shades) and combine the information in those features to detect the presence of different facial expressions of emotion (Lawrence, Giles, Tsoi, & Back, 1997). Not only is big data suited for studying emotion because of how it is conveyed through our language and faces but also because of the temporal and contextual aspects of emotion that would otherwise be difficult to study in a prompted setting. Because emotion is typically defined as a response to a specific target or stimulus, the velocity of big data allows researchers to examine users' emotions in response to unexpected events and the change that occurs before, during, and after the event.

Lewinski (2015) used automated facial coding of emotion from videos on YouTube. The researcher collected 16 different videos from YouTube that featured different speakers in relatively homogenous speaking conditions. The author then used a neural network-based emotion classification software, FaceReader, to code the presence of six discrete emotions (i.e., happiness, sadness, surprise, disgust, anger, fear) expressed throughout the video. Using all six emotions as well as the prior number of views the video had received in a regression model predicting the future number of views a speaker will receive, the author explained 86% of the total variance in the number of future views videos received. The coded expressed emotions explained an additional 25% of variance beyond the prior number of views. In addition, the authors found that disaffiliating facial emotions (i.e., anger, fear, disgust) did not relate to the future performance of social media content, and only expressed happiness, sadness, and surprise were strong predictors of future views.

Motivation

Social psychologists infer people's motivation through a variety of ways using big data. One example is the examination of county-level goal orientation and HIV prevalence reduction (Ireland, Chen, Schwartz, Ungar, & Albarracín, 2016). This research borrowed from the goal-action literature, which ties the structure of speech to the mind-set that people have. The researchers created an "action" dictionary by combining dictionaries related to motion and verb categories, as well as words related to action (e.g., *go, plan, think*), and coded the words in terms of general motor and cognitive activity. Using geolocation information from the message, they coded the proportion of tweets originating from 2,079 U.S. counties mentioning action-related words and regressed each county's HIV prevalence on its action word prevalence. Results showed that more frequent action word usage on Twitter was associated with lower HIV rates.

Prosociality

Often, big data provides a context for users to engage in prosocial behavior. Kraus and Callaghan (2016) examined whether upper class Twitter users would engage in more public prosocial behaviors, such as publicly sending tweets about the ALS ice bucket challenge (via the #ALSicebucketchallenge hashtag), than relatively lower class ones. They coded the user's social class based on the user's indicated occupation. Dichotomizing users into lower and upper class backgrounds, they found that, relative to base-rate Twitter demographics, a much higher proportion of people tweeting about the ALS challenge came from higher social class occupations than from lower ones.

Aggression

Aggression is typically delineated into physical, verbal, and relational forms, depending on whether the harm occurs through bodily contact, communication, or manipulating social standing or relationships. Due to the emphasis of remote communication in online contexts, and the greater anonymity provided, big data is especially suited for examining the latter two forms. For example, examining the different ways of ending communication with people online can allow researchers to study the antecedents and the consequences of negative behaviors directed toward others.

Colaneri, Cooperstein, and Hernandez (2018) collected a sample of "negative tie" (*n* = 23,251) and "control" tweets (*n* = 21,043) over a 2-week period on Twitter. The "negative tie" tweets contained statements reflecting one of the three network relational change options available to Twitter users—"blocking," "unfollowing," or "muting" someone. The "control" tweets were a random sample of English language tweets during that same period. Using the automated text analysis tool, Linguistic Inquiry Word Count, the authors coded each tweet's emotionality (positive and negative emotion words) and power (*ambition, bully, force, bossed, inferior, superior*) language content and then compared the proportions across negative tie types. They found that among those who experience negative ties, emotion has a greater role compared with power in the focus of negative ties, especially from the sender of the tie. They also found evidence for a distinct typology of negative ties, where muting was associated with the most expressed emotional negativity, and unfollowing, where the tie is completely broken, had the least association with power compared with simply terminating communication.

Relationships

Dyadic interactions, such as friendships and romantic relationships, often manifest in online contexts. Researchers find contexts where these interactions occur and can examine their outcomes and antecedents and how they develop to understand processes within close relationships better. Online dating websites provide users a way to find romantic relationships, which allow researchers to examine a multitude of relationship research questions, including "What factors do people seek in partners?" "How do people portray themselves to potential partners?" and "What variables are associated with interest and commitment between individuals?"

Xia, Ribeiro, Chen, Liu, and Towsley (2013) analyzed 200,000 individuals sampled from the Chinese dating website baihe.com, which has over 60 million registered users. For each user, the researchers had records of his or her sent and received messages, as well as the profile information of the user and all the users with whom he or she had communicated. Each profile specifies the user's gender, age, current location (city and province), home town location, height, weight, body type, blood type, occupation, income range, education level, religion, astrological sign, marriage and children status, number of photos uploaded, homeownership, car ownership, interests, smoking and drinking behavior, and a self-description essay, among others. Each user also provides his or her preferences for potential romantic partners in terms of age, location, height, education level, income range, marriage and children status, and so forth. The researchers used this information to examine gender differences in relationship initiation and interests, finding that men tend to send far more messages but get fewer replies than women. Women are more likely to receive unsolicited messages and less likely to reply. They also found convergent findings to cross-cultural research on gender differences in mate preferences (Buss, 1994). Males tended to look for younger females. Females placed more emphasis on socioeconomic status, such as the income and education level of a potential partner. In addition, when comparing the attribute preferences men and women stated in their profiles with the attributes of the people they message, women tended to have larger differences between their stated preferences and the attributes of the people they message than men. These deviations were especially true for attributes such as age, height, and location. Therefore, big data can both provide supportive evidence for relationship theories and also facilitate discovering novel phenomena for further study.

Wearable sensors provide another rich source of information regarding relationships. Pentland and Madan (2005) recorded the activity of individuals wearing sociometric badges as they conversed in various settings. The sociometric badges could record the percentage of time each person spoke in the conversation, the influence of the other person on turn taking, the variation in pitch and amplitude, and verification during a conversation (e.g., Speaker 1: "Okay?" Speaker 2: "Okay!"). With these variables from the sociometric badges, researchers could accurately predict which participants in a speed dating event showed mutual interest, which conference attendees exchanged business cards, and the amount of reported interest in conversation a person had.

Language occurs in many different modalities during relationships. Researchers examined the instant messages sent during couples' romantic relationships to understand the factors associated with positive relationship outcomes (Ireland et al., 2011). Researchers analyzed couples' instant message conversations over 10 days. Following these 10 days, each partner completed the Relationship Assessment Scale (Hendrick, 1988). Three months later, researchers followed up with the couples, asking whether they were still dating. For each couple, the researchers coded how similar their function word usage was into a single measure of "language style matching" (LSM). LSM significantly predicted relationship stability, where, for every standard deviation increase in LSM, couples were approximately twice as likely to be together 3 months later. These effects were independent of the average word count or relationship satisfaction.

Groups

Groups such as political and religious affiliations can be examined through the lens of big data by inferring membership based on the user's network. Barberá (2015), matched Twitter users' names and location to political party registration records and found that Twitter users' political ideologies could be estimated from the individuals they followed. In addition, resulting ideology estimates could accurately predict campaign contributions and the party under which they were registered. Twitter users on the right of the median voter's political ideology donated to republican candidates; Twitter users on the left donated to democratic candidates. The correlation between ideal points estimated using Twitter networks and contribution records was $r = 0.80$.

Ritter, Preston, and Hernandez (2014) inferred religious group membership (Christian vs. atheist) from the people that users follow. Prominent religious (e.g., Joel Osteen, Joyce Meyer) and atheist figures (e.g., Richard Dawkins, Monica Salcedo) were identified, and the researchers recorded the number of friends their followers had, as well as their followers' tweets. The researchers then coded the affective and cognitive content of the tweets from the Christian and atheist followers. Replicating prior research on religious groups, Christians were more socially connected and expressed more positive affect relative to atheist users. Further, the path between Christianity and positive emotion was mediated by the user's social connections via the number of friends in that user's network, whereas that path was mediated by analytic content expressed within one's tweets for atheists. This mediator between atheism and positive affect had not been discussed in the past literature and, therefore, demonstrates the ability for big data to both support existing and develop new theories.

Big data also offers the opportunity to study members of groups that are difficult to sample using in-person methods. Hernandez, Bashir, Jeon, and Bohr (2014) measured users who were enthusiasts of the cryptocurrency Bitcoin, which was then still a developing currency alternative. By sampling people who followed Bitcoin-related accounts and a control group of a random sample of Twitter users, they recorded the users' entire tweet history and coded the percentage of content that related to various predefined topics in the Linguistic Inquiry Word Count. They found that Bitcoin users spoke less about socially related topics such as family and humans and used fewer pronouns. They were also less likely to talk about either home or sexually related topics. From these results, researchers inferred that Bitcoin users might be less socially oriented in their daily conversations and perhaps interests.

Social Influence

Social influence describes the many ways that people affect changes in attitudes, beliefs, feelings, and behavior in others via their comments, actions, and mere presence. Due to the interconnected nature of online interactions, big data also offers social psychologists the opportunity to study how people's behavior is affected by the behaviors of those around them. Users on social media inherently have explicit connections with others who are referred to as "friends" or "followers." By examining the content and behavior of a person's friends and then examining the subsequent content posted and behavior of the user, researchers can study contagion, homophily, and other social influence processes.

In one study conducted by Facebook, over 60 million users saw a "get out the vote" message at the top of their news feeds on November 2, 2010, accompanied by images of their friends who had voted (Bond et al., 2012). Other users on the site received the message without the friend information, whereas another random set of users received no political information at all. The direct effect of the Facebook social message on users who saw it generated an additional 60,000 votes in 2010. The effects of the extended social network— of social contagion spreading from the user to the user's friends—yielded another 280,000 more, they estimated, for a total of 340,000. The researchers estimated that Facebook yielded an additional four voters for every one voter that was directly mobilized. Friends of users who received the "get out the vote" message, regardless of whether they were themselves recipients, were more likely to vote. The researchers also showed that the message affected people at two degrees of separation: The friends of the friends of social message recipients were also more likely to click on the "I voted" button, yielding an additional 1 million instances of voting expression.

Social Cognition

Social cognition research focuses on the thought processes people have as they reason about and perceive the social world. Because of the emphasis on the social environment in social cognitive research, big data offers a realistic context for exploring people's perceptions and judgments of external stimuli. Specifically, social cognitive research has used big data to obtain data sets on individuals who come from varied backgrounds and use that data as stimuli for person perception studies.

Social class research provides one example of deriving real-life stimuli from big data. Because social class is a property of being in a society, it is important to have socially applicable (i.e., noncontrived) stimuli. To examine whether a person's social class is visually perceptible in society, a study needs images that reflect actual social class. In one study, hypothesis-blind research assistants collected face stimuli from Internet dating advertisements of people between the ages of 18 and 35 in major U.S. cities (Bjornsdottir & Rule, 2017). As part of the dating profiles, users reported their incomes, and researchers were able to acquire images of people with reported annual incomes over $150,000 and below $35,000. Participants were able to infer a person's social class using only the images, even when all non-face related information (e.g., hair, jewelry) was removed. Similarly, researchers acquired images from participants by downloading the user's Facebook photos and self-reported income to examine whether class could be perceived from images (Becker, Kraus, & Rheinschmidt-Same, 2017).

Like social class research, research that seeks to understand whether a company's profitability can be perceived in the facial features of its leaders requires people to examine images of individuals tied to successful and nonsuccessful companies. By scraping data from websites of various Fortune 500 companies, researchers presented authentic images of CEOs to participants. Participants then rated their subjective perception of each CEO's power, warmth, and leadership ability. Researchers found that a CEO's perceived power had a positive linear association with the company's average profits, $r(41) = .36$, $p < .05$, from the previous 3 fiscal years (Rule & Ambady, 2008). In addition, a CEO's perceived leadership also positively related to the company's profits, $r(41) = .30$, $p < .05$. Therefore, using a large collection of data provided from online sources, researchers were able to examine the real-life association between facial features on actual positive company outcomes.

Self-Esteem and Identity

Big data has been helpful for understanding people's self-presentation and impression management via the profiles that individuals create. Social media allows its users to shape and tailor the information provided to their network. These deliberate choices, such as the text content and the images used, have allowed researchers to examine how individuals seek to be portrayed.

One study examined how users reveal their self and identity via their profile photo choices on social media (Liu, Preotiuc-Pietro, Riahi Samani, Moghaddam, & Ungar, 2016). Researchers collected tweets from 66,502 Twitter users. The researchers then coded each user's personality using their 3,200 most recent tweets. These personality predictions used prevalidated linear regression models that related tweet content to personality traits. By also coding each user's profile picture in terms of different content, the researchers found that each personality trait has a specific type of profile picture posting. Users that are either high in openness or neuroticism post fewer photos of people, and when these photos are present, they tend not to express positive emotions. The difference between the groups is in the aesthetic quality of the photos—higher for openness and lower for neuroticism. Users high in conscientiousness, agreeableness, or extraversion were more likely to use pictures with at least one face and preferred presenting positive emotions through their facial expressions. Highly conscientious users posted more what is expected of a profile picture, a picture of one face that expresses the most positive emotion out of all traits. Highly extraverted and highly agreeable people regularly posted colorful pictures that convey emotion.

Synthesis: Taxonomy of the Role Big Data Plays in Social Psychology

On the basis of the aforementioned research, big data offers social psychologists the ability to study their questions in a variety of novel ways. Specifically, researchers have used the many forms of big data to conceptualize their outcomes (thoughts, feelings, and behavior), as well as predictor variables, more conveniently, realistically, and statistically powerfully than possible through traditional methods.

Table 10.1 synthesizes the different operationalizations that social psychologists incorporating big data have used to examine various constructs. This

TABLE 10.1. Summary of How Measures From Big Data Have Been Translated to Social Psychological Constructs

Social psychological construct variable	Measured with
Attitudes	• Content analysis of text messages • Ratings of stimuli • Profile information
Motivation and intentions	• Action words in the content of messages • Rate of discussion • Search trace data
Feelings (affect or emotion)	• Sentiment analysis of text • Emotion classification of text • Emotion classification of images
Impression management	• Choice of profile photo and information
Culture or region	• Geolocation of messages • Reported location of profile
Group membership	• Subscription/following of topics and users related to the group • Profile self-report
Social influence	• Messages posted by reported friends in network
Relationship ties and partner attributes	• Network friends and followers • Messages between partners • Profile information of friends and followers
Prosociality	• Content of messages • Use of hashtags for prosocial topic • Following of prosocial groups
Aggression	• Content of messages sent to others • Blocking, muting, and unfollowing others
Physical characteristics	• Photographs from websites

summarization makes the role that big data has in psychology, and how readers can apply it to their questions, clearer. This taxonomy is based only on the research described and, therefore, only represents a baseline for the many conceptualizations. As researchers develop new methods, the list further expands. For social psychologists who seek to integrate these data into their current topic framework, this collection may simplify how to make the transition.

Challenges When Using Big Data in Social Psychology

One important caution to issue is that although researchers have operationalized their constructs in the ways previously described, our psychometric understanding of the different methods varies widely. For certain text analytic methods, the reliability and convergent validity are often established by prior studies but often using text samples from contexts that differ from briefer versions used in social media. For other measures, such as group membership via followership or subscription, reliability, convergent validity, and unidimensionality are not typically reported. Rather, the group membership is simply assumed. In addition, demographic measures (e.g., age, location, education) typically have a direct correspondence to constructs measured through the survey-based measures but are listed in a public context and, therefore, may reflect an idealized or normative image, rather than their actual value. This potential for self-presentation bias may be more severe in an online context because there is a wider social circle to impress than in the lab but also may be diminished for publicly verifiable traits, which would be falsified by the person's social circle if posted incorrectly. Therefore, much more psychometric work is needed to establish the measurement properties of measures derived from big data. Through subsequent psychology analysis, researchers can better integrate findings from big data and traditionally collected studies.

FUTURE OF BIG DATA WITHIN SOCIAL PSYCHOLOGY

Future Roles of Industry

If big data lends itself to studying a greater variety of social phenomena in more precise ways, the industries holding that information are privy to unique insights that benefit social psychology. One possibility the future holds is that there will be greater collaboration between academic researchers and technology firms, such as Facebook, Twitter, LinkedIn, and Google. Indeed, such partnerships have been realized with researchers such as academic Jason Rentfrow teaming with Jeff Potter of Atof, Inc. to translate 7 years of data collected by Potter's website, http://www.outofservice.com, into new cultural insights about the United States (Rentfrow et al., 2013). Thousands of websites and apps exist with data perfectly suited for studying particular hypotheses but without the appropriate theoretical or analytical skills to distill it. These partnerships merge complementary skills from social psychologists, who are adept at studying data, and industry and engineers, who are adept are developing data collection systems. Open challenges presented by embracing these opportunities are the negative public perceptions of companies exploiting their user base, concerns about protecting user privacy, and concerns over experimental manipulation (Sullivan, 2014). As seen with the Cambridge Analytica scandal, even data collected for academic research can be applied for political and ideological purposes far outside the scope of the original intention (Graham-Harrison & Cadwalladr, 2018). Researchers collected data from thisisyourdigitallife, which provided insights into users' personality and was used to develop profiles of individual U.S. voters, serving to target them later with personalized political advertisements. Therefore, although social psychology may try to develop partnerships with industry in the future, they must address hesitations by those in industry for potentially damaging ways the data could be used by others and the liability incurred.

Future of Analyzing Subtle Effects

Social psychology studies many subtle but reliable effects. A meta-analysis examining 100 years of social psychological effects found a highly positively skewed distribution, with the median effect size equal to $r = .18$ and with approximately 76% of effect sizes less than .30, the typical cutoff for a "small effect" (Richard, Bond, & Stokes-Zoota, 2003). Further, about 30% of effect sizes are less than $r = .10$. Therefore, social psychology tends to study small effects, and this emphasis could be problematic because point estimates and their confidence intervals are fairly imprecise, leading to null-hypothesis significance testing being more emphasized. Simonsohn (2014) demonstrated that when studying even medium-sized effects ($r = .5$), the sample sizes typically observed in social psychological studies produce confidence intervals that span three qualitatively different effect size categories. He argued that sample sizes of at least 3,000 are needed for informative point estimates. Given the small effect sizes in social psychology, researchers who transition to big data may provide informative confidence intervals that address open arguments regarding the true effect size of a relationship. This adoption of big data to create point estimates may be problematic for meta-analyses within the field. The sample sizes of big data research overwhelmingly weight those findings more compared with traditional designs, and therefore, social psychological meta-analysts may adopt different norms in the future for addressing the sample size disparity.

Future of Experimental Manipulation

Because big data research tends to be largely correlational, as described in the prior sections, it differs greatly from the experimental paradigm social psychologists tend to invoke. Social psychologists who value experimental manipulation and internal validity may emphasize examining natural experiments within big data or developing designs that can experimentally manipulate the stimuli that users experience. Examples of these big data experimental designs have been used by Kramer, Guillory, and Hancock (2014), who experimentally manipulated the affective content shown to users on their Facebook timeline to measure their subsequent emotional affect and the subsequent affect of their social network. In the age of "nudges" (Thaler & Sunstein, 2008), big data offers a way for social psychologists to examine social manipulations at their maximal influence (referred to as a *hypernudge*; Yeung, 2017). The ability to alter the social environment of hundreds or thousands of people raises questions of consent that social psychologists must address in tandem when deciding to incorporate experimental designs in big data (Flick, 2016).

CONCLUSION

Big data can provide valuable insights into complex social psychological processes. As people increasingly live their lives online, big data becomes an even more powerful tool for social scientists. Social psychologists have used their unique challenges as an impetus for utilizing big data. Its incorporation has not supplanted the use of traditional data because its properties serve as a complement to many of the limitations of traditional data, providing a richer understanding of social behavior than previously possible.

REFERENCES

Ashton, K. (2009). That 'internet of things' thing. *RFID Journal, 22*(7), 97–114.

Asur, S., & Huberman, B. A. (2010, September). *Predicting the future with social media.* Paper Presented at the 2010 IEEE/WIC/ACM International Conference on Web Intelligence and Intelligent Agent Technology, Toronto, Canada.

Back, M. D., Stopfer, J. M., Vazire, S., Gaddis, S., Schmukle, S. C., Egloff, B., & Gosling, S. D. (2010). Facebook profiles reflect actual personality, not self-idealization. *Psychological Science, 21,* 372–374. http://dx.doi.org/10.1177/0956797609360756

Barberá, P. (2015). Birds of the same feather tweet together: Bayesian ideal point estimation using Twitter data. *Political Analysis, 23,* 76–91. http://dx.doi.org/10.1093/pan/mpu011

Baumeister, R. F., Vohs, K. D., & Funder, D. C. (2007). Psychology as the science of self-reports and finger movements: Whatever happened to actual behavior? *Perspectives on Psychological Science, 2,* 396–403. http://dx.doi.org/10.1111/j.1745-6916.2007.00051.x

Becker, J. C., Kraus, M. W., & Rheinschmidt-Same, M. (2017). Cultural expressions of social class and their implications for group-related beliefs and behaviors. *Journal of Social Issues, 73,* 158–174. http://dx.doi.org/10.1111/josi.12209

Bjornsdottir, R. T., & Rule, N. O. (2017). The visibility of social class from facial cues. *Journal of Personality and Social Psychology, 113,* 530–546. http://dx.doi.org/10.1037/pspa0000091

Bond, R. M., Fariss, C. J., Jones, J. J., Kramer, A. D., Marlow, C., Settle, J. E., & Fowler, J. H. (2012). A 61-million-person experiment in social influence and political mobilization. *Nature, 489,* 295–298. http://dx.doi.org/10.1038/nature11421

Buss, D. M. (1994). Mate preferences in 37 cultures. In W. J. Lonner & R. Malpass (Eds.), *Psychology and culture* (pp. 415–436). Boston, MA: Allyn & Bacon.

Carneiro, H. A., & Mylonakis, E. (2009). Google Trends: A web-based tool for real-time surveillance of disease outbreaks. *Clinical Infectious Diseases, 49,* 1557–1564. http://dx.doi.org/10.1086/630200

Cohen, D. (1998). Culture, social organization, and patterns of violence. *Journal of Personality and Social Psychology, 75,* 408–419. http://dx.doi.org/10.1037/0022-3514.75.2.408

Colaneri, A. S., Cooperstein, J. N., & Hernandez, I. (2018). Tweeting about negative ties: A linguistic analysis and typology of dyadic relational change. In A. Speer (Chair), *Using text analytics to advance understanding of workplace behavior and outcomes.* Symposium conducted at the meeting of the Society for Industrial and Organizational Psychology, Chicago, IL.

Csikszentmihalyi, M., Larson, R., & Prescott, S. (1977). The ecology of adolescent activity and experience. *Journal of Youth and Adolescence, 6,* 281–294. http://dx.doi.org/10.1007/BF02138940

Diesner, J., Frantz, T. L., & Carley, K. M. (2005). Communication networks from the Enron email corpus "It's always about the people. Enron is no different." *Com-*

putational & Mathematical Organization Theory, *11*, 201–228. http://dx.doi.org/10.1007/s10588-005-5377-0

Eagle, N., & Pentland, A. S. (2006). Reality mining: Sensing complex social systems. *Personal and ubiquitous computing*, *10*, 255–268. http://dx.doi.org/10.1007/s00779-005-0046-3

Eagly, A. H., & Chaiken, S. (1993). *The psychology of attitudes*. Fort Worth, TX: Harcourt Brace Jovanovich.

Eid, M., & Diener, E. (2001). Norms for experiencing emotions in different cultures: Inter- and intranational differences. *Journal of Personality and Social Psychology*, *81*, 869–885. http://dx.doi.org/10.1037/0022-3514.81.5.869

Ekman, P. (1993). Facial expression and emotion. *American Psychologist*, *48*, 384–392. http://dx.doi.org/10.1037/0003-066X.48.4.384

Ekman, P., & Friesen, W. V. (1971). Constants across cultures in the face and emotion. *Journal of Personality and Social Psychology*, *17*, 124–129. http://dx.doi.org/10.1037/h0030377

Facebook. (2019). *Facebook platform policy*. Retrieved from https://developers.facebook.com/policy

Flick, C. (2016). Informed consent and the Facebook emotional manipulation study. *Research Ethics Review*, *12*, 14–28. http://dx.doi.org/10.1177/1747016115599568

Fraley, R. C., & Vazire, S. (2014). The N-pact factor: Evaluating the quality of empirical journals with respect to sample size and statistical power. *PLoS ONE*, *9*(10), e109019. http://dx.doi.org/10.1371/journal.pone.0109019

Gelman, A. (2018). The failure of null hypothesis significance testing when studying incremental changes, and what to do about it. *Personality and Social Psychology Bulletin*, *44*, 16–23. http://dx.doi.org/10.1177/0146167217729162

Gilovich, T., Keltner, D., Chen, S., & Nisbett, R. E. (2016). *Social psychology*. New York, NY: Norton.

Ginsberg, J., Mohebbi, M. H., Patel, R. S., Brammer, L., Smolinski, M. S., & Brilliant, L. (2009). Detecting influenza epidemics using search engine query data. *Nature*, *457*, 1012–1014. http://dx.doi.org/10.1038/nature07634

Golder, S. A., & Macy, M. W. (2011). Diurnal and seasonal mood vary with work, sleep, and daylength across diverse cultures. *Science*, *333*, 1878–1881. http://dx.doi.org/10.1126/science.1202775

Gosling, S. D., Augustine, A. A., Vazire, S., Holtzman, N., & Gaddis, S. (2011). Manifestations of personality in online social networks: Self-reported Facebook-related behaviors and observable profile information. *Cyberpsychology, Behavior, and Social Networking*, *14*, 483–488. http://dx.doi.org/10.1089/cyber.2010.0087

Graham-Harrison, E., & Cadwalladr, C. (2018, March 17). Revealed: 50 million Facebook profiles harvested for Cambridge Analytica in major data breach. *The Guardian*. Retrieved from https://www.theguardian.com/news/2018/mar/17/cambridge-analytica-facebook-influence-us-election

Gray, K., & Wegner, D. M. (2010). Blaming God for our pain: Human suffering and the divine mind. *Personality and Social Psychology Review*, *14*, 7–16. http://dx.doi.org/10.1177/1088868309350299

Gubbi, J., Buyya, R., Marusic, S., & Palaniswami, M. (2013). Internet of Things (IoT): A vision, architectural elements, and future directions. *Future Generation Computer Systems*, *29*, 1645–1660. http://dx.doi.org/10.1016/j.future.2013.01.010

Hamamura, T., Meijer, Z., Heine, S. J., Kamaya, K., & Hori, I. (2009). Approach–avoidance motivation and information processing: A cross-cultural analysis. *Personality and Social Psychology Bulletin*, *35*, 454–462. http://dx.doi.org/10.1177/0146167208329512

Hendrick, S. S. (1988). A generic measure of relationship satisfaction. *Journal of Marriage and Family*, *50*, 93–98. http://dx.doi.org/10.2307/352430

Henrich, J., Heine, S. J., & Norenzayan, A. (2010, June 30). Most people are not WEIRD. *Nature, 466*(7302), 29. http://dx.doi.org/10.1038/466029a

Hernandez, I., Bashir, M., Jeon, G., & Bohr, J. (2014, June). Are Bitcoin users less sociable? An analysis of users' language and social connections on Twitter. In *Proceedings of the International Conference on Human-Computer Interaction* (pp. 26–31). Cham, Switzerland: Springer.

Hutchings, J., Bywater, T., Davies, C., & Whitaker, C. (2006). Do crime rates predict the outcome of parenting programmes for parents of high-risk preschool children? *Educational and Child Psychology, 23*(2), 15–24.

Ireland, M. E., Chen, Q., Schwartz, H. A., Ungar, L. H., & Albarracín, D. (2016). Action tweets linked to reduced county-level HIV prevalence in the United States: Online messages and structural determinants. *AIDS and Behavior, 20*, 1256–1264. http://dx.doi.org/10.1007/s10461-015-1252-2

Ireland, M. E., Slatcher, R. B., Eastwick, P. W., Scissors, L. E., Finkel, E. J., & Pennebaker, J. W. (2011). Language style matching predicts relationship initiation and stability. *Psychological Science, 22*, 39–44. http://dx.doi.org/10.1177/0956797610392928

Kosinski, M., Stillwell, D., & Graepel, T. (2013). Private traits and attributes are predictable from digital records of human behavior. *PNAS, 110*, 5802–5805. http://dx.doi.org/10.1073/pnas.1218772110

Kramer, A. D., Guillory, J. E., & Hancock, J. T. (2014). Experimental evidence of massive-scale emotional contagion through social networks. *PNAS, 111*, 8788–8790. http://dx.doi.org/10.1073/pnas.1320040111

Kraus, M. W., & Callaghan, B. (2016). Social class and prosocial behavior: The moderating role of public versus private contexts. *Social Psychological and Personality Science, 7*, 769–777. http://dx.doi.org/10.1177/1948550616659120

Laney, D. (2001). *3D data management: Controlling data volume, velocity, and variety.* Retrieved from https://blogs.gartner.com/doug-laney/files/2012/01/ad949-3D-Data-Management-Controlling-Data-Volume-Velocity-and-Variety.pdf

Lawrence, S., Giles, C. L., Tsoi, A. C., & Back, A. D. (1997). Face recognition: A convolutional neural-network approach. *IEEE Transactions on Neural Networks, 8*, 98–113. http://dx.doi.org/10.1109/72.554195

Leung, A. K. Y., & Cohen, D. (2011). Within- and between-culture variation: Individual differences and the cultural logics of honor, face, and dignity cultures. *Journal of Personality and Social Psychology, 100*, 507–526. http://dx.doi.org/10.1037/a0022151

Lewinski, P. (2015). Don't look blank, happy, or sad: Patterns of facial expressions of speakers in banks' YouTube videos predict video's popularity over time. *Journal of Neuroscience, Psychology, and Economics, 8*, 241–249. http://dx.doi.org/10.1037/npe0000046

Liu, L., Preotiuc-Pietro, D., Riahi Samani, Z., Moghaddam, M. E., & Ungar, L. (2016, May). *Analyzing personality through social media profile picture choice.* Paper presented at the Tenth International AAAI Conference on Web and Social Media, Cologne, Germany.

Marr, B. (2018, May). How much data do we create every day? The mind-blowing stats everyone should read. *Forbes.* Retrieved from https://www.forbes.com/sites/bernardmarr/2018/05/21/how-much-data-do-we-create-every-day-the-mind-blowing-stats-everyone-should-read/#69e7fb9460ba

Mehl, M. R., Pennebaker, J. W., Crow, D. M., Dabbs, J., & Price, J. H. (2001). The Electronically Activated Recorder (EAR): A device for sampling naturalistic daily activities and conversations. *Behavior Research Methods, Instruments, & Computers, 33*, 517–523. http://dx.doi.org/10.3758/BF03195410

Mitchell, G. (2012). Revisiting truth or triviality: The external validity of research in the psychological laboratory. *Perspectives on Psychological Science, 7*, 109–117. http://dx.doi.org/10.1177/1745691611432343

Nai, J., Narayanan, J., Hernandez, I., & Savani, K. (2018). People in more racially diverse neighborhoods are more prosocial. *Journal of Personality and Social Psychology, 114*, 497–515. http://dx.doi.org/10.1037/pspa0000103

Nowak, A., Gelfand, M. J., Borkowski, W., Cohen, D., & Hernandez, I. (2016). The evolutionary basis of honor cultures. *Psychological Science, 27*, 12–24. http://dx.doi.org/10.1177/0956797615602860

Olguin, D. O., & Pentland, A. S. (2007, October). *Sociometric badges: State of the art and future applications.* Paper presented at the IEEE 11th International Symposium on Wearable Computers, Boston, MA.

O'Reilly, T. (2005). *What is Web 2.0?* Retrieved from https://www.oreilly.com/pub/a/web2/archive/what-is-web-20.html

Oyserman, D., & Sorensen, N. (2009). Understanding cultural syndrome effects on what and how we think: A situated cognition model. In R. Wyer, Y. Hong, & C. Chiu (Eds.), *Understanding culture: Theory, research and application* (pp. 25–52). New York, NY: Psychology Press.

Pelham, B. W., Shimizu, M., Arndt, J., Carvallo, M., Solomon, S., & Greenberg, J. (2018). Searching for God: Illness-related mortality threats and religious search volume in Google in 16 nations. *Personality and Social Psychology Bulletin, 44*, 2 90–303. http://dx.doi.org/10.1177/0146167217736047

Pennebaker, J. W., Boyd, R. L., Jordan, K., & Blackburn, K. (2015). *The development and psychometric properties of LIWC2015.* Austin: University of Texas at Austin.

Pentland, A., & Madan, A. (2005, October). *Perception of social interest.* Paper presented at the IEEE International Conference on Computer Vision, Workshop on Modeling People and Human Interaction, Beijing, China.

Rentfrow, P. J., Gosling, S. D., Jokela, M., Stillwell, D. J., Kosinski, M., & Potter, J. (2013). Divided we stand: Three psychological regions of the United States and their political, economic, social, and health correlates. *Journal of Personality and Social Psychology, 105*, 996–1012. http://dx.doi.org/10.1037/a0034434

Richard, F. D., Bond, C. F., Jr., & Stokes-Zoota, J. J. (2003). One hundred years of social psychology quantitatively described. *Review of General Psychology, 7*, 331–363. http://dx.doi.org/10.1037/1089-2680.7.4.331

Ritter, R. S., Preston, J. L., & Hernandez, I. (2014). Happy tweets: Christians are happier, more socially connected, and less analytical than atheists on Twitter. *Social Psychological and Personality Science, 5*, 243–249. http://dx.doi.org/10.1177/1948550613492345

Robinson, W. S. (1950). Ecological correlations and the behavior of individuals. *American Sociological Review, 15*, 351–357. http://dx.doi.org/10.2307/2087176

Ruggles, S., Genadek, K., Goeken, R., Grover, J., & Sobek, M. (2017). *Integrated public use microdata series, current population survey: Version 7.0* [Machine-readable database]. Minneapolis: University of Minnesota.

Rule, N. O., & Ambady, N. (2008). The face of success: Inferences from chief executive officers' appearance predict company profits. *Psychological Science, 19*, 109–111. http://dx.doi.org/10.1111/j.1467-9280.2008.02054.x

Schlenker, B. R. (1974). Social psychology and science. *Journal of Personality and Social Psychology, 29*, 1–15. http://dx.doi.org/10.1037/h0035668

Schwartz, H. A., & Ungar, L. H. (2015). Data-driven content analysis of social media: A systematic overview of automated methods. *Annals of the American Academy of Political and Social Science, 659*, 78–94. http://dx.doi.org/10.1177/0002716215569197

Simonsohn, U. (2014). We cannot afford to study effect size in the lab. *Data Colada*. Retrieved from http://datacolada.org/20

Smith, A. (2014). What people like and dislike about Facebook. *Pew Research Center*. Retrieved from http://pewresearch.org/fact-tank/2014/02/03/what-people-like-dislike-about-facebook

Stillwell, D. J., & Kosinski, M. (2004). *myPersonality project: Example of successful utilization of online social networks for large-scale social research.* Retrieved from https://www.gsb.stanford.edu/sites/gsb/files/conf-presentations/stillwell_and_kosinski_2012.pdf

Sullivan, G. (2014, July 2). Angry mood manipulation subjects seize on interview with Facebook researcher Adam Kramer. *The Washington Post*. Retrieved from https://www.washingtonpost.com/news/morning-mix/wp/2014/07/02/angry-mood-manipulation-subjects-seize-on-interview-with-facebook-researcher-adam-kramer/

Tausczik, Y. R., & Pennebaker, J. W. (2010). The psychological meaning of words: LIWC and computerized text analysis methods. *Journal of Language and Social Psychology, 29,* 24–54. http://dx.doi.org/10.1177/0261927X09351676

Tay, L., Woo, S. E., & Vermunt, J. K. (2014). A conceptual and methodological framework for psychometric isomorphism: Validation of multilevel construct measures. *Organizational Research Methods, 17,* 77–106. http://dx.doi.org/10.1177/1094428113517008

Thaler, R., & Sunstein, C. (2008). *Nudge: Improving decisions about health, wealth, and happiness*. New Haven, CT: Yale University Press.

West, S. G., & Brown, T. J. (1975). Physical attractiveness, the severity of the emergency and helping: A field experiment and interpersonal simulation. *Journal of Experimental Social Psychology, 11,* 531–538. http://dx.doi.org/10.1016/0022-1031(75)90004-9

Wyer, R., Chiu, C., & Hong, Y. (2009). *Understanding culture: Theory, research, and application*. New York, NY: Psychology Press.

Xia, P., Ribeiro, B., Chen, C., Liu, B., & Towsley, D. (2013). A study of user behavior on an online dating site. In *Proceedings of the 2013 IEEE/ACM International Conference on Advances in Social Networks Analysis and Mining* (Vol. 1, pp. 243–247). New York, NY: ACM. http://dx.doi.org/10.1145/2492517.2492659

Yeung, K. (2017). 'Hypernudge': Big Data as a mode of regulation by design. *Information Communication and Society, 20,* 118–136. http://dx.doi.org/10.1080/1369118X.2016.1186713

11

Big Data in Health Care Delivery

Mohammad Adibuzzaman and Paul M. Griffin

The role of big data and supporting analytics has been transforming many industries for well over a decade, and their use in health care delivery is no different in that regard. Health care data is generated from several sources, including imaging, lab tests, and physiological monitoring, and is growing exponentially. It was estimated that in 2011, the U.S. health care system held 150 exabytes of data. It is projected that this system will exceed two zettabytes (1000^7 bytes) by 2020 and shortly thereafter will exceed a yottabyte (1000^8 bytes; Raghupathi & Raghupathi, 2014).

Big data holds significant promise in health care, particularly in helping to understand what factors influence patient outcomes and how corresponding treatments and processes can be changed at the point of care to improve patient health and wellness. Some of the areas that are receiving significant attention are clinical operations—particularly in the area of comparative effectiveness; research—through predictive modeling and improving clinical trial design through analytics and learning; public health—analyzing disease pattern, targeting resources, and analyzing policies; evidence-based medicine—using the various forms of health data to better stratify risk, match treatments with outcomes, and improve efficiency (we discuss this point in particular in later sections); genomics—using genomic analysis as a part of medical care;

We thank Drs. Ananth Grama, Elias Bareinboim, and Jeremiah Blocki for their input. We also acknowledge many research efforts by graduate and undergraduate students for their ongoing research activities at the Regenstrief Center for Healthcare Engineering, to whom we are deeply indebted for the preparation of this chapter.

http://dx.doi.org/10.1037/0000193-012
Big Data in Psychological Research, S. E. Woo, L. Tay, and R. W. Proctor (Editors)

fraud analysis—identifying fraud in the billing and claims process; remote monitoring—collecting and analyzing data (often in real time) at the point of care; and personalized care—using patient profile data to define effective segmentations for prevention and care (Raghupathi & Raghupathi, 2014).

Additional data sources that are specifically of interest to the psychological sciences are social network data, such as from Facebook and Twitter, for analyzing changes in health behavior in the era of social network platforms, analyzing behavioral data to understand the impact of health behavior on the cost of health care, and examining discrimination and bias in mental and behavioral health for minority and underrepresented groups.

McKinsey estimated that over $300 billion to $450 billion could be saved each year in U.S. health care costs from the use of big data in the categories of data management, direct intervention, retrospective insight, and predictive power (Kayyali, Knott, & Van Kuiken, 2013). Despite the promise of big data, however, health care delivery has lagged most other industries in its effective use. The purpose of this chapter is to discuss some important reasons why this is the case, discuss what we believe to be the important big data challenges in this space, and present a path forward to help to meet these challenges. Our key focus is on the development of effective data platforms to support the use of big data in health care delivery systems. Through this explication, we hope that psychologists doing research in the areas of health and well-being will be able to better understand and utilize big data uniquely within health care delivery systems and recognize its limitations.

We first present a brief history of health care data, including the development of the electronic health record (EHR), patient claims, and the health information technology environment. We then describe some of the important structural conditions that lead to agency issues and their impact on data usage and sharing. Next, we describe what is perhaps the most challenging aspect of big data usage in health care delivery—namely, the generation of evidence. This is a particularly important topic because the whole foundation of health care evidence is based on the randomized controlled trial (RCT), and there has historically been a reluctance to rely on evidence derived from retrospective observational data. Finally, we discuss the limitations of current data platforms in health care and the challenges that have to be addressed to move beyond these limitations.

It is worth mentioning up front that there are several distinguishing features of big data in health care delivery compared with other industries. Some of the most important features include patient privacy and the improvement of safety and outcome and that it is a value-driven system (Kayyali et al., 2013).

Health care data are held in many different places. Patient data can be held at different hospitals, in different departments within a hospital (e.g., imaging, lab), in patient registries, and in payer claims databases, with virtually no interoperability between systems. A recent survey from KLAS Research found that only 6% of providers said that information obtained from outside of their organization can be located within their workflow, and less than 33% said that they can easily access data from different EHRs (Conn, 2014).

Terms and definitions are not consistent. Different providers use different definitions for a condition (e.g., what type of asthma a child has), procedure, or drug. An illustrative example is that the Regenstrief Center for Healthcare Engineering receives smart infusion pump uploads from roughly 330 hospitals across the United States (Witz et al., 2014). We found that there were over 200 different entry terms for a basic saline bag, and in many cases, the same hospital would use multiple terms. As a result, data sharing alone without interoperability and standardization is not enough for evidence generation.

Data are both structured and unstructured. Most hospitals and clinics store data in EHRs. Even in the EHR, data can be structured as in *International Classification of Diseases* (*ICD*; World Health Organization, 2018) codes, or they can be unstructured, as in clinical notes. To complicate matters, *ICD–10* (as we discuss later) only provides a certain level of granularity. For this reason, two physicians may enter data in different ways for the same diagnosis if it does not perfectly match one of the codes. One physician may choose the closest match, whereas another physician may choose a wild card and then clarify in the clinical notes. This makes analyses of data extremely difficult.

Data are incomplete. The granularity of health care makes it difficult to put together an entire picture of the patient. If we look at patient claims, for example, we only know whether there was a need for a particular service (e.g., a carious tooth that had to be filled) if the patient used the service. Further, although the EHR collects a longitudinal record of patient health, from a population health perspective, patients in the EHR may not be representative of the population at large (i.e., selection bias). Further, because real-time information is typically not captured, it is challenging to describe a patient's care pathway over time accurately. Similarly, less than 6% of U.S. hospitals have their medical devices integrated with their EHR, which means that it is typically not possible to understand the impact of a process change (e.g., the timing of a drug infusion) on patient outcomes. Developing real-time capture of clinical data in the EHR is an active area of study (Bodagh et al., 2018).

There are changing regulations. There have been several regulatory and financial changes that the health care delivery industry has been subjected to over the last decade, as we discuss later. These include regulations about how EHR data are used (i.e., meaningful use) and how providers are paid (e.g., a move from fee-for-service to value-based care). The constantly changing landscape leads to an increase in the effort required for reporting.

We discuss some of these in further detail later in the chapter.

A BRIEF HISTORY OF HEALTH CARE DATA

The use of health care data has changed dramatically in recent years. For example, 10 years ago, roughly 90% of office-based physicians manually updated patient records and stored them in color-coded paper files. Today, well over 90% of these physicians use EHRs. Further, there has been an increasing level of sophistication of standardized data through the following levels (Griffin et al., 2016): (a) nondigital data (paper forms); (b) unstructured, viewable digital data (scans of paper forms); (c) structured, viewable digital data (electronically entered data that cannot be computed by other systems); and (d) computable digital data (electronically entered data that can be computed by other systems). Before discussing why this happened, it is worth providing some background on the key sources of health data and supporting infrastructure.

Electronic Health Record

The EHR is, at its most basic, defined as a digital record of the health of the patient. In this chapter, we use the term synonymously with *electronic medical record*. The EHR is held by the provider (though parts may be accessed by the patient through a portal) and includes several types of information, such as demographic and socioeconomic data (e.g., sex, age, race), patient vital signs, patient management (e.g., registration, admission, transfer), patient lab results (which may stand alone from the EHR), radiology information (imaging), billing information, and physician notes.

The EHR can help simplify the workflow of a physician through records access, which can lead to improved patient safety and care. Some examples include sharing records between clinicians to help coordinate care; allowing quick access to records to support timely decision making; supporting safer prescribing practices (e.g., by identifying potentially harmful drug interactions); ensuring the accuracy of records, compared with written notes; supporting clinician–patient communications; and supporting integration of data from multiple sources to improve clinical decision making by having a "complete" record (Griffin et al., 2016).

The standard of coding used by the vast majority of U.S. health care systems for diagnosis or reason for seeking care is the *ICD*, developed by the World Health Organization (WHO). Although lagging behind most other WHO member countries, the current standard used by U.S. providers is *ICD–10* (or *ICD–10–CM*). This standard includes over 70,000 diagnosis and procedure codes and may be found at http://apps.who.int/classifications/icd10/browse/2016/en. Note that currently *ICD–11* is being adopted by different countries. The standard is an alphanumeric code made up of seven characters (XXX.XXX X), where the first three characters define the category (general type of injury or disease), the second three characters define the subcategory (anatomic site, severity, etiology), and the last character defines whether it was an initial encounter, subsequent encounter, or sequela. The following is an example for a finger wound:

- *S61*—{Open wound of wrist, hand, and fingers}
  - *S61.2* Open wound of other finger without damage to nail
    - ○ *S61.20* Unspecified open would of other finger without damage to nail

- *S61.201* Unspecified open wound of left index finger without damage to nail
- *S61.201 A* Unspecified open wound of left index finger without damage to nail, initial encounter

It is easy to see that even with this scheme, there are several injury types that would satisfy this coding.

The other key coding system is for procedures, services, devices, or treatments and is used for billing. The Current Procedural Terminology (CPT) codes are maintained by the American Medical Association. Each CPT code is five digits long and belongs to one of three categories. Category I is the most common category and includes the following six sections: evaluation and management, anesthesiology, surgery, radiology, pathology and laboratory, and medicine. An example is 41899, which is the CPT code for a dental extraction.

EHRs date back to the 1970s. Figure 11.1 illustrates the timeline. Some of the earliest systems include PROMIS (Patient-Reported Outcomes Measurement Information System), by the Medical Center Hospital of Vermont, and RMRS, developed by the Regenstrief Medical Record System. The Institute of Medicine strongly recommended their use in 1991, and in 2003, released a letter report describing eight key capabilities that should be present (Clancy, 2003): accuracy—both information and data; result management—quick access for care coordination; order management—computerized provider

FIGURE 11.1. Timeline of Key Electronic Health Record (EHR) Events

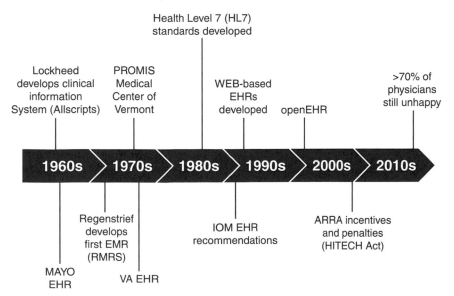

ARRA = American Recovery and Reinvestment Act; EMR = electronic medical record; HITECH = Health Information Technology for Economic and Clinical Health; IOM = Institute of Medicine; PROMIS = Patient-Reported Outcomes Measurement Information System; RMRS = Regenstrief Medical Record System.

order entry to reduce errors; decision support—provide alerts and reminders; electronic communication and connectivity—secure messaging, text messaging, web portals, and so forth; patient support—patient education and telemonitoring; administrative processes and reporting—electronic scheduling, claims submission, eligibility verification, and so forth, reporting, and population health.

The American Recovery and Reinvestment Act (ARRA; Steinbrook, 2009) included both revenues and penalties for demonstrated EHR use by providers in 2009 (discussed later in this section). Today, the majority of the market share is made up of Cerner, MEDITECH, and Epic Systems, though it is worth noting that many physicians are unhappy with current EHR systems. A recent survey of 6,880 physicians (Sinsky et al., 2017) showed that frustration with the EHR was a key reason over 20% of them will either reduce their clinical hours or leave their profession.

An important component of EHRs is the assurance of the protection of patient information. The Health Insurance Portability and Accountability Act (HIPAA; 1996) requires providers to establish several safeguards (physical, administrative, and technical) to protect patient data in the EHR, including data encryption, access control (e.g., passwords), and audit trails. As we discuss later, current methods are woefully inadequate.

Given the wealth of information collected in the EHR, these records have been used in studies of interest to psychology that include a time-series analysis of the EHR to understand the trajectories of autism spectrum disorder patients in terms of comorbidities (Doshi-Velez, Ge, & Kohane, 2014), an examination of how EHR default settings can affect laboratory test ordering practices (Probst, Shaffer, & Chan, 2013), and surveillance for public health (Birkhead, Klompas, & Shah, 2015). Given recent interests in including more dimensions, such as health behaviors and psychosocial functioning (Glasgow, Kaplan, Ockene, Fisher, & Emmons, 2012), the EHR may become an important data touchpoint for psychologists interested in health behaviors.

Meaningful Use and the Medicare Access and CHIP Reauthorization Act

To encourage the adoption of EHR technology, the Health Information Technology for Economic and Clinical Health (HITECH) Act (2009) outlined what is called *meaningful use* (MU), which requires providers to demonstrate they are using their EHR technology to improve patient outcomes. As part of ARRA, a program was established by the Centers for Medicare and Medicaid Services (CMS) based on a set of incentives and penalties that supported MU through three phases: (a) using EHRs for data capture and sharing (e.g., tracking key clinical conditions, using a standardized format for electronic health information), (b) advancing clinical practice (e.g., providing patient-controlled data, transmitting electronic records over multiple settings), and (c) improving outcomes (e.g., improving quality, safety, efficiency). Providers that do not meet MU requirements are penalized up to 3%, starting in 2019. Over $25 billion in incentives have been paid by CMS between 2011 and 2018.

Although HITECH has certainly led to widespread adoption of the EHR by providers, there has been widely reported provider dissatisfaction with its usefulness; many providers state that it adds to their workload. This may be due to the relative short-term focus of HITECH, which emphasizes compliance rather than innovation. In addition, physicians were not properly prepared for the program, and the metrics for electronic clinical quality measures were not ready (Basch & Kuhn, 2016).

It is important to mention that MU was absorbed into the Medicare Access and CHIP Reauthorization Act (MACRA) in 2015. In addition to MU, MACRA also includes the Physician Quality Reporting System, Value-Based Payment Modifier, and Merit-Based Incentive Payment System.

Improving outcomes, such as patient experience and improvement in health, along with increasing innovation and satisfaction with the EHR systems, will require collaborations with social scientists and psychologists to go beyond monetary incentives. The utility of big data analysis of the EHR will only be useful insofar as there is widespread standardized adoption of EHRs.

Claims and Other Data Sources

There are many other important data sources. One source is claims data that result from a bill sent to a payer (e.g., an insurance company or Medicaid or Medicare), which typically arises from services provided. Billing requirements established by Medicaid and Medicare have incentivized most practices to file their claims electronically. Claims data are also coded (i.e., structured) data, though they also suffer from many limitations in their use, like the EHR. Some of the key issues include that claims are organized around a billing event, and it can be difficult to infer unique visits; duplicate records can arise due to claims adjustments; there are missing data from unfiled claims; inference is required in the case of care management organizations because billing is not done by each service provided; claims serve as a lower bound on actual demand for services because only those individuals that use services show up in claims, and it is impossible to determine factors such as medication adherence because we only know whether or not the prescription was filled and not whether the patient took it as intended.

In addition to claims, there are many other sources of individual health data, and this area is growing. Many health systems, such as Geisinger, are collecting and analyzing the DNA of patient participants (e.g., MyCode Community Health Initiative). There have also been significant advancements in the so-called -omics fields—genomics (genetic data), proteomics (the study of proteomes), and transcriptomics (the study of transcriptomes)—and other sources of data, which are helping to lead the way toward the development of precision medicine. Further, the use of wearables, injectables, and implantables is exploding and generating massive amounts of real-time monitoring data. For example, Verily Life Sciences is currently conducting a health-monitoring study on 10,000 people that is generating 6 terabytes of data per person. The advancement of wearable technology brings up a whole range of security, privacy, and ethical issues, beyond the scope of this chapter, largely because, at this point, it all currently exists outside the health care delivery system. We direct readers to the later chapters in this book in which the security and privacy of these big data technical systems are discussed (e.g., Chapter 18, this volume).

Social Network and Behavioral Data

Another recent development in social sciences and psychological sciences is the rise of social networks and how they are impacting people's interaction with each other and what the implications are for individual and the collective health of the society. These interactions have profoundly changed the way we communicate and make decisions, the impact of which we are just starting to understand. There are many potential research opportunities in this domain that require critical thinking and an interdisciplinary approach of psychology, data science, social science, economics, computer science, and methodologies (Harlow & Oswald, 2016). For example, a recent study using Twitter data showed how to successfully predict mortality related to heart disease (Eichstaedt et al., 2015). Many other such examples show how behavioral cues can be identified from social network data to identify insights from the network.

Health Information Exchange

An important component of health information is the ability to share information electronically across organizations. The Health Information Exchange (HIE) allows providers and patients to securely access and share a patient's medical information. The HIE can help better inform the patient and provider and facilitate care coordination. Potential benefits include a reduction in medication errors and duplicate testing, improved diagnosis, and reduced readmissions. At present, there are three key forms of HIE (HealthIT. gov, n.d.):

- directed exchange—sends and receives electronic information between care providers to support coordinated care,

- query-based exchange—allows providers to request and obtain information on a patient from other providers, and

- consumer-mediated exchange—allows patients to control the use of their information among providers.

The 21st Century Cures Act was passed in 2015 to provide resources in support of HIE. Much of the recent efforts in HIE has been including newer technologies such as Internet of Things devices, where all devices are connected to the Internet; cloud services; and mHealth (mobile health or telehealth) applications. There is also significant effort to better include social determinants and behavior health through HIEs in the EHR.

THE ROLE OF FINANCING

Historically, reimbursement for health care has been built on the "fee-for-service" model. In this case, the patient receives a set of services from the provider, and the services are paid for by a third party. The third party is made up of one or more of out-of-pocket payment by the patient, private insurance, or public insurance (Medicare, Medicaid, government). The fact that the patient does not directly pay for the services in this mechanism leads to potential moral hazards (i.e., a party takes an action because they do not internalize the full cost of that action):

- Because the patient does not directly pay for their care, they may "consume" in excess of their need; this may be particularly true in end-of-life care where treatments with a low probability of success may be sought well beyond their expected usefulness.

- Because the provider is paid for each service rendered, they may provide more services than is necessary (supplier-induced demand).

In an effort the address the potentially high costs that result from fee for service, there has been a recent move to value-based care. In this case, payments for care delivery are based on the "quality" of care provided. These models have arisen in both the public and private sectors. For example, CMS has introduced the Medicare Shared Savings Program and Pioneer Accountable Care Organization Model. Further, private insurers have introduced a variety of pay-for-performance programs. Although there are many variations, Figure 11.2 shows a general model that shares the savings between provider and payer.

In theory, value-based care models incentivize providers to deliver the best set care (including prevention) to the population they serve, which helps control costs and improve outcomes. In practice, however, the literature has shown that the results are, at best, mixed. A recent survey of 1,492 practices found that EHR measurement functionality was "insufficient to support federal initiatives that tie payment to clinical quality measures" (Cohen et al., 2018, para. 1).

An additional problem is likely the outcome measures themselves. It is extremely difficult to measure outcomes at the individual level with current processes. Further, there is not always clear evidence that the metrics used actually mean that improvement in them is equivalent to the health and wellness of the population for whom they are measured. In the next section, we discuss the role of evidence in health care and the role that big data can play in generating it.

FIGURE 11.2. Value Based Care Model (Shared Savings)

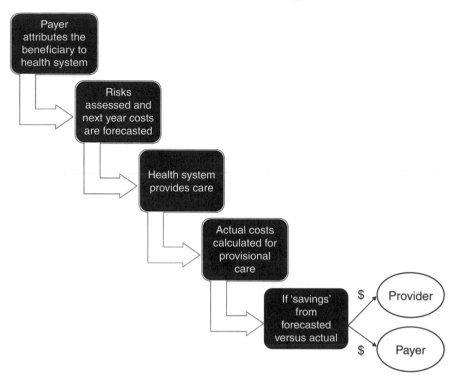

EVIDENCE IN HEALTH CARE

Establishing whether an intervention will work for a certain population is one of the key challenges in the health sciences and biomedical research. The process of gathering empirical evidence to support new interventions is highly nontrivial due to the complexity of human biology and its intricate interactions with the underlying environment.

The enactment of the 1962 Amendments to the Food, Drug, and Cosmetic Act required that new treatments be proven efficacious in "adequate and well-controlled investigations" (Greene & Podolsky, 2012, para. 6). In the 1970s, the Food and Drug Administration translated this into the requirement that an RCT is needed to validate the causal link between a new treatment (causal intervention) and a clinical outcome. The rationale for adopting RCTs as the means of gathering scientific evidence is that spurious associations due to factors extraneous to the relationship between the treatment and the outcome can be controlled for by randomizing the treatment assignment.

RCT-based procedures are currently considered the gold standard for supporting evidence generation in the empirical sciences, and thousands of trials are conducted each year just in the medical domain. Despite a host of benefits, it is widely acknowledged that RCTs are far from perfect. The limitations of RCTs are that they are, for example, usually slow and time consuming, expensive, sometimes not entirely ethical, and often applicable to only a specific subgroup of the population. In contrast to the RCT-based approach, scientists have been collecting increasing amounts of observational (non-experimental) data or big data. Unfortunately, these big data also have limitations, such as confounding biases, and do not solve all the problems either. Psychological research has shown that stronger causal inferences from observational data require careful research design, as well (e.g., Cole & Maxwell, 2003). Consequently, the current generation of biomedical researchers faces a challenge—to understand how to leverage the vast, but imperfect, amounts of data and translate them into new insights about causal interventions.

Significant research activities in theoretical computer science are generating evidence from observational data, such as EHRs, for the identification of causal inference using graphical models (Halpern, 2000; Pearl, 1995, 2009), commonly known as *structural causal models*. This is one of the traditions of causal modeling that does not necessarily prefer randomized controlled experiments and focuses on the mediating or moderating mechanisms of the causal chain (see Shadish & Sullivan, 2012). The grand challenge is to integrate biased and heterogeneous data coming from various populations, the task known as *data fusion* (Bareinboim & Pearl, 2016). It is worth noting that this is beyond the current integrated EHR or HIE systems because those systems barely consider the physical and software integration for interoperability and not the fundamental methodological issues. In structural causal modeling, domain knowledge (e.g., clinical expertise) is encoded in a causal graph, where nodes represent random variables (e.g., treatment, outcome, covariates), and arrows represent causal relations (Pearl, 2009). The challenge in using structural causal modeling is the use of imprecise causal graphs for approximate causal inference. Another challenge is engaging the clinical and psychological science community for wider adoption of the methodologies developed in recent years in structural causal modeling for evidence generation from observational and experimental studies.

DATA PLATFORMS IN HEALTH CARE

Widespread recognition of the potential of data analytics solutions to important socioeconomic and health problems has motivated the development of curated data repositories and analytics frameworks in various application domains, including health care (Gutiérrez-Sacristán et al., 2018; Hripcsak et al., 2015; Kohane, Churchill, & Murphy, 2012; Margolis et al., 2014; Murphy, Castro, & Mandl, 2017; Murphy et al., 2010; Ohno-Machado et al., 2012; Scheufele et al., 2014). These first-generation systems typically collect, curate, and present data in a mediated schema or federate access across databases using conventional web services technologies. Analytics solutions in these frameworks rely on batch systems such as MapReduce and dataflow and event processing systems, such as Storm and Spark, among others. Such systems have been deployed and used with considerable success in various domains.

However, one key issue that remains to be solved is reproducibility. Reproducibility of scientific research has recently garnered much attention, though there remain many challenges in terms of reproducibility, robustness, and verifiability of scientific claims (Gehr, Weiss, & Porzsolt, 2006; Ioannidis, 2005a, 2005b; Open Science Collaboration, 2015). This is particularly true for data-driven research in health care and related to evidence generation, where the data is often biased, cannot be generalized to a broader population, and cannot be easily shared due to privacy and security reasons. The issue of reproducibility is an important one in psychological research, given recent concerns about the lack of reproducibility of many key psychological findings. In psychology, there is a practice of using multiple analyses to examine the same data set (Silberzahn et al., 2018) or using graphical descriptives to showcase aggregate data patterns without revealing raw data (Tay, Parrigon, Huang, & LeBreton, 2016). In the following section, we discuss different systems in light of reproducibility.

Current Platforms and Limitations

Research networks of hospital systems have accumulated large amounts of data and developed systems for analyzing them. These systems are being widely used by researchers. However, questions remain about the validity of the results because, in general, they do not provide a physical (shareability of analytic workflow) and methodological (e.g., causal inference, external validity, generalizability) framework for reproducibility. We provide a brief overview of existing research networks of observational data, primarily EHR-based, in terms of these features.

Informatics for Integrating Biology and the Bedside

Informatics for Integrating Biology and the Bedside, i2b2 (Abend, Housman, & Johnson, 2009; Hong et al., 2016; Johnson et al., 2014; McMurry et al., 2013; Murphy, Castro, & Mandl, 2017; Murphy et al., 2007, 2010; Segagni et al., 2011), is an open-source software system for easy access and basic statistical analysis on large EHR systems. The system is designed for tasks such as cohort identification and retrospective data analysis. It is built with two components: (a) the hive, a back-end infrastructure for data privacy, security, and management; and (b) the workbench, a query builder and analysis tool. Data from any EHR have to be transformed into i2b2's star schema (a specific representation of a database) to provide a common structure for different EHR data sources (Post et al., 2016; Waitman, Warren, Manos, & Connolly, 2011). Data requests that include complex temporal conditions regarding inclusion and exclusion criteria require some amount of pre- and/or postprocessing (Deshmukh, Meystre, & Mitchell, 2009). i2b2 provides privacy features by de-identification of patients by stripping the data of the HIPAA identifiers and providing different levels of access to the researchers (Murphy, Gainer, Mendis, Churchill, & Kohane, 2011). Although the system is useful for simple analysis and cohort selection, it does not provide the features for sharing analytic workflow and methods for reproducibility, generalizability, and transferability.

Observational Health Data Science and Informatics

Observational Health Data Science and Informatics (OHDSI) is a network of care providers that share and use observational health data for evidence generation in medicine (Hripcsak et al., 2015, 2016). It was created to provide a suite of data analytic tools for exploring data and generating evidence to improve health outcomes. OHDSI was initiated by the Observational Medical Outcomes Partnership (OMOP; Hripcsak et al., 2015; Overhage, Ryan, Reich, Hartzema, & Stang, 2012), and it adopted and maintained the OMOP Common Data Model (CDM; Makadia & Ryan, 2014). Each participant in the OHDSI network must translate their data to the OMOP CDM format, as well as map each element to the approved vocabulary; in comparison, the data have to be transformed into a star schema for i2b2. Although a particular analytics workflow can be shared with OHDSI, it is nontrivial to reproduce results with a different data set considering the biases across populations and cohorts. Because of the use of OMOP CDM, OHDSI researchers have been able to replicate analyses across multiple OMOP data sources to produce a consistent set of results (Reisinger, 2016).

Patient-Centered Informatics Common: Standard Unification of Research Elements

Patient-Centered Informatics Common: Standard Unification of Research Elements (PIC-SURE; Gutiérrez-Sacristán et al., 2018; Murphy et al., 2017) is developing an open-source infrastructure to incorporate multiple heterogeneous patient-level data, including clinical, omics, and environmental data. The core idea of PIC-SURE is to utilize distributed data resources of various types and protocols by a single communication interface to perform queries and computations across different resources. For this purpose, PIC-SURE developed the Inter Resource Communication Tool, which is resource-driven and allows new resources to be integrated quickly. PIC-SURE API provides multiple resources to define and run a query. Results generated by a user can be available only for the user. PIC-SURE API is not responsible for authentication and governance for individual access and is defined by resources. The system does not provide support for reproducibility and generalizability.

Use Cases

There are hundreds of publications that used big data captured during routine health care for evidence generation and new methods development for artificial intelligence techniques, among others. For example, a recent publication showed how artificial intelligence techniques can be used for optimal treatment for sepsis in the intensive care unit (Komorowski, Celi, Badawi, Gordon, & Faisal, 2018). Another study showed how observational data can be used to emulate a randomized trial for identifying the effect of hormone therapy in postmenopausal women (Hernán et al., 2008). A recent Google publication showed how deep learning techniques can be used for predicting events from EHR data (Rajkomar et al., 2018). Although considerable progress has been made, as illustrated by these examples, it still will require much analysis and further work for these techniques to be adapted in health care delivery for safety reasons. For example, the sepsis study was criticized for failing in some cases where the optimal treatment is obvious to the clinicians (Jeter, Josef, Shashikumar, & Nemati, 2019).

KEY BIG DATA CHALLENGES IN HEALTH CARE

Even as these analytics systems become commonplace, there is an increasing need for higher level functionality supported within these systems. As analytics kernels operate on increasingly heterogeneous dynamic data sets, with complex dependencies across software components, on ever-changing hardware platforms, reproducibility becomes an important and complex objective (Bui & Van Horn, 2017; Goodman, Fanelli, & Ioannidis, 2016). Reproducibility takes the form of hard reproducibility, which supports complete recreation of the data, software, and execution environment to arrive at the same result, or soft reproducibility, which allows the analytics task to execute on potentially different data (drawn from the same distribution) in different computational environments to arrive at statistically identical results. Hard reproducibility poses significant systems challenges by way of version control for data (data checkpoints), archiving data experiments, and recreating an identical computational environment. Soft reproducibility, however, poses challenging statistical problems in modeling input distributions, deriving concentration bounds, and quantifying statistical identity of analytics results. Current analytics frameworks provide minimal support for such tasks.

Once an analytics result is deemed reproducible, issues of transportability and generalizability are important. We illustrate these concepts using examples derived from clinical applications. Consider two distinct health record repositories—one from South Carolina, and another from Iowa. The states have been selected because of the differences in their demographic composition by race. It is relatively straightforward to select a cohort of individuals in South Carolina with sickle cell disease and correlate pathology with variants of the HBB gene with high statistical significance. However, the same result will likely be much harder to replicate on the data set from Iowa. This is because one in 12 individuals of African American origin carries the HBB variant. This rate is much lower in Caucasian Americans. For this reason, it would be much harder to get statistical power in such correlations on the Iowa cohort, compared with the South Carolina cohort. The general problem highlighted by this example is one of transportability, where a result derived from one sample does not transfer to another sample, due to latent differences in distributions. A related concept is one of generalizability—wherein the goal is to generalize learned models from selected cohorts to general populations. The goal is to provide support for transportability and generalizability within the data analytics system—as opposed to relegating it to applications, where assumptions of distributions, their stationarity, and statistical power may confound any inferences.

Although a result may be reproducible, generalizable, and transportable, it may not be verifiable and/or statistically significant. An example of this is commonly encountered when correlating genomic variants with observed phenotype. It is well known that although significant parts of our genome are shared, a small number of variants (e.g., single nucleotide polymorphisms [SNPs]) predispose us toward phenotype. In typical association studies, one has a small number of samples (say a cohort of 1,000) that a display phenotype and a similar number that do not. This cohort has a few million cataloged SNPs, most of which are unrelated to the phenotype. Given this large number of SNPs and the small number of samples, it is typically possible to find perfect correlations with completely unrelated SNPs. Such correlations are not verifiable and have low statistical power (i.e., with respect to any meaningful prior, their p-value is high). This raises two important questions—how we quantify the verifiability of the result and how we support measures of statistical significance within the analytics framework. Ideally, the system should support both parametric as well as nonparametric priors, coupled with analytical as well as empirical calculations of statistical significance.

A critical aspect of analytics systems is its support for privacy and security (Ness, 2007; Pröell, Mayer, & Rauber, 2015). Specifically, public release of any sensitive data must be suitably de-identified to ensure the privacy of individuals. At the same time, there is significant interplay between privacy and security on the one hand and issues of reproducibility, generalizability, transportability, and verifiability on the other. Traditional approaches to privacy range from the use of research unique identifiers (RUIDs) to index records after identifiable data have been scrubbed to techniques such as differential privacy. RUIDs, although commonly used to de-identify health records, are highly susceptible to 20-questions type attacks (the set of individuals with Southeast Asian genomic variants, with markers for myocardial infarction and having been prescribed blood thinners, in the town of West Lafayette, is rather small). However, although differential privacy is commonly used in various applications (including the forthcoming census), its use in health-related applications is not judicious. This is because typical analytics queries relate to high statistical significance (low *p*-value) artifacts. These are precisely the queries that are washed out by differential privacy—rendering differentially private databases relatively unusable for such applications. This raises several important questions: Can we simultaneously satisfy exacting requirements for privacy while supporting critical analytics tasks? Furthermore, can we provide a computational sandbox for secured execution of analytics workflows on private data while using public domain services and tools, providing suitable authentication and audit trails? We argue that these important higher order functionalities must be supported within the analytics framework, rather than at the application level, to ensure consistent and standardized quantification of critical measures. Furthermore, these functionalities must be developed in ways that they can be seamlessly integrated with existing data repositories through a powerful, yet concise, API into the repository.

A PATH FORWARD

Right Incentive: Financial and Regulatory

A right incentive to reduce cost is critical to create the domino effect in downstream applications, research, and delivery. In the current fee-for-service model, redundant treatment and tests are often encouraged, whereas the shift to the value-based care in effect will ensure the profitability of the health care delivery systems for the right treatment and tests. One emerging trend in this regard is the increasing integration of the providers and insurers, such as the Kaiser Permanente and Geisinger Health System. This vertical integration of the stakeholders will optimize the quality of care and outcome instead of the quantity of care. Another key incentive may come from more competition and transparency. For example, currently, it is almost impossible for a patient to compare costs across providers for best care, and hence there is wide variability of costs across providers. However, this may eliminate inefficient systems from the market and may require a regulatory mandate to be implemented.

Software-Hardware-Data-Methods Ecosystem

The current federated system for integrated analysis is not sufficient to take advantage of the big data. A new generation of software-hardware-data ecosystem is needed for key analytics and query tasks:

- *Cohort selection.* Given a defining set of characteristics, identify a sample from the repository, which serves as a representative for a data study. The system must provide support for statistically and physically identical cohorts through cohort objects. Statistically identical cohorts generate samples with identical (within prescribed bounds) within and across statistical properties. Physically identical cohorts must archive data samples to generate the same cohort when reinstantiated.

- *Querying and statistical characterization.* Given a sequence of queries (statistical as well as traditional database queries), the new generation of systems must support composite query objects that capture query sessions that can be reinstantiated on the same data object at a later time. This will allow for a sequence of queries to be replayed on specific versions of data, with the goal of supporting reproducibility.

- *Support for core analytics tasks.* Common analytics tasks, such as correlation, clustering, association, and classification, must be encapsulated in analytics objects that can be replayed on specified versions of data. Their statistical power must be verified through various statistical tests and their generalizability verified through sampling experiments.

- *Methods for causal inference, generalizability, and transportability.* Causal inference is particularly susceptible to cohort selection, models and methods for statistical power, and generalizability of the study. To this end, our proposed system will quantify these parameters of generalizability drawn from data studies.

We note two important aspects of such advanced analytic systems at this point: (a) The system and its proposed functionality are largely independent of the technologies used to architect the data repositories. It is designed to operate on top of data stores—and we will explicitly support its integration atop commonly used data repositories. (b) Such a system must also be largely independent of the analytics techniques and underlying methods. For instance, the algorithm used for identifying associations or constructing a classifier is orthogonal to the goals of supporting reproducibility, quantifying its statistical validity, generalizability, and robustness. We believe that this layered approach is particularly important given the rich and continually evolving landscape of both the data architecture, as well as the analytics infrastructure. Finally, these systems must evolve to be real-time or near real-time systems for effective adaption and translation.

Privacy

Although data sharing is extremely important for big data–driven research for evidence generation, it is also up to the researchers to respect the privacy of individual patients, specifically in accordance with the Privacy Rule of HIPAA. One key property of the data analytics platform must be the privacy-preserving analysis. Emerging systems must provide analytical support for causal inference and statistical significance while maintaining patient privacy. However, this creates additional research questions—for example, how much information is lost, and how does it affect the validity of inferences from private data (or de-identified data)? Can we quantify the loss of confidence for such reasons? The careful balance between loss of information and preserving privacy is a challenging task that requires a sophisticated algorithmic and social and ethical understanding of the models and systems.

CONCLUSION

We outlined the issues related to big data in health care delivery in this chapter. We started with the data sources and the recent history of data-capturing technologies and their evolution, including financing for the implementation of the technologies. Next, we pivoted to how evidence is generated in medicine and what the challenges are to generate evidence in medicine from big data with a deep understanding of the risk of such approaches. Finally, we concluded with a path forward for a future where big data can be used for quality evidence generation, improved care delivery, and efficient health care for the betterment of human health and longevity. Our focus in this chapter has been the technological issues, and in no way does it capture the myriad policy-making, regulatory, financing, and economic assessments related to big data in health care delivery.

REFERENCES

Abend, A., Housman, D., & Johnson, B. (2009). Integrating clinical data into the i2b2 repository. *Summit on Translational Bioinformatics, 2009*(1), 1–5.

Bareinboim, E., & Pearl, J. (2016). Causal inference and the data-fusion problem. *PNAS, 113*, 7345–7352. http://dx.doi.org/10.1073/pnas.1510507113

Basch, P., & Kuhn, T. (2016, January). It's time to fix meaningful use. *Health Affairs*. Retrieved from https://www.healthaffairs.org/do/10.1377/hblog20160114.052678/full/

Birkhead, G. S., Klompas, M., & Shah, N. R. (2015). Uses of electronic health records for public health surveillance to advance public health. *Annual Review of Public Health, 36*, 345–359. http://dx.doi.org/10.1146/annurev-publhealth-031914-122747

Bodagh, N., Archbold, R. A., Weerackody, R., Hawking, M. K. D., Barnes, M. R., Lee, A. M., . . . Timmis, A. (2018). Feasibility of real-time capture of routine clinical data in the electronic health record: A hospital-based, observational service-evaluation study. *BMJ Open, 8*(3), e019790. http://dx.doi.org/10.1136/bmjopen-2017-019790

Bui, A. A. T., & Van Horn, J. D. (2017). Envisioning the future of 'big data' biomedicine. *Journal of Biomedical Informatics, 69*, 115–117. http://dx.doi.org/10.1016/j.jbi.2017.03.017

Clancy, C. (2003). *Key capabilities of and electronic health record system: Letter report.* Retrieved from https://www.nap.edu/read/10781/chapter/2

Cohen, D. J., Dorr, D. A., Knierim, K., DuBard, C. A., Hemler, J. R., Hall, J. D., . . . Balasubramanian, B. A. (2018). Primary care practices' abilities and challenges in using electronic health record data for quality improvement. *Health Affairs, 37*, 635–643. http://dx.doi.org/10.1377/hlthaff.2017.1254

Cole, D. A., & Maxwell, S. E. (2003). Testing mediational models with longitudinal data: Questions and tips in the use of structural equation modeling. *Journal of Abnormal Psychology, 112*, 558–577. http://dx.doi.org/10.1037/0021-843X.112.4.558

Conn, J. (2014). *Interoperability isn't keeping many providers up at night, survey indicates.* Retrieved from https://www.modernhealthcare.com/article/20141106/NEWS/311069945

Deshmukh, V. G., Meystre, S. M., & Mitchell, J. A. (2009). Evaluating the informatics for integrating biology and the bedside system for clinical research. *BMC Medical Research Methodology, 9*. http://dx.doi.org/10.1186/1471-2288-9-70

Doshi-Velez, F., Ge, Y., & Kohane, I. (2014). Comorbidity clusters in autism spectrum disorders: An electronic health record time-series analysis. *Pediatrics, 133*, e54–e63. http://dx.doi.org/10.1542/peds.2013-0819

Eichstaedt, J. C., Schwartz, H. A., Kern, M. L., Park, G., Labarthe, D. R., Merchant, R. M., . . . Weeg, C. (2015). Psychological language on Twitter predicts county-level heart disease mortality. *Psychological Science, 26*, 159–169. http://dx.doi.org/10.1177/0956797614557867

Gehr, B. T., Weiss, C., & Porzsolt, F. (2006). The fading of reported effectiveness. A meta-analysis of randomised controlled trials. *BMC Medical Research Methodology, 6*, 25. http://dx.doi.org/10.1186/1471-2288-6-25

Glasgow, R. E., Kaplan, R. M., Ockene, J. K., Fisher, E. B., & Emmons, K. M. (2012). Patient-reported measures of psychosocial issues and health behavior should be added to electronic health records. *Health Affairs, 31*, 497–504. http://dx.doi.org/10.1377/hlthaff.2010.1295

Goodman, S. N., Fanelli, D., & Ioannidis, J. P. (2016). What does research reproducibility mean? *Science Translational Medicine, 8*(341), 341ps12. http://dx.doi.org/10.1126/scitranslmed.aaf5027

Greene, J. A., & Podolsky, S. H. (2012, October 18). Reform, regulation, and pharmaceuticals—The Kefauver-Harris Amendments at 50. *The New England Journal of Medicine, 367*(16), 1481–1483. http://dx.doi.org/10.1056/NEJMp1210007

Griffin, P. M., Nembhard, H. B., DeFlitch, C. J., Bastian, N. D., Kang, H., & Muñoz, D. A. (2016). *Healthcare systems engineering*. Hoboken, NJ: Wiley.

Gutiérrez-Sacristán, A., Guedj, R., Korodi, G., Stedman, J., Furlong, L. I., Patel, C. J., . . . Avillach, P. (2018). Rcupcake: An R package for querying and analyzing biomedical data through the BD2K PIC-SURE RESTful API. *Bioinformatics, 34*, 1431–1432. http://dx.doi.org/10.1093/bioinformatics/btx788

Halpern, J. Y. (2000). Axiomatizing causal reasoning. *Journal of Artificial Intelligence Research, 12*, 317–337. http://dx.doi.org/10.1613/jair.648

Harlow, L. L., & Oswald, F. L. (2016). Big data in psychology: Introduction to the special issue. *Psychological Methods, 21*, 447–457. http://dx.doi.org/10.1037/met0000120

Health Information Technology for Economic and Clinical Health (HITECH) Act, Title XIII of Division A and Title IV of Division B of the American Recovery and Reinvestment Act of 2009 (ARRA), Pub. L. No. 111-5, 123 Stat. 226 (Feb. 17, 2009), codified at 42 U.S.C. §§300jj et seq.; §§17901 et seq.

The Health Insurance Portability and Accountability Act of 1996, Pub. L. No. 104-191, 110 Stat. 1938. (1996).

HealthIT.gov. (n.d.). *What is HIE?* Retrieved from https://www.healthit.gov/topic/health-it-and-health-information-exchange-basics/what-hie

Hernán, M. A., Alonso, A., Logan, R., Grodstein, F., Michels, K. B., Willett, W. C., . . . Robins, J. M. (2008). Observational studies analyzed like randomized experiments: An application to postmenopausal hormone therapy and coronary heart disease. *Epidemiology, 19*, 766–779. http://dx.doi.org/10.1097/EDE.0b013e3181875e61

Hong, N., Li, Z., Kiefer, R. C., Robertson, M. S., Goode, E. L., Wang, C., & Jiang, G. (2016). Building an i2b2-based integrated data repository for Cancer research: A case study of ovarian cancer registry. In *VLDB Workshop on Data Management and Analytics for Medicine and Healthcare* (pp. 121–135). Cham, Switzerland: Springer. http://dx.doi.org/10.1007/978-3-319-57741-8_8

Hripcsak, G., Duke, J. D., Shah, N. H., Reich, C. G., Huser, V., Schuemie, M. J., . . . Ryan, P. B. (2015). Observational Health Data Sciences and Informatics (OHDSI): Opportunities for observational researchers. *Studies in Health Technology and Informatics, 216*, 574–578.

Hripcsak, G., Ryan, P. B., Duke, J. D., Shah, N. H., Park, R. W., Huser, V., . . . Perotte, A. (2016). Characterizing treatment pathways at scale using the OHDSI network. *PNAS, 113,* 7329–7336. http://dx.doi.org/10.1073/pnas.1510502113

Ioannidis, J. P. (2005a). Contradicted and initially stronger effects in highly cited clinical research. *JAMA, 294,* 218–228. http://dx.doi.org/10.1001/jama.294.2.218

Ioannidis, J. P. (2005b). Why most published research findings are false. *PLoS Medicine, 2*(8), e124. http://dx.doi.org/10.1371/journal.pmed.0020124

Jeter, R., Josef, C., Shashikumar, S., & Nemati, S. (2019). Does the "Artificial Intelligence Clinician" learn optimal treatment strategies for sepsis in intensive care? *Point 85.* Retrieved from https://point85.ai/artificial-intelligence-clinician/

Johnson, E. K., Broder-Fingert, S., Tanpowpong, P., Bickel, J., Lightdale, J. R., & Nelson, C. P. (2014). Use of the i2b2 research query tool to conduct a matched case-control clinical research study: Advantages, disadvantages and methodological considerations. *BMC Medical Research Methodology, 14,* 16. http://dx.doi.org/10.1186/1471-2288-14-16

Kayyali, B., Knott, D., & Van Kuiken, S. (2013, April 7). *The big-data revolution in US health care.* Retrieved from https://www.mckinsey.com/industries/healthcare-systems-and-services/our-insights/the-big-data-revolution-in-us-health-care

Kohane, I. S., Churchill, S. E., & Murphy, S. N. (2012). A translational engine at the national scale: Informatics for integrating biology and the bedside. *Journal of the American Medical Informatics Association, 19,* 181–185. http://dx.doi.org/10.1136/amiajnl-2011-000492

Komorowski, M., Celi, L. A., Badawi, O., Gordon, A. C., & Faisal, A. A. (2018). The Artificial Intelligence Clinician learns optimal treatment strategies for sepsis in intensive care. *Nature Medicine, 24,* 1716–1720. http://dx.doi.org/10.1038/s41591-018-0213-5

Makadia, R., & Ryan, P. B. (2014). Transforming the Premier Perspective® hospital database into the OMOP common data model. *EGEMS, 2*(1), 15. http://dx.doi.org/10.13063/2327-9214.1110

Margolis, R., Derr, L., Dunn, M., Huerta, M., Larkin, J., Sheehan, J., . . . Green, E. D. (2014). The National Institutes of Health's Big Data to Knowledge (BD2K) initiative: Capitalizing on biomedical big data. *Journal of the American Medical Informatics Association, 21,* 957–958. http://dx.doi.org/10.1136/amiajnl-2014-002974

McMurry, A. J., Murphy, S. N., MacFadden, D., Weber, G., Simons, W. W., Orechia, J., . . . Kohane, I. S. (2013). SHRINE: Enabling nationally scalable multi-site disease studies. *PLoS ONE, 8*(3), e55811. http://dx.doi.org/10.1371/journal.pone.0055811

Medicare Access and CHIP Reauthorization Act of 2015, Pub. L. 114-10, 129 Stat. 87, 2015.

Murphy, S., Castro, V., & Mandl, K. (2017). Grappling with the future use of big data for translational medicine and clinical care. *Yearbook of Medical Informatics, 26,* 96–102. http://dx.doi.org/10.15265/IY-2017-020

Murphy, S. N., Gainer, V., Mendis, M., Churchill, S., & Kohane, I. (2011). Strategies for maintaining patient privacy in i2b2. *Journal of the American Medical Informatics Association, 18,* i103–i108. http://dx.doi.org/10.1136/amiajnl-2011-000316

Murphy, S. N., Mendis, M., Hackett, K., Kuttan, R., Pan, W., Phillips, L. C., . . . Kohane, I. (2007). Architecture of the open-source clinical research chart from informatics for integrating biology and the bedside. In *AMIA Annual Symposium Proceedings* (pp. 548–552). Bethesda, MD: American Medical Informatics Association.

Murphy, S. N., Weber, G., Mendis, M., Gainer, V., Chueh, H. C., Churchill, S., & Kohane, I. (2010). Serving the enterprise and beyond with informatics for integrating biology and the bedside (i2b2). *Journal of the American Medical Informatics Association, 17,* 124–130. http://dx.doi.org/10.1136/jamia.2009.000893

Ness, R. B. (2007). Influence of the HIPAA Privacy Rule on health research. *JAMA, 298,* 2164–2170. http://dx.doi.org/10.1001/jama.298.18.2164

Ohno-Machado, L., Bafna, V., Boxwala, A. A., Chapman, B. E., Chapman, W. W., Chaudhuri, K., . . . Vinterbo, S. A., & the iDASH team. (2012). iDASH: Integrating data for analysis, anonymization, and sharing. *Journal of the American Medical Informatics Association, 19,* 196–201. http://dx.doi.org/10.1136/amiajnl-2011-000538

Open Science Collaboration. (2015). Estimating the reproducibility of psychological science. *Science, 349,* aac4716. http://dx.doi.org/10.1126/science.aac4716

Overhage, J. M., Ryan, P. B., Reich, C. G., Hartzema, A. G., & Stang, P. E. (2012). Validation of a common data model for active safety surveillance research. *Journal of the American Medical Informatics Association, 19,* 54–60. http://dx.doi.org/10.1136/amiajnl-2011-000376

Pearl, J. (1995). Causal diagrams for empirical research. *Biometrika, 82,* 669–688. http://dx.doi.org/10.1093/biomet/82.4.669

Pearl, J. (2009). *Causality: Models, reasoning, and inference* (2nd ed.). Cambridge, England: Cambridge University Press. http://dx.doi.org/10.1017/CBO9780511803161

Post, A. R., Pai, A. K., Willard, R., May, B. J., West, A. C., Agravat, S., . . . Stephens, D. S. (2016). Metadata-driven clinical data loading into i2b2 for clinical and translational science institutes. *AMIA Joint Summits on Translational Science Proceedings, 2016,* 184–193.

Probst, C. A., Shaffer, V. A., & Chan, Y. R. (2013). The effect of defaults in an electronic health record on laboratory test ordering practices for pediatric patients. *Health Psychology, 32,* 995–1002. http://dx.doi.org/10.1037/a0032925

Pröell, S., Mayer, R., & Rauber, A. (2015). Data access and reproducibility in privacy sensitive eScience domains. In *Proceedings of the 11th IEEE International Conference on eScience* (pp. 255–258). Piscataway, NJ: IEEE.

Raghupathi, W., & Raghupathi, V. (2014). Big data analytics in healthcare: Promise and potential. *Health Information Science and Systems, 2*(1), 3. http://dx.doi.org/10.1186/2047-2501-2-3

Rajkomar, A., Oren, E., Chen, K., Dai, A. M., Hajaj, N., Hardt, M., . . . Dean, J. (2018). Scalable and accurate deep learning with electronic health records. *npj Digital Medicine, 1,* 18. http://dx.doi.org/10.1038/s41746-018-0029-1

Reisinger, S. (2016, May). The future of real-world evidence technology. *The Evidence Forum.* Retrieved from https://www.evalytica.com/wp-content/uploads/2016/11/05-The-Future-of-Real-World-Evidence-Technology-2016.pdf

Scheufele, E., Aronzon, D., Coopersmith, R., McDuffie, M. T., Kapoor, M., Uhrich, C. A., . . . Palchuk, M. B. (2014). tranSMART: An open source knowledge management and high content data analytics platform. *AMIA Joint Summits on Translational Science Proceedings, 2014,* 96–101.

Segagni, D., Ferrazzi, F., Larizza, C., Tibollo, V., Napolitano, C., Priori, S. G., & Bellazzi, R. (2011). R engine cell: Integrating R into the i2b2 software infrastructure. *Journal of the American Medical Informatics Association, 18,* 314–317. http://dx.doi.org/10.1136/jamia.2010.007914

Shadish, W. R., & Sullivan, K. J. (2012). Theories of causation in psychological science. In H. Cooper (Ed.), *APA handbook of research methods in psychology* (Vol. 1, pp. 23–52). Washington, DC: American Psychological Association.

Silberzahn, R., Uhlmann, E. L., Martin, D. P., Anselmi, P., Aust, F., Awtrey, E., . . . Nosek, B. A. (2018). Many analysts, one data set: Making transparent how variations in analytic choices affect results. *Advances in Methods and Practices in Psychological Science, 1,* 337–356. http://dx.doi.org/10.1177/2515245917747646

Sinsky, C. A., Dyrbye, L. N., West, C. P., Satele, D., Tutty, M., & Shanafelt, T. D. (2017). Professional satisfaction and the career plans of US physicians. *Mayo Clinic Proceedings, 92,* 1625–1635. http://dx.doi.org/10.1016/j.mayocp.2017.08.017

Steinbrook, R. (2009). Health care and the American recovery and reinvestment act. *The New England Journal of Medicine, 360,* 1057–1060. http://dx.doi.org/10.1056/NEJMp0900665

Tay, L., Parrigon, S., Huang, Q., & LeBreton, J. M. (2016). Graphical descriptives: A way to improve data transparency and methodological rigor in psychology. *Perspectives on Psychological Science, 11,* 692–701. http://dx.doi.org/10.1177/1745691616663875

21st Century Cures Act, H.R. 34, 114th Cong. (2015).

Waitman, L. R., Warren, J. J., Manos, D. L., & Connolly, D. W. (2011). Expressing observations from electronic medical record flowsheets in an i2b2 based clinical data repository to support research and quality improvement. *AMIA Symposium Proceedings, 2011,* 1454–1463.

Witz, S., Buening, N. R., Catlin, A. C., Malloy, W., Kindsfater, J. L., Walroth, T., . . . Zink, R. (2014). Using informatics to improve medical device safety and systems thinking. *Biomedical Instrumentation & Technology, 48,* 38–43. http://dx.doi.org/10.2345/0899-8205-48.s2.38

World Health Organization. (2018). *International classification of diseases* (11th rev.). Retrieved from https://icd.who.int/browse11/l-m/en

12

The Continued Importance of Theory

Lessons From Big Data Approaches to Language and Cognition

Brendan T. Johns, Randall K. Jamieson, and Michael N. Jones

Big data approaches to cognition have become increasingly popular, coinciding with the continued collection and curation of extremely large collections of human behavior (Jones, 2017). The study of natural language has been particularly impacted by the growth in this area, due to the rise of large and realistic corpora of text and the corresponding development of cognitive models that can learn from this text.

It is now possible to build large-scale computational models of language, train those models with a similar amount of linguistic experience to which an average human may have been exposed to, and determine whether the models have extracted knowledge comparable to the average human. We gain insights into learning processes by determining how closely the model's behavior maps onto empirical data collected from human subjects (Landauer & Dumais, 1997). Or we can use the representations extracted from the models as the basis for modeling other cognitive processes, including lexical organization (Hsiao & Nation, 2018; Jones, Johns, & Recchia, 2012; for a review, see Jones, Dye, & Johns, 2017), episodic memory (Johns, Jones, & Mewhort, 2012; Mewhort, Shabahang, & Franklin, 2018), lexical-perceptual integration (Andrews, Vigliocco, & Vinson, 2009; Johns & Jones, 2012; Lazaridou, Marelli, & Baroni, 2017), decision (Bhatia & Stewart, 2018), and sentence processing (Johns & Jones, 2015). In addition, the development of big data approaches to cognition has led to significant applied solutions in cognitive science, such as determining the changes occurring in lexical semantic memory during aging (Taler, Johns, & Jones, 2019) or in the behavior

http://dx.doi.org/10.1037/0000193-013
Big Data in Psychological Research, S. E. Woo, L. Tay, and R. W. Proctor (Editors)

of patients who are developing a memory disorder (Johns et al., 2018). More-over, there are many applied uses for these models, such as automated essay grading (see Jones & Dye, 2018, for a review). Theoretically, this research area has demonstrated the large and systematic connection between the natural language environment and human lexical behavior (Landauer & Dumais, 1997; Johns, Jones, & Mewhort, 2019; Jones & Mewhort, 2007).

The insights offered by big data approaches to natural language did not emerge in a vacuum. Much of current theory emerging from big data approaches to cognition mimics early work in the cognitive sciences that called for a systematic evaluation of the connection between human behavior and the environments that humans occupy (Estes, 1955, 1975; Simon, 1956, 1969). Specifically, Herbert Simon (1956, 1969) proposed that understanding cognition requires an examination and understanding of the organism, its environment, and the interaction of the two: "The apparent complexity of our behavior over time is largely a reflection of the complexity of the environment in which we find ourselves" (Simon, 1969, p. 53). Earlier, William Estes (1955) proposed that theories of behavior should shift "the burden of explanation from hypothesized processes in the organism to statistical properties of environmental events" (p. 145).

As an example of the importance of understanding the external environment to understand behavior, Simon (1969) described an ant walking on a beach. Although the path that the ant takes seems complicated, the complexity in the ant's behavior reflects a series of simple local adjustments to maneuver around the obstacles in its way. If one examines the ant's path without considering its environment, one might misattribute the complexity of the path to the ant rather than the environment.

Big data approaches to natural language heed Estes's and Simon's warnings by acknowledging and quantifying the natural language environment in which people are embedded. With the advance of big data, it is no longer necessary to blindly approximate the information structures to which people are exposed: The information can be directly estimated. Indeed, research has shown that the approximations that have been made in the past have not been accurate, such as in representational assumptions that were made in the cognitive modeling of memory (Johns & Jones, 2010). The availability of large-scale data sources means that making these assumptions is no longer necessary. For example, researchers can estimate the frequency with which different syntactic constructions occur and determine the effect of that exposure on people's behavior (e.g., Reali & Christiansen, 2007). Or properties of texts can be examined to determine how language changes by the demographic characteristics of authors to examine how lexical experience changes lexical behavior (Johns & Jamieson, 2019). More generally, advances in big data approaches to cognitive science have allowed for a systematic analysis of the connection between the statistical structure of the environment and human behavior, especially in the study of how people learn, organize, and use natural language (Johns, Jones, & Mewhort, 2019; Johns, Mewhort, & Jones, 2019; Jones et al., 2017; Jones, Willits, & Dennis, 2015).

Two of the best examples of how big data are being used in the cognitive sciences are given by the fields of lexical organization and lexical semantics. Lexical organization is the problem of how words are stored and retrieved in the mental lexicon. Early in the investigation of the problem, researchers focused on the impact that environmental variables had on word recognition. The first and still widely used variable is word frequency in written language (e.g., Kučera & Francis, 1967). Word frequency effects are ubiquitous across studies on language processing. For example, high-frequency words are easier to process than low-frequency words (e.g., Broadbent, 1967; Forster & Chambers, 1973; for a recent review, see Brysbaert, Mandera, & Keuleers, 2018). Due to these findings, word frequency has become a central component in models of lexical access (e.g., Goldinger, 1998; Murray & Forster, 2004) and is a standard variable used to control and select stimuli.

In this chapter, the importance of word frequency is how it is calculated. Initially, the values were calculated from the analysis of small corpora—for example, the widely used Kučera and Francis (1967) word counts derived from the Brown corpus of 1 million words. However, the advent of the Internet and powerful computers has allowed better, larger, and more diverse sources of language to be assembled, such as school-age textbooks (Landauer & Dumais, 1997), online encyclopedias (Shaoul & Westbury, 2010), television and movie subtitles (Brysbaert & New, 2009), social media (Herdağdelen & Marelli, 2017), crowdsourced dictionaries (Johns, 2019), and fiction and nonfiction books (Johns & Jamieson, 2018; Johns, Jones, & Mewhort, 2019), among many others. The collection of these different language sources has enabled a closer correspondence between the language that people experience and how language is stored and retrieved. Moreover, it has led to the ability to quantify aspects of our language environment to examine issues such as gender or racial bias (e.g., Caliskan, Bryson, & Narayanan, 2017; Johns & Dye, 2019). As detailed later in this chapter, the availability of large corpora has also enabled the development of new models of lexical strength (e.g., Adelman, Brown, & Quesada, 2006; Hoffman, Lambon Ralph, & Rogers, 2013; Jones et al., 2012), allowing for substantial theoretical growth in this research area.

Like the rise of new language sources, the field of lexical semantics has also seen rapid change due to both the growing availability of algorithms that can learn from these large sources of language. Models of this type are referred to as *distributional models of semantic memory* and propose that word meaning can be inferred from the patterns in which words are used (Griffiths, Steyvers, & Tenenbaum, 2007; Jamieson, Avery, Johns, & Jones, 2018; Jones & Mewhort, 2007; Landauer & Dumais, 1997; Mikolov, Sutskever, Chen, Corrado, & Dean, 2013). Although the models differ in significant ways—typically designed to explain particular aspects of linguistic behavior—they all stem from a similar theoretical basis: Simple learning mechanisms applied to language experience establish a sufficient basis for the acquisition of word meanings (Jones, Willits, & Dennis, 2015). In short, they all propose an account of language learning in which a word's meaning derives from the company it keeps—consistent with a more general approach dating back to Wittgenstein (1953), who stated, "The meaning of a word is its use in the language" (p. 43).

More recently, cognitive scientists have leveraged the semantic representations derived from corpus-based models to make sense of behavior and linguistic knowledge (e.g., Chubala, Johns, Jamieson, & Mewhort, 2016; Hills, Jones, & Todd, 2012; Hoffman et al., 2013; Johns & Jones, 2015; Johns, Jones, & Mewhort, 2012, 2019; Taler, Johns, Young, Sheppard, & Jones, 2013). In those accounts, the language representations derived from a distributional model are imported and used in a theory that presents an account of lexical processing, episodic memory, and decision. This exciting program of research aimed at integrating theories of knowledge representation with models of cognitive processing has pushed the borders of psychological theory by allowing for a more complete approach to theory and model development because it allows for both the process and representational components of a model to be fully specified. Moreover, it simplifies the modeling framework by allowing assumptions about the structure of language in memory to be greatly reduced (Johns & Jones, 2010; Johns, Mewhort, & Jones, 2017). Furthermore, it allows for the simulation of empirical fields that rely on the semantic content of linguistic stimuli to manipulate behavior, such as proactive interference (Mewhort et al., 2018) and false memory (Johns, Jones, & Mewhort, 2012, 2014).

Another exciting aspect of corpus-based models is that they enable an examination of model performance at the item level. For example, using a distributional model of semantics, one could take the similarity between the words *dog* and *wolf* and determine how closely that similarity maps onto people's similarity judgments for those same words. Ideally, this would be analyzed over hundreds or thousands of word pairs, enabling a systematic analysis of how closely a model's representation of word meaning maps onto human behavior. This would allow for a determination of whether the learning mechanism that a model uses successfully captures the required lexical behavior. Fortunately, the field was forward looking enough, and a number of large-scale data collection projects have enabled just this type of analysis, meaning that the impact of big data on the cognitive sciences has both a theoretical and empirical component.

MEGA DATA SETS OF HUMAN BEHAVIOR

Both lexical organization and lexical semantics have been targets for large-scale data collection, an exercise that has had a major impact on both fields. In the field of lexical organization, the English Lexicon Project (ELP; Balota et al., 2007) has allowed the field to account for lexical behaviors at an item level. The ELP collected lexical decision and naming reaction time performance for over 40,000 words from over 800 subjects at sites around the United States. The major impact of this work, apart from providing empiricists with a more refined ability to control stimuli, is that it has allowed a number of new models on lexical organization to be tested at the item level (e.g., Adelman et al., 2006; Jones et al., 2012). Indeed, the ELP proved so successful that parallel projects have been conducted for a number of different languages and dialects, including British English (Keuleers, Lacey, Rastle, & Brysbaert, 2012), French (Ferrand et al., 2010), Dutch (Brysbaert, Stevens, Mandera, & Keuleers, 2016b), Chinese (Tse et al., 2017), and Malay (Yap, Liow, Jalil, & Faizal, 2010). The availability of lexical information across so many different languages is an underutilized resource, but there are some ways these data sets have been exploited, such as demonstrating that lexical organization models generalize across different languages (Jones et al., 2017). Other studies have expanded on the ELP by publishing related but different measures of lexical processing (e.g., the semantic decision project; Pexman, Heard, Lloyd, & Yap, 2017). Overall, the existence of so many different lexicon projects demonstrates the use that researchers have found from the original ELP and the promise that many researchers recognize in conducting large-scale item-level analyses of lexical behavior.

Lexical semantics has an even older and arguably richer history of using mega data sets to examine item-level properties of word meaning. Nelson, McEvoy, and Schreiber (2004) published the University of South Florida free-association norms, which contains association data for 72,000 word pairs and has been used to both examine the nature of free association (Nelson, McEvoy, & Dennis, 2000) and develop new models of lexical semantics (e.g., Griffiths, Steyvers, & Tenenbaum, 2007).

Similarly, McRae, Cree, Seidenberg, and McNorgan (2005) published a large set of feature production norms, where subjects were asked to generate as many defining features about a noun as they could. This method is unique in defining semantic representation because it collects information on people's mental representations that might not be encoded directly in text (Cree & McRae, 2003) and, thereby, has served an important role for the development of models that integrate lexical and perceptually grounded representations (e.g., Andrews et al., 2009; Johns & Jones, 2012; Riordan & Jones, 2011). Vinson and Vigliocco (2008) published a similar set of norms but with events included along with objects.

Taking a similar approach to the ELP, the Semantic Priming Project (Hutchison et al., 2013) collected semantic priming data for both lexical decisions and naming time for thousands of words across hundreds of subjects. Although the Semantic Priming Project has not been the target for as much theoretical work as the ELP, it has provided a good deal of information about the nature of semantic priming, such as the impressive range of individual differences in semantic associations (Yap, Hutchison, & Tan, 2016).

This quick summation of available large-scale data sets demonstrates the importance that researchers are placing on item-level analyses of human behavior. Indeed, the item-level data available to researchers span many areas across the study of language and cognition, including such diverse data types as idiomatic processing (Bulkes & Tanner, 2017), word associations (De Deyne, Navarro, Perfors, Brysbaert, & Storms, 2019), taboo words (Roest, Visser, & Zeelenberg, 2018), modality norms (Lynott & Connell, 2009, 2013), humor (Engelthaler & Hills, 2018), and body–object interaction ratings (Bennett, Burnett, Siakaluk, & Pexman, 2011; Pexman, Muraki, Sidhu, Siakaluk, & Yap, 2019; Tillotson, Siakaluk, & Pexman, 2008). A particularly noteworthy project is the Canadian Longitudinal Study of Aging (Raina et al., 2009; Tuokko et al., 2019), which is collecting both demographic and behavioral data on a cohort of 50,000 participants across the aging spectrum on a yearly basis and has become a target for distributional models of semantics (Taler et al., 2019).

The multi-lab effort to collect large sources of data across different tasks signals the growing belief in the power that item-level analysis holds for developing and evaluating new theories of cognition, and especially the cognitive processes underlying language and memory. Critically, it not only offers new resources with which to control experiments but also signals new pathways to theory development. Particularly, large-scale data collection is complementary to the rise of corpus-based modeling; the large-scale analysis of the language environment allows for the training of cognitive models at a scale of language experience that is comparable to what a person might encounter. Secondly, empirical big data allows for hundreds or thousands of word-specific data points to be used in model tests. However, this form of theory development offers a significant divergence from the traditional hypothetico-deductive method that is standard practice in the psychological sciences.

CLASSIC AND BIG DATA APPROACHES TO THEORY DEVELOPMENT

In the field of experimental psychology, and particularly in the cognitive sciences, the hypothetico-deductive method has served as the dominant paradigm for theory development (Hayes, 2000; Laudan, 1981). In practice, the method involves using a theory to produce a priori predictions about the influence of a particular experimental manipulation on human behavior. These predictions are then tested in controlled target experiments designed to test the prediction by a criterion of falsification. To the extent that the data match the a priori theoretical predictions, the theory remains tenable. When data contradict the theory, the data prevail, and the theory is ruled out or, more often, is modified to accommodate the discrepancy. This leads to an iterative process in which a theory is proposed, predictions are generated, data are collected, and the theory is evaluated. The hope is that, across experiments, more powerful and robust theories of human cognition are developed. Clearly, this is an oversimplification of the complexities associated with modern scientific work, but experimental psychology does hold to the foundations of this approach (cf. Rozeboom, 1999).

In contrast to the hypothetico-deductive approach emphasized in experimental psychology, theory development in big data relies more on abduction, a form of reasoning not without its champions in the methodology literature (see Haig, 2005; Rozeboom, 1999; see also Chapter 1, this volume; this approach is also popular in grounded approaches to psychological theory, see Rennie, Phillips, & Quartaro, 1988). As Haig (2005) stated, abductive reasoning "involves reasoning from phenomena, understood as presumed effects, to their theoretical explanation in terms of underlying causal mechanisms" (pp. 372–373). That is, the data are first collected, and then theories of those data are formed from knowledge in the domain. These theories can then be contrasted with other theories in terms of their goodness of fit to relevant data and can be subject to the same empirical testing that traditional approaches use. Theory development thus emerges from data that are already collected, not from the necessity of testing a hypothesis. Much of the large-scale data collection projects outlined here were collected with this strategy in mind— once the data are available to researchers, new theories that can explain the variance in the data are constructed. That is, serious resources are being devoted not to test a given theory but with the hope that new theories can emerge from collected data.

As an illustration of the success of the abductive approach to cognition, consider the development of contextual diversity and semantic diversity models of lexical organization (for a recent review of this area, see Jones et al., 2017). The first work in this area was an article put forth by Adelman et al. (2006), who demonstrated that a contextual diversity (CD) count provided a better fit to lexical decision and naming time (taken mainly from the ELP) data than a word frequency (WF) count. A CD count was operationalized as the number of different documents in which a word occurs across a corpus, not just the number of times that a word occurs in the corpus. The advantage of a context count has been replicated across a number of corpora and data sets (see Adelman & Brown, 2008; Brysbaert & New, 2009).

Jones et al. (2012) agreed with many of the proposals of Adelman et al. (2006) but hypothesized that the semantic construction of a context should also be important in building a word's strength in memory (see Hoffman et al., 2013, for a similar proposal). Specifically, they hypothesized that words that occur in many different contexts (e.g., *occasion*) should be stored in memory more strongly than words that appear in mainly redundant contexts (e.g., *molecule*). To test this hypothesis, Jones et al. developed a distributional model that learns from the semantic context a word occurs in, entitled the semantic distinctiveness model (SDM). Crucially, the SDM uses an expectancy-congruency mechanism such that the strength that a given context is stored in memory for a word is based on how unique that context is compared with the past contexts that the word occurred in, with more unique contexts being given a stronger representation in memory, relative to words that occur in more redundant contexts. Using this learning mechanism, the SDM provided better fits than CD and WF measures to lexical decision and naming time data from the ELP. The analysis demonstrates the importance of acknowledging and considering the semantic rather than text-derived definition of a context when explaining patterns of lexical organization.

Furthermore, it has been demonstrated that the SDM provided an advantage over WF and CD in spoken word recognition (Johns, Gruenenfelder, Pisoni, & Jones, 2012) and could account for results in controlled natural language learning (Johns, Dye, & Jones, 2016); the model also generalized to alternative populations, such as bilinguals and older adults (Johns, Sheppard, Jones, & Taler, 2016). That is, several models (Adelman et al., 2006; Jones et al., 2012) were derived to explain patterns in the ELP mega data set, which were then contrasted and validated using a mix of targeted experimentation and abductive fits. The result of this research program was a new and powerful model of lexical organization, the development of which would have been impossible without access to large-scale sets of data before model development. The exercise shows how abductive and deductive reasoning can be combined productively and carefully: Abductive reasoning is used to develop insightful new models that are then tested in targeted experiments designed to evaluate and refine those models through the use of abductive reasoning. The ultimate goal of abduction in the scientific reasoning process is inference to the best explanation—that is, the model that can explain the relevant data better than any known alternative.

The mechanisms of the SDM are rooted in the structure of the natural language environment. That is, the performance of the model is dependent on information gleaned from large text databases. This means that the explanatory power of the model comes from the systematic connection between the structure of the language environment and the patterns contained in large sets of behavioral data. As stated previously, corpus-based models are uniquely suitable to the abductive approach to model development because the outputs of these models can take place at the group (Johns, Dye, & Jones, 2016), individual (Johns & Jamieson, 2018), or item level (Jones et al., 2012), meaning that the plausibility and power of these theories can be tested and validated with both abductive and deductive empirical approaches.

However, corpus-based models are not the only type of theories built by abductive reasoning. Other researchers have been using large-scale collections of data to explain variance in other large-scale sets of data. We believe this approach represents an error in reasoning, with Jones, Hills, and Todd (2015) labeling these approaches *Turk problems*.

TURK PROBLEMS

The Turk was a chess-playing machine developed in 1770 by Wolfgang von Kempelen to impress the Empress of Austria. It was purported to be an automaton that could play a realistic game of chess against a human opponent. However, in reality, the machine was an illusion—there was a human chess master housed inside the machine who controlled the operation of the Turk.

Given this illusion, it is clear that to understand how the Turk works, it would be first necessary to understand how a human plays chess. Jones, Hills, and Todd (2015) used this analogy to describe models that use human behavioral data (e.g., free association values) as underlying representations. In cognitive modeling, a Turk problem arises when a model's representation is derived from human behavioral data, hiding the complexity of the model within the model's representation.

To understand the behavior of a model that uses a representation derived from human behavior, it is necessary to understand the data that the model is using as its representation. Model behavior is not independent of its choice in representation, as Hummel and Holyoak (2003) noted: "All models are sensitive to their representations, so the choice of representation is among the most powerful wild cards at the modeller's disposal" (p. 247). In some cases, the underlying data used to form a representation can be more complicated than the data that are being modeled. This means that the complexity of a model is significantly undervalued and that the understanding derived from a model is muddled at best.

We believe that Turk problems represent an error in abductive reasoning. The goal of abductive reasoning in this context is to find patterns in data that point to better theories, such as Adelman et al. (2006) did to determine that CD provides a better explanation of lexical behavior than WF. There is knowledge gained from such an analysis about the nature of the cognition under question, and the results spurred new ideas for additional empirical and computational research (e.g., Jones et al., 2012). However, demonstrating that one kind of data provide a good fit to another kind of data offers little theoretical progress, unless one kind of data are already completely understood (which is rarely the case in the cognitive sciences). As an example, consider free association norms.

Free Association Norms

Semantic verbal fluency is a common task used in both clinical and theoretical settings to explore memory search and semantic memory performance (see Taler & Phillips, 2008, for a review). The most common version of this task involves naming as many items from a category as possible (e.g., animals) within a set time limit (typically 1 minute). Traditionally, behavior in this task is assessed by a count of how many category items a subject produced. However, Hills et al. (2012) used a memory search model over a representation of word knowledge from a distributional model of semantics (i.e., BEAGLE [Bound Encoding of the Aggregate Language Environment]; Jones & Mewhort, 2007) to confirm that critical features in people's pattern of recall were consistent with critical features in animals' food-foraging behavior. This work shed light on the generality of cognitive search mechanisms across species

(Hills, Todd, & Jones, 2015) and has been adapted to explore memory search in bilinguals (Taler, Johns, Young, Sheppard, & Jones, 2013) and patients who are developing cognitive impairment (Johns et al., 2018).

Abbott, Austerweil, and Griffiths (2015) questioned this work and proposed that a random walk model (a model type that has had success in the past; e.g., Griffiths, Steyvers, & Firl, 2007) could provide an equivalent explanation of verbal fluency behavior. However, their model did not capture the appropriate patterns when using the BEAGLE representation but could when it used a semantic network derived from the free association norms of Nelson et al. (2004). Free association norms had been used previously to drive models of semantics (e.g., Steyvers, Shiffrin, & Nelson, 2004).

As Jones, Hills, and Todd (2015) pointed out, the use of free association norms subverts traditional accounting of model complexity. The representations derived from BEAGLE come from an articulate and well-understood computational model applied to stable statistical properties of the natural language environment. In contrast, free association data represent patterns of human behavior from a cognitive process that is not well understood. However, by a simple accounting of the parameter space of the two models, the approach of Abbott et al. (2015) could be seen as equal to or better than the approach of Hills et al. (2012) when representational complexity is not considered.

If we accept Abbott et al.'s (2015) account, there is an additional question of what has actually been understood about verbal fluency. If verbal fluency performance is no more than a random walk over free association strength, it is necessary first to understand the cognitive underpinnings of free association. Given that computational models of semantics give a poor accounting to item-level effects in free association (see Maki, McKinley, & Thompson, 2004), it is difficult to accept that this is a well-understood data type. Thus, the model has simply shifted the theoretical goals from understanding verbal fluency to understanding free association. However, verbal fluency performance is quite well captured by searching mechanisms over representations derived from distributional models (e.g., Hills et al., 2012; Johns et al., 2018; Taler et al., 2013), suggesting that verbal fluency performance can be accounted for without a need to first understand the cognitive processes that underpin free association.

Internal Versus External Theories of Language

Like Abbott et al. (2015), De Deyne, Perfors, and Navarro (2016) proposed that a model based on word association data provides a better fit than distribution models to people's lexical behavior—similar to the notion of using free association data to derive semantic representations (Steyvers et al., 2004). Specifically, they proposed that internal models of language provide a better account than external models of language. De Deyne, Perfors, and Navarro defined an *external model of language* as being one that learns from the natural language environment, such as distributional models. In contrast, internal models of language are models that learn language from the knowledge of speakers of that language. Their internal language models were derived from a large set of word association values, where over 80,000 subjects were given a word association task (De Deyne, Navarro, Perfors, & Storms, 2016; De Deyne, Navarro, & Storms, 2013; De Deyne, Perfors, & Navarro, 2016). The specific word association task used in these studies asked subjects to produce three associates to a given cue word.

To compare the performance of external and internal language models, De Deyne, Perfors, and Navarro (2016) contrasted the performance of these model types on word similarity and relatedness tests, where subjects were asked to rate the similarity (or relatedness) of a word pair, a standard data type within computational linguistics (see Finkelstein et al., 2001). De Deyne, Perfors, and Navarro showed that similarity metrics derived from their word association data outperformed a variety of different distributional model types.

The conceptualization of internal versus external models of language effectively characterizes a Turk problem. A word similarity task almost certainly relies on similar cognitive mechanisms as a word association task. Just as explaining lexical decision response times with naming response time would provide little theoretical insight into the nature of lexical retrieval, the finding that word association data provide a good fit to word similarity data also provides little theoretical insight into lexical semantics, other than that the two tasks bear some relation. To understand how humans judge the similarity of words in this approach requires an understanding of how humans perform word associations, similar to the problems seen with Abbott et al. (2015).

The goal of distributional models is to explain how people acquire the knowledge they have (Landauer & Dumais, 1997). From this perspective, an internal model of language is not a competing model to distributional models (i.e., an external model), but instead, it is what this model class was designed to explain (i.e., the knowledge that people have acquired). Thus, it is inappropriate to compare the performance of these model types against one another. Instead, a more productive route would be to determine how well the knowledge gained by external models of language map onto the patterns of knowledge seen in internal models, the original goal of Landauer and Dumais (1997).

Although the distributional models did not perform as well on tests of word similarity and relatedness, they do still provide theoretical insight by demonstrating that people's semantic similarity judgments are systematically related to the statistical patterns of word occurrence in the natural language environment. However, as De Deyne, Perfors, and Navarro (2016) showed, these models are far from perfect and, like all theories, have to be improved or modified to fit human lexical behavior better. The data collected and used by De Deyne, Perfors, and Navarro provide a promising pathway to examining the failures of distributional models by determining where the models diverge from word association data on a large scale. However, word association data are still data that have to be understood and explained with theoretical accounts of language processing, not used as a replacement for a theory.

CONCLUSION

Big data approaches to cognition have been transformative because they allow for an examination of human behavior at a level of precision and scale that was not previously possible. It is now possible to propose a cognitive model, train that model with a similar history of language experience that an adult human might have, and test how well that model's behavior maps onto human behavior at the item level. Big data approaches to natural language have been particularly valuable. There have been two main developments that have proved influential on the understanding of language. The first is the collection of large text bases of natural language and models that can exploit them, such as Latent Semantic Analysis (Landauer & Dumais, 1997). The second is the collection of mega data sets of human behavior, such as the ELP (Balota et al., 2007). These two developments are interdependent; large-scale cognitive models must be evaluated at the item level, and those are the precision of data that the mega collections of human behavior provide.

However, theoretical development using big data does not always follow traditional methodologies. Specifically, much of psychological science has used the hypothetico-deductive method of theory development, where theories are used to generate hypotheses about human behavior that are tested in target experiments and evaluated against the match between prediction and observation. In contrast, much of theory development using big data approaches has proceeded by abduction: Data are collected, and theories are developed to capture variance in the data. Although abduction is an important part of the scientific process, insights reached by abduction are not equivalent to conclusions reached by deductive experimental verification. For the big data approach to science to succeed, the field has to translate curious abductive insights into clear deductive conclusions (although others have different opinions about the outcome of abductive reasoning; see Chapter 1, this volume).

There are dangers to relying only on abduction in theory development, however. One of these dangers is the Turk problem (Jones, Hills, & Todd, 2015), in which behavioral data are used to explain other behavioral data (e.g., using free association norms to explain verbal fluency). Showing that one type of data predicts another offers no clarity toward theoretical progress. Data are not theory (see Chapter 1, this volume, for a different perspective on this issue).

Although we have mainly focused on two particular problems of cognitive psychology, lexical organization and lexical semantics, the developments in big data have an increasingly wide-ranging impact in the cognitive sciences. The biggest advantage that corpus-based approaches to cognition offer is that they allow for content to be placed in memorial representations. For example, the classic approach in the computational cognitive modeling of language is to use randomly generated representations of words (Johns & Jones, 2010). This is no longer necessary (see Johns et al., 2017, for a longer discussion of this issue). It is now possible to use a model of distributional semantics (e.g., latent semantic analysis, BEAGLE, Topics, or a related model) as the representation that can be fed into a process model, allowing for an integration of the knowledge and process components of cognition. Multiple models of cognition have been developed using this integrative approach, such as in episodic memory (Johns, Jones, & Mewhort, 2012; Mewhort et al., 2018), implicit learning (Chubala et al., 2016), and decision making (Bhatia & Stewart, 2018). Moreover, the models can be used to determine the underlying cognitive differences in clinical populations—for example, in patients with memory disorders (Johns et al., 2018) or patients with schizophrenia (Minor, Willits, Marggraf, Jones, & Lysaker, 2019; Willits, Rubin, Jones, Minor, & Lysaker, 2018).

There are a number of challenges facing theoretical development in big data approaches to cognition. One area relevant to the discussion of Turk problems is model complexity. Traditional methods of model comparison use an accounting of a model's parameter space to account for differences in model complexity (e.g., Akaike's Information Criterion; Akaike, 1974). Jones, Hills, and Todd (2015) pointed out that models that use representations derived from human behavior hide complexity due to the cognitive processes of the subjects used to collect the data inside the representation. There are also complexity issues with distributional models. For example, Recchia and Jones (2009) demonstrated that a simple model of distributional semantics (pointwise mutual information; Bullinaria & Levy, 2007) can exceed the performance of a more computationally complex model (latent semantic analysis; Landauer & Dumais, 1997) when the simpler model is given more training materials. However, there are two sources of complexity in this analysis: the computational complexity of the cognitive model, as well as corresponding issues of cognitive plausibility and the amount of training materials that a model requires to learn from. To continue developing better, more cognitively plausible large-scale models of cognition, it will be necessary to develop formal frameworks that can accommodate these different sources of complexity to enable better model comparison techniques. New empirical work, such as the results of Brysbaert, Stevens, Mandera, and Keuleers (2016a), which measured the amount of linguistic experience young adults likely have had, provides useful guidelines to perform more cognitively plausible model training.

Big data is a young but maturing field in the cognitive and psychological sciences. Just like any developing field, there are methodological and theoretical challenges to be faced. However, as this chapter outlines, the continued construction of large-scale models of cognition, together with the collection of mega data sets of human behavior, provides a promising foundation for the development of increasingly powerful theories of human behavior.

REFERENCES

Abbott, J. T., Austerweil, J. L., & Griffiths, T. L. (2015). Random walks on semantic networks can resemble optimal foraging. *Psychological Review, 122*, 558–569. http://dx.doi.org/10.1037/a0038693

Adelman, J. S., & Brown, G. D. (2008). Modeling lexical decision: The form of frequency and diversity effects. *Psychological Review, 115*, 214–227. http://dx.doi.org/10.1037/0033-295X.115.1.214

Adelman, J. S., Brown, G. D. A., & Quesada, J. F. (2006). Contextual diversity, not word frequency, determines word-naming and lexical decision times. *Psychological Science, 17*, 814–823. http://dx.doi.org/10.1111/j.1467-9280.2006.01787.x

Akaike, H. (1974). A new look at the statistical model identification. *IEEE Transactions on Automatic Control, 19*, 716–723. http://dx.doi.org/10.1109/TAC.1974.1100705

Andrews, M., Vigliocco, G., & Vinson, D. (2009). Integrating experiential and distributional data to learn semantic representations. *Psychological Review, 116*, 463–498. http://dx.doi.org/10.1037/a0016261

Balota, D. A., Yap, M. J., Hutchison, K. A., Cortese, M. J., Kessler, B., Loftis, B., . . . Treiman, R. (2007). The English Lexicon Project. *Behavior Research Methods, 39*, 445–459. http://dx.doi.org/10.3758/BF03193014

Bennett, S. D., Burnett, A. N., Siakaluk, P. D., & Pexman, P. M. (2011). Imageability and body–object interaction ratings for 599 multisyllabic nouns. *Behavior Research Methods, 43*, 1100–1109. http://dx.doi.org/10.3758/s13428-011-0117-5

Bhatia, S., & Stewart, N. (2018). Naturalistic multiattribute choice. *Cognition, 179*, 71–88. http://dx.doi.org/10.1016/j.cognition.2018.05.025

Broadbent, D. E. (1967). Word-frequency effect and response bias. *Psychological Review, 74*, 1–15. http://dx.doi.org/10.1037/h0024206

Brysbaert, M., Mandera, P., & Keuleers, E. (2018). The word frequency effect in word processing: An updated review. *Current Directions in Psychological Science, 27*, 45–50. http://dx.doi.org/10.1177/0963721417727521

Brysbaert, M., & New, B. (2009). Moving beyond Kučera and Francis: A critical evaluation of current word frequency norms and the introduction of a new and improved word frequency measure for American English. *Behavior Research Methods, 41*, 977–990. http://dx.doi.org/10.3758/BRM.41.4.977

Brysbaert, M., Stevens, M., Mandera, P., & Keuleers, E. (2016a). How many words do we know? Practical estimates of vocabulary size dependent on word definition, the degree of language input and the participant's age. *Frontiers in Psychology, 7*, 1116. http://dx.doi.org/10.3389/fpsyg.2016.01116

Brysbaert, M., Stevens, M., Mandera, P., & Keuleers, E. (2016b). The impact of word prevalence on lexical decision times: Evidence from the Dutch Lexicon Project 2. *Journal of Experimental Psychology: Human Perception and Performance, 42*, 441–458. http://dx.doi.org/10.1037/xhp0000159

Bulkes, N. Z., & Tanner, D. (2017). "Going to town": Large-scale norming and statistical analysis of 870 American English idioms. *Behavior Research Methods, 49*, 772–783. http://dx.doi.org/10.3758/s13428-016-0747-8

Bullinaria, J. A., & Levy, J. P. (2007). Extracting semantic representations from word co-occurrence statistics: A computational study. *Behavior Research Methods, 39*, 510–526. http://dx.doi.org/10.3758/BF03193020

Caliskan, A., Bryson, J. J., & Narayanan, A. (2017). Semantics derived automatically from language corpora contain human-like biases. *Science, 356*, 183–186. http://dx.doi.org/10.1126/science.aal4230

Chubala, C. M., Johns, B. T., Jamieson, R. K., & Mewhort, D. J. K. (2016). Applying an exemplar model to an implicit rule-learning task: Implicit learning of semantic structure. *Quarterly Journal of Experimental Psychology, 69*, 1049–1055. http://dx.doi.org/10.1080/17470218.2015.1130068

Cree, G. S., & McRae, K. (2003). Analyzing the factors underlying the structure and computation of the meaning of chipmunk, cherry, chisel, cheese, and cello (and many other such concrete nouns). *Journal of Experimental Psychology: General, 132,* 163–201. http://dx.doi.org/10.1037/0096-3445.132.2.163

De Deyne, S., Navarro, D. J., Perfors, A., Brysbaert, M., & Storms, G. (2019). The "Small World of Words" English word association norms for over 12,000 cue words. *Behavior Research Methods, 51,* 987–1006. http://dx.doi.org/10.3758/s13428-018-1115-7

De Deyne, S., Navarro, D. J., Perfors, A., & Storms, G. (2016). Structure at every scale: A semantic network account of the similarities between unrelated concepts. *Journal of Experimental Psychology: General, 145,* 1228–1254. http://dx.doi.org/10.1037/xge0000192

De Deyne, S., Navarro, D. J., & Storms, G. (2013). Better explanations of lexical and semantic cognition using networks derived from continued rather than single-word associations. *Behavior Research Methods, 45,* 480–498. http://dx.doi.org/10.3758/s13428-012-0260-7

De Deyne, S., Perfors, A., & Navarro, D. J. (2016). Predicting human similarity judgments with distributional models: The value of word associations. In Y. Matsumoto & R. Prasad (Eds.), *Proceedings of COLING 2016, the 26th International Conference on Computational Linguistics: Technical Papers* (pp. 1861–1870). Cambridge, MA: Association for Computational Linguistics.

Engelthaler, T., & Hills, T. T. (2018). Humor norms for 4,997 English words. *Behavior Research Methods, 50,* 1116–1124. http://dx.doi.org/10.3758/s13428-017-0930-6

Estes, W. K. (1955). Statistical theory of distributional phenomena in learning. *Psychological Review, 62,* 369–377. http://dx.doi.org/10.1037/h0046888

Estes, W. K. (1975). Some targets for mathematical psychology. *Journal of Mathematical Psychology, 12,* 263–282. http://dx.doi.org/10.1016/0022-2496(75)90025-5

Ferrand, L., New, B., Brysbaert, M., Keuleers, E., Bonin, P., Méot, A., . . . Pallier, C. (2010). The French Lexicon Project: Lexical decision data for 38,840 French words and 38,840 pseudowords. *Behavior Research Methods, 42,* 488–496. http://dx.doi.org/10.3758/BRM.42.2.488

Finkelstein, L., Gabrilovich, E., Matias, Y., Rivlin, E., Solan, Z., Wolfman, G., & Ruppin, E. (2001). Placing search in context: The concept revisited. In *Proceedings of the 10th international conference on World Wide Web* (pp. 406–414). New York, NY: ACM.

Forster, K. I., & Chambers, S. M. (1973). Lexical access and naming time. *Journal of Verbal Learning and Verbal Behavior, 12,* 627–635. http://dx.doi.org/10.1016/S0022-5371(73)80042-8

Goldinger, S. D. (1998). Echoes of echoes? An episodic theory of lexical access. *Psychological Review, 105,* 251–279. http://dx.doi.org/10.1037/0033-295X.105.2.251

Griffiths, T. L., Steyvers, M., & Firl, A. (2007). Google and the mind: Predicting fluency with PageRank. *Psychological Science, 18,* 1069–1076. http://dx.doi.org/10.1111/j.1467-9280.2007.02027.x

Griffiths, T. L., Steyvers, M., & Tenenbaum, J. B. (2007). Topics in semantic representation. *Psychological Review, 114,* 211–244. http://dx.doi.org/10.1037/0033-295X.114.2.211

Haig, B. D. (2005). An abductive theory of scientific method. *Psychological Methods, 10,* 371–388. http://dx.doi.org/10.1037/1082-989X.10.4.371

Hayes, N. (2000). *Doing psychological research.* Abingdon, England: Taylor & Francis.

Herdağdelen, A., & Marelli, M. (2017). Social media and language processing: How Facebook and Twitter provide the best frequency estimates for studying word recognition. *Cognitive Science, 41,* 976–995. http://dx.doi.org/10.1111/cogs.12392

Hills, T. T., Jones, M. N., & Todd, P. M. (2012). Optimal foraging in semantic memory. *Psychological Review, 119,* 431–440. http://dx.doi.org/10.1037/a0027373

Hills, T. T., Todd, P. M., & Jones, M. N. (2015). Foraging in semantic fields: How we search through memory. *Topics in Cognitive Science, 7,* 513–534. http://dx.doi.org/10.1111/tops.12151

Hoffman, P., Lambon Ralph, M. A., & Rogers, T. T. (2013). Semantic diversity: A measure of semantic ambiguity based on variability in the contextual usage of words. *Behavior Research Methods, 45,* 718–730. http://dx.doi.org/10.3758/s13428-012-0278-x

Hsiao, Y., & Nation, K. (2018). Semantic diversity, frequency and the development of lexical quality in children's word reading. *Journal of Memory and Language, 103,* 114–126. http://dx.doi.org/10.1016/j.jml.2018.08.005

Hummel, J. E., & Holyoak, K. J. (2003). A symbolic-connectionist theory of relational inference and generalization. *Psychological Review, 110,* 220–264. http://dx.doi.org/10.1037/0033-295X.110.2.220

Hutchison, K. A., Balota, D. A., Neely, J. H., Cortese, M. J., Cohen-Shikora, E. R., Tse, C. S., . . . Buchanan, E. (2013). The semantic priming project. *Behavior Research Methods, 45,* 1099–1114. http://dx.doi.org/10.3758/s13428-012-0304-z

Jamieson, R. K., Avery, J. E., Johns, B. T., & Jones, M. N. (2018). An instance theory of semantic memory. *Computational Brain & Behavior, 1,* 119–136. http://dx.doi.org/10.1007/s42113-018-0008-2

Johns, B. T. (2019). Mining a crowdsourced dictionary to understand consistency and preference in word meanings. *Frontiers in Psychology, 10,* 268. http://dx.doi.org/10.3389/fpsyg.2019.00268

Johns, B. T., & Dye, M. (2019). Gender bias at scale: Evidence from the usage of personal names. *Behavior Research Methods, 51,* 1601–1618. http://dx.doi.org/10.3758/s13428-019-01234-0

Johns, B. T., Dye, M., & Jones, M. N. (2016). The influence of contextual diversity on word learning. *Psychonomic Bulletin & Review, 23,* 1214–1220. http://dx.doi.org/10.3758/s13423-015-0980-7

Johns, B. T., Gruenenfelder, T. M., Pisoni, D. B., & Jones, M. N. (2012). Effects of word frequency, contextual diversity, and semantic distinctiveness on spoken word recognition. *The Journal of the Acoustical Society of America, 132,* EL74–EL80. http://dx.doi.org/10.1121/1.4731641

Johns, B. T., & Jamieson, R. K. (2018). A large-scale analysis of variance in written language. *Cognitive Science, 42,* 1360–1374. http://dx.doi.org/10.1111/cogs.12583

Johns, B. T., & Jamieson, R. K. (2019). The influence of place and time on lexical behavior: A distributional analysis. *Behavior Research Methods.* Advance online publication. http://dx.doi.org/10.3758/s13428-019-01289-z

Johns, B. T., & Jones, M. N. (2010). Evaluating the random representation assumption of lexical semantics in cognitive models. *Psychonomic Bulletin & Review, 17,* 662–672. http://dx.doi.org/10.3758/PBR.17.5.662

Johns, B. T., & Jones, M. N. (2012). Perceptual inference through global lexical similarity. *Topics in Cognitive Science, 4,* 103–120. http://dx.doi.org/10.1111/j.1756-8765.2011.01176.x

Johns, B. T., & Jones, M. N. (2015). Generating structure from experience: A retrieval-based model of language processing. *Canadian Journal of Experimental Psychology/ Revue canadienne de psychologie expérimentale, 69,* 233–251. http://dx.doi.org/10.1037/cep0000053

Johns, B. T., Jones, M. N., & Mewhort, D. J. K. (2012). A synchronization account of false recognition. *Cognitive Psychology, 65,* 486–518. http://dx.doi.org/10.1016/j.cogpsych.2012.07.002

Johns, B. T., Jones, M. N., & Mewhort, D. J. K. (2014). A continuous source reinstatement model of true and illusory recollection. In P. Bello, M. Gurarini, M. McShane, & B. Scassellayi (Eds.), *Proceedings of the 36th Annual Cognitive Science Conference* (pp. 248–253). Austin, TX: Cognitive Science Society.

Johns, B. T., Jones, M. N., & Mewhort, D. J. K. (2019). Using experiential optimization to build lexical representations. *Psychonomic Bulletin & Review, 26*, 103–126. http://dx.doi.org/10.3758/s13423-018-1501-2

Johns, B. T., Mewhort, D. J. K., & Jones, M. N. (2017). Small worlds and big data: Examining the simplification assumption in cognitive modeling. In M. N. Jones (Ed.), *Big data in cognitive science: From methods to insights* (pp. 227–245). New York, NY: Taylor & Francis.

Johns, B. T., Mewhort, D. J. K., & Jones, M. N. (2019). The role of negative information in distributional semantic learning. *Cognitive Science, 43*, e12730. http://dx.doi.org/10.1111/cogs.12730

Johns, B. T., Sheppard, C. L., Jones, M. N., & Taler, V. (2016). The role of semantic diversity in word recognition across aging and bilingualism. *Frontiers in Psychology, 7*, 703–714. http://dx.doi.org/10.3389/fpsyg.2016.00703

Johns, B. T., Taler, V., Pisoni, D. B., Farlow, M. R., Hake, A. M., Kareken, D. A., . . . Jones, M. N. (2018). Cognitive modeling as an interface between brain and behavior: Measuring the semantic decline in mild cognitive impairment. *Canadian Journal of Experimental Psychology/Revue canadienne de psychologie expérimentale, 72*, 117–126. http://dx.doi.org/10.1037/cep0000132

Jones, M. N. (2017). Developing cognitive theory by mining large-scale naturalistic data. In M. N. Jones (Ed.), *Big data in cognitive science* (pp. 1–12). New York, NY: Taylor & Francis.

Jones, M. N., & Dye, M. W. (2018). Big data methods for discourse analysis. In M. F. Schober, D. N. Rapp, & M. A. Britt (Eds.), *Handbook of discourse processes* (2nd ed., pp. 117–124). New York, NY: Routledge.

Jones, M. N., Dye, M., & Johns, B. T. (2017). Context as an organizational principle of the lexicon. In B. Ross (Ed.), *The psychology of learning and motivation* (Vol. 67, pp. 239–283). Amsterdam, Netherlands: Elsevier.

Jones, M. N., Hills, T. T., & Todd, P. M. (2015). Hidden processes in structural representations: A reply to Abbott, Austerweil, and Griffiths (2015). *Psychological Review, 122*, 570–574. http://dx.doi.org/10.1037/a0039248

Jones, M. N., Johns, B. T., & Recchia, G. (2012). The role of semantic diversity in lexical organization. *Canadian Journal of Experimental Psychology/Revue canadienne de psychologie expérimentale, 66*, 115–124. http://dx.doi.org/10.1037/a0026727

Jones, M. N., & Mewhort, D. J. K. (2007). Representing word meaning and order information in a composite holographic lexicon. *Psychological Review, 114*, 1–37. http://dx.doi.org/10.1037/0033-295X.114.1.1

Jones, M. N., Willits, J. A., & Dennis, S. (2015). Models of semantic memory. In J. R. Busemeyer, Z. Wang, J. T. Townsend, & A. Eidels (Eds.), *Oxford handbook of mathematical and computational psychology* (pp. 232–254). New York, NY: Oxford University Press.

Keuleers, E., Lacey, P., Rastle, K., & Brysbaert, M. (2012). The British Lexicon Project: Lexical decision data for 28,730 monosyllabic and disyllabic English words. *Behavior Research Methods, 44*, 287–304. http://dx.doi.org/10.3758/s13428-011-0118-4

Kučera, H., & Francis, W. N. (1967). *Computational analysis of present-day American English*. London, England: Dartmouth.

Landauer, T. K., & Dumais, S. T. (1997). A solution to Plato's problem: The latent semantic analysis theory of the acquisition, induction, and representation of knowledge. *Psychological Review, 104*, 211–240. http://dx.doi.org/10.1037/0033-295X.104.2.211

Laudan, L. (1981). *Science and hypothesis*. Dordrecht, Netherlands: Reidel. http://dx.doi.org/10.1007/978-94-015-7288-0

Lazaridou, A., Marelli, M., & Baroni, M. (2017). Multimodal word meaning induction from minimal exposure to natural text. *Cognitive Science, 41*, 677–705. http://dx.doi.org/10.1111/cogs.12481

Lynott, D., & Connell, L. (2009). Modality exclusivity norms for 423 object properties. *Behavior Research Methods, 41*, 558–564. http://dx.doi.org/10.3758/BRM.41.2.558

Lynott, D., & Connell, L. (2013). Modality exclusivity norms for 400 nouns: The relationship between perceptual experience and surface word form. *Behavior Research Methods, 45*, 516–526. http://dx.doi.org/10.3758/s13428-012-0267-0

Maki, W. S., McKinley, L. N., & Thompson, A. G. (2004). Semantic distance norms computed from an electronic dictionary (WordNet). *Behavior Research Methods, Instruments & Computers, 36*, 421–431. http://dx.doi.org/10.3758/BF03195590

McRae, K., Cree, G. S., Seidenberg, M. S., & McNorgan, C. (2005). Semantic feature production norms for a large set of living and nonliving things. *Behavior Research Methods, 37*, 547–559. http://dx.doi.org/10.3758/BF03192726

Mewhort, D. J. K., Shabahang, K. D., & Franklin, D. R. J. (2018). Release from PI: An analysis and a model. *Psychonomic Bulletin & Review, 25*, 932–950. http://dx.doi.org/10.3758/s13423-017-1327-3

Mikolov, T., Sutskever, I., Chen, K., Corrado, G. S., & Dean, J. (2013). Distributed representations of words and phrases and their compositionality. In C. J. C. Burges, L., Bottou, M., Welling, Z., Ghahramani, & K. Q. Weinberger (Eds.), *Advances in neural information processing systems* (Vol. 26, pp. 3111–3119). Red Hook, NY: Curran Associates.

Minor, K. S., Willits, J. A., Marggraf, M. P., Jones, M. N., & Lysaker, P. H. (2019). Measuring disorganized speech in schizophrenia: Automated analysis explains variance in cognitive deficits beyond clinician-rated scales. *Psychological Medicine, 49*, 440–448. http://dx.doi.org/10.1017/S0033291718001046

Murray, W. S., & Forster, K. I. (2004). Serial mechanisms in lexical access: The rank hypothesis. *Psychological Review, 111*, 721–756. http://dx.doi.org/10.1037/0033-295X.111.3.721

Nelson, D. L., McEvoy, C. L., & Dennis, S. (2000). What is free association and what does it measure? *Memory & Cognition, 28*, 887–899. http://dx.doi.org/10.3758/BF03209337

Nelson, D. L., McEvoy, C. L., & Schreiber, T. A. (2004). The University of South Florida free association, rhyme, and word fragment norms. *Behavior Research Methods, Instruments & Computers, 36*, 402–407. http://dx.doi.org/10.3758/BF03195588

Pexman, P. M., Heard, A., Lloyd, E., & Yap, M. J. (2017). The Calgary semantic decision project: Concrete/abstract decision data for 10,000 English words. *Behavior Research Methods, 49*, 407–417. http://dx.doi.org/10.3758/s13428-016-0720-6

Pexman, P. M., Muraki, E., Sidhu, D. M., Siakaluk, P. D., & Yap, M. J. (2019). Quantifying sensorimotor experience: Body–object interaction ratings for more than 9,000 English words. *Behavior Research Methods, 51*, 453–466. http://dx.doi.org/10.3758/s13428-018-1171-z

Raina, P. S., Wolfson, C., Kirkland, S. A., Griffith, L. E., Oremus, M., Patterson, C., . . . Brazil, K. (2009). The Canadian longitudinal study on aging (CLSA). *Canadian Journal on Aging, 28*, 221–229. http://dx.doi.org/10.1017/S0714980809990055

Reali, F., & Christiansen, M. H. (2007). Processing of relative clauses is made easier by frequency of occurrence. *Journal of Memory and Language, 57*, 1–23. http://dx.doi.org/10.1016/j.jml.2006.08.014

Recchia, G., & Jones, M. N. (2009). More data trumps smarter algorithms: Comparing pointwise mutual information with latent semantic analysis. *Behavior Research Methods, 41*, 647–656. http://dx.doi.org/10.3758/BRM.41.3.647

Rennie, D. L., Phillips, J. R., & Quartaro, G. K. (1988). Grounded theory: A promising approach to conceptualization in psychology? *Canadian Psychology/Psychologie canadienne, 29*, 139–150. http://dx.doi.org/10.1037/h0079765

Riordan, B., & Jones, M. N. (2011). Redundancy in perceptual and linguistic experience: Comparing feature-based and distributional models of semantic representation. *Topics in Cognitive Science, 3*, 303–345. http://dx.doi.org/10.1111/j.1756-8765.2010.01111.x

Roest, S. A., Visser, T. A., & Zeelenberg, R. (2018). Dutch taboo norms. *Behavior Research Methods, 50,* 630–641. http://dx.doi.org/10.3758/s13428-017-0890-x

Rozeboom, W. W. (1999). Good science is abductive, not hypothetico-deductive. In L. L. Harlow, S. A. Mulaik, & J. H. Steiger (Eds.), *What if there were no significance tests?* (pp. 335–391). Hillsdale, NJ: Erlbaum.

Shaoul, C., & Westbury, C. (2010). Exploring lexical co-occurrence space using HiDEx. *Behavior Research Methods, 42,* 393–413. http://dx.doi.org/10.3758/BRM.42.2.393

Simon, H. A. (1956). Rational choice and the structure of the environment. *Psychological Review, 63,* 129–138. http://dx.doi.org/10.1037/h0042769

Simon, H. A. (1969). *The sciences of the artificial.* Cambridge, MA: MIT Press.

Steyvers, M., Shiffrin, R. M., & Nelson, D. L. (2004). Word association spaces for predicting semantic similarity effects in episodic memory. In A. Healy (Ed.), *Experimental cognitive psychology and its applications: Festschrift in honor of Lyle Bourne, Walter Kintsch, and Thomas Landauer* (pp. 237–249). Washington, DC: American Psychological Association.

Taler, V., Johns, B. T., & Jones, M. N. (2019). A large scale semantic analysis of verbal fluency across the aging spectrum: Data from the Canadian longitudinal study on aging. *The Journals of Gerontology: Series B. Psychological Sciences and Social Sciences.* Advance online publication. http://dx.doi.org/10.1093/geronb/gbz003

Taler, V., Johns, B. T., Young, K., Sheppard, C., & Jones, M. N. (2013). A computational analysis of semantic structure in bilingual verbal fluency performance. *Journal of Memory and Language, 69,* 607–618. http://dx.doi.org/10.1016/j.jml.2013.08.004

Taler, V., & Phillips, N. A. (2008). Language performance in Alzheimer's disease and mild cognitive impairment: A comparative review. *Journal of Clinical and Experimental Neuropsychology, 30,* 501–556. http://dx.doi.org/10.1080/13803390701550128

Tillotson, S. M., Siakaluk, P. D., & Pexman, P. M. (2008). Body–object interaction ratings for 1,618 monosyllabic nouns. *Behavior Research Methods, 40,* 1075–1078. http://dx.doi.org/10.3758/BRM.40.4.1075

Tse, C. S., Yap, M. J., Chan, Y. L., Sze, W. P., Shaoul, C., & Lin, D. (2017). The Chinese Lexicon Project: A megastudy of lexical decision performance for 25,000+ traditional Chinese two-character compound words. *Behavior Research Methods, 49,* 1503–1519. http://dx.doi.org/10.3758/s13428-016-0810-5

Tuokko, H., Griffith, L. E., Simard, M., Taler, V., O'Connell, M. E., Voll, S., . . . Raina, P. (2019). The Canadian longitudinal study on aging as a platform for exploring cognition in an aging population. *The Clinical Neuropsychologist, 30,* 1–30. http://dx.doi.org/10.1080/13854046.2018.1551575

Vinson, D. P., & Vigliocco, G. (2008). Semantic feature production norms for a large set of objects and events. *Behavior Research Methods, 40,* 183–190. http://dx.doi.org/10.3758/BRM.40.1.183

Willits, J. A., Rubin, T., Jones, M. N., Minor, K. S., & Lysaker, P. H. (2018). Evidence of disturbances of deep levels of semantic cohesion within personal narratives in schizophrenia. *Schizophrenia Research, 197,* 365–369. http://dx.doi.org/10.1016/j.schres.2017.11.014

Wittgenstein, L. (1953). *Philosophical investigations.* Hoboken, NJ: Wiley.

Yap, M. J., Hutchison, K. A., & Tan, L. C. (2016). Individual differences in semantic priming performance: Insights from the Semantic Priming Project. In M. N. Jones (Ed.), *Big data in cognitive science* (pp. 203–226). New York, NY: Taylor & Francis.

Yap, M. J., Liow, S. J. R., Jalil, S. B., & Faizal, S. S. B. (2010). The Malay Lexicon Project: A database of lexical statistics for 9,592 words. *Behavior Research Methods, 42,* 992–1003. http://dx.doi.org/10.3758/BRM.42.4.992

13

Big Data in Developmental Psychology

Kevin J. Grimm, Gabriela Stegmann, Ross Jacobucci, and Sarfaraz Serang

Developmental research is dependent on longitudinal data. With longitudinal data, the developmental process can be visualized, analyzed, and understood. Longitudinal data can be characterized as data measured from the same entity over a period, and historically, the majority of longitudinal data in psychology were panel data. Longitudinal panel data are often considered p-dimensional data ($p > 100$) collected on a fairly large sample ($N > 200$) measured over several time points ($T < 8$). Thus, panel data are only considered big, based on the number of variables collected. Given this, data mining methods that are relevant for longitudinal panel data include variable selection methods, such as extensions of classification and regression trees (Breiman, Friedman, Olshen, & Stone, 1984; Morgan & Sonquist, 1963), lasso regression (Tibshirani, 1996), tabu regression (Drezner, Marcoulides, & Salhi, 1999), neural networks (Smith, 1993), and genetic algorithms (Eiben & Smith, 2003), that can account for the clustered nature of longitudinal data.

An example data set that fits this mold is the National Institute of Child Health and Human Development's Study of Early Child Care and Youth Development (National Institute of Child Health and Human Development Early Child Care Research, 2005). The study tracked 1,364 children from birth through age 15. Approximately 20 assessments took place. Information was collected about the child's home environment, preschool environment (if applicable), and school environment. Over the course of the study, tens of thousands of variables were collected. Another example is the Health and

http://dx.doi.org/10.1037/0000193-014
Big Data in Psychological Research, S. E. Woo, L. Tay, and R. W. Proctor (Editors)

Retirement Study (Juster & Suzman, 1995). In the study, longitudinal data were collected on more than 20,000 participants. Assessments took place biannually from 1992 through 2016, and tens of thousands of data points were collected over the course of this study.

More recently, developmentalists have collected intensive longitudinal data—also referred to as *ecological momentary assessment (EMA) data*—of a variety of types. For example, Hedman (2010) collected physiological arousal data through the use of electrodermal activity (EDA) sensors from children with sensory processing disorder and their therapists during two therapy sessions. In this study, the therapy sessions lasted approximately one hour, and EDA levels were recorded every 0.5 seconds.

In a similar vein, Ferrer and Helm (2013) assessed coregulation between measurements of heart rate and respiration among adult romantic partners during an experimental study. In this study, there were upward of 3,500 observations of heart rate and respiration per dyad. These EMA data allow for the modeling of complex developmental patterns (Ram & Diehl, 2015) on a short-term time scale and can be integrated into the longer term study of human development (see Gerstorf, Hoppmann, & Ram, 2014).

Developmentalists have long collected video recordings of interpersonal interaction, such as those between infants and parents, as well as between romantic couples. In the 1980s and 1990s, these video recordings were often coded and summarized; however, recent studies have implemented more intensive data collection strategies to examine coordination and coregulation (e.g., Liu & Palumbo, 2013). Data mining strategies for use with EMA data may search for level shifts in behavior with extensions of multivariate adaptive regression splines (Friedman, 1991), search for consistent lead-lag patterns in the time series, and similarities in the lead-lag patterns in time series across individuals (see Gonzales & Ferrer, 2014).

In this chapter, we focus our attention on the analysis of longitudinal panel data using growth curve models to examine trajectories of development over time and two data mining approaches that attempt to isolate important explanatory variables associated with the trajectories. We begin by discussing the primary research objectives when collecting longitudinal data presented by Baltes and Nesselroade (1979) and then describe the growth modeling framework from a general latent variable modeling point of view. Here, we make connections to both the mixed-effects and structural equation modeling frameworks, highlighting the confirmatory nature of modeling of both the within-person change trajectory and sources of between-person differences. We then discuss machine learning or big data methods that have been developed in regression and expanded to identify key sources of between-person differences in change. Last, we present exploratory analyses of longitudinal mathematics trajectories from kindergarten through fifth grade and attempt to identify key determinants of these trajectories. We feel that these methods should and will transform how researchers analyze developmental data.

OBJECTIVE OF LONGITUDINAL RESEARCH

In 1979, Baltes and Nesselroade described five objectives for longitudinal research. Given the importance of longitudinal data for understanding developmental processes, these objectives are also objectives for developmental research. The first, and most important, objective is the study of within-person change. The study of within-person change, or tracking how a construct changes over time for an individual, requires longitudinal data—the repeated assessment of that construct. Developmental research, by its nature, requires the repeated assessment of individuals (children, adolescents, adults) over time, and the vast majority of developmental studies are interested in the examination of within-person change. For example, Cameron, Grimm, Steele, Castro-Schilo, and Grissmer (2015) analyzed mathematics and reading scores from two large-scale longitudinal studies to examine the patterns of individual changes in these constructs during elementary school and middle school.

The second objective, outlined by Baltes and Nesselroade (1979), is the assessment of between-person differences in within-person change. Following the first objective to examine individual change processes, this objective seeks to understand how change processes differ across individuals. These differences may be present in the patterns of within-person changes (some individuals' rate of change may be constant [linear change], whereas other individuals' rate of change may not be constant [e.g., quadratic change]), or the individual rates of change and the timing of relative changes that vary over individuals when the patterns of change are consistent across individuals. Cameron et al. (2015) examined the differences in the mathematics and reading trajectories by allowing the parameters of the trajectory model to vary over children. The children were found to differ in three aspects of the change trajectory—the relative rate of development, the timing of optimal changes, and the total amount of change. These three aspects of change were able to capture the extent of between-child differences in change.

The third objective focuses on the study of multiple change processes. The idea of this objective is to recognize that multiple constructs are changing at the same time as the focal construct. Moreover, the changes in multiple constructs may be interdependent. That is, the changes in one construct may depend on or be a precursor to changes in another construct, changes may co-occur, and changes may have the same or different determinants or consequents. In line with this objective, McArdle and Hamagami (2001) examined the development of reading and antisocial behaviors for a sample of school-age children. In their analysis, McArdle and Hamagami found a dynamic relationship between reading skills and antisocial behaviors, where reading was a protective factor. That is, reading was a leading indicator of subsequent changes in antisocial behaviors with higher prior reading scores leading to more negative changes in antisocial behaviors.

The fourth objective is to study the determinants of within-person change processes. Here, researchers should identify time-varying or dynamic variables (in addition to the timing variable) that have a direct or indirect effect on the within-person change processes. In line with this fourth objective, Skibbe, Grimm, Bowles, and Morrison (2012) examined the changes in a variety of reading-related measures in a sample of children from preschool through second grade. Skibbe et al. examined these changes over grade but also accounted for whether the assessment took place during the fall or spring semester. The findings indicated that there was overall positive growth in reading-related skills; however, there was a negative summer effect, such that changes from the spring to fall were smaller than expected.

The fifth objective is the study of determinants of between-person differences in within-person change. Following up on the second objective to study how individuals differ in their change patterns, this objective encourages the study of why individuals differ in their change patterns. The variables under consideration here are person-level variables, or variables that only vary between individuals. These variables are often referred to as *time invariant*. In line with this objective, Cameron et al. (2015) studied achievement gaps based on socioeconomic status. That is, the socioeconomic status of the children was associated with the three between-child aspects describing the variations in mathematics and reading change patterns.

These objectives are omnipresent in every study of development. Thus, longitudinal data are necessary to obtain an accurate representation of developmental processes. The modeling of longitudinal data is complex and requires much thought before, during, and after data collection. The main analytic technique for the study of within-person change, between-person differences in change, the study of multivariate change, and the determinants of change is the growth modeling framework (Grimm, Ram, & Estabrook, 2017; Laird & Ware, 1982; McArdle, 1988; Meredith & Tisak, 1990; Singer & Willett, 2003). The majority of growth models can be estimated using mixed-effects software or structural equation modeling (SEM) software; however, some growth models do require nonlinear mixed-effects software or nonlinear constraints in the structural equation modeling framework (see Browne & du Toit, 1991; Grimm & Ram, 2009; Grimm, Ram, & Hamagami, 2011).

GROWTH MODELS FOR STUDYING CHANGE

Growth models are latent variable models that conceive repeated measures data as coming from a smooth trajectory plus noise. The smooth trajectory is often an a priori chosen parametric function (e.g., linear, quadratic, exponential), and the between-person differences enter the model by allowing different individuals to have different parameters of the same trajectory function. The growth model can be written as

$$y_{ti} = f(b_i, x_{ti}) + e_{ti} \tag{1}$$

where y_{ti} is the outcome for case i assessed at time t, $f(b_i, x_{ti})$, is the within-person change function with x_{ti} as the chosen timing variable (e.g., age, time in study, wave) with random coefficients in b_i, and e_{ti} as the time-dependent residual (noise). The time-dependent residual is often assumed to be independent and identically distributed across time and people, with a zero mean and unknown variance, $e_{ti} \sim N(0, \sigma_e^2)$. The random coefficients or latent variables, b_i, are assumed to follow a multivariate normal distribution with estimated means and estimated covariance matrix, $b_i \sim N(\beta, \psi)$.

Once an appropriate trajectory function (i.e., $f(b_i, x_{ti})$) is determined, researchers turn their attention to examining determinants of the between-person differences in the trajectory function. This equates to studying determinants of the random coefficients in b_i. Two approaches are commonly used to examine determinants of b_i. These approaches are the multiple group framework, which is common in the SEM framework, and the latent variable regression framework, which is common in both the SEM and multilevel modeling (MLM) frameworks.

In the multiple group approach, the data are partitioned into two or more groups (usually not more than three), the same type of growth model is fit to each group, and equality constraints are used to determine which, if any, parameters are significantly different across groups. The multiple group approach allows for the study of mean, variance, and covariance differences across groups, which is a major benefit. Moreover, parameters are separately estimated for each group, which makes interpretation simple; however, understanding group differences in change is more complex. The main limitation of the multiple groups approach is that it is often limited by the number of groups. That is, this approach is typically employed with a single grouping variable with few (i.e., two or four) levels. Although including multiple grouping variables is possible, this is often not done. Thus, the multiple group approach may not be able to identify independent effects—akin to running separate univariate regression models instead of a single multiple regression model. Moreover, if the researcher is interested in a continuous predictor, the researcher would have to create groups based on the continuous variable. In this situation, the number of groups and the cut points used to create the groups are often arbitrary and difficult to justify.

The latent variable regression approach, often referred to as the multiple indicators multiple causes model in the SEM framework, treats the random coefficients as outcomes of a multiple linear regression model. This can be written as

$$b_i = \beta + \gamma X_i + d_i \tag{2}$$

where β is a $q \times 1$ vector of latent variable intercepts, γ is a $q \times r$ matrix of latent variable regression parameters, where r is the number of predictor or explanatory variables, X_i is an $r \times 1$ vector of predictor or explanatory variables for person i, and d_i is a $q \times 1$ vector of latent variable disturbance variables. Here, the primary interest is on the γ matrix, which contains the regression parameter estimates indicating the strength of the association between the explanatory variables and the latent variables.

Compared with the multiple groups approach, the latent variable regression approach enables the study of multiple explanatory variables simultaneously, which allows for the estimation of independent effects. Furthermore, the interpretation of parameters is familiar, given the connections with multiple regression analysis. However, this approach is also limited in certain respects. These limitations include the following: (a) researchers often restrict themselves to linear associations and do not examine nonlinear or interactive effects; (b) given the ability to include multiple explanatory variables, researchers may include many predictors, which increases the likelihood of including several unimportant explanatory variables and makes interpretation of parameter estimates unnecessarily complex; (c) the latent variable regression approach only focuses on mean differences in the random effects and, therefore, does not allow for the evaluation of whether there are differences in the variances and covariances of the random coefficients; and (d) the scaling of variables is extremely important (e.g., categorical and ordinal predictor variables should be dummy or effect coded).

The goal of this chapter is to illustrate how predictors of change can be examined in more flexible ways to potentially consider nonlinear and interactive effects and only include variables that are necessary for prediction. For this, we consider machine learning techniques from regression that have been adapted for the analysis of longitudinal data.

MACHINE LEARNING METHODS

Machine learning methods are a collection of statistical methods with the goal of creating reliable and replicable prediction models from data sets that may have a large number of variables. With a large number of variables, traditional approaches, such as multiple regression, may not yield reliable models, and when the number of variables is larger than the number of participants, there is not a unique solution when using multiple regression (i.e., the model cannot be estimated). To handle the large number of variables efficiently, machine learning algorithms can be used to search the predictor space and highlight variables with explanatory power. Although the methods do not guarantee that an optimal model is found, they have been found to perform well under a variety of conditions. Given the exploratory nature of these approaches, internal cross-validation methods are needed to prevent overfitting. *Overfitting* occurs when the model fits too closely to a given data set, such that the model accounts for the unique features of the data, which makes the model less useful when applied to a new data set.

The two machine learning methods that have been adapted for longitudinal change analyses are recursive partitioning (Breiman et al., 1984; Morgan & Sonquist, 1963) and lasso regression (Tibshirani, 1996). *Recursive partitioning* was initially proposed by Morgan and Sonquist (1963) and became popular when Breiman and colleagues (1984) published their book on classification and regression trees (CART). The recursive partitioning algorithm follows a series of steps to develop a prediction model. For a continuous outcome, the residual sum of squares (RSS) is calculated for the sample, with the mean of the outcome used as the predicted value for all participants. This RSS is termed the *root RSS*. Next, the data are partitioned into two groups (often referred to as *nodes*) based on each unique value of every explanatory variable. With the mean of the outcome for the node serving as the predicted value for participants in the same node, the RSS is calculated and summed over the two nodes. The split that yields the greatest reduction in RSS is chosen to partition the data into two child nodes. This process continues independently in each of the two child nodes and subsequently in all child nodes until a stopping criterion is met. Commonly used stopping criteria include a minimum reduction in RSS (or related measure like R^2), a minimum number of participants in a node, and/or a minimum number of participants to split a node. Recursive partitioning can handle a categorical outcome by using the modal response as the predicted value and using the misclassification rate as the measure of node homogeneity.

The results from recursive partitioning can be organized into an upside-down tree–like structure where the root node (full sample) is at the top, and every partition splits the data into two nodes that grow down the tree. The final model can be read like a series of decision rules (conditional statements), which lead to different predictions. Recursive partitioning can identify variables that are important for prediction, and the nature of the algorithm inherently searches for nonlinear effects (linear effects can be approximated) and multiway interactive effects.

Although recursive partitioning has established itself as a popular machine learning algorithm, the algorithm is not without its limitations. The algorithm uses a *greedy* approach by selecting the split that maximizes node homogeneity and never revisits previous splits. This approach may not lead to the optimal tree structure because the optimal first split may not be the optimal first split when considering subsequent splits. Second, the algorithm tends to be unstable. That is, small perturbations in the data can lead to substantially different tree structures. This is partly due to the greedy nature of the algorithm. Third, the algorithm favors variables with more unique values because more unique values equal more ways to partition the data. Because of these limitations, researchers have proposed alternative algorithms that maintain the ideas behind recursive partitioning. For example, Hothorn, Hornik, and Zeileis (2006) proposed *conditional inference trees*, which use permutation tests and significance values based on the permutation tests to determine which variable to select for partitioning. The goal of this approach is to reduce the variable selection issue of the CART algorithm, where variables with more unique values are more likely to be selected. In a similar vein, Grubinger, Zeileis, and Pfeiffer (2014) developed *evolutionary trees*, in which the goal is to create globally optimal models instead of locally optimal models. Thus, this approach does not use a greedy algorithm because it considers the entire tree structure when making splits.

Lasso regression is another machine learning method that attempts to identify important variables necessary for prediction. As opposed to examining significance levels in a large multiple regression model, lasso regression can shrink regression parameters to zero, which effectively eliminates the predictor variable from the model. This often leads to greater stability in the parameter estimates, higher replicability, and simpler interpretation. Furthermore, Jacobucci, Brandmaier, and Kievit (2019) indicated that examining significance levels in a large multiple regression model is only appropriate when the ratio of sample size to the number of estimated parameters is large.

Lasso regression parameters are found by minimizing the following loss function:

$$\sum_{i=1}^{N}\left(y_i - b_0 - \sum_{i=1}^{p}(b_j \cdot x_{ij})\right)^2 + \lambda\sum_{j=1}^{p}|b_j|. \tag{3}$$

The first part of the loss function is the typical ordinary least squares (OLS) loss function, which encourages the parameters to minimize the RSS. The second part of the loss function is a penalty for the size of the regression parameters. In the penalty, λ is a *tuning* parameter, which controls the strength of the penalty, and $\sum_{j=1}^{p}|b_j|$ is the sum of absolute values of the regression parameters. Because the penalty is on the size of the regression parameters, the explanatory variables are often standardized to make their regression parameters more comparable. When $\lambda = 0$, there is no penalty and the estimated regression parameters are equal to those obtained through OLS regression, and when $\lambda = \infty$, the regression parameters are shrunken to zero. The tuning parameter is often chosen through internal cross-validation, in an attempt to balance bias and variance. There have been extensions of this lasso approach to allow for interactive effects (Bien, Taylor, & Tibshirani, 2013) and to account for the scale of the variables (Zou, 2006), making standardization unnecessary.

MACHINE LEARNING METHODS AND GROWTH ANALYSES

As noted, growth analyses are typically conducted in the SEM or MLM framework. The two frameworks have their benefits and limitations (Ghisletta & Lindenberger, 2004); however, the majority of growth models can be specified in both frameworks, and both frameworks should give identical parameter estimates (see Grimm, Ram, & Estabrook, 2017). Thus, machine learning methods available in these frameworks are viable approaches to using machine learning methods for growth analysis.

Recursive partitioning was combined with the SEM framework by Brandmaier, von Oertzen, McArdle, and Lindenberger (2013) and is referred to as *SEM trees*. In SEM trees, the data are partitioned into two nodes based on every unique value of the covariate set. A researcher-provided SEM is fit to each node, and the summed −2 log-likelihood (−2*LL*) is calculated and serves as the measure of homogeneity. The split that minimizes the −2*LL* is retained, and the process is repeated within each node until a stopping criteria is reached. SEM trees can be estimated in R using the `semtree` package (Brandmaier & Prindle, 2018), which allows for greedy and fair (i.e., conditional inference) splitting algorithms. The default stopping rule is based on an estimated *p*-value comparing the –2*LL* from the model estimated in the parent node to the summed –2*LL* from the models estimated in the child nodes. Splits with *p*-values less than .05 are retained by default; however, this default can be changed.

In MLM, recursive partitioning was first introduced by Abdolell, LeBlanc, Stephens, and Harrison (2002) and recently extended to nonlinear MLM by Stegmann, Jacobucci, Serang, and Grimm (2018). The algorithm described by Abdolell et al. and Stegmann et al. is identical to that of SEM trees. The only difference is that a researcher-provided linear or nonlinear MLM is fit to the data from each node. This algorithm is implemented in the `longRPart2` package (Jacobucci, Stewart, Abdolell, Serang, & Stegmann, 2018). In the package, the algorithm stops when the improvement in –2*LL* is less than 1% of the –2*LL* obtained for the root node (where data from all participants are present); however, this stopping criterion can be changed. SEM trees and the MLM recursive partitioning algorithms retain the benefits of the multiple groups model for studying differences in change and handle some of its inherent limitations. That is, many variables (> 100) can be considered, as opposed to a single grouping variable chosen a priori, and the split on the chosen variable that creates models that are the most different (based on the summed –2*LL*) is the split that is retained.

In a similar vein to how recursive partitioning has been combined with the SEM and MLM framework, lasso regression has been combined with both the SEM (Jacobucci, Grimm, & McArdle, 2016) and MLM (Schelldorfer, Bühlmann, & van de Geer, 2011) frameworks. In both cases, a penalty is added to the maximum likelihood fit function to shrink particular model estimates. Lasso regression in SEM is available through the `regsem` package (Jacobucci, Grimm, Brandmaier, Serang, & Kievit, 2018), which allows for the adaptive lasso, which takes the scale of the variable into account, as well as extensions of ridge regression and the elastic net. Lasso regression in MLM is available through the `lmmlasso` package (Schelldorfer, 2015), which allows researchers-chosen fixed-effects parameters to be penalized.

ILLUSTRATIVE EXAMPLE

Data

Longitudinal data from the Early Childhood Longitudinal Study—Kindergarten Cohort of 1998/1999 (ECLS-K; see https://nces.ed.gov/ecls/kindergarten.asp) were analyzed to illustrate the use of these machine learning methods for studying determinants of change. The ECLS-K is a sample of more than 21,000 students who were in kindergarten in the 1998–1999 school year. The ECLS-K is not a random sample, but a multistage, stratified sample that was clustered within schools. Furthermore, certain subpopulations of children were over-sampled. The study included direct assessments of the children and questionnaires that were answered by the child's parents, teachers, and school administrators. Assessments took place during fall 1998 (kindergarten), spring 1999 (kindergarten), fall 1999 (first grade; 30% subsample of schools), spring 2000 (first grade), spring 2002 (third grade), spring 2004 (fifth grade), and spring 2007 (eighth grade).

The outcome of interest was the repeated assessment of the child's mathematics ability—the mathematics theta score. The mathematics assessment was a two-stage adaptive test. In the first stage, questions were asked that ranged in difficulty. The child's responses to this first stage were used to determine the second stage test, which was used to fine-tune the child's estimated mathematics ability. The theta scores were generated from an item response model and the child's responses to the questions asked of the child. These theta scores were then linearly transformed to have positive values at all time points. This linear transformation does not affect the results but makes their discussion simpler.

The 15 predictor variables included to explain the between-child differences in the growth of mathematics skills included demographic (e.g., gender, paternal education, disability status, English home language, health) and school-readiness indicators (e.g., motor skills, attention, behavior ratings). All these variables were assessed in the fall of kindergarten. Because some of the packages required complete input and output data, a nonrandom subsample from the ECLS-K data set was selected. The sample included 2,887 children who were assessed at the first four measurement occasions and had complete data on the explanatory variables measured in the fall of kindergarten.

Longitudinal Models

The longitudinal mathematics data were organized according to time since the beginning of kindergarten (scaled in years). A longitudinal plot of a subsample of these observed trajectories appears in Figure 13.1. The mathematics trajectories over this time scale are fairly linear; however, there appear to be substantial between-student differences in mathematics ability at each time point and in the rate of change in mathematics ability. Thus, a linear change model was considered. The linear change model can be written as

$$y_{ti} = b_{0i} + b_{1i}(x_{ti} - .3) + e_{ti} \tag{4}$$

where y_{ti} is the outcome of interest (mathematics ability), b_{0i} is the random intercept centered at $x_{ti} = .3$, and represents the student's predicted mathematics score at this point in time (this is approximately equal to the time in the fall of kindergarten when assessments began), b_{1i} is the random slope and represents the student's rate of change in mathematics over kindergarten and first grade, and x_{ti} is the timing variable (time since the beginning of

FIGURE 13.1. Longitudinal Plot of the Longitudinal Mathematics Data (Subsample With *N* = 500)

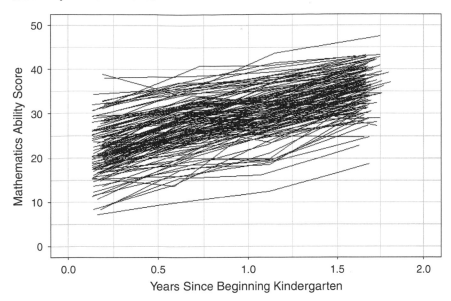

kindergarten scaled in years). Lastly, e_{ti} is the time-dependent residual, which is assumed to be normally distributed with a mean of 0 and a time- and person-invariant variance σ_e^2. The two random coefficients, b_{0i} and $b_{1i'}$ are assumed to follow a multivariate normal distribution with means, β_0 and β_1, variances, ϕ_{00} and $\phi_{11'}$ and covariance, ϕ_{10}.

Recursive partitioning with a linear growth model was fit using the `longRPart2` (Jacobucci, Stewart, et al., 2018) package in R. The stopping rule in `longRPart2` is a user-specified minimum improvement in the $-2LL$. We set this minimum difference to 215 units. Although this minimum amount of improvement is somewhat arbitrary, there is a rationale for its choice. The description of this rationale is reserved for the Discussion section.

Lasso regression with a linear growth model was fit using the `lmmlasso` package in R. In lasso regression, several models are fit and compared to select an optimal tuning parameter. In our application, we used a modified version of the Bayesian information criterion (BIC). The BIC combines the $-2LL$ with a penalty for the number of estimated parameters. Using the BIC to compare two models leads to using the difference in the $-2LL$ and the difference in the number of estimated parameters. In our application, the difference in the number of estimated parameters depends on how many parameters are shrunk to 0. We use a modified version of the BIC because, in large samples, the BIC does not adequately balance the difference in the $-2LL$ and the difference in the number of estimated parameters.

One challenge to using lasso regression with growth models is that the random intercept and slope are in two different scales. Thus, we do not want to use lasso regression on the parameters from the predictor set to the random intercept and slope simultaneously. There are a couple of approaches to consider in this situation. First, we can penalize the effects to the intercept separately from the effects to the slope. That is, we can include the effects to both the intercept and slope but only penalize the effects to the intercept. Once those effects are determined, we can then penalize the effects to the slope. If penalizing the effects to the intercept and slope simultaneously is desired, it is necessary to scale the intercept and slope in a similar metric. This can be done by dividing the time metric by a constant, such that the estimated variance of the intercept and slope are as close as possible when estimating the unconditional model (model without any explanatory variables for the intercept and the slope). Alternatively, the adaptive lasso (Zou, 2006) can be used; however, the adaptive lasso is not available in the `lmmlasso` package.

Recursive partitioning and lasso latent variable models were also estimated in the SEM framework. We report on models obtained using R packages that connect with multilevel modeling packages (`longRPart2` and `lmmlasso`). Programming scripts for all models, including SEM specifications, can be found at https://sites.google.com/site/longitudinalmethods/downloads.

RESULTS

The results section is composed of two parts. First, we review the findings for performing recursive partitioning with a linear growth model for the longitudinal mathematics data. Second, we review the findings for performing lasso regression with a linear growth model for the longitudinal mathematics data.

Recursive Partitioning

The recursive partitioning algorithm with a linear growth model specified, with a minimum improvement in the $-2LL$ of 215 units to retain a partition, first partitioned the data based on the student's fine motor skills. This was the only split retained in the exhaustive search. The root $-2LL$ was 60,817, and splitting the data based on fine motor skills reduced the $-2LL$ to 60,174, a reduction of 642 units. The split on the fine motor skills variable was -0.30, making it slightly below the mean on the fine motor skills measure. The trajectories for children in the two terminal nodes are plotted in Figure 13.2. These plots contain the mean trajectory (solid heavy line) and approximate 95% confidence intervals (dotted heavy lines) of the between-person differences in the trajectories. From this figure, it is apparent that children who had fine motor skills scores less than -0.30 tended to have lower intercept scores; however, these students tended to have a slightly faster linear rate of change over the kindergarten and first-grade years, on average. The parameters of the linear growth model for the two terminal nodes are contained in Table 13.1. From the growth parameters, it is clear that the main difference in the parameters for the participants in the two nodes was the fixed-effect estimate for the intercept. The fixed-effect parameter for the intercept was approximately 4.40 points higher for the students who had higher fine motor skills

FIGURE 13.2. Longitudinal Plots of the Observed Mathematics Trajectories by Terminal Node

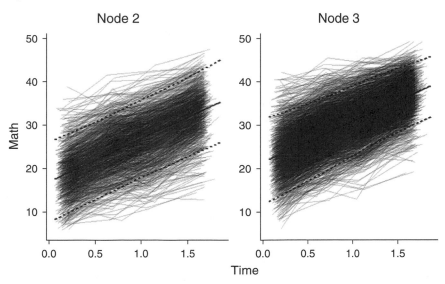

compared with the students who had lower fine motor skills at kindergarten entrance. Given the standard deviation of the random intercept in the two groups $\left(\sqrt{\phi_{00\,pooled}} = 4.71\right)$, this translates to an effect size of $d = 0.93$, suggesting a large effect size based on Cohen's (1988) criteria.

Lasso Regression

Lasso regression was conducted with the `lmmlasso` package in R. The continuous variables were scaled to have a mean of 0 and a standard deviation of 1.

TABLE 13.1. Parameter Estimates of the Linear Growth Model for the Terminal Nodes

Parameter	Fine motor < -0.3 (N = 990)		Fine motor ≥ -0.3 (N = 1,897)	
	Estimate	Standard error	Estimate	Standard error
Fixed-effects				
β_0	19.99	0.16	24.39	0.11
β_1	9.81	0.08	9.40	0.06
Random-effects				
$\sqrt{\Psi_{00}}$	4.66	—	4.73	—
$\sqrt{\Psi_{11}}$	1.59	—	1.48	—
$\Psi_{10}\big/\sqrt{\Psi_{00}\cdot\Psi_{11}}$	−0.20	—	−0.69	—
σ_e	2.28	—	2.16	—

Note. Standard errors are not available for random-effects parameters.

All the dichotomous variables were coded 0 or 1 and were not standardized. First, the effects from the explanatory variables to the random intercept were penalized. An optimal value of the tuning parameter (λ) was chosen by varying the tuning parameter from 0 (no penalty) to a high number ($\lambda = 300$) where all the penalized effects were shrunken to 0. For each value of the tuning parameter, a modified version of the BIC was output, and the model with the smallest BIC was retained. In the second step, the nonzero effects to the intercept were retained and not penalized, and the effects from the explanatory variables to the random slope were penalized. Similarly, an optimal value of the tuning parameter (λ) was chosen by varying the tuning parameter from 0 (no penalty) to a high number ($\lambda = 300$) where all the penalized effects were shrunken to 0. The modified version of the BIC was used to determine the optimal value of the tuning parameter. A final model was then specified with all nonzero effects to the intercept and slope retained and not penalized.

The model with the lowest modified BIC retained several effects from the explanatory variables to the random intercept. These effects were from age at kindergarten entrance, maternal education, paternal education, teacher-rated attention, poverty status, and fine motor skills. These effects were then retained when the effects from the explanatory variables to the random slope were penalized. The model with the lowest modified BIC did not retain any of the effects from the explanatory variables to the random slope. Thus, the final model only included effects from age at kindergarten entrance, maternal education, paternal education, teacher-rated attention, poverty status, and fine motor skills to the intercept. Parameter estimates for this final model (with no penalties) are contained in Table 13.2. Maternal and paternal education, attention, age at kindergarten entrance, and fine motor skills all had positive effects on the intercept for mathematics ability, whereas poverty status had a negative effect. The largest effect appeared to be from the fine motor skills variables.

DISCUSSION

Differential Change

Adequately modeling and examining differential change is challenging. Researchers often consider theory-driven approaches, involving multiple group models or latent variable regression models. As discussed, these approaches are common but do have limitations when considering many potential predictor variables. Multiple group models consider one explanatory variable at a time and do not statistically adjust for correlated variables, which can lead to overestimates of the importance of the explanatory variable considered. Latent variable regression models have fewer limitations when considering the number of explanatory variables; however, researchers often only consider demographic variables that are thought to be important or necessary control variables and the particular variable(s) that are of interest. In both cases, the

TABLE 13.2. Parameter Estimates From the Relaxed Lasso

Parameter	Estimate	Standard error
Fixed-effects		
β_0	21.15	0.22
β_1	9.54	0.05
γ_{01} (age)	0.69	0.07
γ_{02} (attention)	0.59	0.07
γ_{03} (mom education)	0.71	0.09
γ_{04} (dad education)	0.73	0.09
γ_{05} (poverty status)	−1.95	0.23
γ_{06} (fine motor)	1.75	0.07
Random-effects		
$\sqrt{\phi_{00}}$	3.96	—
$\sqrt{\phi_{11}}$	1.53	—
$\phi_{10} / \sqrt{\phi_{00} \cdot \phi_{11}}$	−0.47	—
σ_e	2.21	—

number of explanatory variables can be considered limited. Furthermore, interactive and nonlinear effects are not often considered. Given the limitations of these approaches for examining the determinants of between-person differences in change, exploratory approaches should be considered. Such approaches can be used to purely explore change differences or after using a confirmatory approach.

The exploratory approaches discussed are built on the multiple group and latent variable regression approaches to examining differences in change; however, the approaches can better handle many predictor variables. The recursive partitioning algorithm for longitudinal change models is an exploratory form of multiple group growth modeling. Thus, the particular variable chosen to partition the data is the variable from which two groups can be created that have the most different change trajectories. Because these groups could then be partitioned again by a different variable or the same variable, the recursive partitioning algorithm inherently considers nonlinear and interactive effects among the explanatory variables. The extension of lasso regression discussed here allows researchers to consider more explanatory variables (more than they would typically consider) and then lets the estimation process determine which variables are important for accounting for differences in the change trajectories.

These approaches have several benefits over the inclusion of many explanatory variables to account for differences in change. For example, these approaches are systematic search algorithms, which means they can be repeated, the model selection decisions are clean, and the approaches are exhaustive given the predictor set. These approaches also have limitations.

The lasso approach, as currently implemented in available software, does not search for interactive and nonlinear effects (unless programmed, which would require significant programming when there is a large number of variables). Recent extensions of lasso regression (Bien et al., 2013) allow for nonlinear (squared terms) and interactive effects, and we expect these approaches to be incorporated into using the lasso in latent variable models. Another limitation is the handling of missing data. As currently implemented, the lasso and recursive partitioning approaches for latent variable models do not handle missing data in the explanatory variables. The lasso can be extended to use full information maximum likelihood estimation, which can handle missing data in the exogenous variables. The recursive partitioning approach can use surrogate splits to handle missing data in the exogenous variables. Both approaches can benefit from using multiple imputation; however, summarizing results over imputations can be challenging.

Machine Learning Methods and Developmental Psychology

Over the past few years, more machine learning methods have been applied to developmental studies. We highlight four such studies here.

Tuarob et al. (2017) proposed a method that used random forests to predict the mental state of individuals using multivariate time series data. Here, the methods used data from the past and present to predict future observations. As discussed earlier, the machine learning methods were more flexible than traditional multivariate time series techniques, which require traditional statistical assumptions (stationary, linear relationships). Developmental studies are increasingly relying on the collection of data through participants' cell phones. Individuals use digital devices to interact with the world. Therefore, screenshots of individuals' phones provide great insight into their interactions with the world, accurate timing of events, and insight into how individuals interact with technology. Chiatti et al. (2017, 2018) highlighted how these large-scale developmental studies can be implemented and analyzed using machine learning methods. Data from 900,000 smartphone screenshots were collected from 52 participants (screenshots were taken every 5 seconds).

In a similar vein to our work here, Brandmaier, Ram, Wagner, and Gerstorf (2017) used SEM trees and SEM forests (an extension of SEM trees) to identify predictors of well-being during the terminal phase of life. Information on participants' well-being was collected across time, in addition to sociodemographic variables, physical health characteristics, and psychosocial characteristics. SEM forests was used to further explore important variables in predicting the trajectory of well-being. Brandmaier et al. found that having a disability, hospitalizations, social participation, and perceived control were important variables in identifying groups of individuals following different latent growth curve models of well-being during their terminal years.

In addition to analyzing developmental data using machine learning methods, machine learning methods have also been used to address challenges during the design and analysis stages of developmental research. Brick, Koffer, Gerstorf, and Ram (2018) used machine learning methods as a way to select important variables in longitudinal research to reduce participant burden and the cost of carrying out the longitudinal study. That is, longitudinal studies involve intensive study designs with a large number of potential measures, which can result in a substantial burden for the participants and high cost. Therefore, selecting a small and optimal set of features to measure each time is essential to reduce participant burden and potentially reduce participant dropout. Brick et al. provided guidelines for selecting features in an optimal manner, and they illustrated their proposed approach using random forests on an empirical data set from the German Socio-Economic Panel.

Model Selection

A major challenge that needs greater scrutiny is the process of *model selection*. In both the extension of recursive partitioning and the extension of lasso regression, we relied on a modified version of the BIC. The BIC combines the −2LL, which is a measure of how well the model accounts for the data, and a penalty for the number of estimated parameters. In the BIC, the penalty is $\ln(N) \cdot p$, where N is the sample size and p is the number of estimated parameters. The BIC will choose the proper model to the extent to which the penalty can balance the amount of information present in the −2LL. The challenge to this balance is that the −2LL is dependent on sample size. Generally, the −2LL increases linearly with sample size holding the number of time points per person constant. The penalty for the BIC also increases with sample size according to $\ln(N)$, which leads to a nonlinear association between sample size and the size of the penalty.

Because the association between sample size and −2LL is linear, and the association between sample size and the penalty is nonlinear, there may only be a small range of sample sizes where the −2LL and the penalty in the BIC are appropriately balanced. In a cursory review of the simulation literature that evaluated the BIC as a method of model comparison, it seemed as though the BIC penalty is too strong for smaller sample sizes ($N < 200$), appropriate for moderate sample sizes ($N \sim 500$), and too small for larger sample sizes ($N < 1{,}000$). Given our sample size ($N > 2{,}000$), we expected that the BIC would lead to an overparameterized model. Thus, we modified the BIC and attempted to scale the BIC as if it were based on a sample size of 500—the sample size where it appears (from our cursory review) that the −2LL may be appropriately balanced with the penalty. Thus, we retained the −2LL for each model, divided the −2LL by the sample size, and multiplied this quotient by 500 to obtain an estimate of what the −2LL would have been if we had a sample size of 500. We then added $\ln(500) \cdot p$, which is the value of the penalty that would be added if our sample size was 500. We used this modified BIC to select a model when using the lasso, and we used a similar criterion when determining the minimum improvement in the −2LL for retaining a split with recursive partitioning.

In machine learning methods, a large number of models are considered, and a method to select the most appropriate model is needed. With regression-based methods, the model with the lowest cross-validated mean square error is chosen, or the simplest model with a cross-validated mean square error that is within one standard error of the best model (model with the lowest cross-validated mean square error) is chosen (Hastie, Tibshirani, & Friedman, 2009). With multivariate data and models, model selection is often based on a fit index, such as the BIC and the Generalized Cross-Validation Index. This is because cross-validation is more challenging (especially when the model contains variance components); however, it is possible to use cross-validation with multivariate data and models (see Grimm, Mazza, & Davoudzadeh, 2017). More research is needed on this topic, and the discussion of this topic can revolve around the development of effect size measures (e.g., change in the $-2LL$) for the comparison of multivariate models.

Alternative Approaches

Machine learning extensions of recursive partitioning and lasso regression estimated in the multilevel modeling framework were used in our illustrative example. As noted, similar models can be estimated using the SEM framework. Although not presented here, our illustrative example was run using the `semtree` and `regsem` packages in R. In these runs, the timing metric was measurement occasion, with the intercept centered at the first measurement occasion. `semtree` partitioned the data many more times than `longRPart2` because of the criterion used to retain a split (minimum deviance vs. Bonferroni corrected p-value). However, if the same criterion were used, the same split would have been made, and this split would have been the only split retained. In `regsem`, the adaptive lasso (Zou, 2006) was used. The adaptive lasso accounts for the different scaling of explanatory variables. Thus, the explanatory variables were not standardized before running the model. The results from `regsem` were highly similar to those obtained from `lmmlasso`; however, `regsem` retained age at kindergarten entry as a predictor of the rate of change. This variable was negatively associated with the rate of change in mathematics skills through kindergarten and first grade.

CONCLUSION

Although machine learning methods can be atheoretical, these methods can and should be combined with the thoughtful selection of explanatory variables. That is, in certain situations, prediction is important, and a clear understanding of the mechanisms is less important. We do not think this is the situation in psychology. Thus, researchers should carefully select the set of explanatory variables with the goal of being more flexible in their selection. The machine learning methods can then isolate important predictors and examine the nature of their association (nonlinear and interactive effects). Machine learning methods should be used in psychology even though our data may not be large by convention. At the very least, these methods should be considered after a purely theory-driven approach to examine what, if anything, was missed. We look forward to seeing their greater use in psychological research.

REFERENCES

Abdolell, M., LeBlanc, M., Stephens, D., & Harrison, R. V. (2002). Binary partitioning for continuous longitudinal data: Categorizing a prognostic variable. *Statistics in Medicine, 21,* 3395–3409. http://dx.doi.org/10.1002/sim.1266

Baltes, P. B., & Nesselroade, J. R. (1979). History and rationale of longitudinal research. In J. R. Nesselroade & P. B. Baltes (Eds.), *Longitudinal research in the study of behavior and development* (pp. 1–39). New York, NY: Academic Press.

Bien, J., Taylor, J., & Tibshirani, R. (2013). A lasso for hierarchical interactions. *Annals of Statistics, 41,* 1111–1141. http://dx.doi.org/10.1214/13-AOS1096

Brandmaier, A. M., & Prindle, J. J. (2018). semtree (R package ver. 0.9.12) [Computer software]. Retrieved from http://cran.nexr.com/web/packages/semtree/semtree.pdf

Brandmaier, A. M., Ram, N., Wagner, G. G., & Gerstorf, D. (2017). Terminal decline in well-being: The role of multi-indicator constellations of physical health and psychosocial correlates. *Developmental Psychology, 53,* 996–1012. http://dx.doi.org/10.1037/dev0000274

Brandmaier, A. M., von Oertzen, T., McArdle, J. J., & Lindenberger, U. (2013). Structural equation model trees. *Psychological Methods, 18,* 71–86. http://dx.doi.org/10.1037/a0030001

Breiman, L., Friedman, J. H., Olshen, R. A., & Stone, C. J. (1984). *Classification and regression trees.* Belmont, CA: Wadsworth Statistical Press.

Brick, T. R., Koffer, R. E., Gerstorf, D., & Ram, N. (2018). Feature selection methods for optimal design of studies for developmental inquiry. *The Journals of Gerontology: Series B. Psychological Sciences and Social Sciences, 73,* 113–123. http://dx.doi.org/10.1093/geronb/gbx008

Browne, M. W., & du Toit, S. H. C. (1991). Models for learning data. In L. M. Collins & J. L. Horn (Eds.), *Best methods for the analysis of change* (pp. 47–68). Washington, DC: American Psychological Association.

Cameron, C. E., Grimm, K. J., Steele, J. S., Castro-Schilo, L., & Grissmer, D. W. (2015). Nonlinear Gompertz curve models of achievement gaps in mathematics and reading. *Journal of Educational Psychology, 107,* 789–804. http://dx.doi.org/10.1037/edu0000009

Chiatti, A., Cho, M.-J., Gagneja, A., Yang, X., Brinberg, M., Roehrick, L., . . . Giles, C. L. (2018). Text extraction and retrieval from smartphone Screenshots: Building a repository for life in media. In *Proceedings of the 33rd ACM/SIGAPP Symposium on Applied Computing* (pp. 948–955). New York, NY: ACM.

Chiatti, A., Yang, X., Brinberg, M., Cho, M.-J., Gagneja, A., Ram, N., . . . Giles, C. L. (2017). Text extraction from smartphone screenshots to archive in situ media behavior. In *Proceedings of the 9th International Conference on Knowledge Capture* (K-CAP 2017). New York, NY: ACM. http://dx.doi.org/10.1145/3148011.3154468

Cohen, J. (1988). *Statistical power analysis for the behavioral sciences.* Mahwah, NJ: Erlbaum.

Drezner, Z., Marcoulides, G. A., & Salhi, S. (1999). Tabu search model selection in multiple regression analysis. *Communications in Statistics—Simulation and Computation, 28,* 349–367. http://dx.doi.org/10.1080/03610919908813553

Eiben, A., & Smith, J. (2003). *Introduction to evolutionary computing.* New York, NY: Springer. http://dx.doi.org/10.1007/978-3-662-05094-1

Ferrer, E., & Helm, J. L. (2013). Dynamical systems modeling of physiological coregulation in dyadic interactions. *International Journal of Psychophysiology, 88,* 296–308. http://dx.doi.org/10.1016/j.ijpsycho.2012.10.013

Friedman, J. (1991). Multivariate adaptive regression splines. *Annals of Statistics, 19*, 1–67. http://dx.doi.org/10.1214/aos/1176347963

Gerstorf, D., Hoppmann, C., & Ram, N. (2014). The promise and challenges of integrating multiple time-scales in adult developmental inquiry. *Research in Human Development, 11*, 75–90. http://dx.doi.org/10.1080/15427609.2014.906725

Ghisletta, P., & Lindenberger, U. (2004). Static and dynamic longitudinal structural analyses of cognitive changes in old age. *Gerontology, 50*, 12–16. http://dx.doi.org/10.1159/000074383

Gonzales, J. E., & Ferrer, E. (2014). Individual pooling for group-based modeling under the assumption of ergodicity. *Multivariate Behavioral Research, 49*, 245–260. http://dx.doi.org/10.1080/00273171.2014.902298

Grimm, K. J., Mazza, G., & Davoudzadeh, P. (2017). Model selection in finite mixture models: A *k*-fold cross-validation approach. *Structural Equation Modeling, 24*, 246–256. http://dx.doi.org/10.1080/10705511.2016.1250638

Grimm, K. J., & Ram, N. (2009). Nonlinear growth models in Mplus and SAS. *Structural Equation Modeling, 16*, 676–701. http://dx.doi.org/10.1080/10705510903206055

Grimm, K. J., Ram, N., & Estabrook, R. (2017). *Growth modeling: Structural equation and multilevel modeling approaches.* New York, NY: Guilford Press.

Grimm, K. J., Ram, N., & Hamagami, F. (2011). Nonlinear growth curves in developmental research. *Child Development, 82*, 1357–1371. http://dx.doi.org/10.1111/j.1467-8624.2011.01630.x

Grubinger, T., Zeileis, A., & Pfeiffer, K.-P. (2014). evtree: Evolutionary learning of globally optimal classification and regression trees in R. *Journal of Statistical Software, 61*, 1–29. http://dx.doi.org/10.18637/jss.v061.i01

Hastie, T., Tibshirani, R., & Friedman, J. (2009). *The elements of statistical learning: Data mining, inference, and prediction.* New York, NY: Springer. http://dx.doi.org/10.1007/978-0-387-84858-7

Hedman, E. B. (2010). *In-situ measurement of electrodermal activity during occupational therapy* (Unpublished master's thesis). Massachusetts Institute of Technology, Cambridge.

Hothorn, T., Hornik, K., & Zeileis, A. (2006). Unbiased recursive partitioning: A conditional inference framework. *Journal of Computational and Graphical Statistics, 15*, 651–674. http://dx.doi.org/10.1198/106186006X133933

Jacobucci, R., Brandmaier, A. M., & Kievit, R. A. (2019). A practical guide to variable selection in structural equation modeling by using regularized multiple-indicators, multiple-causes models. *Advances in Methods and Practices in Psychological Science, 2*, 55–76. http://dx.doi.org/10.1177/2515245919826527

Jacobucci, R., Grimm, K. J., Brandmaier, A. M., Serang, S., & Kievit, R. A. (2018). Regsem (R package ver. 1.1.2) [Computer software]. Retrieved from https://cran.r-project.org/web/packages/regsem/regsem.pdf

Jacobucci, R., Grimm, K. J., & McArdle, J. J. (2016). Regularized structural equation modeling. *Structural Equation Modeling, 23*, 555–566. http://dx.doi.org/10.1080/10705511.2016.1154793

Jacobucci, R., Stewart, S., Abdolell, M., Serang, S., & Stegmann, G. (2018). longRPart2 (R package ver. 0.2.3) [Computer software]. Retrieved from https://cran.r-project.org/web/packages/longRPart2/longRPart2.pdf

Juster, F., & Suzman, R. (1995). An overview of the Health and Retirement Study. *The Journal of Human Resources, 30*, S7–S56. http://dx.doi.org/10.2307/146277

Laird, N. M., & Ware, J. H. (1982). Random-effects models for longitudinal data. *Biometrics, 38*, 963–974. http://dx.doi.org/10.2307/2529876

Liu, S., & Palumbo, R. (2013). Dynamic modeling of interpersonal electrodermal activity using cointegration methodology. *Psychophysiology, 50*(Suppl 1), S19.

McArdle, J. J. (1988). Dynamic but structural equation modeling of repeated measures data. In J. R. Nesselroade & R. B. Cattell (Eds.), *Handbook of multivariate experimental psychology* (Vol. 2, pp. 561–614). New York, NY: Plenum Press. http://dx.doi.org/10.1007/978-1-4613-0893-5_17

McArdle, J. J., & Hamagami, F. (2001). Linear dynamic analyses of incomplete longitudinal data. In L. Collins & A. Sayer (Eds.), *Methods for the analysis of change* (pp. 139–176). Washington, DC: American Psychological Association. http://dx.doi.org/10.1037/10409-005

Meredith, W., & Tisak, J. (1990). Latent curve analysis. *Psychometrika, 55,* 107–122. http://dx.doi.org/10.1007/BF02294746

Morgan, J. N., & Sonquist, J. A. (1963). Problems in the analysis of survey data, and a proposal. *Journal of the American Statistical Association, 58,* 415–434. http://dx.doi.org/10.1080/01621459.1963.10500855

National Institute of Child Health and Human Development Early Child Care Research (Ed.). (2005). *Child care and development: Results from the NICHD Study of Early Child Care and Youth Development.* New York, NY: Guilford Press.

Ram, N., & Diehl, M. (2015). Multiple time-scale design and analysis: Pushing towards realtime modeling of complex developmental processes. In M. Diehl, K. Hooker, & M. Sliwinski (Eds.), *Handbook of intraindividual variability across the lifespan* (pp. 308–323). New York, NY: Routledge.

Schelldorfer, J. (2015). lmmlasso (R package ver. 0.1-2) [Computer software]. Retrieved from https://cran.r-project.org/web/packages/lmmlasso/lmmlasso.pdf

Schelldorfer, J., Bühlmann, P., & van de Geer, S. (2011). Estimation for high-dimensional linear mixed-effects models using l_1-penalization. *Scandinavian Journal of Statistics, 38,* 197–214. http://dx.doi.org/10.1111/j.1467-9469.2011.00740.x

Singer, J. D., & Willett, J. B. (2003). *Applied longitudinal data analysis: Modeling change and event occurrence.* New York, NY: Oxford University Press. http://dx.doi.org/10.1093/acprof:oso/9780195152968.001.0001

Skibbe, L., Grimm, K., Bowles, R., & Morrison, F. (2012). Literacy growth in the academic year versus summer from preschool through second grade: Differential effects of schooling across four skills. *Scientific Studies of Reading, 16,* 141–165. http://dx.doi.org/10.1080/10888438.2010.543446

Smith, M. (1993). *Neural networks for statistical modeling.* New York, NY: Van Nostrand Reinhold.

Stegmann, G., Jacobucci, R., Serang, S., & Grimm, K. J. (2018). Recursive partitioning with nonlinear models of change. *Multivariate Behavioral Research, 53,* 559–570. http://dx.doi.org/10.1080/00273171.2018.1461602

Tibshirani, R. (1996). Regression shrinkage and selection via the lasso. *Journal of the Royal Statistical Society: Series A (Statistics in Society), 58,* 267–288.

Tuarob, S., Tucker, C. S., Kumara, S., Giles, C. L., Pincus, A. L., Conroy, D. E., & Ram, N. (2017). How are you feeling? A personalized methodology for predicting mental states from temporally observable physical and behavioral information. *Journal of Biomedical Informatics, 68,* 1–19. http://dx.doi.org/10.1016/j.jbi.2017.02.010

Zou, H. (2006). The adaptive lasso and its oracle properties. *Journal of the American Statistical Association, 101,* 1418–1429. http://dx.doi.org/10.1198/016214506000000735

14

Applying Principles of Big Data to the Workplace and Talent Analytics

Q. Chelsea Song, Mengqiao Liu, Chen Tang, and Laura F. Long

In the current workplace, big data are more relevant and accessible than ever. Big data describe the amount and complexity of the data, as well as the analytical technique and tools revolving around it. As the volume, velocity, and variety of organizational data increase, workplace researchers and practitioners have to adapt to nontraditional approaches that harness the data at an unprecedented level. For example, a company that wants to predict future turnover on the basis of previous turnover rates might find themselves working with tens of thousands of data points that are scattered across hundreds of teams and multiple years. Such a data set could be difficult to analyze using traditional methods but is readily approachable using big data methods. Further, the development of statistical, computational, and data management methods allows us to gain additional insight by applying novel methods to investigate familiar topics with "big" and "small" data. For example, interactive visualization methods allow organizations to efficiently gauge employee satisfaction, needs, and feedback for effective communication and organizational changes.

Not surprisingly, there is growing enthusiasm among practitioners (e.g., talent analytics) and scholars in fields such as industrial and organizational (I/O) psychology, organizational behavior, and human resource management to apply principles of big data to better understand and improve the workplace (Chamorro-Premuzic, Akhtar, Winsborough, & Sherman, 2017; Rienties, Cross, Marsh, & Ullmann, 2017; Tonidandel, King, & Cortina, 2015). In this chapter, we provide an overview of the research and practice of big data in the workplace.

http://dx.doi.org/10.1037/0000193-015
Big Data in Psychological Research, S. E. Woo, L. Tay, and R. W. Proctor (Editors)

Big data have drawn significant and increasing attention in the academic community. For example, at the 2013 annual meeting of the Society for Industrial and Organizational Psychology, there were only four sessions with *big data* or *analytics* in the title. That number nearly increased four times in 2018 to a total of 15 sessions. The topics of the sessions ranged from best practices in establishing human resource (HR) analytics functions within organizations to research findings in organizational sciences that were made possible by big data analytics. To systematically examine the research trend, we conducted a quantitative summary of the number of publications in the past 10 years using the PsycINFO database. Our results, shown in Figure 14.1, suggest that there was a dramatic increase in the number of publications that used big data approaches. Among them, some of the most common topics include personnel assessment, job performance, and personality.

A further examination (see Figure 14.2) showed that publications can be found in research outlets from various fields. The majority of the studies were published in journals of psychology and management (e.g., *Journal of Applied Psychology*), where familiar topics (e.g., job satisfaction) were examined with novel big data approaches, whereas a nonnegligible number of relevant studies were published in outlets that were not traditionally focused on workplace research (e.g., conferences in computer science). Big data is, indeed, an interdisciplinary topic. After all, a vast majority of individuals conducting research in big data initially came from fields such as computer science and statistics, rather than organizational sciences. To have a more comprehensive knowledge of related research, we have to expand our focus to interdisciplinary outlets.

FIGURE 14.1. Growth Trajectory of the Number of Scholarly Publications That Used Big Data Methods to Study Workplace Topics Over the Past 10 Years

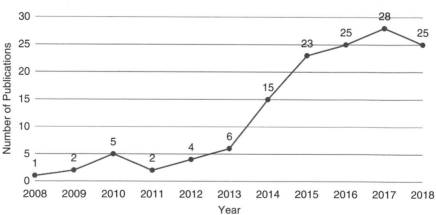

We searched PsycINFO for papers published between January 2008 and December 2018. Only publications written in English were included in the search. The final list included peer-reviewed articles, editorials, chapters, reviews, dissertations, retractions, and conference proceedings. A supplementary material with a list of all publications included is available from the corresponding author on request.

FIGURE 14.2. Proportion of Papers Published in Psychology and Nonpsychology Journals

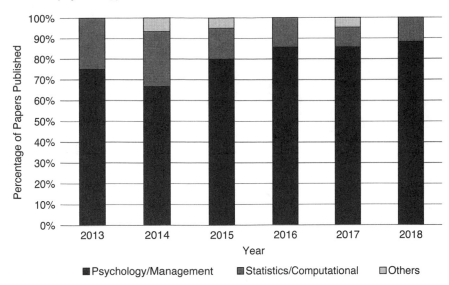

The shading indicates whether the publication source is primarily associated with the field of psychology or management, statistics or computational, or neither categories. The figure only includes the years with more than five publications (2013–2018), for reliable interpretation.

Big data provide a rich opportunity for interdisciplinary collaboration and innovative efforts to forward our understanding of the workplace.

In parallel to the enthusiasm in academia, there is also a growing trend among practitioners (e.g., I/O consultants) to explore big data applications in the workplace, as reflected by a steady increase in related employment reported by the Bureau of Labor Statistics (BLS; see Figure 14.3). According to BLS (2017), between 2016 and 2026, the number of job positions for analytics-related occupations is expected to increase by 33.8%—more than 4 times the average growth across all occupations (7.4%). Further, a recent survey of human resources professionals suggested that, in 2016, a majority of organizations (82%) will have or are projected to have positions that require data analysis skills, and more than half (59%) of the surveyed organizations expect to increase the number of such positions over the next 5 years (Society of Human Resource Management, 2016). Organizations are investing significantly in their research and analytic capabilities, employing in-house experts to extract constructive insights from data.

We see great potential in the future for big data to play a key role in understanding and improving the workplace. In light of this, in this chapter, we strive to showcase current trends and discuss future potentials for big data to advance workplace science and practice. The chapter is organized into three primary sections. First, we discuss content areas where big data has contributed to (a) the study of the workplace and (b) application in talent analytics. Second,

FIGURE 14.3. Change in Total Number of Employment (Unit: 1,000) for Big Data Related Jobs by Occupation

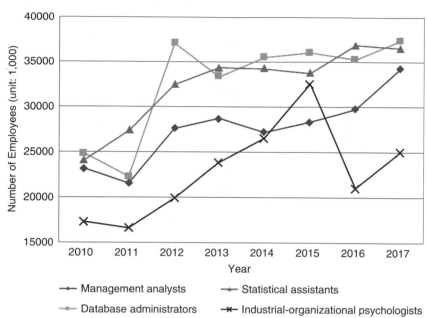

Data obtained from Bureau of Labor Statistics (2017).

we provide a survey of related big data sources, methodology, and tools that could potentially be used by interested readers. Finally, we discuss challenges of, and provide recommendations for, incorporating big data in workplace research and practice.

BIG DATA IN THE WORKPLACE: RESEARCH AND APPLICATIONS

Research Topics

Big data have enabled researchers to examine existing problems from new angles. Moreover, technological advances have fundamentally changed many day-to-day activities in the workplace, thus introducing exciting, contemporary research topics that were not possible to study with traditional methodologies.

Recruitment

Recruitment has seen one of the biggest revolutions over the past years: The accessibility, magnitude, and speed of Internet information have pushed the once-dominant newspaper ads to the side stage, introducing platforms and applications that swiftly close the distance between applicants and employers. Although exciting, such change also brought about new questions for employers (Ployhart, Schmitt, & Tippins, 2017): Do different online platforms influence application decisions differently? How can we guarantee fair access to opportunities among potential applicants? Most of the current research on Internet recruiting examines features of online recruitment that influence outcomes, such as the perception of organizational attraction and intent to pursuit (e.g., Allen, Mahto, & Otondo, 2007; Dineen, Ling, Ash, & DelVecchio, 2007; Dineen & Noe, 2009). Other studies have explored the use of text mining techniques to supplement traditional job analytic methods and improve job advertisements (e.g., Kobayashi et al., 2018). It is important to point out that most of the research was published nearly a decade after online recruitment became common practice (Ployhart et al., 2017). This demonstrates a lag between research and practice and significant potential for research on contemporary recruitment methods. Future possibilities include adaptive recruitment by bridging adaptive testing in education with job recruitment.

Selection

Currently, the most common applications of big data methods in personnel selection include (a) improving the scoring of selection predictors (e.g., resume information, interview performance) and (b) using advanced analytics to achieve better prediction of workplace outcomes (e.g., job performance, turnover). For example, researchers assessed the reliability and validity of computer-based scoring of candidate essays (Campion, Campion, Campion, & Reider, 2016) and explored multiobjective optimization techniques to help make hiring decisions that simultaneously optimize multiple selection objectives (e.g., job performance, diversity; De Corte, Lievens, & Sackett, 2007). Further, researchers are exploring potential alternative sources of data (e.g., social media) to predict job-related individual differences (e.g., Back et al., 2010; Park et al., 2015). For example, machine learning models are trained to predict self-reported Big Five personality traits using digital footprints such as social media posts and images. A recent meta-analytic review (Azucar, Marengo, & Settanni, 2018) showed that the correlation between the scores obtained from digital footprints and self-reported Big Five personality scores ranged from .29 (Agreeableness) to .40 (Extraversion). The predictive accuracy of the digital footprints improved when demographic information and multiple types of digital footprints were included in the models.

Consistent with the recent trends in recruitment, social media platforms such as Facebook and LinkedIn have also been used broadly in selection practice. Although research in this area has been limited, recent psychometric evaluation of LinkedIn (Roulin & Levashina, 2019) showed that there was an acceptable level of consistency between others' ratings of perceived skills, personality, and cognitive ability based on LinkedIn profile and corresponding self-ratings. Factors such as profile length, profile picture, and the number of connections influenced others' ratings. Such studies provide exciting insights for predicting employee attitude and behavior in the workplace. However, the use of social media information in selection has to be based on established evidence for job relatedness and validity, as well as voluntary consent from the applicants.

We envision that the big data approach conveys exceptional capabilities for understanding and predicting the fit between a person and a job. For example, future research in selection could leverage the interdisciplinary toolbox of big data analytics to develop innovative selection methods in personnel assessment (e.g., automatic item generation in tests combined with adaptive testing; Harrison, Collins, & Müllensiefen, 2017), explore the use of nontraditional predictors or alternative sources of data in selection (e.g., using wearable sensors in work sample tests), and use big data analytics to improve the local and global validity of decisions (e.g., regularization methods to minimize model overfitting). However, the use of big data methods in selection also introduces unprecedented and pressing challenges, such as issues of personal privacy, evaluation of job relatedness of the predictors from novel data sources, and legal concerns when using alternative approaches to make hiring decisions (McDonald, Thompson, & O'Connor, 2016; Ployhart et al., 2017). These potential challenges are discussed toward the end of this chapter.

Job Attitudes

The big data approach has expanded the scope of job attitude research by introducing alternative operationalization of attitudes. Instead of using traditional self-response scales to measure job attitudes, we are now able to examine organic expressions of attitudes through sources such as message boards and e-mails. For example, Hernandez, Newman, and Jeon (2015) analyzed the regional variability in job satisfaction expressed in Twitter feeds. In another example, Ford, Jebb, Tay, and Diener (2018) explored the potential of Internet search patterns as an indicator of subject well-being. They found that Internet search frequency correlated with self-reported emotions and indicators of cardiovascular health and depression.

Big data approaches have also allowed a more in-depth understanding of job attitudes. For example, much of the dynamics between emotion and attitudes has been uncovered using longitudinal data collected using sociometric sensors and analyzed with the help of big data analytics (see review by Wang, Zhou, & Zhang, 2016). In another example, Zuccolotto (2010) used a random forest algorithm to examine mechanisms that influence job satisfaction, contributing to the theoretical understanding of the development of job attitudes.

Teams

Nontraditional data sources such as audio and video have started to play a key role in team research. For example, Kim, Chang, Holland, and Pentland (2008) used social interaction data captured via sociometric sensors to facilitate brainstorming sessions and group problem-solving processes. The method had a significant effect on increasing interactivity among members, partially through reducing the behavioral differences among dominant and non-dominant individuals in the team. More recently, Kozlowski, Chao, Chang, and Fernandez (2015) used team interaction patterns, captured with wearable sensors, to study team dynamics and effectiveness. Future research in this area could incorporate multimedia data collection methods (e.g., visual and audio sensors) and longitudinal study designs to understand how team interaction changes during the initial and later stages of team formation. Location and distance information could also be used to study effective space designs that optimize collaborations among team members (e.g., to increase the efficiency of communications). Moreover, the interactivity of big data methods could potentially facilitate real-time intervention and coaching for effective team building—the possibilities are unlimited.

Diversity and Inclusion

There is great potential for using big data approaches to study diversity and inclusion in the workplace, such as minimizing group differences in selection and enhancing inclusion climate in the organizations. For example, Thelwall and Stuart (2018) investigated user activities in a social media site, Reddit, to assess gender differences of interests toward discussion topics. The findings could potentially be used to enhance diversity through online recruitment. Multiobjective optimization techniques were also applied in personnel selection to quantitatively incorporate diversity in hiring decision making to enhance diversity among new hires (i.e., reduce adverse impact; e.g., De Corte et al., 2007; Song, Wee, & Newman, 2017). At this juncture, however, not many studies have used big data methods to directly examine inclusion in the workplace and elements that influence the career pipeline for diverse talents. Morgan, Dunleavy, and DeVries (2015) provided some ideas to leverage big data methods in that regard. For example, recommendation systems can be developed to identify employees to form diverse and effective teams; natural language processing techniques can help monitor communication systems to avoid discrimination and prejudice.

Big data analytics are naturally equipped to deal with the problems faced in diversity and inclusion research. By nature, diversity information is often nested within a multilevel structure in organizations. For example, to study whether the gender composition of a team differentially influences job satisfaction for men and women, we have to work with data embedded in at least two levels: individual-level gender and team-level gender composition. If there are multiple teams within an organization, the level of analysis increases accordingly. Many big data techniques (e.g., deep learning) have advantages in analyzing complex multilevel data, which could potentially help organizational scientists and practitioners better understand and improve diversity in aspects such as recruitment, selection, and teams. Further, knowledge in big data analytics can also help better evaluate group differences when statistical significance testing offers limited implications due to a large sample size.

New Opportunities

Not surprisingly, organizational scholars have shown enthusiasm toward the future possibilities that big data methods could bring to the field, which are reflected in the continuous discussions and proposals for future research (e.g., George, Haas, & Pentland, 2014; George, Osinga, Lavie, & Scott, 2016; King, Tonidandel, Cortina, & Fink, 2015; McAbee, Landis, & Burke, 2017). We highlight one unprecedented opportunity that big data have made possible: the platform for interdisciplinary communication.

Big data could be considered the great "equalizer" in terms of interdisciplinary research (Guzzo, Fink, King, Tonidandel, & Landis, 2015). Big data sources that are of interest to organizational researchers (e.g., I/O psychologists, management scholars) are often also of interest to researchers from other disciplines (e.g., computer science, information science). Shared interests in the same data sources provide a natural birthplace for interdisciplinary research and grounds for researchers to gain insights from different fields. For example, the data on internal e-mail exchanges among employees could help organizational researchers examine topics such as team communication and leader–member exchange. The same data could be used by information scientists to understand how information and knowledge were created, retrieved, and shared within an organization. Further, the knowledge gained by the information scientists could help organizational researchers introduce ways to optimize communications among team members, whereas insights from organizational research could help information scientists better understand information development and flow.

Analytical methods developed in one field can also often be adapted to solve problems in other fields. Take multiobjective optimization techniques, for example—the technique was mainly used in economics and engineering to find solutions that optimize various objectives of interest (e.g., cost, profit). De Corte et al. (2007) innovatively adapted the idea to the study of personnel selection to optimize multiple selection objectives (e.g., job performance and diversity). We expect to see similar examples as the disciplines and publication outlets become less segregated, evidenced by our review of publications discussed earlier in this chapter. It is inevitable that big data research will foster many exciting interdisciplinary collaborations, and we look forward to seeing more great works in the future.

Applied Settings

In the applied world, the use of big data to produce insights into the workforce has also surged over the last few years. According to the *2018 Deloitte Global Human Capital Trends*, 84% of the respondents see people analytics as a high priority in their organizations (second-highest ranked trend in importance), whereas 69% of companies are building integrated systems that capture and analyze workforce data, marking the arrival of the "people data revolution" (Abbatiello et al., 2018, p. 89). In this section of the chapter, we introduce people analytics and its trends and applications.

People analytics—also known as *talent analytics*, *workforce analytics*, and so forth—is "the attempt to understand patterns in an organization's workforce through analysis of employee-related data" (Kaur & Fink, 2017, p. 1). Driven by business needs and relying on the explosion of big data, advanced capabilities via artificial intelligence (AI), and analytics tools and cloud systems from technology vendors, people analytics is shifting from an HR technical group to a critical business function. This fundamental shift is driven from the top down and has manifested itself in five trends.

First, the players are shifting from HR to include senior stakeholders across different business functions. The C-suite (e.g., CEOs, CFOs), in collaboration with HR and information technology, is now demanding answers to business problems from analytics. At the same time, they are also playing a significant role in driving people-data initiatives and coming up with strategies to ensure value-added, effective, and secure people analytics. Second, the purpose of people analytics is shifting from HR-driven issues to the entirety of the business. It is now becoming a business function that seeks to tie a variety of data and metrics with management and operational issues to drive employee performance and well-being. This requires highly integrated data systems and real-time analytics that enable leaders at all levels to make informed business decisions. Third, data are being harvested internally and externally throughout the entire workforce cycle and from every part of a business operation, coming from both traditional (e.g., employee surveys, financial data) and nontraditional (e.g., social media, e-mails, microexpressions) sources. Fourth, the breadth and depth of analytical demands require people analytics teams to be diverse and multidisciplinary. Nowadays, it is common to see a combination of I/O psychologists, HR professionals, data scientists, software engineers, and computer scientists working together to come up with analytical processes and solutions (Bersin, 2018). Fifth, people analytics functions are increasingly incorporating advanced analytical techniques, such as machine learning and natural language processing, in solving people-related issues in the workplace.

A mature talent analytics team has three common subfunctions: (a) data infrastructure and reporting, (b) advanced analytics, and (c) organizational research (Kaur & Fink, 2017). A strong data infrastructure that helps source and maintain high-quality data is the foundation for scalable analytics projects, whereas a systematic and user-friendly reporting mechanism can enable data monitoring and data-driven business decisions to be made. Unfortunately, building such an integrated system is a challenge for most organizations— it requires a good understanding of all the data sources; efficient ways to clean, aggregate, and analyze the data; and collaboration across different teams. It has been estimated that more than 75% of the effort in talent analytics is invested in performing ad hoc and proactive reporting, even before strategic and predictive analytics can be done (Bersin, 2013).

Today, people analytics teams are tasked to solve real-world business problems pertaining to productivity, turnover, retention, customer satisfaction, and so on, and the (big) data that help support these decisions include demographics, personality, financial records, and employee feedback, among others.

Big data are used in all aspects of a business and through the employment life cycle. In the following paragraphs, we discuss a few examples of people analytics projects (organized by topic) where organizations leveraged data to solve business issues.

Productivity

One of the key criteria for people analytics is employee performance. In a case study with a global quick-service restaurant chain, Arellano, DiLeonardo, and Felix (2017) demonstrated how data insights can drive business performance. By clearly defining the business problems and curating more than 10,000 data points from diverse sources (from individuals, shifts, and restaurants), the company was able to build algorithms that help determine the key drivers to store performance. Changes were made based on the findings: In just 4 months, the company saw significant increases in sales, customer service, and employee retention.

Job Analysis

Job analysis serves as the foundational piece for most HR practices. It provides necessary information for recruitment, selection, compensation, promotion, and so forth. Traditionally, job analyses relied mainly on the ratings of subject matter experts (SMEs), which often include time-consuming procedures such as focus groups and surveys. Recently, Putka (2018) used text analysis and sparse partial least-squares method to predict and replace SME ratings, making it possible to conduct thousands of job analyses in an hour—far exceeding the capability of (human) expert rating. Expert judgment is still crucial for job analysis, and it is recommended to conduct checks by SMEs on the machine-generated job analysis results, but we see an unlimited possibility of the text analysis application.

Recruitment

Companies, especially the fast-growing ones, are increasingly relying on big data to gain insights into the effectiveness of their recruitment processes and talent pipeline. During its 40% rapid growth period, LinkedIn was under pressure to keep up with the hiring demand. To better predict staffing needs, the Talent Analytics function combined existing data from hiring plans, attrition rates, and expected internal transfer rates and built a forecast model (with only a 5% margin of error) to predict expected hires by business units and regions, which saved the company 15% of its recruiting budget in a year. This team also built dashboards in Tableau to make these data transparent and readily accessible, which ensured accountability in the recruiting function (White, 2016).

To attract talent, online recruitment services (e.g., LinkedIn, Indeed, Glassdoor) are leveraging machine learning techniques to streamline the application process to increase the number of applications companies receive. In addition, recommender systems are developed for these platforms to match job seekers with jobs based on users' data (e.g., experience, expertise, clicks, searches) and job information (e.g., tasks, requirements).

Selection

In the selection space, several attempts were made to extract information from resumes and social media (e.g., education, job experience, GPA) to predict who is likely to become a good performer, while minimizing potential biases (Forbes Human Resources Council, 2018; e.g., IBM Watson Recruitment). Although traditional assessment centers and interviews rely heavily on human assessors and evaluators, machine learning algorithms have been developed to decode text and video data and identify the top candidates (Campion et al., 2016; Hill, 2016).

Learning and Development

Big data and emerging technologies are transforming the learning and development (L&D) space. For example, to initiate the L&D process, recommender systems are trained to help employees find suitable coaches or identify the types of training programs they should engage in based on their skills, behaviors, and preferences (e.g., BetterUp, Workday). Google Analytics, for example, can be embedded into a learning platform and track data such as time spent watching a video or viewing a page, the learners' journey, what learners are searching for, learning engagement by location, and devices and browsers used to access the platform (Lowenthal, 2018). These data allow organizations to evaluate L&D efforts using objective metrics and identify factors that correlate with effective learning.

Career Mobility

Retention is a top priority for many organizations, and a key driver of retention comes from perceived career mobility within the company. Microsoft faced this business challenge—employees seemed to think that career mobility is greater outside the company than inside. To further understand this problem, Microsoft's HR Business Insights team gathered and analyzed data from historical transfer rates, employee engagement surveys, attrition rates, and exit surveys. By surfacing a linkage between internal mobility and engagement and retention, this team was able to implement organizational changes to simplify the job transfer process that led to increased internal mobility (Green, 2016).

Turnover

To detect and minimize attrition risk, many organizations and start-ups can use algorithms to analyze data based on employee (e.g., demographic, performance, income) and environmental (e.g., unemployment rate, company performance) factors to predict who is likely to leave, which helps with workforce planning and employee retention (Alexander, 2015). In fact, because turnover (not turnover intention) is usually considered as a binary variable (i.e., stay in or leave the job), it is one of the most simply defined prediction problems that are ready to be studied using big data methods. For example, in 2018, at the first machine learning competition in the I/O community, teams of I/O psychologists and data experts competed in building the most accurate model focused on predicting one metric: voluntary turnover. The data (over 30,000 cases) came from a global pharmaceutical company and consisted of 162 variables that spanned 5 years, including demographics, high-potential indicators, job performance ratings, job functions, pay grade, and so on. Over the course of a month, the competing teams built a diverse set of machine learning models and identified topic factors leading to voluntary turnover, which included location (e.g., country), performance, demographics (e.g., tenure, age), income, and economic indicators (e.g., unemployment rate).

Employee Experience

With employee experience becoming an increasingly important theme for HR and management, more companies are finding ways to better understand the contributors to employee satisfaction, well-being, and engagement. Ford Motor Company is one of the leading companies going through this transformation. With the implementation of innovative digital apps, the company collected open feedback via employee polls and workshops globally; insights from these data, in turn, informed a series of changes aimed to improve employee engagement and innovation (Schwartz, Collins, Stockton, Wagner, & Walsh, 2017). To monitor and promote employee well-being and engagement, AI tools have also been developed (e.g., Limeade, Culture Amp) to identify and understand positive and negative behaviors, sentiment, and feedback from different sources of data (e.g., employee surveys, social media).

Diversity and Inclusion

According to the *2017 Deloitte Global Human Capital Trends* (Deloitte, 2017), 69% of executives see diversity and inclusion as an organizational priority, with more companies starting to use analytics to identify gaps and measure progress. Cisco, one of the top-rated technology companies on diversity and inclusion (Ansari, 2018), has developed a suite of digital solutions that leverage data and analytics to drive toward a more diverse and equal workforce, including monitoring equality in pay, measuring diversity in the recruitment and emergence of leaders, and tracking inclusion from employee satisfaction surveys (Cisco, 2018).

Leadership

In 2008, the People Innovation Lab at Google embarked on Project Oxygen, a multiyear program aimed at answering one question: "Do managers matter?" Instead of adopting generic management models based on research or conventional wisdom, this team of statisticians leveraged Google's People Analytics—they collected more than 10,000 observations across more than 100 variables related to managers at Google from employee surveys, performance ratings, interviews, and employee feedback. On the basis of these data,

Project Oxygen identified eight common qualities shared by the most effective managers and used them to guide management development programs for the years to come. In just 4 years, the program led to significant improvements in managerial effectiveness and performance (Bryant, 2011; Garvin, Wagonfeld, & Kind, 2013).

BIG DATA METHODS IN THE WORKPLACE

Leading scholars and practitioners of big data are combining effective data management with sophisticated algorithms and insightful visualization. Previous chapters in this edited volume have given us a broad illustration of such examples. In this section, we briefly highlight the data sources, algorithms, and data visualization that are at the forefront of workplace practice and research.

Data Sources

Enterprise (Private) Data
Private enterprise data are the data held by individual firms and organizations that are not freely available to the public. Examples of enterprise data include interview scores of job candidates, number of employees in each team, and compensation, as well as inventory record, sales data, internal e-mail exchanges among employees, and so forth. Such data are usually organization specific, reflecting the characteristics (e.g., industry, business model, number of employees, national vs. international) of the organization. Many organizations collect data periodically (e.g., annual surveys, quarterly performance evaluations), which allows for the examination of longitudinal trends and comparison among repeated measures. These data also have the advantage of largely being housed within a single organization, allowing for data merging and linkage (e.g., individual performance data linking to training data). However, as data in an organization are often collected and managed by various teams (e.g., sales team, HR team), sometimes due to temporary business needs and events (e.g., layoffs), they might also be fragmented.

Nonprofit and Research (Public) Data
Many public data sets are made available by government agencies, nonprofit organizations, enterprises, and research labs. For example, the U.S. federal government makes available more than 100,000 data sets on the website, https://www.data.gov; the Bureau of Statistics of various countries (mostly developed countries) periodically releases national censorship and longitudinal survey data (e.g., job search, turnover, income, personality); and the Open Science Framework allows researchers to publish data sets they collected. Furthermore, Google Dataset Search provides a powerful tool for users to obtain publicly available data sets.

Publicly available data often encompass information on a broad scale (e.g., multiple regions, industry), and it is also possible to link multiple data sets using common variables (e.g., zip code). Moreover, national surveys and censors commonly adapt sampling methods that enhance the representation of the data and the generalizability of the analytic results. However, as publicly available data are also usually archival, they could be static and outdated, and analysts might not be able to find variables that exactly match their needs and thus have to use proxy variables (i.e., variables that convey similar meaning as the desired variables).

Social Media and Other Web-Based Data

Big data methods make it possible to obtain insights from a wide scope of nontraditional data. So far, perhaps the most mined nontraditional data is web-based data, such as social media (Kern et al., 2016; see McFarland & Ployhart, 2015, for a theoretical contextual framework for social media research). Web-based data include information on individuals' search behavior, Twitter communications, Facebook likes, endorsement patterns (e.g., "This review was helpful"), and so forth. Such data capture individuals' organic and dynamic web-based activities, compared with their behaviors and perceptions in controlled, research settings (e.g., laboratory experiments, online research tasks), thus allowing for a broader level of generalizability.

Web-based data often convey a rich amount of information; they are generally unstructured, user-generated, and come in multiple formats, such as text, numeric, image and video, and possibly multilingual content. They could illustrate individual-level (e.g., identified by username) and group-level (e.g., identified by geographic location) characteristics; they could also capture dynamic, often event-based patterns (e.g., communication and interaction among people). Such data include simple tracking of viewing or clicking activity, geographical representation of trends, and the social network pattern of communications among web users. In practice, social media could potentially be used to obtain cues for employee sentiment and signals of turnover intention. Moreover, web-based information influences recruitment because applicants are affected by reviews on sites such as Glassdoor and LinkedIn; at the same time, organizations can and do use social media information to search and vet potential candidates. Various tools have been developed to allow for mining web-based data, which includes open-source methods. Interested readers could refer to tutorials and examples such as Munzert, Rubba, Meißner, and Nyhuis (2014), and Mitchell (2018).

Images, Audios, and Videos

Whereas traditional quantitative analysis relied mainly on numerical data,[1] big data analytics allow for directly working with multimedia data sources

---

[1]Including numeric data converted from nonnumeric information based on human judgment, such as counting how many interpersonal communications took place in a video.

such as images, audio files, and videos. In the workplace, interview and presentation videos could be used for selection, promotion, and training (e.g., leadership training; see Barsade, Ramarajan, & Westen, 2009), and audio file and videos on team interaction could help understand team performance (e.g., Tripathi & Burleson, 2012). Some platforms (e.g., Expimetrics) allow for the collection of multimedia information using an experience sampling and longitudinal design, adding on additional dimensions of time and events. Multimedia data bring an important addition to understanding individuals in the workplace as they convey objective, nonlinguistic social signals such as emotion (e.g., microexpression), and some could also provide relative location cues (e.g., wearable cameras).

Sociometric Sensors

Sociometric sensors (e.g., Fitbit, cell phones) are wearable devices that can collect a variety of highly linked, objective, and person-specific data (e.g., time, temperature, movement, distance from others) from users and the environment around them. Data are usually collected continuously, capturing longitudinal and dynamic processes. Leveraging these data, researchers have examined topics such as team process dynamics (e.g., Kozlowski et al., 2015) and organizational citizenship behavior (e.g., Ilies, Scott, & Judge, 2006).

Algorithms

The complexity of big data demands advanced analytic approaches. Although the purpose of our chapter is not to provide a comprehensive description of the big data methods (see Oswald & Putka, 2015, and Putka, Beatty, & Reeder, 2018, for reviews), we briefly introduce three sets of methods from the machine learning literature (i.e., supervised learning, unsupervised learning, reinforcement learning) and techniques of text mining, focusing on their potential applications in the workplace.

Supervised Learning

Supervised learning is used when a data set contains both input (predictor) and output (criterion) variables, and a chosen algorithm is used to optimize the prediction from the data (Hastie, Tibshirani, & Friedman, 2009), such as using personality to predict job performance. Supervised learning algorithms can be further categorized to solve either classification or regression problems. *Classification problems* pertain to categorical outcomes (e.g., turnover), whereas *regression problems* pertain to those where the criterion variable is continuous (e.g., performance ratings).

There are hundreds of algorithms—logistic regression (LR), Naive Bayes, support vector machines (SVM), random forest (RF), *k*-nearest neighbors, to name a few (see Fernández-Delgado, Cernadas, Barro, & Amorim, 2014)—and it turns out that we do not need all of them to solve real-world problems. For instance, after evaluating 179 classifiers from 17 families on 121 data sets, Fernández-Delgado and colleagues (2014) found the top, most accurate classifiers to be RF, SVM, neural networks, and boosting ensembles. According to machine learning and data mining competitions such as Kaggle and Knowledge Discovery and Data Mining Cup, boosting ensembles (e.g., XGBoost) tend to achieve the best results in both classification and regression problems, especially when there is a large number of weak predictors.

Unsupervised Learning

Unsupervised learning is used when a data set does not include criterion data (and therefore does not pertain to prediction). The goal of unsupervised learning is to reveal the data's underlying structure and patterns (Hastie et al., 2009), such as uncovering employee personality profiles. Unsupervised learning models can be understood as clustering or dimension reduction methods. Clustering pertains to algorithms that look for subgroups within a data set that share common characteristics (e.g., categorizing customers according to their needs and preferences; see Berkhin, 2006, for a comprehensive review on clustering techniques); the *k*-means algorithm (Hartigan, 1975; Hartigan & Wong, 1979) is the most popular clustering technique used in research and practice. Dimension reduction deals with the curse of dimensionality (i.e., the sample size requirement grows exponentially as the number of variables increases; Bellman, 1961) and aims to extract a smaller set of variables that can be used to describe a larger data set (see Carreira-Perpinán, 1997, and Fodor, 2002, for reviews on dimension reduction techniques); the most popular techniques include principal components analysis and factor analysis.

Reinforcement Learning

Rooted in the intersection of computer science, statistics, psychology, and neuroscience, reinforcement learning has attracted increasing interest in the last decade. Reinforcement learning uses feedback (i.e., rewards and punishments) from an interactive environment to learn optimal solutions that maximize cumulative reward (see Kaelbling, Littman, & Moore, 1996, for a review). Although a limited number of organizations have deployed reinforcement learning for real-world applications (as of 2019), many are actively researching and experimenting with these techniques for applications such as robotics and industrial automation (e.g., Levine, Pastor, Krizhevsky, Ibarz, & Quillen, 2018).

Text Mining and Natural Language Processing

Text mining describes the process of automatically extracting information from text and has wide applications for analyzing and understanding human language (for a review on text mining techniques, see Gupta & Lehal, 2009, and Banks, Woznyj, Wesslen, & Ross, 2018). It encompasses tasks that deal with text data collection, cleaning, transformation, and analysis (Kobayashi et al., 2018). In organizational research and practice, text mining can be used in conjunction with machine learning techniques to solve different types of problems, such as topic tracking, summarization, categorization, emotion detection, and question answering.

Machine learning and text mining are increasingly used to solve problems in the workplace, and it is not uncommon to leverage different techniques simultaneously. For instance, when analyzing resumes, one has to first clean and preprocess the raw text data so it can be used for machine learning algorithms. From there, supervised learning algorithms (e.g., LR, SVM) can be used to predict job performance or turnover, whereas unsupervised learning algorithms (e.g., *k*-means) can help search for commonalities and categorize different job candidate profiles. In general, we have seen the most applications, whether on numeric- or text-based data, leveraging supervised learning algorithms, followed by unsupervised learning, and we look forward to seeing more mature use cases of reinforcement learning in the workplace in the future.

Data Visualization

What Is Data Visualization?

Most of us are not new to data visualization—we have been creating histograms, scatterplots, and so forth, long before we heard the term *big data*. In general, *data visualization* is a set of methods for graphically and accurately displaying data in a way that is easy to understand (Sinar, 2015). The analytical understanding of data is the basis of data visualization, but equally important, the perceived aesthetics of data visualizations can influence efficiency and effectiveness (Cawthon & Moere, 2007).

For example, an organization could map employees' job satisfaction survey results on their hierarchical organizational chart, using the size of the chart elements to represent the number of individuals within a job function; using color to represent the level of satisfaction (e.g., a continuum from green, very satisfied, to red, very unsatisfied); and using shape to differentiate job role (e.g., marketing). The audience could immediately capture which groups of employees are satisfied with their work and where there might be problems. In another example, using an individual's work-related connections, we could construct a visualization of social networks where each contact is represented by a colored dot (node) and classified by types of connection (e.g., alumnus, colleagues of the current employer), and each connection is represented by lines between the dots.[2] Such data visualization could help the audience immediately recognize the individual's main types of contacts and how different groups are connected to each other. Individuals could use this information to grow their network, and recruiters could use this information to reach out to potential job candidates.

Why Do We Visualize Data?

Advancements in both hardware and software have enabled computers to store and analyze massive amounts of data that often have high dimensionality. However, we, humans, live in a low-dimensional world by nature and can

---

[2]Examples include the LinkedIn InMaps application and similar applications by http://www.socilab.com.

only make sense of a small amount of data with low dimensionality (e.g., 3-D space). We often struggle to intuitively understand data that are high in both volume and dimensionality (Fayyad, Wierse, & Grinstein, 2002)—this is a key barrier to many people who want to generate insights directly from big data (Sinar, 2015). Moreover, understanding data analysis results takes time and effort. For example, when making time-sensitive managerial decisions, managers need easily accessible information to guide their judgments. Graphic displays of data, when properly designed, are effective and efficient at communicating information (Unwin, Chen, & Härdle, 2007) and can provide more accessibility to valuable information that is "hidden" in the data.

In general, data visualization has two main functions: exploration and explanation (Sinar, 2015). The exploration function of data visualization can help us identify underlying relationships that are buried in raw data; the explanatory function can help us answer research questions or fulfill business objectives. Recent developments in data visualization have allowed us to combine various modes of data (e.g., qualitative and quantitative) to reveal unprecedented insights into relationships among variables, enable real-time display of data in a time-sensitive manner, and empower an increasingly diverse audience to explore data sets to accommodate their needs and interests (e.g., Tay et al., 2018). These advancements have enhanced the capability of organizational researchers and practitioners to reveal, understand, and further solve problems in the workplace. Data visualization plays a key role in both research and practice in the workplace.

How to Visualize Data

Data visualization techniques are fast developing (see reviews in Chapter 7, this volume, and Chen, Härdle, & Unwin, 2007). A variety of data visualization methods are available in commercial statistical software (e.g., Statistical Package for the Social Sciences, Stata, Statistical Analysis System), as well as open-source packages such as ggplot2 in R and Matplotlib, seaborn, and plotly in Python. In addition, many software applications that specialize in data visualization are available, providing navigable displays (allowing focused observation within the visualization) and monitoring dynamic change in real time. Some even allow for the multimodal display of data, using sound (e.g., audio and image sonification) and touch (e.g., touch interfaces), in addition to visual displays (Stanton, 2015). Among the tools, Tableau is considered by many as the "grand master" of data visualization software (e.g., Marr, 2017). It is simple to use, has compatibility with major database solutions, and can produce accurate and aesthetically pleasing visualizations.

CHALLENGES AND RECOMMENDATIONS FOR BIG DATA IN THE WORKPLACE AND TALENT ANALYTICS

Despite its richness and capabilities, big data also bring challenges and concerns. Here, we briefly describe some of the main challenges in applying big data principles in the workplace and provide recommendations.

Preparing Data

Organizational data are often collected at different sites, with different tools, and by different people. For example, the data from employee surveys, HR information systems, performance management, and employee social interactions represent some of the data variety that organizations may wish to leverage. Unfortunately, these different types of data are often stored in less-structured formats and separated by incompatible interfaces (King et al., 2015), introducing significant challenges to data preparation and integration. In addition, there is also a concern about the quality of data—in most cases, workplace data are collected without consideration for appropriate sampling, reliability, and validity. Quality of data also depends on the source via which data are being collected. For example, the reliability of sociometric censors partly depends on the accuracy of the device, which might vary among different products and manufacturers.

Further, we should note that web-based data, especially social media data, has limited and biased sampling because they only capture those who use specific web services and leave traces online. Nonetheless, because of the seemingly unlimited capacity of the data, it is sometimes difficult to set a boundary for web-based data collection: Reviewers of academic studies frequently request additional data collection, without a consensus of when the data collection is "adequate." To effectively utilize big data, further efforts are needed to reevaluate existing standards (that are largely adaptable for "small data") and build corresponding guidelines (Adjerid & Kelley, 2018).

Analyzing Data

"Traditional" statistical training for workplace researchers and practitioners (e.g., with education in I/O psychology, organizational behavior, and human resource management) is generally based on "small data," and thus, many of the statistical models that we are familiar with are not necessarily suitable for analyzing big data in the workplace. For example, when we are analyzing a large number of variables in an organization (e.g., turnover, performance), missing data is a common issue (e.g., performance ratings are not available for newcomers; sales teams and products team have different performance measures)—the resulting data set is large yet sparse. As the missing values might result from systematic reasons during data collection (e.g., different performance criteria among teams), it would be inaccurate to "treat" the missing values might using methods such as multiple imputation, and alternative methods should be used.

Although advanced analytic methods for big data serve as powerful tools to solve real-world problems, they are not the solution for all cases: One has to carefully examine the problem and data at hand to determine the most appropriate algorithm(s), instead of directly applying the "best" algorithm from previous research or practice. The choice of unsuitable methods makes it difficult to interpret results or, worse, leads to the wrong conclusions. Further, issues associated with overfitting could arise when a complex algorithm captures the training data too well, and the solution for the training data does not generalize to other data sets (e.g., lower prediction rate). For example, scholars (e.g., Yarkoni & Westfall, 2017) pointed out that the problem of research replicability (i.e., the failure of many scientific results to replicate across multiple research settings) is due in part to relying on conclusions drawn from small samples with large effect sizes that have low generalizability. Model overfitting and generalizability have to be carefully examined and controlled via techniques such as regularization (i.e., techniques that prevent overfitting by controlling the model complexity) and k-fold cross-validation (i.e., a resampling technique that trains and test the model k times on subsets of the data).

Moreover, big data analytics is experiencing fast development, with cutting-edge algorithms and tools being continuously introduced all the time. Relying on static knowledge in statistics (that we mainly gained in schools) is not sufficient, and we have to constantly keep up to date with the most recent techniques. It is both a challenge and an opportunity to reevaluate statistical training to adapt to the world of big data.

Interpreting Data

Interpretability is a key to obtaining information from data—researchers interpret results to inform theory, and practitioners interpret results to advise businesses. However, many big data approaches tend to produce predictive models that could not be easily interpreted (Mahmoodi, Leckelt, van Zalk, Geukes, & Back, 2017). In machine learning, interpretability can be improved through techniques such as feature selection (i.e., selecting predictors that are most relevant to the criterion; e.g., least absolute shrinkage and selection operator regression) and feature extraction (i.e., transforming existing predictors to some new predictors; e.g., principal component analysis). Effective data visualization could also largely increase the interpretability of data analysis results. Although complex models (e.g., those based on the nonlinear feature extraction methods) are not always easy to interpret, recent research has shed light on techniques to better address model interpretability. As an example, Ribeiro, Singh, and Guestrin (2016) introduced Local Interpretable Model-Agnostic explanations, an explanation technique, which improves the interpretation of models by focusing on local results and using visualization.

Legal and Ethical Concerns

The increased popularity of big data has raised awareness of data privacy and ethics in the general public. One of the highest risks in the use of big data is data security and author (re-)identification. For example, Perry (2011) showed that 87% of the U.S. population can be identified by the combination of seemingly "anonymous" information such as zip code, gender, and date of birth. Because of such concerns, the European Union (EU) passed the General Data Protection Regulation (GDPR; The European Parliament and the Council of the European Union, 2016) that took effect on May 25, 2018. GDPR affords rights to all EU citizens on data privacy and applies to a variety of individuals and organizations (The European Parliament and the Council of the European Union, 2016). In the United States, the California legislature recently passed the California Consumer Privacy Act of 2018, protecting a number of data privacy rights of individual consumers. With these changes, companies are making necessary adjustments in data systems, and we believe more data security concerns will be addressed in institutional review boards. It is our responsibility as researchers and practitioners to keep ourselves informed of the legal and ethical concerns, while advancing our knowledge and practice through the exciting promises of big data.

CONCLUSION

Big data have indeed opened up the door for a new era of data-driven organizational research and practice. As big data principles increasingly become essential in understanding and improving the workplace, organizational researchers and practitioners have an undeniable role to play in the interdisciplinary practice of big data. After all, much of the big data phenomenon takes place in, and revolves around, the workplace. Equipped with the expertise in work, organizational scholars and practitioners could advance the interpretability, applicability, and techniques of big data. Through innovation, communication, and adaptation to emerging technologies and appropriate guidelines, we are sure to see a promising future for big data in the workplace.

REFERENCES

Abbatiello, A., Agarwal, D., Bersin, J., Lahiri, G., Schwartz, J., Volini, E. (2018). *The rise of the social enterprise: 2018 Deloitte global human capital trends*. Retrieved from https://www2.deloitte.com/content/dam/insights/us/articles/HCTrends2018/2018-HCtrends_Rise-of-the-social-enterprise.pdf

Adjerid, I., & Kelley, K. (2018). Big data in psychology: A framework for research advancement. *American Psychologist, 73*, 899–917. http://dx.doi.org/10.1037/amp0000190

Alexander, F. (2015). *Watson Analytics use case for HR: Retaining valuable employees*. Retrieved from https://www.ibm.com/blogs/business-analytics/watson-analytics-use-case-for-hr-retaining-valuable-employees/

Allen, D. G., Mahto, R. V., & Otondo, R. F. (2007). Web-based recruitment: Effects of information, organizational brand, and attitudes toward a Web site on applicant attraction. *Journal of Applied Psychology, 92*, 1696–1708. http://dx.doi.org/10.1037/0021-9010.92.6.1696

Ansari, K. (2018). *Diversity & inclusion at 10 top tech companies*. Retrieved from https://linkhumans.com/diversity-inclusion-tech-companies/

Arellano, C., DiLeonardo, A., & Felix, I. (2017). *Using people analytics to drive business performance: A case study*. Retrieved from https://www.mckinsey.com/business-functions/mckinsey-analytics/our-insights/using-people-analytics-to-drive-business-performance-a-case-study

Azucar, D., Marengo, D., & Settanni, M. (2018). Predicting the Big 5 personality traits from digital footprints on social media: A meta-analysis. *Personality and Individual Differences, 124*, 150–159. http://dx.doi.org/10.1016/j.paid.2017.12.018

Back, M. D., Stopfer, J. M., Vazire, S., Gaddis, S., Schmukle, S. C., Egloff, B., & Gosling, S. D. (2010). Facebook profiles reflect actual personality, not self-idealization. *Psychological Science, 21*, 372–374. http://dx.doi.org/10.1177/0956797609360756

Banks, G. C., Woznyj, H. M., Wesslen, R. S., & Ross, R. L. (2018). A review of best practice recommendations for text analysis in R (and a user-friendly app). *Journal of Business and Psychology, 33*, 445–459. http://dx.doi.org/10.1007/s10869-017-9528-3

Barsade, S. G., Ramarajan, L., & Westen, D. (2009). Implicit affect in organizations. *Research in Organizational Behavior, 29*, 135–162. http://dx.doi.org/10.1016/j.riob.2009.06.008

Bellman, R. E. (1961). *Adaptive control processes: A guided tour*. Princeton, NJ: Princeton University Press. http://dx.doi.org/10.1515/9781400874668

Berkhin, P. (2006). A survey of clustering data mining techniques. In J. Kogan, C. Nicholas, & M. Teboulle (Eds.), *Grouping multidimensional data* (pp. 25–71). Berlin/Heidelberg, Germany: Springer. http://dx.doi.org/10.1007/3-540-28349-8_2

Bersin, J. (2013). The datafication of human resources. *Forbes*. Retrieved from https://www.forbes.com/sites/joshbersin/2013/07/19/the-datafication-of-human-resources/#2177308e3318

Bersin, J. (2018). The geeks arrive in HR: People analytics is here. *Forbes*. Retrieved from https://www.forbes.com/sites/joshbersin/2015/02/01/geeks-arrive-in-hr-people-analytics-is-here/#1ae94dd973b4

Bryant, A. (2011, March 12). Google's quest to build a better boss. *The New York Times*. Retrieved from https://www.nytimes.com/2011/03/13/business/13hire.html?mtrref=www.fruitbox.io&gwh=D05A6F9AF91465B77014D54527FD21FD&gwt=pay&assetType=REGIWALL

Bureau of Labor Statistics. (2017). *Projections of occupational employment, 2016–2026*. Retrieved from https://www.bls.gov/careeroutlook/2017/article/occupational-projections-charts.htm

California Consumer Privacy Act of 2018. Assembly Bill No. 375. An act to add Title 1.81.5 (commencing with Section 1798.100) to Part 4 of Division 3 of the Civil Code, relating to privacy. (2018). Retrieved from https://leginfo.legislature.ca.gov/faces/billTextClient.xhtml?bill_id=201720180AB375

Campion, M. C., Campion, M. A., Campion, E. D., & Reider, M. H. (2016). Initial investigation into computer scoring of candidate essays for personnel selection. *Journal of Applied Psychology, 101*, 958–975. http://dx.doi.org/10.1037/apl0000108

Carreira-Perpinán, M. A. (1997). *A review of dimension reduction techniques* (Technical Report CS-96-09). Retrieved from http://www.pca.narod.ru/DimensionReductionBrifReview.pdf

Cawthon, N., & Moere, A. V. (2007). The effect of aesthetic on the usability of data visualization. In *Proceedings of the 11th International Conference on Information Visualization* (pp. 637–648). Washington, DC: IEEE.

Chamorro-Premuzic, T., Akhtar, R., Winsborough, D., & Sherman, R. A. (2017). The datafication of talent: How technology is advancing the science of human potential at work. *Current Opinion in Behavioral Sciences, 18*, 13–16. http://dx.doi.org/10.1016/j.cobeha.2017.04.007

Chen, C. H., Härdle, W. K., & Unwin, A. (Eds.). (2007). *Handbook of data visualization*. Berlin/Heidelberg, Germany: Springer Science+Business Media.

Cisco. (2018). *Inclusion and collaboration: The power of people—connected*. Retrieved from https://www.cisco.com/c/en/us/about/inclusion-diversity.html

De Corte, W., Lievens, F., & Sackett, P. R. (2007). Combining predictors to achieve optimal trade-offs between selection quality and adverse impact. *Journal of Applied Psychology, 92*, 1380–1393. http://dx.doi.org/10.1037/0021-9010.92.5.1380

Deloitte. (2017). *Rewriting the rules for the digital age: 2017 Global human capital trends.* Retrieved from https://www2.deloitte.com/content/dam/Deloitte/global/Documents/ About-Deloitte/central-europe/ce-global-human-capital-trends.pdf

Dineen, B. R., Ling, J., Ash, S. R., & DelVecchio, D. (2007). Aesthetic properties and message customization: Navigating the dark side of web recruitment. *Journal of Applied Psychology, 92,* 356–372. http://dx.doi.org/10.1037/0021-9010.92.2.356

Dineen, B. R., & Noe, R. A. (2009). Effects of customization on application decisions and applicant pool characteristics in a web-based recruitment context. *Journal of Applied Psychology, 94,* 224–234. http://dx.doi.org/10.1037/a0012832

The European Parliament and the Council of the European Union. (2016, Apri 5). Regulation (Eu) 2016/679 of the European Parliament and of the Council of 27 April 2016 on the protection of natural persons with regard to the processing of personal data and on the free movement of such data, and repealing Directive 95/46/EC (General Data Protection Regulation) (Text with EEA relevance). *Official Journal of the European Union, 119,* 1–88. Retrieved from https://eur-lex.europa.eu/ eli/reg/2016/679/oj

Fayyad, U. M., Wierse, A., & Grinstein, G. G. (2002). Introduction. In U. Fayyad, G. G. Grinstein, & A. Wierse (Eds.), *Information visualization in data mining and knowledge discovery* (pp. 1–18). San Francisco, CA: Morgan Kaufmann.

Fernández-Delgado, M., Cernadas, E., Barro, S., & Amorim, D. (2014). Do we need hundreds of classifiers to solve real world classification problems? *Journal of Machine Learning Research, 15,* 3133–3181.

Fodor, I. K. (2002). *A survey of dimension reduction techniques.* Livermore, CA: U.S. Department of Energy. http://dx.doi.org/10.2172/15002155

Forbes Human Resources Council. (2018, July 9). 11 ways AI can revolutionize human resources. *Forbes.* Retrieved from https://www.forbes.com/sites/ forbeshumanresourcescouncil/2018/07/09/11-ways-ai-can-revolutionize-human-resources/#6cbd605ce304

Ford, M. T., Jebb, A. T., Tay, L., & Diener, E. (2018). Internet searches for affect-related terms: An indicator of subjective well-being and predictor of health outcomes across U.S. states and metro areas. *Applied Psychology: Health and Well-Being, 10,* 3–29. http://dx.doi.org/10.1111/aphw.12123

Garvin, D. A., Wagonfeld, A. B., & Kind, L. (2013, April). Google's Project Oxygen: Do managers matter? *Harvard Business Review.* Retrieved from https://www.hbs.edu/ faculty/Pages/item.aspx?num=44657

George, G., Haas, M. R., & Pentland, A. (2014). Big data and management. *Academy of Management Journal, 57,* 321–326. http://dx.doi.org/10.5465/amj.2014.4002

George, G., Osinga, E. C., Lavie, D., & Scott, B. A. (2016). Big data and data science methods for management research. *Academy of Management Journal, 59,* 1493–1507. http://dx.doi.org/10.5465/amj.2016.4005

Green, D. (2016, October 16). The HR Analytics journey at Microsoft. *LinkedIn.* Retrieved from https://www.linkedin.com/pulse/people-analytics-interviews-3-dawn-klinghoffer-microsoft-green/

Gupta, V., & Lehal, G. S. (2009). A survey of text mining techniques and applications. *Journal of Emerging Technologies in Web Intelligence, 1,* 60–76. http://dx.doi.org/ 10.4304/jetwi.1.1.60-76

Guzzo, R. A., Fink, A. A., King, E., Tonidandel, S., & Landis, R. S. (2015). Big data recommendations for industrial–organizational psychology. *Industrial and Organizational Psychology: Perspectives on Science and Practice, 8,* 491–508. http://dx.doi.org/ 10.1017/iop.2015.40

Harrison, P. M. C., Collins, T., & Müllensiefen, D. (2017). Applying modern psychometric techniques to melodic discrimination testing: Item response theory, computerised adaptive testing, and automatic item generation. *Scientific Reports, 7,* 3618. http:// dx.doi.org/10.1038/s41598-017-03586-z

Hartigan, J. A. (1975). *Clustering algorithms*. New York, NY: Wiley.

Hartigan, J. A., & Wong, M. A. (1979). Algorithm AS 136: A k-means clustering algorithm. *Journal of the Royal Statistical Society: Series C. Applied Statistics, 28*, 100–108.

Hastie, T., Tibshirani, R., & Friedman, J. (2009). Overview of supervised learning. In T. Hastie, R. Tibshirani, & J. Friedman (Eds.), *The elements of statistical learning* (pp. 9–41). New York, NY: Springer. http://dx.doi.org/10.1007/978-0-387-84858-7_2

Hernandez, I., Newman, D. A., & Jeon, G. (2015). Twitter analysis: Methods for data management and a word count dictionary to measure city-level job satisfaction. In S. Tonidandel, E. B. King, & J. M. Cortina (Eds.), *Big data at work: The data science revolution and organizational psychology* (pp. 78–128). New York, NY: Routledge.

Hill, E. (2016, August 5). *Introducing HireVue's IO psychology and assessment experts.* Retrieved from https://www.linkedin.com/pulse/people-analytics-interviews-3-dawn-klinghoffer-microsoft-green/

Ilies, R., Scott, B. A., & Judge, T. A. (2006). The interactive effects of personal traits and experienced states on intraindividual patterns of citizenship behavior. *Academy of Management Journal, 49*, 561–575. http://dx.doi.org/10.5465/amj.2006.21794672

Kaelbling, L. P., Littman, M. L., & Moore, A. W. (1996). Reinforcement learning: A survey. *Journal of Artificial Intelligence Research, 4*, 237–285. http://dx.doi.org/10.1613/jair.301

Kaur, J., & Fink, A. A. (2017). *Trends and practices in talent analytics*. Alexandria, VA: Society for Industrial and Organizational Psychology.

Kern, M. L., Park, G., Eichstaedt, J. C., Schwartz, H. A., Sap, M., Smith, L. K., & Ungar, L. H. (2016). Gaining insights from social media language: Methodologies and challenges. *Psychological Methods, 21*, 507–525. http://dx.doi.org/10.1037/met0000091

Kim, T., Chang, A., Holland, L., & Pentland, A. S. (2008). Meeting mediator: Enhancing group collaboration using sociometric feedback. In *Proceedings of the 2008 ACM conference on Computer supported cooperative work* (pp. 457–466). New York, NY: ACM.

King, E. B., Tonidandel, S., Cortina, J. M., & Fink, A. A. (2015). Building understanding of the data science revolution and IO psychology. In S. Tonidandel, E. B. King, & J. M. Cortina (Eds.), *Big data at work: The data science revolution and organizational psychology* (pp. 15–30). New York, NY: Routledge.

Kobayashi, V. B., Mol, S. T., Berkers, H. A., Kismihók, G., & Den Hartog, D. N. (2018). Text mining in organizational research. *Organizational Research Methods, 21*, 733–765. http://dx.doi.org/10.1177/1094428117722619

Kozlowski, S. W., Chao, G. T., Chang, C. H., & Fernandez, R. (2015). Team dynamics: Using "big data" to advance the science of team effectiveness. In S. Tonidandel, E. B. King, & J. M. Cortina (Eds.), *Big data at work: The data science revolution and organizational psychology* (pp. 273–309). New York, NY: Routledge.

Levine, S., Pastor, P., Krizhevsky, A., Ibarz, J., & Quillen, D. (2018). Learning hand-eye coordination for robotic grasping with deep learning and large-scale data collection. *The International Journal of Robotics Research, 37*, 421–436. http://dx.doi.org/10.1177/0278364917710318

Lowenthal, S. (2018, January 22). *How data transforms learning and development, part 2: Google Analytics*. Retrieved from https://elearningindustry.com/data-transforms-learning-and-development-part-2-google-analytics

Mahmoodi, J., Leckelt, M., van Zalk, M. W., Geukes, K., & Back, M. D. (2017). Big Data approaches in social and behavioral science: Four key trade-offs and a call for integration. *Current Opinion in Behavioral Sciences, 18*, 57–62. http://dx.doi.org/10.1016/j.cobeha.2017.07.001

Marr, B. (2017). *Data strategy: How to profit from a world of big data, analytics and the Internet of Things*. London, England: Kogan Page.

McAbee, S. T., Landis, R. S., & Burke, M. I. (2017). Inductive reasoning: The promise of big data. *Human Resource Management Review, 27*, 277–290. http://dx.doi.org/10.1016/j.hrmr.2016.08.005

McDonald, P., Thompson, P., & O'Connor, P. (2016). Profiling employees online: Shifting public–private boundaries in organisational life. *Human Resource Management Journal, 26*, 541–556. http://dx.doi.org/10.1111/1748-8583.12121

McFarland, L. A., & Ployhart, R. E. (2015). Social media: A contextual framework to guide research and practice. *Journal of Applied Psychology, 100*, 1653–1677. http://dx.doi.org/10.1037/a0039244

Mitchell, R. (2018). *Web scraping with Python: Collecting more data from the modern web.* Sebastopol, CA: O'Reilly.

Morgan, W. B., Dunleavy, E., & DeVries, P. D. (2015). Using big data to create diversity and inclusion in organizations. In S. Tonidandel, E. B. King, & J. M. Cortina (Eds.), *Big data at work: The data science revolution and organizational psychology* (pp. 310–335). New York, NY: Routledge.

Munzert, S., Rubba, C., Meißner, P., & Nyhuis, D. (2014). *Automated data collection with R: A practical guide to web scraping and text mining.* New York, NY: Wiley. http://dx.doi.org/10.1002/9781118834732

Oswald, F. L., & Putka, D. J. (2015). Statistical methods for big data: A scenic tour. In S. Tonidandel, E. B. King, & J. M. Cortina (Eds.), *Big data at work: The data science revolution and organizational psychology* (pp. 57–77). New York, NY: Routledge.

Park, G., Schwartz, H. A., Eichstaedt, J. C., Kern, M. L., Kosinski, M., Stillwell, D. J., . . . Seligman, M. E. P. (2015). Automatic personality assessment through social media language. *Journal of Personality and Social Psychology, 108*, 934–952. http://dx.doi.org/10.1037/pspp0000020

Perry, C. (2011). You're not so anonymous. *Harvard Gazette.* Retrieved from https://news.harvard.edu/gazette/story/2011/10/youre-not-so-anonymous/

Ployhart, R. E., Schmitt, N., & Tippins, N. T. (2017). Solving the Supreme Problem: 100 years of selection and recruitment at the *Journal of Applied Psychology. Journal of Applied Psychology, 102*, 291–304. http://dx.doi.org/10.1037/apl0000081

Putka, D. J. (2018, September). 10,000 job analyses per hour: A language-based approach to synthesizing KSA and interest ratings. Presentation at the *Personnel Testing Council Metropolitan Washington.*

Putka, D. J., Beatty, A. S., & Reeder, M. C. (2018). Modern prediction methods: New perspectives on a common problem. *Organizational Research Methods, 21*, 689–732. http://dx.doi.org/10.1177/1094428117697041

Ribeiro, M. T., Singh, S., & Guestrin, C. (2016, August). Why should I trust you? Explaining the predictions of any classifier. In *Proceedings of the 22nd ACM SIGKDD International Conference on Knowledge Discovery and Data Mining* (pp. 1135–1144). New York, NY: ACM.

Rienties, B., Cross, S., Marsh, V., & Ullmann, T. (2017). Making sense of learner and learning Big Data: Reviewing five years of data wrangling at the Open University UK. *Open Learning, 32*, 279–293. http://dx.doi.org/10.1080/02680513.2017.1348291

Roulin, N., & Levashina, J. (2019). LinkedIn as a new selection method: Psychometric properties and assessment approach. *Personnel Psychology, 72*, 187–211. http://dx.doi.org/10.1111/peps.12296

Schwartz, J., Collins, L., Stockton, H., Wagner, D., & Walsh, B. (2017). *Rewriting the rules for the digital age: 2017 Deloitte global human capital trends.* Retrieved from https://www2.deloitte.com/content/dam/Deloitte/us/Documents/human-capital/hc-2017-global-human-capital-trends-us.pdf

Sinar, E. F. (2015). Data visualization. In S. Tonidandel, E. B. King, & J. M. Cortina (Eds.), *Big data at work: The data science revolution and organizational psychology* (pp. 129–171). New York, NY: Routledge.

Society of Human Resource Management. (2016). *Jobs of the future: Data analysis skills.* Retrieved from https://www.shrm.org/hr-today/trends-and-forecasting/research-and-surveys/pages/data-analysis-skills.aspx

Song, Q. C., Wee, S., & Newman, D. A. (2017). Diversity shrinkage: Cross-validating pareto-optimal weights to enhance diversity via hiring practices. *Journal of Applied Psychology, 102*, 1636–1657. http://dx.doi.org/10.1037/apl0000240

Stanton, J. (2015). Sensing Big data: Multimodal information interfaces for exploration of large datasets. In S. Tonidandel, E. B. King, & J. M. Cortina (Eds.), *Big data at work: The data science revolution and organizational psychology* (pp. 172–192). New York, NY: Routledge.

Tay, L., Ng, V., Malik, A., Zhang, J., Chae, J., Ebert, D. S., . . . Kern, M. (2018). Big data visualizations in organizational science. *Organizational Research Methods, 21*, 660–688. http://dx.doi.org/10.1177/1094428117720014

Thelwall, M., & Stuart, E. (2018). She's Reddit: A source of statistically significant gendered interest information? *Information Processing & Management, 56*, 1543–1558. http://dx.doi.org/10.1016/j.ipm.2018.10.007

Tonidandel, S., King, E. B., & Cortina, J. M. (Eds.). (2015). *Big data at work: The data science revolution and organizational psychology*. New York, NY: Routledge.

Tripathi, P., & Burleson, W. (2012). Predicting creativity in the wild: Experience sample and sociometric modeling of teams. In *Proceedings of the ACM 2012 Conference on Computer Supported Cooperative Work* (pp. 1203–1212). New York, NY: ACM.

Unwin, A., Chen, C. H., & Härdle, W. K. (2007). Introduction. In C. H. Chen, W. K. Härdle, & A. Unwin (Eds.), *Handbook of data visualization* (pp. 3–12). Berlin/Heidelberg, Germany: Springer.

Wang, M., Zhou, L., & Zhang, Z. (2016). Dynamic modeling. *Annual Review of Organizational Psychology and Organizational Behavior, 3*, 241–266. http://dx.doi.org/10.1146/annurev-orgpsych-041015-062553

White, R. (2016, December 19). How building out a talent analytics function saved LinkedIn recruiting considerable time and money. *LinkedIn Talent Blog.* Retrieved from https://business.linkedin.com/talent-solutions/blog/recruiting-strategy/2016/how-building-out-a-talent-analytics-function-saved-linkedin-recruiting-considerable-time-and-money

Yarkoni, T., & Westfall, J. (2017). Choosing prediction over explanation in psychology: Lessons from machine learning. *Perspectives on Psychological Science, 12*, 1100–1122. http://dx.doi.org/10.1177/1745691617693393

Zuccolotto, P. (2010). Evaluating the impact of a grouping variable on job satisfaction drivers. *Statistical Methods and Applications, 19*, 287–305. http://dx.doi.org/10.1007/s10260-010-0141-0

IV

RECOMMENDATIONS FOR RESPONSIBLE AND RIGOROUS USE OF BIG DATA

15

The Belmont Report in the Age of Big Data

Ethics at the Intersection of Psychological Science and Data Science

Alexandra Paxton

Forty years before the publication of this chapter, the U.S. National Institutes of Health released the Belmont Report (National Commission for the Protection of Human Subjects of Biomedical and Behavioral Research, 1979) to establish ethical guidelines for researchers working with human subjects. Since then, the Belmont Report has not only guided ethical principles but has also shaped federal policy for biomedical and psychological research (Protection of Human Subjects, 2018). In many ways, psychological science today still strongly resembles psychological science from 40 years ago. Researchers are still captivated by understanding many of the same affective, behavioral, and cognitive phenomena. Participants still largely consist of undergraduate student volunteers. Research methods still include self-report surveys and painstaking observation, along with ever-improving dynamics-focused equipment such as eye trackers (Cornsweet & Crane, 1973) and accelerometers (Morris, 1973).

My thanks to Tom Griffiths for conversations about related issues during our work together on Data on the Mind; to Julia Blau for invaluable feedback on this chapter; to Aaron Culich for thoughtful discussions about securing computational pipelines; to audiences at the University of Cincinnati's Center for Cognition, Action, & Perception Colloquium and University of Connecticut's Perceiving-Acting Workshop for insightful questions and comments during presentations of earlier versions of this chapter; to R. Stuart Geiger for sharing his thoughts on this work from a data-ethics perspective outside of psychological science; and to attendees and organizers of the 2018 Moore-Sloan Data Science and Data Science Leadership Summits (Park City, UT) for discussions about algorithmic justice.

http://dx.doi.org/10.1037/0000193-016
Big Data in Psychological Research, S. E. Woo, L. Tay, and R. W. Proctor (Editors)

However, technological innovations over the intervening decades have opened doors that the authors of the Belmont Report likely never imagined. Humans now generate quintillions of gigabytes of data every day (James, 2018). These digital traces of human activity are incredibly useful to private corporations and government agencies, but they also hold immense promise for understanding psychological phenomena outside the laboratory. This promise has drawn in pioneering researchers from psychology (e.g., Goldstone & Lupyan, 2016) to network science (e.g., Vespignani, 2009) in the hopes of tapping these data to reconstruct and predict the human behavioral, affective, and cognitive processes that generated them.

The increasing popularity of this approach—along with the increasing richness of the underlying data[1]—has prompted increasingly pressing new questions about ethics. This poses a particular concern to psychological scientists, who often lack the technological or methodological expertise to appreciate the extent of these ethical concerns fully. Despite these novel ethical challenges, I argue that the core principles of the Belmont Report are broad enough to encompass any medium of human subjects research, whether in the lab or the wild.

This chapter is intended to provide an overview of the ethical issues facing psychological scientists—and other human-focused researchers—as they embrace these new data. After situating the ethics of large-scale human-derived data use in a historical context, I discuss how the fundamental principles of the Belmont Report can be expanded to address the emerging research landscape. The chapter then ends with a consideration of open questions that pose some of the biggest concerns for ensuring the continuing protection of human subjects.

At the outset of this chapter, it is important to stress that the concerns noted here are not limited to any particular type of data. Although the majority of examples given here focus on social media or user behavior data, this focus is a natural byproduct of the kinds of data that have been available for study to date. However, as society's online interactions become more complex—and as it becomes cheaper to store and share the complex data that result from those interactions—it will be important for psychological scientists to apply these principles to all forms of human data and to carefully consider what new privacy and security challenges richer data may pose (e.g., video data; cf. Chapter 18, this volume).

This chapter does not prescribe specific solutions for every case. The specific actions needed to keep our general ethical commitments must be continually reevaluated as the type, scope, and usage of large-scale human-derived data evolves. As a result, I instead outline how foundational ethical principles should be considered in the face of new data and technology, providing a

---

[1]Although this chapter is most directly interested in exploring large-scale data use, many researchers who use smaller-scale naturally occurring or online data may also find these questions useful to consider.

basis for evaluating individual-use cases and supporting future action to expand ethical guidelines.

A BRIEF HISTORY OF THE ETHICAL LANDSCAPE FOR PSYCHOLOGICAL SCIENCE

To understand the challenges facing our field, we should first examine why our ethical and legal frameworks for human subjects research ethics exist and how they manifest themselves today.

The Belmont Report and the Common Rule

Egregious violations of human rights in the mid-20th century led the U.S. Congress to enact legislation that was pivotal in creating the current U.S. system of human subjects research ethics. A comprehensive recounting of the emergence of this history is outside the scope of this chapter, but a brief sketch of what ethical historians consider to be the three most influential experiments will be helpful for framing this discussion. (For more on the historical, ethical, and philosophical contexts of these events—including other, less well-known horrors from the biomedical and behavioral sciences—see Baker, 2001; Beauchamp, 2011; Drewry, 2004; Rice, 2008.)

The first two experiments were biomedical atrocities. First, the Nazi human experiments on unwilling prisoners in the 1940s—exposed to the world during the Nuremberg trials—catalyzed the development of worldwide ethical principles for human biomedical research (see Annas & Grodin, 1992). Second, the Tuskegee Study of Untreated Syphilis tracked the progression of untreated syphilis from 1932 to 1972 in hundreds of poor African American men who were unaware of the experiment and uninformed of eventual treatment options, and its existence shocked the American public when a whistle-blower brought it to light (see Farmer, 2003; Reverby, 2009).

The third experiment was by no means equivalent in the magnitude of harm caused by the first two experiments, but it nevertheless demonstrated the potential risks posed to participants by behavioral research. U.S. psychologist Stanley Milgram (1963)—directly inspired by the Nuremberg Trials—deceived and coerced participants into delivering what they believed would be painful electric shocks to another individual. The study's methods raised ethical questions for social and behavioral research, especially for the use of deception (Baumrind, 1964, 1979; Englehardt & Englehardt, 2013; Schlenker & Forsyth, 1977).

Although the Nazi and Tuskegee experiments were incomparably different from Milgram's (1963) experiment in the type, duration, and level of harm they caused, these and other patently immoral and unethical studies sparked efforts to create legal and moral frameworks for human subjects research around the world. In 1947, the Nuremberg Code emerged as a result of the

Nuremberg Trials (reprinted in Annas & Grodin, 1992). The 10 ethical principles included in the Nuremberg Code formed the basis for the medical research ethics outlined by the World Medical Association (WMA) in the Declaration of Helsinki nearly two decades later in 1964. The United States immediately signed onto the Declaration of Helsinki and ostensibly adopted its standards for biomedical research. However, 10 years later, public outcry at the Tuskegee syphilis experiment—along with increasing questions about the potential dangers of behavioral research (cf. Baumrind, 1964)—led Congress to create the National Commission for the Protection of Human Subjects of Biomedical and Behavioral Research to explore options for improving human subjects research safety (National Research Act of 1974).

Five years later, the committee's work culminated in the publication of the Belmont Report (National Commission for the Protection of Human Subjects of Biomedical and Behavioral Research, 1979). The Belmont Report was intended to be a nonlegislative statement of core values for human subjects research. It laid out three foundational principles with clear ties to specific requirements at various stages of the research process.

- *Respect for persons* upholds the dignity and autonomy of all human research subjects. From it, we have requirements for informed consent, for additional constraints for researchers who intend to recruit participants from protected populations, for maximizing voluntariness, and for strict guidelines on any research involving deception.

- *Beneficence* is a conceptual extension of the "do no harm" principle. It explicitly mandates that researchers maximize potential benefits and minimize potential harm to individual research subjects. From this principle, we have the obligations to balance the ratio of individual risks to potential social benefits, to assess the severity and probability of individual risks, and to more carefully weigh risks to protected populations.

- *Justice* calls for the equal distribution of potential benefits and potential risks across all groups who could potentially benefit from the research. From it, we have the duty to equitably select research subjects from the broader population by minimizing individual or systemic biases that would shift potential risks onto a subset of the population (especially members of protected populations or underrepresented groups) while allowing society at large to benefit.

The U.S. Department of Health and Human Services formally incorporated the Belmont Report's guidelines into binding policies under the Common Rule in 1981 (revised again in 1991 and 2018; Protection of Human Subjects, 2018). Today, the Common Rule applies to human subjects research that falls under the purview of 16 U.S. federal agencies and departments, from the Department of Agriculture to the Social Security Administration. Perhaps the most visible contribution of the Common Rule is the creation of Institutional Review Boards (IRBs), ethical bodies that oversee human subjects research, directly or indirectly supported by U.S. government funds.

Current Ethical Oversight for Federally Funded Research

Crucially, activity must meet two specific requirements to be subject to IRB review: It must be (a) research involving (b) human subjects. *Research* is defined as "systematic investigation, including research development, testing, and evaluation, designed to develop or contribute to generalizable knowledge" (Protection of Human Subjects, 2018, Section 46.102(l)). In its most recent revision, the Common Rule has been explicitly updated to exclude certain categories of activities that could have been construed as research—specifically, "scholarly and journalistic activities (e.g., oral history, journalism, biography, literary criticism, legal research, historical scholarship)," "public health surveillance activities," "collection and analysis of information . . . for a criminal justice agency," and "authorized operational activities . . . in support of . . . national security" (Protection of Human Subjects, 2018, Section 46.102(l)(1-4)). A *human subject* is defined as

> a living individual about whom an investigator (whether professional or student) conducting research:
>
> (i) Obtains information or biospecimens through intervention or interaction with the individual, [*sic*] and uses, studies, or analyzes the information or biospecimens; or
>
> (ii) Obtains, uses, studies, analyzes, or generates identifiable private information or identifiable biospecimens. (Protection of Human Subjects, 2018, Section 46.102(e))

Under these definitions, most psychological scientists in academia have engaged with IRBs through their work collecting and analyzing laboratory-based scientific data. For these scientists, it would seem only natural that the collection of new data from participants—whether online or in person—would require researchers to submit their protocols (i.e., formal research plans) for review and approval by their IRB before beginning their research. Such researchers may also know that IRB approval is required to conduct research on certain kinds of existing laboratory-based data sets.

Despite their awareness of ethical protocols for laboratory-derived data sets, many researchers who are first considering working with nonlaboratory data sets may not think to seek approval from their IRBs. However, federal guidelines do require oversight for certain kinds of nonexperimental data sets. Currently, IRBs can make one of four determinations on research projects using big data and naturally occurring data sets. First, the research could be considered not human subjects research, meaning that the IRB does not have to review it. Second, it could fall under Category 4 ("reanalysis of existing data") of the exempt IRB classification—somewhat of a misnomer given that it still falls under a lighter form of IRB review. Finally, it could receive an expedited or full-board classification, both of which require a higher level of review.

Taking a simplified view of the regulations, we can essentially classify the review of existing data sets by answering four questions: (Q1) whether

FIGURE 15.1. Simplified Flow Chart of the Regulations Used to Determine the Level of Oversight Required for Existing Data Sets in Federally Funded Research

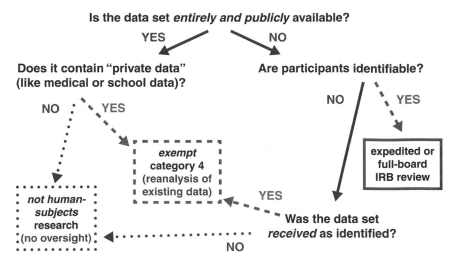

However, all final decisions about institutional review board (IRB) reviews are made by IRBs, not by individual researchers. (Dotted lines lead to a nonhuman subjects–research determination. Dashed lines lead to a determination requiring IRB oversight. Solid lines indicate a path that could end in either determination.)

the data set is entirely available to the public (without any restrictions whatsoever, including registering for free accounts),[2] (Q2) whether the data set contains "private data" (e.g., medical or school data),[3] (Q3) whether the data includes identifiers or possible identifiers, and (Q4) whether the data were received first by the researcher as identifiable. (See Figure 15.1 for flow chart.)

A nonhuman subjects research determination can be made either (a) when the data set (Q1) is publicly available and (Q2) contains no private data or (b) when the data set (Q1) is publicly available, (Q2) contains private data, (Q3) currently contains no participant identifiers, and (Q4) was never sent to the current researchers with any identifiers. This is possible because of the definition of a *human subject* in the Protection of Human Subjects act (2018;

---

[2]However, requiring payment to access the data set is generally considered permissible, as long as there are no restrictions designating eligible purchasers.

[3]According to the Common Rule, the question of whether data are "private" essentially refers to whether there could be a reasonable expectation of privacy regarding the data. Simply including personally identifiable information is not sufficient to be considered private. For example, a photograph is inherently personally identifiable information, but a photograph that is shared publicly on a social media website would not necessarily be considered private data. Issues of privacy are discussed more in the Open Questions section at the end of this chapter.

e.g., University of California Berkeley Committee for the Protection of Human Subjects, 2016; University of Chicago Social and Behavioral Sciences Institutional Review Board, 2014). However, individual universities may decide to systematically limit nonhuman subjects research determinations (Interuniversity Consortium for Political and Social Research [ICPSR], n.d.).

A determination of exempt Category 4 can be made when data sets—either (a) (Q1) entirely publicly available data sets (Q2) with private information or (b) (Q1) nonpublicly available data sets—have (Q3) no identifiers because (Q4) the identifying data were removed from the data set by the current researchers. Interestingly, the 2018 Common Rule now includes prospective data acquisition under exempt Category 4, whereas the pre-2018 Common Rule required the data already exist before the current researcher's involvement (Protection of Human Subjects, 2018). Generally, this means that data sets with (Q2) private and (Q3) identifiable data will be subject to expedited or full board review.

Whether a project is "human subjects research" (and, if so, its specific classification) may only be decided by an IRB: No individual researcher can make any classification determination on their own. Although the IRB process may be natural to researchers in psychology, it is important to note that some academic researchers are engaged in IRB-eligible activity without being aware of it (e.g., Dittrich & Kenneally, 2012). This is especially likely to occur in computer science, mathematics, statistics, and other fields that have not traditionally conducted human subjects research but are now interested in big data or data science (e.g., Metcalf & Crawford, 2016). Accordingly, all researchers—especially those conducting federally funded research or who work at public U.S. institutions—should consult their IRB before beginning work on any human-derived data.

BELMONT PRINCIPLES IN THE 21ST CENTURY

Keeping our field's legal and ethical framework (and its history) in mind, let us move on to consider how our current challenges can fit within our existing framework. To do so, however, we must also discuss what these data are and how they can be used.

Ethics Lessons From Recent Studies of "Wild" Data

Big data or naturally occurring data sets (BONDS; Paxton & Griffiths, 2017) allow psychological scientists to test, expand, and refine theories by analyzing human behavior in the real world. BONDS are typically not created for general scientific purposes but can, with a bit of careful thinking and the right computational tools, provide crucial insights into psychological science and complement rigorous lab-based experimental inquiry. These data sets could include government records, sports data, large image databases, and more (for more examples, see Goldstone & Lupyan, 2016; Paxton & Griffiths, 2017).[4]

Keeping in mind the proper awareness of limitations, messiness, and potential biases of these data (e.g., Ioannidis, 2013; Lazer, Kennedy, King, & Vespignani, 2014), real-world data—especially from social media or other social platforms—have been increasingly seen as another valuable tool for psychological scientists to add to their research tool kits (e.g., Goldstone & Lupyan, 2016; Jones, 2016; Lazer et al., 2009). To be clear, BONDS research should not be seen as rebuking or replacing traditional experimental psychological methods: Rather, the clearest value of BONDS to psychological science lies in their ability to complement these traditional methods, creating a "virtuous cycle of scientific discovery" (Paxton & Griffiths, 2017, p. 1631).

Along with the promising theoretical and empirical contributions of BONDS research, however, some scientific[5] BONDS research has raised ethical concerns. In one example, academic researchers scraped over 700,000 profiles from a dating website and then published the entire data set—including highly identifiable information such as usernames—in an open-access repository (Kirkegaard & Bjerrekaer, 2016). The resulting public outcry over the breach in participant privacy without participant consent or IRB oversight eventually caused the repository to remove both the data and manuscript preprint (see Zimmer, 2018).

In a second example, researchers scraped over 35,000 profile pictures and corresponding sexual orientation data[6] from the publicly available online dating profiles of nearly 15,000 users (Wang & Kosinski, 2018). These data were used to create various classifiers that could identify a person's sexual orientation from a photograph with 71% to 91% accuracy. In addition to scientific concerns about the study's methodology and interpretation (e.g., that the classifier likely picked up on other markers of self-presented sexual orientation and gender identity, such as hairstyles or photo filters; Gelman, Mattson, & Simpson, 2018), the public and LGBTQ+ advocates raised concerns about potential implications for the physical and social well-being for gay men and women (e.g., Anderson, 2017).

Although the first two examples used existing data, one final example was an experimental study conducted on social networks (Kramer, Guillory, &

---

[4]Although most experimental data sets shared on data-sharing repositories would not be considered BONDS data sets, some experimental data can achieve BONDS status—for example, when many individual experiments are combined in large-scale experimental data-sharing efforts in the pursuit of novel insights (e.g., Wordbank; Frank, Braginsky, Yurovsky, & Marchman, 2017). However, data sets are not BONDS simply because they are shared openly, and not all BONDS data sets are shared openly.
[5]Importantly, there are equally or more problematic nonscientific uses of BONDS data (e.g., the Cambridge Analytica scandal; Granville, 2018; Laterza, 2018). To the extent that these uses intersect with scientific concerns, they are discussed later in the chapter. Otherwise—although they present serious legal, social, and personal concerns—an in-depth discussion of them is outside the scope of the current chapter.
[6]By comparing the user's self-stated gender with the stated gender of their desired partners.

Hancock, 2014). Specifically, by manipulating over 689,000 users' news feeds to show either more positive-emotion or more negative-emotion posts from their Facebook friends, these researchers were the first to demonstrate that real-time in-person contact was not necessary for emotional contagion (i.e., one's emotion becoming more similar to another person's displayed emotion). Despite this novel scientific finding, general public alarm at the study—especially because users were unaware of their participation in the study, were not given the opportunity to provide informed consent, and could not withdraw their participation—led Facebook to establish new internal principles for research review (see Jackman & Kanerva, 2016). However, public and scientific scrutiny over the process raised significant questions about how Cornell University (the collaborating academic institution) justified its decision to claim that its researchers were not involved in human subjects research (e.g., Meyer, 2014), despite a vague statement from Cornell that the researchers had been involved in "initial discussions" about the study (cf. quoted Cornell press release in Sullivan, 2014, para. 1).[7]

Each of these scientific projects presents a mix of unique and overlapping ethical concerns. The opportunities from new data sources are incredibly exciting, but without clear ethical guidelines for today's changing data landscape, even the most well-intentioned researchers can make mistakes. Although the researchers on these projects may not have been fully aware of the potential ethical implications of their work, lessons from these projects can inform not only the ethical considerations for BONDS research in psychology but also ongoing conversations about BONDS ethics more broadly. Critically, because of psychology's long-standing concerns with human subjects ethics, psychological scientists are well-poised to influence BONDS ethics policies even outside of human subjects research.

Belmont Today

Although the writers of the Belmont Report could not have anticipated the new challenges brought by 21st-century technology and data, the principles underlying the Belmont Report are broad enough to apply to research in any century. For example, the Menlo Report (Bailey, Dittrich, & Kenneally, 2013; Dittrich & Kenneally, 2012) sought to apply Belmont principles to "information and communication technology" researchers and gave some prescient insights into problems facing such researchers at the dawn of BONDS research. Building on the Belmont and Menlo Reports, I extend the three core Belmont principles to apply to human-focused BONDS research (especially in academia) today.

Many of these issues target data collection—a particular challenge that many researchers who use existing data sets may not directly face. However,

---

[7]The original version is no longer available through Cornell University's website. An archived version from November 2017 is available through the WayBack Machine on the Internet Archive: https://web.archive.org/web/20171114194825/http://mediarelations.cornell.edu/2014/06/30/media-statement-on-cornell-universitys-role-in-facebook-emotional-contagion-research/.

as ethics-bound researchers, we should consider how data were collected before using it: The fact of data availability does not immediately confer the ethicality of analysis, and researchers should seriously consider refraining from using unethically collected or unethically shared data sets. Nevertheless, some researchers may be in a position to effect change through direct collaboration with the entities creating BONDS data sets. Whether or not they were engaged in the data collection, each researcher should take it upon themselves to safeguard public trust and individual rights. Public trust in science is a precious shared resource, and taking advantage of that resource for personal fame, notoriety, or career advancement will lead to its marked depletion to the detriment both of the remainder of the scientific community and society at large (cf. tragedy of the commons; Lloyd, 1883).

In this section, I outline some of the major hurdles to Belmont-compatible behavior in using BONDS research, along with some ways that psychological scientists could begin to address them.

Respect for Persons

Under this principle, individuals' autonomy should be upheld throughout the research process by giving them enough information to make an informed decision about participation and allowing them to withdraw that consent at any time. Today, BONDS-based researchers are increasingly questioning how compatible the principle of informed consent is with opaque, overly broad terms of service and with rampant dragnet data collection (e.g., Flick, 2016; Zimmer, 2018). An increasing proportion of daily activity occurs online on forums with mandatory terms of service—long, convoluted, and dense documents that a minuscule percentage of people read (e.g., approximately 2% of users; Obar & Oeldorf-Hirsch, 2018). How voluntary and informed, then, is consent under these conditions?

To more fully embrace the respect for persons principle in BONDS research, researchers should move to opt-in models of data collection and research participation, outlining explicitly how and to what end their data will be used if they choose to participate. Alternatively, in situations where opt-in models are judged infeasible or impossible by their ethics board, researchers should work with their ethics board to create an opt-out model with clear and frequent reminders to participants of their rights to drop out of the study at any time. All information shared with participants should be easily obtainable and accessibly written, especially as it pertains to the technical details surrounding the storing and use of their data.

Beneficence

Although individuals may not benefit directly from their participation in BONDS research (as is true with most laboratory-based psychological science research), researchers must protect their participants from modern-day financial, reputational, and other harms. Today, beneficence requires a keen awareness of issues around data privacy and data breaches. Even dealing strictly with public-domain data, massive data-gathering and data-sharing efforts allow researchers to gather dangerous quantities of data about specific individuals (e.g., Metcalf & Crawford, 2016; Rivers & Lewis, 2014; Zimmer, 2018), raising serious questions about whether de-identified data can ever be truly free from the possibility of reidentification (cf. reidentification of data from the Netflix challenge in Narayanan & Shmatikov, 2008; see also Ohm, 2010). Moreover, some of the most valuable data to companies and researchers today—namely, video and audio data—are inherently and inextricably identifiable (see, e.g., Chapters 5 and 6, this volume). Given the potential risks that even public data pose, the potential risk posed by breaches to sensitive data is nearly unimaginable even if the data do not include financial records or government identification (e.g., ransomed data from a social media site facilitating extramarital affairs; Mansfield-Devine, 2015). How protected, then, are individuals from potential harms of not only participation itself but also from the potential misuse or mismanagement of the associated data?

To more fully embrace the beneficence principle in BONDS research, researchers should minimize harm to individual participants by exercising extreme caution when deciding what data to collect, aggregate, or record. No data are free from the possibility of a hack or other form of breach, no matter how secure or well-designed data protections are. Therefore, researchers should minimize the type and amount of data collected from individual participants, with extra consideration given to any data that could be considered potentially sensitive or private. For large-scale data collection, the best protection for participants' long-term data security is, quite simply, to not collect the data in the first place. In addition to enduring commitments to data security, researchers should reconsider their motivations in data collection and be judicious in what data are gathered: Just because the data can be collected does not mean that they should be collected.

Complementarily, to maximize the benefits to individual participants, researchers should more freely share data and deliverables with participants. Questions of data ownership have been on the rise in industry and medicine for some time (e.g., Cios & Moore, 2002), and members of the public have been expressing interest in having access to their data (e.g., Ritzer & Jurgenson, 2010; Tene & Polonetsky, 2013). One tangible benefit to participation in BONDS research could be in helping to satisfy participants' curiosity about themselves and their digital lives. Given how much easier open science tools (e.g., apps and data exploration tools) have made sharing data and deliverables among researchers and the public, the additional effort required by the researcher to provide these insights would be relatively minimal relative to the potential value to participants.

Justice

The principle of justice calls for an equal distribution of benefits and risks across the population. Today, psychological scientists must ensure that the risks of BONDS data do not fall on the limited and nonrepresentative subset of the population who engage with entities and services collecting the data (e.g., Vitak, Shilton, & Ashktorab, 2016) and that groups of people—especially vulnerable groups—are not further disadvantaged by data nor by products created with those data (e.g., O'Neil, 2017). Although issues regarding algorithmic justice for women, communities of color, and other underrepresented groups have been gaining some attention over the past few years (e.g., Hamilton, 2018; O'Neil, 2017), concerns for justice are especially sharp as they relate to data from and about children—a population that is not considered capable of giving consent themselves for traditional laboratory experiments (Protection of Human Subjects, 2018) but that often has data shared about them (e.g., on social media) without their knowledge or assent by caregivers and others (Berman & Albright, 2017). How representative or biased, then, are our data sets and results?

To more fully embrace the principle of justice in BONDS research, researchers should be as concerned with questions of representation among their BONDS participants as they would be for traditional laboratory paradigms. Explicit demographics information may not be available (or advisable to always collect, as discussed in the Beneficence subsection), but when possible, efforts should be made to ensure that data are representative. Issues of self-selection and online access may make this particularly difficult to achieve with certain groups (e.g., rural communities, lower socioeconomic status individuals, older individuals). Researchers using existing data could remedy this by subsampling their data set to statistically overrepresent underrepresented groups and underrepresent overrepresented groups in the final sample; researchers collecting new data could additionally improve the representativeness of their sample by improving recruitment to overrepresent underrepresented groups. Subsampling data to reduce the impact of participants from overrepresented groups on the results could result in lower statistical power, but it could also increase the applicability and validity of findings. This is especially true when researchers are working with data that are linked with and potentially contain human biases and structural inequalities (e.g., arrest records, hiring records, housing records) to create deliverables that could exacerbate those inequalities (e.g., Hamilton, 2018; O'Neil, 2017).

Questions of fairness and equity should also significantly influence researchers' selection of data and research questions. Again, the simple fact that a data set is available does not mean that a researcher is ethically legitimized to use it, and taking advantage of existing (even public) data could cause certain groups of people to bear an unnecessary share of risk. For example, when creating their classifier to identify gay and straight men and women from facial images, Wang and Kosinski's (2018) stated desire to show the limitations of human perception and the superiority of computer algorithms put a greater share of the risk of participation on gay men and women who could face economic, social, and even physical harm by being identified against their will. This risk falls not only on the gay men and women who were included in the sample but also potentially all gay men and women worldwide; because there is no obvious additional benefit to gay men and women for having been included, this is a significant cause for concern for the principle of justice. To improve this, researchers should be acutely aware of the real-world implications for the groups included in and potentially affected by their research, and researchers who are unsure of the potential implications could solicit advocacy groups for feedback and input on how using BONDS data from their groups could help or harm them.

BEYOND THE BELMONT REPORT: OPEN QUESTIONS FOR TODAY'S PSYCHOLOGICAL SCIENTISTS

Today's technological, legal, and social milieus present new challenges for psychological scientists using BONDS. Here, I outline some new considerations that have not yet been neatly addressed by our ethical framework. Although this section provides suggestions on how to address some of them, careful thought and collaboration among all stakeholders will be essential to tackling the new ethical challenges of 21st-century human subjects research.

Balancing Open Science With Participant Rights

Psychological science—like other scientific areas—has been increasingly focused on adopting open-science practices, including open data (Kidwell et al., 2016). Intriguingly, the Menlo Report (Dittrich & Kenneally, 2012) advocated explicitly for forward-thinking improved transparency as part of its principle of respect for law and public interest. Transparency—not only in information and communication technologies research but also in all scientific work—helps improve public trust in science by facilitating access to the scientific process and products.

However, although some principles of open science can be readily embraced by BONDS researchers (e.g., open materials, open access), the principle of open data should be carefully considered, given the potential privacy ramifications for the individuals in the data set. As mentioned in the Respect for Persons subsection, serious concerns exist about the limits of de-identification and the real risks of reidentification (even of sparse data sets) in a cultural moment of extensive data sharing (Narayanan & Shmatikov, 2008; Ohm, 2010). This risk of reidentification becomes more concerning to individual participants' rights as researchers use potentially sensitive data and as researchers derive potentially impactful deliverables from those data. This is especially true for BONDS researchers who are working with naturally occurring data sets, heterogenous data sets, or data sets that are not entirely public (although even entirely public data sets should not be used without consideration, as discussed later).[8]

---

[8]Data-sharing is still important even for researchers using naturally occurring BONDS because data may change over time. Finding some way to share the specific data included in scientific work (e.g., by sharing frozen versions of the entire data set, by providing unique ID codes for the records) is crucial to computational reproducibility. However, the extent and nature of data sharing should be informed foremost by participant ethics.

Encouragingly, the tools for sharing data from laboratory experiments could provide a model for BONDS data. For example, the ICPSR (https://www.icpsr.umich.edu/) has a special class of "gated" repositories for sensitive data. These *restricted-use repositories* are freely available to any ICPSR-verified researcher, blending a commitment to open data with dedication to participant rights. Although appropriate de-identification should take place to the maximal extent possible, such a vehicle for sharing BONDS data could help minimize the impact of open data on individual participants.

In any case, specific questions of open data must be evaluated according to the unique needs and risks of each data set. The value of open BONDS data could also be weighed according to whether we see open data as public goods or common goods, a debate that can be informed by similar questions within genomics (e.g., Bialobrzeski, Ried, & Dabrock, 2012). Briefly, a *public good* is like clean air—something that everyone should be entitled to use and that cannot be used up in a zero-sum way. By contrast, a *common good* is like a public park or universal health care—something that should be shared by all because it can help improve general well-being but that is subject to terms of use set by group deliberation. A model of participant data as a public good would mandate data access to every (valid) researcher but would also require that every researcher contribute their data. By contrast, a model of participant data as a common good allows for more flexibility for participants and researchers in what, how, and with whom data are shared, with compliance emerging from a common conviction of the utility and power of data sharing.

In light of the respect for persons principle, it seems most reasonable to treat BONDS research in psychological science as a common good. Such a perspective affords flexibility in data sharing while fostering a community commitment to the value of open data. For example, Bialobrzeski and colleagues (2012) proposed that genetics repositories could work with patients to provide them with options for how they would share their data and for how long it could be kept on file. A similar model could be considered in BONDS research, allowing participants to decide how much (if any) of their data they want to have publicly shared, rather than simply requiring participants to share their data as a condition of their participation.

Contextualizing Human Data Use Outside Academia

The Common Rule applies only to research conducted using federal funds, but companies and private organizations also explore human behavior and cognition through their users' data. Most of this would not fall under the definition of human subjects research because it often does not seek to find "generalizable knowledge" (Protection of Human Subjects, 2018, 46.102(d)) and focuses instead on corporate goals such as improving user experience. However, even projects that are intended to contribute generalizable findings would not be bound by these requirements if they are not federally funded.

This clear gap between the expectations for human data use inside versus outside of academia is concerning for ethicists and data experts. Although peer-reviewed scientific journals increasingly require authors to confirm in their manuscripts that their protocol was approved by an appropriate ethics board (e.g., Graf et al., 2007), a plurality of industry-focused research is never ultimately published. To that end, Calo (2013) proposed an analog to IRBs for industry—consumer subject review boards (CSRBs). Although CSRBs have not been widely adopted, interest in these and similar entities has increased as the line between research and corporate activity blurs (e.g., Jackman & Kanerva, 2016; Polonetsky, Tene, & Jerome, 2015; Tene & Polonetsky, 2016). With the volume and heterogeneity of companies' user data collection on the rise, data scientists and big data researchers using human-derived data are grappling with whether and how to provide oversight to corporate research. Future solutions for resolving the disparity in the treatment of research inside versus outside academia may include expanding legal frameworks and combining technical and ethical training for data scientists.

Combining BONDS and Institutional Ethics

The current provisions in the Common Rule (Protection of Human Subjects, 2018) were originally developed to handle existing or public data sets that were dramatically different from the options today. The Belmont Report and original Common Rule emerged from a time when large-scale data collection was only possible through massive organizational initiatives (e.g., government records, academic research) and a handful of corporate entities (e.g., insurance companies). Now, hundreds of thousands of organizations collect and share data on hundreds of millions of individuals worldwide.

Despite the significant concerns about the gaps in ethical oversight at the intersection of academic and industry research that rose to prominence following the Facebook affective contagion study (e.g., Flick, 2016; Sullivan, 2014), the 2018 revisions to the Common Rule make it clear that there is still relatively little understanding of the unique risks posed by BONDS, especially when combining multiple public data sets (cf. Metcalf & Crawford, 2016). Industry researchers are grappling with their own questions of oversight (as noted earlier), but academic researchers should think carefully about the risks of BONDS collaborations in light of their potential impact.

As academic researchers collaborate more with companies on interesting and complex data sets, the ethics boards governing academic research must begin to raise real questions about the risks posed even by data collected by businesses as a matter of course or through internal experimental work. Under the current terms of IRB review, academic researchers could simply claim no ethical responsibility for the data collection and proceed to work with those data, but in the face of current skepticism over science and scientific practices, it seems shortsighted to divorce considerations of ethical data collection from ethical data use.

Researchers should have a duty—not only to specific participants in a study but also to the scientific community and the public—to conduct ethical research: Using ethically obtained data (no matter who obtained it) must remain a pillar of that ethical obligation. However, at present, individual researchers—not an ethics board—would make such a decision about whether a nonhuman-subjects data set should be ethically used. Moving forward, academic researchers and ethical bodies should consider whether it would be more prudent to formalize the process to provide additional oversight.

Securing Computational Pipelines

The increasing complexity of data collection and analysis necessitates increasing the scale in our computational and storage capacity, and the ease of cloud-based options is attractive to many scientists working on collaborative projects. The necessity of these resources has grown to the point where the National Science Foundation has funded national cyberinfrastructure for researchers in the United States (e.g., Extreme Science and Engineering Discovery Environment [XSEDE]; Towns et al., 2014). Because these computational pipelines are growing faster than most psychological scientists can learn them, systems administrators and other cyberinfrastructure personnel are essential to ensuring the smooth (and secure) functioning of the hardware and software.

Despite the heavy reliance on the computational and human systems enabling discovery using BONDS, relatively less attention has been paid to the ethical oversight of these systems. For example, say that a researcher is working with a cloud computing platform to analyze sensitive large-scale data. If that researcher were planning to analyze patient medical files, those files would be protected by Health Insurance Portability and Accountability Act (HIPAA) regulations throughout the pipeline, and the researcher could turn to guidelines from the Department of Health and Human Services (HHS. gov, n.d.). However, if that researcher were planning to run computer vision algorithms over videos of people in nonmedical contexts, the researcher would have significantly fewer formal guidelines; much less consensus exists on how to secure computational pipelines for inherently identifiable data that are not HIPAA-protected. It is important to note that this extends beyond simply hardware and software: Questions of what ethical regulations, training, or approvals might apply to systems administrators are similarly important and as yet unsettled.

Redefining "Minimal Risk" and "Private" Data

Given the power of connecting multiple data sets—even those that are entirely publicly available—data scientists themselves are increasingly arguing for oversight of big data (Metcalf & Crawford, 2016). A requirement of expedited and exempt IRB categories is that projects under these designations pose no more than *minimal risk*, defined as research in which "the probability and magnitude of harm or discomfort anticipated in the research are not greater in and of themselves than those ordinarily encountered in daily life or during the performance of routine physical or psychological examinations or tests" (Protection of Human Subjects, 2018, Section 46.102(j)). The paramount importance of minimizing risk to participants is, at first glance, consistent with why entirely public data is not considered human subjects research: Because the data are already public, there is an assumption that no additional risk would be incurred if the data were used for scientific purposes.

However, the vast quantities of available data can—when woven together—produce insights that could have the power to harm specific individuals. For example, Hauge, Stevenson, Rossmo, and Le Comber (2016) used only freely available data in an attempt to uncover the real identity of the artist known as Banksy, but the project still uncovered a massive amount of information about the person singled out (for more, see Metcalf & Crawford, 2016). This is also related to concerns about the reidentification of private data discussed earlier (e.g., Narayanan & Shmatikov, 2008; Ohm, 2010)—for example, if researchers leverage open data sets to reidentify de-identified data sets that include private information. Understanding the true potential for harm in these data—especially when using open data to conduct research on underrepresented or potentially vulnerable groups (e.g., gay men and women; Wang & Kosinski, 2018)—should give researchers and ethical bodies pause when considering whether research activities using open data truly pose "minimal risk" simply by virtue of their openness.

Dovetailing with concerns about what should count as "minimal risk" are questions about what data should count as "private." According to current federal regulations,

> *private information* includes information about behavior that occurs in a context in which an individual can reasonably expect that no observation or recording is taking place, and information that has been provided for specific purposes by an individual and that the individual can reasonably expect will not be made public (*e.g.,* a medical record). (Protection of Human Subjects, 2018, Section 46.102(e)(4))

An essential part of this definition is the concept of whether the individual has a reasonable expectation that their activity will not be recorded or observed. This is, for example, one reason why research that relies on observation of public behavior is considered minimal risk and falls under an exempt category. Again, the assumption is that—because the behavior itself was executed in public—there would be no additional risk to participants if data on the public behavior were used for scientific purposes.

Therefore, a crucial question is whether individuals acting online expect that they are acting publicly or privately. The majority of people do not read privacy policies or understand the legality of broad tracking initiatives online (e.g., Hoofnagle, Urban, & Li, 2012; Martin, 2015). This unfortunate reality could explain the *privacy paradox* (i.e., the widespread prevalence of sharing data despite widespread stated concerns about privacy; Smith, Dinev, & Xu, 2011) and presents concerns for researchers using online data. By contrast, ethics boards would be appalled if the majority of participants in a laboratory-based experiment failed to understand what data they were giving to researchers.

Even in the cases of outright sharing (e.g., on social media), many IRB professionals have expressed extreme reservations with considering such data as public, citing concerns about whether the individuals truly understood the impact of their sharing (Woelfel, 2016). Others have suggested that social media sites present a sort of public–private hybrid that has no real face-to-face or in-person analog (e.g., Strauß & Nentwich, 2013). Put simply, if the major-ity of people are not aware that their behavior could be (and likely is) tracked extensively on a single online platform or across the Internet—regardless of whether a researcher or ethics board finds that lack of awareness to be reasonable—we should be hypervigilant about perceptions of violations of privacy. Moreover, although traditional classes of "private" data included medical and educational records, this lapse in the general understanding of tracking suggests that we might move to align our concepts of private data to better conform to the general public's understanding of what data could reasonably be considered private. This is especially true in an age when data shared online are likely to exist in perpetuity.

To complicate matters further, even when participants do voluntarily share data with researchers, the data often have a life far beyond the original use. For example, the myPersonality data set (Kosinski, Stillwell, & Graepel, 2013) was created by aggregating Facebook data from tens of thousands of users who opted to share their data with researchers as part of a personality quiz. Although the brief consent document[9] told participants that their data could be used in a variety of ways (including research), it included no specifics about the potential risks and benefits of participating nor any detailed expla-nation about how their data could be used. The data were eventually shared with a wide variety of researchers and led to dozens of publications—with findings likely revealing far more than any participant could have imagined (as noted in the original paper's discussion of privacy implications; Kosinski et al., 2013). For cases in which these rich data sets may find uses far beyond a single study, it would be particularly useful for researchers to consider pro-viding even more information to participants about any limits on access or use on the data, along with specific resources for participants to see how their data were used (e.g., a list of published articles with high-level summaries).

Despite surface parallels with in-person observation, researchers should grapple with questions of scope of observation and tracking in online settings.

---

[9]The consent document is no longer available through myPersonality's website (https://sites.google.com/michalkosinski.com/mypersonality). An archived version from March 2018 is available through the WayBack Machine on the Internet Archive: https://web.archive.org/web/20180318230401/http://mypersonality.org/wiki/doku.php?id=disclaimer

In real-world settings, a crowd can provide a form of anonymity through obscurity by presenting too many targets for a single person to track; however, in online arenas, both the virtual crowd and its constituent members can be simultaneously tracked with high fidelity in real time. Online data collection affords passive, dragnet data collection at a scale and precision that would be unimaginable to attain using human observers. The scale of observation through BONDS data collection—especially when combining multiple data sets (e.g., Metcalf & Crawford, 2016)—is so striking as to feel qualitatively different from observations performed by note-taking humans or even by passive video cameras. This difference in perception should drive us to reevaluate whether our consideration of behavior in digital "public spaces" is truly equivalent to behavior in real-life public spaces. However, as observation of private and public spaces through large-scale video analysis becomes more prevalent and more computationally tractable, similar questions may come to be asked even of real-world behavior (cf. Chapter 5, this volume).

LIMITATIONS

This chapter—like all scientific works—has its own set of limitations, including noting that several interesting and important questions fall outside its scope. First, this chapter has focused on concerns both for researchers involved in new BONDS data collection and for researchers (re-)analyzing existing BONDS. This, of course, does not completely address the unsettling collection and use of data by companies in the first place—a problem that has been increasingly recognized in the United States and around the world. As psychological scientists, we often have less direct control over that problem. Instead, our consideration of ethical questions for data sets can guide our choices of which data sets to use, which companies to collaborate with (or work for), what curricula to teach, and what ethical and legal structures to advocate.

Second, legal and ethical questions about what companies can and should be doing with users' data are being raised worldwide as the public becomes increasingly aware of companies' collection, tracking, and use of user data. The lines between *scientific research* (for identifying generalizable knowledge about human behavior) and *company testing* (for improving a specific business's or industry's performance) are legally distinct in the United States— even if many users (and researchers) might see them as nearly identical. Large-scale collection by companies, of course, is not unique to this time—for example, actuarial research by insurance companies have long aggregated data as a core part of their business—but today's data collection and application occur at an unprecedented granularity and pace. Addressing such questions would require interrelated legal and ethical frameworks regarding data collection, use, and ownership. Although important, such proposals are outside the scope of this chapter.

Third, this chapter has largely centered on the U.S. legal and ethical framework, but the formalization of human subjects research ethics was born out of international concern. The Nuremberg Code (see a reprint in Annas & Grodin, 1992) and the Declaration of Helsinki (WMA, 1964) both originated outside the United States and laid the groundwork for the principles in the current U.S. system. The European Union General Data Protection Regulation (GDPR, 2016) recently enacted sweeping reforms to data collection and use in the European Union, prompting some ancillary changes in the United States as international entities shifted their business practices. Among other things, the GDPR reinforced the "right to be forgotten" (Ausloos, 2012)—which itself could present new challenges to researchers aggregating and storing naturally occurring data—and mandated that all user-focused research be explicitly opt-in. These reforms address some of the concerns outlined in this chapter, and similar reforms should be seriously considered (and supported) by U.S. researchers.

Finally, as of the time of writing this chapter, the 2018 revision to the Common Rule still contains several gaps that the U.S. Department of Health and Human Services has yet to fill, some of which will be relevant to BONDS researchers. (One of the most notable is a flow chart to determine whether a project will require IRB oversight.) However, additional guidance and documentation may emerge that could alter the landscape of ethical review for BONDS researchers. As these and other changes take effect, BONDS researchers should continue to educate themselves about their ethical responsibilities—and to call for stronger legal and ethical frameworks to protect human subjects, science, and society.

AN INEXHAUSTIVE LIST OF QUESTIONS FOR NEW RESEARCH

This chapter has offered questions, recommendations, and suggestions that psychological scientists should consider when evaluating their research. Underlying all of them is the reality that changing technology will necessarily shape our evaluation of the risks that a given study or data set might pose to individuals, groups, and societies. This nuance makes it difficult to distill these recommendations into a simple checklist or questionnaire that researchers can easily apply to assess a given data set.

However, psychological scientists who are just beginning to embark on work with big data and naturally occurring data sets face a challenge: Although they have robust ethical training to appreciate human subjects concerns in the abstract and in the lab, they often lack the technological expertise to critically evaluate important questions about these data sets—or even to know which questions they should ask. Although I urge readers to read the chapter closely for a deeper exploration of these issues, I provide a few basic questions that can serve as a starting point for researchers who are new to this perspective.

- *Respect for persons. Were the principles of autonomy and informed consent preserved in the creation of the data set?* (a) Were the individuals in the data set aware that their data were being collected, and were they truly aware that their data could be used for scientific purposes? More subtly, researchers may also ask whether the participants could have considered the data pertaining to private matters. That is, even if the data were shared or posted openly, could the participants have reasonably felt as though their data were private? This is not formally a consideration under the current definition of private data (as discussed earlier), but researchers may nevertheless wish to consider it before proceeding. (b) Were the individuals truly free to choose whether to be involved in the data collection, or were there coercive components to the data collection? This is especially important to consider as public life increasingly requires engagement in online forums with mandatory terms of service. In such cases, it may be technically true that the individuals could have stopped using the data-collecting service, but the opportunity cost of leaving the (virtual) public square could be considered coercive. These questions should apply as much to opt-in models as they do to opt-out models of data collection.

- *Beneficence. How might the data set (and the proposed use of it) impact the specific people included in it?* (a) If the raw or processed data somehow became publicly available (e.g., through leaks, hacks, open data), how would individual participants in your data set be affected (e.g., socially, economically)? A complete answer to this question should include evaluations of (i) whether the scope or depth of the data collection or sharing were warranted for the current question, (ii) what harm could be posed if the data were combined with other existing data, and (iii) how robust the de-identification procedures were (or can be). (b) Could the data and/or deliverables be turned into actionable insights that would benefit the participants? For example, could an interface be provided that would allow participants included in the data set to understand aspects of their behavior, cognition, or emotion better? (This should not simply be an attempt to entice more people to share their data; instead, this should be a way to concretely benefit the participants included in the data set.)

- *Justice. How might the data set (and the proposed use of it) impact groups of people both inside and outside the data set?* (a) Is the data set representative of the entire target population, or is it biased through self-selection toward members of certain groups or people with certain identities? Researchers may consider using statistical or sampling means to balance the sample. However, each researcher should carefully consider whether post hoc means of rebalancing can adequately address issues of representativeness in their specific case, especially for questions touching on issues of social inequity and systemic bigotry. (b) Does the data set or analysis bring risk to a specific group of people without commensurate benefit? Thoroughly answering this question may require reaching out to advocacy organizations because individual researchers may not be aware of important issues facing specific communities.

I urge researchers to think beyond these few questions when evaluating their work. This short list cannot account for the variety of all current and future data sets, and the specific questions offered here may be rendered obsolete as technology rapidly changes. However, by continuing to think carefully about these issues, our ethical frameworks can grow to provide more robust guidance for BONDS research, grounded within the Belmont principles and informed by evolving technological realities.

CONCLUSION

Psychological scientists today have an unprecedented opportunity to expand our field of study into more natural arenas through capitalizing on big data and naturally occurring data sets. By adopting the tools of data science and staying grounded in rich theoretical and experimental traditions, we can use these data as a window into real-world behavior, cognition, and emotion to help us test, expand, and refine psychological theory. Despite these promising avenues, this paradigm presents new ethical challenges to individuals and society. However, our core ethical principles—the Belmont principles of respect for persons, beneficence, and justice—can be expanded to address the risks and benefits of today's data, not only protecting the rights and dignity of our individual participants but also preserving the public's faith and trust in psychological science.

REFERENCES

Anderson, D. (2017). *GLAAD and HRC call on Stanford University & responsible media to debunk dangerous & flawed report claiming to identify LGBTQ people through facial recognition technology.* Retrieved from https://www.glaad.org/blog/glaad-and-hrc-call-stanford-university-responsible-media-debunk-dangerous-flawed-report

Annas, G. J., & Grodin, M. A. (1992). *The Nazi doctors and the Nuremberg Code: Human rights in human experimentation.* New York, NY: Oxford University Press.

Ausloos, J. (2012). The "right to be forgotten"—Worth remembering? *Computer Law & Security Review, 28,* 143–152. http://dx.doi.org/10.1016/j.clsr.2012.01.006

Bailey, M., Dittrich, D., & Kenneally, E. (2013). *Applying ethical principles to information and communication technology research.* Retrieved from https://www.caida.org/publications/papers/2013/menlo_report_companion_actual_formatted/menlo_report_companion_actual_formatted.pdf

Baker, R. (2001). Bioethics and human rights: A historical perspective. *Cambridge Quarterly of Healthcare Ethics, 10,* 241–252. http://dx.doi.org/10.1017/S0963180101003048

Baumrind, D. (1964). Some thought on ethics of research: After reading Milgram's "Behavioral Study of Obedience." *American Psychologist, 19,* 421–423. http://dx.doi.org/10.1037/h0040128

Baumrind, D. (1979). IRBs and social science research: The costs of deception. *IRB, 1*(6), 1–4. Retrieved from https://www.jstor.org/stable/3564243

Beauchamp, T. L. (2011). Codes, declarations, and other ethical guidance for human subjects research: The Belmont Report. In E. J. Emanuel, C. Grady, R. A. Crouch, R. K. Lie, F. G. Miller, & D. Wendler (Eds.), *The Oxford textbook of clinical research ethics* (pp. 149–155). New York, NY: Oxford University Press.

Berman, G., & Albright, K. (2017). *Children and the data cycle: Rights and ethics in a big data world*. Retrieved from https://www.unicef-irc.org/publications/907/

Bialobrzeski, A., Ried, J., & Dabrock, P. (2012). Differentiating and evaluating common good and public good: Making implicit assumptions explicit in the contexts of consent and duty to participate. *Public Health Genomics, 15*, 285–292. http://dx.doi.org/10.1159/000336861

Calo, R. (2013). Consumer subject review boards: A thought experiment. *Stanford Law Review Online, 66*(97), 97–102.

Cios, K. J., & Moore, G. W. (2002). Uniqueness of medical data mining. *Artificial Intelligence in Medicine, 26*, 1–24. http://dx.doi.org/10.1016/S0933-3657(02)00049-0

Cornsweet, T. N., & Crane, H. D. (1973). Accurate two-dimensional eye tracker using first and fourth Purkinje images. *Journal of the Optical Society of America, 63*, 921–928. http://dx.doi.org/10.1364/JOSA.63.000921

Dittrich, D., & Kenneally, E. (2012). *The Menlo Report: Ethical principles guiding information and communication technology research*. Retrieved from https://www.caida.org/publications/papers/2012/menlo_report_actual_formatted/

Drewry, S. (2004). The ethics of human subjects protection in research. *The Journal of Baccalaureate Social Work, 10*, 105–117. http://dx.doi.org/10.18084/1084-7219.10.1.105

Englehardt, E. E., & Englehardt, R. K. (2013). The Belmont Commission and a progression of research ethics. *Ethics in Biology, Engineering & Medicine, 4*, 315–326.

Farmer, P. (2003). *Pathologies of power: Health, human rights, and the new war on the poor*. Berkeley: University of California Press.

Flick, C. (2016). Informed consent and the Facebook emotional manipulation study. *Research Ethics Review, 12*, 14–28. http://dx.doi.org/10.1177/1747016115599568

Frank, M. C., Braginsky, M., Yurovsky, D., & Marchman, V. A. (2017). Wordbank: An open repository for developmental vocabulary data. *Journal of Child Language, 44*, 677–694. http://dx.doi.org/10.1017/S0305000916000209

Gelman, A., Mattson, G., & Simpson, D. (2018). Gaydar and the fallacy of decontextualized measurement. *Sociological Science, 5*, 270–280. http://dx.doi.org/10.15195/v5.a12

General Data Protection Regulation of the European Union. (2016). *Official Journal* L119, 4 May 2016, pp. 1–88.

Goldstone, R. L., & Lupyan, G. (2016). Discovering psychological principles by mining naturally occurring data sets. *Topics in Cognitive Science, 8*, 548–568. http://dx.doi.org/10.1111/tops.12212

Graf, C., Wager, E., Bowman, A., Fiack, S., Scott-Lichter, D., & Robinson, A. (2007). Best practice guidelines on publication ethics: A publisher's perspective. *International Journal of Clinical Practice, 61*(152), 1–26. http://dx.doi.org/10.1111/j.1742-1241.2006.01230.x

Granville, K. (2018, March 19). Facebook and Cambridge Analytica: What you need to know as the fallout. *The New York Times*. Retrieved from https://www.nytimes.com/2018/03/19/technology/facebook-cambridge-analytica-explained.html

Hamilton, I. A. (2018, October 10). Amazon built AI to hire people, but it discriminated against women. *Business Insider*. Retrieved from https://amp.businessinsider.com/amazon-built-ai-to-hire-people-discriminated-against-women-2018-10

Hauge, M. V., Stevenson, M. D., Rossmo, D. K., & Le Comber, S. C. (2016). Tagging Banksy: Using geographic profiling to investigate a modern art mystery. *Journal of Spatial Science, 61*, 185–190. http://dx.doi.org/10.1080/14498596.2016.1138246

HHS.gov. (n.d.). *Guidance on HIPAA & cloud computing*. Retrieved from https://www.hhs.gov/hipaa/for-professionals/special-topics/cloud-computing/index.html

Hoofnagle, C. J., Urban, J. M., & Li, S. (2012). *Privacy and modern advertising: Most US internet users want "Do Not Track" to stop collection of data about their online activities*. Retrieved from http://ssrn.com/abstract=2152135

Inter-university Consortium for Political and Social Research. (n.d.). *Institutional Review Boards (IRBs)*. Retrieved from https://www.icpsr.umich.edu/icpsrweb/ICPSR/irb/

Ioannidis, J. P. A. (2013). Informed consent, big data, and the oxymoron of research that is not research. *The American Journal of Bioethics, 13*(4), 40–42. http://dx.doi.org/10.1080/15265161.2013.768864

Jackman, M., & Kanerva, L. (2016). Evolving the IRB: Building robust review for industry research. *Washington and Lee Law Review Online, 72*, 442–457.

James, J. (2018). *Data never sleeps 6.0*. Retrieved from https://www.domo.com/blog/data-never-sleeps-6/

Jones, M. N. (2016). Developing cognitive theory by mining large-scale naturalistic data. In M. N. Jones (Ed.), *Big data in cognitive science* (pp. 1–12). New York, NY: Routledge. http://dx.doi.org/10.4324/9781315413570

Kidwell, M. C., Lazarević, L. B., Baranski, E., Hardwicke, T. E., Piechowski, S., Falkenberg, L.-S., . . . Nosek, B. A. (2016). Badges to acknowledge open practices: A simple, low-cost, effective method for increasing transparency. *PLoS Biology, 14*(5), e1002456. http://dx.doi.org/10.1371/journal.pbio.1002456

Kirkegaard, E. O. W., & Bjerrekaer, J. D. (2016). The OKCupid dataset: A very large public dataset of dating site users. *Open Differential Psychology*. Retrieved from https://pdfs.semanticscholar.org/fabe/35049b1b8a0be052ef8c1647e5b6cb2d8cf0.pdf

Kosinski, M., Stillwell, D., & Graepel, T. (2013). Private traits and attributes are predictable from digital records of human behavior. *PNAS, 110*, 5802–5805. http://dx.doi.org/10.1073/pnas.1218772110

Kramer, A. D. I., Guillory, J. E., & Hancock, J. T. (2014). Experimental evidence of massive-scale emotional contagion through social networks. *PNAS, 111*, 8788–8790. http://dx.doi.org/10.1073/pnas.1320040111

Laterza, V. (2018). Cambridge Analytica, independent research and the national interest. *Anthropology Today, 34*(3), 1–2. http://dx.doi.org/10.1111/1467-8322.12430

Lazer, D., Kennedy, R., King, G., & Vespignani, A. (2014). The parable of Google Flu: Traps in big data analysis. *Science, 343*, 1203–1205. http://dx.doi.org/10.1126/science.1248506

Lazer, D., Pentland, A., Adamic, L., Aral, S., Barabási, A.-L., Brewer, D., . . . Van Alstyne, M. (2009). Computational social science. *Science, 323*, 721–723. http://dx.doi.org/10.1126/science.1167742

Lloyd, W. F. (1883). *Two lectures on the checks to population*. Oxford, England: Oxford University Press.

Mansfield-Devine, S. (2015). The Ashley Madison affair. *Network Security, 2015*(9), 8–16. http://dx.doi.org/10.1016/S1353-4858(15)30080-5

Martin, K. (2015). Privacy notices as tabula rasa: An empirical investigation into how complying with a privacy notice is related to meeting privacy expectations online. *Journal of Public Policy & Marketing, 34*, 210–227.

Metcalf, J., & Crawford, K. (2016). Where are human subjects in Big Data research? The emerging ethics divide. *Big Data & Society , 3*, 1–14. http://dx.doi.org/10.1177/2053951716650211

Meyer, R. (2014, June 28). Everything we know about Facebook's secret mood manipulation study. *The Atlantic*. Retrieved from https://www.theatlantic.com/technology/archive/2014/06/everything-we-know-about-facebooks-secret-moodmanipulation-experiment/373648/

Milgram, S. (1963). Behavioral study of obedience. *The Journal of Abnormal and Social Psychology, 67*, 371–378. http://dx.doi.org/10.1037/h0040525

Morris, J. R. W. (1973). Accelerometry—A technique for the measurement of human body movements. *Journal of Biomechanics, 6*, 729–736. http://dx.doi.org/10.1016/0021-9290(73)90029-8

Narayanan, A., & Shmatikov, V. (2008). Robust de-anonymization of large sparse datasets. *IEEE Symposium on Security and Privacy*, 111–125. Retrieved from https://www.cs.utexas.edu/~shmat/shmat_oak08netflix.pdf

National Commission for the Protection of Human Subjects of Biomedical and Behavioral Research. (1979). *The Belmont Report: Ethical principles and guidelines for the protection of human subjects of research*. Retrieved from https://www.hhs.gov/ohrp/regulations-and-policy/belmont-report/read-the-belmont-report/index.html

National Research Act of 1974, PL 93-348 (1974).

Obar, J. A., & Oeldorf-Hirsch, A. (2018). The biggest lie on the Internet: Ignoring the privacy policies and terms of service policies of social networking services. *Information Communication and Society*. http://dx.doi.org/10.1080/1369118X.2018.1486870

Ohm, P. (2010). Broken promises of privacy: Responding to the surprising failure of anonymization. *UCLA Law Review, 57*, 1701–1777.

O'Neil, C. (2017). *Weapons of math destruction: How big data increases inequality and threatens democracy*. New York, NY: Broadway Books.

Paxton, A., & Griffiths, T. L. (2017). Finding the traces of behavioral and cognitive processes in big data and naturally occurring datasets. *Behavior Research Methods, 49*, 1630–1638. http://dx.doi.org/10.3758/s13428-017-0874-x

Polonetsky, J., Tene, O., & Jerome, J. (2015). Beyond the Common Rule: Ethical structures for data research in non-academic settings. *Colorado Technology Law Journal, 13*(101), 333–337.

Protection of Human Subjects, 45 C.F.R. § 46 (2018).

Reverby, S. M. (2009). *Examining Tuskegee: The infamous syphilis study and its legacy*. Chapel Hill: University of North Carolina Press.

Rice, T. W. (2008). The historical, ethical, and legal background of human-subjects research. *Respiratory Care, 53*, 1325–1329.

Ritzer, G., & Jurgenson, N. (2010). Production, consumption, prosumption: The nature of capitalism in the age of the digital "prosumer." *Journal of Consumer Culture, 10*, 13–36. http://dx.doi.org/10.1177/1469540509354673

Rivers, C. M., & Lewis, B. L. (2014). Ethical research standards in a world of big data. *F1000 Research*. http://dx.doi.org/10.12688/f1000research.3-38.v2

Schlenker, B. R., & Forsyth, D. R. (1977). On the ethics of psychological research. *Journal of Experimental Social Psychology, 13*, 369–396. http://dx.doi.org/10.1016/0022-1031(77)90006-3

Smith, H. J., Dinev, T., & Xu, H. (2011). Information privacy research: An interdisciplinary review. *Management Information Systems Quarterly, 35*, 989–1015. http://dx.doi.org/10.2307/41409970

Strauß, S., & Nentwich, M. (2013). Social network sites, privacy and the blurring boundary between public and private spaces. *Science & Public Policy, 40*, 724–732. http://dx.doi.org/10.1093/scipol/sct072

Sullivan, G. (2014, July 1). Cornell ethics board did not pre-approve Facebook mood manipulation study. *The Washington Post*. Retrieved from https://www.washingtonpost.com/news/morning-mix/wp/2014/07/01/facebooks-emotional-manipulation-study-was-even-worse-than-you-thought/

Tene, O., & Polonetsky, J. (2013). Big data for all: Privacy and user control in the age of analytics. *Northwestern Journal of Technology and Intellectual Property, 11*, 240–273.

Tene, O., & Polonetsky, J. (2016). Beyond IRBs: Ethical guidelines for data research. *Washington and Lee Law Review Online, 72*, 458–471. Retrieved from https://scholarlycommons.law.wlu.edu/wlulr-online/vol72/iss3/7

Towns, J., Cockerill, T., Dahan, M., Foster, I., Gaither, K., Grimshaw, A., . . . Wilkins-Diehr, N. (2014). XSEDE: Accelerating scientific discovery. *Computing in Science & Engineering, 16*(5), 62–74. http://dx.doi.org/10.1109/MCSE.2014.80

University of California Berkeley Committee for the Protection of Human Subjects. (2016). *Research involving the secondary use of existing data.* Retrieved from https://cphs.berkeley.edu/secondarydata.pdf

University of Chicago Social and Behavioral Sciences Institutional Review Board. (2014). *Investigator guidance.* Retrieved from https://sbsirb.uchicago.edu/investigatorguidance/

Vespignani, A. (2009, July 24). Predicting the behavior of techno-social systems. *Science, 325*(5939), 425–428. http://dx.doi.org/10.1126/science.1171990

Vitak, J., Shilton, K., & Ashktorab, Z. (2016). Beyond the Belmont principles: Ethical challenges, practices, and beliefs in the online data research community. In *Proceedings of the 19th ACM Conference on Computer-Supported Cooperative Work & Social Computing* (pp. 941–953). New York, NY: ACM. http://dx.doi.org/10.1145/2818048.2820078

Wang, Y., & Kosinski, M. (2018). Deep neural networks are more accurate than humans at detecting sexual orientation from facial images. *Journal of Personality and Social Psychology, 114*, 246–257. http://dx.doi.org/10.1037/pspa0000098

Woelfel, T. (2016). *Behind the computer screen: What IRB professionals really think about social media research* (Master's thesis). Retrieved from https://digital.lib.washington.edu/researchworks/bitstream/handle/1773/36448/Woelfel_washington_0250O_16207.pdf

World Medical Association. (1964). *Declaration of Helsinki 1964.* Retrieved from https://www.wma.net/what-we-do/medical-ethics/declaration-of-helsinki/doh-jun1964/

Zimmer, M. (2018). Addressing conceptual gaps in big data research ethics: An application of contextual integrity. *Social Media and Society.* http://dx.doi.org/10.1177/2056305118768300

16

Promoting Robust and Reliable Big Data Research in Psychology

Joshua A. Strauss and James A. Grand

Imagine being tasked with constructing the table of contents for a book whose goal was to summarize the trends, developments, and themes that defined psychological science over the past 50 years. When considering how to describe the past decade, one would be hard pressed to choose between the rise of computational social science (including big data research) and matters of robust and reliable science as the titular focus. In some respects, these topics have found themselves intertwined. For example, the accumulation and analysis of largescale replication data sets has been used as a tool for demonstrating concerns regarding the robustness of published findings in psychology (e.g., Camerer et al., 2018; Klein et al., 2014; Open Science Collaboration, 2015). However, increasing the volume of data used to examine psychological phenomena hardly registers on the scale of what excites most about the advent of big data and a more computationally oriented social science. Interest in these new frontiers is encapsulated by the promise of new discoveries, insights, and the development of predictive tools for understanding human affect, behavior, and cognition that can be used to shape future knowledge generation and policy decisions.

Unfortunately, the excitement and potential of big data analytics and computational social science makes it all too easy to lose sight of the issues that have contributed to worries regarding the reliability and robustness of psychological research in general. Lazer, Kennedy, King, and Vespignani (2014) coined the term *big data hubris* to reflect the implicit belief that the use of large data sets and sophisticated analyses provides researchers license to relax

http://dx.doi.org/10.1037/0000193-017
Big Data in Psychological Research, S. E. Woo, L. Tay, and R. W. Proctor (Editors)

principles of scientific rigor such as accurate measurement, construct validity, and reliability. Similar concerns have also been raised regarding replicability and reproducibility in big data research. For example, Leetaru (2017) recounted the many methodological challenges faced in attempting to replicate big data research, such as determining whether an original and a replication data set are equivalent and whether or how the decisions/algorithms used by a researcher to collect, organize, and analyze big data can even be effectively reproduced. Still others have raised concerns regarding the transparency of big data research, in addition to more complex issues regarding societal and technical infrastructures (ever-changing government policies and business practices that influence data quality, programmers/developers dynamically restructuring data and data access protocols, etc.; Boyd & Crawford, 2012; Lazer et al., 2014).

These points should give pause to even the strongest advocates of big data analytics to consider how the unique strengths of big data can be leveraged to advance psychological science and practice without repeating the sins of our past. The focus of this chapter thus concerns a critical question—what can big data and computational social science do to improve the likelihood that research meets emerging criteria for robust and reliable psychological science? In reflecting on this topic, we have elected not to debate the merits of specific methodologies and analyses available to big data researchers or when computational approaches may be more or less appropriate. These are clearly important matters; however, our intention is to discuss and provide guidance applicable to establishing norms and standardized practices for the conduct, reporting, and dissemination of big data research. We begin by first describing what we believe are the characteristics of a robust big data science and some of the more significant challenges for meeting these demands. The remainder of the chapter then focuses on three issues related to scientific credibility that have been frequent topics of discussion in psychology (i.e., hypothesizing after results are known [HARKing], questionable research practices [QRPs], and replicability/reproducibility), describing their relevance to big data research, and offering recommendations for facilitating reliable and robust contributions of big data science to psychology.

WHAT MAKES A SCIENCE ROBUST?

Although the replicability and reproducibility of findings in the social and psychological sciences has seemingly received the most widespread attention (Camerer et al., 2018; Fanelli, 2010b; Klein et al., 2014; Open Science Collaboration, 2015), virtually all disciplines of science wrestle with similar issues (e.g., Fanelli, 2009, 2012; Ioannidis, 2005a, 2005b; Marcus, 2014; Rubin, 2011). A great deal has already been written regarding the purported causes of the "credibility crisis" in science, including how both top-down/environmental forces (e.g., "publish or perish" norms and incentive structures in academia) and bottom-up/individual behaviors (e.g., engaging in research practices to "game" the system) across a variety of stakeholders in the scientific enterprise can collectively affect the trustworthiness of research (National Academies of Sciences, Engineering, & Medicine, 2017). Rather than reiterate those points again, we adopt a more aspirational lens that elaborates what we believe constitutes a robust and reliable scientific field of inquiry and consider what that vision entails for research involving big data methods and analytics.

To frame this discussion, we rely on the defining characteristics of a robust science proposed by Grand, Rogelberg, Allen, et al. (2018). As opposed to a checklist or set of standards for judging individual researchers or pieces of scholarship, these characteristics are intended to distill the values that reflect "better science" (Grote, 2017) and serve as markers for evaluating how decisions, policies, resources, and practices intended to improve scientific credibility contribute to that goal. In the sections following, we define and apply these characteristics to research conducted using big data approaches. Table 16.1 provides a summary of this discussion.

Robust Big Data Science Should Be Relevant

Grand, Rogelberg, Allen, et al. (2018) characterized relevance with respect to the utility of the research generated by a science. Specifically, a more robust science is one in which the knowledge produced by a discipline improves understanding of the natural world, can be used to address important needs, and builds towards contributions that benefit society. In many ways, the principle of relevance concerns the extent to which scientific outputs are problem-focused, solution-oriented, and attempt to "do good." Big data applications should seemingly adhere to this principle well, given that they are frequently described as tools for extracting evidence-based insights into complex and often intractable problem domains (e.g., Kim, Trimi, & Chung, 2014; Ryan & Herleman, 2015). However, when the generation of such insights occurs through inductive and exploratory methods (e.g., unsupervised learning techniques) and through the use of data sources and models not designed with an eye toward drawing the intended inferential claims or maintaining individual protections, the relevance and applicability of such knowledge should be appropriately vetted.

Lazer et al. (2014) provided an excellent commentary and case study on this challenge for big data research in the context of using Google search activity to estimate the prevalence of flu cases. Developing a model capable of predicting flu outbreaks automatically and in near-real time is an admirable scientific pursuit with clear implications for positively influencing healthcare practice and policies. However, the big data model resulted in systematically biased overestimations and was frequently outperformed by existing models that used and analyzed data with more traditional methods (e.g., local laboratory surveillance reports collected by the Centers for Disease Control and Prevention, simple time-lagged regression). Lazer et al. suggested that this case study offers a number of important lessons for ensuring the relevance, utility,

TABLE 16.1. Defining Principles of Robust Science and Their Implications for Big Data Research

Robust science is . . .	Description	Implications for big data research
Relevant	Generation and application of research is intended to improve understanding of the natural world, address contemporary needs and issues, and contribute to beneficial societal outcomes.	• Goals, purpose, and focus of research are made explicit. • Exploratory, insight-driven research is presented as such.
Rigorous	Theoretical and empirical activities emphasize careful operationalization of core concepts and use of diverse methodological and analytical approaches to explore research questions.	• Consideration is directed toward validity, reliability, and psycho-metric properties of data. • Appropriateness (rather than size) of data source for examining relationships is justified. • Big data are used in addition to, rather than as replacement for, existing methodologies.
Replicated	Collection of multiple and repeated observations of primary relationships are pursued and recognized as critical to establishing confidence in scientific claims and evidence-based practice.	• Sensitivity of inferences to alternative models and specifications is examined and reported. • Examination of relationships described in previous data is valued and pursued with new data sources.
Accumulative and cumulative	Cumulative knowledge and efforts to establish confi-dence in the strength of scientific understanding are pursued in a manner that balances generation and incremental vetting of new ideas.	• Relationships identified in previous data are integrated into or accounted for in new data. • Big data approaches are used in both confirmatory and exploratory manners.
Transparent and open	Activities related to conduct-ing, reporting, and disseminating research are undertaken in ways that facilitate understanding of the processes involved and products created during research.	• Data sources, methods, and analyses are shared. • All data processing, wrangling, and recording decisions are shared. • Researchers participate in registered reporting, preregistra-tion, and other mechanisms that emphasize research process.
Theory oriented	Outputs of all scientific research contribute to the development of increasingly accurate, useful, evidence-based, and precise explana-tions for natural phenomena observed in the world.	• Big data are used to bound, revise, and falsify in addition to advancing new claims. • Big data are used to improve precision of process-level accounts for phenomena.

Note. From "A Systems-Based Approach to Fostering Robust Science in Industrial–Organizational Psychology," by J. A. Grand, S. G. Rogelberg, T. D. Allen, R. S. Landis, D. H. Reynolds, J. C. Scott, S. Tonidandel, and D. M. Truxillo, 2018, *Industrial and Organizational Psychology*, *11*, p. 16. Copyright 2017 by the Society for Industrial and Organizational Psychology. Adapted with permission.

and trustworthiness of big data research and applications, including the need to establish whether, how, and why the insights produced by these techniques improve upon existing knowledge. We echo this sentiment and the position that ensuring the relevance of a robust big data science requires that researchers explicate and monitor the purpose of their investigations (e.g., confirmatory vs. exploratory) and make concerted efforts to verify the veracity of proposed conclusions through multiple means.

Robust Big Data Science Should Be Rigorous

Rigor is reflected by the extent to which core constructs and variables are operationalized with precision, the methodologies used to gather observations are free from error and bias, data are acquired from samples that are representative and appropriate for desired inferences, and the analytical techniques used to model relationships within data meet required assumptions. Concerns with the rigor of big data science are among the most commonly discussed issues in the academic literature, with numerous authors citing the need for big data practitioners to evaluate more carefully the quality, appropriateness, and psychometric properties of data used to generate inferences (e.g., Boyd & Crawford, 2012; Braun & Kuljanin, 2015; Guzzo, Fink, King, Tonidandel, & Landis, 2015; Hilbert, 2016; Whelan & DuVernet, 2015). Guidance for promoting more rigorous big data research is beginning to emerge (e.g., Cai & Zhu, 2015; Landers, Brusso, Cavanaugh, & Collmus, 2016), and we suspect the rigor of big data approaches will continue to mature as standards and best practices emerge. Nevertheless, big data hubris (Lazer et al., 2014) and the failure to scrutinize the rigor of computational social science applications represent clear threats to promoting a robust big data science because they compound the risk of generating inferences that are unreliable, unreproducible, and untrustworthy.

Robust Big Data Science Should Be Replicated and Accumulative/Cumulative

Although there are subtle and important distinctions between research that is replicated and research that is accumulative/cumulative, we discuss these issues collectively because they are both relevant to the assumption that bigger or more data necessarily implies higher quality inferences (e.g., Boyd & Crawford, 2012; Guzzo et al., 2015; Landers et al., 2016; Lazer et al., 2014). Though many have opined that the replication of findings is the cornerstone of all science (e.g., Simons, 2014), what it means to replicate research is a more complicated issue than many assume (Anderson & Maxwell, 2016; see also the exchange between Gilbert, King, Pettigrew, & Wilson, 2016, and Anderson et al., 2016). The use of relatively small, underpowered sample sizes in psychological research is a common reason that meta-scientists have so strongly advocated for replication studies in the past. Although big data applications are much less likely to suffer from low statistical power, random error is not the only potential source of variance that replication efforts may address. Psychologists have long recognized that human affect, behavior, and cognition are responsive to situation, context, time, and myriad other factors that may vary across a set of observations. From this perspective, then, even a single big data study may represent an *n* of 1 (albeit a large *n* of 1). Furthermore, if research is "poorly designed" (e.g., questionable operationalization of core constructs, use of psychometrically deficient measures, failing to consider the representativeness of a sample for inferences), replicating or collecting vast amounts of data adds rather than reduces uncertainty around inferences. If a critical goal of science is to advance understanding of the natural world, replication should be viewed as an effort to accumulate as many high-quality observations as possible. That effort allows us to establish the degree of confidence we should place in our cumulative knowledge. Big data methods can clearly play an important and unique role in helping psychological science accumulate such knowledge, but direct and conceptual replications both are needed to ensure the reliability and reproducibility of the results.

Robust Big Data Science Should Be Transparent and Open

Transparency and openness in science are most directly embodied by efforts to share with the scientific community by disclosing all data, materials, analyses, and hypotheses that comprise a research study (Nosek et al., 2015). Many available platforms have made sharing and accessing these items easy for both primary investigators and secondary consumers (e.g., Open Science Framework, https://osf.io; GitHub, https://github.com; Dataverse, https://dataverse.org), and the available features, interconnectivity among, and support for such outlets has continued to increase as more users adopt these technologies. However, fostering a transparent and open science goes beyond sharing data and materials; it also involves concerted efforts to detail the precise processes (i.e., methods and analyses) involved in the procurement and analysis of data, rather than only the final outcomes of the research (Grand, Rogelberg, Banks, Landis, & Tonidandel, 2018). This is a particularly important target for promoting a robust big data science because many decisions in the collection, aggregation, processing, wrangling, recording, storage, and analysis of data can be ambiguous or opaque (Boyd & Crawford, 2012). To this end, we think it likely that big data science would benefit from participating in preregistration, registered reporting, and other similar mechanisms that place emphasis on how research questions will be addressed and inferences drawn (Cumming, 2014; Open Science Collaboration, 2015). Even when such options may be unavailable to the researcher, big data practitioners should make every effort to document accurately and completely all procedures that affect what goes into and out of analyses and to make those data and computations available. Although this principle is relevant to all empirical research, we believe it carries even greater weight for big data analytics that rely heavily on data rather than theory for insight generation (cf., Landers et al., 2016).

Robust Big Data Science Should Be Theory Oriented

A defining feature of science, in contrast to other epistemological perspectives, is the pursuit of evidence that helps bound, revise, falsify, and advance explanatory claims about the natural world. This definition does not mean that descriptive and correlational research (as might be pursued using unsupervised learning methods) are or should be valued less than research geared toward hypothesis testing or confirmation (as might be pursued using supervised learning methods). Instead, a theory-oriented science is one that builds toward a precise understanding of the magnitude, form, processes, and conditions that account for observed relationships (Edwards & Berry, 2010; Kozlowski, Chao, Grand, Braun, & Kuljanin, 2013). This goal is clearly served by both inductive and deductive perspectives. That said, we believe there is great and untapped potential for big data analytics to play a more significant role in efforts to develop and test theory in the psychological sciences than we have seen thus far. There are many examples in which big data analytics have demonstrated their unique power to extract intriguing signals from noisy data, but efforts to guide and situate this knowledge in the broader context of previous theory often occur in a more retrospective, abductive manner or not at all. Leveraging the strengths of computational science methods to generate and to evaluate theory would greatly improve the capacity for a robust big data science. One area where we envision particularly exciting potential is the use of big data techniques for advancing theory on the dynamic processes that unfold over time within persons and at other levels of analysis (e.g., dyads, networks, teams, organizations; Braun & Kuljanin, 2015; Kozlowski et al., 2013; Lazer et al., 2009; see Kennedy & McComb, 2014; and Kozlowski, Chao, Chang, & Fernandez, 2015, for examples at the team level).

In sum, creating and sustaining a robust scientific field of inquiry is facilitated when its contributors and stakeholders share similar aspirational values (Grand, Rogelberg, Allen, et al., 2018). Given that big data analytics is not a field owned or developed by a particular discipline, the users and producers of big data research have a significant responsibility for ensuring that the knowledge generated through these methods is credible, reliable, and relevant. This is likely to be particularly important in the psychological sciences, where we suspect big data and computational social science techniques will be intriguing to many but actively pursued and well understood by only a small subset of researchers (Aiken & Hanges, 2015). As a result, the opportunities for self-correction, oversight, and peer evaluation—the traditional safeguards for ensuring scientific integrity—are likely more limited. Consequently, we next direct our attention to issues that researchers who are not working with big data frequently cite as threats to the reliability and credibility of science. We believe that when big data researchers in psychology attend to these issues, they increase the likelihood that their work will actively contribute to a more robust psychological science.

AVOIDING PITFALLS AND ENCOURAGING A ROBUST BIG DATA SCIENCE IN PSYCHOLOGY

Many stakeholders contribute to the reliability and credibility of any scientific field (Grand, Rogelberg, Allen, et al., 2018; National Academies of Sciences, Engineering, & Medicine, 2017). However, researchers arguably hold the most central role as the first-line producers, disseminators, reviewers, and consumers of a field's knowledge. We consider three concerns commonly discussed in the broader psychological research literature—HARKing, QRPs, and replicability or reproducibility—by describing how these concerns might manifest and offering suggestions for minimizing their proliferation in big data research.

Hypothesizing After Results Are Known (HARKing)

HARKing was originally characterized as adding or removing predictions from a research paper after the researcher is aware of the pattern of findings in collected data (Kerr, 1998). This conceptualization has expanded more broadly in recent years to encompass attempts to change or redevelop one's hypotheses or proposed theoretical rationale for hypotheses after seeing the results of statistical analyses. For example, a commonly described form of HARKing involves "cherry-picking" statistically significant results and then weaving together (post hoc) a convincing narrative in the introduction to a paper that implies such findings were predicted, were consistent with theoretical rationale, and can be packaged into a coherent whole (Banks et al., 2016; Hollenbeck & Wright, 2017).

HARKing has numerous negative consequences for a scientific discipline. Most notably, the practice can inflate the false positive rate of published findings by increasing the likelihood that the inferential conclusions and claims advanced in a paper are the result of chance or spurious relationships in a study's sample. To be clear, the issue with HARKing is not a statistical one— the presence of a significant relationship in a sample does not change based on whether it was predicted a priori. Rather, the concern stems from the philosophy and principles of logic from which the epistemological framework of scientific deduction is rooted. Hypothesis testing implies that a researcher believes a relationship should exist in the natural world on the basis of a theoretical rationale. A methodology is then devised and implemented to gather observations of this relationship and (often) to control or rule out alternative explanations. Finally, the observations are fit to an inferential (i.e., statistical) framework to evaluate the likelihood of the theoretical claim relative to other claims (e.g., null hypothesis significance testing, interpreting Bayes factors or Bayesian credibility intervals). This process maintains the logical consistency and underpinnings of deductive reasoning (i.e., theory → hypothesis → inference). In contrast, HARKing covertly reverses this process (i.e., inference → hypothesis → theory) and thus undermines the argumentative strength on which the support for an inferential conclusion and any associated theoretical considerations is derived.

Beyond the direct epistemological concerns for science, HARKing also has the potential for a number of indirect harms (Hollenbeck & Wright, 2017; Kerr, 1998). For example, HARKing can result in theories that do not offer viable causal explanations for relationships becoming entrenched in the science. As a result, a field could be misled and its explanatory foundations weakened as others use those spurious claims to generate and integrate new theory. Additionally, valuable researcher time and resources may be expended on efforts to replicate and evaluate the veracity of HARKed findings that emerged through chance variation in a sample. Although such replication efforts are warranted and are critical means of correcting such erroneous conclusions, they are regrettable in the case of HARKed results because the originating research knowingly advanced misguided claims. An even more extreme scenario can be envisioned if one considers that "supportive" results tend to be published more frequently than null results (Fanelli, 2010b, 2012; Ioannidis, 2005b). Thus, papers that end up reproducing HARKed findings—either purposefully or by chance—may be more likely to be published than those that do not, thus further embedding the erroneous inference in the literature.

Relevance and Recommendations for Big Data Research

Because big data analytics have a natural inclination toward quantitative empiricism, the underlying philosophy often encourages data mining—probing data for unplanned or unanticipated relationships—to generate insights post hoc. For example, a researcher might apply one or more unsupervised learning techniques to identify novel or previously unknown groupings in a data set, leverage various supervised learning techniques to identify potential predictors or covariates of cluster membership, and then produce an interpretation or explanatory rationale for notable relationships (i.e., "generate insight") while ignoring those that appear less promising. In many respects, this process closely resembles the much maligned practice of HARKing described previously—particularly if the big data researcher subsequently develops a conceptual narrative that neatly fits the particular clusters, predictors, and relationships observed in the data set and poses it in the introduction of a research paper as the theoretical foundation for the study.

The most critical recommendation for avoiding the pitfalls of HARKing in big data research is that researchers should clearly differentiate relationships that were anticipated a priori from substantive theory from relationships that were unanticipated, observed post hoc, and relationships for which the researchers had no explicit intention to infer the veracity of particular theoretical claims (see Hollenbeck & Wright, 2017, for similar conclusions in general psychological research). In cases where one intends to use big data methods or techniques in a deductive fashion to evaluate theory-driven hypotheses, the researcher should explicate the conceptual model and rationale for all hypotheses in the Introduction section of a paper and evaluate the degree of support for those theoretical claims in the subsequent Results and Discussion sections (similar to the format commonly used in the majority of published psychological research). In cases where one intends to use big data methodologies in an inductive fashion to explore, identify, and discover potential relationships in a data set, the researcher should communicate the decisions, choices, rationale, and accompanying justification for the ways in which data were gathered, processed, and analyzed in the Introduction and Method sections of the paper. The results and discussion sections should subsequently focus on interpreting the generative mechanisms, possible reasons for the observed findings, and the implications for developing new theoretical claims. Finally, in the (potentially more common) case in which one uses big data techniques to both deductively test hypotheses and inductively probe additional or alternative relationships, the researcher should clearly delineate these foci in the introduction, methods, and results portions of a paper. The inclusion of one or more sections dedicated to exploratory analysis and interpretation is recommended so that consumers and reviewers can easily identify these distinctions and apply the appropriate intellectual skepticism when interpreting and building on findings from the published work (Grand, Rogelberg, Banks, et al., 2018).

Questionable Research Practices

Although the scientific method and empirical research process are often described as highly standardized and systematic approaches to studying the natural world, anyone who has performed research recognizes that scientific research involves a series of judgment calls for which there are often no clearly defined rules or guidelines. For example, researchers decide how to measure and operationalize constructs; where, when, and how to sample participants; when to terminate data collection; how to treat outliers; and which (if any) control variables to include in an analysis. Simmons, Nelson, and Simonsohn (2011) characterized these choice points as "researcher degrees of freedom" and discussed the profound impact they can have on the outcomes and inferences drawn from a research project. Though researcher degrees of freedom open the door for a wide degree of variability in scientific practices, they are largely unavoidable and not inherently threats to the robustness of science (e.g., McGrath, 1982). However, they become clear causes for concern when researchers make such judgment calls in ways that present only favorable evidence for proposed claims or hypotheses. Decisions and associated actions of this nature are commonly referred to as questionable research practices (QRPs; cf. Banks et al., 2016).

It should be noted that all but the most egregious of QRPs (e.g., falsifying or fabricating data) are likely not motivated by malicious intent of a researcher to disseminate misinformation or misrepresent their data and claims. Simmons et al. (2011) intimated that participation in QRPs is more likely a result of ambiguity in how to resolve researcher degrees of freedom coupled with the researcher's optimism and hope of finding results that support the hypotheses. Others cite the influence of norms within academia (e.g., publish or perish) and the broader research enterprise (e.g., journal criteria that emphasize "novel" or "counterintuitive" findings) as relevant contributing factors (e.g., Anderson, 2007; Fanelli, 2010a; Rawat & Meena, 2014). Regardless of the cause, the negative implications of QRPs are clear and are similar to those described for HARKing (e.g., inflated false positive rate of published findings, erroneous inferential conclusions, ambiguous theoretical evidence). Potentially more insidious is the precedent that QRPs set for future methodological practices. Whereas HARKing encourages "creative storytelling" and the development of post hoc rationalizations for observed findings, engaging in QRPs additionally encourages playing with data and statistics until desired relationships are found.

Relevance and Recommendations for Big Data Research

Research utilizing big data methodologies is likely to be just as susceptible to QRPs as any other form of research. However, the specific ways in which they manifest may differ. Additionally, the techniques, standards, and affordances related to collecting large data sets (e.g., web scraping, trace data, wearable sensors) and the analytic practices used to model such data are still emerging and further contribute to uncertainties regarding how to resolve researcher degrees of freedom in big data applications.

With respect to data gathering and collection, *subsetting* (i.e., removing or focusing on specific observations from a data set on the basis of particular characteristics) and *fusing* (i.e., complementing data with other properties of the data source or observations from a secondary data source) are common practices in big data research (Braun & Kuljanin, 2015; Cheung & Jak, 2016; Hilbert, 2016). For example, suppose a researcher is interested in studying political echo chambers and predicts that the ideology of journalists' social media networks and the news content they produce are correlated (e.g., those who follow more liberal [conservative] Twitter accounts write more liberal [conservative] articles).[1] Upon gathering the initial data set of more than 500,000 articles from 1,000 journalists, the researcher finds that the results seem close to supporting the prediction, but there are a number of unusual observations (e.g., highly prolific authors, small number of Twitter follows). The researcher elects to remove those data points from the analysis and observes that the subsetted data set—which still includes roughly 300,000 articles from 750 journalists—brings the findings directly in line with the predictions.

---

[1]This example is based on a study by Wihbey, Coleman, Joseph, and Lazer (2017). We make no claims about the methodological practices or presence of potential QRPs in this work and use the research question explored by the authors only for pedagogical purposes.

The reduced data set is subsequently reported in the final research product with little discussion of outlier removal or its effects on the study interpretations. Alternatively, suppose the researcher finds that operationalizing the ideology of a person's social media networks using only Twitter data does not reveal the predicted trend. However, the hypothesis is supported when those data are combined with a data set tracking journalists' "likes" on Facebook posts about political events. The composite metric is subsequently used for the researchers' analyses and is the only one reported in the final research product. Although each decision seems innocuous and arguments defending those choices could be made, such decisions venture dangerously close to the territory of QRPs as they make it difficult to evaluate the generalizability (in the case of data subsetting) and validity (in the case of data fusion) of the final inferences faithfully.

Related QRPs can emerge in a variety of big data analytic techniques as well. For example, most machine learning techniques depend heavily on the quality of the training samples used to inform their prediction and classification routines (Oswald & Putka, 2015). Consequently, different sizes or compositions within one's holdout samples (i.e., samples set aside from the training and testing samples) could result in different patterns of results that could be knowingly or unknowingly leveraged to support particular claims. Additionally, many analyses contain parameters that can be tweaked to produce different results and thus represent additional researcher degrees of freedom. For example, determining the number of nodes, layers, and connections among nodes in artificial neural networks is described by some as more art than science and can result in different conclusions about predictor–criterion relationships (e.g., Jain, Mao, & Mohiuddin, 1996). Similarly, decision tree or random forest models can be adjusted to account for more global versus local optimization of predictors (Oswald & Putka, 2015). In both cases, the results produced under different configurations are no less correct than other parameterizations and can be explored to identify conditions under which particular inferences or conclusions are justifiable. Although we suspect that criteria or rules of thumb for such choices are likely to emerge as big data analyses continue to mature, a large majority of psychologists will not possess the requisite expertise to evaluate the significance of such choices (Aiken & Hanges, 2015), and detecting these potential QRPs will remain difficult.

In many respects, recommendations for limiting the impact and prevalence of QRPs in big data research are similar to those proposed for improving the robustness of more general psychological research. These suggestions largely revolve around improving the transparency with which researcher degrees of freedom are resolved and journal reporting standards that necessitate these discussions in published materials (e.g., Nosek et al., 2015; Simmons et al., 2011). We also encourage big data researchers to explore the use of preregistration and alternative publication mechanisms (e.g., registered reports, results-blind reviews; Cumming, 2014; Grand, Rogelberg, Banks, et al., 2018; Open Science Collaboration, 2015). Though it may be difficult to adapt big data research that is more inductive and exploratory in nature to these avenues, encouraging researchers to consider their measurement, data gathering, and analysis plans carefully and explicitly prior to collecting or observing any data should be beneficial. For example, explicitly declaring what, how much, and from where data will be collected can help prevent the introduction of QRPs once a study is underway. Any deviations from this plan can still be made without stifling creativity and innovation; the key is simply to be transparent, explaining where any deviations occur and why they are justifiable.

On a related note, we suggest big data researchers who use archival or scraped data adhere to Landers et al.'s (2016) recommendation to construct and refer to a data source theory throughout all aspects of their research. A data source theory describes the assumptions a researcher must make about a prospective data source to be able to extract meaningful inferences from it. For example, researchers make assumptions about what the available data represent (e.g., Do Facebook "likes" indicate agreement with or acknowledgment of the original content?), the individuals who have access to and are likely to participate in the data source (e.g., Is a website for seeking social support or sharing opinions?), and where or how data are structured (e.g., Is information located on private profile pages or in open forums?). These assumptions facilitate understanding of the context and provide useful information for determining construct validity (Boyd & Crawford, 2012; Braun & Kuljanin, 2015; Guzzo et al., 2015; Hilbert, 2016; Whelan & DuVernet, 2015). Data source theories can also be used to help elaborate why particular data collection or analytic strategies were not chosen or were deemed less desirable. In sum, the goal of practices to combat QRPs in big data research is to provide information that allows readers and reviewers to determine more accurately the extent to which a study's inferences hinge on the researcher's methodological and statistical decisions and to consider whether the conclusions change depending on how variables are operationalized.

Replicability and Reproducibility

As noted previously, many have expressed concerns over the replicability and reproducibility of research across the sciences in general and the psychological sciences in particular. Although the terms are often used interchangeably, replication and reproduction should be differentiated in discussions of robust science because they carry different implications for establishing confidence in scientific results (Bollen, Cacioppo, Kaplan, Krosnick, & Olds, 2015). Furthermore, efforts to examine replicability and reproducibility of scientific claims often rely on different methodologies and sources of evidence to judge. It is thus useful to distinguish between these concepts when considering their significance in big data applications.

Replicability is generally defined as the capacity to "duplicate the results of a prior study if the same procedures are followed but new data are collected" (Bollen et al., 2015, p. 4). In this sense, efforts to replicate research findings most often involve determining whether similar findings, conclusions, and interpretations presented in an existing study can be observed in a new study. However, Anderson and Maxwell (2016) noted that replication studies can serve many purposes; they highlighted methodological and analytical strategies and criteria for evaluating replication success. For example, a replication study could be carried out to infer whether an observed effect exists, in which case the replication researcher should attempt to conduct the exact analyses of the original study and evaluate whether the new finding is in the same direction and significant. Alternatively, a replication study could be performed to assess whether a finding is inconsistent with the original observation, in which case the researcher should rely on evaluating confidence intervals or effect size differences. Other researchers have debated the merits of and differences between direct replications (e.g., efforts to reach the same conclusion using identical procedures) and conceptual replications (e.g., efforts to reach the same conclusion using different procedures; Simons, 2014; Stroebe & Strack, 2014). Regardless of form, though, the focus of most replication efforts concerns establishing the generalizability of inferential claims (i.e., how much confidence should be placed in the veracity and robustness of an empirical conclusion or theoretical claim).

In contrast, *reproducibility* is usually defined as the capacity to "duplicate the results of a prior study using the same materials and procedures as were used by the original investigator" (Bollen et al., 2015, p. 3). Reproducing research findings thus typically involves determining whether the findings, conclusions, and interpretations presented in an existing study can be recreated using the materials, data, and analyses from the same study. Goodman, Fanelli, and Ioannidis (2016) expanded this definition to differentiate three considerations of reproducibility. The first, *methods reproducibility*, considers whether the procedures, steps, and choices used in the original study can be exactly repeated or reconstructed and is typically evaluated by the extent to which the data collection and measurement process, data processing, and analytical reporting are sufficiently detailed in a published product. Goodman et al. equated their second form of reproducibility, *results reproducibility*, with direct replication. However, this criterion can also represent the degree to which an independent researcher can use the same raw data to run the same statistical analysis and produce the same statistical result presented in a published research study (Bollen et al., 2015). Finally, *inferential reproducibility* describes whether the same interpretations of an original study can be reached under different assumptions about the data, statistical models used, or evaluative criteria. In sum, the primary focus of reproducibility evaluations tends to concern the internal validity of the procedures used to generate inferential claims (i.e., can the methodological steps be determined, are they robust to different researcher decisions, and do they lead to the stated conclusions).

Relevance and Recommendations for Big Data Research

Although both replicability and reproducibility provide value for establishing the robustness of scientific research, they also offer unique costs and benefits that hold important implications for big data researchers. Many scientists acknowledge that direct replication of results is the definitive standard and that reproduction of results is a minimal standard for establishing the veracity of scientific claims (e.g., Bollen et al., 2015; Peng, 2011; Sandve, Nekrutenko, Taylor, & Hovig, 2013; Simons, 2014). However, replication efforts are usually much more time and resource intensive because they require a researcher to acquire new data sources that are equated with the original study on as many methodological factors as possible (e.g., operationalization and measurement of critical constructs, sample and contextual characteristics). This demand may render direct replication of big data research infeasible at best, near impossible at worst. Further, some data scientists have argued that direct replication efforts may be antithetical to the inherent strengths and uses that big data techniques offer for generating unique insights (e.g., Drummond, 2009).

Though efforts to directly replicate big data research face a litany of unique and difficult complications, we believe that big data researchers can take important actions toward this end. Specifically, we recommend that big data researchers participate in data sharing and open science practices to facilitate cumulative verification of results. As Anderson and Maxwell (2016) noted, the goals of replication can be much broader than attempts to conclude whether the findings from a particular study hold. Instead, replication efforts can contribute to the broader goal of improving the veracity and degree of confidence a field should place in generated knowledge (Grand, Rogelberg, Allen, et al., 2018). Poldrack and Gorgolewski (2014) summarized how this philosophy is being adopted by a growing number of neuroscientists and the subsequent development of open access repositories for sharing neural imaging data. As more researchers contribute to these repositories—the majority of whom are not attempting to replicate a particular study directly but have gathered observations of relevant phenomena—the capacity to evaluate and verify brain activation differences among healthy controls and individuals with clinical diagnoses (in a true or quasi-Bayesian manner) has improved. We suspect that the construction, maintenance, and regulation of such repositories will be idiosyncratic for some time as more individuals begin to dabble in big data techniques. However, good models (such as those cited by Poldrack & Gorgolewski, 2014) and first principles for how to manage and grow these repositories are becoming available and are expected to improve in the coming years.

Though not without its own challenges, improving the methods, results, and inferential reproducibility of big data research appears to be a more attainable and oft discussed goal by big data researchers. The most common recommendation discussed for achieving this standard involves improving the documentation, disclosure, and dissemination of the procedures used in the collection, processing, and analysis of big data research. For example, Sandve and colleagues (2013) offered 10 rules for improving the reproducibility of computational science, with suggestions ranging from maintaining accurate version control of scripts and analytical software to keeping records of how results were produced from start to finish. Peng (2011) also described a useful heuristic, the *reproducibility spectrum,* that provides authors, reviewers, and editors a classification system for characterizing and suggesting ways to enhance the reproducibility of published research products. At the lowest end of this spectrum is the basic journal article in which methods and analyses are described in the manuscript text, appendices, and other supplemental documents. From there, reproducibility can be increasingly improved by providing (a) all computer code used to process, analyze, and produce data; (b) all code plus all the raw data used in the reported analyses; and (c) fully executable code and data that link directly to the conclusions and inferences in the manuscript. We also recommend that demonstrating or including the means to evaluate more readily the degree to which inferences do not change when alternative analytic parameters are applied as part of submitted code would make a useful and positive contribution to the reproducibility of big data research.

CONCLUSION

The use and potential of big data and computational methodologies for furthering psychological research on human affect, behavior, cognition, and relationships is both thought provoking and energizing. The impetus of this chapter was consideration of what big data and computational social scientists could do to improve the likelihood that big data research meets emerging criteria for robust and reliable psychological science. In many ways, it is serendipitous that interest in big data techniques has coincided with the most recent surge of calls to action for safeguarding the credibility and trustworthiness of scientific research. The psychological sciences have taken their share of bumps and bruises in this domain. However, new norms, standards of practice, and tools for countering potential threats to the robustness of psychological research are emerging more rapidly than ever before and are incrementally changing how research is performed, reviewed, and disseminated. We believe these developments are equally applicable and critical to the burgeoning areas of computational social science, and we hope that conversations regarding how to promote robust and reliable big data research in psychology continue to unfold.

REFERENCES

Aiken, J. R., & Hanges, P. J. (2015). Teach an I-O to fish: Integrating data science into I-O graduate education. *Industrial and Organizational Psychology: Perspectives on Science and Practice, 8,* 539–544. http://dx.doi.org/10.1017/iop.2015.80

Anderson, C. J., Bahník, Š., Barnett-Cowan, M., Bosco, F. A., Chandler, J., Chartier, C. R., . . . Zuni, K. (2016). Response to Comment on "Estimating the reproducibility of psychological science." *Science, 351,* 1037–1039. http://dx.doi.org/10.1126/science.aad9163

Anderson, G. (2007). *Experiences in academic governance and decision-making of full-time nontenure track faculty in communications fields* (Doctoral dissertation). Retrieved from http://digitallibrary.usc.edu/cdm/ref/collection/p15799coll127/id/550411

Anderson, S. F., & Maxwell, S. E. (2016). There's more than one way to conduct a replication study: Beyond statistical significance. *Psychological Methods, 21*, 1–12. http://dx.doi.org/10.1037/met0000051

Banks, G. C., O'Boyle, E. H., Jr., Pollack, J. M., White, C. D., Batchelor, J. H., Whelpley, C. E., . . . Adkins, C. L. (2016). Questions about questionable research practices in field of management: A guest commentary. *Journal of Management, 42*, 5–20. http://dx.doi.org/10.1177/0149206315619011

Bollen, K., Cacioppo, J. T., Kaplan, R. M., Krosnick, J. A., & Olds, J. L. (2015). *Social, behavioral, and economic sciences perspectives on robust and reliable science*. Arlington, VA: National Science Foundation.

Boyd, D., & Crawford, K. (2012). Critical questions for big data. *Information, Communication & Society, 15*, 662–679. http://dx.doi.org/10.1080/1369118X.2012.678878

Braun, M. T., & Kuljanin, G. (2015). Big data and the challenge of construct validity. *Industrial and Organizational Psychology: Perspectives on Science and Practice, 8*, 521–527. http://dx.doi.org/10.1017/iop.2015.77

Cai, L., & Zhu, Y. (2015). The challenges of data quality and data quality assessment in the big data era. *Data Science Journal, 14*, 2–10. http://dx.doi.org/10.5334/dsj-2015-002

Camerer, C. F., Dreber, A., Holzmeister, F., Ho, T. H., Huber, J., Johannesson, M., . . . Wu, H. (2018). Evaluating the replicability of social science experiments in *Nature* and *Science* between 2010 and 2015. *Nature Human Behaviour, 2*, 637–644. http://dx.doi.org/10.1038/s41562-018-0399-z

Cheung, M. W., & Jak, S. (2016). Analyzing big data in psychology: A split/analyze/meta-analyze approach. *Frontiers in Psychology, 7*, 738. http://dx.doi.org/10.3389/fpsyg.2016.00738

Cumming, G. (2014). The new statistics: Why and how. *Psychological Science, 25*(1), 7–29. http://dx.doi.org/10.1177/0956797613504966

Drummond, C. (2009). Replicability is not reproducibility: Nor is it good science. In L. Bottou & M. Littman (Eds.), *Proceedings of the 26th International Conference on Machine Learning*, Montreal, CA. Retrieved from http://cogprints.org/7691/7/ICMLws09.pdf

Edwards, J. R., & Berry, J. W. (2010). The presence of something or the absence of nothing: Increasing theoretical precision in management research. *Organizational Research Methods, 13*, 668–689. http://dx.doi.org/10.1177/1094428110380467

Fanelli, D. (2009). How many scientists fabricate and falsify research? A systematic review and meta-analysis of survey data. *PLoS One, 4*, e5738. http://dx.doi.org/10.1371/journal.pone.0005738

Fanelli, D. (2010a). Do pressures to publish increase scientists' bias? An empirical support from US states data. *PLoS One, 5*, e10271. http://dx.doi.org/10.1371/journal.pone.0010271

Fanelli, D. (2010b). "Positive" results increase down the Hierarchy of the Sciences. *PLoS One, 5*, e10068. http://dx.doi.org/10.1371/journal.pone.0010068

Fanelli, D. (2012). Negative results are disappearing from most disciplines and countries. *Scientometrics, 90*, 891–904. http://dx.doi.org/10.1007/s11192-011-0494-7

Gilbert, D. T., King, G., Pettigrew, S., & Wilson, T. D. (2016). Comment on "Estimating the reproducibility of psychological science." *Science, 351*, 1037b.

Goodman, S. N., Fanelli, D., & Ioannidis, J. P. A. (2016). What does research reproducibility mean? *Science Translational Medicine, 8*(341), ps12.

Grand, J. A., Rogelberg, S. G., Allen, T. D., Landis, R. S., Reynolds, D., Scott, J. C., . . . Truxillo, D. M. (2018). A systems-based approach to fostering robust science in industrial–organizational psychology. *Industrial and Organizational Psychology: Perspectives on Science and Practice, 11*, 4–42. http://dx.doi.org/10.1017/iop.2017.55

Grand, J. A., Rogelberg, S. G., Banks, G. C., Landis, R. S., & Tonidandel, S. (2018). From outcome to process focus: Fostering a more robust psychological science through registered reports and results-blind reviewing. *Perspectives on Psychological Science, 13*, 448–456. http://dx.doi.org/10.1177/1745691618767883

Grote, G. (2017). There is hope for better science. *European Journal of Work and Organizational Psychology, 26*, 1–3. http://dx.doi.org/10.1080/1359432X.2016.1198321

Guzzo, R. A., Fink, A. A., King, E., Tonidandel, S., & Landis, R. S. (2015). Big data recommendations for industrial–organizational psychology. *Industrial and Organizational Psychology: Perspectives on Science and Practice, 8*, 491–508. http://dx.doi.org/10.1017/iop.2015.40

Hilbert, M. (2016). Big data for development: A review of promises and challenges. *Development Policy Review, 34*, 135–174. http://dx.doi.org/10.1111/dpr.12142

Hollenbeck, J. R., & Wright, P. M. (2017). HARKing, sharking, and tharking: Making the case for post hoc analysis of scientific data. *Journal of Management, 43*(1), 5–18.

Ioannidis, J. P. A. (2005a). Contradicted and initially stronger effects in highly cited clinical research. *JAMA, 294*, 218–228. http://dx.doi.org/10.1001/jama.294.2.218

Ioannidis, J. P. A. (2005b). Why most published research findings are false. *PLoS Medicine, 2*, 0696–0701.

Jain, A. K., Mao, J., & Mohiuddin, K. M. (1996). Artificial neural networks: A tutorial. *Computer, 29*, 31–44. http://dx.doi.org/10.1109/2.485891

Kennedy, D. M., & McComb, S. A. (2014). When teams shift among processes: Insights from simulation and optimization. *Journal of Applied Psychology, 99*, 784–815. http://dx.doi.org/10.1037/a0037339

Kerr, N. L. (1998). HARKing: Hypothesizing after the results are known. *Personality and Social Psychology Review, 2*, 196–217.

Kim, G. H., Trimi, S., & Chung, J. H. (2014). Big data applications in the government sector. *Communications of the ACM, 57*, 78–85. http://dx.doi.org/10.1145/2500873

Klein, R. A., Ratliff, K. A., Vianello, M., Adams, R. B., Jr., Bahník, Š., Bernstein, M. J., . . . Nosek, B. A. (2014). Investigating variation in replicability. *Social Psychology, 45*, 142–152. http://dx.doi.org/10.1027/1864-9335/a000178

Kozlowski, S. W. J., Chao, G. T., Chang, C.-H., & Fernandez, R. (2015). Team dynamics: Using "big data" to advance the science of team effectiveness. In S. Tonidandel, E. King, & J. Cortina (Eds.), *Big data at work: The data science revolution and organizational psychology* (pp. 272–309). New York, NY: Routledge.

Kozlowski, S. W. J., Chao, G. T., Grand, J. A., Braun, M. T., & Kuljanin, G. (2013). Advancing multilevel research design: Capturing the dynamics of emergence. *Organizational Research Methods, 16*, 581–615. http://dx.doi.org/10.1177/1094428113493119

Landers, R. N., Brusso, R. C., Cavanaugh, K. J., & Collmus, A. B. (2016). A primer on theory-driven web scraping: Automatic extraction of big data from the Internet for use in psychological research. *Psychological Methods, 21*, 475–492. http://dx.doi.org/10.1037/met0000081

Lazer, D., Kennedy, R., King, G., & Vespignani, A. (2014). The parable of Google Flu: Traps in big data analysis. *Science, 343*, 1203–1205. http://dx.doi.org/10.1126/science.1248506

Lazer, D., Pentland, A. S., Adamic, L., Aral, S., Barabasi, A. L., Brewer, D., . . . Jebara, T. (2009). Life in the network: The coming age of computational social science. *Science, 323*, 721–723. http://dx.doi.org/10.1126/science.1167742

Leetaru, K. (2017). A case study in big data and the replication crisis. *Forbes*. Retrieved from https://www.forbes.com/sites/kalevleetaru/2017/09/01/a-case-study-in-big-data-and-the-replication-crisis/#281f1c045105

Marcus, E. (2014). Credibility and reproducibility. *Cell, 159*, 965–966. http://dx.doi.org/10.1016/j.cell.2014.11.016

McGrath, J. E. (1982). Dilemmatics: The study of research choices and dilemmas. In J. E. McGrath, J. Martin, & R. A. Kulka (Eds.), *Judgment calls in research* (pp. 69–102). Beverly Hills, CA: Sage.

National Academies of Sciences, Engineering, & Medicine. (2017). *Fostering integrity in research*. Washington, DC: The National Academies Press.

Nosek, B. A., Alter, G., Banks, G. C., Borsboom, D., Bowman, S. D., Breckler, S. J., . . . Yarkoni, T. (2015). Promoting an open research culture. *Science, 348*, 1422–1425. http://dx.doi.org/10.1126/science.aab2374

Open Science Collaboration. (2015). Estimating the reproducibility of psychological science. *Science, 349*, aac4716. http://dx.doi.org/10.1126/science.aac4716

Oswald, F. L., & Putka, D. J. (2015). Statistical methods for big data: A scenic tour. In S. Tonidandel, E. King, & J. Cortina (Eds.), *Big data at work: The data science revolution and organizational psychology* (pp. 57–77). New York, NY: Routledge.

Peng, R. D. (2011). Reproducible research in computational science. *Science, 334*, 1226–1227. http://dx.doi.org/10.1126/science.1213847

Poldrack, R. A., & Gorgolewski, K. J. (2014). Making big data open: Data sharing in neuroimaging. *Nature Neuroscience, 17*, 1510–1517. http://dx.doi.org/10.1038/nn.3818

Rawat, S., & Meena, S. (2014). Publish or perish: Where are we heading? *Journal of Research in Medical Sciences, 19*, 87–89.

Rubin, M. B. (2011). Fraud in organic chemistry. *Chemistry in New Zealand, 78*, 128–132.

Ryan, J., & Herleman, H. (2015). A big data platform for workforce analytics. In S. Tonidandel, E. King, & J. Cortina (Eds.), *Big data at work: The data science revolution and organizational psychology* (pp. 19–42). New York, NY: Routledge.

Sandve, G. K., Nekrutenko, A., Taylor, J., & Hovig, E. (2013). Ten simple rules for reproducible computational research. *PLoS Computational Biology, 9*, e1003285. http://dx.doi.org/10.1371/journal.pcbi.1003285

Simmons, J. P., Nelson, L. D., & Simonsohn, U. (2011). False-positive psychology: Undisclosed flexibility in data collection and analysis allows presenting anything as significant. *Psychological Science, 22*, 1359–1366. http://dx.doi.org/10.1177/0956797611417632

Simons, D. J. (2014). The value of direct replication. *Perspectives on Psychological Science, 9*, 76–80. http://dx.doi.org/10.1177/1745691613514755

Stroebe, W., & Strack, F. (2014). The alleged crisis and the illusion of exact replication. *Perspectives on Psychological Science, 9*, 59–71. http://dx.doi.org/10.1177/1745691613514450

Whelan, T. J., & DuVernet, A. M. (2015). The big duplicity of big data. *Industrial and Organizational Psychology: Perspectives on Science and Practice, 8*, 509–515. http://dx.doi.org/10.1017/iop.2015.75

Wihbey, J., Coleman, T. D., Joseph, K., & Lazer, D. (2017). Exploring the ideological nature of journalists' social networks on Twitter and associations with news story content. *ArXiv*, abs/1708.06727.

17

Privacy and Cybersecurity Challenges, Opportunities, and Recommendations

Personnel Selection in an Era of Online Application Systems and Big Data

Talya N. Bauer, Donald M. Truxillo, Mark P. Jones, and Grant Brady

Data in the 21st Century is like Oil in the 18th Century: an immensely untapped valuable asset. Like oil, for those who see Data's fundamental value and learn to extract and use it there will be huge rewards.

—JORIS TOONDERS, *WIRED* (2014)

As with the oil industry, there are potential societal opportunities and associated costs to be paid for generating and extracting data assets. As you read this chapter, thousands—if not millions—of people are updating their social media profiles while "web crawlers" continually search the Internet to analyze and compile personal information into vast data sets (Bauer, Erdogan, Caughlin, & Truxillo, 2018). The resulting collection of massive amounts data can be useful for predictive purposes, often referred to as *big data*, which is characterized as being high in volume, velocity, and variety. Such data may also vary a great deal in terms of its accuracy or veracity. This burgeoning field of analytics poses extraordinary opportunities for individuals and organizations

This work is based in part on funding from the SHRM Foundation, SIOP Foundation, and National Science Foundation EAGER Grant No. 1544535 (Cyber-security and Social Sciences) to Donald M. Truxillo (PI) and Mark P. Jones and Talya N. Bauer (Co-PIs). During much of the funded research referenced in this paper, Donald M. Truxillo was in the Department of Psychology, Portland State University. He is now at the Kemmy Business School, University of Limerick. The author team wishes to thank Autumn Krauss, Michael Baysinger, Alexa Garcia, and Sylvia Lisman-Broetje for their help with our work in this area.

http://dx.doi.org/10.1037/0000193-018
Big Data in Psychological Research, S. E. Woo, L. Tay, and R. W. Proctor (Editors)
Copyright © 2020 by the American Psychological Association. All rights reserved.

but is accompanied by concerning new realities and new risks—especially for users in terms of privacy concerns—that have been brought to light by numerous recent incidents of cyberattacks, data breaches, and/or blatant misuses of private information. These incidents include the theft of 117 million customer passwords at LinkedIn; the exposure of credit card information of 70 million Target customers; and the discovery that hackers had managed to gain access to the names, Social Security numbers, and dates of birth of 26.5 million veterans through the Veterans Administration (Abrams, 2017; Hackett, 2016; Vijayan, 2007).

With the surge in data being collected, it has never been easier to monitor, track, and identify individuals around the world. This explosion of online data collection and storage, and its accompanying risks, now applies to the job application process as well. For example, in 2018 over 3,000 cases of recruiting scams, which prey on job seekers applying to online job postings, were filed with the Better Business Bureau (Porter, 2018). Despite these risks, the majority of job seekers are now using online job applications when searching for a new position, with 79% reporting that they used online information during their most recent job search (Smith, 2015). When we apply to jobs online, our personal information is transported, stored, and backed up on servers, potentially removing our control over our personal information. Organizations use social media profiles to recruit applicants and infer characteristics about individuals who apply for open positions (Caers & Castelyns, 2011; Mulvey, Esen, & Coombs, 2016; Perrin, 2015) or to identify individuals with a skill set the company is searching for, often without the knowledge of the applicants themselves. Taken together, these rapid advances mean that maintaining the privacy of job applicants and employees in this "brave new world" is a significant challenge.

Although technological advances and the use of big data can be concerning, they have also facilitated remarkable advances for job applicants, employees, and employers. Instead of paper application forms and in-person interviews, many, if not most, organizations now rely on web-based systems to collect personal details from prospective employees and in many cases to complete online assessments that evaluate job suitability. Information collected through these online mechanisms is then leveraged to make human resource (HR) decisions more data driven. Further, the practice of web crawling allows recruiters to identify and proactively reach out to candidates who may not be aware of relevant job opportunities. This procedure benefits organizations by identifying highly qualified professionals while conveniently presenting people with employment opportunities for which they may not have applied.

Clearly, the collection and use of massive amounts of data brings about a host of new possibilities regarding personnel selection, but it also raises substantial privacy concerns. This chapter addresses these issues by providing an overview of the potential benefits of utilizing online job application systems in personnel selection; discussing major concerns about big data within the hiring context; and offering practical recommendations for job applicants, employers, developers, and policy makers to leverage big data while engaging in ethical practices that protect the privacy of personal data. The next section addresses potential benefits of these developments in the online selection context for a variety of stakeholders, starting with employers.

THE ONLINE SELECTION CONTEXT

Online Job Application Systems: Benefits for Employers

Online job application systems are attractive to employers because they can handle large numbers of applicants, automatically filtering and prioritizing candidates to match the needs of specific openings. The resulting selection processes are potentially faster and more efficient than those of a traditional hiring process, with substantial cost savings. Further, once an individual's data have been captured in an online system, they can be kept on file, establishing an applicant pool that can be accessed at any time and shared across multiple locations or branches, all of which may help to reduce the hiring time as new positions open up. An applicant's data can also be embedded into an applicant tracking system and into an employee tracking system if the applicant is hired. From an employer's perspective, avoiding a traditional, labor-intensive hiring process means that they have more time and resources to focus on their primary business goals.

In addition to information that is directly provided by applicants, *web crawlers*—which automatically find and organize information from publicly accessible websites, such as details about people with desirable skills and abilities—are increasingly being used to expand and monetize valuable information and sell it to organizations in need of talent (Landers, Brusso, Cavanaugh, & Collmus, 2016; Tonidandel, King, & Cortina, 2018). While not data "breaches" in a classical sense, these data collection methods lead to the creation of profiles of individuals based on news articles, social media profiles, company web pages, and a host of other online sources without the individuals' awareness of this use of their online data. This aggregated information can be used for good reasons. For example, it can be particularly helpful for sourcing "passive" job applicants—workers who may be interested in finding a new job but are not actively looking. These methods provide an avenue for organizations to identify candidates with an appropriate skill set who are likely to fit with their organizational values and to begin recruiting them, potentially with the advantage of knowing their hobbies, interests, and personal values.

In addition, employers wishing to reduce bias and achieve particular recruitment goals through their job postings and job descriptions can take advantage of big data through the use of machine learning, making adjustments to their recruitment materials to better achieve recruitment goals. For example, job descriptions are often reused as positions reopen, without a critical analysis of how that posting may influence applicants' perceptions of the job posting. The health care company Johnson & Johnson found their job postings could be substantially improved and has been using the writing platform Textio to scan its job postings and job descriptions for word usage that may not feel welcoming to some candidates, particularly those who do not fit the stereotypes of a given position (Klahre, 2017). As an example, a job description for a leadership position that includes more masculine descriptors may unintentionally deter women from applying for the position, stifling diversity-related efforts and potentially driving top talent out of the applicant pool. As such, this example highlights an opportunity for using big data techniques to broaden the perceived accessibility of job postings to a wider, more diverse range of applicants.

Big data is also being used to evaluate applicants. Machine learning algorithms can be used to "read" and evaluate résumés, form personality profiles based on social media pages, and potentially reduce bias while retaining their predictive validity (Feldman, Friedler, Moeller, Scheidegger, & Venkatasubramanian, 2015). However, there are concerns that these big data algorithms can be contaminated with human biases (Caliskan, Bryson, & Narayanan, 2017) and that these algorithms could then be used as justification for hiring practices that may be biased. Amazon recently shuttered a program aimed at developing a machine learning algorithm for this exact reason—the algorithm was biased against female applicants for software engineer positions (Dastin, 2018). Further, there are concerns that the information presented in résumés by applicants is not consistent and may not even be accurate. Despite these challenges, as organizations continue to develop strategies for interpreting the data they collect and identify ways it can improve various organizational functions, big data will play a significant role in this process for years to come.

Online Job Application Systems: Benefits for Applicants

Prospective employees can also benefit from the automated job search and application functionality of online hiring systems. That is, technology has made applying for jobs more convenient, more efficient, and less dependent on location. Social media engagement, which is a significant source of information for some web crawlers, provides an excellent opportunity for applicants to increase their visibility and marketability. Candidates can maintain profiles on social media and professional networking sites in ways that likely improve their ratings according to these machine learning techniques. Furthermore, big data tools continually search and store potential employee information, whether the person has applied or not. As such, a candidate can be notified of an opening without taking any direct action on their part or can set up job alerts that notify them when jobs fitting a given set of criteria are added to the database.

Big data also has the potential to create better person–job and person–organization fits. By taking the information stored about applicants and matching it to open positions, the fit between an individual's skills, interests, and abilities and the demands of the job should be improved, at least in theory. Improving person–job and person–organization fits therefore benefits the employee through increased job satisfaction and reduced strain (Kristof-Brown, Zimmerman, & Johnson, 2005). Thus, big data has the potential to provide an individual with benefits beyond the work environment itself.

At this point, it should be clear that big data is not going away, and it is not a fad or fleeting trend. It is fundamentally changing how organizations make decisions. The question remains, what can be done to help leverage big data in ways that are ethical and respectful of individuals' rights to privacy of their personal information during selection? The following section approaches issues of big data and privacy concerns from two points of view: first, a human-centered perspective regarding privacy concerns; and second, a technical perspective about the systems used to collect, store, and analyze applicant data.

DATA PRIVACY AND SECURITY CONCERNS FOR ONLINE APPLICATION SYSTEMS

Privacy concerns surrounding the collection and storage of sensitive information, and the need to protect that information from unauthorized use, are a direct source of tension in online application systems. The use of online systems exposes both applicants and employers to new risks, and these risks must be identified, understood, and managed in appropriate ways.

Human-Centered Perspectives on Privacy and Security

In this section, we focus specifically on potential interactions between online application systems and applicant concerns about *privacy*. These concerns focus on general privacy issues, the use of information collected from social media, and the use of big data algorithms for HR decisions.

Nobody who applies for work using an online system will be surprised to find that they are required to provide personal details, such as an address and other contact information; after all, how would an employer be able to provide a job offer or request an interview without such details? Similarly, at some point in the process, an applicant will likely be asked to provide additional information, such as their Social Security number (as evidence of authorization to work) or details of education, previous pay, and past work history. Job seekers have a strong motivation to share sensitive personal information like this, and to ensure it is accurate, especially when they recognize it as a necessary step toward employment. Of course, applicants have shared such private information with employers for decades. However, the risks associated with sharing information through an online application portal are far greater than when it is shared via paper, as was the case throughout most of the 20th century. Those who have seen media coverage about data breaches, third-party data sharing, and identity theft are right to feel concerned about the security of their data. Moreover, those concerned about being discriminated against based on demographic characteristics may also feel uncomfortable with these requirements and may be eager for assurances that their information will be transmitted and stored securely, and also that it will be used solely for the intended purpose.

Although applicants are accustomed to sharing personal information during the application process, how much is too much? What if an employer requests an applicant's social media login information? Or asks to pull an applicant's credit report? Research shows that individuals generally do not appreciate having personal information from their social media pages used in selection decisions (Nikolaou, Bauer, & Truxillo, 2015; Stoughton, Thompson, & Meade, 2015). Use of this information, even when it is publicly available, may be considered a violation of privacy by individuals. In turn, these privacy concerns are related to a host of negative outcomes in terms of how individuals view the application process itself, as well as organizations using these practices (Bauer et al., 2006). For example, individuals may be more likely to litigate against a company, rate the company as less attractive, and be less likely to rate an application process as fair when personal information from social media pages is used in the assessment of candidates. After all, social media profiles contain an abundance of information that is not job relevant (e.g., race, religion, gender, age, marital status, number of children) but could be used to discriminate against individuals. Applicants perceive the inappropriate use of this information as an important privacy concern. Indeed, numerous scholars have argued that organizations should be cautious about using information from social media profiles to make selection decisions due to the risk of potential legal action (Nikolaou et al., 2015; Roth, Bobko, Van Iddekinge, & Thatcher, 2016; Van Iddekinge, Lanivich, Roth, & Junco, 2016).

Algorithms that incorporate big data techniques also pose privacy concerns for individuals. For example, if historical data from an organization is used to create an algorithm, the algorithm itself may inherit many of the same decision-making characteristics, including biases, as those held by the human raters (Barocas & Selbst, 2016; Caliskan et al., 2017). On the other hand, researchers have demonstrated the ability to remove bias against certain groups (e.g., women, ethnic minorities) using algorithms, but they also acknowledge that the process to remove bias is similar to processes deemed illegal in previous court rulings (Feldman et al., 2015). The substantial concerns with using these algorithm-based techniques have even led to adoption of the "right to explanation" within the General Data Protection Regulation (GDPR) of the European Union, which provides individuals rated by these algorithms with the right to an explanation about how the decision was made (Politou, Alepis, & Patsakis, 2018; Tankard, 2016).

For big data to be leveraged and its utility to be fully realized, large data sources are needed to develop predictive algorithms. That is, without having large sources of data available, algorithms cannot reasonably be expected to identify useful trends or patterns in the data. Take, for example, machine learning to evaluate résumés. To validate such an assessment, the algorithm may "read" the résumés of hundreds of successful employees and from that develop an algorithm that can be used to identify applicants that have similar qualities. To modify the algorithm, additional data would be needed, and these accumulating sources of information are often stored in centralized systems online.

One critical drawback to storing large sources of data in a centralized online location is that they are attractive targets for hackers. In addition, anyone with access to those databases, such as a disgruntled employee or coworker, could use that data in nefarious ways. Combined with concerns about privacy and the inappropriate use of personal information (e.g., demographic information) for selection purposes, failure to properly protect applicant information could lead to a data breach that inflicts serious damage on individuals. That is, applicants, as well as employees and customers, are put at risk of having their identity stolen by relying on organizations to properly store their personal information. These types of data breaches could broadly damage an employer's brand and reputation among consumers and potential job applicants, expose them to expensive legal challenges or other punitive actions, and thus impede an employer's ability to hire new workers (cf. McCarthy et al., 2017). Furthermore, there is the distinct possibility that well-qualified candidates would be deterred from applying for a position if the employer is unable to provide credible guarantees that steps have been taken to protect applicant data. As such, it is essential that employers have not only a commitment to ethical and transparent practices, but also the technical know-how, systems, and tools to ensure personal information is protected.

Technical Mechanisms for Protecting Data

The general tasks and challenges of protecting electronic data from unauthorized access are often referred to as *cybersecurity* and have motivated the development of numerous technologies, algorithms, and protocols for securing computer systems. At a high level, the broad discipline of cybersecurity is often presented as a combination (e.g., Bishop, 2002) of three primary concerns—confidentiality, integrity, and availability—that are conveniently remembered using the mnemonic "CIA":

- *Confidentiality* refers to the ability to protect information so that it can be seen and used only by authorized parties. *Encryption*, for example, is one of the most widely used technical mechanisms for providing confidentiality, allowing information to be encoded in a way that makes it practically impossible for somebody to read unless they know (or can guess) the associated key that was used to encrypt it. Technologies like this can be useful in the context of online application systems as a way to conceal applicant personal data, both when it is stored on servers and when it is transmitted between sites. However, the level of protection that is provided in practice depends critically on the strength of the encryption and on the extent to which passwords or access keys are themselves protected from unauthorized access. To address these concerns, it is common to introduce additional tools, such as password managers, multifactor authentication techniques, or hardware tokens that communicate via USB or near-field wireless connections. Each of these, if used properly, allows controlled access to data for legitimate users, while significantly increasing the barrier for unauthorized third parties.

- *Integrity* refers to the ability to trust that information provided by a source is legitimate and that it has not been modified when it is delivered to a recipient. In much the same way that handwritten signatures have been used as evidence of authorship on paper communications, modern computer systems often rely on cryptographic signatures (or "hashes"), which are a function of the document's contents and its author's identity, as an integrity mechanism. A recipient will be able to determine that a document has been modified, either by mistake or by some malicious action, if it does not have a matching signature. In an online application system, integrity is important in ensuring, for example, that applicant information is communicated accurately to the people who are involved in making hiring decisions.

- Finally, *availability* refers to the importance of ensuring that information and services are available for legitimate user access whenever they are needed. For example, "denial of service" is a common form of attack that attempts to compromise availability by overloading a website with a flood of invalid requests, thereby preventing or significantly degrading its intended use. In an online application system, availability is important to ensure that applicants are able to access and upload their information to the system, but also to ensure that those details can be accessed by the appropriate staff members in the hiring company.

These descriptions demonstrate, unsurprisingly, that all aspects of computer security are important in the design and operation of online application systems. In this chapter, however, we focus primarily on confidentiality and, more specifically, on *privacy*, which relates to the ability of users to control the ways in which their information is used or further distributed. For example, "Privacy can be defined in terms of having control over the extent, timing, and circumstances of sharing oneself (physically, behaviorally, or intellectually) with others" (Hicks, 2004, quoting from *IRB Guidebook*, United States Department of Health and Human Services Office for Human Research Protections, 1993).

As an example of privacy considerations, social media websites often provide users with features to limit the visibility of their posts or to delete their account completely. From a technical standpoint, these features provide the opportunity for individuals to protect their information, but doing so generally requires an uncommon level of active participation on the part of the user. And, unfortunately, even for people who do use these features, it can be difficult to predict the privacy implications of their actions online. In part, this is an inevitable result of the large, complex, and constantly changing systems that power modern websites. But the resulting misunderstandings can lead to compromised systems and unintended sharing by job applicants. Although many sites link to an explicit privacy policy—which could potentially guide users in making more informed choices in this area—users often do not read these documents because they are long and written in complex legal language. Further, organizations often sell personal information to other sources, including advertisers and partner sites, and they are incentivized to keep these lines of data sharing open.

THE GAP IN USER UNDERSTANDING OF CYBERSECURITY THREATS

Although researchers argue that policy-level changes need to be made to better protect users online, as noted, other concerns are that end users of online technology may not understand the cybersecurity threats they may face or be uncertain about how much they should care about the privacy of their information (Acquisti, Brandimarte, & Loewenstein, 2015). For example, Pfleeger and Caputo (2012) argued that technological advances alone are unsuited to improve cybersecurity and that human behavior needs to be integrated, especially teaching people how to use computer systems securely and responsibly. These authors presented "next steps" to aid the integration of technological and behavioral components into cybersecurity, including organizing workshops to bring together different disciplines, conducting empirical evaluations, and building a repository of findings.

As evidence of this knowledge-gap problem, Ion, Reeder, and Consolvo (2015) compared the online security behavior of experts and nonexperts. They found that while both groups considered the use of strong and unique passwords to be highly important, their responses differed in important ways. Experts stated the importance of updating software often, using a password manager, and using two-factor authentication. Nonexperts, on the other hand, relied on antivirus software, visiting only trusted websites, and changing passwords often. The authors concluded that three practices could be recommended for more widespread use by nonexperts: installing updates, using a password manager, and using two-factor authentication. However, getting end users to adopt these safer practices can be challenging in the trade-off between convenience and security. Indeed, Ion et al. found that many nonexperts expressed distrust in password managers and were concerned that software updates might install malware along with the actual software. Thus, from a technical standpoint, there are tools available that would greatly improve security of personal information, but this knowledge gap leads to only a small percentage of users actually using these tools to protect their information.

Data from a Pew Research Center study of 461 American adults suggest that Americans are neither entirely open nor entirely opposed to sharing some personal information if they perceive a potential benefit (Chong, Xiong, & Proctor, 2018; Rainie & Duggan, 2016), and they are also influenced by how such information is primed/presented to them (e.g., Chong, Ge, Li, & Proctor, 2018). Thus, assessment by applicants depends predominantly on the conditions of the offer, their trust in the collection and storage of the data, and what the aftermath of data sharing might look like (e.g., stolen identity, third-party selling, telemarketer calls). Researchers in this study encouraged the development and use of centralized update managers, comparable to those already used for mobile phone apps, to deliver security updates separately from those installing new features. In addition, the researchers recommended that more needs to be done to explain concepts such as password managers and two-factor authentication methods in a digestible way to non–tech-savvy users.

RECOMMENDATIONS AND FUTURE RESEARCH NEEDS

Practical Recommendations for Stakeholders

Based on our review of the literature on privacy concerns in online job applications and the use of big data, we provide the following recommendations for online job applicants, employers, developers of online job application tools, and policy makers. These sections are followed by recommendations for research.

Online Job Applicants

Applicants should be aware that the landscape of applying for jobs is changing rapidly and will continue to do so in the foreseeable future. This change brings substantial speed and convenience for applicants when applying for jobs, but also includes some significant trade-offs in terms of privacy and what information is shared with and stored by employers. For example, logging in to one's social media page as part of an online application process may help to speed up the process, but it can also give employers access to information that you may not have intended to share with them. Not only might employers use personal information about individuals (e.g., friends, hobbies, what they do in their private lives) when they make hiring decisions, but this personal data might also be inadvertently shared with others via a data breach on the part of the employers or their representatives charged with collecting and storing the data. Any job applicant should be conscious of the trade-off between convenience and privacy, deciding what information they would like potentially shared and safeguarding personal data that already exists online.

Several technical recommendations can be made for job applicants. When using an online job application portal, applicants should check that the site is secure (for example, by confirming the appearance of a padlock icon in their browser), use a complex password that is not shared with other sites (preferably in conjunction with a password manager), and take advantage of two-factor authentication when possible. Additionally, applicants should refrain from providing sensitive information, such as a Social Security number, prior to being offered a position. By being mindful of data being collected and the risks of sharing personal information in a big data environment, applicants can reduce the risk of having their information stolen, hacked, or used inappropriately or by parties that they had not intended to have access to their information. This is consistent with advice given by cybersecurity experts (Mele, 2018).

Employers

The use of online job applications and screening provides tremendous value to employers in terms of speed and convenience. With that, however, comes ethical and legal responsibilities to maintain the security of systems that collect and manage job applicant data. For example, although big data algorithms have shown promise in reducing adverse impact, we note that there are substantial, and untested, concerns regarding the legality of using algorithms that manipulate hiring data to remove adverse impact, which appears to be strikingly similar to the illegal practice of within-group norming. Thus, we caution employers to consider these legal implications before implementing the use of a complex algorithm that will influence staffing decisions.

The security of online applicant data is a source of significant ethical issues, but it also has ramifications for an employer's brand and reputation. Moreover, we caution employers about the use of job applicants' nonprofessional social media pages (e.g., Facebook, Twitter) in making hiring decisions, noting that the use of that information is likely to be perceived poorly by job applicants and that there are potential legal concerns and questions regarding their use. Further, as data-driven solutions are sought out, we note that social media pages often include a host of personal information that organizations are legally barred from asking applicants directly (e.g., parenthood status, race/ethnicity, disability status, and religious affiliation). In fact, different types of information provided as well as social media use and engagement may vary by personality factors (Bachrach, Kosinski, Graepel, Kohli, & Stillwell, 2012; Saef, Woo, Carpenter, & Tay, 2018). Organizations should heed legal restrictions as a guideline when seeking out and using information from social media pages, even those publicly available, and HR staff should be thoroughly trained in the practical, ethical, and legal issues involved in the implementation of online systems for screening job applicants (Beyer & Brummel, 2015).

Developers and Providers of Online Job Application Tools

The developers of online job application tools have significantly streamlined the online job application process, and there is continued promise of using big data to efficiently assess applicants' job-related characteristics and behavioral tendencies. But developers also have ethical and professional responsibilities to job applicants and employers. These include developing secure systems that protect applicant data and ensuring that they promote only the collection of data that is legal (and does not entail legal exposure for the employer) and that research has shown is relevant to the selection process (Nikolaou et al., 2015; Zhang, Van Iddekinge, Roth, & Lanivich, 2017).

Organizations can see the repercussions of the misuse of personal information, including that of third-party services with access to their data, such as in the Facebook and Cambridge Analytica scandal (Granville, 2018). As a consequence of the privacy-related misuse of data in this case, Facebook was asked to testify regarding their knowledge and role in the issue, and Cambridge Analytica has announced their intent to close their business operation entirely. This leads to a central question for future investigation: For technologists, how can current methods for the design and deployment of online systems be changed to ensure stronger protection for both the privacy of users and the interests of developers, while at the same time fulfilling the promise of using big data algorithms for effective applicant assessment?

Policy Makers

The technology used to screen job applicants is moving rapidly and will pose challenges to policy makers wishing to protect the rights of applicants while also supporting business needs. We suggest that policy makers carefully examine developments in this arena with an eye toward protecting the rights of the public and the use of individuals' online data. An important role includes educating the public about how to best protect their personal data. Other considerations include looking at how nations across the globe (e.g., the recently adopted GDPR in the European Union) are implementing security-related regulations and determining how those might be adapted to the local regulatory systems. For example, within the GDPR, users have the right to receive an explanation as to how they were evaluated when algorithms are used. This emphasizes the importance of fairness and transparency in algorithm design and use and may ease applicants' concerns about the use of algorithms in the hiring process.

Recommendations for Research

Research on how to harness big data to develop algorithms to predict job behavior will boost the effectiveness with which employers can predict the performance of potential employees. In addition, our review of the literature and our own research on privacy concerns in online application systems has uncovered a wide range of issues that should be examined by future research.

First, the research shows that online job applicants may not (a) understand the risks involved in applying for jobs online, (b) value the protection of their privacy, and (c) know the best ways to protect themselves. These gaps present several avenues for future work. Research should examine the most effective methods for teaching job applicants the importance of protecting their private information online. This includes an examination of which methods are most effective for communicating the risks of online security, which have the greatest effect on applicants' online behavior, and which are most relevant to different applicant groups (e.g., job types, education). As examples of research questions, applicants may read shorter explanations more carefully with greater effects on their understanding and behavior. Or job applicants applying for retail jobs versus executive positions may have different expectations regarding the treatment of their data and the types of questions asked. Another question is whether applicants accept privacy explanations that are explained in ways that are low key versus those that provide "scary" explanations of all the things that could go wrong when providing private information online.

Second, research should assess general levels of online security "fluency" and examine ways of increasing the general population's knowledge of security issues. Importantly, as technology-related security knowledge rapidly changes, it is critical for users to continually keep up with current best practices, as opposed to engaging in a one-time effort to learn a single set of best practices. Thus, research is needed to understand the most effective ways for increasing knowledge of this topic and for disseminating that knowledge in the most straightforward ways possible to a general audience. Doing so will allow researchers to determine what, if any, interventions are needed in this space to help individuals and organizations remain aware of the challenges and opportunities related to online selection in terms of privacy and cybersecurity.

Third, future studies should examine the actual security behaviors of online applicants and how security behaviors can be promoted. That is, while learning a set of best practices is important, it is perhaps more important that changes in behaviors are made to promote safer behaviors online. One opportunity for behavior change may be when applicants are asked to create "accounts" with each organization when applying for a job online. Often these application portals require some form of creating a user ID and password, which is a perfect setting for using a password manager as a secure way to generate, save, and protect those credentials. Other worthwhile research questions in this area include the following: Do specific employer practices during the hiring process cause applicants not to share highly personal information about themselves? Also, do certain employer practices cause applicants to conceal information that employers need from applicants, such as their education and work history, or drop out of the application process entirely?

Fourth, applicants' perceptions of different methods of collecting online information about them should be examined closely, as this may also affect their willingness to apply for jobs. This is an important issue: Applicants may feel compelled to provide their information because it is a required part of the application process but may be substantially uneasy and unhappy with certain practices. Examples of what might make applicants uncomfortable include a request for information from an applicant's social media pages; alignment of the depth of personal history information actually required to assess a candidate versus the information being requested; and the use of centralized application portals where third-party vendors are actually collecting information about the applicant, even though the individual has no desire to share their information with the third party.

Fifth, we agree with Beyer and Brummel (2015), who presented recommendations for the effective implementation of online security training in companies, emphasizing the importance of end users in online security that included advocating for an interdisciplinary approach involving the multiple expertise areas of HR, IT, computer science, and industrial–organizational psychologists. As an interdisciplinary team, we have found that the multiple perspectives approach is effective in ensuring that the work is representative of both the front end and back end parts of the selection system operations.

Finally, how does an employer's reputation for online security affect applicant behavior? For example, applicants may choose not to apply for jobs with, or not to accept offers from, employers who have a poor reputation. These effects may be particularly strong for the best applicants, who naturally have a broader range of opportunities (Ryan & Ployhart, 2000), causing employers to lose the best talent. This may be particularly important in the rapidly growing tech industry, where highly trained and qualified software engineers and computer science professionals are needed to drive the growth of technology platforms; however, these professionals are also the most capable of seeing holes in security systems and may feel more strongly about poor security practices than more naive users.

CONCLUSION

We set out to describe the use of online systems and big data in the context of the job application process, with an emphasis on online privacy and cybersecurity issues. First, we provided an overview of the use of online systems and big data in organizations and in the application context. Second, we discussed the benefits to employers and individuals of using big data methods. Third, we outlined major concerns with using big data in the selection context, with an emphasis on the privacy concerns of applicants and security concerns of those managing security systems. Fourth, we offered specific recommendations for stakeholders likely affected by the issues associated with online privacy in a selection context. Finally, we identified several gaps in the literature that hinder recommendations for best practices, providing several avenues for future research. Our hope is that this work will highlight key questions to be addressed in the future and spur new research in this important area.

REFERENCES

Abrams, R. (2017, May 23). Target to pay $18.5 million to 47 states in security breach settlement. *The New York Times.* Retrieved from https://www.nytimes.com/2017/05/23/business/target-security-breach-settlement.html

Acquisti, A., Brandimarte, L., & Loewenstein, G. (2015). Privacy and human behavior in the age of information. *Science, 347*, 509–514. http://dx.doi.org/10.1126/science.aaa1465

Bachrach, Y., Kosinski, M., Graepel, T., Kohli, P., & Stillwell, D. (2012). Personality and patterns of Facebook usage. In *Proceedings of the 4th Annual ACM Web Science Conference* (pp. 24–32). New York, NY: ACM. http://dx.doi.org/10.1145/2380718.2380722

Barocas, S., & Selbst, A. D. (2016). Big data's disparate impact. *California Law Review, 104*(3) 1–62.

Bauer, T., Erdogan, B., Caughlin, D., & Truxillo, D. (2018). *Human resource management: People, data, and analytics.* Thousand Oaks, CA: Sage.

Bauer, T. N., Truxillo, D. T., Tucker, J. S., Weathers, V., Bertolino, M., Erdogan, B., & Campion, M. A. (2006). Selection in the information age: The impact of privacy concerns and computer experience on applicant reactions. *Journal of Management, 32*, 601–621. http://dx.doi.org/10.1177/0149206306289829

Beyer, R. E., & Brummel, B. J. (2015). *Implementing effective cyber security training for end users of computer networks.* Retrieved from https://www.shrm.org/hr-today/trends-and-forecasting/special-reports-and-expert-views/Documents/SHRM-SIOP%20Role%20of%20Human%20Resources%20in%20Cyber%20Security.pdf

Bishop, M. (2002). *Computer security: Art and science.* Boston, MA: Addison-Wesley Professional.

Caers, R., & Castelyns, V. (2011). LinkedIn and Facebook in Belgium: The influences and biases of social network sites in recruitment and selection procedures. *Social Science Computer Review, 29*, 437–448. http://dx.doi.org/10.1177/0894439310386567

Caliskan, A., Bryson, J. J., & Narayanan, A. (2017). Semantics derived automatically from language corpora contain human-like biases. *Science, 356*, 183–186. http://dx.doi.org/10.1126/science.aal4230

Chong, I., Ge, H., Li, N., & Proctor, R. W. (2018). Influence of privacy priming and security framing on mobile app selection. *Computers & Security, 78*, 143–154. http://dx.doi.org/10.1016/j.cose.2018.06.005

Chong, I., Xiong, A., & Proctor, R. W. (2018). Human factors in the privacy and security of the Internet of things. *Ergonomics in Design, 27*(3), 5–10. http://dx.doi.org/10.1177/1064804617750321

Dastin, J. (2018, October 9). Amazon scraps secret AI recruiting tool that showed bias against women. Retrieved from https://www.reuters.com/article/us-amazon-com-jobs-automation-insight/amazon-scraps-secret-ai-recruiting-tool-that-showed-bias-against-women-idUSKCN1MK08G

Feldman, M., Friedler, S. A., Moeller, J., Scheidegger, C., & Venkatasubramanian, S. (2015). Certifying and removing disparate impact. In *Proceedings of the 21st ACM SIGKDD International Conference on Knowledge Discovery and Data Mining* (pp. 259–268). New York, NY: ACM.

Granville, K. (2018, March 19). Facebook and Cambridge Analytica: What you need to know as fallout widens. *The New York Times.* Retrieved from https://www.nytimes.com/2018/03/19/technology/facebook-cambridge-analytica-explained.html

Hackett, R. (2016, May 18). LinkedIn lost 167 million account credentials in data breach. *Fortune.* Retrieved from http://fortune.com/2016/05/18/linkedin-data-breach-email-password/

Hicks, L. (2004). *Privacy and confidentiality.* Retrieved from https://eppla.sites.stanford.edu/sites/g/files/sbiybj6561/f/citi_-_privacy_and_confidentiality.pdf

Ion, I., Reeder, R., & Consolvo, S. (2015, July). *". . . No one can hack my mind": Comparing expert and non-expert security practices.* Paper presented at the Symposium on Usable Privacy and Security, Ottawa, Canada. Abstract retrieved from https://www.usenix.org/conference/soups2015/proceedings/presentation/ion

Klahre, A.-M. (2017, August 29). *3 ways Johnson & Johnson is taking talent acquisition to the next level*. Retrieved from https://eppla.sites.stanford.edu/sites/g/files/sbiybj6561/f/citi_-_privacy_and_confidentiality.pdf

Kristof-Brown, A. L., Zimmerman, R. D., & Johnson, E. C. (2005). Consequences of individuals' fit at work: A meta-analysis of person–job, person–organization, person–group, and person–supervisor fit. *Personnel Psychology, 58*, 281–342. http://dx.doi.org/10.1111/j.1744-6570.2005.00672.x

Landers, R. N., Brusso, R. C., Cavanaugh, K. J., & Collmus, A. B. (2016). A primer on theory-driven web scraping: Automatic extraction of big data from the Internet for use in psychological research. *Psychological Methods, 21*, 475–492. http://dx.doi.org/10.1037/met0000081

McCarthy, J. M., Bauer, T. N., Truxillo, D. M., Anderson, N. R., Costa, A. C., & Ahmed, S. M. (2017). Applicant perspectives during selection: A review addressing "so what?", "what's new?", and "where to next?" *Journal of Management, 43*, 1693–1725. http://dx.doi.org/10.1177/0149206316681846

Mele, C. (2018, August 1). Data breaches keep happening. So why don't you do something? *The New York Times*. Retrieved from https://www.nytimes.com/2018/08/01/technology/data-breaches.html

Mulvey, T., Esen, E., & Coombs, J. (2016, January 7). *SHRM survey findings: Using social media for talent acquisition—recruitment and screening*. Retrieved from https://www.shrm.org/hr-today/trends-and-forecasting/research-and-surveys/Documents/SHRM-Social-Media-Recruiting-Screening-2015.pdf

Nikolaou, I., Bauer, T. N., & Truxillo, D. M. (2015). Applicant fairness reactions to selection methods: An overview of recent research and suggestions for the future. In I. Nikolaou & J. K. Oostrom (Eds.), *Employee recruitment, selection, and assessment: Contemporary issues for theory and practice* (pp. 80–96). London, England: Routledge/Psychology Press.

Perrin, A. (2015, October 8). *Social media usage: 2005–2015*. Retrieved from http://www.pewinternet.org/2015/10/08/social-networking-usage-2005-2015/

Pfleeger, S. L., & Caputo, D. D. (2012). Leveraging behavioral science to mitigate cyber security risk. *Computers & Security, 31*, 597–611. http://dx.doi.org/10.1016/j.cose.2011.12.010

Politou, E., Alepis, E., & Patsakis, C. (2018). Forgetting personal data and revoking consent under the GDPR: Challenges and proposed solutions. *Journal of Cybersecurity, 4*(1), tyy001.

Porter, K. (2018, December 13). *Recruiting scams are on the rise*. Retrieved from https://www.shrm.org/resourcesandtools/hr-topics/talent-acquisition/pages/recruiting-scams-are-on-the-rise.aspx

Rainie, L., & Duggan, M. (2016, January 14). *Privacy and information sharing*. Retrieved from http://www.pewinternet.org/2016/01/14/privacy-and-information-sharing/

Roth, P. L., Bobko, P., Van Iddekinge, C. H., & Thatcher, J. B. (2016). Social media in employee-selection-related decisions: A research agenda for uncharted territory. *Journal of Management, 42*, 269–298. http://dx.doi.org/10.1177/0149206313503018

Ryan, A. M., & Ployhart, R. E. (2000). Applicants' perceptions of selection procedures and decisions: A critical review and agenda for the future. *Journal of Management, 26*, 565–606. http://dx.doi.org/10.1177/014920630002600308

Saef, R., Woo, S. E., Carpenter, J., & Tay, L. (2018). Fostering socio-informational behaviors online: The interactive effect of openness to experience and extraversion. *Personality and Individual Differences, 122*, 93–98. http://dx.doi.org/10.1016/j.paid.2017.10.009

Smith, A. (2015, November 19). *Searching for work in the digital era*. Retrieved from http://www.pewinternet.org/2015/11/19/searching-for-work-in-the-digital-era/

Stoughton, J. W., Thompson, L. F., & Meade, A. W. (2015). Examining applicant reactions to the use of social networking websites in pre-employment screening.

Journal of Business and Psychology, 30(1), 73–88. http://dx.doi.org/10.1007/s10869-013-9333-6

Tankard, C. (2016). What the GDPR means for businesses. *Network Security, 2016*(6), 5–8.

Tonidandel, S., King, E. B., & Cortina, J. M. (2018). Big data methods: Leveraging modern data analytic techniques to build organizational science. *Organizational Research Methods, 21*, 525–547. http://dx.doi.org/10.1177/1094428116677299

Toonders, J. (2014, July). Data is the new oil of the digital economy. *Wired*. Retrieved from https://www.wired.com/insights/2014/07/data-new-oil-digital-economy/

United States Department of Health and Human Services Office for Human Research Protections. (1993). *IRB Guidebook*. Rockville, MD: Author.

Van Iddekinge, C. H., Lanivich, S. E., Roth, P. L., & Junco, E. (2016). Social media for selection? Validity and adverse impact potential of a Facebook-based assessment. *Journal of Management, 42*, 1811–1835.

Vijayan, J. (2007, June 1). One year later: Five lessons learned from the VA data breach. *ComputerWorld*. Retrieved from https://www.computerworld.com/article/2541516/

Zhang, L., Van Iddekinge, C., Roth, P. L., & Lanivich, S. E. (2017). What's in applicants' social media profiles? Effects on recruiter ratings and job performance. *Academy of Management Proceedings, 2017*(1), 11322. Retrieved from https://journals.aom.org/doi/abs/10.5465/ambpp.2017.322

18

Privacy Enhancing Techniques for Security

Elisa Bertino

Recent technological advances and novel applications, such as sensors, cyber-physical systems, smart mobile devices, cloud systems, data analytics, and social networks, are making it possible to capture, process, and share huge amounts of data—referred to as *big data*—and to extract useful information from these data and predict trends and events (Bertino, 2013). Big data are useful to psychological scientists for many purposes and are particularly critical for security-related tasks (Bertino, 2014). For example, by analyzing and integrating data collected in social networks, one can identify connections and relationships among individuals that may inform social psychological theory or help with homeland protection. By collecting and mining data concerning user travels and disease outbreaks, one can predict the spread of disease across geographical areas. In cybersecurity, big data technologies can help with system and network security monitoring, situation awareness, anomaly detection, user monitoring, protection from insider

The contents of the Research Agenda Section are partially based on the results of the privacy session (which I chaired) organized as part of the National Science Foundation Big Data Security and Privacy Workshop, September 16–17, 2014 (National Science Foundation, 2014). I thank the workshop chair, Professor Bhavani Thuraisingham, the chair of the workshop security session, Professor Murat Kantarcioglu, and the workshop participants for the discussions during the workshop that led to an initial draft agenda for privacy research for big data.

I thank the editors of this book for the comments and corrections that led to a much better version of this chapter.

http://dx.doi.org/10.1037/0000193-019
Big Data in Psychological Research, S. E. Woo, L. Tay, and R. W. Proctor (Editors)

threat (Bertino, 2012), continuous user authentication, and context-based access control—all of which involve human interactions with the cyber system. And those are just a few examples; many other domains exist in which big data technologies can play a major role in providing test beds and enhancing security.

The use of data for research purposes or security tasks, however, raises major privacy concerns. Collected data, even if anonymized by removing identifiers such as names or Social Security numbers and using generalization techniques (Dai, Ghinita, Bertino, Byun, & Li, 2009), when linked with other data may enable reidentification of the individuals to which specific data items are related. Also, because organizations such as governmental agencies often collaborate on security tasks, data sets are exchanged across different organizations, resulting in these data sets being available to many different parties, thus increasing the data exposure to privacy breaches. Security tasks such as authentication and access control may require detailed information about users. An example is multifactor authentication that, in addition to a password or a certificate, may require user biometrics (Dasgupta, Roy, & Nag, 2017). Recently proposed continuous authentication techniques extend user authentication to include information such as user keystroke dynamics to verify user identity constantly (Kołakowska, 2018). Another example is location-based access control (Damiani, Bertino, Catania, & Perlasca, 2007), which requires users to provide the access control system with information about their current location. As a result, detailed user location information may be collected over time by the access control system. This information, if misused or stolen, can lead to privacy breaches.

It would thus seem that privacy and use of data for security and research tasks are conflicting requirements. If we want to achieve security or use the data for research, we must give up privacy; although if we are keen on assuring privacy, we may undermine security and research. However, this may not be necessarily the case. Recent advances in applied cryptography are making it possible to work on encrypted data—for example, for performing analytics on encrypted data (Liu, Bertino, & Yi, 2014; Yi, Rao, Bertino, & Bouguettaya, 2015). However, much more has to be done because the choice of data privacy techniques heavily depends on the specific use of data and the security tasks at hand. Also, current techniques are still not able to meet the efficiency requirement of many applications. Moreover, recent events such as the Facebook Cambridge Analytica data scandal, wherein personal data from millions of Facebook users were used without consent (Datoo, 2018), have emphasized the need for increased transparency with respect to data uses by parties collecting user data as part of their business operations. Transparency is, however, a broader notion and has to be properly articulated.

In this chapter, I first present a few examples of privacy enhancing techniques that help in reconciling the use of data for research or security tasks and privacy. I then discuss a research agenda for allowing one to use data for research or security tasks while assuring data privacy.

PRIVACY ENHANCING TECHNIQUES

Many privacy enhancing techniques have been proposed over the last 15 years, ranging from cryptographic techniques, such as oblivious data structures (Wang et al., 2014) that hide data access patterns, to data anonymization techniques that transform the data to make it more difficult to link specific data records to specific individuals (Byun, Kamra, Bertino, & Li, 2007). The problem of location privacy has also been the focus of extensive research both in the past and present (Damiani, Bertino, & Silvestri, 2010; Ghinita, Kalnis, Khoshgozaran, Shahabi, & Tan, 2008; Paulet, Kaosar, Yi, & Bertino, 2014). More recently, research efforts have been devoted to investigating privacy-preserving techniques for data in the cloud (Nabeel & Bertino, 2014b; Seo, Nabeel, Ding, & Bertino, 2014), on smartphones (Shebaro, Oluwatimi, Midi, & Bertino, 2014), and on social networks (Carminati, Ferrari, & Viviani, 2013). I refer the reader to specialized conferences, such as the Privacy-Enhancing Symposium[1] series, and journals, such as *Transactions on Data* Privacy[2] and *IEEE Transactions on Dependable and Secure Computing*,[3] for further references. However, it is important to note that most proposed privacy enhancing techniques only focus on privacy and do not address the key problem of reconciling security with privacy. There are a few notable exceptions, and in what follows, I focus on some of these approaches.

Privacy-Preserving Data Matching

Record matching is typically performed across different data sources to identify common information shared among these sources. An example is matching a list of passengers on a flight with a list of suspicious individuals. However, record matching from different data sources is often in conflict with privacy requirements concerning the records to be matched. Cryptographic approaches, such as secure set intersection protocols (Freedman, Nissim, & Pinkas, 2004), may alleviate such concerns. *Secure set intersection protocols* allow two parties, each owning a set, to privately compute the intersection of these sets without requiring each party to disclose to the other party its own set. The only information that is shared between the two parties is the set of elements in the intersection. Many protocols have been developed for computing secure set intersection. However, those protocols currently do not scale for large data sets. Experimental results from Cao, Rao, Bertino, and Kantarcioglu (2015) showed that on a single Intel Core i7-2600 CPU machine, it takes 974.4 hours to execute the private linkage of two data sets, each having 6,000 records and five attributes.

A recent matching protocol (Cao et al., 2015) combining secure multi-party computation (SMC) techniques and differential privacy (Dwork & Roth,

2014) addressed the scalability and security issues of previous protocols. *Differential privacy* is a statistical technique that seeks to accurately enable others to query the database while protecting privacy. This matching protocol is based on a hybrid strategy by which each party partitions its data set into subsets and releases a synopsis of each subset (i.e., the subset extent and size) to the other party. Record matching between "faraway" subsets is then pruned, and thus efficiency is greatly improved. To protect the privacy of the records in each subset, the subset size is randomized by differential privacy (inserting statistical noise into the data; Dwork & Roth, 2014) before being released, which ensures that the presence or absence of any individual record does not affect the released subset size significantly.

More specifically, the matching protocol includes three parties: Alice and Bob are the data set owners, and Charlie is a third party (Cao et al., 2015). The three parties are *honest but curious* (Goldreich, 2004). Alice and Bob partition their data sets into subsets and send Charlie the differentially private synopses of the subsets. Charlie coordinates the record matching between Alice and Bob. Based on the received synopses, Charlie prunes the record matching between subsets with a distance beyond a threshold specified by Alice and Bob. During the entire protocol, Charlie does not access any record value. At the end of the protocol, its knowledge remains limited to the private synopses of the subsets released to it by Alice and Bob. At the same time, Alice and Bob obtain the matching records. But they neither learn the attribute values of nonmatching records nor the private synopses of the subsets.

Such a hybrid protocol thus separates the differentially private synopses from the matching records. The protocol has been formally proved to comply with differential privacy. The protocol also uses a private indexing scheme to enhance the effectiveness of data partitioning. The indexing scheme hierarchically partitions a data set, forming a tree. Whenever a node in the tree has to be split, a privacy budget is dynamically allocated based on the basis of the node size, in such a way that the magnitude of added noise does not dominate the node size. In other words, the indexing scheme optimizes the accuracy of the noisy node size in relative terms. Experimental results show that such a hybrid protocol is superior to existing approaches with respect to both recall and efficiency in the context of private record linkage. The execution of the hybrid protocol for computing the privacy-preserving record matching for two data sets, each having 6,000 records and five attributes, takes 20.17 hours, which is an improvement of two orders of magnitude compared with the 974.4 hours required with a conventional private matching protocol.

However, even though such an approach represents an important step, research is needed in several directions. Privacy-preserving techniques must be designed that are suited for complex matching techniques, based, for example, on semantic matching where similar nodes can be matched on the basis of equivalent network structures. Security models and definitions also have to be developed to support security analysis and proofs for solutions combining different security techniques, such as SMC and differential privacy.

Privacy-Preserving Collaborative Data Mining

Conventional data mining aimed at discovering patterns in big data is typically performed on big centralized data warehouses collecting all the data of interest. However, centrally collecting all data poses several privacy and confidentiality concerns when data belong to different organizations. An approach to address such concerns is based on distributed collaborative approaches by which the organizations retain their data sets and cooperate to learn the global data mining results without revealing the data in their individual data sets.

Fundamental work in this area includes (a) techniques allowing two parties to build a decision tree without learning anything about each other's data sets except for what can be learned by the final decision tree (Lindell & Pinkas, 2000) and (b) specialized collaborative privacy-preserving techniques for association rules, clustering, and *k*-nearest neighbor classification (Vaidya, Zhu, & Clifton, 2006). Usually most of the approaches proposed for privacy-preserving collaborative data mining are based on cryptographic tools that leave one or more parties unaware of some aspect of the data, such as oblivious transfer protocols (Even, Goldreich, & Lempel, 1985; Naor & Pinkas, 2001), oblivious evaluation of protocols (Naor & Pinkas, 2006), and oblivious circuit evaluation (Yao, 1986). In computer science, a circuit is a model of computation in which input values proceed through a sequence of gates, each of which computes a function. Examples of functions include conjunction, disjunction, and negation of Boolean values. The evaluation of a circuit refers to the execution of the functions in the circuit, according to their sequence in the circuit, for a given input. These oblivious-type protocols and circuit evaluations fundamentally seek to be unaware of what information is transferred or evaluated.

These tools are, however, still inefficient. Recent research has thus been focusing on more efficient implementation techniques for basic cryptographic tools. Notable recent examples include approaches to enhance the efficiency and scalability of secure function computation by circuit evaluation (Demmler, Schneider, & Zohner, 2015; Kreuter, Shelat, Mood, & Butler, 2013). However, research is needed on how to efficiently use such novel implementations in the context of data mining. Novel approaches based on cloud computing and new cryptographic primitives (i.e., basic cryptographic algorithms used to build cryptographic protocols) also have to be investigated. Notable recent work includes an efficient approach to perform clustering on data stored in a cloud (Liu et al., 2014). This approach, however, has to be extended for use in collaborative settings.

Privacy-Preserving Biometrics Authentication

Conventional approaches to biometrics authentication require recording biometrics templates of enrolled users and then using these templates for matching with the templates provided by users during authentication (Jain & Ross,

2008). Templates of user biometrics represent sensitive information that has to be strongly protected. In distributed environments in which users have to interact with many different service providers, the protection of biometric templates becomes even more complex. The main problem is how to support strong authentication via biometrics without revealing the biometric template to the identity verifier. Notice that in a distributed system supporting decentralized authentication, multiple verifiers may have to have available such templates.

A recent approach addresses this issue by using a combination of perceptual hashing techniques, classification techniques, and zero-knowledge proof of knowledge (ZKPK) protocols (Gunasinghe & Bertino, 2014). Under such approach, the image of the biometrics—for example, the image of a retina scan—of the user is processed to extract from it a string of bits through the use of a perceptual hash function (Klinger & Starkweather, 2008–2010) based on the discrete cosine transform. This string of bits is then processed through a support vector machine (SVM) classifier. The label of the class returned by the SVM classifier is then combined with a secret S derived from a user's password. The result of such a combination is the biometric identifier (BID) of the user. The class label is an integer represented by 32 bits, and S is 128 bits. The generated BID (which is 160 bits) is then used together with a random number to generate a Pedersen cryptographic commitment (Pedersen, 1992), which represents an identification token that does not reveal anything about the original input biometrics. The commitment is then used in the ZKPK protocol to authenticate the user. To enhance accuracy, Hadamard error-correcting codes are also used. The approach has been engineered for secure use on mobile phones. Experimental results show that the accuracy of the proposed biometric-based authentication is at 90% when 16-bit Hadamard codes are used. In other words, biometric information is transformed and combined in such a way that it becomes unique for identifying an individual for authentication but does not reveal the original biometrics.

Much work has to be done, however, to increase accuracy. Different approaches to authentication have to be investigated based on recent homomorphic encryption techniques that allow computing and analytics on encrypted data themselves. Also, recent trends in authentication suggest the use of multimodal biometric authentication, by which multiple biometrics are used to authenticate the users, and continuous authentication, by which the system learns features from the behavior of the users and then compares the actual user behavior with the learned features. An example of such a feature is the speed with which the user types at a computer keyboard. However, those advanced forms of authentication further increase the need for collecting detailed data about each user. Privacy-preserving techniques have to be devised to support such forms of authentication, such as techniques similar to the technique described in this subsection or based on recent homomorphic encryption techniques.

Privacy-Preserving Fine-Grained Access Control for Cloud Data

Cloud technology allows a large variety of organizations to store and manage large amounts of data at a cost lower than was possible before. However, the confidentiality of data stored in a cloud is a critical requirement, especially when the cloud is public and manages data and applications by different customers. Encryption is a commonly adopted approach to protect the confidentiality of the data. Encryption alone, however, is not sufficient because organizations often have to enforce fine-grained access control on the data. *Fine-grained access control* is one of the most critical security functions that establishes who can view or use specific data. Such control is often based on attributes of data users, referred to as *identity attributes*, such as the roles of users in the organization, projects on which users are working, and so forth. These access control systems are usually referred to as *attribute-based access control (ABAC) systems*. The well-known eXtensible Access Control Markup Language standard (34) is an example of an ABAC model. I refer the reader to Bertino, Ghinita, and Kamra (2011) for a survey of access control, including the ABAC model. Therefore, an important requirement is to support fine-grained access control, based on ABAC policies, over encrypted data stored in the cloud.

A major issue in addressing this requirement is that the identity attributes used in the ABAC policies often reveal privacy-sensitive information about users and leak confidential information about the data content. The confidentiality of the content and the privacy of the users are, thus, not fully protected if the identity attributes are not protected. Further, privacy, both individual as well as organizational, is a key requirement in all solutions, including cloud services, for digital identity management. Further, because insider threats (Bertino, 2012) are one of the major sources of data theft and privacy breaches, identity attributes must be strongly protected even from access within organizations. With the adoption of cloud technology, the scope of insider threats is no longer limited to physical organizational perimeters. Therefore, protecting the identity attributes of the users while enforcing attribute-based access control both within the organization, as well as in the cloud, is crucial.

An approach to address this requirement is based on encryption. *Encryption* consists of transforming data by using a secret input, referred to as a *symmetric encryption key*, into some random data. The original data can only be recovered by parties that have the original secret; this form of encryption is known as *symmetric encryption*. Symmetric encryption is widely used to protect data stored in files and databases. Another well-known form of encryption is *asymmetric encryption* by which data are transformed using some publicly known information, referred to as a *public key*. The original data can be recovered by applying to the transformed data another key, which is secret; this key is thus referred to as a *secret key*. Asymmetric encryption is often used when having to protect messages to be sent across computer networks so that only the intended recipients can decrypt the messages.

To address these requirements, different portions of the data are encrypted with different symmetric encryption keys. The use of different encryption keys for different portions of a given data set is often referred to as *fine-grained encryption*. Such an approach allows one to share the data with different parties selectively. Suppose that a file is divided into two portions, P_1 and P_2, encrypted with symmetric encryption keys K_1 and K_2, respectively. Suppose that user Bob can access both portions; he will then receive both keys K_1 and K_2. Suppose now that user Alice can only access P_1; she will then receive only key K_1. The use of fine-grained encryption requires, however, a mechanism to send the symmetric encryption keys to the users based on the access permissions these users have. A possible approach to distribute such keys is the *attribute-based broadcast group key management* (AB-BGKM) scheme (Nabeel, Shang, & Bertino, 2013).

Fine-grained encryption thus allows one to encrypt different portions of the data with different symmetric encryption keys while minimizing the number of symmetric encryption keys required; which portions of the data are encrypted with which keys is based on ABAC policies (Nabeel et al., 2013). The AB-BGKM scheme (Nabeel & Bertino, 2014a) allows one to share encryption keys among a group of users. Keys are shared according to user identity attributes so that each user in a group of users receives only the encryption keys for the data portions he or she is authorized to access. The AB-BGKM scheme has several relevant properties. When the group changes, the rekeying operations do not affect the private information of existing group members, and thus the AB-BGKM scheme eliminates the need to establish private communication channels. The scheme provides the same advantage when the group membership conditions change. Furthermore, the group key derivation is efficient because it only requires a simple vector inner product and/or polynomial interpolation. Moreover, the AB-BGKM scheme is resistant to collusion attacks. Multiple group members are unable to combine their private information in a useful way to derive a group key, which they cannot derive individually.

The AB-BGKM scheme is based on the access control vector technique (Shang, Nabeel, Paci, & Bertino, 2010) and Shamir's threshold scheme (Shamir, 1979). The access control vector technique allows one to hide a secret—that is, a data encryption key—in some publicly available information, referred to as an *access control vector*. Only users with certain secrets can extract the information from this vector, which can thus be published in the cloud. Users receive these secrets by engaging in an oblivious envelop transfer protocol with the identity issuer. The oblivious envelop transfer protocol assures that a user can extract the secret from the envelope only if his or her identity attributes verify the conditions associated with the envelope.

To summarize, under the approach in Nabeel and Bertino (2014b), fine-grained encrypted data are stored in the cloud together with access control vectors hiding the encryption keys. From the access control vectors, the cloud cannot learn the keys hidden in the vectors nor any information about the user identity attribute. When a user wants to access some data items from the cloud, the user downloads the encrypted data items and the corresponding access vectors. The user then uses his or her secret to extract the encryption keys from the vectors. Notice that if a user does not have the authorization to access the downloaded encrypted data items, the user will not be able to extract the encryption keys from the access control vectors because the access control vectors are generated only on the basis of the secrets held by the users authorized to access the data items. If policies change or a user is not any longer authorized to access certain data items, it is sufficient to reencrypt the data with some new encryption keys, generate new access control vectors, and upload them to the cloud. No specific actions or communications are required with users. I refer the reader to Nabeel et al. (2013) and Nabeel and Bertino (2014b) for details and performance evaluation.

Even though the approach described in Nabeel et al. (2013) is an effective and efficient approach to support fine-grained access control based on identity attributes, while assuring the privacy of identity attributes of users, several issues still have to be addressed. The first issue is related to the problem of hiding data access patterns. By looking at the data access patterns, it is possible to derive useful information (Islam, Kuzu, & Kantarcioglu, 2012) from the data. Therefore, it is critical to devise effective approaches to hide such access patterns. In addition, it is critical to develop approaches able to support context and content-based access control that can be enforced in a cloud without leaking information about context and content.

Privacy Enhancing Techniques

Several privacy enhancing techniques have been developed over the years, including oblivious random-access memory (RAM), security multiparty computation, multi-input encryption, homomorphic encryption. A *RAM* is a form of computer data storage device that allows data items to be read or written in almost the same amount of time irrespective of the physical location of data inside the memory. Other types of storage devices, such as hard disks, do not have such property. An *oblivious RAM* (Goldreich & Ostrovsky, 1996) is a RAM that hides its access pattern—that is, for each input, the memory locations accessed are similarly distributed. An oblivious RAM prevents an observer from learning which data are read or written in memory by observing the memory access patterns. However, oblivious RAM and the other privacy enhancing techniques mentioned at the beginning of this paragraph are not yet practically applicable to large data sets.

RESEARCH AGENDA

Despite initial solutions to the problem of security with privacy that have been proposed—some of which were outlined in the previous section—comprehensive solutions require addressing many research challenges, especially when dealing with big data. In what follows, I outline relevant research directions.

Data Confidentiality

Many data confidentiality techniques have been proposed, including access control and encryption, and included in access control systems that are part of database management systems and operating systems. However current access control systems have several shortcomings, including the inability to merge large numbers of access control policies; lack of automatic administration of authorization; inability to enforce access control policies for multimedia data and big data stores, such as Hadoop MapReduce (https://hadoop.apache.org/docs/r1.2.1/mapred_tutorial.html); and lack of tools for automatic evolution and adaptation of access control policies. We refer the reader to Bertino (2016) for a detailed discussion of these shortcomings and preliminary approaches to address them.

Data Privacy

A major issue arising from big data is that by correlating many (big) data sets, one can extract unanticipated information. Relevant issues and research directions that have to be investigated include techniques to control what is extracted and to check that data are used for the intended use, support for both personal and population privacy, efficient and scalable privacy enhancing techniques, usability of data privacy policies, privacy risk models, data ownership, and data life cycle framework. I refer the reader to Bertino (2016) for a detailed discussion of those research directions that require multidisciplinary approaches across psychology and computer science to achieve solutions that can be adopted in practice. For example, designing usable data privacy policies requires understanding how best to communicate these policies to users so that they can assess the implications on their privacy and decide which of their personal data to share. Risk models are another example; there are different types of relationships of risks with big data: (a) big data can increase privacy risks, and (b) big data can reduce risks in many domains (e.g., national security). However, risks are also related to personal perception and risk tolerance, which may be different for different individuals. It is critical to develop models for these two types of risk to identify tradeoffs suitable for different "types" of users and develop related privacy enhancing techniques.

TRANSPARENCY

As discussed by Bertino, Merrill, Nesen, and Utz (2019), the use of big data combined with powerful machine learning algorithms raises major concerns because such technologies, if not used properly, may lead to many adverse effects. For example, machine learning algorithms would allow one to infer much more privacy-sensitive information than expected by users providing their data. For example, by analyzing the social network activities of users, machine learning algorithms would allow other parties to learn the political preferences of the users. In addition to privacy, the use of machine learning algorithms can lead to unfair decisions and discriminatory practices if the original data are biased (O'Neil, 2016). Data transparency is thus emerging as a critical requirement for many data-intensive applications.

Bertino et al. (2019) proposed a preliminary high-level definition of *data transparency*: the ability of a subject to effectively gain access to all information related to data used in processes and decisions that affect the subject. This definition emphasizes the principle that processes are executed and decisions are made based on data, and these processes and decisions have an impact on the subject. Therefore, this definition covers two important cases: (a) the case in which data about the subject were collected and used in a process or decision that has affected the subject and (b) the case in which data, other than the data related to the subject, were used in a process or decision that has affected the subject.

However, making such a definition an operational one requires addressing several challenges, including the definition of transparency policies, both internal and external to organizations, comprehensive logging systems, trading-off transparency, and business confidentiality. I refer the reader to Bertino et al. (2019) for a comprehensive discussion about the notion and dimensions of data transparency and a comprehensive research road map.

CONCLUSION

In this chapter, I discussed the difficult problem of reconciling security with privacy. I showed initial examples of technologies that pave the way toward effective approaches to this problem. I also identified a number of key challenges that arise when trying to use big data, as psychologists desire to do, while maximizing the use of the data and preserving data privacy and confidentiality. Addressing the challenges requires multidisciplinary research drawing from many different areas, including computer science and engineering, information systems, statistics, risk models, economics, social sciences, political sciences, human factors, and psychology. I believe that all these perspectives are needed to achieve effective solutions to the problem of privacy in the era of big data and how to reconcile security with privacy.

REFERENCES

Bertino, E. (2012). *Data protection from insider threats: Synthesis lectures on data management.* San Rafael, CA: Morgan & Claypool. http://dx.doi.org/10.2200/S00431ED1V01Y201207DTM028

Bertino, E. (2013). Big data—Opportunities and challenges. In *Proceedings of the 2013 IEEE 37th Annual Computer Software and Applications Conference* (pp. 479–480). Piscataway, NJ: IEEE. http://dx.doi.org/10.1109/COMPSAC.2013.143

Bertino, E. (2014). Security with privacy—Opportunities and challenges. In *Proceedings of the 2014 IEEE 38th Annual International Computers, Software and Applications Conference* (pp. 436–437). Piscataway, NJ: IEEE. http://dx.doi.org/10.1109/COMPSAC.2014.98

Bertino, E. (2016, December). *Big data security and privacy*. Paper presented at the 2016 IEEE International Conference on Big Data, Washington, DC.

Bertino, E., Ghinita, G., & Kamra, A. (2011). Access control for databases: Concepts and Systems. *Foundations and Trends in Databases, 3*(1–2), 1–148. http://dx.doi.org/10.1561/1900000014

Bertino, E., Merrill, S., Nesen, A., & Utz, C. (2019). Redefining data transparency—a multi-dimensional approach. *Computer Magazine, IEEE, 52*, 16–26.

Byun, J.-W., Kamra, A., Bertino, E., & Li, N. (2007). Efficiently k-anonymization using clustering techniques. In R. Kotagiri, P. R. Krishna, M. Mohania, & E. Nantajeewarawat (Eds.), *Advances in databases: Concepts, systems and applications* (Vol. 4443, pp. 188–200). New York, NY: Springer-Verlag.

Cao, J., Rao, F.-Y., Bertino, E., & Kantarcioglu, M. (2015, April). A hybrid private record linkage scheme: Separating differentially private synopses from matching records. In *Proceedings of the 31st International Conference on Data Engineering* (pp. 1011–1022). Washington, DC: IEEE.

Carminati, B., Ferrari, E., & Viviani, M. (2013). *Security and trust in online social networks*. San Rafael, CA: Morgan & Claypool. http://dx.doi.org/10.2200/S00549ED1V01Y201311SPT008

Dai, C., Ghinita, G., Bertino, E., Byun, J.-W., & Li, N. (2009). TIAMAT: A Tool for Interactive Analysis of Microdata Anonymization Techniques. *The Proceedings of the VLBD Endowment, 2*, 1618–1621. http://dx.doi.org/10.14778/1687553.1687607

Damiani, M., Bertino, E., Catania, B., & Perlasca, P. (2007). GEO-RBAC: A spatially aware RBAC. *ACM Transactions on Information and System Security, 10*, 29–37. http://dx.doi.org/10.1145/1210263.1210265

Damiani, M. L., Bertino, E., & Silvestri, C. (2010). The PROBE framework for the personalized cloaking of private locations. *Transactions on Data Privacy, 3*, 123–148.

Dasgupta, D., Roy, A., & Nag, A. (2017). *Advances in user authentication*. Cham, Switzerland: Springer. http://dx.doi.org/10.1007/978-3-319-58808-7

Datoo, A. (2018). Data in the post-GDPR world. *Computer Fraud & Security, 2018*(9), 17–18. http://dx.doi.org/10.1016/S1361-3723(18)30088-5

Demmler, D., Schneider, T., & Zohner, M. (2015). ABY—a framework for efficient mixed-protocol secure two-party computation. In *Proceedings of the 2015 Network and Distributed System Security (NDSS) Symposium* (pp. 1–15). Reston, VA: Internet Society. http://dx.doi.org/10.14722/ndss.2015.23113

Dwork, C., & Roth, A. (2014). The algorithmic foundations of differential privacy. *Foundations and Trends in Theoretical Computer Science, 9*(3–4), 211–407. http://dx.doi.org/10.1561/0400000042

Even, S., Goldreich, O., & Lempel, A. (1985). A randomized protocol for signing contracts. *Communications of the ACM, 28*, 637–647. http://dx.doi.org/10.1145/3812.3818

Freedman, M., Nissim, K., & Pinkas, B. (2004). Efficient private matching and set intersection. In C. Cachin & J. L. Camenisch (Eds.), *Lecture notes in computer science: Vol. 3027. Advances in cryptology—EUROCRYPT 2004* (pp. 1–19). New York, NY: Springer-Verlag. http://dx.doi.org/10.1007/978-3-540-24676-3_1

Ghinita, G., Kalnis, P., Khoshgozaran, A., Shahabi, C., & Tan, K.-L. (2008). Private queries in location based services: Anonymizers are not necessary. In *Proceedings of the 2008 ACM SIGMOD International Conference on Management of Data* (pp. 121–132). New York, NY: ACM. http://dx.doi.org/10.1145/1376616.1376631

Goldreich, O. (2004). *The foundations of cryptography: Vol. II. Basic applications*. Cambridge, England: Cambridge University Press.

Goldreich, O., & Ostrovsky, R. (1996). Software protection and simulation on oblivious RAMs. *Journal of the Association for Computing Machinery, 43*, 431–473. http://dx.doi.org/10.1145/233551.233553

Gunasinghe, H., & Bertino, E. (2014). Privacy preserving biometrics-based and user centric authentication protocol. In M. H. Au, B. Carminati, & C. C. J. Kuo (Eds.),

Lecture notes in computer science: Vol. 8792. Network and system security (pp. 389–408). Cham, Switzerland: Springer. http://dx.doi.org/10.1007/978-3-319-11698-3_30

Islam, M. S., Kuzu, M., & Kantarcioglu, M. (2012). *Access pattern disclosure on searchable encryption: Ramification, attack and mitigation.* Retrieved from https://pdfs. semanticscholar.org/9614/87973d4b33f96406fddbfcf1235dc587571f.pdf

Jain, A. K., & Ross, A. (2008). Introduction to biometrics. In A. K. Jain, P. Flynn, & A. Ross (Eds.), *Handbook of biometrics* (pp. 1–22). New York, NY: Springer. http:// dx.doi.org/10.1007/978-0-387-71041-9_1

Klinger, E., & Starkweather, D. (2008–2010). *pHash: The open source perceptual hash library.* Retrieved from http://www.phash.org/

Kołakowska, A. (2018). Usefulness of keystroke dynamics features in user authentication and emotion recognition. In Z. Hippe, J. Kulikowski, & T. Mroczek (Eds.), *Human–computer systems interaction* (pp. 42–52). Cham, Switzerland: Springer. http:// dx.doi.org/10.1007/978-3-319-62120-3_4

Kreuter, B., Shelat, A., Mood, B., & Butler, K. (2013). PCF: A portable circuit format for scalable two-party secure computation. In *Proceedings of the 22nd USENIX Conference on Security* (pp. 321–336). Berkeley, CA: USENIX Association.

Lindell, Y., & Pinkas, B. (2000). Privacy preserving data mining. In M. Bellare (Ed.), *Advances in cryptology* (pp. 36–54). New York, NY: Springer-Verlag.

Liu, D., Bertino, E., & Yi, X. (2014). Privacy of outsourced K-means clustering. In *Proceedings of the 9th ACM Symposium on Information, Computer and Communication Security* (pp. 123–134). New York, NY: ACM.

Nabeel, M., & Bertino, E. (2014a). Attribute based group key management. *Transactions on Data Privacy, 7,* 309–336.

Nabeel, M., & Bertino, E. (2014b). Privacy preserving delegated access control in public clouds. *IEEE Transactions on Knowledge and Data Engineering, 26,* 2268–2280. http:// dx.doi.org/10.1109/TKDE.2013.68

Nabeel, M., Shang, N., & Bertino, E. (2013). Privacy-preserving policy-based content sharing in public clouds. *IEEE Transactions on Knowledge and Data Engineering, 25,* 2602–2614. http://dx.doi.org/10.1109/TKDE.2012.180

Naor, M., & Pinkas, B. (2001). Efficient oblivious transfer protocols. In *Proceedings of the twelfth annual symposium on discrete algorithms* (pp. 448–457). Philadelphia, PA: Society for Industrial and Applied Mathematics.

Naor, M., & Pinkas, B. (2006). Oblivious polynomial evaluation. *SIAM Journal on Computing, 35,* 1254–1281. http://dx.doi.org/10.1137/S0097539704383633

National Science Foundation. (2014, September). *NSF Workshop on Big Data Security and Privacy* (B. Thuraisingham, Chair), The University of Texas at Dallas, Richardson, TX. Retrieved from http://csi.utdallas.edu/events/NSF/NSF%20workshop%202014.htm

O'Neil, C. (2016). *Weapons of math destruction: How big data increases inequality and threatens democracy.* New York, NY: Crown/Archetype.

Paulet, R., Kaosar, M., Yi, X., & Bertino, E. (2014). Privacy-preserving and content-protecting location based queries. *IEEE Transactions on Knowledge and Data Engineering, 26,* 1200–1210. http://dx.doi.org/10.1109/TKDE.2013.87

Pedersen, T. P. (1992). Non-interactive and information-theoretic secure verifiable secret sharing. In *Proceedings of 11th annual international cryptology conference on advances in cryptology* (pp. 129–140). London, England: Springer-Verlag.

Seo, S.-H., Nabeel, M., Ding, X., & Bertino, E. (2014). An efficient certificateless encryption for secure data sharing in public clouds. *IEEE Transactions on Knowledge and Data Engineering, 26,* 2107–2119. http://dx.doi.org/10.1109/TKDE.2013.138

Shamir, A. (1979). How to share a secret. *Communications of the ACM, 22,* 612–613. http:// dx.doi.org/10.1145/359168.359176

Shang, N., Nabeel, M., Paci, F., & Bertino, E. (2010). A privacy-preserving approach to policy-based content dissemination. In *Proceedings of the 26th International Conference on Data Engineering* (pp. 944–955). Washington, DC: IEEE.

Shebaro, B., Oluwatimi, O., Midi, D., & Bertino, E. (2014). IdentiDroid: Android can finally wear its anonymous suit. *Transactions on Data Privacy, 7*(1), 27–50.

Vaidya, J., Zhu, Y., & Clifton, C. (2006). *Privacy preserving data mining*. New York, NY: Springer.

Wang, H. X., Nayak, K., Liu, C., Chan, T.-H., Shi, E., Stefanov, E., & Huang, Y. (2014). Oblivious data structures. In G.-J. Ahn, M. Yung, & N. Li (Eds.), *Proceedings of the 21st Conference on Computers and Communications Security* (pp. 215–226). New York, NY: ACM.

Yao, A. C. (1986). How to generate and exchange secrets. In *Proceedings of the 27th annual symposium on foundations of computer science* (pp. 162–167). Washington, DC: IEEE.

Yi, X., Rao, F., Bertino, E., & Bouguettaya, A. (2015). Privacy-preserving association rule mining in cloud computing. In *Proceedings of the 10th ACM symposium on information, computer and communication security* (pp. 439–450). New York, NY: ACM.

V

CONCLUDING REMARKS

19

Future Research Directions for Big Data in Psychology

Frederick L. Oswald

This brief concluding chapter allows me the privilege and opportunity to draw on the collective scholarship, useful and cutting-edge insights, and hard work contributed by all the authors of this book addressing the nature and role of big data in psychology. Also, the conclusion of this chapter allows me to offer a list of future research directions (immodestly abbreviated FReDs) that summarize how psychology can be more strategically and actively involved in the big data research arena, alongside other disciplines already strongly engaged in this arena (e.g., applied statistics, computer science). Most FReDs will be obvious, but the idea is that the list as a whole might be appreciated as a broad systemic approach for the psychological sciences to take. Moreover, this book, in its entirety, should inspire psychologists to incorporate additional big data–related strategies, ideas, and knowledge into their research and thinking, regardless of their level of analytic training or career stage.

DEFINING BIG DATA PROBLEMS AND PROJECTS IN TERMS OF PSYCHOLOGY AND ITS SUBFIELDS

Defining big data problems and projects appropriately and understanding their broad nature and implications is not only good science but it also helps address both ethical and legal concerns. To this end, the social science disciplines (e.g., psychology, sociology, economics, political science), as well as other disciplines (e.g., philosophy, ethics, history), can enter usefully and critically into the

http://dx.doi.org/10.1037/0000193-020
Big Data in Psychological Research, S. E. Woo, L. Tay, and R. W. Proctor (Editors)

development phase of big data projects, before they become fully executed. This book is incredibly timely in this respect because many big data projects like those described herein involve collecting data relevant to psychology in the attempt to address problems involving complex human behavior at the levels of individuals, society, and everything in between (Foster, Ghani, Jarmin, Kreuter, & Lane, 2017).

Related to these psychology-related developments in the big data arena is the fact that the U.S. labor market has witnessed a major influx of venture capital–backed startup companies that are developing psychology-related, big data–oriented applications at a rapid pace, involving teams of people, largely in the technology sector, who are extremely knowledgeable and committed to their work and their missions. To exercise their full responsibility to the success of these psychological applications, such teams might usefully collaborate with expert psychologists to receive multiple benefits coming from (a) their solid base of psychometrics and measure development expertise; (b) their research and theoretical expertise in how they understand psychological phenomena and collect behavioral and attitudinal data on them; (c) their extensive practical experience in how to implement technologies successfully in schools, work, home, or wherever people and teams are involved; and (d) their legal expertise, such as when industrial-organizational (I/O) psychologists who specialize in personnel selection help consider and troubleshoot artificial intelligence (AI) tools so that they address job relevance, validity, and fairness by avoiding discrimination against protected classes. In short, just as is true with scientific research projects of all sorts, big data research projects can benefit greatly from multidisciplinary efforts involving researchers in the psychological sciences.

A prime example of a societal big data problem where multiple disciplines can continue to be actively involved is the following: The aging U.S. population is leading to great financial strain in the health care industry, on the order of trillions of dollars (Centers for Medicare & Medicaid Services, 2018). Thus, any big data efforts that stand to improve human health, increase economic and labor efficiencies, and reduce demographic inequities in health outcomes are vitally needed. Such efforts include improvements in systems that involve integrated data platforms, electronic health records, and appropriate medical interventions with their risk–benefit profiles—all of which have been the targets of big data tools and technologies (see Chapter 11, this volume). Given that humans are involved as both the users and the beneficiaries of these big data systems in the health care arena, it seems obvious and critical to involve psychological research and researchers in understanding what human factors psychologists might call the "human in the system." Health care workers, along with patients and their families, interact with this system, and that human–system interaction, in turn, will affect people's knowledge, their motivation and collaboration, their goal-setting capabilities, and, of course, the health outcomes themselves, ultimately.

A second critical area where big data and AI or machine learning algorithms have had a heavy focus in psychology is the talent management arena, which is relevant to the domain of I/O psychology (Putka & Oswald, 2016; see also Chapter 14, this volume). Test vendors in this arena are developing and selling a variety of new tools that make claims—with varying degrees of supportive data—pertaining to (a) increasing job applicant engagement, (b) understanding the job-relevant characteristics via novel measurement (e.g., virtual reality or video games, neuroscientific measures, physiological expressions), and (c) measuring the applicant naturally and unobtrusively to get at the "real" self (e.g., through video recordings of behaviors, facial and bodily expressions, and verbal conversations). These big data and AI assessment tools include, but are not limited to, cognitive measures (e.g., measures of working memory, processing speed) and video games (e.g., virtual reality games) and video- and audio-based interactive assessments (e.g., interviews with avatars), and they might incorporate online material (e.g., resumes, social media profiles and posts). In addition to these tools gathering big data, machine learning is then applied to the database, and finally, personnel decisions are made, often on a large scale (i.e., big data across applicants, not just within each applicant).

These two examples, from the health care and talent management arenas, are simply two out of an infinite variety of big data problems that are relevant to the psychological sciences; later, I refer to two more from this book to serve as prime examples. But note that even for big data problems that do not seem directly relevant to social sciences, many big data research projects and enterprises require employing, deploying, and managing diverse teams of experts, which itself is inherently a social sciences problem where research-backed findings from psychology can provide great benefit. Specifically, researchers studying the "science of team science" have assembled over a decade of accumulated research findings about how to coordinate, communicate, and set individual and shared research goals effectively (Bisbey, Reyes, Traylor, & Salas, 2019; National Research Council, 2015). Related to this is how one of the major benefits of today's "big data revolution" is its creation of data-oriented projects and teams, with its critical effect on the culture of collaborative and interdisciplinary work. In some ways, "big data" is a more professional version of "happy hour," given that both often bring people together from diverse job roles and bases of expertise in a larger institution (university, hospital, school, organization) to discuss and solve problems in meaningful ways that they never would have otherwise.

In the educational setting, big data certainly has brought visionary initiatives and wide-ranging disciplinary perspectives together. As a personal example, at my institution, Rice University, a recent large financial investment has stimulated multiyear university-wide faculty hiring and the development of a data science undergraduate minor relevant to all majors. This university-wide conversation has been rewarding for everyone involved: for learning how psychological sciences can inform and be informed by other disciplines; and for discussing how critical data science skills include communication, visualization, and ethical sensemaking and decision making (in addition to data management and analysis skills). The shared knowledge and friendships developed in this process have been extremely valuable for stimulating future ideas, collaborations, institutional support, and large-scale grant initiatives addressing important big data research questions. Hopefully, positive developments and outcomes such as these continue to happen and be further cultivated in psychology and the social sciences, writ large.

BIG DATA IN THE CONTEXT OF THE RESEARCH PROCESS WITHIN PSYCHOLOGY

Reflecting on the research process in psychology can help illuminate how big data play a role within it, such as in the substantive illustrations that were just provided. The reader likely appreciates that the research enterprise reflects an iterative process informed by (a) top-down theory and confirmatory modeling approaches, where data are more structured and directly relevant to testable hypotheses, and (b) bottom-up inductive and abductive approaches, where the data set may be relatively unstructured and the models and algorithms used are subject to systematic exploration. In both cases, theory and reasoning work toward the best explanation from the findings obtained, which then may inform subsequent theory testing and evaluation (Chapter 1, this volume; also see Janssen & Kuk, 2016). Any given research project may occupy all or part of this research process where, to the extent such projects involve big data, they will usually take on this latter bottom-up approach because they address the opportunity—and challenge—of dealing with relatively unstructured data that are laden with the three Vs (volume, variety, velocity). Both within and across research projects, big data approaches can usefully be complemented by research focused on theory-driven deductive approaches (Mahmoodi, Leckelt, van Zalk, Geukes, & Back, 2017). As aptly noted in Chapter 1 of this volume, science is a problem-oriented endeavor at its heart, where basic and applied problems must call for many solutions, and this book is a testament to the fact that big data platforms and analytic tools are now part of the essential toolbox of social scientists as they work with other disciplines.

It is important to note that big data and traditional methods do not need to exist in separate silos in the aforementioned research cycle. Through the powers of inference and abduction, big data approaches can be used to detect the "signals in the noise" of complex data that subsequently are amplified through future measurement and research designs of smaller data projects that are more top down in terms of data collection, modeling and analysis, and interpretation (Chapter 10, this volume). Conversely, traditional deductive and confirmatory research can be open to subsequent exploratory phases, where any empirical surprises can then be followed up on with big data exploratory research. The traditional deductive–inductive research cycle in psychology is thus expanded through the implementation of big data methods.

In addition to the place of big data within a larger research cycle, it is also useful to discuss the nature of big data–oriented analyses in contrast with "smaller data" and more traditional analyses. Big data may have not only millions of cases but also the "$p \gg N$" situation, meaning that the number of variables far exceeds the number of cases (e.g., voxels in a functional magnetic resonance imaging scan of the brain; daily or even hourly fitness tracker data). By contrast, traditional research teams entering into smaller data projects may have a more limited budget of finances, staff, and participants, where such teams may have greater motivation to think more carefully about and prioritize which research designs, measures, experimental manipulations, and sampling plans seem worth the investment.

This is not to say that big data projects lack advanced planning or that having more data is not generally better. Also, there is no clear demarcation between "big data" and "smaller data." But even having said all this, big data projects often extract algorithmic predictions from unstructured and/or conveniently available data (e.g., Twitter posts), which is generally not the case for smaller data. The point, then, is that resource constraints on data collection have traditionally forced our science into greater theory-driven and measure-driven planning in the effort to "stretch" and do more with less data (see the popular press book *Stretch*, by Sonenshein, 2017, for real-world analogies in the business world).

Ultimately, the research process itself can be usefully informed by big data projects and findings just as much as big data findings inform the research question at hand. There has been some fear expressed that the scale and automation of big data and related analyses might somehow automate research and supplant the sort of traditional thoughtful study design, intervention, and measurement that leads to stronger interpretation, such as those pertaining to causal inference. But quelling those fears, the opposite seems to have been the case: Through big data research projects, researchers have been encouraged to engage in "smaller data" thinking, meaning to think even harder about how theory-driven causal insights and algorithm-driven predictive insights might combine to serve the problems at hand (Chapter 9, this volume). Even if we cannot infer theoretical models from big data predictions, perhaps we can at least place realistic constraints on hypotheses that involve causality, the more that incoming big data predictions help triangulate on the mechanisms that give rise to them. This book provides many valuable insights from psychology on how one might do this.

INTENTIONAL VERSUS INCIDENTAL MEASUREMENT IN PSYCHOLOGY

In rough alignment with the aforementioned contrast between traditional research and big data approaches is the contrast or continuum of intentional measurement versus incidental measurement. *Intentional measurement* reflects the traditional testing and measurement approach within psychology, where the item content is developed and refined to be construct driven and standardized (the same questions are asked of all respondents). By contrast, *incidental measurement* is relatively natural, unobtrusive, and unstandardized, as found in Twitter and Facebook posts and likes, Internet searches, video capture, wearable sensors, and actions from gamification and virtual reality (e.g., Chapters 5 and 6). At least in lower-stakes measurement settings, it has been found that incidental measures of text can be supported, empirically and conceptually, as reliable and valid psychologically driven signals in the noise of big data and analyses—especially with the help of factor analysis combined with corpora of external information to help extract sentiments, belief, knowledge, or other thematic information (see Chapter 8). When scored and aggregated appropriately, incidental data have the potential to provide reliable measures of psychological characteristics (knowledge, personality, motivation, interests) and social characteristics (social and occupational networks). But again, one should consider a wide range of practical, technical, and legal issues should incidental data be used in employment testing, college admissions, or other high-stakes settings. Professional standards have been developed and refined from decades of applied testing, and those standards remain quite relevant in the big data era (e.g., American Educational Research Association, American Psychological Association, National Council on Measurement in Education, Joint Committee on Standards for Educational and Psychological Testing, 2014; Principles for the Validation and Use of Personnel Selection Procedures, 2018).

Critically, with incidental data such as those in the examples provided, subjects also might be unaware of the purpose of data collection—or even that data are being collected at all. Thus, ethical obligations to informed consent, beneficence, and data privacy have become especially important, as is discussed further in conclusion. As one ethical approach to collecting natural data, crowdsourced experiments can take advantage of both intentional measurement and design, as well as informed consent, yet examine variations in natural environments on a big data scale (see Chapter 2).

PSYCHOMETRICS AND MEASURE-DEVELOPMENT EXPERTISE IN PSYCHOLOGICAL SCIENCE

Obviously, big data projects aim for making high-quality predictions; hopefully, those predictions will improve even further as the conceptual, measurement, and algorithmic foundations of such projects become stronger and more well established. In the planning and analysis phases of big data projects, what should be appreciated—and not overlooked—is how over a century of research in psychology has been intensely focused on developing psychological measures and psychometrically quantifying and understanding their reliability and validity, all in the service of effective and fair measurement. Psychometrics is just as relevant to big data and incidental measurement as it has been to "smaller data" and traditional measurement—perhaps even more so, given the messiness of big data and the opacity of big data algorithms (see Chapter 3). Because big data analyses focus squarely on the goal of prediction (i.e., the *what* of big data), any attendant insights can be confounded, mistakenly interpreted, or ignorant of their potential biases and other undesired implications (i.e., the *why* of big data; O'Neil, 2017).

On these fronts, psychological research can be of great help. Although big data algorithms focus on prediction, the psychological and behavioral research designs and data themselves can also be used more rigorously to test causal theories and multilevel theories, and to suggest future interventions. For example, a wide range of characteristics at the level of schools, teachers, peer groups, and students can be measured over time to see how and when they interact over time to influence student learning (see Chapter 10 for several other interesting examples). Big data can also enrich mixed methods, such that qualitative data and trends can support or qualify quantitative modeling and predictions—and vice versa.

There is the rising promise that incidental measures might be more revealing and reliable in some aspects than traditional measures, such as personality measures (e.g., Facebook likes as indicators of personality traits—Kosinski, Stillwell, & Graepel, 2013; Internet searches indicating religious and political preferences—Chapter 4, this volume). Or perhaps there are commonalities and uniquenesses to incidental and intentional measures of the same constructs, where each type of measure triangulates on both understanding and prediction. To address questions of this nature, psychologists from all of its subdisciplines have a longstanding tradition of measuring and statistically modeling patterns of convergent and discriminant validity (e.g., via multitrait–multimethod analysis; Eid, 2000; Widaman, 1985). Given real-time, high-volume big data measurement, such pattern detection could be done on a dynamic and roughly real-time basis (e.g., Ippel, Kaptein, & Vermunt, 2019) to (a) understand the meaning and value of incidental versus intentional measurement and (b) to inform theories that may have been largely historically informed (and perhaps limited) by cross-sectional data and/or self-report data.

Of course, reliable dynamics have to be disentangled from transient error in longitudinal analysis frameworks, and within those reliable dynamics, construct relevance has to be disentangled from systematic errors (e.g., Le, Schmidt, & Putka, 2009). Psychological theories, concepts, and sophisticated dynamic modeling approaches have developed over the long history of developmental psychology (e.g., going back to Baltes & Nesselroade, 1979) and can bring themselves to bear on this thorny problem that big data can address through careful data collection, such that big data analyses are more interpretable and useful in fulfilling their intended purposes (Chapter 13, this volume). And certainly, big data will be needed because complex relationships will require large sample sizes to be estimated with high precision and with the hope of being generalizable.

For example, one can certainly appreciate the many affordances of online testing when selecting job applicants: convenient locations (e.g., at home, on one's cell phone), increased applicant engagement (e.g., video games), larger scale testing (online access vs. physical testing rooms), and faster processing of testing and obtaining test scores. All these affordances can result in efficiencies for organizations and applicants alike. However, all these aspects should also be subject to reasonable lines of questioning and reasonable support from data. For instance, are employee hiring tools claiming to take advantage of things such as AI technologies, neuroscience, video capture, and sophisticated big data analyses offering actual improvements in terms of reliability, validity, and fairness when compared with traditional methods, and how do we know? Are such tools measuring the job-relevant constructs that test vendors claim, are random and systematic errors minimized, and how do we know?

As a specific example, imagine that applicants engage in a video game consisting of interactions in a fictitious retail store. The test vendor claims that the video game measures customer service, and this might make sense by all appearances—but how would you know from the data themselves? First, if the customer service measure is comprehensive, customer service video game scores should reflect repeated interactions across all major aspects of a customer service environment (e.g., welcoming a customer, asking about their needs, handling conflict). That way, the job applicant's score is more likely to be both a representative and stable representation of the complex construct of customer service. Second, the aspects of customer service being selected for are presumed to be needed at the point of hire. If applicants receive formal and/or informal training on aspects of customer service that are being selected for, such as welcoming a customer, it is possible that this aspect of selection is unnecessary (it is possible the training is also unnecessary).

Third, the stability of customer service scores should be demonstrated over time, meaning that a job applicant should get roughly the same score if she or he were to play the customer service video game a week later or within a relatively short period (assuming the applicant did not actually learn customer service from the game itself or between testing occasions). This temporal stability is important; otherwise, applicants could essentially be rolling dice to produce a random or highly variable score. Fourth, the customer service scores should demonstrate *convergent validity*, being correlated with external outcomes that experts would agree reflect customer service (e.g., supervisory ratings of customer service, average ratings of service provided by random samples of customers), as well as other measures also thought to relate to customer service (e.g., an employee's measured standing on agreeableness, conscientiousness, and social interests; Frei & McDaniel, 1998). And fifth and finally, a solid measure should also demonstrate *discriminant validity*, or meaningful patterns of low correlation where it is expected (e.g., customer service does not correlate with cognitive ability or arm strength).

It is through empirical evidence for reliability and patterns of convergent and discriminant validity that one understands why a measure predicts outcomes of interest, in hopes that job applicant scores vary due to construct-relevant reasons and not due to irrelevant effects, such as the type of method used it never hurts to review the classic (Campbell & Fiske, 1959). Again, the big data approach focuses on the what of prediction, the fact that data and algorithms, together, can effectively predict outcomes of interest; however, it is through the psychological science traditions of measure development, along with psychometric analysis and evaluation, that one also learns the why of prediction. Understanding the why of prediction is becoming increasingly important in today's big data era where, for ethical, legal, and scientific reasons, one seeks to avoid bias and other irrelevant effects on the road to obtaining reliable, valid, and fair talent management tools and systems.

BIG DATA RESEARCH, ALGORITHMS, AND THE PSYCHOLOGICAL SCIENCES

Two specific examples from this book reflect big data research projects and insights that, together, support the aforementioned integration of big data–oriented research design with longstanding traditional measurement approaches in psychology. The first example comes from cognitive psychology, where researchers have used real-world corpora with big data to model natural language production, as well as changes in language production with memory and cognitive aging. Such models can be productively compared with top-down theoretical predictions about cognition (see Chapter 12). The second example is from developmental psychology in examining the development of mathematical skills in kindergarten through eighth grade (see Chapter 13) and involves bottom-up big data approaches (recursive partitioning and lasso regression) in combination with top-down multilevel modeling and structural growth models in a manner that explores theoretically relevant data for relevant control variables, nonlinearities, and interactive effects—all the while using methods that seek to avoid overfitting models to the data (e.g., cross-validation, regularization of model coefficients, using model-fit indices to select models that balance fit with parsimony). These are two excellent substantive examples of taking a hybrid approach, as mentioned earlier, such that abduction from big data contributes to the research cycle, theories get informed and revised, and perhaps new theories arise that explain the data and promote future large-scale and smaller scale inductive and deductive modeling, data collection, and testing.

When invoking big data analyses, as we find in these examples, a full data set comprising thousands of variables, cases, and time points might be used in the service of prediction and classification. Big data technologies measure behaviors and their sequences (e.g., Markov chains analytically measure the progressive mastery of calculus concepts), networks (e.g., wearable sensors measure proximity between coworkers), processes and their correlates (e.g., experience sampling methods to measure smoking cessation), images and text (e.g., analyzing personality themes from Facebook posts), and psychophysiological responses (e.g., galvanic skin response, heart rate variability).

Whether measurements are related to social sciences or not, big data may not only be "messy" but the associated analyses can also provide multiple predictions for each case. These multiple predictions may come out of repeated bootstrapped samples and even out of entirely different algorithms, where multiple predicted values for each case are averaged (e.g., model ensemble techniques). This averaging is an attempt to produce a robust and unbiased prediction, analogous to how political forecasters (e.g., https://fivethirtyeight.com) average predictions across multiple voting models in an attempt to average out the biases for any given model and provide better political forecasts as a result.

In this way, big data algorithms might be forcing psychology into a new form of "dustbowl empiricism," where we obtain predictive findings that are robust, and in this sense are better than those from traditional methods—yet, we may not know exactly how we achieved them. The old form of dustbowl empiricism tended to overfit models to data (e.g., small-sample analysis of variance or multiple linear regression), which then leads to quirky results that might be statistically significant but do not replicate. By contrast, in the service of prediction, big data algorithms work hard not to capitalize on chance, whether that is through using methods that perturb the sample (e.g., via bootstrapping or k-fold cross-validation), perturb the variables available (e.g., sampling from the variable set in the random forest algorithm), or by averaging predictions across different models. As a result of this big data approach, as noted previously, how improved prediction is achieved is often unknown (e.g., random forests average across a large number of predictive trees, neural nets have uninterpretable network properties, and support vector machines use the "kernel trick" to take advantage of complex multidimensionality without having to model its functional form).

To be clear, improving predictions through the use of big data algorithms has shown great promise and has already solved challenging problems. In general, we all can appreciate improved prediction through deep learning and other AI algorithms in cases where society has largely embraced the problem and its solutions (e.g., winning at chess, Go, or Jeopardy!; recognizing handwriting on envelopes processed by the postal service). Other predictions, however, clearly have to be avoided in the future (e.g., biases regarding who is to receive a loan or a traffic ticket), and still other predictions may be more nuanced in terms of their predictions and implications (e.g., modeling drug dosages when the resulting quality versus quantity of life is something of a trade-off that doctors and patients must decide). Understanding and navigating these nuances of prediction are yet another way the psychological sciences can inform big data, through the ethical considerations that are raised.

BIG DATA ETHICS IN PSYCHOLOGY

Today's known ethical issues and concerns about big data have been vitally important in suggesting and stimulating greater thoughtfulness and planning when defining big data problems and implementing solutions. Through their training, psychologists are adept at quantitatively synthesizing relevant past empirical research findings (e.g., via meta-analysis or multilevel modeling); creating solid research designs involving data on human cognition, affect, and behaviors (e.g., based on training in individual differences and experimental design); and considering the human subjects implications of research projects that involve psychological testing and experimentation (e.g., given their extensive experience with institutional review boards in conducting studies involving human subjects). Psychologists' input can be essential to assuring some of the fundamentals of ethical practice using big data—for example, respect for persons, maximizing benefit while minimizing harm (in line with the Belmont Report—National Commission for the Protection of Human Subjects of Biomedical and Behavioral Research, 1979), adhering to the range of federal and international laws that enforce data privacy (e.g., Fair Credit Reporting Act, General Data Protection Regulation), and collecting data by intention, not the mere convenience that the data are simply available (Chapter 15, this volume). Regarding this latter point, people may feel that it is innocuous when offering single data points (e.g., posting a tweet or blog post), yet those same people may take issue with extensive data harvesting of those single data points that would lead to a large database containing convergent identifying information.

Thus, with big data technologies come critical privacy, security, and use issues that are of special consideration by researchers in their responsibilities. Also, these issues should be clearly communicated and understood by individuals who are providing and using the data (e.g., organizations and job applicants; Chapter 17, this volume). Privacy technologies embedded into big data analyses (e.g., de-identification, secure distributed collaboration), big data sharing (e.g., cloud-based encryption, differential privacy), and big data transparency (e.g., informing subjects about data-driven decisions and policies) continue to evolve as much as the big data techniques themselves (see Chapter 18). Psychologists can help address attendant ethical issues about data privacy and use, not only because of their deep experience in dealing with human subjects committees and human subjects research but also because psychologists have developed these policies themselves. Psychologists have also been at the forefront of the open science movement, generating and following practices that deliberately seek to balance privacy needs with the need for the transparency and reproducibility of their research, which involves dealing with competing ethical concerns (see Chapter 16).

In addition to privacy versus transparency, the open science movement can be usefully tied to other critical ethical issues regarding big data, such as preregistration. The preregistration of a research project can specify which variables, samples, and big data algorithms will be used (and R or Python code could be provided with those preregistration plans). Obviously, preregistration never precludes any researcher from conducting additional analyses that were not specified. Instead, preregistration can serve to enhance the ethical integrity of research by distinguishing planned big data analyses from exploratory follow-up analyses that depart from those plans (e.g., for a simple and useful preregistration approach, see https://aspredicted.org). These latter exploratory analyses might have been informed by the results that were obtained and, therefore, may carry a greater need for replication.

Finally, new ethics and fairness issues might also come to the forefront with big data technologies, such as with the previously mentioned talent assessment tools, where, for example, one can see how a traditional measure could be read out loud to a blind job applicant; yet, it is more difficult to come up with accommodations for the same applicant given a video game assessment

438 *Frederick L. Oswald*

that collects big data and applies sophisticated scoring algorithms to them. Or older job applicants may have slower reflexes that might impair their video game playing (Verhaeghen & Salthouse, 1997) and thus create differences in applicant scores, even though reaction time in the game may be irrelevant to what the game intends to measure and to the job itself. Thinking about these accommodation issues more broadly, however, perhaps job applicants of the future could be widely accommodated via human–computer collaborative decision making (HCCD), where the hybrid environment ends up resembling a key subset of the actual job that is relevant for personnel selection (vs. relevant after post-hire training). Selection would then be somewhat analogous to how they would be accommodated via HCCD as employees, which has already been demonstrated for making high-stakes decisions in cybersecurity or the military or for power-grid operators (see Chapter 7).

CONCLUSION

Today's big data era moves psychology away from the shores of its substantive and methodological research past into exciting waters previously uncharted by the discipline, as seen in the set of complementary, insightful, and compelling chapters presented in this book. Yet as the discipline of psychology evolves in the era of big data, perhaps it should not sail too far away from its moorings. Why? The messiness of big data—for example, incidental data combined with relatively opaque algorithms and predictions applied to them—has sounded the ethical alarms in terms of (a) the potential lack of substantive models with interpretability, (b) the potential for making stable predictions based partially on unknown algorithmic irrelevancies (bias), and (c) the use of incidental data that might invade privacy due to lack of consent or due to the characteristics they reveal in their aggregation and analysis.

But with perils come promise: It is with exactly these three big data limitations that psychology and psychological measurement can vitally contribute to big data projects and collaborations—for example, psychologists have over a century of developing, statistically modeling, and testing a wide range of psychological measures and interventions, where (unlike the typical big data analysis) one stands to gain more of a substantive understanding from modeling based on those data, which can greatly help when interpreting model-based predictions. From this foundation, combined with open science principles and practices, results might be more conceptually, legally, and ethically defensible than in many big data scenarios, where the reasons (both variables and algorithms) driving predictive results can be much more inscrutable. This not to say that there are not interpretable approaches to big data (e.g., dimension reduction, regression-based approaches) or that approaches to "explainable AI" are making meaningful advances (e.g., Ribeiro, Singh, & Guestrin, 2016). But overall, as noted, top-down modeling efforts and bottom-up big data approaches should better integrate and iterate with one another, as should the psychological sciences with other disciplines.

The field of psychology is shaping a combination of influences coming usefully together—for example, open science advancements, innovations and insights reflected in this book, and the hard-won expertise, experience, and training of psychologists in developing measures, experiments, and project teams. These elements (and more) suggest a future of psychology-based big data projects and applications that are coupled with intentional measurement and top-down modeling. One exciting area involves tailored dynamic responses to social behaviors (e.g., quickly identifying academically at-risk children at school; providing real-time notifications that improve health-related behaviors or protect neighborhoods) or the appropriate large-scale processing and modeling of psychological data (e.g., appropriately developing and modeling big data sets that comprise a vast number of relevant psychological and situational characteristics on tens of thousands of job seekers, college applicants, or military recruits). See Table 19.1 for a list of future research directions. The future is now.

TABLE 19.1 Future Research Directions (FReDs) for Big Data in Psychology

Key question	Details
FReD 1: "If a traditional data analysis project is the baseline approach, how much do big data projects improve on the baseline?"	Conduct research across a wide range of informative areas of psychology—developmental, personality and social, cognitive, industrial and organizational (I/O), and quantitative psychology—that helps quantify the utility and effectiveness of big data projects in terms of improved measurement and interpretation of individual and group-level characteristics (e.g., measures of knowledge, conscientiousness, teamwork, communication, empathy).
FReD 2: "How do we know whether data science teams are effective, and how they can be made more effective?"	Conduct research on the effectiveness of recruiting, selecting, developing, training, and evaluating data science teams. Such research can be informed and conducted by experts in I/O and consulting psychology.
FReD 3: "How can research experts help get better data (and not just big data) into our databases?"	Research from human factors, I/O, and educational psychology that can improve applied big data projects via design and data collection codeveloped by psychologists (e.g., projects addressing educational and occupational training, safety in medical settings, training and program outcomes in diversity and inclusion).
FReD 4: "How can we promote open science in big data projects?"	Research from all subdisciplines of psychology on how the psychological sciences formulates and adopts principles and practices of open science (e.g., transparency, reproducibility) influence and improve big data projects (e.g., maximize scientific benefits to researchers, minimize privacy threats or other forms of harm to participants). Pursuing this future research direction can usefully address many key scientific, ethical, and legal concerns associated with big data projects.

REFERENCES

American Educational Research Association, American Psychological Association, National Council on Measurement in Education, Joint Committee on Standards for Educational and Psychological Testing. (2014). *Standards for educational and psychological testing* (5th ed.). Washington, DC: American Educational Research Association.

Baltes, P. B., & Nesselroade, J. R. (1979). History and rationale of longitudinal research. In J. R. Nesselroade & P. B. Baltes (Eds.), *Longitudinal research in the study of behavior and development* (pp. 1–39). New York, NY: Academic Press.

Bisbey, T. M., Reyes, D. L., Traylor, A. M., & Salas, E. (2019). Teams of psychologists helping teams: The evolution of the science of team training. *American Psychologist, 74*, 278–289. http://dx.doi.org/10.1037/amp0000419

Campbell, D. T., & Fiske, D. W. (1959). Convergent and discriminant validation by the multitrait-multimethod matrix. *Psychological Bulletin, 56*, 81–105. http://dx.doi.org/10.1037/h0046016

Centers for Medicare & Medicaid Services. (2018). *National health expenditures 2017 highlights*. Retrieved from https://www.cms.gov/Research-Statistics-Data-and-Systems/Statistics-Trends-and-Reports/NationalHealthExpendData/Downloads/highlights.pdf

Eid, M. (2000). A multitrait-multimethod model with minimal assumptions. *Psychometrika, 65*, 241–261. http://dx.doi.org/10.1007/BF02294377

Foster, I., Ghani, R., Jarmin, R. S., Kreuter, F., & Lane, J. (Eds.). (2017). *Big data and social science: A practical guide to methods and tools*. Boca Raton, FL: CRC Press/Taylor & Francis.

Frei, R. L., & McDaniel, M. M. (1998). Validity of customer service measures in personnel selection: A review of criterion and construct evidence. *Human Performance, 11*, 1–27. http://dx.doi.org/10.1207/s15327043hup1101_1

Ippel, L., Kaptein, M. C., & Vermunt, J. K. (2019). Estimating multilevel models on data streams. *Psychometrika, 84*, 41–64. http://dx.doi.org/10.1007/s11336-018-09656-z

Janssen, M., & Kuk, G. (2016). Big and open linked data (BOLD) in research, policy, and practice. *Journal of Organizational Computing and Electronic Commerce, 26*, 3–13. http://dx.doi.org/10.1080/10919392.2015.1124005

Kosinski, M., Stillwell, D., & Graepel, T. (2013). Private traits and attributes are predictable from digital records of human behavior. *PNAS, 110*, 5802–5805. http://dx.doi.org/10.1073/pnas.1218772110

Le, H., Schmidt, F. L., & Putka, D. J. (2009). The multifaceted nature of measurement artifacts and its implications for measuring construct-level relationships. *Organizational Research Methods, 12*, 165–200. http://dx.doi.org/10.1177/1094428107302900

Mahmoodi, J., Leckelt, M., van Zalk, M. W., Geukes, K., & Back, M. D. (2017). Big Data approaches in social and behavioral science: Four key trade-offs and a call for integration. *Current Opinion in Behavioral Sciences, 18*, 57–62. http://dx.doi.org/10.1016/j.cobeha.2017.07.001

National Commission for the Protection of Human Subjects of Biomedical and Behavioral Research. (1979). *The Belmont report: Ethical principles and guidelines for the protection of human subjects of research*. Retrieved from https://www.hhs.gov/ohrp/regulations-and-policy/belmont-report/read-the-belmont-report/index.html

National Research Council. (2015). *Enhancing the effectiveness of team science*. Washington, DC: National Academies Press.

O'Neil, C. (2017). *Weapons of math destruction: How big data increases inequality and threatens democracy*. New York, NY: Broadway Books.

Principles for the validation and use of personnel selection procedures. (2018). *Industrial and Organizational Psychology: Perspectives on Science and Practice, 11*(S1), 1–97. http://dx.doi.org/10.1017/iop.2018.195

Putka, D. J., & Oswald, F. L. (2016). Implications of the big data movement for the advancement of I-O science and practice. In S. Tonidandel, E. King, & J. Cortina

(Eds.), *Big data at work: The data science revolution and organizational psychology* (pp. 181–212). New York, NY: Routledge.

Ribeiro, M. T., Singh, S., & Guestrin, C. (2016). Why should I trust you? Explaining the predictions of any classifier. In *Proceedings of the 22nd ACM SIGKDD International Conference on Knowledge Discovery and Data Mining* (pp. 1135–1144). New York, NY: ACM.

Sonenshein, S. (2017). *Stretch: Unlock the power of less-and achieve more than you ever imagined.* New York, NY: HarperCollins.

Verhaeghen, P., & Salthouse, T. A. (1997). Meta-analyses of age–cognition relations in adulthood: Estimates of linear and nonlinear age effects and structural models. *Psychological Bulletin, 122*, 231–249. http://dx.doi.org/10.1037/0033-2909.122.3.231

Widaman, K. F. (1985). Hierarchically nested covariance structure models for multitrait-multimethod data. *Applied Psychological Measurement, 9*, 1–26. http://dx.doi.org/10.1177/014662168500900101

INDEX

ABOUT THE EDITORS

Sang Eun Woo, PhD, is an associate professor in the Department of Psychological Sciences at Purdue University. She received her doctorate in industrial and organizational psychology from University of Illinois at Urbana-Champaign with a minor in quantitative psychology.

Dr. Woo's substantive research so far has focused on how people's personality and motivation can help explain various psychological phenomena in the workplace. Particular outcomes of interest include work attitudes (e.g., satisfaction and commitment), withdrawal behaviors (e.g., turnover), and interpersonal relationships (e.g., networking and social networks). Dr. Woo's overall research program is motivated by her desire to understand, harness, and/or foster openness in academia as well as the rest of the world—openness to new ideas and experiences, to people with different opinions and cultural backgrounds, to important life lessons and opportunities for growth, and to novel and underutilized scientific methods (e.g., inductive and abductive, person centered and configural, big data, Bayesian, qualitative).

Dr. Woo has extensive experience in conducting research in the area of psychological measurement in both public and private sectors. Her focal expertise lies in developing and validating techniques of assessing personality and individual differences for various organizational and educational purposes (e.g., selection, diagnosis, training and development, retention), as well as in clarifying the theoretical underpinnings and implications of such techniques. Dr. Woo actively contributes to the international community of psychology and social sciences more broadly: She has produced a number of high-quality journal articles and conference presentations within and across multiple disciplines, including industrial and organizational psychology, personality psychology, management (organizational behavior and human resources), organizational methods, sociology, education, careers and vocational psychology, and engineering.

Dr. Woo recently guest-edited a special issue on inductive approaches to organizational science for *Human Resource Management Review* (2017) and is currently serving on the editorial board for *Organizational Research Methods, Journal of Applied Psychology, Journal of Management, Journal of Business and Psychology*, and *Human Resource Management Review*. Dr. Woo is also serving on the American Psychological Association Committee on Psychological Tests and Assessment (2019–2021).

Louis Tay, PhD, is an associate professor in industrial–organizational (I-O) Psychology at Purdue University. He received his psychology undergraduate training at the National University of Singapore and the University of Melbourne. He holds a doctorate in I-O psychology from the University of Illinois at Urbana-Champaign. He is also an associate editor at *Organizational Research Methods*.

As an I-O psychologist embedded within the broader field of psychology, Dr. Tay seeks to programmatically pursue cross-disciplinary lines of inquiry in methodology (i.e., measurement, continuum specification, latent class modeling, big data and data science) and well-being (i.e., societal well-being, wellness programs, work–leisure [e.g., arts and humanities activities] interface). His goal is to contribute more broadly beyond I-O psychology to enhance measurement and methodology research for psychology and develop science-based well-being policies at organizational and societal levels.

Dr. Tay is the coeditor of several books and books in progress that include the *Handbook of Well-Being, The Oxford Handbook of Positive Psychology on the Arts and Humanities*, and *Handbook of Positive Psychology Assessment*. He has published more than 100 articles that have appeared in journals such as *Nature Human Behavior, Psychological Bulletin, Perspectives on Psychological Science, Journal of Personality and Social Psychology, Psychological Science, Journal of Applied Psychology*, and *Organizational Research Methods*. Several of these works have been featured in news outlets such as *The Wall Street Journal, Time, Scientific American, The Washington Post, U.S. News & World Report, Science Daily, Business Insider, Newsweek*, and the *World Economic Forum*.

Dr. Tay is the founder of Expimetrics (https://www.expimetrics.com), which is an experience sampling software company that currently serves more than 1,500 researchers around the world. He seeks to help researchers in practical ways to develop cutting-edge ways of collecting experience data through participant mobile devices in a simple but rigorous manner.

For his contributions to the field, he was awarded the 2015 Association for Psychological Science Rising Star Award, the 2016 Ruut Veenhoven Award from the Erasmus Happiness Economics Research Organization, the 2016 Academy of Management Sage Publications/RMD/CARMA Early Career Achievement Award, the 2018 Early Career Research Award from Health and Human

Sciences College at Purdue University, and the 2020 Society for Personality and Social Psychology Sage Young Scholars Award.

Robert W. Proctor, PhD, is Distinguished Professor in the Department of Psychological Sciences at Purdue University, with a courtesy appointment in the School of Industrial Engineering. He received his doctorate in psychology from the University of Texas at Arlington.

Dr. Proctor is an experimental cognitive psychologist whose research focuses on basic and applied aspects of human performance. His primary emphasis is on response, or action, selection. Much of his research in that area involves stimulus–response compatibility effects, which are factors that influence performance with different display-control mappings. He coedited the first book devoted to that topic with T. Gilmour Reeve in 1990, *Stimulus–Response Compatibility: An Integrated Perspective*, and coauthored the first authored book with Kim-Phuong L. Vu in 2006, *Stimulus–Response Compatibility Principles: Data, Theory, and Application*.

Dr. Proctor also conducts research in human factors, training, human–computer interaction, human aspects of cybersecurity, and psychology of science. He is the coauthor with Trisha Van Zandt of the text *Human Factors in Simple and Complex Systems*, which is currently in its third edition. Over the past decade, he has co-led interdisciplinary research programs examining various user-centric issues in the domain of cybersecurity (with Ninghui Li) and training for operation of heavy construction equipment (with Phillip Dunston).

Recently, Dr. Proctor guest-edited (with Kim-Phuong L. Vu) special issues of the *American Psychologist* (2019) on multidisciplinary research teams and the *International Journal of Human–Computer Interaction* (2017) on foundations of cognitive science for the design of human-computer interactive systems. He is the editor of the *American Journal of Psychology*, founded in 1887 by G. Stanley Hall, and is on the editorial boards of the journals *Acta Psychologica, Human Factors, International Journal of Human–Computer Interaction, Memory & Cognition, Psychological Research,* and *Technology, Mind, and Behavior*. Dr. Proctor is a fellow of the American Psychological Association, Association for Psychological Science, Psychonomic Society, and Human Factors and Ergonomics Society. He is recipient of the 2018 Paul M. Fitts Education Award for outstanding contributions to the education and training of human factors and ergonomics specialties from the latter society and the 2013 Franklin V. Taylor Award for Outstanding Contributions in the Field of Applied Experimental/ Engineering Psychology from Division 21 of the American Psychological Association.